PROGRAMMING WITH OBJECTS

PROGRAMMING WITH OBJECTS

A Comparative Presentation of Object-Oriented Programming With C++ and Java

AVINASH C. KAK

Purdue University

WILEY-INTERSCIENCE

A JOHN WILEY & SONS, INC., PUBLICATION

Library of Congress Cataloging-in-Publication Data:

Kak, Avinash C.
    Programming with objects : a comparative presentation of object-oriented programming
with C++ and Java / Avinash C. Kak.
        p. cm.
    "A Wiley-Interscience publication."
    Includes bibliographical references and index.
    ISBN 0-471-26852-6 (cloth)
        1. Object-oriented programming (Computer science)   2. C++ (Computer program
langruage)   3. Java (Computer program language)   I. Title.

    QA76.64 .K355 2003
    005.13'3—dc21   2002033108

Printed in the United States of America.

10 9 8 7 6 5 4 3 2 1

To
my daughter
Maura

Contents in Brief

Contents

Preface

This book presents object-oriented programming with C++ and Java, which are to-day's two dominant languages for such programming. The presentation format is mostly comparative, all the way from the basic language constructs to application-level issues dealing with graphics programming, network programming, and database programming. This book is intended for a reader who is well-conversant with the important features of C: pointers, strings, arrays, and structures.

The author strongly believes in the notion that, in addition to the syntax, it is essential to also show a programming language through its applications to fully establish its beauty and power. Teaching a programming language divorced from its applications – not uncommon in many educational programs – would be like teaching English through just its grammar.

This book grew out of an attempt to meet a specific academic need for a comprehensive educational program in object-oriented programming. We wanted a program that would not be too indoctrinating with regard to any one style (or any one language, since language often dictates style) of object-oriented programming. While programming skill could have been taught by focusing on a single language, education in its larger sense demanded that we provide a broader menu of styles and concepts. The result was what the reader sees in this book: An integrated presentation of C++ and Java. There is educational value in comparing and contrasting the two languages, from basic language constructs to how the languages are used in application-level programming. Such comparisons may even inspire an enterprising student to think of new and more powerful object-oriented languages of the future. To further enhance the educational value of this comparative approach, this book also includes treatment of simulated object-orientation in plain C, with GNOME/GTK+ presented as a major example of this approach.

This book is based on the philosophy that learning by comparison is very efficient and can be a lot of fun. Sometimes we find it easier to remember and learn things if we can anchor our memory and comprehension in interesting differences and similarities between supposedly similar objects, structures, and situations. Learning C++ and Java together can exploit this aspect of human cognition. Students find it interesting to compare C++ and Java programming constructs for doing the same thing.

Teaching and learning C++ and Java together have some unique advantages. First, because both C++ and Java were born out of C, they have much in common at the level of basic language structures. Teaching these structures together saves time. For example, once the concept of a vector in C++ is made clear and some of the more useful functions associated with C++ vectors are elucidated, the discussion of the Java ArrayList takes hardly any time. The Java discussion consists mostly of pointing out the Java functions that do the same thing as the previously discussed C++ functions.

Then there is also the unique process of learning by coding up a program in C++ that does the same thing as a given program in Java, or vice versa. My experience is that this approach enables the students to tackle more difficult projects in both C++ and Java than would otherwise be the case under the time constraints of a course.

Learning two large languages together does have its down side. One can get confused as to what feature belongs to which language. Fortunately, this difficulty is minimized by the modern programming practice of keeping one eye on the on-line documentation in one terminal window while programming in another terminal window. Both Java and C++ have become so large that it would be impossible for anyone to commit to memory all of the classes and all of the functions and attributes defined for the classes. So even if one were not learning two languages simultaneously, one would still need to refer to documentation while writing programs.

The book contains more material than can be accommodated in a typical one-semester course. In my experience, the book works well for a sequence of two back-to-back courses, the first focusing on the basic language constructs as presented in the first fifteen chapters, and the second focusing on application- and design-level issues. For the second course, I complement the material in the last five chapters with a book on design patterns.

It would be naive of me to assume that a manuscript as large as this would be free of errors. I'd be much grateful to the readers who would bring the errors to my attention at kak@purdue.edu. All corrections will be made available online at www.programming-with-objects.com, and the authors of the corrections will be duly acknowledged. The same applies to any slip-ups on my part in giving proper attributions to authors. Where my example programs were inspired directly by what I saw in other sources, I have acknowledged their authors in the "Credits and Suggestions for Further Reading" section at the end of each chapter.

The author will be glad to make available to the prospective instructors the solutions to the homework problems.

Finally, the book should also be useful to those who are transitioning from C++ to Java, or vice versa.

AVINASH C. KAK

West Lafayette, Indiana
January, 2003

Acknowledgments

Whatever merit this book has should go in large measure to the stalwarts of the object-oriented programming movement, to those who created C++ and Java, and to those who have been the chief expositors of these two languages over the last several years (see the references at the end of the book).

This book would not have been possible without the help of the following people:

- Guilherme DeSouza, a man with insights that are as deep as they are broad and for whom Linux is a religion to which he has converted many, this author included. Guilherme's insights in multiprocessing and multithreading played an important role in the revamping of Chapter 18.

- Elvia Suryadi, who can spot from a mile the slightest flaw in a logical argument, the minutest weakness in an explanation. Her constant feedback helped with the cleanup of many sections of the book, too numerous to be listed here individually. The homework problems in Chapters 13 and 20 are by Elvia.

- Malcolm Slaney, with an uncanny eye for rigor and precision, for providing critical feedback on the first five chapters.

- Carl Crawford, never a man to mince words, who insisted that my earlier version of the front matter did not do justice to the rest of the book.

- Susan Gottschlich, with deep insights in the software development cycles of industry, for her careful reading and feedback of the first 11 chapters.

- Robert Cromwell, who has always had his ear to the ground for the latest happenings in the world of software and hardware, for looking carefully at the C-related material in the book and suggesting improvements.

- Sarah Sellke, with many years of object-oriented software design and development experience for telecom and other applications, for her feedback on Chapter 19.

- Christina Pavlopoulou, as a source of great help in the early stages of my putting together this book.

- Prathima Venkatesan, who proofread and caught many errors in the draft copies of Chapters 4, 5, 6, and 7.

- Bob Mulvey, for helping me better understand the various shortcomings associated with the use of `setjmp`–`longjmp` macros for achieving multilevel return in C.

- Brett Maden, for creating the final versions of the figures in Chapters 15 and 17. He also contributed to the homework section of Chapter 17; the Qt and GNOME/GTK+ problems were supplied by him.

- Kheng Tan, for many of the final production figures for Chapters 14 and 16. Kheng also supplied the problems for the homework section of Chapter 14.

Thanks also go to the anonymous reviewers of the book; many of the comments I received through the review process helped in the revision of much material. Of the publisher reviews received nonanonymously, I wish to thank Simon Gray in particular for catching many errors in Chapter 2, 8, 10, 14, and 19 and suggesting improvements.

Many additional sources of help and information that proved important to the writing of this book are acknowledged near the end of each chapter in a section entitled "Credits and Suggestions for Further Reading," or sometimes just "Suggestions for Further Reading." Occasionally, I have also used a footnote for the same purpose.

I am also grateful to Subhash Kak, whose powers of exposition border on the lyrical, for his many wonderful suggestions for smoothing out the text at various places.

Finally, and most importantly, many thanks go to Carla for her loving friendship, support, and understanding, all things that give true meaning to life. Thanks also go to Carla for her direct contributions to the book by way of critical reading of its various sections.

A.C.K.

PROGRAMMING
WITH OBJECTS

1

Why OO Programming – Some Parallels with Things at Large

What is object-oriented programming?

Although the answer to this question will reveal itself as you work your way through this book, at this juncture it might be useful to draw parallels between object-oriented programming (OO) and the world around us. You are unlikely to dispute the assertion that during the last half century the following facts about societies have become amply clear: Societies function best when centralized control is kept to a minimum; when the intelligence needed for the smooth functioning of a society is as distributed as possible; when each person is sufficiently smart to know for himself or herself how to make sense of the various norms and mores of the society for the common good; and when the higher-level organizational structures, often organized in the form of hierarchies, facilitate the propagation of society-nurturing messages up and down the hierarchies.

Large object-oriented programs are no different. The idea is to think of large software (sometimes consisting of millions of lines of code) as consisting of a society of objects: objects that possess sufficient intelligence to interpret messages received from other objects and to then respond with appropriate behavior; objects that inherit properties and behaviors from higher-level objects and permit lower-level objects to inherit properties and behaviors from them; and so on. Just as decentralization of human organizations makes it easier to extend and maintain the various societal structures (because the intelligence needed for such maintenance and extension resides locally in the structures), a decentralized organization of software allows it to be extended and maintained more easily. If as a programmer you are not happy with the objects supplied to you by a software vendor, in most cases you'd be able to extend those objects with relative ease and customize them to your particular needs. And if any problems developed in one of the components of a large decentralized organization of objects, your troubleshooting would be easier because of its localized nature – this would apply as much to a society of people as it would to a society of software objects.

A discourse concerning societies is made more efficient if we group together all those objects that share common characteristics. We could then refer to such groups as classes. For example, all people engaged in the delivery of healthcare have to have certain common professional attributes. We could say that these common attributes define the class *health-care professional*. All medical doctors — the class *medical doctor* being a subclass of the class *health-care professional* — must possess the attributes of all health-care professionals; they must also possess additional attributes by way of specialized education and training.

This analogy carries over directly to software design based on objects. All objects that possess the same attributes and exhibit the same behaviors are grouped into a single class. In fact, we first define a class and then create individual objects by a process known as *instantiating a class*. All objects that possess the attributes and behaviors of a previously defined class, possessing at the same time additional more-specialized attributes and behaviors, are represented as a subclass of the previously defined class.

What good does OO do?

Over the years, object-oriented programming has become the preferred style of programming for graphical user interfaces (GUI) — so much so that even when using languages that do not directly support object orientation (such as C), programmers create software structures that simulate OO for GUI programming. Probably the most famous example of this is the GNOME/GTK+ toolkit for GUI design; it's all in C, yet it is "very OO" in its programming style and structuring. For purposes of comparative presentation, we discuss GNOME/GTK+ in Chapter 17 on GUI programming, where the main focus is, of course, on C++ and Java. OO is also making strong inroads into database and network programming.

How do I master it?

It takes a three-pronged strategy to master the OO paradigm for solving actual problems involving large and complex systems. You must, of course, learn the syntax specific to the languages. Clearly, without a working level familiarity with all the major constructs of a language, you may not be able to bring to bear the most effective tools on a problem. This, however, does not mean that you must memorize all of the syntax. For example, it would be impossible to commit to memory all of the different Java classes and the attributes and the functions associated with each of the classes. Fortunately, it is not necessary to do so in this age of web-based documentation. A standard approach to Java programming is to display in one window the extremely well-organized on-line Java documentation while you are constructing your own program in another window.

In addition to the syntax, you must master for each language the concepts of encapsulation, inheritance, and polymorphism, as these three concepts form the cornerstones of a truly OO language. How each concept works varies in subtle ways from language to language. For example, C++ permits multiple inheritance which gives a programmer certain freedoms, but with an increased risk of writing buggy code. On the other hand, Java forbids multiple inheritance in the sense permitted by C++, but allows for a class to inherit from any number of *interfaces*. Similarly, the *access modifiers* that allow you to encapsulate information in a class with different levels of access work slightly differently in C++ and Java. Additionally, Java has the concept of a `package` that has a bearing on access control – a concept that does not exist in C++. Polymorphism allows a subclass type to be treated like a superclass type. Although it works essentially the same in all major OO languages, the manner in which it is invoked can place important constraints on programming. In C++, for example, polymorphism can only be invoked through pointers, a fact that can have a large bearing on how you might refer to an object in a program.

The last of the three-pronged strategy deals with learning OO design. As with all design activity, there is a certain mystique associated with it. This is not surprising, because it would be impossible to enunciate the design principles that would span all possible problems, those already solved and those yet to be solved. Much of learning how to design an OO solution to a large and complex problem is a matter of experience, aided perhaps by examining good OO code written by other people. Nonetheless, the accumulated wisdom over the years now dictates the following approach to the development of expertise in OO design: (1) mastering a "meta" language, such as the Unified Modeling Language (UML), that allows you to express your design visually at a conceptual level; and (2) learning the *design patterns*, these being template solutions to a host of subproblems likely to be encountered during the evolution of an OO program. This book contains an abbreviated introduction to UML in Chapter 14. Regarding design patterns, there is no specific chapter devoted to it, although the example code presented includes the implementation of some of the patterns. For a reader wanting to pursue more deeply both UML and the topic of design patterns, there are excellent books available on both [7, 13, 20, 21].

2

Baby Steps

The main goal of this chapter is to help the reader make a connection between his/her C background and some of the beginning constructs in C++ and Java. This will be accomplished by comparing simple programs in C with equally simple programs in C++ and Java that do the same thing.

The author requests the reader to be indulgent when encountering unfamiliar terms in our explanations of the C++ and Java examples in this chapter. The presence of these terms — "class," "object," "exception" — will not hinder the reader in seeing parallels between the C programs and their equivalent C++ and Java programs. On the contrary, the C++ and Java programs, and their accompanying explanations, should make the reader curious about these terms, making it easier to formally introduce them in subsequent chapters. The idea is to use the easily-established conceptual parallels between the C programs and their equivalent C++ and Java programs as a pedagogical vehicle for giving the reader a first introduction to the rudiments of OO vocabulary.

A second goal of this chapter is to familiarize the reader with command-line compilation of C++ and Java programs, as well as with the *-classpath* option that sometimes must be specified for Java compilation.

2.1   SIMPLE PROGRAMS: SUMMING AN ARRAY OF INTEGERS

Let's say you want to add 10 integers that are stored in an array. A C program for doing this would look like

```
/* AddArray1.c */

#include <stdio.h>

int addArray( int [], int );

main()
{
    int data[] = {4,3,2,1,0,5,6,7,8,9};                        /* (A) */
    int size = sizeof(data)/sizeof(data[0]);                   /* (B) */
    printf("sum is %d\n", addArray( data, size ));             /* (C) */
    return 0;
}

int addArray( int a[], int n ) {                               /* (D) */
    int sum = 0;
    int i;
    for(i=0; i<n; i++ )
        sum += a[i];                                           /* (E) */
    return sum;
}
```

Line (A) of main declares an integer array data and initializes it as shown. Line (B) figures out the size of the array. The function addArray is called in line (C) to sum up all the integers in the array.

If there is anything noteworthy about this program at all, it lies in the fact that an array name in C (and also in C++) is treated like a pointer in some contexts. Whereas data is an array name when supplied as an argument to the operator sizeof in line (B), it is a pointer to the first element of the array when supplied as an argument to the function addArray in line (C).

Contrast this with the fact that the array name a in the called function addArray in line (D) is merely a pointer, in the sense that sizeof(a) computed anywhere inside the function addArray will return 4 for the four bytes it takes to store a memory address on many modern machines. On the other hand, sizeof(data) in line (B) will return 40 for the 40 bytes that it takes to store the 10 integers of the array `data`, assuming that your machine allocates 4 bytes for an `int`.[1]

So when `main` calls `addArray` in line (C), the memory address that is the value of `data` when treated as a pointer is assigned to the parameter `a` in line (D) and that the array itself is not copied. Subsequently, the function `addArray` visits each element of the array in line (E) through the memory address assigned to `a` and adds the element to the sum.

A more explicitly pointer version of the `addArray` function is shown in the following program that does the same thing:

```
/* AddArray2.c */

#include <stdio.h>

int addArray( int*, int );

main()
{
    int data[] = {4,3,2,1,0,5,6,7,8,9};
    int size = sizeof(data)/sizeof(data[0]);
    printf("Pointer Version: sum is %d\n", addArray( data, size ));
    return 0;
}

int addArray( int* a, int n ) {
    int sum = 0;
    int i;
    for(i=0; i<n; i++ )
        sum += *a++;
    return sum;
}
```

The two programs shown above are essentially identical because, as mentioned already, declaring a function parameter to be an array (the first program) is the same as declaring it to be a pointer (the second program).

Now let's consider a C++ program for doing the same thing:

---

[1]It is important to bear in mind that while an array name can "decay" into a pointer, it is not a pointer. The extent to which an array name decays into a pointer depends, among other things, on whether an array name is the name of a parameter of a callable function. So, whereas the array name `data` in `main` will act like a pointer in some contexts only, the array name `a` in the function `addArray` of the program `AddArray1.c` will act like a pointer in practically all contexts.

```
//AddArray.cc

#include <iostream>                                              //(A)
using namespace std;                                             //(B)

int addArray( int*, int );

int main()
{
    int data[] = {4,3,2,1,0,5,6,7,8,9};
    int size = sizeof(data)/sizeof(data[0]);
    cout << "C++ version: sum is "                               //(C)
        << addArray( data, size ) << endl;
    return 0;
}

int addArray( int* a, int n) {
    int sum = 0;
    int i;
    for(i=0; i<n; i++ )
        sum += *a++;
    return sum;
}
```

This program shows this book's first use of an "object" in C++. The object is cout in line (C). This is an output stream object whose name is usually pronounced "c-out" as an abbreviation for "console out." This object knows how to send information to the standard output stream, which would generally be directed to the window of the terminal screen in which you are running your program. All objects in OO programming belong to some object class. The output stream object cout belongs to the class basic_ostream that is defined in the library header file iostream included in the program in line (A)..

The header iostream is one of the many header files that constitute the C++ Standard Library.[2] This library is a culmination of the effort of the International Standards Organization (ISO) and the American National Standards Institute (ANSI) for the standardization of the C++ language. A significant portion of the C++ Standard Library includes what is informally referred to as the *Standard Template Library*

---

[2]The C++ *Standard Library* consists of these header files: algorithm, bitset, complex, deque, exception, fstream, functional, iomanip, ios, iosfwd, iostream, istream, iterator, limits, list, locale, map, memory, new, numeric, ostream, queue, set, sstream, stack, stdexcept, streambuf, string, typeinfo, utility, valarray, vector. Of these, the following are informally referred to as the *Standard Template Library* (STL): algorithm, bitset, deque, functional, iterator, list, map, queue, set, stack, valarray and vector.

(STL). STL consists of container classes for holding collections of objects and classes that play supporting roles for using the container classes. The Standard Library also includes the header file `string` that we will be using very frequently in this book for representing and processing C++ strings. Other header files in the C++ Standard Library contain classes for memory management (`new` and `memory`); representing exceptions (`exception` and `stdexcept`); representing complex numbers (`complex`); run-time type identification (`typinfo;`) and so on.

Although this point will become clearer after we have presented the idea of a *namespace* in Chapter 3, the *directive*

```
using namespace std;
```

in line (B) of the program takes account of the fact that all the identifiers (meaning the names of classes, functions, objects, etc.) used in the C++ Standard Library are defined within a special namespace known as the *standard namespace* and designated `std`. If we did not invoke this directive, we would need to call the output stream object by using the syntax `std::cout`.

The symbol '`<<`' in line (C) is called the *output operator* or the *insertion operator*. This operator, defined originally as the left bitwise shift operator, has been overloaded in C++ for inserting data into output stream objects when used in the manner shown here.[3] The '`<<`' operator does formatted insertions into an output stream object. What that means is that if the operator is asked to insert an `int` into an output stream object, it will translate the four bytes of the `int` into its printable character representation and then insert the character bytes into the output stream object.

You can comment code in C++ the way you do it in C, that's by using the delimiters `/* .... */`. You can also comment individual lines, or the trailing part of a line, by `//`. The compiler will not see on that line any characters past `//`.

Note that, as indicated by the commented out statement at the beginning of the program, Unix-like platforms require the name of a file containing the C++ source code to end in the suffix `.cc`. One can also use the suffix `.C` or the suffix `.cpp`. To compile this program, you'd say

```
g++ filename
```

The compiler will deposit an executable file called `a.out` or `a.exe` in your directory. This assumes that you are using the GNU C++ compiler. This compiler comes prepackaged with Unix and Linux distributions, although, if needed, you could download the latest version from the Free Software Foundation (*www.gnu.org*). If you are using a PC and you do not have access to a pre-loaded C++ compiler, you can download the GNU compiler (and other very useful Unix-emulation utilities for Windows)

---

[3]Operator overloading, discussed in detail in Chapter 12, allows the same operator to be used in different ways. The operands determine as to which meaning of such an operator applies in a given context.

from the site *sourceware.cygnus.com/cygwin/*. For Solaris platforms, you should also be able to use the CC compiler via the invocation

```
CC filename
```

where, again, the name of the file must end in either '.C' or '.cc' or '.cpp'. As with g++, the compiler will deposit an executable file called a.out or a.exe in your directory.

For another point of difference — a difference regarding style — between the C programs we showed at the beginning of this section and the C++ program above is in the header of main. The main in both C and C++ programs returns a status code, which is 0 if the program terminates normally and a nonzero integer to indicate abnormal termination. By tradition, the return type of main in C programs is left unmentioned — it being int by default. On the other hand, C++ requires a program to explicitly mention the return type int of main.

Now let's see how one would write a Java program for doing the same thing:

```
//AddArray.java

public class AddArray {                                   //(A)

    public static void main( String[] args )              //(B)
    {
        int[] data = { 0, 1, 2, 3, 4, 5, 9, 8, 7, 6 };    //(C)
        System.out.println( "The sum is: "                //(D)
                                    + addArray(data) );
    }

    public static int addArray( int[] a ) {               //(E)
        int sum = 0;
        for ( int i=0; i < a.length; i++ )
            sum += a[i];
        return sum;
    }
}
```

As shown in the commented out line at the beginning of the program, this source code resides in a file called

```
AddArray.java
```

The program begins with a class declaration:

```
public class AddArray {
    ....
    ....
```

In Java, functions can exist only inside classes. So even though using a class for the simple task for which we are writing the program seems rather excessive, there is no choice.

Note that the name of the file before the suffix java is the same as the class name, AddArray. Ordinarily, this is necessary only if a class is declared to be public. A file containing Java classes is allowed to have no more than one public class. If no classes in a file are public, the file can be given any name, but, of course, it must end in the suffix .java. To compile this file, you invoke the Java compiler by

```
javac AddArray.java
```

The compiler outputs what's known as the *bytecode* for the class and, in this case, deposits it in a file called

```
AddArray.class
```

This bytecode is machine-independent, unlike the executables for C or C++ programs, and can be run by another program called the *Java Virtual Machine* (JVM). A JVM will execute the program either in the interpreted mode or by first converting the bytecode into a machine-dependent executable using a second round of what is known as *just-in-time* (JIT) compilation and then executing the binaries thus obtained. The latter is the default mode and results in a tenfold increase in execution speed over the interpreted mode. For the bytecode file named AddArray.class, a Java Virtual Machine is invoked by

```
java AddArray
```

Before you can compile and run a Java program, you may have to tell the system how to find the classes you created with your program. The default is your current directory. But if you wanted to compile a class that was stored in some other directory, you have to tell both javac and java tools how to locate the class. The preferred way to do this is by using the *-classpath* option when invoking the javac compiler or the java application launcher. The *-classpath* option is also needed even if you are trying to compile a Java program in the directory in which it resides if your program uses other Java classes, your own or written by a third party, that reside in other directories.[4]

Suppose your program uses third-party classes that are stored in directories *directory_1* and *directory_2*,[5] you'd want to invoke javac and java with the following syntax on Unix and Linux platforms:

```
javac -classpath .:directory_1:directory_2  sourceCode.java

java  -classpath .:directory_1:directory_2  className
```

---

[4]You do not need to specify the classpath for the classes that come with the Java platform. Both the compiler and the application launcher can locate those automatically.

[5]By directory name here is meant the pathname to the directory.

and on Windows platforms by[6]

```
javac -classpath .;directory_1;directory_2  source.java

java  -classpath .;directory_1;directory_2  className
```

where the symbol '.' is used to designate the current directory where presumably the main application resides. Note that the delimiter between the directories for Unix and Linux platforms is the character ':' and for the Windows platform the character ';'. The third-party classes, or, for that matter, even your previously programmed classes may come packaged in the form of an archive called the JAR archive.[7] If that's the case, you'd need to specify the pathname to such archives in your classpath specification, as for example in

```
javac -classpath .:/path_to_archive/archive.jar  your_program.java

java -classpath .:/path_to_archive/archive.jar  your_class_name
```

If the classpath strings become too long, you can create shell files containing the above invocations on Unix and Linux platforms. On Windows platforms, the same is accomplished by using batch files. On Unix and Linux platforms, it is also possible to set up aliases for the compiler and the application launcher that include the classpath string.

On Unix and Linux platforms and on some of the older Windows platforms, instead of using the classpath option as shown above, it is also possible to set the CLASSPATH environment variable. For example, if you are using either the csh or the tcsh shells, you can define a classpath by, say, including the following in a .cshrc file,

```
setenv CLASSPATH .:directory_1:directory_2:....
```

---

[6]If you are using a Cygnus emulation of Unix on Windows, you may need to place the classpath string between double quotes.

[7]A JAR file in Java is an archive file, just like a Unix *tar* (tape archive) file. Jar files are created and manipulated by using the Java *jar* tool. To create a JAR archive of all your classes, including the sources, in your current directory, you'd say

```
jar  cvf  archiveName.jar  *.class  *.java
```

To list the contents of a JAR file, you'd say

```
jar tvf archiveName.jar
```

and to unpack a jar archive, you'd say

```
jar xvf archiveName.jar
```

If you don't want to unpack the entire archive, but would like to extract a single class, you'd say

```
jar xf archiveName.jar className.java
```

or

```
jar xf archiveName.jar className.class
```

as the case may be.

which would create the same classpath setting as our earlier examples. If, on the other hand, you are using either sh, ksh, or bash, you can achieve the same effect by including the following strings in your *.profile* file:

```
CLASSPATH=.:directory_1:directory_2:....
export CLASSPATH
```

If desired, you can "unset" the value of the environmental variable by invoking *unsetenv CLASSPATH* in csh and tcsh and by invoking *unset CLASSPATH* in sh and ksh.

Even if you use the CLASSPATH environment variable, you may still have to use the *-classpath* option as shown previously to customize the classpath for a particular application. The classpath as set by the *-classpath* option overrides the classpath as set by the environmental variable. Note again the importance of including the character '.' in the CLASSPATH environment variable since, as was the case with the *-classpath* option, setting the environment variable overrides the default.

Getting to the program itself, the code that is inside the class definition is very much like the C or the C++ code we showed earlier. We have the function main() in line (B) and the method[8] addArray() inside the class definition in line (E). In Java, any class can include main(). When a class includes main(), the class becomes executable as an application. Since main() does not return anything in Java, its return type is declared as void. The significance of the labels public and static in the header for main will be explained in Chapter 3. In the body of main, we declare the identifier data as an array of ints and initialize it at the same time, very much like we did for C and C++.

The invocation System.out.println(...) in line (D) is a call to the println() method that is defined for the output stream object out. More precisely, out is a field of type OutputStream defined in the class System. System is a class that comes with the java.lang package.[9] This package is loaded in automatically by the Java compiler. println() is a method defined for the class OutputStream. One could also use the method print() via the invocation System.out.print(...) if it is not necessary to display the output in a separate line of text. The println and the print methods are as defined for the PrintStream class. The argument to these methods must either be a string or a type that Java would know how to convert into a string for display. In our example, the second part of the argument, of type int, gets converted into a string automatically.

The rest of the program consists of the method addArray() in line (E), which is very much like the C++ function of the same name in the earlier program, except for the manner in which the size of the array is determined inside the function. For both C

---

[8]All Java functions (and some C++ functions) are known as methods. The distinction between method and function in OO programming is explained in Chapter 9.

[9]The notion of a package in Java is explained in the next chapter.

and C++, the size of the array had to be passed explicitly to the function. But in Java, that is not necessary. Arrays in Java are objects that have data members[10] associated with them. The data member that is associated with an array object is `length`. When we access this data member through the call `data.length`, we can determine the length of the array `data`.

Also note from the above examples that C++ and Java have exactly the same way of commenting code. You can either use the C-style comment delimiters `/*` .... `*/` or `//`. However, the latter can only be used for comments on a single line, because the compiler will not see any characters past `//`.

With regard to comments in Java programs, a special tool called `javadoc` can automatically generate documentation for your program using text that is delimited by `/**` and `*/`. This tool generates HTML files that can be viewed with a browser.

2.2   SIMPLE PROGRAMS: TERMINAL I/O

Let's now compare simple C, C++, and Java programs for eliciting information from a user and then printing something out in response on the terminal.

Here is a C program that asks the user to type in a sequence of integers, all in one line. The integers are allowed to be anywhere in a line, not necessarily starting at the beginning, and the entry of the data is considered completed when the user presses 'Enter' on the keyboard. The program sums up all the integers and types out the sum. Therefore, if a user types in

```
####3#######56##20#1#####19########<Enter>
```

where # stands for a space, the program should print out 99. The following C program does the job.

```
/* TermIO.c */

#include <stdio.h>

main()
{
    int i;
    int sum = 0;
    char ch;

    printf("Enter a sequence of integers:   ");
```

---

[10]The concept of a `data` member of a class type object is introduced in Section 3.1.

```
    while (  scanf( "%d", &i ) == 1 ) {                    /* (A) */
        sum += i;                                          /* (B) */
        while ( ( ch = getchar() ) == ' ' )               /* (C) */
            ;
        if ( ch == '\n' ) break;
        ungetc( ch, stdin );                              /* (D) */
    }
    printf( "The sum of the integers is: %d\n", sum );
    return 0;
}
```

The integers are read in by the `scanf()` function call in line (A) and the summing of the numbers done in line (B). Lines (C) through (D) take care of the following property of `scanf`: Most conversion specifiers for this function skip over the white-space characters — meaning the tabs, the space, the newline character, and so on — before the beginning of an input item (and not after). Therefore, after consuming an integer, `scanf` will simply wait for the next integer, ignoring any blank spaces and the end of the data entry line. This creates a problem at the end of the data line when the user hits "Enter" — `scanf` will simply gobble up the newline character and wait for the next integer. The statements in lines (C) through (D) peek ahead, while consuming blank spaces, and look for the newline character in case the user has hit "Enter" on the keyboard. If the character found after all the blank spaces have been consumed does not turn out to be a newline character, we put it back in the input stream in line (D).

Here is a C++ program that does the same thing:

```
//TermIO.cc

#include <iostream>
using namespace std;

int main()
{
    int sum = 0;
    cout << "Enter a sequence of integers: ";
    int i;
    while ( cin >> i ) {                                  //(A)
        sum += i;
        while ( cin.peek() == ' ' ) cin.get();           //(B)
        if ( cin.peek() == '\n' ) break;                 //(C)
    }
    cout << "Sum of the numbers is: " << sum << endl;
    return 0;
}
```

This program uses the *input stream* object `cin` whose name is usually pronounced "c-in" for "console-in." This object is of type `istream` and it knows how to read data from a user's terminal. The expression in line (A)

```
cin >> i;
```

causes the *input operator* '`>>`', which is also known as the *extraction operator*, to extract one `int` at a time from the input stream object `cin`. As the user makes keystrokes, the corresponding characters are entered into the operating system's keyboard buffer and then, when the user hits the "Enter" key on the keyboard, the operating system transfers the contents of the keyboard buffer into the `cin` stream's internal buffer. The operator '`>>`' then extracts the needed information from this buffer. Clearly, the program will block if the user did not provide the necessary keystrokes.[11] The operator '`>>`', originally defined to be the right bitwise shift operator, has been overloaded in C++ for extracting information from input stream objects when used in the manner shown here. Because the operator has been overloaded for all the built-in data types, it can be used to extract an `int`, a `float`, a `double`, a `string`, and so on, from an input stream object.

To understand the controlling expression in line (A) of the `while` loop:

```
while ( cin >> i )
```

the expression

```
cin >> i
```

returns the input stream object itself, meaning `cin`. However, the returned `cin` will evaluate to `false` when either the end-of-file is encountered or when the extraction operator runs into an illegal value. As an example of the latter case, if you were trying to read a floating point number into an `int` variable, the extraction operator, when it runs into the decimal point, would place the input stream object in an error state and cause `cin` to evaluate to `false`.

Lines (B) and (C) deal with the fact that the default behavior of the extraction operator '`>>`' skips over the white space characters, which includes blank space, tabs, newlines, and so on. So the controlling expression in line (A) will not by itself stop the `while` loop when the user hits "Enter" after entering the desired number of integers in a line. We invoke[12] `peek()` on the object `cin` in lines (B) and (C) to ascertain the

---

[11]This is an example of *blocking* I/O. The other I/O modes are *nonblocking* and *asynchronous*. A nonblocking read will fetch the information if it is available or report immediately that the information is not available. In an asynchronous communication link, the information source puts out the information at its convenience and the consumer of the information reads the information at its convenience.

[12]In object-oriented programming, you can *invoke a function on an object* if that function is either defined for the class of the object or inherited by such a class. Since the function `peek()` is defined for the class `istream` in the header file `iostream` and since `cin` is an object of type `istream`, we can invoke `peek()` on `cin` in the manner shown.

character immediately after the most recently consumed integer. If it's a blank space, we consume it in line (B) by invoking get() on the object cin; and do the same to all the successive blank spaces until there are no more blank spaces left. If the next character is a newline, it would be trapped in line (C) and the while loop of line (A) exited. Otherwise, we continue reading the data in the next iteration of the loop.

This program also demonstrates that, unlike in C, C++ allows you to declare a variable anywhere in a program. We declared the variable i after the cout statement asking the user to enter data.[13] This feature improves the readability of large C++ programs as one can declare variables just before they are actually needed.

We will now show an equivalent Java program:

```java
//TermIO.java

import java.io.*;

class TermIO {

    static boolean newline;                             //(A)

    public static void main( String[] args ) {
        int sum = 0;
        System.out.println( "Enter a sequence of integers: " );
        while ( newline == false ) {
            String str = readString();                  //(B)
            if ( str != null ) {
                int i = Integer.parseInt( str );        //(C)
                sum += i;
            }
        }
        System.out.println( "Sum of the numbers is: " + sum );
    }

    static String readString() {                        //(D)
        String word = "";
        try {
            int ch;
            while ( ( ch = System.in.read() ) == ' ' )  //(E)
                ;
            if ( ch == '\n' ) {                         //(F)
                newline = true;                         //(G)
                return null;                            //(H)
            }
```

---

[13] As we will explain further in Chapter 7, all such local variables have *block scope*.

```
        word += (char) ch;                                      //(I)
        while ( ( ch = System.in.read() ) != ' '
                && ch != '\n' )                                 //(J)
            word += (char) ch;                                  //(K)
        if ( ch == '\n' ) newline = true;                       //(L)
    } catch( IOException e ) {}
    return word;                                                //(M)
  }
}
```

Since Java does not provide a function that can directly read an integer value into an int variable, the logic of the program is slightly more complex than that of the C and the C++ programs shown earlier. To make sense of this program, recall that the program is supposed to extract the integer values from the numbers entered by a user in a single line and the user is allowed to place any number of spaces before the first integer, between the integers, and after the last integer. In other words, we want our program to be able to extract integer numbers from the following sort of a line entered by a user:

####3#######56##20#1#####19########<Enter>

where the symbol # stands for a space. To explain the working of the program:

The program reads each integer value entered by the user as a string which is of type String, a Java class we will discuss in detail in Chapter 4. This is done by invoking the method readString() in line (B). Therefore, for the data entry line shown above, the first string read will correspond to the number 3, the second to the number 56, and so on.

If the string read in the previous step is not null, we invoke the method parseInt of the Integer class in line (C) to convert the string into its integer number value, assuming that the reader did not try to fool the system by typing nondigit characters.[14]

With regard to the readString() method, we strip off all the empty spaces before a string in the while loop in line (E). Each character is read from the user's terminal in this loop by the read() method that of the java.io.InputStream class. The standard input stream System.in is an object of type java.io.InputStream. We invoke the method read() inside a try–catch block since it throws an exception of type IOException that must either be caught or rethrown, as we will explain in Chapter 10.

If the last character read in the while loop in line (E) is the newline character, the test in line (F) causes readString to terminate with null for the returned value in

---

[14]If the user does enter nondigit characters, the method parseInt will throw a NumberFormatException. Exceptions are discussed in Chapter 10.

line (H). We also set the `newline` variable to `true` in line (G) to tell `main` that the data entry has come to an end. If the last character read in the `while` loop in line (E) is not the newline character, we then start a new word with this character in line (I).

The `while` loop that starts in line (J) keeps on adding fresh characters to the word started in line (I) as long as a new character is neither a space nor a newline. If the latest character read in the `while` loop of line (J) is a newline, we set our flag `newline` to true in line (L).

The reader is probably wondering about the qualifier `static` for the `boolean` variable `newline` in line (A) and for the header of the method `readString()` in line (D). The purpose of `static` will be explained briefly in Chapter 3 and more fully in Chapter 11.

2.3 SIMPLE PROGRAMS: FILE I/O

Let's now compare programs in C, C++, and Java for copying one file into another file. The input file may be a text file or a binary file. We will first show the C implementation. We will assume that the executable for this program would be invoked with a command line like

```
copy  sourceFile  destFile
```

where copy is the name of the file containing the executable. Here is the source code:

```
/* FileCopy.c */

#include <stdio.h>
#include <stdlib.h>

main(int argc, char* argv[])                              /* (A) */
{
    FILE *in, *out;                                       /* (B) */
    int ch;

    if ( argc != 3 ) {                                    /* (C) */
        fprintf( stderr, "usage: copy in_file out_file\n" );
        exit( EXIT_FAILURE );
    }

    if ( ( in = fopen(argv[1], "rb" ) ) == NULL ) {       /* (D) */
        fprintf( stderr, "Can't open %s\n", argv[1] );
        exit( EXIT_FAILURE );
    }
```

```
    if ( ( out = fopen(argv[2], "wb" ) ) == NULL ) {          /* (E) */
        fprintf( stderr, "Can't open %s\n", argv[2] );
        fclose( in );
        exit( EXIT_FAILURE );
    }

    while ( ( ch = getc( in ) ) != EOF )                      /* (F) */
        if ( putc( ch, out ) == EOF )                         /* (G) */
            break;

    if ( ferror( in ) )                                       /* (H) */
        printf( "Error while reading source file.\n" );
    if ( ferror( out ) )                                      /* (I) */
        printf( "Error while writing into dest file.\n" );

    fclose( in );                                             /* (J) */
    fclose( out );                                            /* (K) */
    return 0;
}
```

With the command line for invoking the executable of this program as shown previously, the parameter argc in line (A) will be set to 3 and the parameter argv will denote an array of character pointers, each pointer pointing to one of the strings in the command line. So the value stored in argv[0] will point to the string copy, the value stored in argv[1] to the string sourceFile, and the value stored in argv[2] to the string destFile.

In line (B), we declare two file pointers to serve as two I/O streams, each of type FILE*, a type declared in the header file stdio.h. We will use one of these, in, for reading the characters from a file and the other, out, for writing those same characters into another file.

Line (C) guarantees that the program will not inadvertently be called with a wrong number of command-line arguments given to copy. The macro EXIT_FAILURE is defined in the header stdlib.h with its value implementation dependent, although typically 1. The invocation of exit in the block that starts in line (C) will cause the program to terminate.

In line (D), we open the source file in the *read binary* mode.[15] The function fopen() returns a file pointer that becomes the value of in. In this line, we also ensure that the file is opened successfully by checking the value of the file pointer returned. If the file was not successfully opened, a message is sent to the standard

---

[15]The undesirable consequences of reading a binary file in character mode are discussed in Section 6.8.3.

error stream `stderr`. The block of code that begins in line (E) does the same for the destination file.

The actual job of copying from the source file to the destination file is done by the statements in lines (F) and (G). The `getc()` function gets one character at a time from the input stream, and the `putc()` function deposits the character into the output stream. If `getc()` returns EOF, it could be either because the end of file was reached, or because an error occurred during the process of reading the input stream.[16] Note also that we read what's returned by `getc()` into an `int`, since `ch` is of that type, and not into a `char`. This is to enable the detection of the EOF condition.

To make sure that if either the `getc()` or the `putc()` function returns EOF, it is not because of an error condition encountered, we test the error indicators associated with the two streams in lines (H) and (I). Finally, we close the streams in lines (J) and (K).

Shown below is a C++ program for doing the same thing – copying one file into another:

```
//FileCopy.cc

#include <fstream>                                        //(A)
#include <cstdlib>
using namespace std;                                      //(B)

void print_error(const char*, const char* = " ");        //(C)

int main(int argc, char* argv[])                          //(D)
{
    if (3 != argc)
        print_error("usage: copy source dest");

    ifstream in( argv[1], ios::binary );                  //(E)
    if (!in)
        print_error( "can't open", argv[1] );

    ofstream out( argv[2], ios::binary );                 //(F)
    if (!out)
        print_error( "can't open", argv[2] );

    char ch;                                              //(G)
    while ( in.get(ch) )                                  //(H)
        out.put( ch );                                    //(I)
```

---

[16]To refresh the memory of the reader, EOF, a macro defined in the header file `<stdio.h>`, is a negative integer constant, usually −1.

```
    if ( !in.eof() )                                          //(J)
        print_error("something strange happened");
    return 0;
}

void print_error(const char* p, const char* p2) {             //(K)
    cerr << p << ' ' << p2 << '\n';                           //(L)
    exit(1);                                                  //(M)
}
```

In line (A), we include the header file fstream.[17] This file includes the classes ifstream and ofstream that are needed for setting up the input and the output streams. The using directive in line (B) takes care of the fact that the identifiers used in the header fstream are defined in the namespace std.[18]

Line (C) declares the function prototype for the print_error function. This function has a default argument for its second parameter, the default argument being the empty string.[19]

The header of main() in line (D) is the same as the header of the C program shown before. Then, after we make sure that the program is called with the correct number of command line arguments, in line (E) we create an input stream by making an object named in of class ifstream. The file name associated with this object is the string pointed to by the pointer argv[1]. The object in will evaluate to false if the file cannot be opened for some reason. Similarly, in line (F) we construct an output stream object named out for the destination file in a manner similar to what was done for the input stream object.[20]

The actual file-to-file copy takes place in lines (H) and (I). In line (G), the function get() returns the iostream stream object on which the function is invoked, unless it has reached the end of the file, in which case the invocation get returns false.[21]

---

[17]The fstream header file includes the iostream header file. See Chapter 6 for the C++ iostream library.

[18]Namespaces are discussed in Chapter 3.

[19]The *default arguments* feature of C++ will be discussed in Chapter 9. Suffice it here to say that we have the choice of calling the function print_error() with only one argument. That argument will become the value of the first parameter. The second parameter in such a case will be set to an empty string.

[20]The classes ifstream and ofstream are subclasses of the class iostream. They inherit all the public attributes of the parent class iostream and in addition have their own specialized attributes for file I/O. See Chapter 6 for a treatment of the C++ iostream library.

[21]An alternative would be to use the following invocation in line (G):

```
    int ch = in.get();
```

since at the end of the file the function get() returns EOF that is defined in the header file iostream to be -1. Chapter 6 presents further details.

Line (J) checks the state of the input stream object. The function eof() will return true if the stream to which it is applied has encountered the end of file. So, if the flow of control has reached line (J) without the input stream having reached the end of the file, !eof() will return true and the error message in line (K) will be printed out on the standard terminal.

That leaves us with the definition of the print_error() function in line (K). The only thing new here is the cerr object in line (L) for printing out the error messages on the user's terminal. While the object cout introduced in the previous section defines the *standard output* stream, the object cerr defines the *standard error* stream. Most shells allow the standard output and the standard error streams to be redirected independently. You could, for example, redirect the standard output into a file or a pipe while the standard error keeps on going to the user's terminal or into some log file. The invocation of exit() in line (M) causes immediate program termination with its argument as the value that is returned by the program to the operating system. A value of 0 means that the program finished successfully without encountering any error conditions.[22]

The reader will note that, unlike in the C program, we did not explicitly close the streams. In C++, as the streams go out of scope, their destructors are invoked; the destructors automatically close the streams. However, there do arise situations when we may need to explicitly close a stream. This can be done by invoking the function close() on the stream. For example, if we wanted to close the in input stream, we would say

```
in.close();
```

We will now show a Java program that does the same thing:

```
//FileCopy.java

import java.io.*;                              //(A)

class FileCopy {                               //(B)

    public static void main( String[] args )   //(C)
    {
        int ch = 0;
        FileInputStream in = null;             //(D)
```

---

[22]The execution of a C++ program can also be terminated immediately by calling abort(). The advantage of exit() is that it can close any open output streams and invoke the destructors for any constructed static objects before actually terminating the program. As we will see in Chapter 10, the execution of a program can also be terminated by throwing an exception that is not caught by the program. For large and complex OO programs, throwing an exception is the way to go if immediate termination of program execution is needed. The reasons for this will become clear after the reader has gone through Chapter 10.

```
        FileOutputStream out = null;                                //(E)

        if ( args.length != 2 ) {                                   //(F)
            System.err.println( "usage: java FileCopy source dest" );
            System.exit( 0 );
        }
        try {
            in = new FileInputStream( args[0] );                    //(G)
            out = new FileOutputStream( args[1] );                  //(H)

            while ( true ) {
                ch = in.read();                                     //(I)
                if (ch == -1) break;
                out.write(ch);                                      //(J)
            }
            out.close();                                            //(K)
            in.close();                                             //(L)
        } catch (IOException e) {
            System.out.println( "IO error" );
        }
    }
}
```

In line (A), we import the package java.io because it contains the classes we need to create the input and output streams. Since a function in Java can reside only inside classes, in line (B) we define a class FileCopy inside which we will write the file copying function. The syntax in line (C) is the same as for the main() function in Java shown before, except that now the parameter args will actually be bound to an array of Strings corresponding to our command line arguments. We will use the following command line invocation of this program:

```
java fileIODemo sourceFile destinationFile
```

With this command line invocation, args[0] will be bound to the String sourceFile and args[1] to destFile.

With the declarations in lines (D) and (E), in can be used as an input stream and out as an output stream. The input and the output streams are bound to the respective files in lines (G) and (H). The function read() associated with the class FileInputStream reads one byte at a time in line (I). And the function write() writes that byte into the output stream in line (J). In between, we check whether or not the input stream has encountered the end of the source file. Finally, we close the two streams in lines (K) and (L).

In the program shown, setting up of the input and output streams and reading the input stream and writing to the output stream have all been carried out inside a try–catch block. This is necessitated by the fact that these Java methods are capable of throwing an exception of type `IOException` if something were to go awry during their execution. In Java, if an invoked function is capable of throwing an exception, then that exception must either be caught with a `catch` block or the calling function must rethrow the exception. [23]

2.4 SUGGESTIONS FOR FURTHER READING

For a reader needing a more thorough review of pointers and arrays in C, the book by King [45] is highly recommended. In flavor and style, the C related discussion in this chapter follows closely the explanations provided by King.

The basic reference for C++ is the book by the creator of the language, Stroustrup [54]. The C++ operators and functions used in this chapter are presented in detail in Chapters 6 and 10 of this book. The reader is also referred to [54, pp. 605–656] and [50, pp. 1063–1121] for this material. For a very readable and helpful source of information related to the C++ Standard Library, the reader is referred to the book by Josuttis [42]. Helpful online sources for the same are Brokken's C++ Annotations [10], Rogue Wave *Standard C++ Library User Guide and Tutorial* [38], and the *Standard C++ Library Class Reference* [37].

The basic references for Java are the books coauthored by the creator of the language, Gosling [2, 23], and the voluminous online information at the `java.sun.com` site [24, 33]. The specific Java language constructs used in this chapter are presented further in Chapters 6 and 10 of this book. The reader is also referred to [26, pp. 1–71].

2.5 HOMEWORK

1. The following code fragment is legal in C++, but not so in C. Why? What would it take to make the code legal in C? Also, what's the value of the variable y?

```
double x[10] = {5.1, 7.3};
x[0] = 3.12;
*x = 4.13;
double y;
y = x[0];
```

---

[23]As we will explain in Chapter 10, this requirement applies strictly to what are known as *checked* exceptions.

2. Write programs in C++ and Java for reading just one integer, just one string, and just one double from the console.

3. Write programs in C++ and Java for finding the maximum of an array of `ints`. Your C++ program should use the object `cout` and the operator '`<<`' for displaying the result. Your Java program should use the `System.out.println` method for doing the same.

4. Write programs in C++ and Java that read a text file containing 100 or fewer words and store all the words read into an array of strings.

   Suggestions for the C++ solution:

   (a) You can declare an array of string pointers by

   ```
   const int N = 100;
   string* wordList[ N ]
   ```

   Each word read from the text file can be stored in the form of a `string` and a pointer to the string deposited in the array `wordList`.

   (b) Create an input stream for reading words from the file by something like

   ```
   ifstream readFromFile( sourceFile );
   ```

   Now you can read one word at a time by

   ```
   string buffer;
   readFromFile >> buffer
   ```

   A pointer to this word can then be deposited in the array by

   ```
   wordList[ i ] = new string( buffer );
   ```

   Suggestions for the Java solution:

   (a) Be prepared to browse the on-line Java documentation at `java.sun.com` as you go through the rest of the suggestions here.

   (b) The author recommends that you read all the characters in the text file into one single string and then break the string into individual words using a `StringTokenizer` class.

   (c) You can use the `while` loop shown below to read the file one character at a time into one long string called `allChars`:

   ```
   String allChars = "";
   int ch;
   ```

```
Reader in = new FileReader( fileName );
while ( -1 != ( ch = in.read() ) )
    allChars += (char) ch;
```

Check out the on-line documentation on the class FileReader in the java.io package. As the documentation says, it is a convenient class for reading character files. Its read() method reads one character at a time into an int. The value read can be compared against −1 to test for the end-of-file condition. For reasons that will be explained in Chapter 6, you must cast the value to char before appending it to allChars.

(d) Now use the StringTokenizer class to break allChars into the individual words. The on-line documentation presents a simple example illustrating how to use this class. We have used same logic in the following code fragment. By invoking hasMoreTokens() and nextToken() alternately on the StringTokenizer object, you can extract all the words from the allChars string.

```
String[] wordList = new String[100];
StringTokenizer st = new StringTokenizer( allChars );
int i = 0;
while ( st.hasMoreTokens() )
    wordList[i++] = st.nextToken();
```

(e) As was the case with the Java code in this chapter, the I/O functions above throw exceptions. So you must invoke them inside try–catch blocks. For the same pattern as used in the chapter examples.

3

The Notion of a Class and Some Other Key Ideas

Every branch of knowledge has its special words and phrases that capture the essence of that knowledge. The following words/phrases represent the concepts that are most central to OO programming:

- Class

- Encapsulation

- Inheritance

- Polymorphism

Objects in object-oriented programming (OO) are made from classes. At a high level of conceptualization, a class can be thought of as a category or a type. We may think of "Cat" as a class. A specific cat would then be an *object* or an *instance* of this class. At the level of programming, a class is a data structure with *data members* for representing the various properties of the different object instances of the class, and with *member functions* for representing the *behavior* of the class. For example, the class Cat could be given the following definition:

```
class Cat {
    string name;
    double weight;
    // other data members
```

```
void meow() {
   // code for sounding out a meow
}

void purr() {
   // code for sounding out a purr
}

// code that would allow a specific
// cat to be instantiated from this class,
// etc.
}
```

In this definition, name and weight are the data members of the class Cat, and meow() and purr() its member functions. The data members of a class are also known as the *fields* of the class and the member functions as *methods*.[1]

So the concept of a class essentially helps us pull together the various properties and behaviors important to a certain category of objects.

In object-oriented programming, there often arises a need to "hide" some of the implementation detail of a class and to also control access to some of the data members and the member functions of a class. If direct access to a data member or a member function has the potential of putting an object in an undesirable or an erroneous state, then obviously you would not allow direct access to such data members and member functions. If the implementation code for meow() for a Cat object requires that we define another function regulateExhale(), we probably would not want other objects in a program to access regulateExhale() directly. Before invoking regulateExhale(), the function meow() probably has to place the cat in a state where it has inhaled. An outsider having an unfettered access to regulateExhale() could cause the cat to exhale on an empty lung.

Hiding, or controlling the access, of the implementation-related data members and member functions of an object is called *encapsulation*. With appropriate data encapsulation, each object will present a well-defined public interface for its clients (the users of the object). A client would only be able to access those data members and invoke those members functions that are in the public interface.

The other two concepts, polymorphism and inheritance, rely on us being able to establish a hierarchy of classes for the different objects needed by a program. To illustrate the notion of a *hierarchy* of classes, let's start with the class Animal which stands for what it means. This class can be extended into a more specialized class FourLegged representing just the four-legged animals. The class Animal could also be extended to a more specialized class TwoLegged. When a class A is extended to

---

[1] Strictly speaking, a member function can be called a method only under certain conditions having to do with polymorphism. The distinction will be clarified in Chapters 9 and 15.

create a class B, we say that class B is a *subclass* of class A and that A is a *superclass* of B. We can also say that class A is the *base class* and class B the *derived class*.

A set of classes related through such superclass–subclass relationships forms a *hierarchy*, as illustrated by the example in Figure 3.1. In particular, a class hierarchy

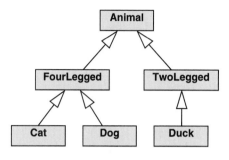

Fig. 3.1

formed in the manner shown in the figure is an *IsA hierarchy*, in the sense every Cat IsA FourLegged, every Dog IsA FourLegged, every FourLegged IsAn Animal, and so on.

Inheritance in object-oriented programming allows a subclass to inherit some or all of the data members and functions of its superclass(es). This is one of the most important reasons for why object-oriented code is more easily extensible than other kinds of code. If a vendor-supplied class does not fit the bill exactly, you can extend it by creating a subclass that would inherit the properties and the behavior of the vendor-supplied class and then you can add to it additional properties and behaviors as needed.

That brings us to the notion of polymorphism. Polymorphism basically means that a given category of objects can exhibit multiple identities at the same time, in the sense that a Cat object is not only of type Cat, but also of types FourLegged and Animal, all at the same time. What does that gain us? Since every Cat is a FourLegged and every FourLegged is an Animal, it should be possible to "manipulate" the Cat objects through the functions defined for the Animal class. As an example of what we mean by manipulation here, suppose we have a function calculateIQ() defined for all of the classes in the animal hierarchy shown above. Obviously, the actual implementation of calculateIQ() for a Cat would be very different from its implementation for a Dog or a Duck. So, presumably, all we can do is to declare calculateIQ() for the root Animal class, have each subclass inherit the function declaration from the root class, and, if at all possible, provide its own implementation. We will also make sure that calculateIQ() is accessible to the users of the animal hierarchy of classes.[2]

---

[2]This would allow us to say that calculateIQ() is a part of the *public interface* of the class hierarchy.

Now let's make an array of animals as follows:

```
Animal[] animals = {kitty, fido, tabby, quacker, spot};
```

where `kitty` and `tabby` are `Cat` objects, `fido` and `spot` `Dog` objects, and `quacker` a `Duck` object. So even though the objects in the array are of different actual types, we want to be able to invoke those functions on them that are defined for the `Animal` class since all the objects are after all of type `Animal` also. Polymorphism lets us do exactly that. It lets us treat `kitty` as a `Cat`, as a `FourLegged`, and as an `Animal`, all at the same time. Thus, through polymorphism, we can write object-oriented code like

```
int i;
for ( i = 0; i < animals.length; i++ )
    animals[i].calculateIQ();
```

Polymorphism would cause the correct implementation code for `calculateIQ()` to be automatically invoked for each of the animals. The function invoked for `kitty` would be the `calculateIQ()` defined for the `Cat` class, for `fido` the same function but defined for the `Dog` class, and so on.

So, in a nutshell, polymorphism allows us to manipulate objects belonging to the different classes of a hierarchy through a common interface defined for a root class. Polymorphism allows for different definitions for functions of the same name to reside in different class and for automatic invocation of object-specific definitions of such functions at run time. This, as we will see later, can lead to great efficiencies in programming.

It is time for the reader to become acquainted more formally with what's meant by a class in C++ and Java. At this time, our explanations and examples will be elementary, their primary role being to facilitate introduction of other ideas in the chapters that immediately follow this one. Later in the book, after we have gone through many other associated ideas, we will revisit the concept of a class in Chapter 11 and provide richer examples there.

3.1 DEFINING A CLASS IN C++

Here is a simple example of a C++ class:

```
class User {
    string name;
    int age;
};
```

We have defined the class `User` with two variables, `name` and `age`. As mentioned before, these are usually referred to as *members*, *data members*, or *fields*. The former is of type `string` and the latter of type `int`. Note that a C++ class needs a semicolon at the end to terminate the definition.

The reader who is not already familiar with the system-supplied classes in C++ is probably perplexed by the type `string`. An introduction to the C++ `string` type will be provided in the next chapter. All we want to say here is that while in C a string of characters is represented by a null-terminated array of `char`'s, as in

```
char str[] = "hello";
```

or by a pointer to type `char`, as in

```
char* str = "hello";
```

where the right hand side is a string literal, it is more common in C++ to use the `string` type. Of course, one also has the option of using the C-style strings in C++, but these don't come with the same protections as the `string` type, as we will see in the next chapter.

A class defines a new type. It may be system supplied, or can be programmer defined. With the `User` class defined as above, we are allowed to declare variables of type `User`. For example, we could declare the name u to be a variable of type `User` by

```
User u;
```

just as you might declare the name i to be a variable of type `int` by

```
int i;
```

or the name ch to be a variable of type `char` by

```
char ch;
```

One is immediately faced with the following question for a user-defined class: How does one initialize variables of such types? How would one initialize the variable u for a `User` whose name is "Zaphod" and whose age is 119? What we really want to do is to create a specific object of type `User` whose `name` member is set to Zaphod and whose `age` member is set to 119. An object is constructed by instantiating a class with the help of a class *constructor*. A constructor sets aside a part of the memory for the object that one wants to create and sets the various members of the object according to the arguments supplied to the constructor. If the arguments for some or all of the data members are not supplied, the constructor may use default values.

Here is a more useful definition of the `User` class with a constructor included:

```
class User {
    string name;
    int age;
public:
    User( string str, int yy ) { name = str;   age = yy; }
};
```

The use of the keyword `public` as shown places the constructor in the public section of the class. (The data members `name` and `age` are implicitly in the private section of the class.) This, as further explained in Section 3.11, allows the rest of your program to create objects of type `User`. Also note that there is no return type specified for the constructor. That's because a constructor is really not a function; its job is to appropriate the memory needed and build an object therein.

Now that we have available to us a constructor for the class `User`, we can create objects of this type by invoking one of the following forms in C++

```
User u( "Zaphod", 119 );                                    //(A)
```

```
User* p = new User( "Zaphod", 119 );                        //(B)
```

The constructor invocation in line (A), in the form of a declaration/initialization for the variable u, allocates memory for the new object on the stack. This memory gets freed up automatically when the variable u goes out of scope. In the constructor invocation in line (B), the operator `new` allocates fresh memory for the object on the heap and then returns a pointer to this memory. This memory can only be freed up under program control by explicit invocation of the `delete` operator, as in line (C) below:

```
User* p = new User( "Zaphod", 119 );
delete p;                                                   //(C)
```

When invoked on a pointer to a class-type object, the `delete` operator invokes the class's destructor. We will have more to say about destructors in Section 3.8 of this chapter and in Chapter 11.

Since we would also want to see the objects we create, let's include in the class definition a print function:

```
class User {
    string name;
    int age;
public:
    User( string str, int yy ) { name = str;   age = yy; }

    void print() {                                          //(D)
        cout << "name: " << name << " age: " << age << endl;  //(E)
    }
};
```

In Section 2.1 of the previous chapter, we briefly discussed the purpose served by the insertion operator '<<' and by the output stream object `cout` used in line (E).

A member function, such as `print()` in line (D) above, is *invoked on* a specific object. The syntax of this invocation depends on whether the function is invoked directly on an object or on a pointer to an object, as shown in the following two examples:

```
    User u( "Zaphod", 119 );
    u.print();                      // name: Zaphod    age: 119           //(F)

    User* p = new User( "Zaphod", 119 );
    p->print();                     // name: Zaphod    age: 119           //(G)
```

where '.' in line (F) and '->' in line (G) are known as the *member access operators*.

Here is a working C++ program that uses the class definition provided above:

```
//User1.cc

#include <iostream>
#include <string>
using namespace std;

class User {
    string name;
    int age;
public:
    User( string str, int yy ) { name = str;   age = yy; }

    void print() {
        cout << "name: " << name << "   age: "   << age << endl;
    }
};

int main()
{
    User u( "Zaphod", 119 );
    u.print();
    return 0;
}
```

C++ allows the implementation code for a class to reside outside the definition of the class itself. Shown below is the same program as above, but with the constructor and the print function definition outside the class definition:

```
//User2.cc

#include <iostream>
#include <string>
using namespace std;

class User {
```

```
    string name;
    int age;
public:
    User( string str, int yy );                                  //(H)
    void print();                                                //(I)
};

User::User( string str, int yy ) {                               //(J)
    name = str;  age = yy;
}

void User::print() {                                             //(K)
    cout << "name: " << name  << "  age: "  << age << endl;
}

int main()
{
    User u( "Zaphod", 119 );
    u.print();
    return 0;
}
```

So whereas the constructor is declared in line (H) inside the class definition, the implementation code for the constructor is provided in line (J) outside the class. Same for the print function; the declaration as a member function is in line (I) and the definition at line (K). Note the use of the scope operator ':::' in lines (J) and (K) to help the compiler figure out that the definitions being provided are for the class User. This usage of the scope operator is as a *class scope operator*.[3] As we will explain in Chapter 11, one has no choice but to resort to the class scope operator in the manner shown and provide definitions external to a class when classes are interleaved in a C++ program. This is necessitated by the fact that, unlike what happens in Java compilation, a C++ compiler does not possess a look-ahead capability.

There is yet another variation on how a class is defined in C++. This variation concerns how the data members of a class instance are initialized by a constructor. The program shown below is identical to the program User1.cc, except that in line (L) below the constructor now uses the *member initialization syntax* for the initialization of the data members of an object. Strictly speaking, as will be explained in Chapter 7, it is necessary for only the const and the reference data members of a class to be initialized in this manner. But it is common to see code in which this sort of initialization is carried out for other types of data members also.

---

[3]A C++ class member function whose implementation code is provided inside the class definition is considered to be an *inline* function. Whether or not a function is inline can affect a compiler's ability to perform certain types of optimizations. A member function defined outside a class can also be made inline through explicit declaration. See Section 9.5 of Chapter 9 for details.

```
//User3.cc

#include <iostream>
#include <string>
using namespace std;

class User {
    string name;
    int age;
public:
    User( string str, int yy ) : name( str ), age( yy ) {}        //(L)
    void print() {
        cout << "name: " << name << "  age: "  << age << endl;
    }
};

int main()
{
    User u( "Zaphod", 119 );
    u.print();
    return 0;
}
```

Please refer back to the previous chapter on how to compile and run the working programs shown in this section.

3.2 DEFINING A CLASS IN JAVA

Paralleling our class definitions for C++ in the previous section, here is a simple example of a Java class:

```
class User {
    private String name;
    private int age;
}
```

As for C++, we define the class User with two data members, name and age. As mentioned before, these are usually referred to as *members*, *data members*, or *fields*. The string type in Java is named String — the data type we use for the member name above.[4] Note that, unlike C++, a class definition in Java does not need a terminating semicolon.

Whereas for C++, leaving the access control modifier unmentioned meant that the data members were in the private section of the class. For achieving the same effect in Java, the modifier `private` must be made explicit in the manner shown.

As was the case with the C++ example of the previous section, in order to create objects from a class, the class needs a constructor. Here is a more useful definition of the User class in Java with a constructor included:

```
class User {
    private String name;
    private int age;

    public User(String str, int yy) {name = str;   age = yy;}  //(A)
}
```

The access control modifier `public` in line (A) serves the same purpose as it did for C++ — it allows the rest of your program to create objects of type User. As before, no return type is specified for the constructor.

Now that we have available to us a constructor for the class User, we can create objects of this type by invoking the following form

```
User u = new User( "Zaphod", 119 );
```

The invocation on the right creates a new object of type User and then returns a *reference* to the newly created object. Subsequently, the assignment operation causes the variable u to hold this reference.

We will now include in the class definition a print function:

```
class User {
    private String name;
    private int age;

    public User( String str, int yy ) { name = str;   age = yy; }

    public void print() {                                      //(B)
        System.out.println( "name: " + name + "   age: " + age );
    }
}
```

---

[4]Java also provides the `StringBuffer` type for strings that need to be modified after they are created. Further details on the `String` and the `StringBuffer` types are in the next chapter.

In the previous chapter, we briefly alluded to the Java method `System.out.println` for displaying information on your terminal.

As was the case with C++, a member function such as `print()` in line (B) above is *invoked on* an object, as in the following example:

```
User u = new User( "Zaphod", 119 );
u.print();                      // name: Zaphod    age:  119        //(C)
```

where '.' in line (C) is the member access operator. This is the only operator available for member access in Java.

Here is a working Java program that does the same thing as the C++ programs of the previous section:

```
//User.java

class User {                                                    //(D)
    private String name;
    private int age;

    public User( String str, int yy ) { name = str;   age = yy; }
    public void print() {
        System.out.println( "name: " + name + "  age: " + age );
  }
}

class Test {                                                    //(E)
    public static void main( String[] args ) {
        User u = new User("Zaphod", 23 );
        u.print();
    }
}
```

Note that we now have two classes, in lines (D) and (E), defined in the same file called `User.java`. In keeping with our explanation in the last chapter, we compile this file by using the invocation

```
javac User.java
```

The compilation will deposit the bytecode for the classes `User` and `Test` in the files

```
User.class
```

and

```
Test.class
```

Of the two classes, only `Test` is executable since it contains `main`. We execute the class by

```
java Test
```

3.3 CONSTRUCTING OBJECTS: DIFFERENCES AND SIMILARITIES BETWEEN C++ AND JAVA

The left column of Table 3.1 shows the two most common ways of constructing a C++ object and the right column the only way a Java object can be constructed. The question now is, which of the two C++ ways for object construction is similar to how an object is constructed in Java?

C++	Java

Class definition:
    `class User { ..... };`
	Class definition:
	    `class User { ..... }`

Object construction: (1)
    `User u(.... );`
 	
Object construction: (2)
    `User* p = new User(.... );`
	
	Object construction:
	    `User q = new User( .... );`

Table 3.1

Consider first the C++ case: With the constructor invocation labeled as (1), we can think of u itself as the `User` object. The constructor invocation fills up a block of memory that could be called the u object, as depicted in Figure 3.2. On the other hand, the constructor invocation labeled as (2) in the C++ column results in the creation of a memory location where p's value — a memory address — is stored and in the filling up of a block of memory where the `User` object created on the right-hand side of the assignment operator is stored. The memory address stored in p points to the block of memory where the `User` object resides, as depicted in Figure 3.3.

Consider now the Java case. The constructor invocation shown in the Java column again reserves a memory location where q's value is stored and in the filling up of a block of memory where the `User` object resides. In this case, the memory location

u:

Fig. 3.2

reserved for q's value holds the object reference for the User object, as depicted in Figure 3.4. Think of the object reference stored in q as a disguised pointer (a disguised memory address), disguised in the sense that you cannot dereference it in the same sense that you can dereference a C++ pointer.

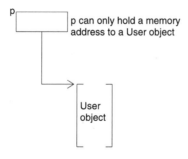

Fig. 3.3

Obviously then the construction invocation labeled (2) for C++ in Table 3.1 is very similar to the construction invocation for Java. The only difference is that for the case of C++ the variable p holds a pointer (a memory address) to the object, whereas for the case of Java the variable q holds a pointer (in the form of an object reference) to the object.

Does this imply that an object reference in Java is identical to a pointer in C++? They are similar but not identical. For the case of Java, if the JVM decided to move the User object to a different place in the memory for reasons of memory management, the object reference held by q would still be able to find the object. On the other hand, if the object pointed to by p were to be shifted to some other place in the memory, the value of p would need to be changed explicitly under program control.

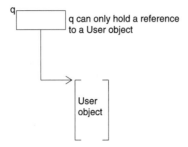

Fig. 3.4

3.4   DEFINING A SUBCLASS IN C++

As was mentioned before, being able to extend a class by defining its subclasses is one of the central features of object oriented programming. Here is the User class again and a subclass called StudentUser:

```
class User {
    string name;
    int age;
public:
    User(string nm, int a) {name=nm; age=a;}
    void print() { cout << ''Name: '' << name << "  Age: " << age; }
};

class StudentUser : public User {                                    //(A)
    string schoolEnrolled;
public:
    StudentUser(string nam, int y, string school) : User(nam, y){ //(B)
        schoolEnrolled = school;
    }
    void print() {                                                 //(C)
        User::print();                                             //(D)
        cout << "School Enrolled:  " << schoolEnrolled << endl;
    }
};
```

In accordance with the terminology already presented, User is a base class or a superclass and StudentUser a subclass, a derived class, or an extended class. The reader should note the following special features of the definitions given above:

- Note the class header for the definition of the StudentUser class in line (A). The colon followed by the keyword public followed by the class name User means that StudentUser is a subclass of the class User, or, equivalently, User is a superclass of StudentUser. The subclass will inherit all the members of the superclass but may or may not have direct access to them. In our example, since name and age are in the private section of User, they will be inherited by StudentUser but will not be directly visible to any functions defined for StudentUser. Issues related to what parts of a superclass are visible in a subclass will be taken up in Section 3.11.

- In line (B), the constructor for the StudentUser subclass was defined as

```
StudentUser( string nam, int y, string school ) : User(nam, y) {
    schoolEnrolled = school;
}
```

The header of the constructor contains a colon followed by an invocation of the constructor of the parent class User. Thus the constructor for the subclass invokes the constructor of the superclass for assigning values to those data members that are only accessible to functions defined for the superclass. As explained more fully in Chapter 15, a derived class constructor must invoke a base class constructor before it does anything else. If a base-class constructor is not called explicitly in a derived class constructor, the system tries to invoke what's known as the *no-arg* constructor for the base class. No-arg constructors are discussed in Chapters 9, 11, and 15.

- Next we turn our attention to how we defined the print() function for the subclass StudentUser in line (C)

```
void print() {
    User::print();
    cout << "schoolEnrolled:  " << schoolEnrolled << endl;
}
```

Note how the subclass print() invokes in line (D) the print() defined for the parent class User to print out those member values that are not directly accessible in the subclass. Suppose we create an instance of StudentUser by

```
StudentUser* p = new StudentUser( "Zaphlet", 10, "cosmology" );
```

and then if we invoke the print() function for uptr by

```
p->print();
```

the following would be printed out on a standard terminal:

```
Zaphlet 10  cosmology
```

the first two items here are the output of the `print()` function defined for the superclass and the last one directly by the rest of the `print()` function for the subclass.

Since the `print()` function defined for the base class `User` is inherited by the derived class `StudentUser` and since we have provided `StudentUser` with its own `print()` method, does there exist an ambiguity between the two `print()` definitions for a `StudentUser` object. No, not at all. As far as a `StudentUser` object is concerned, it is the `StudentUser` definition of `print()` that holds. The general rule here, as explained further in Chapter 15, is that a function of a given name in a derived class hides all functions of the same name in the base class. Base class functions that are hidden in a derived class through this name hiding mechanism can still be accessed in the derived class through the ':::' operator, as in line (D) of the program above.

3.4.1   A Small Demonstration of Polymorphism in C++

Now that we have a small class hierarchy, consisting of the `User` base class and the `StudentUser` derived class, we can give a small demonstration of polymorphism. This demonstration will consist of constructing an array of `User` objects, some of which are actually `StudentUser` objects. (Recall from the introduction to this chapter, a `StudentUser` IsA `User`.) We will then invoke `print()` on all the elements of this array, with the expectation that polymorphism will cause object-specific definitions of `print()` to be invoked on each of the elements.

For a C++ program to take advantage of polymorphism, the following two conditions must hold true:

- The objects must be manipulated through pointers or references.[5]

- The functions that are expected to behave polymorphically must be declared *virtual*[6] in the base class. An inherited virtual function remains virtual.

These two conditions are satisfied by the program shown below. Line (E) declares `print()` to be virtual in the base class and line (F) provides an *override definition* for `print()` in the derived class. In lines (G) through (J) of `main`, we first declare an array of `User*` elements and then fill this array with pointers to a mixture of objects, two of type `User` and one of type `StudentUser`. Since `print()` is virtual, object-specific definition of `print()` for each element of the array is automatically invoked at run time. As a result, the output of the program is

```
Name: Buster Dandy    Age: 34
Name: Missy Showoff    Age: 25    School Enrolled:  Math
```

---

[5]The concept of a reference in C++ is discussed in Chapter 8.

[6]Virtual functions in C++ and associated concepts like virtual tables are discussed in detail in Chapter 15.

```
Name: Mister Meister  Age: 28
```

Here is the source code for the demonstration:

```
//Polymorph.cc

#include <iostream>
#include <string>
using namespace std;

class User {
    string name;
    int age;
public:
    User(string nm, int a) {name=nm; age=a;}
    virtual void print() {                                  //(E)
        cout << "Name: " << name << "  Age: " << age;
    }
};

class StudentUser : public User {
    string schoolEnrolled;
public:
    StudentUser(string nam, int y, string school) : User(nam, y){
        schoolEnrolled = school;
    }
    void print() {                                          //(F)
        User::print();
        cout << "  School Enrolled:  " << schoolEnrolled;
    }
};

int main()
{
    User* users[3];                                         //(G)

    users[0] = new User( "Buster Dandy", 34 );              //(H)
    users[1] = new StudentUser("Missy Showoff", 25, "Math");  //(I)
    users[2] = new User( "Mister Meister", 28 );            //(J)

    for (int i=0; i<3; i++) {                               //(K)
        users[i]->print();                                  //(L)
        cout << endl;
    }
    // this program has a memory leak; ignore it for now    //(M)
    return 0;
}
```

Since we did not deallocate the memory that was acquired with the `new` operator in lines (H), (I), and (J), the program has a memory leak, as indicated by the comment line (M). We could eliminate the leak by invoking `delete` directly on the pointers `users[0]` and `users[1]` and on the pointer `users[1]` after it is cast down to be of type `StudentUser*`. However, a more efficient way to deallocate memory in this example would be to define a virtual destructor for the base class `User` even if it has a do-nothing implementation. Now the memory occupied by the array `users` can be freed up with a single invocation of the `delete[]` operator, as in

```
delete[] users;
```

Virtual destructors are discussed in Chapter 15. Chapter 8 presents further discussion on the `delete` and the `delete[]` operators for memory deallocation.

Our demonstration of polymorphism defined a virtual `print()` function in the base class and then provided an override definition for the function in the derived class. In general, there are restrictions on the syntax of an overriding function in a derived class vis-à-vis the syntax of the overridden function in a base class. These restrictions are presented in Chapter 15.

3.5 DEFINING A SUBCLASS IN JAVA

To parallel the C++ discussion in Section 3.4, here is how one can extend the class `User` and define a subclass `StudentUser` in Java:

```
class User {
    private String name;
    private int age;

    public User( String str, int yy ) { name = str; age = yy; }
    public void print() {
        System.out.print( "name: " + name + "   age: " + age );
    }
}

class StudentUser extends User {                              //(A)
    private String schoolEnrolled;

    public StudentUser( String nam, int y, String sch ) {     //(B)
        super(nam, y);                                        //(C)
        schoolEnrolled = sch;
    }
```

```
    public void print() {                                        //(D)
        super.print();                                           //(E)
        System.out.print( "    School: " + schoolEnrolled );
    }
}
```

As with C++, we refer to `User` as a base class or a superclass, and to `StudentUser` as a subclass, a derived class, or an extended class. Note the following important features of this subclass definition:

- In the header of the subclass definition in line (A), the phrase `StudentUser extends User` makes `StudentUser` a subclass of `User`, or, equivalently, `User` is a superclass of `StudentUser`. The subclass will inherit all the members of the superclass, but only the non-private members of the base class will be directly visible in the functions defined for the subclass, as explained further in Section 3.11.

- In line (B), the constructor for the subclass is defined as

```
    StudentUser( String nam, int y, String sch ) {
        super(nam, y);
        schoolEnrolled = sch;
    }
```

  Note the invocation `super()` in line (C) which invokes the constructor for the superclass `User`. So, as with C++, a part of the job in the subclass constructor is done by the constructor for the superclass. Again paralleling C++, if a superclass constructor is not invoked explicitly via `super()` or, for the case of Java, if another one of the subclass's constructor is not invoked, then the system will try to invoke the superclass's *no-arg* constructor. These ideas are discussed in detail in Chapter 15.

- In the definition of `print()` for the subclass in line (D)

```
    void print() {
        super.print();
        System.out.print( "    School: " + schoolEnrolled );
    }
```

  again part of the work of `print()` for the subclass is done by calling in line (E) the `print()` function defined for the parent class. The definition of `print()` for the `StudentUser` class overrides the definition of the same function inherited from `User` for objects of type `StudentUser`.

3.5.1   A Small Demonstration of Polymorphism in Java

Nothing special needs to be done to demonstrate polymorphism in Java. That is, we do not need to manipulate Java objects in any special way. Neither do we need to give functions any special designators in order to make them behave polymorphically. Recall that in the C++ example in Section 3.4.1, we had to manipulate the objects created there through pointers and had to declare the function `print()` virtual to demonstrate polymorphism. In Java, all objects are polymorphic and all functions behave polymorphically.

To drive home this point, the following Java program is an exact parallel of the C++ program `Polymorph.cc` of Section 3.4.1. The classes `User` and `StudentUser` are exactly the same as shown earlier in this section. As already mentioned, the `print()` of the derived class in line (G) overrides the `print()` of the base class in line (F). We have added a `Test` class to demonstrate polymorphism. In the `main` of `Test`, we first declare an array of three `User` objects in line (H). The elements of the array are initialized in lines (I), (J), and (K). One of the three elements is actually a `StudentUser`. When the function `print()` is invoked on the elements of this array in the loop in lines (L), (M), and (N), the object-specific definitions of `print()` are automatically used in each case. As a result, the output is the same as shown earlier in Section 3.4.1, that is

```
name: Buster Dandy    age: 34
name: Missy Showoff    age: 25    School: Math
name: Mister Meister    age: 28
```

Here is the source code for this exercise:

```java
//Polymorph.java

class User {
    private String name;
    private int age;

    public User( String str, int yy ) { name = str; age = yy; }
    public void print() {                                         //(F)
        System.out.print( "name: " + name + "   age: " + age );
    }
}

class StudentUser extends User {
    private String schoolEnrolled;

    public StudentUser( String nam, int y, String sch ) {
        super(nam, y);
```

```
            schoolEnrolled = sch;
    }
    public void print() {                                    //(G)
        super.print();
        System.out.print( "   School: " + schoolEnrolled );
    }
}

class Test {
    public static void main( String[] args )
    {
        User[] users = new User[3];                          //(H)

        users[0] = new User( "Buster Dandy", 34 );           //(I)
        users[1] = new StudentUser("Missy Showoff",25,"Math"); //(J)
        users[2] = new User( "Mister Meister", 28 );         //(K)

        for (int i=0; i<3; i++) {                            //(L)
            users[i].print();                                //(M)
            System.out.println();
        }
    }
}
```

As was the case with C++, in general, there are restrictions on the syntax of an overriding function in a derived class vis-à-vis the syntax of the overridden function in a base class. These are presented in Chapter 15.

3.6 BLOCKING INHERITANCE

Sometimes a compiler can do a better job of optimizing the function calls and data access if it is told in advance that a class will not be extended. Security considerations may also dictate that a user not be allowed to extend a vendor-supplied class.

Java gives you a convenient way to prevent a class from being extended. If the keyword final is used as a prefix in the header of a class, that class cannot be extended. We use this mechanism in line (A) of the following example to keep StudentUser from being extended in line (B).

```
//BlockInheritance.java

class User {
    private String name;
```

```
        private int age;
        public User( String str, int yy ) { name = str;   age = yy; }
        public void print() {
            System.out.print( "name: " + name + "  age: " + age );
        }
}

//StudentUser cannot be extended
final class StudentUser extends User {                          //(A)
        private String schoolEnrolled;
        public StudentUser( String nam, int y, String sch ) {
            super(nam, y);
            schoolEnrolled = sch;
        }
        public void print() {
            super.print();
            System.out.println( "  school: " + schoolEnrolled );
        }
}

//Wrong:
//class UndergradStudentUser extends StudentUser { }             //(B)

class Test {
        public static void main( String[] args ) {
            StudentUser us = new StudentUser(
                            "Zaphlet", 10, "Cosmology" );
            us.print();
        }
}
```

In Java, we can also be selective in controlling inheritance by declaring only certain methods to be `final`. When a method of a superclass is declared to be `final`, it cannot be overridden in a subclass. The subclass inherits the method alright, but it cannot provide its own implementation code for the method. Consider the following example in which `print` of `User` is `final` in line (C). Any attempt to override this function by providing a definition in the derived class `StudentUser`, as in line (E), will elicit an error report from the compiler.

```
//BlockInheritance2.java

class User {
        private String name;
        private int age;
        public User( String str, int yy ) { name = str;   age = yy; }
```

```
        //cannot be overridden:
        final public void print() {                              //(C)
            System.out.print( "name: " + name + "  age: " + age );
        }
}

//cannot be extended:
final class StudentUser extends User {                           //(D)
    private String schoolEnrolled;

    public StudentUser( String nam, int y, String sch ) {
        super(nam, y);
        schoolEnrolled = sch;
    }
/*
    public void print() {                       // ERROR          //(E)
        super.print();
        System.out.println( "school: " + schoolEnrolled );
    }
*/
}

class Test {
    public static void main( String[] args ) {
        StudentUser us = new StudentUser(
                        "Zaphlet", 10, "Cosmology" );
        us.print();                                              //(F)
    }
}
```

The invocation

```
    us.print();
```

in line (F) will now use `print` as inherited from the superclass `User`. As a result,
only the `User` slice of the `StudentUser` object will be printed out:

```
    name: Zaphlet  age: 10
```

The keyword `final` in Java programs has another role also that is similar to the
role played by `const` in C++ programs. If the data member of a class is declared to
be `final`, its value cannot be changed after initialization. By the same token, if a
variable or a function parameter is declared to be `final`, its value cannot be changed
after initialization. This `const` like role of `final` is discussed further in Chapter 7
for variables and in Chapter 11 for the data members of a class.

C++ does not provide a keyword like `final` for keeping a class from being extended
or for blocking the override mechanism on a selective basis. However, a C++ class

can be made non-extendible by placing its constructors in the private section of the class. For illustration, in the following example, class X cannot be extended since the X's constructor needed in class Y is not publically available. Restricting access to constructors in C++ is discussed in greater detail in Chapter 11.

```
//BlockInheritance.cc

class X {
    int n;
    X( int nn ) { n = nn; }           // constructor is private
};

/*
class Y : public X {                  // Error.  X cannot be extended
    int m;
public:
    Y( int nn, int mm ) : X( nn ) { m = mm; }
};
*/

int main() {}
```

3.7 CREATING PRINT REPRESENTATIONS FOR OBJECTS

Every class in Java inherits a method called `toString()` from the root class `Object` that, if overridden, allows a print method such as `System.out.print` to directly print out an object of that class. In the following example, instead of equipping `User` with a `print` method as we did before, we now provide it with an override definition for the `toString` method in line (A).

```
//PrintObj.java

class User {
    private String name;
    private int age;

    public User( String str, int yy ) { name = str;   age = yy; }

    public String toString(){                                    //(A)
        return "Name: " + name + " Age: " + age;
    }
}
```

```
class Test {
    public static void main( String[] args ) {
        User us = new User( "Zaphod", 119 );
        System.out.println( us );    // Name: Zaphod  Age: 119    //(B)
    }
}
```

As a result, we can now directly supply a User argument to the System.out.println method in class Test, as we show in line (B).

We could use the same strategy in a C++ program; that is, equip a class with a toString()-like function that creates a string representation from the values of the data members of the class. The string thus constructed could then be output by, say, the usual output operator '<<'. However, a more common way to create print representations in C++ is to overload the output operator directly for a class, as we do in the example below in line (C). The syntax used will make sense after we have discussed the friend declaration in Section 3.11 of this chapter and operator overloading in Chapter 12. From the syntax shown in line (D), note how the operator overload definition of line (C) allows us to use a User object directly as an operand for the output operator.

```
//PrintObj.cc

#include <iostream>
#include <string>
using namespace std;

class User {
    string name;
    int age;
public:
    User( string str, int yy ) { name = str;  age = yy; }

    friend ostream& operator<<(ostream& os, const User& user) {   //(C)
        os << "Name: " << user.name << " Age: " << user.age << endl;
    }
};

int main()
{
    User us( "Zaphod", 119 );
    cout << us << endl;             // Name: Zaphod  Age: 119          //(D)
    return 0;
}
```

3.8 OBJECT DESTRUCTION

When objects go out of scope[7] in C++, they are automatically destroyed by the invocation of their destructors. A destructor is given the name of the class prefixed with a tilde. It should not return a value, neither should it take a parameter, as in the following example where we have supplied class Y with a destructor of its own in line (C). If a class has not been supplied explicitly with a destructor, the default meaning of the destructor is invoked for objects made from that class. The default meaning is to invoke the destructors for each of the data members of the class. For data members of the primitive types, destruction simply means freeing up the memory occupied by them.

```
//Dest.cc

#include <iostream>
using namespace std;

class X {};

class Y {
    X* p;                                                   //(A)
public:
    Y( X* q ) : p( new X(*q) ){}                            //(B)
    ~Y(){ delete p; }                                       //(C)
};

int main() {
    X* px = new X();                                        //(D)
    Y y( px );                                              //(E)
    delete px;                                              //(F)
    return 0;
}
```

As the variable y in line (D) goes out of scope when the flow of execution hits the right brace of main, Y's destructor in line (C) will be invoked automatically.

As will be explained in greater detail in Chapter 11, programmer-supplied destructors are needed particularly when an object appropriates system resources that need to be freed up before the object is destroyed. In our example here, construction of an object of type Y in line (B) entails allocating memory for an object of type X to which the data member p points. The system supplies a class with a default destructor if

---

[7]See Section 7.7 of Chapter 7 for a discussion on the scope of an identifier in C++. As mentioned there, the scope of an identifier is that part of a program in which an identifier is recognized as declared.

the programmer does not provide one. If we had not supplied Y with a destructor as shown in line (C), its default destructor would have just freed up the four bytes occupied by the pointer data member p, but not the memory to which p points.[8]

Java's object destruction works very differently from C++. If no variables in a Java program are holding references to an object, that object becomes a candidate for what is known as *garbage collection*. The garbage collector runs continuously in the background in a separate but low-priority thread. To somewhat compensate for the fact that it is beyond the control of a programmer to reclaim the memory occupied by an object at the very instant it becomes unreferenced, Java gives the programmer the option of *asking* the garbage collector to make a best effort to right away reclaim the space occupied by all unreferenced objects by invoking

```
System.gc();
```

Before actually destroying an object, the garbage collector executes the code in the `finalize()` method of the object assuming the class was given such a method. The `finalize()` method does for Java what a programmer-supplied destructor does for C++ — it can be used to close I/O connections, files, and so on. Chapter 11 goes more deeply into Java's garbage collection and object finalization.

3.9 PACKAGES IN JAVA

The Java platform consists of packages of related classes and interfaces. For example, all the classes that deal with I/O are in the `java.io` package; the utility classes are all grouped in the `java.util` package; and so on. If you become involved in a large software development project in Java, you'd want to organize your own classes into packages.

In this section, we will first show how a package supplied with the Java platform is used in your own program. Then we will discuss how you can create your own packages.

The following program is a simple demonstration of how a package that comes with the Java platform can be used in your own program. The program first declares and initializes an array of integers in lines (B) and (C). Subsequently, in line (E), this array is sorted by invoking the highly efficient `sort` method defined for the class `Arrays` in the `java.util` package. Finally, the program reports back the time taken for sorting in line (G).

---

[8]The invocation X(*q) in line (B) is actually a call to the *copy constructor* of class X for constructing a new object of type X as a copy of a previously constructed object of the same type. Since X does not possess a programmer-defined copy constructor, its default meaning will be used, which is to make a byte-by-byte copy. The concept of a copy constructor in discussed in detail in Chapter 11.

```
//SortTiming.java

import java.util.*;                                              //(A)

public class Test {
    public static void main( String[] args ) {
        int[] arr = new int[1000000];                           //(B)
        for ( int i=0; i<1000000; i++ )
            arr[i] = (int) ( 1000000 * Math.random() );         //(C)
        long startTime = System.currentTimeMillis();            //(D)
        Arrays.sort( arr );                                     //(E)
        long diffTime = System.currentTimeMillis() - startTime; //(F)
        System.out.println("Sort time in millisecs: " + diffTime);//(G)
    }
}
```

For line (E) to make any sense to the compiler, the program starts in line (A) with the statement

```
import java.util.*;
```

for importing the java.util package that contains the class Arrays. With the import statement as shown in line (A), our program will be able to refer to any class in the java.util package by its name directly. Without the import statement, we would need to replace the statement in line (E) by

```
java.util.Arrays.sort( arr );
```

Therefore, when your program includes an import statement for a certain package, you just make it easier to refer to the classes in that package. If for some reason you decide to use a class without importing the package containing the class, then you have no choice but to use what's known as the *package qualified name* for that class, as, for example, by java.util.Arrays for the Arrays class in the java.util package.

The program also uses a couple of other classes, Math and System. Both these classes are in the java.lang package which gets automatically imported into every Java program. The class Math is needed in line (C) for the invocation of random() to fill up a million-element array with random numbers.[9] And the class System makes available the method currentTimeMillis(), used in lines (D) and (F), which returns the current time in milliseconds from midnight January 1, 1970. A particular run of the program on a 4-processor UltraSparc produced the following output:

---

[9]Math.random() returns a double that is greater than or equal to 0.0 and less than 1.0. The statistical distribution of these pseudorandomly generated numbers is uniform over this range.

```
Sort time in millisecs: 1378
```

The rest of this section is devoted to how you can create and use your own packages. To illustrate the various issues related to package creation and usage, let's say that we want to create the following three packages with classes therein as shown:

```
packageX:        contains classes TestOne and TestTwo
packageY:        contains class   TestOne
testDirectory:   contains class   TestFinal
```

In order to create a name conflict, we have intentionally named one of the classes in `packageX` the same as the sole class in `packageY`. The `TestOne` class in `packageX` is meant to be different from the `TestOne` class in `packageY`.

We will now provide simple definitions for the four classes listed above. As could be the case during code development, for testing purposes you would want to compile and execute the classes in the directories in which they exist. With respect to class definition, compilation, and execution, the reader should note the following:

- How a statement like

  ```
  package packageX;
  ```

  is used at the top of a class file to name the package in which a class resides.

- How a class sometimes needs both a `package` statement of the kind shown above and an `import` statement for the same package. This happens when a class needs to use other classes within the same newly created package.

- Using the `classpath` option for either the `java` command or both the `javac` and the `java` commands when we import a user-created package into a program.

- When two different packages contain classes of the same name, how we can avoid name conflict by using package qualified names for the classes.

We now ask the reader to carry out the following steps:

1. In any directory in which you like to do Java programming, create the following three subdirectories:

   ```
   packageX
   packageY
   testDirectory
   ```

2. In the directory `packageX`, create the class `TestOne` in a file named `TestOne.java`:

```
//TestOne.java
package packageX;                                              //(A)

public class TestOne {
    public void print() {
        System.out.println( "print of packageX.TestOne invoked" );
    }
    public static void main( String[] args ) {
        TestOne testone = new TestOne();
        testone.print();
    }
}
```

Note the statement in line (A) at the top of the class file

```
package packageX;
```

that tells the Java platform that this class will reside in a package named packageX. This class can be compiled by

```
javac TestOne.java
```

If you wanted to execute this class while you are in the directory packageX, you'll have to invoke the Java Virtual Machine with the *-classpath* option, as for example in

```
java -classpath .:/chap3/packageStudy.d  packageX.TestOne
```

which is based on the assumption that the three package directories you created are in the directory packageStudy.d.

3. Create in the same directory, packageX, the following class in a file named TestTwo.java:

```
//TestTwo.java
package packageX;                                              //(B)

import packageX.*;                                             //(C)

public class TestTwo {
    TestOne testone = new TestOne();                          //(D)

    public void print() {
```

```
        System.out.println( "print of packageX.TestTwo invoked" );
    }
    public static void main( String[] args ) {
        TestTwo testtwo = new TestTwo();
        testtwo.print();
        testtwo.testone.print();
    }
}
```

Note that this class contains both a package statement, in line (B), that says that the class resides in package packageX and an import statement in line (C). The import statement is needed because the class has a data member of type TestOne in line (D) which is defined in the package packageX. To compile this class, you'd now need to use the *-classpath* option, as for example in

```
javac -classpath .:/chap3/packageStudy.d  TestTwo.java
```

The classpath tells the compiler how to go about locating packageX needed by the import statement of the class. Executing the class with the java command will also need the *-classpath* option, as for example in

```
java -classpath .:/chap3/packageStudy.d  packageX.TestTwo
```

4. Now switch over to the directory packageY and, in order to create a name conflict with packageX, install in this directory a class named TestOne in a file named TestOne.java:

```
//TestOne.java
package packageY;                                            //(E)

public class TestOne {
    public void print() {
        System.out.println( "print of packageY.TestOne invoked" );
    }
    public static void main( String[] args ) {
        TestOne testone = new TestOne();
        testone.print();
    }
}
```

Note the declaration of packageY in line (E) at the top of the class file. As long as you are in the packageY directory, you can compile this class by

```
javac TestOne.java
```

And you can execute the class by something like this

```
java -classpath .:/chap3/packageStudy.d packageY.TestOne
```

5. Now switch over to the directory `testDirectory` and create in it a class named `TestFinal` in a file called `TestFinal.java`:

```
//TestFinal.java
import packageX.*;                                              //(F)

public class TestFinal {
    packageX.TestOne testone_X = new packageX.TestOne();        //(G)
    packageY.TestOne testone_Y = new packageY.TestOne();        //(H)
    TestTwo testtwo = new TestTwo();                            //(I)

    void print() {
        System.out.println( "print of TestFinal invoked" );
    }

    public static void main( String[] args ) {
        TestFinal tf = new TestFinal();
        tf.print();
        tf.testone_X.print();
        tf.testone_Y.print();
        tf.testtwo.print();
    }
}
```

Note how the package qualified names are used in lines (G) and (H) to tell the compiler which `TestOne` class is used where. Also note that the import statement in line (F) is needed for the unqualified class name in line (I). To compile the file `TestFinal.java`, you'd need to use the *-classpath* option to help the compiler locate the packages `packageX` and `packageY`:

```
javac -classpath .:/chap3/packageStudy.d  TestFinal.java
```

To execute `TestFinal`, you'd again need to use the *-classpath* option, as in

```
java -classpath .:/chap3/packageStudy.d  TestFinal
```

Executing this class produces the expected output:

```
print of TestFinal invoked
print of packageX.TestOne invoked
print of packageY.TestOne invoked
print of packageX.TestTwo invoked
```

3.10 NAMESPACES IN C++

The modularity that one gives to Java software through the mechanism of packages can be given to C++ software through the mechanism of namespaces. The basic syntax for encapsulating code in a namespace is

```
namespace ModuleName {
  // code
}
```

All of the code in a given namespace can be in one file, or distributed over multiple files. If more than one file is involved, the code in each file must be encapsulated in the manner shown above.

As the following example illustrates, basically a namespace creates a scope[10] for the identifiers that are its members. The member identifiers declared in a given namespace cannot ordinarily be accessed directly outside that namespace without the scope resolution operator '::'. For example, the following namespace, named Module1, encapsulates the names foo, bar and T.

```
namespace Module1 {
    void foo() { cout << "Module1 foo() invoked" << endl; }
    int bar( int x ) { return x; }
    typedef string* T;
}
```

To access the function foo() outside the namespace Module1, we must use its *namespace-qualified name*:

```
Module1::foo();
```

Since it can quickly become tedious to always have to use a namespace qualified name in the manner shown above, C++ allows us to employ the *using directive*,as in

```
int main() {
    using namespace Module1;
    foo();
}
```

---

[10]See Section 7.7 of Chapter 7 for a discussion on the scope of an identifier in C++. As mentioned there, the scope of an identifier is that part of a program in which an identifier is recognized as declared.

This would cause foo() of namespace Module1 to be invoked. Obviously, this would only work if there was no name conflict between foo() of Module1 and, say, foo() defined at the global top level, as in

```
void foo() { cout << "Top-level foo() invoked" << endl; }

int main() {
    using namespace Module1;
    foo();                      // ERROR, foo conflict
    return 0;
}
```

The first foo here, defined with a global scope, could be thought of existing in a nameless *global namespace*. The names defined in the global namespace in this manner can be accessed by pre-pending the scope operator to them. For example, if we had a need to invoke both the foo of Module1 and the foo of the global scope in the above code fragment, we could rewrite it as

```
void foo() { cout << "Top-level foo() invoked" << endl; }

int main() {
    Module1::foo();             // invokes foo of Module1
    ::foo();                    // invokes global foo
    return 0;
}
```

The following program brings together these and other aspects of namespaces. Please read the comments carefully as you scan the code.

```
//Namespaces.cc

#include <string>
#include <iostream>
using namespace std;                                            //(A)

namespace Module1 {
    void foo();          // this is only a declaration,
                         // definition will come later in line (D)
}

namespace Module2 {
    void foo() { cout << "Module2 foo() invoked" << endl; }
}

namespace Module3 {
    using namespace Module1;    // has 'foo'                     //(B)
    using namespace Module2;    // also has 'foo', but           //(C)
                                // no problem at this point
```

```cpp
        void bar() { cout << "Module3 bar() invoked" << endl; }
}

namespace Module4 {
        void foo() { cout << "Module4 foo() invoked" << endl; }
}

namespace Module5 {
        void bar() { cout << "Module5 bar() invoked" << endl; }
}

// foo of Module1 defined outside the namespace Module1. Must
// therefore use namespace-qualified name for foo:
void Module1::foo() {cout << "Module1 foo() invoked" << endl;}    //(D)

// The global foo:
void foo() { cout << "top level foo() invoked" << endl; }

//Addition to Module5:
namespace Module5 {
        void hum() { cout << "Module5 hum() invoked" << endl; }
}


int main() {
    //This statement invokes global foo()
    foo();                                                        //(E)

    Module1::foo();                                               //(F)
    Module2::foo();                                               //(G)

    //The following statement, if uncommented, results
    //in compiler error because Module1 and Module2
    //both have foo()
    //  Module3::foo();                                           //(H)

    Module3::bar();                                               //(I)

    using namespace Module4;

    //The following statement, if uncommented, results
    //in compiler error because foo() of Module4
    //conflicts with the global foo()
    //  foo();                                                    //(J)

    //But the following statement is okay since it uses
    //the scope operator for invoking the global foo()
    ::foo();                                                      //(K)
```

```
    using namespace Module5;
    bar();                                                    //(L)
    hum();                                                    //(M)
    return 0;
}
```

The program produces the output shown below to the left of the the symbol `//` in each line:

```
top level foo() invoked          // from line (E)
Module1 foo() invoked            // from line (F)
Module2 foo() invoked            // from line (G)
Module3 bar() invoked            // from line (I)
top level foo() invoked          // from line (K)
Module5 bar() invoked            // from line (L)
Module5 hum() invoked            // from line (M)
```

The *using directives* in lines (A), (B), and (C) of the above program specify that the names in the indicated namespaces can be used as if they were declared directly in the scope in which the directives occur. The using directive does not actually introduce the namespace names into the current scope, but simply makes them available should they be called upon in the current scope. It is for this reason that any name conflicts between two namespaces pulled into the current scope are not discovered unless those names are actually invoked. That's why the compiler has no problem with the definition of Module3 namespace even though it starts out with the using-directives for Module1 and Module2 in line (B) and (C), both containing the name foo. However, if we tried to invoke

```
    Module3::foo();
```

in main, as we have shown in the commented out statement in line (H), the name conflict between the foo of Module1 and Module2 would be flagged down by the compiler. So if two or more namespaces injected into the current scope have common names amongst them, the compiler does not care unless one of those common names is invoked in the current scope.

3.10.1   Using Declaration Versus Using Directive

While a *using directive* makes all its names merely available to the current scope, a *using declaration* actually declares a specific namespace name in the current scope. The syntax of a using-declaration is a little bit different from that for a using-directive, as illustrated in the following example code. The namespaces Module1 and Module2 both encapsulate the programmer-defined types X and Y. To specifically declare X of Module1 inside main, we say

```
    using Module1::X;
```

in line (A) of the program. Once a specific name is declared in the current scope with a using-declaration, an attempt to declare the same name from another namespace would be flagged down by the compiler. The compiler would declare a name conflict in the following example if we uncomment the commented-out statement in line (B) of main.

```
//Namespaces2.cc

namespace Module1 {
    class X {};
    class Y {};
}

namespace Module2 {
    class X {};
    class Y {};
}

int main() {
    using Module1::X;                                        //(A)
    X x1;
    // using Module2::X;        // ERROR, name conflict       //(B)
    X x2;
    return 0;
}
```

3.10.2 Which Namespace Owns Names Imported from Another Namespace?

If one namespace is imported into another named namespace, the member names of the former can be thought of as belonging to the latter. This is made clear by the following example in which we import the namespace Module1 and a specific name, foo, of the namespace Module2 into the namespace Module3. All of the names invoked in main are with respect to Module3, even those that are really owned by the other two modules.

```
//Namespaces3.cc

#include <iostream>
using namespace std;

namespace Module1 {
```

```
        class X {};
}

namespace Module2 {
        void foo(){ cout << "foo of Module2 invoked" << endl; }
        void bar(){ cout << "bar of Module2 invoked" << endl; }
}

namespace Module3 {
        using namespace Module1;
        typedef X Y;
        using Module2::foo;
        class Z {};
}

int main()
{
        Module3::X x;
        Module3::Y y;
        Module3::foo();
        //  Module3::bar();        // ERROR.  No bar in Module3.
        return 0;
}
```

3.10.3   Using Declarations and Directives Have Scope

Just like any other declaration, using directives and declarations have block scope.[11] This fact can be used to localize the visibility of the names introduced into a program by either a using directive or a using declaration. This is illustrated in the following program where we have divided the code in main into four separate blocks. As a result, there is no conflict between the name Type imported into the first block from Module1 and the same name Type imported into the second block from Module2. The third and the fourth blocks show a similar localization of the accessibility of names imported through using declarations.

```
//Namespaces.cc

#include <iostream>
using namespace std;
```

---

[11]A block is a section of code delimited by curly brackets. Chapter 7 discusses this and other aspects of scoping in greater detail.

```
namespace Module1 {
    typedef int Type;
    Type foo( Type arg ) { return arg; }
}

namespace Module2 {
    typedef double Type;
    Type foo( Type arg ) { return arg; }
}

int main()
{
    {
        using namespace Module1;
        Type x = 100;                      // int
        cout << foo( x ) << endl;          // 100
    }
    {

        using namespace Module2;
        Type x = 3.14;                     // double
        cout << foo( x ) << endl;          // 3.14
    }
    {
        using Module1::foo;
        cout << foo( 100 ) << endl;        // 100
    }
    {

        using Module2::foo;
        cout << foo( 3.14) << endl;        // 3.14
    }
    return 0;
}
```

3.10.4 Nesting Namespaces and Namespace Aliases

As with classes, it is possible to nest namespaces to any depth. If an inner namespace contains a name that is identical to an outer namespace, the inner name hides the outer name. Also, the namespace-qualified name of an inner namespace starts with the name of the outermost namespace, followed by the scope operator, followed by the name of the next-to-the-outermost namespace, followed by the scope operator, etc., until reaching the inner namespace. These aspects of namespace nesting are illustrated by the following example in which the namespaces N1 through N4 are nested to a depth of four. Each namespace contains a type Type that means different things in the different namespaces.

```
// NamespaceNested.cc

#include <iostream>
#include <string>
using namespace std;

namespace N1 {
    typedef int Type;
    namespace N2 {
        typedef int* Type;
        namespace N3 {
            typedef string Type;
            namespace N4 {
                typedef string* Type;
            }
        }
    }
}

int main()
{
    using namespace N1;

    Type x = 10;                           // Type is int
    cout << x << endl;                     // 10

    N1::N2::Type p = &x;                   // Type is int*
    cout << *p << endl;                    // 10

    N1::N2::N3::Type str( "hello" );       // Type is string
    cout << str << endl;                   // "hello"

    N1::N2::N3::N4::Type q = &str;         // Type is string*
    cout << *q << endl;                    // "hello"

    namespace N_FOUR = N1::N2::N3::N4;     // namespace alias      //(A)
    N_FOUR::Type ptr = &str;
    cout << *ptr << endl;                  // "hello"

    return 0;
}
```

This example also shows in line (A) how we can define an alias for an unwieldy namespace name. In the example, the namespace qualified name for the innermost namespace is

```
N1::N2::N3::N4
```

Line (A) of the program defines N_FOUR to be an alias for the innermost namespace name:

```
namespace N_FOUR = N1::N2::N3::N4;
```

The general syntax for defining an alias for the complete name of a namespace is

```
namespace new_name = current_name;
```

3.10.5 Unnamed Namespaces

When defining a namespace, you are allowed to omit the name of the namespace:

```
namespace {
    int buffer;
    class X;
    void foo();
    typedef string* T;
}
```

The compiler internally generates a unique name for such a namespace. *Furthermore, a using directive is automatically assumed for an unnamed namespace.* So, in effect, an unnamed namespace declaration is equivalent to

```
namespace ---UNIQUE_NAME--- {
    int buffer;
    class X;
    void foo();
    typedef string* T;
}
using namespace ---UNIQUE_NAME---;
```

So, for internal bookkeeping purposes, the names declared in an unnamed namespace are transformed by the compiler by mangling the names with the internally generated unique name for the namespace, as is done for a regular namespace but with the programmer-supplied namespace name. Additionally, these names possess internal linkage — the same linkage as for a global name that is declared to be static. As you'll recall, when you declare a global name in file A to be static, its scope is limited to file A. It cannot be linked to from a file B by the use of *extern* declaration in file B. That allows you to use the same name in file B for a different purpose without fear of creating a name clash with file A. An unnamed namespace is meant to be a cleaner way of achieving the same effect. The use of the global static in C++ programs for achieving internal linkage for a name is being deprecated.

3.10.6 Koenig Lookup for Unqualified Function Names

So far the reader has seen three different ways in which the namespace definition of a name can be accessed outside the namespace. We can either use a namespace-qualified name, or resort to a `using` declaration, or to a `using` directive in the manner shown earlier.

For unqualified function names, there is yet another way that allows the system to access the namespace definition of a function name — through *Koenig lookup*.

This is demonstrated by the following program. The program defines in line (B) a new type X in namespace `Module1` and then proceeds to define in line (C) a function `foo( X )` in the same namespace. As shown in line (D), another namespace, `Module2`, also contains a function of same name and the same parameter type as the function in namespace `Module1`. Finally, yet another version of the same function, `foo( int )`, is defined in the global scope in line (E).

As you would expect, the call to `foo` in line (G) in `main` invokes the global definition of `foo`. Now let us examine closely the call to `foo( X )` in line (H). In the scope in which `foo` is invoked in line (H), there does not exist a function definition with the required parameter type that could possibly be used for the function call. Nonetheless, the compiler has no problem with the function call in line (H) because it uses what is known as Koenig lookup. Koenig lookup permits the compiler to reach into all the namespaces where the arguments types of a function are defined. If such namespaces contain function definitions that could possibly be used for a given function call, all those function definitions become candidates for possible invocation. The particular function definition chosen for invocation is selected through overload resolution discussed in Chapter 9. In the program shown, because the type of argument in the function call in line (H) is not defined in namespace `Module2`, the version of `foo` in line (D) is not considered for possible invocation.[12]

```
//Koenig.cc

#include <iostream>
using namespace std;

namespace Module1 {                                              //(A)
    class X {};                                                  //(B)
    void foo( X xobj ) { cout << "Module1's foo(X) invoked"; }   //(C)
}

namespace Module2 {
    void foo( Module1::X xobj ) { cout << "X's foo(X) invoked"; } //(D)
}
```

---

[12] Koenig lookup is also known as *argument-dependent name lookup*.

```
void foo( int i ) { cout << "global foo(int) invoked"; }         //(E)

int main() {
    Module1::X xob;                                               //(F)
    foo( 1 );                   // global foo(int) invoked        //(G)
    foo( xob );                 // Module1's foo(X) invoked       //(H)
    return 0;
}
```

3.11 ACCESS CONTROL FOR CLASS MEMBERS

Every member of a class has associated with it an access control property. In C++, a member can be *private*, *protected*, or *public*. In addition to these three, Java also allows for the access control property of a member to be *package*. When the access control modifier is left unspecified for a class member in Java, it is of type *package*.

Before explaining what each of these access control modifiers means, let's first address the issue of why any access control is needed at all. People just getting into OO programming frequently ask: Suppose all of the source code was made available to an application developer, would access control still make sense? If you somehow know or find out about a private data member in a class, what's so private about it?

The basic reason for access control is not to hide the information from the users of the software. On the other hand, it is to prevent direct alteration of a data member or direct invocation of a member function. Sometimes changing a data member entails that the state of the object be changed in other ways also. For example, if you write a window manager program for orchestrating the desktop environment on a workstation, you would not want some other program (or a human agent) to directly change the value of, say, the window_width variable. Changing the width of a window might, for example, also require that any images displayed in the window be resized so that they don't look distorted. So you'd want there to exist some kind of a setWindowWidth function that will take care of all of those additional details as you alter the width of a window. This you could accomplish by making the width data member private to a Window class and then supplying a public setWindowWidth function.

So access control is simply a means to regulate how the state of an object can be changed, making it less likely that when the program is extended by an application developer that it will behave in ways not intended originally.

Access Control in C++:

All members of a C++ class are *private* unless declared explicitly to be otherwise.

As the name implies, the *public* members of a class are accessible to all other classes and functions. Additionally, the *public* members of a class are inherited by its subclasses.

On the other hand, members that are *private* to a class are accessible only to the definitions that are meant specifically for that class. Private members of a class are also accessible to the *friends* of that class. (We will shortly show an example to illustrate the notion of a friend in C++.) While the private members of a class are inherited by its subclasses, they cannot be accessed within the subclasses.

The access control modifier *protected* is used for a member if we wish for that member to be accessible to only the subclasses of that class. In other words, a protected member of a class acts like a public member for the subclasses derived from that class, but like a private member for the rest of the program. We will have more to say about this when we discuss how to extend classes in Chapter 15.

As we mentioned already, the private members of a class are accessible to the friends of that class. The following example illustrates this concept (which does not have a parallel in Java).

The data members m and n are private to the class X. But note that another class Y and a global function print() are declared to be the *friends* of class X in lines (B) and (C). (So that the identifier Y would make sense to the compiler in line (B), we had to declare the class Y partially in line (A).) With Y as a friend of X, line (D) of class Y can directly access the private data members m and n of X. By the same token, in line (E) the global print() can also directly access the private members of X.

```
//Friend.cc

#include <iostream>
using namespace std;

class Y;                                                    //(A)

class X {
    int m;
    int n;
public:
    X( int mm, int nn ) { m = mm; n = nn; }
    friend Y;                                               //(B)
    friend void print( X* );                               //(C)
};

class Y {
    X* x;
    int t;
public:
    Y( X* xobj ) { x = xobj; t = x->m + x->n; }            //(D)
```

```
    int get_t() { return t; }
};

void print( X* ptr ) {cout << ptr->m << "  " << ptr->n << endl;}  //(E)

int main()
{
    X* ptr = new X(100, 200);
    Y y( ptr );
    cout << y.get_t() << endl;          // 300
    print( ptr );                        // 100   200
    return 0;
}
```

A *friend* declaration may be placed in any section of a class, private, protected, or public. It carries the same meaning regardless of where it appears.

Access Control in Java:

As mentioned previously, in addition to the modifiers *public, private*, and *protected*, Java has one more: *package*.

The modifiers *public* and *private* carry the same meaning in Java as they do in C++. The modifier *protected* also carries the same meaning, except that such members are like public members in the same package. In other words, a protected class member will be accessible inside all classes in the same package, but to only the subclasses in other package.

When no access modifier is specified in Java, that means the member has access control of type *package*. Such members are no different from the public members within the same package. But they act like private members with respect to other packages.

What this means is that for a beginning Java programmer, when all of your work is likely to be contained in a single directory, the access modifiers *public, package*, and *protected* in your own code behave very much the same. That is, if you leave a member or a method unadorned by not designating any access modifiers, it will exhibit a *public*-like behavior. The opposite thing to do would be to control its access by using the *private* modifier.

3.12 ABSTRACT CLASSES AND INTERFACES

Abstract classes are very important to object-oriented programming. While the notion of an abstract class is common to both C++ and Java, the latter also supports a variant thereof — *interfaces*. A Java interface is an abstract class that is not allowed to contain any implementation code at all for any of the member functions. An interface is also not allowed any data members that can be given values on a per object basis.[13]

In general, a class is abstract if it is not possible to construct objects from that class. This can happen for a variety of reasons. In C++, if one or more of the member functions of a class is declared to be *pure virtual*, then you cannot make objects from that class. In Java, if you declare a class to be abstract explicitly, you are not allowed to make any objects from that class.

The reader might ask: If you cannot make objects from a class definition, what good is the class? Here are some answers to this question:

- An abstract class can lend organization to the other classes in a class hierarchy.

- An abstract class can represent a specialized behavior, which when mixed with the other classes gives us classes with that behavior.

- Abstract classes can help build up an implementation incrementally.

An abstract class can help with knowledge organization in an OO program by serving as a root class of a hierarchy of other concrete classes and thus pull together what might otherwise be disparate bits of knowledge encapsulated in the subclasses. A classic and frequently used example of this is the Shape hierarchy of classes shown in Figure 3.5. Obviously, while we can construct objects of type Circle, Rectangle,

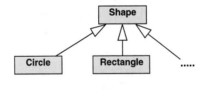

Fig. 3.5

and so on, it would make no sense to construct an object of type Shape. Yet the class Shape serves a critical role, because it pulls together all the other classes into a single hierarchy. What do we mean by "pull together"? This question is actually deeper than it appears at first sight.

What we mean by the Shape class pulling together the other classes has to do with inheritance and polymorphism. Taking advantage of inheritance, we could place in the Shape class all of the code that is common between its various subclasses, making our program more efficient. And, given a list of Shapes, some of which

---

[13]What's meant by "value on a per object basis" will become clear after we have presented the notion of a *static* class member in Section 3.12 of this chapter. The topic of static class members is discussed more fully in Chapter 11.

may actually be `Circles`, some `Rectangles`, and so on, we could invoke a function such as `area()` on the entire list. Polymorphism would then automatically cause the object-specific `area()` to be invoked on each `Shape` in the list. This assumes that we have at least *declared* `area()` as one of the functions for the root class `Shape` and that we have provided implementation code for `area()` in the subclasses.

Here is how you could define an abstract class `Shape` in C++:

```
class Shape {
public:
    virtual double area( ) = 0;                      //(A)
    virtual double circumference() = 0;              //(B)
    //....
};
```

Incorporating the symbol "=0" as we have in lines (A) and (B) tells the compiler that these two functions are *pure virtual*. A C++ class that has at least one pure virtual function is treated as an abstract class by the compiler; the compiler will not allow such a class to be instantiated into objects. The compiler expects no implementation code for a pure virtual function. Chapter 15 explains this point and consequences thereof in much greater detail.

An abstract class in Java is defined in the following manner:

```
abstract class Shape {
    abstract public double area( );
    abstract public double circumference();
    //....
}
```

As you can see, Java requires that the class header start with the keyword *abstract* and, also, if your class includes any methods for which you do not intend to provide implementation code, the method declaration must also include the same keyword.

As we mentioned at the beginning of this section, Java also supports interfaces, which is a class that consists solely of abstract methods and of constants. You might ask: If C++ can make do with just abstract classes, why does Java need both abstract classes and interfaces? The answer to this question, to be given in detail in Chapter 15, basically has to do with the fact that C++ allows for multiple inheritance, while Java does not. A Java class is allowed to inherit implementation code from only one superclass. While this restriction eliminates many difficult programming issues associated with the use of multiple inheritance in C++, it creates its own program design limitations that are gotten around through the concept of an interface. A Java class can be a subclass of any number of interfaces.

Interfaces in Java are mostly used for lending specialized behaviors to classes. To illustrate this point, Figure 3.6 shows how the class `ArrayList`, which is a very useful class for constructing dynamically expandable arrays of objects, is implemented in the Java source code: In this class hierarchy, `ArrayList` is the only concrete

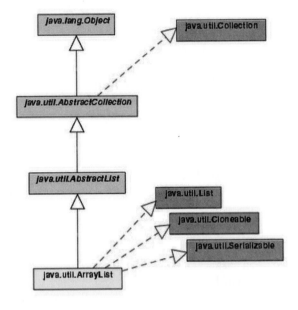

Fig. 3.6

class, meaning a class that can be instantiated to form actual objects. The part of the hierarchy that is shown vertically on the left illustrates how the implementation of ArrayList is built incrementally through the abstract classes AbstractCollection and AbstractList. ArrayList can inherit implementation code only from its superclasses AbstractCollection and AbstractList. In addition to this implementation code, ArrayList inherits "behaviors" directly from the interfaces List, Cloneable, and Serializable. ArrayList must provide implementation code for all the functions declared in all of these interfaces. ArrayList also inherits behaviors indirectly from the interface Collection.

In this manner, every ArrayList object is also a List object. By the same token, every ArrayList object is also a Cloneable object, just as it is also a Serializable object and a Collection object. This implies that objects of type ArrayList can be manipulated polymorphically with respect to the interfaces declared in List, Cloneable, Serializable, and Collection.

Interfaces in Java are also used for grouping together related constants. When a class inherits from such an interface, the constants appear as if locally defined in the class. Such constants defined for interfaces are treated implicitly as final and static.[14]

---

[14]The notion of the static member of a class is discussed briefly in Section 3.14 and in greater detail in Chapter 11. The modifier final, when applied to variables, acts like const in C++. There is a brief

The syntax for declaring a Java interface is

```
interface Collection {
    public boolean add( Object o );
    public boolean remove( Object o );
    // other methods
}
```

The methods declared in an interface are always `public`, implicitly so if their access privilege is not stated. Such methods are also not allowed to be `static`.

We say that a Java class *implements an interface* if the class provides implementation code for all the methods declared in the interface. The header of a class `MyClass` that implements an interface `MyInterface` must include keyword *implements* as shown below

```
class MyClass implements MyInterface {
    // .....
    // implementation code for
    // the methods declared in MyInterface
    // .....
}
```

Java interfaces are discussed in much more detail in Chapter 15.

3.13 COMPARING OBJECTS

Our goal in this section is to talk about comparing objects at a high level and to provide forward pointers to where the reader can find more detailed discussion on the issues involved.

The basic issues in object comparison relate to

- what can be compared; and
- how to compare.

Given the following two classes

```
class Apple {                       class Orange {
    Taste taste;                        Taste taste;
    Size  size;                         Size size;
    Weight wt;                          Weight wt;
    // ...                              //...
};                                  };
```

---

remark concerning this use of `final` in Java at the end of Section 3.6; a fuller discussion can be found in Chapter 7.

it makes no sense to compare apples with oranges in most cases in real life.[15] However, there can be genuine programming needs for comparing apples with apples and oranges with oranges for the purpose of, say, grading them on the basis of either taste, or size, or weight, or any combination of these and other attributes.

It should be obvious to the reader that there is no unique way to compare class type objects, unlike what can be done with primitive types such as integers. In some situations, weight may be irrelevant for comparing apples, and, in others, it may play a most important role. So it falls on the programmer to tell the system how to compare two objects of the same class. When supplying a criterion for comparing objects, the programmer has to bear in mind that there are two kinds of comparisons that one can make for class type objects:

- We may wish to know whether or not two objects are identical on the basis of equal values for one or more of the data members. The result of such a comparison is either true or false.

- Or, we may wish to know whether one object is smaller than, equal to, or greater than another object, again on the basis of the values for one or more data members of the objects involved. Obviously, a function that carries out such a comparison must be capable of returning at least three different symbols, say, -1 when object A is less than object B, 0 when object A is equal to object B, and $+1$ when object A is greater than object B.

In C++, the first kind of comparison is yielded typically by the '==' operator. The programmer has to overload this operator for a given class. It's the overload definition that tells the system that two apples will be deemed to be identical as long as their sizes are the same, regardless of the other attributes. Operator overloading in C++ is discussed in Chapter 12. As discussed in Section 4.3.3, the `string` type supplied by the C++ Standard Library already comes with an overload definition for the '==' operator. Two strings are declared identical by this operator if they are composed of identical character sequences.

The second type of comparison in C++ is implemented by defining an appropriate comparison function that returns the three values needed. For example, as reported in Section 4.3.3, the `string` class of the C++ Standard Library comes with a three-valued function `compare()` that can be invoked to determine whether one string is less than, equal to, or greater than another string; the comparison is typically established on the basis of the ASCII codes associated with the characters.

Object comparisons in C++ are also needed by the various sort functions that come with the C++ container classes. As discussed in Chapter 12 on operator overloading,

---

[15]This does not mean that OO forbids you to compare apples with oranges. If there is a legitimate need to carry out what appear to be cross-class comparisons, we could derive the classes `Apple` and `Orange` from a common root class `Fruit` and equip the root class with a suitable comparator function.

the comparison function needed by a sorting algorithm can be supplied either in the form of a *function object* or by overloading directly the '<' operator.

Our discussion so far on object comparison has been centered primarily on a comparison of two objects on the basis of their *content*, meaning on the basis of the values of one or more the data members of the objects. Java adds an additional twist to this — it allows object comparisons on the basis of *equality of reference*. Two objects are equal on the basis of equality of reference if they are the same object in the memory. This kind of a comparison can also be carried out in C++ by comparing the memory addresses of the two objects.

In Java, comparison of two objects on the basis of equality of reference is carried out by the '==' operator. And a comparison on the basis of content can be carried out by a programmer-supplied definition for the equals() method that every class in Java inherits from the root class Object. A frequent source of confusion for beginning Java programmers is the meaning of the '==' operator vis-à-vis the role of the function equals(). Say, we are given a class X:

```
class X {
    int p;
    X( int m ) { p = m; }
    // ...
}
```

and the following statements

```
X x1 = new X( 10 );
X x2 = x1;
x1 == x2;                    // true
```

Since both x1 and x2 will be holding references to one and the same object, the comparison in the third statement above will return true.[16] On the other hand, the comparison in the third statement below

```
X x1 = new X( 10 );
X x2 = new X( 10 );
x1 == x2;                    // false
```

---

[16]It is interesting to note that for C++ the comparison made in the third statement below

```
X x1;
X x2 = x1;
x1 == x2;                    // true
```

will also return true, *but for a reason that is entirely different from that for Java.* In C++, the second statement will cause the copy constructor of X to be invoked to copy over the data members of x1 into the memory locations reserved for the data members of x2. The objects x1 and x2 will be two different objects, in the sense of residing at two different locations in the memory, even though their data members will have the same values. If overloaded in the usual manner, the operator '==' in C++ will check for the identity of the two objects on the basis of equality of content. Copy constructors in C++ are discussed in Chapter 11 and operator overloading in Chapter 12.

will return a false simply because x1 and x2 are now holding references to two distinct objects — objects located at two different places in the memory.

What's interesting is that, assuming we do not supply our own override definition for equals that X inherits from Object, comparisons using equals behave in exactly the same manner as comparisons using '==:

```
X x1 = new X( 10 );
X x2 = x1;
x1.equals( x2 );               // true
X x3 = new X( 10 );
x1.equals( x3 );               // false
```

That's because for the root class Object both the '==' operator and the equals method are defined to do the same thing — check for equality of reference. But, being a Java operator, while '==' cannot be overridden, the method equals can.

The class X below has its own override definition for the method equals in line (A) that compares two X objects on the basis of the values of the data member p. So even though the two X objects constructed in lines (B) and (C) are very different, the equality test in line (D) reports them to be equal objects.

```
//EqualityTest.java

class  X {
    int p;
    int q;
    X( int m, int n ) { p = m; q = n; }
    boolean equals( X other ) { return p == other.p; }          //(A)
}

class Test {
    public static void main( String[] args ) {
        X x1 = new X( 10, 100 );        // x1 and x2                //(B)
        X x2 = new X( 10, 10000 );      // look very different      //(C)
        System.out.println( x1.equals( x2 ) );   // true           //(D)
    }
}
```

As mentioned in Chapter 4, the String class in Java already comes with an override definition for the equals method that compares strings on the basis of content.

The Java platform also uses the notion of *natural ordering* for comparing class type objects. Some of the container classes in the Java Collections Framework discussed in Chapter 5 store objects according to their *natural order*, unless instructed otherwise by the programmer.

The objects of a Java class exhibit natural ordering if the class has implemented the `java.lang.Comparable` interface. Such a class must provide an implementation for the `compareTo` method — referred to as the class's *natural comparison method* — that can then be used by the algorithms and the data structures for comparing data objects. The `compareTo` method must return a negative integer, a zero, or a positive integer if the object on which it is invoked is less than, equal to, or greater than the argument object.

It is strongly recommended that a class's natural ordering as dictated by the implementation of the `compareTo` method be consistent with `equals`. This consistency is achieved if and only if `e1.compareTo( (Object) e2 ) == 0` has the same boolean value as `e1.equals( (Object) e2 )` for every pair of objects `e1` and `e2` of the class. Lack of this consistency could elicit strange behavior from the data structures that need to compare objects.

Many of the system supplied classes in Java possess natural ordering. These include `String`, `Integer`, `Float`, `Double`, `Date`, `File` and many others. For the `String` class, the natural order is lexicographic; it is chronological for the `Date` class; lexicographic on the pathname for the `File` class, and so on.

3.14 STATIC MEMBERS OF A CLASS

Although a much more detailed discussion of this topic is presented in Chapter 11, we want to quickly introduce the reader here to the basic notion of a static member for a class and the syntax that is employed to access such members.

A static member is global to all the objects of a class. For example, in the C++ class

```
class SavingsAccount {
    string name;
    double balance;
public:
    static double interestRate;                         //(A)
    //....
};
```

all objects of type `SavingsAccount` will have the same value for the static data member `interestRate` of line (A). If the value of this data member is changed at some point, that change will affect all `SavingsAccount` objects — even those that were constructed prior to the change.

In C++, a public static data member can be accessed directly through the class using the scope operator ':::', as in

```
SavingsAccount::interestRate = 6.5;
```

although it could also be accessed through an object of type SavingsAccount (see Chapter 11).

A private static data member may require appropriate access functions. The following example shows the use of static member functions in lines (C) and (D) for retrieving and changing the value of the static data member of line (B): purpose:

```
class X {
    int m;
    static int n;                                    //(B)
public:
    X( int p ) { m = p; }
    static int getn() ( return n; }                  //(C)
    static void setn( int m ) { n = m; }             //(D)
};
```

Now the value of the static member n may be retrieved by invoking it directly against the class, as in

```
X::setn( 20 );
cout << X::getn();
```

This example is not meant to imply that the value of a static data member can only be modified by a static member function; it can also be modified by a nonstatic member function. However, a static member function is *not* allowed to access nonstatic data members of a class.

The static members of a Java class behave in the same manner as the static members of a C++ class; however, the syntax for accessing such members is different since Java does not support the scope operator. For example, for the Java class

```
class SavingsAccount {
    string name;
    double balance;
    public static double interestRate;              //(E)
    //....
}
```

the static data member interestRate of line (E) may be accessed using the usual dot operator, but against the class itself, as in

```
SavingsAccount.interestRate = 6.5;
```

The same would apply to the static method of a Java class. To access it, you'd need to invoke via the dot operator on the class itself.

An abstract class is not allowed to have static member functions.

3.15 TEMPLATE CLASSES

A "templatized" C++ program can work with different types of data types. For example, a templatized C++ linked-list can be used to hold elements of type `int`, `double`, `char`, and so on.

To explain the basic idea behind a template class, let's say that we want the following class to hold a data member whose exact type in not known in advance:

```
class X{
    T datum;                // type T not known in advance
public:
    // constructor, etc.
};
```

We, of course, have the option of defining a different class X for each different data type for the field `datum`, or we can be more efficient in our programming and use the following template class definition for X:

```
template <class T> class X {
    T datum;
public:
    X( T dat ) : datum( dat ) {}
    T getDatum(){ return datum; }
};
```

This parameterizes the definition of the class X by the incorporation of the parameter T in the class header. This one parameterized definition allows us to use in our program the data types `X<int>`, `X<float>`, `X<double>`, `X<char>`, `X<string>`, and so on, all at the same time, as illustrated by the following program:

```
//TemplateX.cc

#include <string>
#include <iostream>
using namespace std;

template <class T> class X {
    T datum;
public:
    X( T dat ) : datum( dat ) {}
    T getDatum(){ return datum; }
};

int main()
{
    int x = 100;
```

```
    X<int> xobj_1( x );

    double d = 1.234;
    X<double> xobj_2( d );

    string str = "hello";
    X<string> xobj_3( str );

    string ret1 = xobj_3.getDatum();
    cout << ret1 << endl;                           // output: ''hello''

    return 0;
}
```

Chapter 13 presents in much greater detail the notion of templatized classes and functions in C++. Chapter 13 also discusses a proposed extension to the standard Java platform that allows for the parameterization of class and method definitions.

3.16 NESTED TYPES

If a class is expected to play a role that is completely subsidiary to another class, it is best to define the former as a member of the latter. A class is called a *nested class* if it is defined as a member of another class, the latter usually referred to as the *enclosing class*. In C++, one can also nest a typedef inside a class. In Java, one can also nest an interface inside another interface or another class, resulting in *nested interfaces*. It is also possible in Java to nest a class inside an interface.

3.16.1 Nested Classes in C++

A nested class can be defined in the private, public, or protected section of the enclosing class. The usual meaning ascribed to these access control modifiers applies.

In the following example, X in line (A) is the enclosing class for a nested class Y defined in line (B). The enclosing class is also provided with a data member of type Y* in line (E). Note that the definition of the nested class starting in line (B) is like any other class definition. It has a data member, a constructor, and a member function. Line (F) provides a constructor for the enclosing class and line (G) a get function for its sole data member.

```
//NestedClass.cc

#include <iostream>
using namespace std;

class X {                                                    //(A)

    class Y{                                                 //(B)
        int m;
    public:
        Y( int mm ) { m = mm; }                             //(C)
        void printY(){ cout << "m of nested class object: "
                            << m << endl; };                //(D)
    };

    Y* yptr;                                                //(E)
public:
    X() { yptr = new Y( 100 ); }                            //(F)
    Y* get_yptr(){ return yptr; }                          //(G)
};


int main() {
    X x;                                                    //(H)
    x.get_yptr()->printY();                                //(I)
    return 0;
}
```

When you run this program, the statement in line (H) will invoke the no-arg constructor of line (F). The invocation in line (I) will call on the print function in line (D) to output

```
m of nested class: 100
```

In the example above, all the member functions were defined inline for both the enclosing class and the nested class. Shown below is the same program as above, but written with all the member function definitions outside the classes. The class scope operator ': : ', introduced in Section 3.1, must now be used as shown to indicate the class for which a definition is being provided.

```
//NestedClassDefsNotInline.cc

#include <iostream>
using namespace std;

class X {                                                    //(A)
    class Y{                                                 //(B)
```

```
        int m;
    public:
        Y( int mm );                                          //(C)
        void printY();                                        //(D)
    };


    Y* yptr;                                                  //(E)
public:
    X();                                                      //(F)
    Y* get_yptr();                                            //(G)
};


//Definitions specific to the enclosing class X:
X::X() { yptr = new Y( 100 ); }                               //(H)
X::Y* X::get_yptr(){ return yptr; }                           //(I)


//Definitions specific to the nested class Y:
X::Y::Y( int mm ) { m = mm; }                                 //(J)
void X::Y::printY(){ cout << "m of nested class object: "
                            << m << endl; }                   //(K)

int main() {
    X x;
    x.get_yptr()->printY();
    return 0;
}
```

Note how in line (I) the return type of the function `get_yptr()` of class X is declared to be `X::Y*`. Also note how in line (J) the constructor for the nested class Y is accessed via `X::Y::Y( int mm )`.[17] Even the definition of a nested class can be taken outside the outermost enclosing class. So the code in lines (A) through (G) in the previous program can be replaced by

```
    class X {
        class Y;
        Y* yptr;
    public:
        X();
        Y* get_yptr();
    };


    class X::Y {
        int m;
```

---

[17]When the implementation code for a nested class member in C++ is not provided inside the class definition, it can only be provided outside the outermost enclosing class using the class scope operator in the manner shown.

```
public:
    Y( int mm );
    void printY();
};
```

Here are some important facts to bear in mind about the relationship between an enclosing class and a nested class:

- An enclosing class cannot directly access the private members of a nested class. The definition of the enclosing class must include a "friend" declaration for the nested class if the former is to have direct access to the private members of the latter.

- A nested class cannot directly access the private data members of the enclosing class. The definition for the nested class must include a "friend" declaration for the enclosing class if the former is to have direct access to the private members of the latter.

- A static member of the enclosing class can be accessed inside a nested class without the intermediary of an object of the enclosing class. (This is to be expected since a static member is global with respect to all the objects of a class.)

- A nonstatic member of the enclosing class can be accessed inside a nested class only through the intermediary of an object of the enclosing type. (This is again to be expected, since a nonstatic class member can only exist on a per-object basis.)

The last two points made above are illustrated by the following program in which the enclosing class X has two data members, one nonstatic and one static, in lines (A) and (B), respectively. The nested class accesses these in lines (C) and (D). The nonstatic data member of the enclosing class is accessed through a pointer to an object of the enclosing class type in line (C). On the other hand, the static member of the enclosing class, initialized in line (F), is accessed directly in line (D).

```
//EnclosingClassAccess.cc

#include <iostream>

class X {
public:
    int regularIntEnclosing;                        //(A)
    static int staticIntEnclosing;                  //(B)

    class Y{
    public:
```

```
        int m;
        int n;
        Y( X* xptr ) {
            m = xptr->regularIntEnclosing;                      //(C)
            n = staticIntEnclosing;                             //(D)
        }
    };

    X( int n ) { regularIntEnclosing = n; }                     //(E)
};

int X::staticIntEnclosing = 300;                                //(F)

int main() {
    X* xptr = new X( 100 );
    X::Y y( xptr );
    return 0;
}
```

For the case of C++, it is also possible (and common) to nest type definitions created by typedef and enumerations inside an enclosing class, as in lines (A) and (B) in the example below:

```
//NestedTypes.cc

class X {};

class Y {
public:
    typedef X Z;                                                //(A)
    enum Weight { light, medium, heavy };                       //(B)
private:
    Z zobj;
    Weight weight;
};

int main() {
    // Z zobj;                      // error
    Y::Z zobj;                      // ok
    // Weight w = medium;           // error
    // Y::Weight w = medium;        // error
    Y::Weight w = Y::medium;        // ok
    return 0;
}
```

Note the fact that the type Z and the enum `Weight` are not directly available in the global namespace in `main`. However, if needed, Z is available in `main` through the class Y via the scope operator. The same is true for the enumeration.

3.16.2 Nested Classes in Java

What a nested class does for C++ is achieved by a *static* nested class in Java.[18] Here is the Java equivalent of the C++ nested classes program `NestedClass.cc` shown in the preceding subsection:

```
//NestedClass.java

class X {                                              //(A)
    static class Y{                                    //(B)
        private int m;
        public Y( int mm ) { m = mm; }
        public void printY(){
            System.out.println( "m of nested class object: " + m );
        }
    }

    private Y yref;

    public X() { yref = new Y( 100 ); }

    Y get_yref(){ return yref; }
}

class Test {
    public static void main( String[] args ) {
        X x = new X();
        x.get_yref().printY();    // m of nested class object: 100
    }
}
```

The class X contains a nested type defined by the class Y in line (B). The definition of class Y is like that of any other class in Java; it is allowed to have its own constructors, data members and methods, with different access privileges, if so desired. Since a static nested class in Java creates a type with respect to the enclosing class, it can only be accessed via the enclosing class. To illustrate this fact, in the following version of the above program, the nested class Y is in the public section of the enclosing class

---

[18]A nested interface in Java is implicitly a static member of the enclosing type.

X. We can use it like any other class to declare variables provided we access it via the X.Y notation, as shown below:

```java
//NestedClassAsType.java

class X {

    public static class Y{                                          //(A)
        private int m;
        public Y( int mm ) { m = mm; }
        public void printY(){
            System.out.println( "m of nested class obj: " + m );
        }
    }

    private Y yref;

    public X() { yref = new Y( 100 ); }

    Y get_yref(){ return yref; }
}


class Test {
    public static void main( String[] args ) {
        X x = new X();
        x.get_yref().printY();  // m of nested class obj: 100

        X.Y y = new X.Y( 200 );                                     //(B)
        y.printY();                 // m of nested class obj: 200
    }
}
```

Note how in line (B) the variable y is declared to be of type X.Y and how the constructor for Y is invoked through the full name of the nested class, X.Y.

The following example parallels (and also illustrates an important difference between C++ and Java) the C++ code of the program EnclosingClassAccess.cc. As with the earlier C++ program EnclosingClassAccess.cc, our enclosing class has a nonstatic data member in line (A) and a static data member in line (B). To access the nonstatic data member in line (C), we must do so through the intermediary of an object of the enclosing type. But, as we show in line (D), the static data member of the enclosing class can be accessed directly.

```
//EnclosingClassAccess.java

class X {
    private int regularIntEnclosing;                        //(A)
    private static int staticIntEnclosing = 300;            //(B)

    public static class Y{
        private int m;
        private int n;
        Y( X xref ) {
            m = xref.regularIntEnclosing;                   //(C)
            n = staticIntEnclosing;                         //(D)
        }
    }

    public X( int n ) { regularIntEnclosing = n; }          //(E)
}

class Test {
    public static void main( String[] args ) {
        X x = new X( 100 );
        X.Y y = new X.Y( x );                               //(F)
    }
}
```

With regard to restrictions on the access to the members of the enclosing class, the main difference between the Java code shown above and the C++ code in the equivalent EnclosingClassAccess.cc is that, for the Java case, we kept the data members of the enclosing class private and were still able to access them inside the nested class. If we had made the data members private for the C++ example, we'd need to also make the nested class a friend of the enclosing class for the C++ and the Java programs to remain logically identical. The important point to note about the Java case is that a nested class is like any other member for the enclosing class; the private members of the enclosing class are visible everywhere, even inside nested classes.

Java also permits you define a nonstatic nested class, called an *inner class*. An inner class is defined on a per object basis with respect to the instances of the enclosing class. In other words, the type corresponding to the inner class will be defined separately for each instance of the enclosing class. For that reason, an inner class can directly access all members of the enclosing class — static as well as nonstatic.

This is illustrated by the following example in which, as before, the enclosing class has a nonstatic and a static data member in lines (A) and (B). Note the nested class is nonstatic, meaning that it is now an inner class. Lines (C) and (D) demonstrate that both the static and the nonstatic members of the enclosing class are directly accessible inside the inner class — without the intermediary of an object of the enclosing type. Since the inner class is public, we should be able to use it outside the enclosing class as a data type and create object of that type. Line (G) demonstrates that to construct an object of the inner type, you have to invoke the operator new on the enclosing object.

```
//InnerClass.java

class X {
    private int regularIntEnclosing;                              //(A)
    private static int staticIntEnclosing = 300;                  //(B)

    public class Y{
        private int m;
        private int n;
        public Y() {
            m = regularIntEnclosing;                              //(C)
            n = staticIntEnclosing;                               //(D)
        }
    }

    public X( int n ) { regularIntEnclosing = n; }               //(E)
}

class Test {
    public static void main( String[] args ) {
        X x = new X( 100 );                                      //(F)
        // X.Y y = new X.Y();               // error
        X.Y y = x.new Y();                  // ok                 //(G)
    }
}
```

If X is the enclosing class for Y, the members of X can also be accessed inside Y by using the X.this prefix. This is illustrated by the following example that is identical to the above program, except that we have used the same names, m and n, for the data members of both the enclosing and the inner classes. Now how the name conflict is avoided in lines (E) and (F) by using appropriate prefixes.

```
//InnerClassThisPrefix.java

class X {
    private int m;                                                //(A)
    private static int n = 300;                                   //(B)

    public class Y{
        private int m;                                            //(C)
```

```
        private int n;                                        //(D)
        public Y() {
            this.m = X.this.m;                                //(E)
            this.n = X.this.n;                                //(F)
        }
        public String toString() {
            return "inner's state: " + this.m + "   " +  this.n;
        }
    }

    public X( int mm ) { m = mm; }                            //(G)
}

class Test {
    public static void main( String[] args ) {
        X x = new X( 100 );
        X.Y y = x.new Y();
        System.out.println( y );                 // 100 300
    }
}
```

As we mentioned at the beginning of this section, a Java interface can also contain nested interfaces and classes. The following example illustrates this idea. The interface Drawable contains a nested class Color. Any class implementing the interface would have available to it the data type Color.

```
//NestedInterface.java

interface Drawable {

    class Color {
        private int red;
        private int green;
        private int blue;
        public Color( int r, int g, int b ) {
            red = r;
            green = g;
            blue = b;
        }
    }

    void setColor( Color c );
    void draw();
}

class Rectangle implements Drawable {
```

```
private Color color;   // Color made available by the interface
private int width;
private int height;

public Rectangle( int w, int h ) {
    width = w;
    height = h;
}

public void setColor( Color c ) { color = c; }

public void draw() {
    System.out.println( "Invoke code for drawing a rectangle" );
}

public static void main( String[] args ) {
    Color col = new Color( 120, 134, 200 );
    Rectangle rect = new Rectangle( 23, 34 );
    rect.setColor( col );
    rect.draw();
}
}
```

When an interface encloses a class, that class is implicitly public and static.[19]

A nested class can have its own nested class and interfaces. If class X encloses class Y and class Y enclosed class Z, the members of X can be accessed inside Z by using the X.this prefix. Finally, an inner class is not allowed to have static members.

3.17 IMPLEMENTING OO BEHAVIOR IN C PROGRAMS

Yes, it is possible to capture, albeit in a somewhat limited sense, the three important elements of OO behavior — encapsulation, inheritance, and polymorphism — in purely C code. It is also educational to see how this can be done, in the same sense that it is educational to build a model airplane to gain insights into the workings of a real airplane. Actually, in their power and functionality the OO programs in C go beyond what would be suggested by this airplane-based analogy. Recent years have seen the emergence of a powerful package of freely available software called

---

[19]Here is a summary of the implicit properties of the various things you can place inside a Java interface: (a) All methods declared inside an interface are implicitly public and nonstatic. (b) All constants in an interface are implicitly public, final, and static. (c) All classes nested inside an interface are implicitly public and static.

GNOME that is based on simulating object-orientation directly in C. GNOME, which stands for GNU Object Modeling Environment, is meant for designing graphical user interfaces for Linux/Unix based platforms.

Before showing how a limited version of object orientation can be captured directly in a C program, we need a data structure that can be used for a class. An obvious candidate for that is a C structure. But, of course, a structure in C does not directly provide us with a mechanism for data encapsulation, since all the data members of a structure object are directly accessible to the rest of the program wherever the object is in scope. Nonetheless, encapsulation with a structure can be achieved by adhering to the convention that a programmer shall access the members of a structure only through functions provided for that purpose. To illustrate this point, consider the following structure

```
typedef struct {
    char* name;
    int age;
} User;
```

We could now write the following functions for setting the values of the data members of User and for retrieving them:

```
void setUserName( User* user, char aName[] ) {
    user->name = malloc( sizeof( strlen( aName ) + 1 ) );
    strcpy( user->name, aName );
}

char* getUserName( User* user ) { return user->name; }

void setUserAge( User* user, int yy ) { user->age = yy; }

int getUserAge( User* user ) { return user->age; }
```

If we now insisted on following the convention that only these functions would be used for setting and/or retrieving the values of the members of User, we have achieved encapsulation. Remember, the purpose of encapsulation in OO is to permit a class to hold certain data members private so that objects belonging to other classes would not be able to access them directly, but only through functions designated for such purpose. Obviously, the approach to encapsulation shown here depends entirely on the cooperation of the programmer and would not be suitable for a general-purpose language for OO.

This brings us to the twin issues of inheritance and polymorphism. They can both be addressed by designating a parent structure as the first data member of a child structure. To illustrate, we will now show how one might program in C the parent-child class relationship of Figure 3.7. Here we wish for StudentUser to be a subclass of User. Using the same definition for User as given previously, we could now define StudentUser by

Fig. 3.7

```
typedef struct {
    User user;                                          /* (A) */
    char** listOfCourses;
    int numCourses;
    int whatYear;
} StudentUser;
```

Through user, defined as the first data member of type User in line (A), a StudentUser object will inherit all of the data members of User. An object of type StudentUser could be stored in the memory in the manner depicted in Figure 3.8. Of course, the data members name and age would not be directly accessible through a pointer of type StudentUser* since they are not directly the data members of the StudentUser type. We have two options to reach those data members:

```
StudentUser* student;
....
....
student->user.name;
```

or

```
StudentUser* student;
....
....
( (User*) student )->name;
```

In the first case, we access the member name through the data member user defined for the type StudentUser and in the second case we do the same by first casting the student pointer to type User* and reaching the name member directly. As depicted in the figure, both a StudentUser* pointer and the pointer obtained by casting it to User* type point to exactly the same location in the memory. Using the second approach, we can set and get the User members of a StudentUser object by using the setUserName, setUserAge, getUserName, getUserAge functions defined previously for the User type, as in the example below:

```
StudentUser* trillianUser;
trillianUser = malloc( sizeof( StudentUser ) );

setUserName( (User*) trillianUser, "Trillian" );
setUserAge( (User*) trillianUser, 38 );
getUserName( (User*) trillianUser );
```

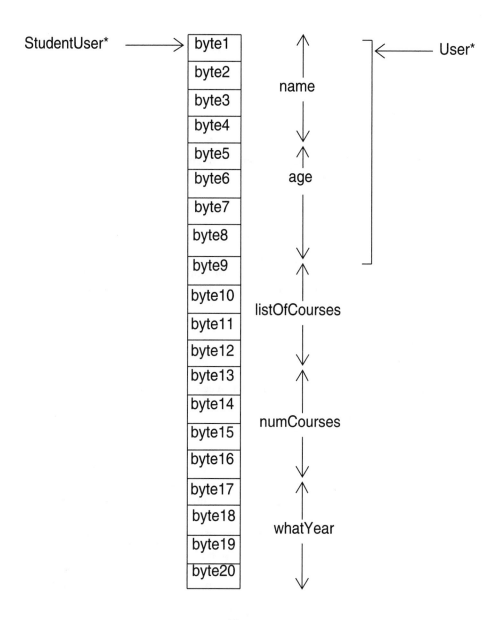

Fig. 3.8

```
getUserAge( (User*) trillianUser );
```

When different structure types are related in the manner shown above, in addition to inheritance they also exhibit polymorphic behavior, provided we use proper casting. Recall, in OO languages polymorphism basically means that we can pass a subclass type where a base class type is needed. In simulated OO in C, if we write a function such as

```
int isSenior( User* usr ) {
    if ( usr->age > 70 ) return 1;
    else return 0;
}
```

we can invoke this function with a `StudentUser` argument provided we cast the argument to its parent type, as in

```
StudentUser* trillianUser;
....
isSenior( (User*) trillianUser );
```

This means that all functions defined for the base-class type will work just the same for the subclass type. In addition, polymorphism implies the subclass type can be *assigned* to a base-class type and the resulting pointer down-cast to the subclass type. For simulated OO in C, these effects can be achieved if we remember to cast as shown below

```
StudentUser* xenonStudentUser;
...
...
User* xenonUser = (User*) xenonStudentUser;
...
...
StudentUser* p = (StudentUser*) xenonUser;
```

In the source code shown below, we have pulled together the various explanations above into a single program. We start by defining a base type in line (A) and its subtype in line (B). Lines (C) through (G) define functions for the base type `User`, and lines (H) through (K) do the same for the subtype `StudentUser`. Note that in line (I1), we need access to a base type data member through a subtype pointer.

In `main`, lines (L) and (M) then declare a base type pointer and a subtype pointer. The base type object declared in line (L) is exercised in the block of statements beginning at line (N). We do the same with the subtype object in the block of statements that begin in line (O). We apply the `isSenior()` predicate to the base type object in line (P) and to the subtype object in line (Q). Note the polymorphic behavior of this predicate in the invocation in line (Q). The last three statements in `main` show that the memory addresses of a subtype object, its base slice, and its first data member are all the same.

```
/* SimulatedOO.c */

#include <stdlib.h>
#include <string.h>
#include <stdio.h>

/* base type: */
typedef struct {                                          /* (A) */
    char* name;
    int age;
} User;

/* subtype */
typedef struct {                                          /* (B) */
    User genericUser;
    char** listOfCourses;
    int numCourses;
    int whatYear;
} StudentUser;

/* function defined for the base type User */
void setUserName( User* user, char aName[] ) {            /* (C) */
    user->name = malloc(
                     sizeof( strlen( aName ) + 1 ) );
    strcpy( user->name, aName );
}

/* function defined for the base type User */
char* getUserName( User* user ) {                         /* (D) */
    printf( "\nName of user: %s\n", user->name );
    return user->name;
}

/* function defined for the base type User */
void setUserAge( User* user, int yy ) {                   /* (E) */
    user->age = yy;
}

/* function defined for the base type User */
int getUserAge( User* user ) {                            /* (F) */
    printf( "%s's age: %d\n", user->name, user->age );
    return user->age;
}

/* function defined for the base type User */
int isSenior( User* usr ) {                               /* (G) */
    if ( usr->age > 70 ) return 1;
```

```
        else return 0;
}


/* function defined for the subtype StudentUser */
void setListOfCourses( StudentUser* student,                    /* (H) */
                    char* listCrs[], int nCourses ) {
    int i;
    char** temp;

    student->numCourses = nCourses;
    temp = malloc( nCourses * sizeof( char* ) );
    student->listOfCourses = temp;

    for (i=0; i<nCourses; i++) {
        *temp = malloc( sizeof( strlen( *listCrs ) + 1 ) );
        strcpy( *temp, *listCrs );
        temp++;
        listCrs++;
    }
}

/* function defined for the subtype StudentUser */
void printListOfCourses( StudentUser* student ) {              /* (I) */
    int i;
    char** temp;

    temp = student->listOfCourses;

    /* Here we access a field of the base type */
    /* in a function defined for the subtype:  */
    printf( "\n%s's courses: \n",
            student->genericUser.name );                      /* (I1) */

    for (i=0; i<student->numCourses; i++)
        printf( "%s\n", *temp++ );
}

/* function defined for the subtype StudentUser */
void setYear( StudentUser* student, int yy ) {                 /* (J) */
    student->whatYear = yy;
}

/* function defined for the subtype StudentUser */
int getYear( StudentUser* student ) {                         /* (K) */
    return student->whatYear;
}
```

```
int main()
{
    User* zaphod;                                        /* (L) */
    StudentUser* trillian;                               /* (M) */

    char* listCourses[] =
            {"physics", "chemistry", "algebra" };
    int numCrs =
       sizeof( listCourses ) / sizeof( listCourses[0] );

    zaphod = malloc( sizeof( User ) );                   /* (N) */
    setUserName( zaphod, "Zaphod" );
    setUserAge( zaphod, 129 );
    getUserName( zaphod );                               /* (N1) */
    getUserAge( zaphod );                                /* (N2) */

    trillian = malloc( sizeof( StudentUser ) );          /* (O) */
    setUserName( (User*) trillian, "Trillian" );
    setUserAge( (User*) trillian, 38 );
    getUserName( (User*) trillian );                     /* (O1) */
    getUserAge( (User*) trillian );                      /* (O2) */
    setListOfCourses( trillian, listCourses, numCrs );
    printListOfCourses( trillian );                      /* (O3) */

    printf( "\nZaphod is senior is %s\n",
      isSenior( zaphod ) ? "true" : "false" );           /* (P) */

    /* polymorphism in action */
    printf( "\nTrillion is senior is %s\n\n",
      isSenior( (User*) trillian ) ? "true" : "false" ); /* (Q) */

    printf( "trillian object starts at address: %p\n", trillian );
                                                         /* (R) */
    printf( "name field of trillian is at address: %p\n",
                          &(trillian->genericUser.name) );
                                                         /* (S) */
    printf( "trillian when cast to User* is at address : %p\n",
                          (User*) trillian );
                                                         /* (T) */
}
```

The program produces the following output

```
Name of user: Zaphod                    /* from line N1 */
Zaphod's age: 129                        /* from line N2 */

Name of user: Trillian                   /* from line O1 */
```

```
Trillian's age: 38                                      /* from line 02 */

Trillian's courses:                                     /* from line 03 */
physics
chemistry
algebra


Zaphod is senior is true                                /* from line P */

Trillion is senior is false                             /* from line Q */

trillian object starts at address: 0x8049b38            /* from line R */
name field of trillian is at address: 0x8049b38         /* from line S */
trillian when cast to User* is at address : 0x8049b38 /* from line T */
```

3.18 SUGGESTIONS FOR FURTHER READING

Within the various sections of this chapter, we have already provided forward pointers to other places in the book where the relevant concepts are discussed in greater detail.

The references cited in the "Suggestions for Further Reading" section of Chapter 2 are also valid for the concepts laid out in this chapter. To add to those sources, the reader is referred to [54, pp. 723-787], [6, pp. 27-80], and [16] for extended discussions related to the fundamental notions of encapsulation, inheritance, and polymorphism; to Section 13.10 of the book by Lippman and Lajoie [50] for a more thorough treatment of nested classes in C++; and to the book by Flanagan [19] for an easy-to-read discussion on the abstract classes and interfaces in Java. The reader will also find the on-line source [10] useful for language-specific details concerning C++. The material on simulating object orientation in C was inspired by the discussion in [25].

3.19 HOMEWORK

1. Will this C++ program compile? If the code shown in not legal, what's wrong with it and how will you fix it?

```cpp
class X {
    int n;
public:
    void X( int i ) { n = i; }
};

int main() { X xobj( 100 ); }
```

2. Will this Java program compile? If the code shown in not legal, what's wrong with it and how will you fix it?

```
class X {
    private int n;
    public void X( int i ) { n = i; }
}

class Test {
    public static void main( String[] args ) {
        X xobj = new X(100);
    }
}
```

3. Do you see any parallels between the children's riddle: "Who is bigger? Mr. Bigger or Mr. Bigger's little baby?" and the question "Which is bigger? A class or a class's little baby (meaning a subclass)?"

4. Provide C++ and Java definitions for an `Account` class that could be used for a bank account. The class would need at least four data members: `name`, `balance`, `accountNumber`, and `interestRate`. Specify a constructor and a print function for the class. Give some thought to whether you'd want these data members to be public, private, or protected. You'd obviously not want to make all the class members public since that'd destroy the privacy of an account.

Let the `Account` class be the parent class of the subclasses named `SavingsAccount` and `CheckingAccount`. The subclass `SavingsAccount` should have an additional data member signifying whether the savings can to be used for short-term high-risk investments or long-term low-risk invest- ments. The subclass `CheckingAccount` would need a data member signifying the minimum balance to be maintained in the account. As with the parent class, your subclasses would also need constructors and print functions.

Your homework should show the class definitions. Your homework should also show some specific objects created from the classes and successful invocations of the print functions for the different types of objects.

5. The following Java class does something rather "peculiar"; in line (A) it sets its data member y equal to the value of the data member x. The class comes with two constructors, in lines (B) and (C). The constructor in line (B) supplies a value for each of the two data members of the class. On the other hand, the constructor in line (C) initializes only the data member x. What will be printed

out by the statements in lines (D) and (E)? [*Note: You'll probably be surprised by the correct answer to the question, which you can find out by compiling and running the program. The discussion in Section 7.3 will help you understand the behavior of the program.*]

```
class X {
    private int x;
    private int y = x;                          //(A)

    X( int xx, int yy ) { x = xx; y = yy; }     //(B)
    X( int xx ) { x = xx; }                     //(C)

    public String toString() { return "" + x + " " + y; };

    public static void main( String[] args ) {
        X xobj = new X( 100, 200 );
        System.out.println( xobj );             //(D)

        xobj = new X( 300 );
        System.out.println( xobj );             //(E)
    }
}
```

6. The `print( X* )` function defined below is not able to do its job because m and n are in the private section of the class X? How can this situation be fixed with a single *additional* declaration in the definition of class X? (You are not allowed to change the access control property for any of the members of X.)

```
class X {
    int m;
    int n;
public:
    X( int mm, int nn ) { m = mm; n = nn; }
};

void print( X* ptr ) {
    cout << ptr->m << "  " << ptr->n << endl;
}
```

7. Here is an example of a nested interface in Java. Would this code fragment compile?

```
interface X {
    interface Y {
        void doSomething_Y();
```

```
    }
    void doSomething_X();
}

class Z implements X {
    public void doSomething_X() {}
    public void doSomething_Y() {}
}
```

8. The following Java program does not compile. The compiler reports a problem with the statement in line (A). How will you fix it? (Let's say that you really need to construct an object of type Y in line (A). So commenting out that statement is not an option.)

```
interface X {
    interface Y {
        void doSomething_Y();
    }
    void doSomething_X();
}

class Z implements X {
    public void doSomething_X() {}
    public void doSomething_Y() {}
    public static void main( String[] args ) {
        X x = new Z();
        Y y = new Z();                          //(A)
    }
}
```

4

Strings

In the teaching of C++ and Java, it is always difficult to decide when exactly to discuss the topic of strings. Consider, for example, the case of C++ strings. To fully understand this data type in C++, one has to have already been exposed to operator overloading, but operator overloading is best discussed after the notion of a class is fully aired. While we did provide a basic introduction to classes in Chapter 3, many more issues related to classes still need to be addressed — issues that sometimes are easier to understand if the string type is used to illustrate the examples (as we did for some of the definitions in Chapter 3).

We will therefore go ahead and and use this chapter to present the strings types in C++ and Java. The goal here is to only provide a level of familiarity with the string types that allows a reader to understand the examples in the chapters that follow. Additional information on the string types will be subsequently provided wherever the ongoing discussion makes it possible to do so.

Since it is possible to implement C++ string processing functions using the more generic C functions from the string.h header file of the C standard library,[1] this chapter will start with a very brief review of how strings are stored and processed in C. We will then discuss some of shortcomings of C-style strings, which will provide us with motivation for learning about strings in C++ and Java.

---

[1]For example, overload definitions for the '==,' '<', and '>' operators used in the C++ string class *could* use the strcmp() function of C for comparing strings.

4.1 STRINGS IN C, A BRIEF REVIEW

A C-style string is defined as an array of characters that terminates in the null character. For example, in a C program the following would declare a string variable str with a storage allocation of 6 characters, the last character being reserved for the terminating null character:

```
char str[6];
```

If we wish to also initialize a string variable at the time it is declared, we can do so by

```
char str[5 + 1] = "hello";
```

or by

```
char str[] = "hello";                                    /* (A) */
```

where we have omitted the length of the array str. The double-quoted string of characters on the right-hand side, "hello", is called a string literal.[2] A string literal is a string *constant*, very much like the number 5 is an integer constant. Since a string literal is stored as an array of chars, the compiler represents it by the memory address of the first character, in the above case the address of the character h. More precisely, the type of a string literal is const char*.

We can also use a character pointer directly to represent a string, as in

```
char* str = "hello";                                     /* (B) */
```

which causes the address of the first character, h, of the string literal "hello" to be stored in the pointer variable str. Note that the declaration in (B) gives you direct access to the block of memory, that is read-only, in which the string literal is stored. On the other hand, the declaration in (A) copies the string literal from wherever it is stored into the designated array.

While we may declare a string variable to be an array of characters, as in the definition in line (A) above, or to be a character pointer, as in the definition in line (B), the two versions are not always interchangeable. In the array version, the individual characters can be modified, as would be the case with an array in general. However, with the pointer version, the individual characters of the string cannot be changed because a string literal, being of type const char*, is stored in a read-only section of the memory. The fact that a statement such as the one shown in line (B) is legal is because the compiler allows you to assign a const char* type to char* type. So whereas the pointer str in line (B) is of type char*, it is pointing to a block of

---

[2]The initialization syntax shown at (A) copies over the string literal stored in a read-only section of the memory into the array. Therefore, effectively, the declaration shown at (A) is equivalent to

```
char str[] = { 'h', 'e', 'l', 'l', 'o', '\0' } ;
```

read-only memory in which the string literal itself is stored.[3] For another difference between the string definitions in lines (A) and (B), the identifier `str` in the array version is the *name* of an array — it cannot be assigned values as it cannot serve as an `lvalue`. On the other hand, in the pointer version in line (B), `str` is a pointer variable that, during program execution, could be given any value of type `char*`.

We will now review briefly the frequently used functions in C that are provided by the `string.h` header file for performing operations on strings. These include `strcmp` whose prototype is given by

```
int strcmp( const char* arg1, const char* arg2 );
```

for comparing two strings that are supplied to it as `arg1` and `arg2`. It returns a value less than, equal to, or greater than 0 depending on whether `arg1` is less than, equal to, or greater than `arg2`. Typically, ASCII character sets are used and strings are compared using the ASCII integer codes associated with the characters. For example, the following inequality is true for the one-character strings shown

```
strcmp( "A", "a" )   < 0
```

because the ASCII code for the character A is 65, whereas the ASCII code for a is 97, making the string literal "A" less than the string literal "a". Given this character by character comparison on the basis of ASCII codes, longer strings are compared using lexicographic ordering — an ordering that is akin to how words are arranged in a dictionary. For example, in lexicographic ordering, the string ''abs'' will occur before the string absent, so the former is less than the latter. However, the string Zebra will occur before the string debra, as the former is less than the latter because the ASCII codes for all uppercase letters, A through Z, occupy the range 65 through 90, whereas the codes for lowercase letters, a through z, occupy the range 97 through 122.

Another frequently used string function from the `string.h` header file is the `strlen` function for ascertaining the length of a string. This function has the following prototype:

```
size_t strlen( const char* arg );
```

---

[3] Some C and C++ compilers do allow a string literal to be modified through a pointer to which the string literal is assigned. For example, the following will work with some compilers:

```
char* str = "hello";
*str = 'j';
```

But modifying a string literal though a pointer in this manner could result in non-portable code. If you must modify a string literal, it is best to first copy it into an array that is stored at a location different from where the string literal itself is stored, as in

```
char str[] = "hello";
str[0] = 'j';
```

String literals being represented by `const char*` allows for code optimization, such as achieved by storing only one copy of each literal.

where the return type, `size_t`, defined in the header file `stddef.h`, is usually either `unsigned int` or `unsigned long int`. For practically all cases, we can simply think of the value returned by `strlen` as an integer. To illustrate,

```
strlen( "hello" )
```

returns 5. Note that the integer count returned by `strlen` does not include the terminating null character.

Another very useful C function for dealing with strings is

```
char* strcpy( char* arg1, const char* arg2 );
```

which copies the characters from the string `arg2` into the memory locations pointed to by `arg1`. For illustration, we could say

```
char str1[6];
char* str2 = "hello";
strcpy( str1, str2 );
```

or, using the C memory allocation function `malloc()`,

```
char* str1 = (char*) malloc( 6 );
char* str2 = "hello";
strcpy( str1, str2 );
```

In both cases above, the string `hello` will be copied into the memory locations pointed to by the character pointer `str1`. The function `strcpy()` returns the pointer that is its first argument. However, in most programming, the value returned by `strcpy()` is ignored. The returned value can be useful in nested calls to this function [45, p. 252].

When one wants to join two strings together, the following function from the `string.h` header comes handy

```
char* strcat( char* arg1, const char* arg2 );
```

This function appends the string pointed to by `arg2` to the string pointed to by `arg1`. For example,

```
char str1[8];
strcpy( str1, ''hi'' );
strcat( str1, ''there'' );
```

will cause the string `hithere` to be stored at the memory locations pointed to by `str1`. As with the `strcpy()` function, the string concatenation function returns the pointer to its first argument. But again as before, the returned value is usually ignored in most programming.

4.2 SOME COMMON SHORTCOMINGS OF C-STYLE STRINGS

C-style strings can be painful to use, especially after you have seen the more modern representations of strings in other languages. For starters, when invoking some of the most commonly used string library functions in C, such as a `strcpy()`, `strcat()`, and so on, you have to ensure that sufficient memory is allocated for the output string. This requirement, seemingly natural to those who do most of their programming in C, appears onerous after you have experienced the convenience of the modern string types.

Consider this sample code for the `string` type from the C++ Standard Library:

```
string str1 = "hi";
string str2 = "there";
string str3;
str3 = str1 + str2;
```

We are joining the strings `str1` and `str2` together and copying the resulting string into the string object `str3`. Using the operator `+` for joining two strings together seems very natural. More particularly, note that we do not worry about whether or not we have allocated sufficient memory for the new longer string. The system automatically ensures that the string object `str3` has sufficient memory available to it for storing the new string, regardless of its length.

Now compare the above code fragment with the following fragment that tries to do the same thing but with C-style strings using commonly used functions for string processing in C:

```
char* str1 = "hi";
char* str2 = "there";
char* str3 = (char*) malloc( strlen( str1 ) + strlen( str2 ) + 1 );
strcpy( str3, str1 );
strcat( str3, str2 );
```

The syntax here is definitely more tortured. A visual examination of the code, if too hasty, can be confusing with regard to the purpose of the code. You have to remind yourself about the roles of the functions `strcpy` and `strcat` to comprehend what's going on. You also have to remember to allocate memory for `str3` — forgetting to do so is not as uncommon as one might like to think. What's worse, for proper memory allocation for `str3` you have to remember to add 1 for the null terminator to the byte count obtained by adding the values returned by `strlen` for the strings `str1` and `str2`. (Just imagine the disastrous consequences if you should forget!)

For another example of the low-level tedium involved and the potential for introducing bugs when using C-style strings, consider the following function:

```
void strip( char* q ) {
    char* p = q + strlen( q ) - 1;                    //(A)
    while ( *p == ' ' && p >= q )                      //(B)
        *p-- = '\0';                                   //(C)
}
```

which could be used to strip off blank space at the trailing end of a string. So in a call such as

```
char* str = (char*) malloc( 10 );
strcpy( str, "hello      " );
strip( str );
```

the function `strip` would erase the five blank space characters after "hello" in the string `str`. Going back to the definition of `strip`, in line (A) we first set the local pointer p to point to the last character in the string. In line (B), we dereference this pointer to make sure that a blank space is stored there and that we have not yet traversed all the way back to the beginning of the string. If both these conditions are satisfied, in line (C) we dereference the pointer again, setting its value equal to the null character, and subsequently decrement the pointer.[4] If someone were to write in a hurry the implementation code for `strip`, it is not inconceivable that they'd write it in the following form:

```
void strip( char* q ) {
    char* p = q + strlen( q ) - 1;
    while ( *p == ' ' )                                //(D)
        *p-- = '\0';
}
```

where in line (D) we have forgotten to make sure that that the local pointer p does not get decremented to a value before the start of the argument string. While this program would compile fine and would probably also give correct results much of the time, it could also cause exhibit unpredictable behavior. In programs such as this, one could also potentially forget to dereference a string pointer resulting in programs that would compile alright, but not run without crashing.

---

[4]Recall from C programming that the unary postfix increment operator, '--', has a higher precedence than the indirection operator '*'. So the expression *ptr-- in line (C) is parsed as *(ptr--). But because the decrement operator is postfix, the expression ptr-- evaluates to ptr. Therefore, what gets dereferenced is ptr. It is only after the evaluation of the expression that ptr is decremented by the postfix decrement operator.

4.3 C++ STRINGS

C++ has a built-in type `string` that avoids the pitfalls of C-style strings.[5] Since many aspects of this type cannot be fully explained until we discuss concepts such as operator overloading, our goal in this section is limited to familiarizing the reader with some rudimentary aspects of this type to the extent that we can use it in some of the examples in this and later chapters. To use the C++ `string` type, you must include its associated header file:

```
#include <string>
```

4.3.1 Constructing a C++ String Object

To declare a string with initialization, we can say

```
string str( "hi there");
```

which is a call to the constructor of the `string` class with "hi there" as its `const char*` argument. An alternative way to initialize a `string` is

```
string str = "hi there";
```

. We can also use the following syntax:

```
string str = string( "hi there" );
```

We can think of the right-hand side here as constructing an *anonymous* `string` object that is then assigned to the variable `str` through what's known as the copy constructor for the `string` class.[6] We also have the option of invoking the `new` operator to obtain a pointer to a string object:

```
string* p = new string( "hi there" );
```

An empty string can be declared in the following manner[7]

```
string str;
```

or as

---

[5]Actually, the built-in string type in C++ is the template class `basic_string`. The C++ `string` class is a `typedef` alias for `basic_string<char>`, which is the `basic_string` template with char as its template parameter. The concept of a template class, introduced briefly in Chapter 3, is presented more fully in Chapter 13.

[6]Copy constructors are discussed in Chapter 11.

[7]Depending on how the `string` type is implemented, a C++ string may not include a null terminator at the end. In that case, an empty C++ can be truly empty, as opposed to a "" string in C which consists of the null terminator.

```
string str = "";
```

These declarations create an object of class string whose name is str.[8] A principal feature of this object is that it stores inside it the string of characters specified by the initialization syntax. The stored string may or may not be null terminated. If in a particular implementation of C++, the string is not null terminated, that does not create a problem because also stored in the object is the exact length of the string. So there is never any question about how many memory locations would need to be accessed in order to read an entire string.

While the string constructor invocations illustrated above show us how to convert a const char* string into a string object, what about the opposite? How does one convert a C++ string object back into a C-style null-terminated string? This is done by invoking the c_str() member function for the string class:

```
string str( "hello" );
const char* c_string = str.c_str();
```

4.3.2 Accessing Individual Characters

The individual characters of a C++ string can be accessed for reading and writing by either using the subscript operator '[]' or the member function at(). The former is not range checked, while the latter is. What that means is that suppose you try to access a character position that does not really exist, what you get with the subscript operator is unpredictable, meaning implementation dependent. On the other hand, if you try to access a nonexistent position with the at() function, the program is guaranteed to abort. This is illustrated by the following program where we have commented out the line in which we invoke the at() function with an argument that is clearly outside the range valid for the "hello" string. If you uncomment this line, the program will abort at run time when the flow of control reaches that line. On the other hand, when we try to reach the same index with the subscript operator, we may see some garbage character displayed on the screen.

```
// StringCharIndexing.cc

#include <string>
using namespace std;

int main()
{
    string str( "hello" );
    char ch = str[0];                 // ch initialized to 'h'
```

---

[8]We could also have said: "This declaration creates an object of *type* string." For nonprimitive types, the characterizations *type* and *class* are used interchangeably in object-oriented programming.

```
str[0] = 'j';                  // str now equals "jello"
ch = str.at( 0 );              // ch's value is now 'j'
str.at(0) = 'h';               // str agains equals "hello"
ch = str[ 1000 ];              // garbage value for ch
// ch = str.at( 1000 );        // program aborts if uncommented
return 0;
}
```

4.3.3   String Comparison

Two strings can be compared for equality (or inequality) on the basis of the ASCII codes associated with the characters using the binary operators '==', '!=', '>', '>=', '<', and '<='. Two strings are equal if and only if they are composed of identical character sequences. A string is less than another string if the former occurs earlier in a lexicographic ordering of the strings on the basis of the ASCII codes associated with the characters.

While the operators listed above are all binary, in the sense that they return either true or false, sometimes it is more useful to employ a 3-valued comparison function, compare(), that is defined for the string class. Given two string objects str1 and str2, the invocation

```
str1.compare( str2 );
```

returns one of three possible values:

> a positive value if str1 is greater than str2
>
> 0 if str1 is equal to str2
>
> a negative value if str1 is less than str2

For example,

```
string str1( "abc" );
string str2( "abc123" );
if ( str1.compare( str2 ) == 0 )   // test returns false
  .....
if ( str1.compare( str2 ) < 0 )    // test returns true
  .....
if ( str1.compare( str2 ) > 0 )    // test rturns false
  ....
```

It is also possible to invoke compare with additional arguments that designate at what character position to start the comparison in the invoking string and how many characters to use from the argument string. In the following example, "hello" is the string that invokes `compare` on the argument string "ellolotion" in line (A). The second argument to `compare` in line (A) — in this case 1 — designates the index at which the start the character comparisons in the string "hello". This means that the string comparison will begin at the letter 'e' of "hello". The third argument to `compare` in line (A) is 4; this is the number of characters from the string "ellolotion" that will be used for string comparison.

```
string str1("hello");
string str2("ellolotion");
if ( str1.compare( str2, 1, 4 ) == 0 )                        //(A)
    cout << "\nThe substring starting at index 1 "
            "of 'hello' is the same as the first "
            "four chars of 'ellolotion'."
        << endl;                                              //(B)
else
    cout << "The compare test failed" << endl;
```

For the example code shown, the comparison test in line (A) returns true and the message in the statement leading up to line (B) is printed out.

In the three-argument version of `compare` shown in line (A) above, the second argument is of type `string::size_type`,[9] which for all practical purposes can be considered to be `int`, and the third argument of type `unsigned int`. There is also a two-argument version of `compare` in which the second argument plays the same role as in the example shown. Now the comparison is with the entire argument string. We should also mention that the `compare` function works just the same if its first argument is a C-style `const char*` string.[10]

A 3-valued string comparison function, such as the `compare` function, is what you'd need for certain kinds of string sorting functions. Let's say we wish to sort an array of string literals as shown below:

```
string wordList[] = {"hello", "halo", "jello", "yellow",     //(C)
                    "mellow", "Hello", "JELLO", "Yello",
                    "MELLOW"};
```

Although later the reader will be introduced to the sorting functions designed expressly for C++, we can sort this array by using the venerated `qsort` function defined originally in the `stdlib.h` header file of the C standard library, but also made available through the header file `string` of C++. The function `qsort`, frequently an implementation of quick-sort, is capable of sorting an array of any data type as long

---

[9]On the basis of the notation explained in Section 3.16.1 of Chapter 3, the syntax `string::size_type` refers to inner type `size_type` defined for the `string` class.

[10]This is actually true of all string member functions. They work the same for both `string` and `const char*` arguments.

as you are able to specify a comparison function for the elements of the array.[11]   The prototype of qsort is

```
void qsort( void* base,                                          //(D)
            size_t nmemb,
            size_t size,
            int (* compar)( const void*, const void* ) );
```

where base is a pointer to the first element of the array to be sorted, nmemb the number of elements to be sorted,[12] size the size of each element in bytes,[13] and, finally, compar a pointer to a user-defined function for comparing any two elements of the array. The user defined comparison function that will be bound to the parameter compar must return an int and must take exactly two arguments, both of type void*. Furthermore, for qsort() to work correctly, the int returned by the comparison function must be positive when the entity pointed to by the first argument is greater than the entity pointed to by the second argument; must be negative when the opposite is the case; and must be zero when the two entities are equal.

Here is a possible comparison function for the fourth argument of qsort for sorting the elements of the array wordList of line (C) above:[14]

```
int compareStrings( const void* arg1, const void* arg2 ) {    //(E)
    return ( *( static_cast<const string*>( arg1 ) ) ).compare(
                        *( static_cast<const string*>( arg2) ) );
}
```

In terms of the return type and the parameter structure, this comparison function corresponds exactly to what is specified for the fourth argument of qsort() in line (D). The actual comparison is carried out by invoking the compare function of the string class.

Shown below is a simple program that pulls together the code fragments shown above into a complete program:

---

[11] In Chapter 5, we discuss the notion of *stable sorting* for class type objects and point out that qsort may not be the best sorting function to invoke in some cases.

[12] We can think of size_t as an unsigned integer.

[13] For the example array shown, each element of the array is a string object that is initialized by the corresponding string literal on the right hand side of the declaration for wordList. So we can use sizeof(string) for the third argument of qsort.

[14] Typical C syntax for the same function would be

```
int compareStrings( const void* arg1, const void* arg2 ) {
    return (*(const string*) arg1).compare(*(const string*) arg2);
}
```

The difference between the C way of writing this function and the C++ syntax shown in line (E) is with regard to casting. What is done by the cast operator (const string*) in the C version here is accomplished by static_cast<const string*>() in the C++ definition in line (E). The static_cast and other C++ cast operators are presented in Chapters 6 and 16.

```
//Qsort.cc

#include <string>
using namespace std;

int compareStrings( const void* arg1, const void* arg2 );
int checkUpperCase( string buffer );

int main()
{
    string wordList[] = {"hello", "halo", "jello", "yellow",
                         "mellow", "Hello", "JELLO", "Yello",
                         "MELLOW"};

    cout << sizeof( wordList ) << endl;              // 36

    int sizeArray = sizeof( wordList ) / sizeof( wordList[ 0 ] );
    cout << sizeArray << endl;                       // 9

    qsort( wordList, sizeArray , sizeof(string), compareStrings);

    int j = 0;
    while ( j < sizeArray )
        cout << wordList[j++] << " ";
            //Hello JELLO MELLOW Yello halo hello jello mellow yellow
    cout << endl;
    return 0;
}

int compareStrings( const void* arg1, const void* arg2 ) {
    return ( *( static_cast<const string*>( arg1 ) ) ).compare(
                      *( static_cast<const string*>( arg2) ) );
}
```

4.3.4 Joining Strings Together

Through the overloading of the '+' operator, the string class makes it very easy to join strings together without having to worry whether or not you allocated sufficient memory for the result string.[15] For example, we can say

---

[15]Obviously, there has to be sufficient free memory available to the memory allocator used by the string class for this to be the case. If the memory needed is not available, the memory allocator will throw an exception.

```
string str1( "hello" );
string str2( "there" );
string str3 = str1 + " " + str2;     // "hello there"
str2 += str1;                        // "therehello"
```

which would result in the object str3 storing the string "hello there" and the object str2 storing the string "therehello". The operator '+' works the same if the second operand is of type const char* or just char as long as the first operand is an object of type string.[16] So while the following will not work

```
string s = "hello" + " there";       // Wrong
```

the following does:

```
string s = string( "hello" ) + " there";
```

It is also possible to use the append member function for joining two strings, or one string with a part of another string, as the following example illustrates:

```
string string1( "hello" );
string string2( " the world at large" );
string string3 = string1;

string3.append( string2 );                                    //(A)
cout << string3;           // "hello the world at large"

string1.append( string2, 3, 6 );                              //(B)
cout << string1;           // "hello world"
```

In the one-argument invocation of append in line (A), the entire argument string is appended to the invoking string. In the three-argument version of append, shown in line (B), a substring from the argument string is appended to the invoking string. The substring begins at the index specified by the second argument, with the third argument specifying its length. The second and the third arguments in the three-argument version are both of type string::size_type, which as mentioned before can be taken to be the same as int for the purpose of program design.

There is also a two-argument version of append in which the second argument is the same as the second argument of the three-argument version. In this case, the entire argument string starting at the specified index is appended to the invoking string.

---

[16]As we will explain in Chapter 12, for class type operands the compiler translates the expression

```
str1 + str2;
```

into

```
str1.operator+( str2 );
```

where the function operator+ contains the overload definition for the '+' operator. That makes str1 the operand on which the function operator+ is invoked and str2 the argument operand. We may loosely refer to str1 as the invoking operand.

As is true of all `string` class member functions, the argument string can also be a C-style `const char*` string.

4.3.5 Searching for Substrings and Characters

A frequent problem in string processing is that we want to know if a given string has particular substrings or particular characters in it. Consider, for example, the problem of isolating words in a text file. Of the many different ways of solving this problem, one would be to read the file one line at a time and to then look for whitespace characters in each line. If not excessively large, we could even read the entire file as a single string and then look for whitespace characters (which include line-feeds and carriage returns) to break the string into individual words.

The C++ `string` library provides a number of functions for searching for substrings and individual characters in a string. These functions are named `find`, `rfind`, `find_first_of`, `find_last_of`, `find_first_not_of`, and `find_last_not_of`. In all there are 24 functions with these six names, the various versions of the functions catering to different types of arguments. In this section, we will explain how one can invoke `find` and `find_first_of` on string type objects with `string` or `char` type arguments. (Their usage on `const char*` type arguments is parallel to the usage on `string` arguments.) The functions `rfind` do the same thing as `find`, except that they start the search from the end of a string towards its beginning. The functions `find_last_of` again do the same thing as `find_first_of`, except that they start their search at the end of a string toward its beginning.

Here is an example that illustrates how one can invoke `find` to search for a substring in a string:

```
string::size_type pos = 0;
string quote(  "Some cause happiness wherever they go,"
               " others whenever they go - Oscar Wilde" );
if ( ( pos = quote.find( "happiness" ) ) != string::npos )     //(A)
    cout << "The quote contains the word 'happiness'" << endl;
```

The function `find` returns the index of the character in the invoking string where it scores a match with the argument string. This index, although officially of type `string::size_type`, can be taken to be an `int` for all practical purposes. If no match is found, `find` returns a symbolic constant `string::npos`, a static data member of the `string` class also of type `size_t`. The actual value of `npos` is such that no actual character index in any valid string would ever correspond to it. In the above program fragment, note how we compare the value returned by `find` with the symbolic constant `npos` to establish the presence or the absence of the substring.

The following program shows a simple demonstration of the use of `find`. It also shows how `replace`, another member function of the `string` class, can be used together with `find` to search for each occurrence of a substring in a string and, when found, how the substring can be replaced with another string. The program produces the output

```
4
32
one armadillo is like any other armadillo
```

where the numbers 4 and 32 are the position indices where the substring "hello" occurs in the larger string "one hello is like any other hello". Here is the program:[17]

```
//StringFind.cc

#include <string>
using namespace std;

int main()
{
    string str( "one hello is like any other hello" );
    string searchString( "hello" );
    string replaceString( "armadillo" );

    assert( searchString != replaceString );

    string::size_type pos = 0;
    while ( (pos = str.find(searchString, pos)) != string::npos ) {
        str.replace( pos, searchString.size(), replaceString );
        pos++;
    }
    cout << str << endl;    //one armadillo is like any other armadillo
    return 0;
}
```

Note the use of the 2-argument version of find in the above program. The second argument tells find where to begin the search for the substring. When you are searching for a character or a substring with find, after you have obtained the first match, you need to increment the index represented by pos so that the search can continue on for the next occurrence. If you don't do that, find will keep on returning the same index ad infinitum.

The above example code also illustrates the use of the 3-argument replace. This function can take up to five arguments. The two additional arguments, both of type

---

[17]Note the use of the assert function in this program. The test stated in the argument to this function must evaluate to true for the thread of execution to proceed beyond the point of this function call.

string::size_type, specify the position in the argument string and the number of characters to be taken starting at that position for the purpose of replacement.

Shown below is an example of how one can use the string library function find_first_of to locate and count some of the more frequently used punctuation marks in a string. We place all the punctuation marks we are looking for in a string called marks, with the original string stored in quote. We invoke find_first_of on quote and supply it with marks as its first argument, the second argument consisting of the position index in quote where we want the search to begin. Note how we increment pos after each hit. If we did not do so, the function find_first_of will keep on returning the same location where it found the first punctuation mark. For the example shown, the program returns a count of five.

```
string quote( "Ah, Why, ye Gods, should two and two "
              "make four? - Alexander Pope" );
string marks( ",.?:;-" );
string::size_type pos = 0;
int count = 0;
while ( ( pos = quote.find_first_of( marks, pos ) )
              != string::npos ) {
    ++pos;
    ++count;
}
cout << count << endl;              // 5
```

4.3.6 Extracting Substrings

The string library offers the function substr for extracting a substring from a source string on which the function is invoked. This function can be invoked with one argument, of type size_type, that designates the index of the character that marks the start of the substring desired from the source string. The extracted substring will extend all the way to the end of the source string. This use is illustrated by the following code fragment. Here the string returned by substr will start at the position indexed 44 and go to the end of the quote. As a result, the output produced by line (B) is "Fiction has to make sense. - Tom Clancy".

```
string quote( "The difference between reality and fiction? "
              "Fiction has to make sense. - Tom Clancy" );
string str = quote.substr( 44 );
cout << str << endl;                            //(A)
```

There is also a two-argument version of substr in which the first argument works the same as in the example shown above. The second argument, also of type size_type, now designates the number of characters to be extracted from the source string. If the number of characters requested exceeds the number remaining in the source string, the extracted substring will stop at the end of the source string. The following code fragment, which will output "Fiction," illustrates this usage.

```
string quote( "The difference between reality and fiction? "
              "Fiction has to make sense. - Tom Clancy" );
string str = quote.substr( 44, 7 );
cout <<  str << endl;                    // Fiction
```

It is also possible to invoke the substr function with no arguments, in which case it simply returns a copy of the string object on which it is invoked.

Substrings can also be extracted by invoking the string constructor with a string argument and with additional optional arguments to specify the starting index for substring extraction and the number of characters to be extracted from the first argument string. In the invocations of the string constructor below that construct the objects str_1 and str_2, the first yields the substring "Fiction has to make sense. - Tom Clancy", and the second just the word "Fiction".

```
string quote( "The difference between reality and fiction? "
              "Fiction has to make sense. - Tom Clancy" );
string str_1( quote, 44 );
string str_2( quote, 44, 7 );
```

4.3.7 Erasing and Inserting Substrings

The string class member function erase can be used to erase a certain number of characters in the string on which the function is invoked. The function can be invoked with zero arguments, with one argument, and with two arguments. When invoked with no arguments, the function erases the string stored in the invoking object and replaces it with the empty string "". When invoked with one argument, which must be of type string::size_type, the string stored in the invoking object is erased from the position indexed by the second argument to the end. When invoked with two arguments, both of typestring::size_type, the second argument designates the number of characters to be erased starting at the position specified by the first argument.

The following code fragment illustrates the two-argument erase. It also illustrates the insert member function which can be used to insert a new substring into a string object. The function insert can be invoked with either two arguments, or three arguments, or four arguments. When invoked with two arguments, the first argument, of type string::size_type, designates the index of the position at which the new insertion is to begin, and the second argument the string to be inserted. In the three-argument version, the additional argument specifies a position in the argument string that designates the start of the substring to be inserted; the substring continues to the end. In the four-argument invocation, the last argument specifies the number of characters to be taken from the argument string for the purpose of insertion.

The example below shows two-argument and four-argument versions of insert.

```
string::size_type pos = 0;
string quote = "Some cause happiness wherever they go, "
               "others whenever they go - Oscar Wilde";
if ( ( pos = quote.find( "happiness" ) ) != string::npos ) {
    quote.erase( pos, 9 );
    quote.insert( pos, "excitement" );
}
cout << quote << endl;                                          //(A)
quote.erase( pos, 10 );
cout << quote << endl;                                          //(B)
quote.insert( pos, "infinite happiness in the air", 9, 9 );
cout << quote << endl;                                          //(C)
```

The code produces the following output:

```
FROM LINE (A):
  Some cause excitement wherever they go, others whenever they go - Oscar Wilde

FOME LINE (B):
  Some cause  wherever they go, others whenever they go - Oscar Wilde

FROM LINE (C):
  Some cause happiness wherever they go, others whenever they go - Oscar Wilde
```

4.3.8 Size and Capacity

The size() (or length(), which does the same thing) member function when invoked on a string object will ordinarily return the number of characters in the string stored in the object. This will also ordinarily be the amount of memory allocated to a string object for the storage of the characters of the string.

```
string str( "0123456789" );
cout << str.size() << endl;     // returns 10
```

When you extend the length of a string by using, say, the '+=' operator, the size of the allocated memory is automatically increased to accommodate the longer length. But if a string is going to be extended in bits and pieces frequently, you can reduce the background memory-allocation work by preallocating additional memory for the string through the resize() member function. If we refer to the total amount of memory currently available to a string for the storage of its characters as the string object's *capacity*, we can use resize to endow a string with any desired capacity. In the code fragment shown below, we initially create a string object of size 10 characters. At this moment the capacity of the string object is also 10. But then we increase the capacity to 20 characters by invoking `resize`, although the number of actual characters in the string is still 10.

```
//StringSize.cc

#include <iostream>
#include <string>

int main()
{
    string str = "0123456789";

    cout << "The current capacity of the string is: "
         << str.size() << endl;                        // 10
    str.resize( 20 );

    cout << "The new capacity of the string is: "
         << str.size() << endl;                        // 20

    cout << "The actual length of the string is: "     // 10
         << strlen( str.c_str() ) << endl;

    cout << "The string object after resizing "
         << "to 20 a 10 character string: "
         << str << endl;                        // "0123456789"
    str += "hello";
    cout << str << endl;                        // "0123456789hello"

    return 0;
}
```

This code shows a one-argument version of `resize`. When supplied with an optional second argument, which must be of type `char`, the designated character is used to initialize the spaces not occupied by the characters in the string, the default being the null character.

While on the subject of size, we also want to clarify the relationship between the size of a `string` object and the size of the string held by a `string` object. The size of a `string` object can be ascertained by invoking `sizeof( string )`, which for g++ returns 4 for all strings (but could return 8 on some systems). Before we go into why `sizeof( string )` returns the same number for all strings on any given system, let's quickly review the nature of `sizeof`.

Remember from C that, despite its appearance, `sizeof` is not a function, but an operator. It is not a function in the sense that it does not evaluate its argument; it only looks at the type of its argument. To illustrate the nature of this operator, all of the following invocations of sizeof[18]

```
int x = 4;
int y = 5;
sizeof(x);
sizeof(x + y);
sizeof x;
sizeof( int );
sizeof int;
```

return on the author's machine the same value, which is 4 for the 4 bytes that it takes to store an int.[19] So if we say

```
string s1 = "hello";
string s2 = "hello there";
```

and then invoke the sizeof operator by

```
sizeof( s1 );        // returns 4 for g++
sizeof( s2 );        // returns 4 for g++
```

we'd get exactly the same answer in both cases, the number 4 (or 8 for some compilers). Compare this with the following case of applying sizeof to the string literals directly:

```
sizeof( "hello" );         // returns 6
sizeof( "hello there" );   // returns 12
```

We get 6 for the string literal "hello" because it is NOT stored as a string object and because its internal representation is a null-terminated array of characters. Similarly for the string literal "hello there".

---

[18]Although the parentheses are not really needed in sizeof(x), in the sense that we could also have said sizeof x, because of operator precedence the compiler would understand sizeof(x + y) and sizeof x + y differently. Since the operator sizeof is a unary operator and since unary operators have higher precedence than binary operators, sizeof x + y; would be interpreted as sizeof(x) + y.

[19]To be precise, the sizeof operator in C++ returns the size of a type-name in terms of the size of a char. However, in most implementations, the size of a char is 1 for the 1 byte that it takes to hold a character in C++. Also as a point of difference between C++ and C, in C sizeof('x') returns 4, whereas sizeof(char) returns 1. On the other hand, in C++, both sizeof('x') and sizeof(char) return 1. The reason for the discrepancy between the two sizeof values for C is that a char argument to the operator is read as an int, as is often the case with char arguments in C. Despite this discrepancy in C, the following idiom in C

```
int size;
char arr[3] = {'x', 'y', 'z'};
size = sizeof( arr ) / sizeof( arr[0] );
```

does exactly what the programmer wants it to do (the value of size is set to 3, the number of elements in the array) because the sizeof operator looks only at the type of arr[0] in the denominator. In other words, even though sizeof('x') returns 4 in C, sizeof(arr[0]) will always return 1.

The constant value of 4 returned by sizeof(string) is easy to understand if we think of the string class as having been provided with a single non-static data member of type char* for holding a character pointer to a null-terminated array of characters.

```
class string {
    char* ptr;
    // static data members if needed
public:
    // string functions
};
```

Then the memory occupied by a string object would be what's needed by its sole nonstatic data member shown — 4 bytes for the pointer. On the other hand, if a compiler returned 8 bytes for sizeof(string), that's because the string class used by that compiler comes with an additional data member — of possibly an unsigned integer type — for holding the size of the string pointed to by the first data member. In this case, it would not be absolutely necessary for the char* string to be null terminated since the second data member would tell us directly how many characters belonged to the string.

Note that if we applied the sizeof operator to any pointer type, we'd get 4 for the four bytes to hold a memory address. For example,

```
sizeof( string* )   ->  4
sizeof( int* )      ->  4
sizeof( char* )     ->  4
```

We have brought the above statements together in the following program:

```
//StringSizeOf.cc

#include <iostream>
#include <string>

int main()
{
  cout << sizeof( "hello" ) << endl;          // 6
  cout << sizeof( "hello there" ) << endl;    // 12

  string str1 = "hello";
  string str2 = "hello there";

  cout << sizeof( str1 ) << endl;             // 4
  cout << sizeof( str2 ) << endl;             // 4

  char* s1 = "hello";
```

```
    char* s2 = "hello there";

    cout << sizeof( s1 ) << endl;                    // 4
    cout << sizeof( s2 ) << endl;                    // 4

    char c_arr[] = "how are you?";
    cout << sizeof( c_arr ) << endl;                 // 13

    return 0;
}
```

Before ending this subsection, we should remind the reader that sizeof() can sometimes show seemingly unexpected behavior. Consider the role of sizeof in the following program that attempts to find the size of the array in a called function by invoking sizeof:

```
//ArraySizeOf.cc

#include <iostream>

int sum( int [], int );

int main()
{
  int data[100] = {2, 3};
  int m = sizeof( data ) / sizeof ( data[0] );      //(A)
  cout << sum( data, 100 ) << endl;
  return 0;
}

int sum( int a[], int arr_size ) {
  //the following value of n is not very useful
  int n = sizeof( a ) / sizeof( a[0] );             // (B)

  int result = 0;
  int* p = a;
  while (p-a<arr_size) result += *p++;
  return result;
}
```

While at (A) the number m will be set to 100, at (B) the number n will be set to 1. The reason for this is that when an array name is a function parameter, it is treated strictly as a pointer. So the numerator on the right-hand side at (B) is synonymous with sizeof(int*) which yields 4.

4.3.9 Some Other String Functions

The `string` library offers a function `swap` that can be used to swap the actual strings stored inside two `string` objects. In the following code fragment, after the execution of the third statement, the object `str1` will store the string "lemonade", whereas the object `str2` will store the string "lemon".

```
string str1 = "lemon";
string str2 = "lemonade";
str1.swap( str2 );
```

A different effect is achieved by the `assign` function. After the execution of the third statement below, both the objects `str1` and `str2` will contain the string "lemonade".

```
string str1 = "lemon";
string str2 = "lemonade";
str1.assign( str2 );
```

4.4 STRINGS IN JAVA

Java provides two classes, `String` and `StringBuffer`, for representing strings and for string processing. An object of type `String` cannot be modified after it is created.[20] It can be deleted by the garbage collector if there are no variables holding references to it, but it cannot be changed. For this reason, string objects of type `String` are called *immutable*. If you want to carry out an *in-place* modification of a string, the string needs to be an object of type `StringBuffer`.

---

[20]Operations on `String` type objects sometimes have the appearance that you might be changing an object of type `String`, but that is never the case. In all such operations, a new `String` object is usually formed. For example, in the following statements the string literal `"jello"` in line (A) did not get changed into `"hello"` in line (B). The string literals `"jello"` and `"hello"` occupy separate places in the memory. Initially, `s1` holds a reference to the former literal and then to the latter literal. After `s1` changes its reference to `"hello"`, the string literal `"jello"` will eventually be garbage collected if no other variable is holding a reference to it. The statement in line (C) results in the creation of a new `String` object whose reference is held by the variable `s2`.

```
String s1 = "jello";                                    //(A)
s1 = "hello";                                           //(B)
String s2 = s1 + " there";                              //(C)
```

By the same token, in lines (D) and (E) below, the object `s2` is a new string object, as opposed to being an extension of the object `s1`:

```
String s1 = "hello";                                    //(D)
String s2 = s1.concat( "there" );                       //(E)
```

The invocation of the `concat` method in line (E) returns a new string that is a concatenation of the string on which the method is invoked and the argument string.

As in C++, a string literal in Java is double-quoted. String literals in Java are objects of type String. As in C++, two string literals consisting of the same sequence of characters are one and the same object in the memory. That is, there is only one String object stored for each string literal even when that literal is mentioned at different places in a program, in different classes, or even in different packages of a Java program.

That a string literal consisting of a given sequence of characters is stored only once in the memory is made clear by the following program. Lines (A) and (B) of the program define two different String variables, strX and strY, in two different classes; both strX and strY are initialized with string literals consisting of the same sequence of characters. Nonetheless, a comparison of the two with the '==' operator in line (D) tests true. Recall, the operator '==' returns true only when its two operands are one and the same object in the memory.

Line (C) of the program illustrates the following string-valued constant expression on the right-hand-side of the assignment operator

```
"hell" + "o"
```

In such cases, the Java compiler creates a new string literal by joining the two string literals "hell" and "o". Being still a literal, the resulting literal is not stored separately in the memory if it was previously seen by the compiler. So in our case, the variable strZ in line (C) will point to the same location in the memory as the variables strX in line (A) and strY in line (B). This is borne out by the fact that the '==' comparison in line (E) tests true.

While joining two string literals together results in a constant expression that is resolved at compile time, the assignment to the variable s3 in the following three instructions can only be made at run time. Therefore, the string hello constructed on the right-hand side in the third statement below will have a separate existence as a String object in the memory even if a string literal consisting of the same sequence of characters was created previously by the program. That should explain why the comparison in line (F) of the program tests false.

```
String s1 = "hel";
String s2 = "lo";
String s3 = s1 + s2;
```

However, Java provides a mechanism through the method intern() defined for the String class that allows a string created at run-time to be added to the pool of string literals (if it was not in the pool already). If the above three instructions are replaced with

```
String s1 = "hel";
String s2 = "lo";
String s3 = (s1 + s2).intern();
```

Java will compare the character sequence in the string object returned by s1 + s2 with the string literals already in store. If a match is found, intern() returns a reference to that literal. If a match is not found, then the string returned by s1 + s2 is added to the pool of string literals and a reference to the new literal returned. That should explain why the '==' comparison in line (G) of the program tests true. The reference returned by (s1 + s2).intern() will point to the same string literal as the data member strx of class X.

Here is the program:

```
//StringLiteralUniqueness.java

class X { public static String strX = "hello"; }               //(A)

class Y { public static String strY = "hello"; }               //(B)

class Z { public static String strZ = "hell" + "o"; }          //(C)

class Test {
    public static void main( String[] args ) {

        // output: true
        System.out.println( X.strX == Y.strY );                //(D)

        // output: true
        System.out.println( X.strX == Z.strZ );                //(E)

        String s1 = "hel";
        String s2 = "lo";

        // output: false
        System.out.println( X.strX == ( s1 + s2 ) );           //(F)

        // output: true
        System.out.println( X.strX == (s1 + s2).intern() );    //(G)
    }
}
```

4.4.1 Constructing String and StringBuffer Objects

String objects are commonly constructed using the following syntax

```
String str = "hello there";
```

or

```
String str = new String( "hello there" );
```

For constructing a `StringBuffer` object, the first declaration does not work because of type incompatibilities caused by the fact that the right hand side would be a `String` object and the left hand side a `StringBuffer` object.

```
StringBuffer strbuf = "hello there";     //WRONG
```

`StringBuffer` objects are commonly constructed using the following syntax

```
StringBuffer strbuf = new StringBuffer( "hello there" );
```

An empty `String` object, meaning a `String` object with no characters stored in it, can be created by

```
String s0 = "";
```

or by

```
String s0 = new String();
```

To create an empty `StringBuffer` object, use either

```
StringBuffer sb0 = new StringBuffer( "" );
```

or

```
StringBuffer sb0 = new StringBuffer();
```

When a `String` object is created with a nonempty initialization, the amount of memory allocated to the object for the storage of the characters equals exactly what's needed for the characters. On the other hand, when a new `StringBuffer` object is created, the amount of memory allocated to the object for actual representation of the string is often 16 characters larger than what is needed. This is to reduce the memory allocation overhead for modifications to a string that add small number of characters to the string at a time. The number of characters that a `StringBuffer` object can accommodate without additional memory allocation is called its *capacity*. The number of characters stored in a `String` or a `StringBuffer` object can be ascertained by invoking the method `length()` and the capacity of a `StringBuffer` object by invoking the method `capacity()`:

```
String str = "hello there";
System.out.println( str.length() );                 // 11

StringBuffer strbuf = new StringBuffer( "hello there" );
System.out.println( strbuf.length() );              // 11
System.out.println( strbuf.capacity() );            // 27
```

One is, of course, not limited to the capacity that comes with the default initialization of a `StringBuffer` object — usually 16 over what is needed for the initialization string. If we invoke the `StringBuffer` with an `int` argument, it constructs a string buffer with no characters in, but a capacity as specified by the argument. So the following invocation

```
StringBuffer strbuf = new StringBuffer( 1024 );
```

would create string buffer of capacity 1024. Characters may then be inserted into the buffer by using, say, the `append` function that we will discuss later in this section.

While we have shown all the different possible constructor invocations for the `StringBuffer` class, the `String` class allows for many more, all with different types of arguments. In the rest of this section, we will show a few more of the `String` constructors. One of the `String` constructors takes a `char` array argument to construct a `String` object from an array of characters, as in the following example:[21]

```
char[] charArr = { 'h', 'e', 'l', 'l', 'o' };
String str4 = new String( charArr );
```

A `String` object can also be constructed from an array of `bytes`, as in

```
byte[] byteArr = { 'h', 'e', 'l', 'l', 'o' };
String str5 = new String( byteArr );        // "hello"
```

Each byte of the byte array `byteArr` will be set to the ASCII encoding of the corresponding character in the initializer. When constructing a `String` from the byte array, the Java Virtual Machine translates the bytes into characters using the platform's default encoding, which in most cases would be the ASCII encoding. Subsequently, the `String` object is constructed from the default encodings for the characters.

If the default encoding will not do the job for constructing a `String` from a byte array, it is possible to specify the encoding to be used.[22] In the following example, the byte array is specified so that each pair of bytes starting from the beginning corresponds to a Unicode representation of the character shown by the second byte of the pair. For example, the 16-bit pattern obtained by joining together one-byte ASCII

---

[21]The reader may wish to read the rest of this subsection after we discuss the different primitive types in Java in Chapter 6.

[22]Java supports the following character encodings that we will discuss further in Chapter 6:

US-ASCII (this is the seven-bit ASCII)

ISO-8859-1 (ISO-Latin-1)

UTF-8 (8-bit Unicode Transformation Format)

UTF-16BE (16-bit Unicode in big-endian byte order)

UTF-16LE (16-bit Unicode in little-endian byte order)

UTF-16 (16-bit Unicode in which the byte order is specified by a mandatory initial byte-order mark)

based representations of '\0' and 'h' is the Unicode in its big-endian representation for the character 'h'. As a result, the string formed by the constructor is again "hello".

```
byte[] byteArr2 = { '\0', 'h', '\0', 'e', '\0', 'l',
                                 '\0', 'l', '\0', 'o' };
String str6 = new String( byteArr2, "UTF-16BE" );  // "hello"
```

If we wanted to specify the byte order in the little-endian representation, we'd need to use the "UTF-16LE" encoding, as shown below:

```
byte[] byteArr3 = { 'h', '\0', 'e', '\0', 'l', '\0',
                               'l', '\0', 'o', '\0' };
String str7 = new String( byteArr3, "UTF-16LE" );   // "hello"
```

The last two invocations of the String constructor throw the UnsupportedEncodingException if the specified encoding is not supported by a JVM. The topic of exceptions and how to deal with them will be discussed in Chapter 10.

4.4.2 Accessing Individual Characters

The individual characters of a Java string can be accessed by invoking the charAt method with an int argument:

```
String str = "hello";
char ch = str.charAt( 1 );                          // 'e'

StringBuffer strbuf = new StringBuffer( "hello" );
ch = strbuf.charAt( 1 );                            // 'e'
```

Since the strings created through the StringBuffer class are mutable, it is possible to write into each character position in such a string, as the following example illustrates:

```
StringBuffer strbuf = new StringBuffer( "hello" );
strbuf.setCharAt( 0, 'j' );
```

which would convert "hello" into "jello".

Indexing for accessing the individual characters of a string is always range checked in Java. If you try to access an index that is outside the valid limits for a string, JVM will throw an exception of type StringIndexOutOfBoundsException:

```
String str = "hello";
char ch = str.charAt( 100 );                        // ERROR

StringBuffer strbuf = new StringBuffer( "hello" );
ch = strbuf.charAt( 100 );                           // ERROR
```

For a `StringBuffer` string, it is a range violation if you try to access an index that is outside the length of the string even if the index is inside the capacity.

```
StringBuffer strbuf = new StringBuffer( "hello" );
System.out.println( strbuf.capacity() );          // 21
ch = strbuf.charAt( 20 );                          // ERROR
```

For a `StringBuffer` string, you can delete a character by invoking `deleteCharAt`:

```
StringBuffer strbuf = new StringBuffer( "hello" );
strbuf.deleteCharAt( 0 );
System.out.println( strbuf.length() );     // 4, was 5
System.out.println( strbuf.capacity() );   // 21, was 21
```

By deleting a character, the `deleteCharAt` method shrinks the length of the string by one, but note that the capacity of the string buffer remains unaltered.

4.4.3 String Comparison

Java strings are compared using the `equals` and `compareTo` methods, and the '==' operator. The method `equals` returns a TRUE/FALSE answer, whereas the method `compareTo` returns an integer that tells us whether the `String` on which the method is invoked is less than, equal to, or greater than the argument `String`. For example, in the following program fragment

```
String str1 = "stint";
String str2 = "stink";
System.out.println( str1.equals( str2 ) );       // false

String str3 = "stint";
String str4 = "stink";
System.out.println( str3.compareTo( str4 ) > 0 ); // true
```

the first print statement outputs `false` because the strings pointed to by `str1` and `str2` are composed of different character sequences. The second print statement outputs `true` because the string `str3` is indeed "greater" than the string `str4`. We'll have more to say on the `compareTo` method later in this subsection when we talk about sorting arrays of strings.

With regard to the '==' operator, as we have already mentioned, the operator can only be used for testing whether two different `String` variables are pointing to the same `String` object. Suppose we have the following statements in a program

```
String s1 = new String("Hello");
String s2 = s1;
```

then s1 == s2 would evaluate to true because both s1 and s2 will be holding references to the same string object, meaning an object that resides at the same place in the memory. On the other hand, if we say

```
String s1 = new String("hello");
String s2 = new String("hello");
```

then s1 == s2 will evaluate to false because we now have two distinct String objects at two different places in the memory even though the contents of both objects are identical in value, since they are both formed from the same string literal.

As was mentioned earlier in Chapter 3, both equals and '==' are defined for the Object class, the root class in the Java hierarchy of classes, and that the system-supplied definitions for both are the same for Object — comparison on the basis of equality of reference. So, as defined for Object, both these predicates tell us whether the two references point to exactly the same object in the memory. However, while equals can be overridden, '==' cannot because it is an operator. The method equals has already been overridden for us in the String class. So it carries out its comparisons on the basis of equality of content for String type strings. But since, in general, operators cannot be overridden in Java, the operator '==' retains its meaning as defined in the Object class.

A word of caution about comparing objects of type StringBuffer: While the system provides us with an overridden definition for the equals method for the String class, it does not do so for the StringBuffer class. In other words, while for the String class you can use the equals method to test for the equality of content, you cannot do so for the StringBuffer class, as borne out by the following code:

```
String s1 = new String( "Hello" );
String s2 = new String( "Hello" );
System.out.println( ( s1.equals( s2 ) ) + "" );      // true

StringBuffer s3 = new StringBuffer( "Hello" );
StringBuffer s4 = new StringBuffer( "Hello" );
System.out.println( ( s3.equals( s4 ) ) + "" );      // false
```

If you must compare two StringBuffer objects for equality of content, you can can do so by first constructing String objects out of them via the toString method, as in

```
StringBuffer sb = new StringBuffer( "Hello" );
if ( ( sb.toString().equals( "jello" ) ) )
    ....
```

We will now revisit the compareTo method for the String class. The String class implements the Comparable interface by providing an implementation for the compareTo method. The compareTo method as provided for the String class compares two strings lexicographically using the Unicode values associated with the characters in the string.[23]   Because the `String` class comes equipped with `compareTo` method, we say that `String` objects possess a *natural ordering*, which implies that we are allowed to sort an array of `Strings` by invoking, say, `java.util.Arrays.sort` without having to explicitly supply a comparison function to the sort method. This is in accord with our Chapter 3 discussion on comparing objects in Java. The following example illustrates invoking `java.util.Arrays.sort` for sorting an array of strings.

If we do not want the array of strings to be sorted according to the `compareTo` comparison function, we can invoke a two-argument version of `java.util.Arrays.sort` and supply for its second argument an object of type Comparator that has an implementation for a method called `compare` that tells the sort function how to carry out comparisons.[24]   If all you want to do is to carry out a case-insensitive comparison, you can use the `Comparator` object `CASE_INSENSITIVE_ORDER` that comes as a static data member of the `String` class. In the code example shown below, the second sort is a case-insensitive sort. The `java.util.Arrays.sort` is based on the merge-sort algorithm.

```java
//StringSort.java

import java.util.*;

class StringSort {
    public static void main( String[] args ) {
        String[] strArr = { "apples", "bananas", "Apricots", "Berries",
                            "oranges", "Oranges", "APPLES", "peaches" };
        String[] strArr2 = strArr;

        System.out.println("Case sensitive sort with Arrays.sort:" );
        Arrays.sort( strArr );
        for (int i=0; i<strArr.length; i++)
            System.out.println( strArr[i] );

        System.out.println("\nCase insensitive sort:" );
        Arrays.sort( strArr2, String.CASE_INSENSITIVE_ORDER );
        for (int i=0; i<strArr2.length; i++)
            System.out.println( strArr2[i] );
    }
}
```

---

[23]For the characters represented in the ASCII code, these comparisons essentially boil down to ASCII-code based comparisons, as was the case earlier with C++ strings. We will have more to say about the Unicode in Chapter 6.

[24]An example of how to set up a `Comparator` object for a sorting function is shown in Chapter 5. `Comparator` is defined as an interface in the `java.util` package. Interfaces, presented briefly in Chapter 3, are discussed more fully in Chapter 15.

The output of this program is

```
Case sensitive sort:
APPLES
Apricots
Berries
Oranges
apples
bananas
oranges
peaches

Case insensitive sort:
APPLES
apples
Apricots
bananas
Berries
Oranges
oranges
peaches
```

4.4.4   Joining Strings Together

In general, Java does not overload its operators. But there is one exception to that general rule, the operator '+' for just the `String` type (and not even for the `StringBuffer` type). The overload definition for this operator will cause the object `str3` in the following code fragment to store the string "hello there".

```
String str1 = "hello";
String str2 = " there";
String str3 = str1 + str2;
```

Strings of type `StringBuffer` can be joined by invoking the `append` method, as in

```
StringBuffer strbuf = new StringBuffer( "hello" );
StringBuffer strbuf2 = new StringBuffer( " there" );
strbuf.append( strbuf2 );
System.out.println( strbuf );            // "hello there"
String str = "!";
strbuf.append( str );
System.out.println( strbuf );            // "hello there!"
```

The capacity of a string buffer is automatically increased if it runs out of space as additional characters are added to the string already there.

In addition to invoking the append method with either the `String` or the `StringBuffer` arguments, you can also invoke it with some of the other types that Java supports, as illustrated by:

```
StringBuffer strbuf = new StringBuffer( "hello" );
int x = 123;
strbuf.append( x );
System.out.println( strbuf );            // "hello123"

double d = 9.87;
strbuf.append( d );
System.out.println( strbuf );            // "hello1239.87"
```

As you can see, append first converts its argument to a string representation and then appends the new string to the one already in the buffer. This permits append to be invoked for any object, even a programmer-defined object, as long as it is possible to convert the object into its string representation. As we saw in Chapter 3, when a class is supplied with an override definition for the `toString` method, the system can automatically create string representations of the objects made from the class.

Going back to the joining of `String` type strings, an immutable string class is inefficient for serial concatenation of substrings, as in

```
String s = "hello" + " there" + " how" + " are" + " you";
```

The string concatenations on the right are equivalent to

```
String s = "hello" + (" there" + (" how" + (" are" + " you")));
```

If the Java compiler had available to it only the immutable `String` class for string processing, each parenthesized concatenation on the right would demand that a new `String` object be created. Therefore, this example would entail creation of five `String` objects, of which only one would be used. And then there would be further work entailed in the garbage collection of the eventually unused `String` objects. Fortunately, the Java compiler does not really use the `String` class for the operations on the right. Instead, it uses the mutable `StringBuffer` class and the append method of that class to carry out the concatenations shown above. The final result is then converted back to a `String`.

4.4.5 Searching and Replacing

One can search for individual characters and substrings in a `String` type string by invoking the `indexOf` method:

```
String str = "hello there";
int n = str.indexOf( "the" );          // 6
```

By supplying indexOf with a second int argument, it is also possible to specify the index of the starting position for the search. This can be used to search for all occurrences of a character or a substring, as the following code fragment illustrates:

```
String mystr = new String( "one hello is like any other hello" );
String search = "hello";
int pos = 0;
while ( true ) {
    pos = mystr.indexOf( search, pos );
    if ( pos == -1 ) break;
    System.out.println( "hello found at: " + pos );   // 4 and 28
    pos++;
}
```

To parallel our C++ program StringFind.cc, we show next a program that searches for all occurrences of a substring and, when successful, it replaces the substring by another string. Since a String is immutable, we'll have to use a StringBuffer for representing the original string. But since there are no search functions defined for the StringBuffer class, we have to somehow combine the the mutability of a StringBuffer with the searching capability of a String. The following program illustrates this to convert "one hello is like any other hello" into "one armadillo is alike any other armadillo".

```
//StringFind.java

class StringFind {
    public static void main( String[] args ) {
        StringBuffer strbuf = new StringBuffer(
                    "one hello is like any other hello" );
        String searchString = "hello";
        String replacementString = "armadillo";
        int pos = 0;
        while ( ( pos = (new String(strbuf)).indexOf(
                            searchString, pos ) )  != -1 ) {
            strbuf.replace( pos, pos +
                        searchString.length(), replacementString );
            pos++;
        }
        System.out.println( strbuf );
    }
}
```

There is also the method lastIndexOf that searches for the rightmost occurrence of a character or a substring:

```
String str = "hello there";
```

```
int n = str.lastIndxOf( "he" );          // 7
```

The methods endsWith and startsWith can be invoked to check for suffixes and prefixes in strings:

```
String str = "hello there";
if ( str.startsWith( "he" ) )            // true
   ....
if ( str.endsWith( "re" ) )              // true
   ....
```

4.4.6 Erasing and Inserting Substrings

The following example shows how we can search for a substring, erase it, and then insert in its place another substring. What erase did for C++ is now done by delete with two int arguments for the beginning index and the ending index of the character sequence to be deleted. Insertion of a substring is carried out with the insert method whose first argument, of type int, specifies the index where the new substring is to be spliced in.

```
// StringInsert.java

class StringInsert {
    public static void main( String[] args ) {
        int pos = 0;
        StringBuffer quote = new StringBuffer(
                "Some cause happiness wherever they go,"
            +   " others whenever they go - Oscal Wilde" );
        String search = "happiness";
        if ( ( pos = ( new String(quote) ).indexOf( search) ) != -1 ) {
            quote.delete( pos, pos + search.length() );
            quote.insert( pos, "excitement" );
        }
        System.out.println( quote );
    }
}
```

4.4.7 Extracting Substrings

Both String and StringBuffer support substring extraction by invoking the substring method with either one int argument or two int arguments. When only one argument is supplied to substring, that is the beginning index for the substring to be extracted. The substring extracted will include all of the characters from the beginning index till the end. When two arguments are supplied, the second argument stands for the ending index of the desired substring. In all cases, for both `String` and `StringBuffer`, the returned object is a new `String`. For illustration:

```
String str = "0123456789abc";
System.out.println( str.substring( 5 ) );        // "56789abc"
System.out.println( str.substring( 5, 9 ) );      // "56789"

StringBuffer stb = new StringBuffer( "0123456789abc" );
System.out.println( stb.substring( 5 ) );         // "56789abc"
System.out.println( stb.substring( 5, 9 ) );      // "56789"
```

4.5 SUGGESTIONS FOR FURTHER READING

For a more detailed review of C-style strings, the book by King [45] is highly recommended. In style and flavor, the discussion presented here regarding C-style strings follows King's treatment of the subject.

For a detailed presentation of how the string class is implemented in C++, the reader is referred to Chapter 20 of the book by Stroustrup [54].

For a detailed presentation of the specifications of Java's `String`, `StringBuffer` and the string literals, the reader is referred to the book by Gosling, Joy, Steele [23].

4.6 HOMEWORK

1. How many `String` objects will be created by the following Java statements:

```
String s1 = "hoity";
String s2 = s1;
s1 = s2 + "toity";
```

2. How many `String` objects are created by the following Java statements:[25]

```
String s1 = "hoity";
String s2 = "hoity";
String s3 = "hoity";
String s4 = "hoity";
char[] charArr = [ 'h', 'o', 'i', 't', 'y' ];
```

---

[25]Based on an example posted at the Java Virtual Machine Forum of the Java Developer Connection.

```
String s5 = new String( charArr );
String s6 = new String( s1 );
```

3. The goal of this homework is to write a Java program to determine whether a string is a palindrome. (A palindrome is a word, phrase, verse, or sentence that reads the same backward or forward.) The string may contain other characters that are not alphanumeric. These characters are to be removed first before determining whether a string is a palindrome. More specifically, your solution should be structured along the following lines:

   (a) Provide implementation for a function `removeAllMarks( String )` that takes the original string as its argument and returns a new string after the original string has been stripped of the punctuation marks.

   [**Suggestion:** A convenient way to do this is by scanning the argument string with the `charAt( int i )` method presented in Section 4.4.2 and checking whether the character at position `i` is alphanumeric or not. This test can be carried out by invoking `Character.isLetterOrDigit(` `char )` on the character. In order to create a clean version of the string, all characters that pass the test can be appended to a `StringBuffer` object with the `append( char )` method defined for the `StringBuffer` class. Finally, the `StringBuffer` object can be converted into a `String` object by using the `toString()` method of the `StringBuffer` class.]

   (b) Provide implementation for `reverseString(String str)` which returns a new string obtained by reversing the argument string.

   [**Suggestion:** You can convert the argument string into a `StringBuffer` object via the latter's constructor and then invoke the `reverse()` method on the `StringBuffer` object.]

   (c) Provide implementation for `isPalindrome( string )` that will return true or false as to whether the argument string is a palindrome. Compare the cleaned up version of the original string with the cleaned up and reversed version using the `compareToIgnoreCase( String )` method of the `String` class.

   You may define and implement other functions to complete this homework. Print out the original string and whether or not it is a palindrome.

4. Both the `StringFind.cc` program of Section 4.3.5 and the `StringFind.java` program of Section 4.4.5 suffer from one major shortcoming that is illustrated by the following example. If we ask the program to replace "ice" by "cream" in the following string,

   ```
   ice and icecream are two different things
   ```

both programs would result in the following string

```
cream and creamcream are two different things
```

This happens because the programs blindly replace the substrings without making certain that the substrings are words. Modify those programs so that this does not happen.

5. Extend the `StringFind.cc` program of Section 4.3.5 so that it prompts a user for the entry of a line of text, a word all of whose occurrences must be replaced in the text, and a replacement word. The program should then display on the terminal the modified line of text.

6. Write a C++ program that reads a text file to accomplish the following

   - As it reads each word into the program, it should drop any punctuations and other non-alphanumeric marks sticking to the words in the text file. In particular, it should detect and drop the following marks

     ```
     , ; : # . * ! " ) ( > < ] [ \ _ - ?
     ```

     if they are attached to either the beginning or the end of a word. Make sure that if there are multiple occurrences of a mark at either the beginning or the end of a words, your program deletes all of them. That is, the word "!!!great!!!" should get cleaned up to just "great".
   - The program should store each cleaned up word in a vector of strings.
   - Finally, the program should sort the cleaned up words by invoking the generic algorithm `sort` and write the words in sorted order into an output text file.

   Use the code shown in Chapter 2 for reading from a text file and writing into a text file. Test your program on the following input

   ```
   !!!Hello!!!
   Where's you??????
   You have not been seen in a >>>>long<<<< time.
   Will you *****ever***** sur-
   face again??????? I can't wait for e-v-e-r!
   I have a question: Should "dirty-words" be
   stored as two words: 'dirty' and 'words',
   or as one word: dirtywords.
   Yours
   ** ### !!!!
   ```

7. Extend the above program by giving special consideration to hyphenations and apostrophes. For hyphenated words, if the hyphenation is at the end of a line, assume that the last word in the line got broken up into two parts. Join the two parts. If the hyphenation is in middle of a line, do not delete it. When you detect an apostrophe, also drop the letter that follows the apostrophe. *Hint: Use the* peek() *function to detect the end of a line.*

8. If you just feed an array of strings to the java.util.Arrays.sort method, it uses the natural order for strings for sorting. This order, which basically amounts to comparing ASCII encodings of the characters, places all the words that begin with uppercase letters before the words that begin with lowercase letters. If you are not happy with this sort result, it is possible to invoke java.util.Arrays.sort with a second argument that is a Comparator object which can tell the sort function to produce its output in the same way you see the words in an English dictionary. The Comparator object must invoke the locale-specific string comparison methods. The locale-specific string comparison methods are defined for the Collator class. The main goal of this homework is to see how the Locale, Collator, and Comparator classes work together to produce a sort that corresponds to English language dictionary order.

   Write a Java program that sorts the words of English in a way that you'd find in an English language dictionary. For the purpose of testing your program, initialize an array of strings within the program with different words.

5

Using the Container Classes

Practically every programmer has used arrays, and many have used linked lists. These are the two most widely used containers for holding multiple items of data in many programming languages. But both these containers suffer from limitations. While an array has the great advantage of giving us constant-time access to its elements, its principal limitation is that you have to know its size in advance — before you start placing data in it. If you did not know in advance the size needed for an array, you would probably declare an array so large as to suffice for the worst possible case. As a consequence, the array could be too large for most runs of the program — leading to inefficient memory utilization — or not large enough because you underestimated the size needed for the worst case — leading to program crash.[1] Another serious limitation of an array is that once an array is declared and initialized, it is not possible to insert new elements into the array or delete any existing elements without writing additional code for creating a new array.

On the other hand, linked lists have the advantage of being perfectly flexible with regard to their size. You do not need to know in advance how much data you'd be storing in a linked list. You can make a linked list larger by inserting a new node anywhere — at the beginning, in the middle, or at the end. And you can cause a linked list to shrink by deleting nodes anywhere you do not need them. But this convenience

---

[1]What if some application required you to place all the words in a text file in an array of strings. If the size of the file was allowed to be arbitrary, how would you know what sized array to declare? You'd probably try to guess the largest size that your program would have to deal with, and then use that number for the array declaration. But what if that guess proved to be wrong at some future time?

of linked lists come at a price. First, insertion of new elements and removal of existing elements requires that you pay close attention to memory allocation and deallocation. Additionally, you are stuck with inefficient access to the data items stored in the nodes of a linked list. Since a linked list does not allow for random access, locating a data item may require searching sequentially starting from the first node and working your way to the end.

The container classes of the C++ Standard Template Library (STL) and those that come with the Java Collections Framework are designed to redress the various shortcomings mentioned above by providing us with a variety of containers that combine the desirable features of arrays with the desirable features of linked lists without exposing the users to memory management issues. For example, a modern container such as a `vector` in C++ or an `ArrayList` in Java can combine the best of a conventional array — constant-time access to the elements — with most of the best of a linked list — insertions and deletions anywhere (although not as efficiently as a pure linked list). So if an application needs a dynamically expandable container for which constant-time access to the elements is of critical importance, but in which you only occasionally need to insert or delete elements, you'd choose a `vector` in C++ or an `ArrayList` in Java. On the other hand, if you had an application in which the insertions and deletions anywhere were of critical importance, and you did not need constant-time array-like access and you did not want to bother with memory allocation and deallocation yourself, you'd use the STL container `list` in C++ and the container `LinkedList` from the Java Collections Framework. This kind of reasoning can be used to choose for an application the container that best suits the application.

In addition to the container classes, the C++ Standard Template Library and the Java Collections Framework also provide algorithms that can be used with the containers for sorting, searching, inserting, deleting, shuffling, and so on. To give the reader a flavor of these algorithms, we will use some of them when we present example code illustrating the various container classes.

The main aim of this chapter is the same as for the last chapter — to provide the reader with an early familiarity with useful objects that can then be used in later chapters to exemplify the more basic ideas in C++ and Java. So it is possible that some of the programming syntax that you will see in this chapter will seem strange. If that's the case, the author hopes that the strange syntax will not be a source of frustration and that it will only raise questions in the mind of the reader that he/she would want to see resolved in the later chapters of the book.

5.1 CONTAINER CLASSES IN C++

The ten main container classes that come with the C++ Standard Template Library (STL) are:

vector: Particularly efficient for random access of data elements using array-like indexing. Also, efficient for addition and deletion of data elements at the back end of a `vector`. A vector can act both like a regular array and like a linked list. If the insertion of new elements into a vector causes the vector to exceed the memory previously allocated to it, the vector simply migrates to a new location in the memory. To minimize the overhead associated with such migration, one must judiciously choose the amount of memory that is allocated to a vector initially and the incremental additions to this memory as the vector runs out of previously allocated memory.

list: Particularly efficient for all kinds of list operations, meaning insertion and deletion of elements anywhere in a list, including the addition and deletion of elements at both its ends. Accessing elements via array-like indexing is not allowed.

deque: (Stands for double-ended queue and rhymes with 'check') Combines the best of `vector` and `list` with regard to subscripting via the '[]' operator and the add/delete operations at *both* ends of a data sequence stored in a `deque`. However, the prototypical list operations (insert/erase anywhere in a list) are not as efficient as for a list.

stack: Only supports storage and retrieval at the back end of a sequence of data. That means that the only data element that can be retrieved is the one that was pushed most recently into the stack.

queue: Only supports retrieval at the front end of a sequence of data while new elements are pushed into the back end. This means that of the data elements currently in the container, it is the oldest that is available next for retrieval.

priority_queue: A priority queue is like a queue except that the element that is available for retrieval next has the highest priority associated with it.

map: This container is used to store a sequence of `<key, value>` pairs. The name `map` implies a mapping from the keys to the values. Particularly efficient for retrieving a 'value' for a given 'key'. The `<key, value>` pairs are stored in a sorted order using a comparison function whose default meaning corresponds to the '<' operator for the key type. As an example, a telephone directory in which any single name can appear only once is an example of a map container. The keys are the names and the values the phone numbers.

set: A set is a degenerate form of a map in that no value need be specified for the keys. Therefore, in contrast with, say, a vector or a list, the list of objects (meaning the keys) is stored in a sorted order.

multimap: A more general form of `map`. While any single 'key' can appear only once in the sequence of `<key, value>` pairs in a `map`, in a `multimap` it is possible to have more than one `<key, value>` pair for the same key. A phone directory in which a name is allowed to appear more than once (because a person is allowed to have more than one phone number) would be an example of a multimap container.

multiset: A multiset is a degenerate form of a multimap in which no value need be specified for the keys.

In addition to these ten, there are other more specialized container classes like bitset, valarray, etc. Our focus will be on the ten main classes listed here. The end of the section includes a few brief comments about the other containers of STL.

Of the main STL containers, vector, list, and deque are known as the *sequence containers*, because they keep their elements in a sequential order. Sequential order does not imply that the elements are necessarily kept in contiguous segments of memory. It only means that the container supports some kind of a next-element operation that would allow one to go from one element to the next until reaching the end of the data sequence.

The sequence containers that do store their elements in contiguous segments of memory are vector and deque. For that reason, these two containers permit array-like random-access through the subscript operator '[]'. The fact these two containers store their data in contiguous segments of memory means that insertions or deletions anywhere except at the two ends of the container must be expensive. Obviously, if you insert a new element in the middle, to create room for the new element you'd need to shuffle all of the existing entries on one side of the new entry. If you delete an entry in the middle, you'd again need to shuffle all of the entries on one side of the deletion point so that there is no gap in the container after the deletion.

Of the two containers with very similar properties, vector and deque, the former has very little memory overhead — meaning memory needed in addition to what is actually required for the storage of data — and has the '[]' type of indexing that is almost as efficient as for arrays. On the other hand, a deque has a slightly higher memory overhead and its array-like indexing via the '[]' operator is slightly less efficient than that for vector. However, a deque is more efficient than a vector for insertions/deletions at the front of the container.

On the other hand, if you were looking for a container that was efficient for insertions and deletions everywhere, especially in the middle, and you did not care about array-like indexing, you'd choose list. A list container consists of doubly linked nodes that facilitate highly efficient insertions/deletions anywhere. Because of the memory needed for all the nodes, a list has the highest memory overhead of the three sequenced containers.

Table 5.1 should help the reader choose the best container for a given application. The notation O(N) used in this table stands for *linear time complexity*; it means that the time taken for the operation listed in the first column is linearly proportional to the number of elements in the container. The notation O(1) stands for *constant time complexity*; it means that the time taken is independent of the number of items already in the container. The '+' symbol means that the operation might occasionally have a significant extra overhead associated with it. For example, inserting an additional element at the back of a vector would ordinarily incur a fixed cost, but if we run out of room to grow the vector and the entire vector has to be migrated to some other location in the memory, there would come into play the overhead of having to copy over all of the vector elements to their new locations. The combined notation O(1)+ is referred to as *amortized constant time*.

Operation and its efficiency	vector	deque	list
Efficiency for array-like access	O(1)	O(1)	O(N)
Efficiency for insert/delete at front	O(N)	O(1)+	O(1)
Efficiency for insert/delete at back	O(1)+	O(1)+	O(1)
Efficiency for insert/delete in middle	O(N)	O(N)	O(1)

Table 5.1

The containers stack, queue, and priority_queue are called *adapters* or *adapter containers* because their role is to restrict the more general interfaces of the basic sequence containers vector, deque, and list. For example, by using the operations push_back and pop_back, it is perfectly possible to use either a vector or a deque directly as a stack. But if you wanted to make sure that a stack in your program was used only as a stack and in no other way that is possible with, say, a vector, you can use a vector through a stack adapter. Similarly, it is possible to use either a list or a deque as a queue data structure, but if you wanted to suppress all the other non-queue functionality of those two containers, you can use them through the queue adapter. The same goes for the priority_queue adapter container.

The remaining four containers — map, set, multimap, and multiset — are known as the *associative containers*. These containers allow us to store and retrieve an object on the basis of a *key* associated with the object. What gets stored in such containers are <key, value> pairs in key-sorted order, usually in the form of a binary tree. Key-order sorting ensures that the object associated with a key can be retrieved in O(log(N)) time, where N is the number of keys in the container. The keys must be unique for a map, meaning that there can be only one <key, value> pair for each key. If it is desired to have multiple entries for the same key, the associative container to use is multimap. The container set is a degenerate form of map in which only the keys are stored. The reason for the name set is that there can be no duplicate keys — a basic requirement of membership in a set in the formal set theory. A multiset is to a multimap what set is to a map. If key-sorted storage of the <key, value> pairs is not necessary, it is also possible to implement a map using a hash table, which is capable of giving a O(1) time retrieval efficiency depending on the data and the hashing function used.[2]

Of the more specialized containers that we will not be discussing in this book, bitset is used for achieving array-like addressing for the individual bits of a data entity in the memory and valarray for holding numerical data and processing thereof.

All container classes support the assignment operator so that a container can be assigned wholesale to a variable of the same type; the '==' operator that returns true if two containers of the same type have the same number of elements and if the elements in corresponding positions in the two containers satisfy the '==' operator for the element type; and the '<' operator if each element in the container on the left of the operator is less than the corresponding element of the container on the right. The meaning of the other comparison operators, '!=, '>', '<=', and '>=', is inferred from the overloadings for '==' and '<'.

When a class type object is inserted into an STL container, there is the question of what actually gets stored in the container. Is it the object itself? Or, is it a copy of the object? The answer is the latter. The container will copy the object using either the copy constructor or the copy assignment operator defined for the element type. Copy constructors and copy assignment operators are presented in Chapter 11.

In the rest of this section, we will show simple examples for all but two of the ten main containers of STL. We do not show examples for multimap and multiset because their interfaces are similar to those for map and set, respectively. Additionally, we will present the class vector in more detail than others because this container type is used more often than others and because much of what we say about the vector container applies to other containers also. For example, the issues that arise when we store programmer-defined class type objects in a vector are identical to such issues for the other containers.

5.1.1 Vector

A vector is like an array that can grow and shrink as elements are added to or removed from the vector. Since vectors allow for array-like indexing, they can be used very much like arrays. In addition, since vectors allow new elements to be inserted anywhere, they can be used very much like linked lists. The random access efficiency of

---

[2]An ideal hashing function will allocate a unique memory address to every single key in an associative container like map. When that can be done, a key and its associated value can be retrieved in constant time (meaning in time that is independent of the number of <key, value> pairs in the container) since one would not have to search through the keys. When this ideal condition cannot be satisfied, two or more keys may get mapped to the same hash code. When that happens, only one such <key, value> pair will be assigned the address corresponding to that hash code. But stored along with the chosen <key, value> pair will be pointers to the other pairs whose keys got assigned the same hash code.

a vector through array like indexing is comparable to that for arrays since — as for arrays — the elements are held in a contiguous block of memory.

The reader might ask: Doesn't holding all the elements of a vector in one contiguous block of memory prevent an indefinite insertion of new elements into the vector? Won't the vector eventually run into the memory allocated to the other objects in a computer program? In a vector, this problem is taken care of by allowing a vector to migrate elsewhere in memory if that is what it takes to keep all its elements in one contiguous block of memory. The elements residing at the current locations are then copied over into the freshly appropriated memory and the currently used memory deallocated.[3]

But then the reader might ask: If a vector is allowed to migrate around in the memory as it grows, does that not create an overhead associated with memory allocation, memory deallocation, the copying of elements from one location to another, etc.? This computational overhead associated with a vector can be alleviated by intelligently preallocating memory when a vector is first created. If despite this memory preallocation, a vector has to move to a different place in the memory occasionally, in many applications the computational overhead associated with that would be a small price to pay for the huge convenience afforded by a vector's array-like random access combined with its highly efficient insert/delete operations at its back end, and its linked-list like flexibility for occasional insertions and deletions everywhere else.

The following statement declares vec to be an empty vector whose elements will be of type T:[4]

```
vector<T> vec;
```

For example, a vector of integers would be declared by

```
vector<int> vec;
```

and a vector of strings by

```
vector<string> s_vec;
```

Basic to the use of a C++ vector is the notion of an *iterator*. What a pointer is to an ordinary array, an STL iterator is to a vector (and to other STL containers). From the standpoint of usage, an important difference between the two is that there is no such thing as a null iterator. That is, an iterator cannot be initialized by setting it equal to 0.

---

[3]Therefore, it makes no sense to write functions that have pointers to vectors or to vector elements. Functions that cause a vector to get resized explicitly or implicitly are capable of moving an entire vector to a new location in the memory. These include resize(), which is an explicit call for resizing a vector, and functions like like push_back() and insert(), which resize a vector implicitly.

[4]The syntax used here is that for a template class, a concept that was introduced in Chapter 3 but is presented more fully in Chapter 13.

The following statement declares p to be an iterator for a vector of `ints`:

```
vector<int>::iterator p;
```

Whereas an array pointer can be initialized by setting it equal to the name of the array, a vector iterator needs more specialized syntax for its initialization. For example, to make the iterator of an integer vector `vec` point to the first element of the vector, you'd need to say

```
vector<int>::iterator p = vec.begin();
```

and to make it point to one past the last element of the vector, you'd say

```
vector<int>::iterator p = vec.end();
```

Using the `begin()` and `end()` function, one can set up a following kind of a `while` loop for printing out the elements of a vector of `ints`:

```
vector<int>::iterator p = vec.begin();
while ( p != vec.end() )
    cout << *p++ << "   ";
```

This construct shows two additional features of vector iterators: (1) They can be dereferenced in exactly the same manner as array pointers — by using the operator '`*`'. (2) They can be incremented (and decremented) in exactly the same manner as array pointers by using the '`++`' (and '`--`') operator. The loop iteration comes to a halt when the value of the iterator p reaches one past the end of the vector, a condition detected by the function `end()`.

C++ provides the functions `push_back()` and `pop_back()` for adding new elements at the back end of a vector and for popping elements off the back end. Both functions return `void` and do their assigned jobs by side effect. For example, if we say

```
vector<int> vec;
vec.push_back( 34 );
vec.push_back( 23 );
vec.pop_back();          //get rid of the last element -- 23
```

that would push the integers 34 and 23 into the vector `vec` and then pop the last entry, 23, off the vector. To determine the size of the vector thus created, we could say

```
cout << vec.size();      // answer: 1
```

Note that `size()` would have returned 2 before we popped off the last entry.

As is the case with array pointers, we could also set the value of a vector element by dereferencing the iterator, as shown below:

```
vector<int> vec;
```

```
    vec.push_back( 34 );
    vec.push_back( 23 );
    vector<int>::iterator p = vec.begin();
    *(p + 1) = 52;
```

The last statement will change the value of the second element from 23 to 52.

As was mentioned at the beginning of this chapter, vectors come with the subscript operator for random access to their elements. So if vec is a vector consisting of N elements, the elements can be designated vec[0], vec[1], ..., vec[N-1]. Therefore, another way to print out all the elements of a vector would be

```
    int i = 0;
    while ( i < vec.size() )
        cout << vec[i++] << "   ";
```

We can even change the value of a vector element by using the subscript operator. For example, if we say

```
    vec[1] = 49;
```

the value stored at the second element will be changed to 49.

The following program shows the above-mentioned features of a vector inside a program that you can run (and modify) for practice:

```
// VectorBasic.cc

#include <iostream>
#include <vector>                                              //(A)
using namespace std;

void print( vector<int> );

int main()
{
    vector<int> vec;                                           //(B)

    vec.push_back( 34 );                                       //(C)
    vec.push_back( 23 );       // size is now 2
    print( vec );              // 34 23

    vector<int>::iterator p;                                   //(D)
    p = vec.begin();                                           //(E)
    *p = 68;                                                   //(F)
    *(p + 1) = 69;                                             //(G)
    //  *(p + 2) = 70;         // WRONG                        //(H)
    print( vec );              // 68 69
    vec.pop_back();            // size is now 1                //(I)
```

```
    print( vec );                    // 68

    vec.push_back(101);                                          //(J)
    vec.push_back(103);      // size is now 3                    //(K)
    // size is now 3
    int i = 0;
    while ( i < vec.size() )                                     //(L)
        cout << vec[i++] << "  ";
    cout << endl;            // 68 101 103

    vec[0] = 1000;                                               //(M)
    vec[1] = 1001;                                               //(N)
    vec[2] = 1002;                                               //(O)
    print( vec );           // 1000 1001 1002

    return 0;
}

void print( vector<int> v ) {
    cout << "\nvector size is: " << v.size() << endl;
    vector<int>::iterator p = v.begin();
    while ( p != v.end() )
        cout << *p++ << "  ";
    cout << endl << endl;
}
```

Note in line (A) the inclusion of the header file `vector`. This file contains the prototypes of all C++ vector related functions. The effect of the statements in lines (B) through (D) has already been explained. In line (E), we initialize the iterator so that it points to the beginning of the vector. In lines (F) and (G), we then show how to alter the values of elements of the vector by dereferencing the iterator. We are able to do so because, by using the `push_back()` function, we have already created a vector of two elements. So the iterators being dereferenced point to valid locations in the vector. That should also explain why the statement in line (H) is illegal. In line (I), we pop the vector and remove the last element from its back end. The `pop_back()` returns void but removes the last element as a side effect. After that, the vector has only one element. The `while` loop in line (L) shows how the elements of a vector can be accessed with the subscript operator. Finally, lines (M) through (O) show how the elements of a vector can be overwritten by using subscript indexing.

It is also possible to declare a vector of a predetermined size, say of size 100 elements, by a declaration like

```
    vector<int> vec(100);
```

In such declarations, each element of the vector is initialized to a zero of the appropriate kind. For the case shown, each element will be initialized to the integer 0.

When applicable, the default initialization can be changed by supplying it as a second argument to the vector constructor. For example, in the declaration

```
vector<int> vec(100, 2);
```

each of 100 elements of the vector will be initialized to the integer 2.

We will use the next program to illustrate the functions `front()` and `back()` and to show the use of the '`&`' operator to obtain the iterator associated with a particular vector element. The functions `front()` and `back()`, when invoked on a vector, return the first and the last elements of the vector. This program also illustrates the use of `resize()` which adds zero-initialized elements to a previously defined vector; and `reserve()` which increases the capacity of a vector by setting aside uninitialized memory for the vector.

Line (A) of the program below declares a vector with preallocated memory for storing 100 integers. Each element of this vector is initialized by default to 0, as evidenced by the output produced by the `sum(v1)` statement. Subsequently, in line (B), we push a new element into the vector. Notice that this step acquires memory in addition to what was allocated in line (A). As a result, the size of the vector is now 101. In line (C), we increase the capacity of the vector by invoking `reserve`; the additional memory allocated to the vector remains uninitialized. Note that increasing the capacity of the vector through `reserve` does not alter what is returned by the `size()` function. Lines (D) and (E) demonstrate the behavior of the `front()` and `back()` functions. Line (F) shows how a vector iterator can be initialized to point directly to a chosen element in the vector.

By creating a vector of predetermined size but with nonzero initialization, lines (H) through (J) show the behavior of `resize` with regard to adding additional initialized elements to a vector. Line (H) creates a vector of 150 integers, each element of the vector initialized to the integer 2. In line (I), we resize this vector so that its new size is 500. But the additional elements that are added are initialized to the zero of the appropriate kind — in this case the integer 0.

Line (K) and the statements that immediately follow show how `clear()` can be used to clear out all the elements of a vector — and the size of the vector made zero — without altering its capacity. As shown in line (L), the same effect can be achieved by invoking `resize(0)` on the vector.

```
//VectorFrontBackResize.cc

#include <iostream>
#include <vector>

int sum( vector<int> vec ) {
    int result = 0;
    vector<int>::iterator p = vec.begin();
```

```
        while ( p != vec.end() ) result += *p++;
            return result;
}

int main()
{
        vector<int> v1(100);                                              //(A)
        cout << v1.size() << endl;              // 100
        cout << sum( v1 ) << endl;              // 0

        v1.push_back( 23 );                                               //(B)
        cout << v1.size() << endl;              // 101
        cout << sum( v1 ) << endl;              // 23

        v1.reserve( 1000 );                                               //(C)
        cout << v1.capacity() << endl;          // 1000
        cout << v1.size() << endl;              // 101
        cout << v1[900] << endl;                // undefined
        cout << sum( v1 ) << endl;              // 23

        cout << v1.front() << endl;             // 0              //(D)
        cout << v1.back() << endl;              // 23             //(E)

        v1.pop_back();

        cout << v1[ v1.size() - 1 ] << endl;    // 0              //(F)

        vector<int>::iterator p = &v1[50];                                //(G)
        cout << *p << endl;                     // 0

        vector<int> v2(150, 2);                                           //(H)
        cout << sum( v2 ) << endl;              // 300

        v2.resize( 500 );                                                 //(I)
        cout << v2.size() << endl;              // 500
        cout << v2[150] << endl;                // 0              //(J)

        v2.clear();                                                       //(K)
        cout << v2.empty() << endl;             // true
        cout << v2.capacity() << endl;          // 500
        cout << v2.size() << endl;              // 0

        v2.resize( 0 );                                                   //(L)
        cout << v2.capacity() << endl;          // 500
        cout << v2.size() << endl;              // 0

        return 0;
}
```

Note that the call `v1[ v1.size() - 1 ]` in line (F) is identical to invoking the function `back()` on a vector.

As mentioned before, the functions

```
begin()
end()
```

return iterators: the former to the first element of the vector, and the latter to one past the last element. On the other hand, the functions

```
front()
back()
```

return the vector elements themselves, the former the first element and the latter the last element.[5]

5.1.1.1 *List Operations on Vectors*

We will now show some operations on vectors that highlight the fact that a vector can also be used in much the same manner as a linked list, meaning that elements can be added or removed at the beginning, anywhere in the middle, or at the end of a vector. But the reader needs to be aware of the fact that it is only at the back end of a vector that the list operations can be carried out efficiently, meaning in constant time. List operations anywhere else run the risk of taking time proportional to the number of elements in the vector. The reason for this is that a vector must keep all its elements in one continuous run of the memory. Given a vector of a sufficiently large capacity, adding an element at the back-end requires only that the new element be placed in the memory segment next to where the vector currently ends. But inserting an element anywhere else would require that all of the downstream elements be shuffled over in order to create space for the new element.

The functions that are used commonly for inserting new elements into a vector and for deleting existing elements are `insert()` and `erase()`. Both these functions take iterator arguments. The iterator must point to the position where a new element is to be inserted or from where an old element is to be deleted. As you would expect, when `insert()` is used for inserting a new element, the size of the vector increases by one; and when `erase()` is used for deleting an element, the size of the vector decreases by one. If the location of an item that needs to be deleted is not known, one can invoke the `find()` function to obtain the iterator that points to the first occurrence of the item. The iterator returned by `find()` can then be passed to the `erase()` function for the deletion of the item.

The next program illustrates the list operations on a vector. Even more importantly, this program shows that when you modify a vector structurally with a list operation,

---

[5]Strictly speaking, the functions `front()` and `back()` return references to the first and the last elements. Object reference in C++ is presented in Chapter 8.

any previous initializations of an iterator become invalid. This is illustrated with lines (A) through (E) of the program below. Line (A) creates a vector of five integers, all initialized to 0. In line (B), we declare and initialize an iterator to the vector. When this iterator is dereferenced in line (C), we obtain the value stored in the first element of the vector — the number 0. We then invoke a list operation in line (D) by inserting a new element, 9, at the location pointed to by the iterator value in the first argument to `insert`. When we dereference the previously initialized iterator again in line (D), we can expect unpredictable behavior from the program, probably some garbage output if not a program crash. When we re-initialize the iterator in line (F), the problem disappears and we see the expected output in line (G).

Line (H) illustrates the invocation of `erase` to delete an element of the vector that is pointed to by the iterator argument to the function — in this case the very first element. Line (I) demonstrates inserting an element in the middle of a vector, and line (J) the deletion of an element in the middle of a vector. Lines (K) and (L) show the same pair of operations at the end of the vector.

Lines (M) through (R) show how `find` can be used in conjunction with `erase` to delete vector elements holding a particular item of data whose location is not known in advance. Each invocation of `find` returns the iterator value pointing to first occurrence of the data item supplied to the function for its last argument.

```
//VectorInsertEraseSort.cc

#include <iostream>
#include <vector>
#include <algorithm>   // for the find() and sort() generic functions
using namespace std;

void print( vector<int> );

int main()
{
    vector<int> vec(5);                                     //(A)
    print( vec );                    // 0 0 0 0 0

    vector<int>::iterator p = vec.begin();                  //(B)

    cout << *p << endl;              // 0                    //(C)

    vec.insert( vec.begin(), 9 );                           //(D)
    print( vec );                    // 9 0 0 0 0 0

    cout << *p << endl;              // ERROR                //(E)

    p = vec.begin();                                        //(F)
    cout << *p << endl;              // 9                    //(G)
```

```
    vec.erase( vec.begin() );                                    //(H)
    print( vec );                           // 0 0 0 0 0

    vec.insert( vec.begin() + 2, 8 );                            //(I)
    print( vec );                           // 0 0 8 0 0 0

    vec.erase( vec.begin() + 2 );                                //(J)
    print( vec );                           // 0 0 0 0 0

    vec.insert( vec.end(),  7 );                                 //(K)
    print( vec );                           // 0 0 0 0 0 7

    vec.erase( vec.end() - 1 );                                  //(L)
    print( vec );                           // 0 0 0 0 0

    vec.insert( vec.begin() + 3, 6 );                            //(M)
    print( vec );                           // 0 0 0 6 0 0
    vec.erase( find( vec.begin(), vec.end(), 6 ) );              //(N)
    print( vec );                           // 0 0 0 0 0

    vec.insert( vec.begin() + 1, 3 );                            //(O)
    vec.insert( vec.begin() + 5, 3 );                            //(P)
    print( vec );                           // 0 3 0 0 0 3 0
    vec.erase( find( vec.begin(), vec.end(), 3 ) );              //(Q)
    vec.erase( find( vec.begin(), vec.end(), 3 ) );              //(R)
    print( vec );                           // 0 0 0 0 0

    vec[0] = 23;                                                 //(S)
    vec[1] = 2;
    vec[2] = 16;
    vec[3] = 45;
    vec[4] = 16;
    print( vec );                           // 23 2 16 45 16

    sort( vec.begin(), vec.end() );                              //(T)
    print( vec );                           // 2 16 16 23 45

    return 0;
}

void print( vector<int> v ) {
    vector<int>::iterator p = v.begin();
    while ( p != v.end() )
        cout << *p++ << "   ";
    cout << endl;
}
```

The above program also illustrates the sorting of a vector by the STL generic algorithm sort declared in the `algorithm` header file of the C++ Standard Library. The two arguments passed to sort in line (T) are the two iterator values, first pointing to the beginning of the vector and the second to one past the end. (We could have sorted just a portion of the vector by supplying appropriate iterator values to sort.).

5.1.1.2 Vector of Class Type Objects   All of our discussion so far, although stated for the case of vectors of integers, carries over to the case of vectors of other data types, including class types. For a class type object to be stored in a container, at the minimum the class should support a no-arg constructor so that memory appropriated for a container can be properly initialized. The class must also possess overload definitions for the '==' and '<' operators so that the objects stored in a container can be compared by the various STL algorithms. STL is capable of inferring the meaning for the other comparison operators from these two.

As an example of a container of a class type object, you could declare a `vector` of strings by

```
vector<string> vec;
```

And then you could push into the vector either `string` objects or objects that the system can covert automatically into `string` objects. For example, you could say

```
vec.push_back( "hello" );
vec.push_back( "hi" );
vec.insert( vec.end(), "greetings" );
```

where the last statement is equivalent to invoking push_back("greetings"). The argument supplied to the push_back function is first converted into a `string` object and then entered into the vector. This works because the function push_back has been suitably overloaded to accept a `const char*` argument.

A vector of strings can be sorted by the sort function declared in the `algorithm` header file of the C++ standard library just as a vector of `ints` was sorted in the previous subsection. We could, for example, say

```
sort( vec.begin(), vec.end() );
```

By default, the system will sort a vector of strings according to the lexicographic order dictated by the ASCII code associated with the characters. A different sorting order can be obtained by supplying one more argument to the sort function that establishes the comparison criterion to be used. To fully appreciate the nature of this third argument, you'd need to first understand operator overloading in C++, a topic that will be discussed in Chapter 12. Sections 12.10 and 12.11 of that chapter discuss sorting of class type objects with the user-specified criteria for sorting supplied through operator overload definitions.

You can also create a vector of a data type that you may define yourself. Given a programmer-defined class

```
class X {
    int p;
public:
    //
};
```

let's say that we want to store objects of type X in a vector. To create a vector of this data type, you would say

```
vector<X> vec;
```

or, if you wanted to create a vector with a preallocated capacity of, say five, you'd say

```
vector<X> vec( 5 );
```

You can push an X object into a vector by

```
vector<X> vec;
X x1(...);
vec.push_back( x1 );
```

where the second statement is a call to one of the constructors of class X. While the invocation of push_back would work fine, as it has in our earlier examples, we are faced with the following interesting question: *What exactly is being inserted into the vector? Is it the object* x1 *itself, or is it a copy of the object?* The answer: A copy of the object.[6]

The following program provides a working example of a vector of a type defined by a programmer in line (A). Lines (B) and (C) provide overload definitions for the operators '==' and '<'. The syntax used for these overload definitions will be explained in Chapter 12.

In main, we first create an empty vector for object of type X in line (F). We then create three X object in lines (G) through (I); these are subsequently pushed into the vector in the next three lines of code.[7]

To demonstrate that what gets stored in the container are the copies of the objects and not the original objects directly, in line (J) we change the state of one of the objects. But this state change is not reflected in the printout statements for the vector elements just before and just after line (J).

---

[6]This copy is made using either a programmer-defined copy constructor or a system-supplied default copy constructor for the class. Copy constructors are discussed in Chapter 11.

[7]More accurately speaking, it is the copies of the three objects that are pushed into the container.

Line (K) demonstrates the declaration of a vector of predetermined size and the initialization of the vector elements by the no-arg constructor for class X. Lines (L) and (M) demonstrate the resizing of a vector and the changing of its capacity, respectively. While the memory acquired through resizing is initialized according to the no-arg constructor for X, the additional memory reserved by changing the capacity of the vector remains uninitialized, as evidenced by the output in line (N).

The sort function invoked in line (O) on a vector of X objects uses the '<' operator that is overloaded for the class in line (B). Another way to invoke sort would be via its 3-argument version, shown in the commented out line (P), that for its third argument requires a function object that knows how to compare objects of type X. The commented out code for X_Comparator in line (D) creates such a function object through the overloading of the '()' operator in line (E). Chapter 12 will explain what is meant by a function object and by the overloading of the overloaded '()' operator.

```
//VectorForClassType.cc

#include <iostream>
#include <vector>
#include <algorithm>          // for sort()
using namespace std;

class X {                                             //(A)
    int p;
public:
    X() { p = 42; }
    X( int q ) { p = q; }
    int getp() const { return p; }
    void changeState( int pp ) { p = pp; }
};

//Chapter 12 explains the syntax shown for the two
//operator overloadings for class X:
bool operator<( const X& x1, const X& x2 ) {          //(B)
        return x1.getp() < x2.getp();
}
bool operator==( const X& x1, const X& x2 ) {         //(C)
        return x1.getp() == x2.getp();
}

// An alternative way of sorting a vector of objects
// of type X would be to invoke a 3-argument sort with
// the third argument set to the function object
// X_Comparator(). This function object would correspond
// to the overloading of the '()' operator.  See Chapter
// 12 for the overloading of this operator.
// class X_Comparator {                               //(D)
```

```
// public:
//     bool operator() ( const X& x1, const X& x2 ) const {        //(E)
//         return x1.getp() < x2.getp();
//     }
// };

void print( vector<X> );

int main()
{
    vector<X> vec;                                                 //(F)

    X x1( 2 );                                                     //(G)
    X x2( 3 );                                                     //(H)
    X x3( 5 );                                                     //(I)

    vec.push_back( x1 );
    vec.push_back( x3 );
    vec.push_back( x2 );

    print( vec );                    // 2 5 3
    x2.changeState( 1000 );                                        //(J)

    //change made to x2 in line (J) does not affect copy of x2 in vec:
    print( vec);                     // 2 5 3

    //vector elements initialized by X's no-arg constructor:
    vector<X> vec_2( 5 );                                          //(K)
    print( vec_2 );                  // 42 42 42 42 42
    vec_2.resize( 7 );                                             //(L)
    print( vec_2 );                  // 42 42 42 42 42 42 42

    //uninitialized increase in the vector capacity:
    vec_2.reserve( 10 );                                           //(M)
    cout << vec_2.capacity() << endl;    // 10
    print( vec_2 );                  // 42 42 42 42 42 42 42
                                     // size still returns 7
    cout << vec_2[ 8 ].getp() << endl;   // undefined              //(N)

    //set up vector for sorting:
    vec_2[0] = X(12);
    vec_2[1] = X(36);
    vec_2[2] = X(3);
    vec_2[3] = X(56);
    vec_2[4] = X(2);

    sort( vec_2.begin(), vec_2.end() );                            //(O)

    // The commented out statement in line (P) below is an
```

```
        // alternative way of sorting a vector of objects of
        // type X.  In the 3-argument invocation of sort, the
        // third argument is a function-object that corresponds
        // to the overloading of the '()' operator for the
        // X_Comparator class.  This overloading was shown earlier
        // in the commented out line (E).
        // sort( vec_2.begin(), vec_2.end(), X_Comparator() );         //(P)

        print( vec_2 );                     // 2 3 12 36 42 42 56

        vec_2.clear();
        print( vec_2 );                                // vec_2 is now empty
        cout << vec_2.capacity() << endl;    // 10

        return 0;
}

void print( vector<X> v ) {
    cout << "\nvector size is: " << v.size() << endl;
    vector<X>::iterator p = v.begin();
    while ( p != v.end() )
        cout << (*p++).getp() << "   ";
    cout << endl << endl;
}
```

Note again that when we create a vector of a designated size, as in

```
    vector<X> vecPresized( 5 );
```

each element of the vector is initialized by invoking the no-arg constructor of the class. Since the no-arg constructor for X sets the data member p to 42, and since we print out the vector by printing out the value of the data member p for each element of the vector, we get the sequences of the number 42, as shown in the output displayed below line (K).

When an element is erased for a vector of class type objects, the destructor for the class is invoked to carry out the erasure. Also, if the erasure of a vector element requires that all the higher-indexed elements be shuffled down in memory (so that all of the vector elements can stay in contiguous segments of memory), it is the *copy assignment operator* for the class that if defined is called upon to do the job. A brief introduction to destructors was provided in Chapter 3. Destructors and copy assignment constructors are fully discussed in Chapter 11.

5.1.1.3 *Using an Array to Initialize a Vector* We will now show how an array can be used to initialize a vector. To initialize a vector with an array, the vector constructor takes two arguments, both pointers, one pointing to the beginning of the array and the other to *one past the end* of the array. So an int array named data:

```
int data[] = {11, 12, 23, 34};
```

can be used to initialize an int vector by

```
vector<int> vec( data, &data[ size ] );                    //(A)
```

Note that the pointer that is the second argument to the constructor points to a position that is past the end of the array. The pointer to the end of the array is given by

```
&data[ size - 1 ]
```

but if you use this for the second argument in the invocation shown at (A) above, you'll be excluding the last element of the array from the vector. The following example shows a small program containing the above statements for vector initialization:

```
//VectorInitArray.cc

#include <iostream>
#include <vector>
using namespace std;

void print( vector<int> );

int main()
{
    int data[] = {11, 12, 23, 34};
    int size = sizeof( data ) / sizeof( data[0] );
    vector<int> vec( data, &data[ size ] );
    print( vec );                               // 11 12 23 34
    return 0;
}

void print( vector<int> vec ) {
    vector<int>::iterator p = vec.begin();
    while ( p < vec.end() )
      cout <<  *p++ << " ";
    cout << endl;
}
```

5.1.2 Deque

A deque has all the functionality of a `vector` and then some. As mentioned before, a `vector` is inefficient for insert/delete operations at the front of the sequence, because if you insert a new element at the front, the vector has to shuffle all the other elements in the memory to their next location. On the other hand, in a deque the insert/delete operations at the front are just as efficient as they are at the back. So, whereas a `vector` provides us with the efficient `push_back` and `pop_back` operations at the back, a deque has these two and also `push_front` and `pop_front` for equally efficient operations at the front. However, note that if an application does not require efficient insert/delete operations at the front of a data sequence, you are better off with a `vector` because of its lower memory overhead and more efficient array indexing.

The main reason for the next program is to illustrate the `push_front` and `pop_front` operations made available for deque and the fact that these two operations work the same way at the front of the container as the `push_back` and `pop_back` operations at the back. The program also shows some of the features of deque that it shares with the `vector` container.

Line (A) of the program below creates an empty deque. Lines (B) and (C) then use `push_back` to place two items in the deque. We then use `push_front` in lines (D) and (E) to push two more items into the deque. Whether the items were pushed in from the front or from the back is reflected in the order in which the items appear when displayed by the print statement next. Lines (F) and (G) demonstrate the popping off of the items from the two ends of the container. Lines (H) through (L) demonstrate list operations on a deque — these work the same way as for a vector. Finally, line (M) shows how a deque can be sorted using the STL algorithm `sort`. All of the remarks we made earlier in the chapter concerning this sort function for the case of vectors apply here also.

```
//DequeFront.cc

#include <string>
#include <deque>
#include <algorithm>              // for sort, find
using namespace std;

void print( deque<string> );

int main()
{
    deque<string> animals;                              //(A)

    animals.push_back( "yak" );                         //(B)
    animals.push_back( "zebra" );                       //(C)
```

```
    animals.push_front( "cat" );                                    //(D)
    animals.push_front( "canary" );                                 //(E)

    print(animals);              //  canary cat yak zebra

    animals.pop_front();                                            //(F)
    animals.pop_back();                                             //(G)

    print(animals);              //  cat yak

    //list operations on a deque:
    animals.erase(find( animals.begin(), animals.end(), "cat" )); //(H)
    print(animals);                 //  yak
    animals.insert( animals.begin(), "canary" );                    //(I)
    print(animals);                 //  canray yak
    int sz = animals.size();        // 2
    animals.resize( 5 );            // size() will now return 5      //(J)
    animals[sz] = "fox";            // animals[2] = "fox"            //(K)
    animals[sz+1] = "elephant";     // animals[3] = "elephant"
    animals[sz+2] = "cat";          // animals[4] = "cat"
    print( animals );               // canary yak fox elephant cat
    animals.erase( animals.begin() + 2 );  // remove "fox"          //(L)
    print( animals );               // canary yak elephant cat

    //sorting a deque:
    sort( animals.begin(), animals.end() );                         //(M)
    print( animals );               // canary cat elephant yak

    return 0;
}

void print( deque<string> d ) {
    typedef deque<string>::const_iterator CI;                       //(N)
    cout << "The number of items in the deque: " <<  d.size() << endl;
    for ( CI iter = d.begin(); iter != d.end(); iter++ )
        cout << *iter << " ";
    cout << endl << endl;
}
```

A couple of additional features to note about the above program are the use of typedef and const_iterator in line (N). The typedef shown allows us to create an abbreviated and more convenient synonym for an existing type.[8] A const_iterator, as

---

[8]We could also have used a macro definition to create a shorthand for a long type name by replacing line (N) with

```
#define CI deque<string>::const_iterator
```

we will mention in Section 13.2.2 of Chapter 13, does not permit any modification of the element it points to, in much the same way as a const pointer will not allow you to change the object it points to.

5.1.3 List

If your application requires frequent insertions of new data items anywhere — front, back, or anywhere else in the middle — in a sequence and array-like indexing for accessing the data items is not important, then you need to use a list. In contrast with a vector and a deque, a list is stored in the form of a linked list, which makes it efficient to insert new elements anywhere — front, back, or in the middle. But because a linked list is not stored in a contiguous run of the memory, array-like indexing is not provided for accessing list elements.

The following program illustrates some of the more common operations on a list of strings, these being

```
push_back     : for attaching a new element at the back
pop_back      : for removing the last element in a list
remove        : for removing an element anywhere (first occ. only)
push_front    : for attaching a new element at the front
pop_front     : for removing the first element
sort          : for sorting
unique        : for removing duplicates
splice        : for splicing one list into another
merge         : for merging two lists
size          : for determining the number of elements
begin         : iterator pointing to the first element
end           : iterator pointing to one past the last element
```

The program starts in line (A) by declaring animals to be an empty list<string>. Lines (B) through (F) push string items into the list, the last intentionally a duplicate to later demonstrate the usefulness of the unique operation. Each call to push_back creates a new list node by side effect while returning a void. Line (H) shows how the last item in the list can be popped off by pop_back, whereas line (I) shows how the first occurrence of a designated item can be gotten rid of by value using the remove function. Both these calls return void and eliminate nodes by side effect. Lines (J) and (K) illustrate the push_front and pop_front operations for attaching a new node at the front of the list and for removing the first node of a list. As with push_back and pop_back, these two operations return void and do their job through side effect. Line (L) shows how a new node can be inserted at a specified place in a list.

---

but a typedef is more appropriate here because a typedef name obeys the same scoping rules as ordinary variables. A typedef name defined inside a function would not be visible outside the function. Besides, as we will mention in Section 7.12 of Chapter 7, the use of macros is discouraged in C++.

An STL list has its own sort function, which is then invoked on animals in line (M). The sort function uses by default the meaning of the '<' operator for the string type for comparing the data items in the list. There is also a two-argument version of sort which can be supplied with your own comparison criterion. The member function unique invoked in line (N) eliminates any duplicates in a list. By default, it uses the '==' operator to compare its argument with the items in a list to identify any duplicates in the list. A two-argument version of unique allows you to specify a predicate for the uniqueness criterion for class type objects. Both sort and unique return void.

The rest of the program illustrates splicing from one list into another and the merging of two lists. For these demonstrations we create a second list in a block of code starting in line (O). The location where the splicing is to occur on the invoked list is specified by the first argument to splice in line (P). The second argument is the name of the list from which an item is to be taken for splicing. And the last argument is the location in the argument list which points to the data item to be spliced in. Note that the argument list loses the node which was spliced into the invoking list. The merge function shown in line (R) assumes that both the list on which it is invoked and the argument list are sorted. The argument list is merged into the invoked list in such a way that the result remains sorted. The argument list will be empty after a merge.

As evidenced by the invocation of begin() and end() in lines (L) and (P), a list supports iterators. As with other containers, begin() returns an iterator to the first item in a list and end() returns it to just beyond the last item. Again, as with other containers, it is an error to dereference the iterator returned by end().

```
//ListOps.cc

#include <string>
#include <list>
using namespace std;

void print( list<string>& );

int main()
{
    list<string> animals;                                    //(A)

    animals.push_back( "cheetah" );                          //(B)
    animals.push_back( "lion" );                             //(C)
    animals.push_back( "cat" );                              //(D)
    animals.push_back( "fox" );                              //(E)
    animals.push_back( "elephant" );                         //(F)
    animals.push_back( "cat" );      // duplicate cat        //(G)

    print( animals );                // cheetah lion cat fox
```

```
                                    // elephant cat

    animals.pop_back();                                        //(H)
    print( animals );              // cheetah lion cat fox
                                   // elephant

    animals.remove( "lion" );      // first occurrence of lion   //(I)
    print( animals );              // cheetah cat fox elephant

    animals.push_front( "lion" );                              //(J)
    print( animals );          // lion cheetah cat fox elephant
    animals.pop_front( );                                      //(K)
    print( animals );              // cheetah cat fox elephant

    animals.insert( animals.end(), "cat" );                    //(L)
    print( animals );              // cheetah cat fox elephant cat

    animals.sort();                                            //(M)
    print( animals );          // cat cat cheetah elephant fox

    animals.unique();                                          //(N)
    print( animals );              // cat cheetah elephant fox

    //another list needed for demonstrating splicing and merging:
    list<string> pets;                                         //(O)
    pets.push_back( "cat" );
    pets.push_back( "dog" );
    pets.push_back( "turtle" );
    pets.push_back( "bird" );

    animals.splice( animals.begin(), pets, pets.begin() );     //(P)
    print( animals );          // cat cat cheetah elephant fox
    print( pets );                 // dog turtle bird

    pets.sort();                   // bird dog turtle           //(Q)

    animals.merge( pets );                                     //(R)

    cout << pets.empty() << endl;  // true                     //(S)

    print( animals );              // bird cat cat cheetah      //(T)
                                   // dog elephant fox
                                   // turtle
    return 0;
}

void print( list<string>& li ) {                              //(U)
    typedef list<string>::const_iterator CI;
    cout << "The number of items in the list: "
```

```
        << li.size() << endl;;
    for ( CI iter = li.begin(); iter != li.end(); iter++ )
        cout << *iter << " ";
    cout << endl << endl;
}
```

The reader will also notice that a `list<string>` object is passed by reference to the print function in line (U) – that is a consequence of declaring the parameter type to be `list<string>&`. As we will explain in Chapter 9, this is a more efficient way to pass a large object to a function (provided this mode of argument passing is used with care). Object reference in C++ is presented in Chapter 8.

5.1.4 Stack

We will now present the first of the sequence container adapters. These are container classes that are basically the same as the sequence containers we have discussed so far, but with restricted interfaces.

To explain what we mean by a "sequence container with a restricted interface", let's say you need the stack data structure in a computer program. A stack works on the principle of "last in, first out" (LIFO), as shown pictorially in Figure 5.1. Based on the earlier discussion on vectors, it should be obvious that we can use a

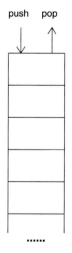

Fig. 5.1

`vector` as a stack. A `vector` provides us with all the necessary operations for a stack: push_back, pop_back, back, and empty — push_back for pushing an item into a stack; pop_back to get rid of the item most recently pushed into a stack; back for retrieving the value of the item at the top of a stack; and, finally, empty for ascertaining whether a stack is empty. But using a vector directly as a stack makes the program somewhat less perspicuous in comparison with a program that uses a container that was called stack.

Now imagine a stack class that in its internals uses a vector to store the data, but only makes available to the programmer the functions push and pop for doing what the names imply, a function top for retrieving the value of the element at the top of the stack, and empty to figure out if the stack is empty. Someone perusing the program would know immediately as to what logic was being implemented through the stack container, making the program easier to understand and maintain. This would amount to using vector with a restricted interface.

The STL stack container class has been defined in such a way that it can act as a wrapper class for any container that supports the operations push_back, pop_back, back, and either empty or size, if not both. What that means is that if you were to write your own container class equipped with these functions, the STL stack container would be able to *adapt* to it (hence the name "adapter class").

Shown below is a program that illustrates how an STL stack can be used. Note the constructor:

```
stack< string, vector<string> > s;
```

This constructor invocation says that the stack object s will use vector<string> as the underlying container. If no underlying container is specified, as for example in

```
stack< string > s;
```

the stack uses a deque by default — deque<string> for the example shown. The functions push and pop perform their duties as side effects — both return void. The function push of stack basically calls push_back on the underlying container, and the function pop calls pop_back on the underlying container. The function top returns a value obtained by invoking back on the underlying container.

```
//StackOps.cc

#include <string>
#include <stack>
#include <vector>
using namespace std;

int main()
{
    stack< string, vector<string> > s;

    s.push( "me" );
    s.push( "to" );
```

```
    s.push( "talk" );

    while ( !s.empty() ) {
        cout << s.top() << " ";              // talk to me
        s.pop();
    }

    return 0;
}
```

5.1.5 Queue

This is the second of the adapter containers. Just as stack can adapt to any underlying container that provided a certain functionality, queue can adapt to any underlying container that supports push_back, pop_front, front, back, size, and empty. The queue itself provides to the user the functions push, pop, front, back, size, and empty. The push of queue invokes push_back of the underlying container and the pop of queue invokes pop_front of the underlying container. The rest of the functions of queue directly invoke functions of the same name on the underlying container. Figure 5.2 captures the control action of a queue.

Fig. 5.2

The following program shows how one can use the queue container. Note the constructor call

```
    queue<string> q;
```

which declares q to be a queue<string> whose underlying container is a deque<string> by default. If you wanted to use some other container, say, a list container as the underlying container, the constructor invocation would become

```
    queue< string, list<string> > q;
```

```
//QueueOps.cc

#include <string>
```

```
#include <queue>
using namespace std;

int main()
{
    queue<string> q;

    q.push( "roses" );
    q.push( "are" );
    q.push( "red" );

    while ( !q.empty() ) {
        cout << q.front() << " ";            // roses are red
        q.pop();
    }

    return 0;
}
```

5.1.6 Priority_Queue

This is the last of the adapter containers. A `priority_queue` works very much like a queue except that the item that will be popped off next is the one with the highest-priority. So whenever anything is pushed into or popped off a `priority_queue`, the item with the highest priority is brought to the front of the queue. The priority of an item is usually established on the basis of a programmer-supplied comparison criterion for the queue items. If a comparison criterion is not explicitly supplied, the system will try to use either the '<' operator if defined for the items in the queue or, if applicable, the `less` *function object* from the `functional` header file of the C++ Standard Library. Function objects, discussed in Chapter 12, correspond to classes for which the operator '()' has been overloaded.

The program shown below stores `pair` objects in a `priority_queue`.[9] Each `pair` consists of a `string` and an `unsigned int`, the latter serving as a priority number for the former. We also define a `Prioritize` function object by overloading the '()' operator. As already stated, the topic of function objects is treated in detail in Chapter 12.

Note the call to the constructor:

---

[9]The `pair` class, actually a `struct`, is convenient for encapsulating a pair of different types that belong together because they stand for two mutually related attributes. It is defined in the `utility` header file of the C++ Standard Library.

```
priority_queue< pair< string, unsigned int >,
    vector <pair< string, unsigned int > >, Prioritize >   pq;
```

which declares pq to be a priority_queue based on a vector< pair<string, unsigned int> > for its underlying container. Since a priority_queue can adapt to any underlying container that supports front, push_back, pop_back, and empty, one can also use a list or a deque for the underlying container.

```
//PriorityQueueOps.cc

#include <string>
#include <queue>
using namespace std;

class Prioritize {
public:
    // As explained in Chapter 12, the overloading of the
    // '()' operator shown below makes available a function
    // object Prioritize() that is subsequenlty supplied as
    // the third argument to the priority_queue constructor.
    int operator() ( const pair<string, unsigned int>& p1,
                     const pair<string, unsigned int>& p2 ) {
        return p1.second < p2.second;
    }
};

int main()
{
    priority_queue< pair< string, unsigned int >,
        vector <pair< string, unsigned int > >, Prioritize >   pq;

    pq.push( pair<string, int>( "go to lunch", 2) );
    pq.push( pair<string, int>( "go to bathroom", 10 ) );
    pq.push( pair<string, int>( "take a nap", 1 ) );

    while ( !pq.empty() ) {                                          //(A)
        cout << pq.top().first << endl;
        pq.pop();
    }

    return 0;
}
```

The output of the program produced by the while loop in line (A) is

```
go to bathroom
```

```
go to lunch
take a nap
```

5.1.7   Map

A C++ map is a sequence of `<key, value>` pairs in which every key is unique. So a phone book in which every name appeared only once could be represented by a map — each distinct name would serve as a key and the phone-number associated with that name would be the corresponding value. A map can be thought of as a *mapping* from the keys to the values.

As mentioned at the beginning of Section 5.1, all the `<key, value>` pairs in a map are stored in a key-sorted ascending order in a binary tree to allow for fast retrieval. The order is maintained as new pairs are added to the container. As one would expect, generating and maintaining a key-sorted order requires that the container have access to a less-than predicate for the key type.[10] This usually is not a problem for the commonly used case of the string type for the keys — since the operator '<' is defined for the string type. But should you decide to use this container with your own class type for the keys, you'd need to make sure that a suitable less-than operation is defined for your class type.[11]

To illustrate how map is used, let's try to write a C++ program that generates a word histogram for a text file.[12] First of all, we must include the header file for this container, as shown in line (A) in the program that follows. The container itself is declared as in line (B), which declares hist to be an empty map to begin with. After the creation of this container (and after setting up an input file stream in line (C)), the histogram itself is constructed by exactly two lines of code in lines (D) and (E), repeated here for convenience:

```
while ( in >> word )
    hist[ word ]++;
```

The logic that is embedded in the second of these two lines is as follows: For a word just read from the source file, we first evaluate hist[word]. If word is not already a key in the histogram, the container would go ahead and create an entry for it, setting its value to 0 of the appropriate kind. In our case, since the *value* part of each `<key, value>` pair is supposed to be an integer, the value set for such a word will be the integer 0. After doing all this work, hist[word] will return 0, which would then get incremented to 1 by the postfix increment operator. Through this mechanism, for

---

[10]This would ordinarily be provided by overloading the '<' operator for the data type of the keys. Overloading of C++ operators is discussed in Chapter 12.

[11]If the overload definition of the '<' is not suitable for the kind of sorting that is desired with a map container, it is also possible to invoke the map constructor with a separate comparison function.

[12]Based on an example provided by Stroustrup [54].

a word that was not already in the histogram, we'd get a count of 1 inserted in the histogram. On the other hand, if the word was already as a key in the histogram, hist[word] would return the current value for that key — meaning the current count. The postfix increment operator would then bump up the count by one.

Lines (H) and (I) print out the contents of the map container. We scan through the sequence of <key, value> pairs in the container and then output the keys and the values in the form of a table. The scanning is accomplished by first defining a local typedef for an iterator to the map container in line (G) and then setting up a for loop for printing out the keys and the corresponding values through the pair data members first and second in line (I). Initializing the iterator and setting up a terminating condition for the loop are very much like what we saw earlier for vectors. Here is the program:

```
//MapHist.cc

#include <string>
#include <map>                                            //(A)
#include <fstream>
using namespace std;

int main()
{
    map<string, int> hist;                                //(B)

    ifstream in( "inFile" );                              //(C)

    string word;
    while ( in >> word )                                  //(D)
        hist[ word ]++;                                   //(E)

    in.close();                                           //(F)

    typedef map<string, int>::const_iterator CI;          //(G)
    for ( CI iter = hist.begin(); iter != hist.end(); ++iter )   //(H)
        cout << iter->first << '\t' << iter->second << endl;     //(I)

    return 0;
}
```

The default choice of the '<' operator as a criterion for key-ordering the elements of a map is not always appropriate. Consider the case when the keys are of type char*. Strings of type char* should not be compared with the '<' operator; instead, they should be compared using the strcmp function. When '<' is not suitable, the programmer must provide an alternative ordering criterion in the form of a function object (see Section 12.10 of Chapter 12). Here is Stroustrup's example of a function object that invokes the strcmp function:

```
class Cstring_less {
public:
    bool operator() ( const char* p, const char* q ) const {
        return strcmp( p, q ) < 0;
    }
};
```

We can now declare a map for holding <C_style_string, value> pairs by

```
map< char*, int, Cstring_less >  assoc_list;
```

For this container, the Cstring_less function object will be used to build a tree representation from the items in the container. When the user defines a comparison function in the form of a function object, all other relational operators are derived from that comparison function. To illustrate, if a user-defined comparison function is denoted cmp(x, y), the following predicate could then be used for testing for an equivalence:

```
!cmp(x,y)  &&  !cmp(y,x)
```

This implies that equivalent keys need not be equal in a map container. For example, as stated by Stroustrup [54], an associative container that uses case-insensitive comparison as its comparison criterion will consider the strings "Last," "last," "lAst," "laSt," and "lasT" equivalent, even though the operator '==' for strings considers them different.

Finally, if it is not necessary for the <key, value> pairs to be stored in a key-sorted order, you may obtain better performance by using a hash-table version of the mapping container called hash_map if the hashing function used is effective for the keys.

5.1.8 Set

Each object can appear only once in a set — no duplicate elements allowed. For example, the names of all of your friends would constitute a set — assuming that the same name was not shared by two or more friends.

The following example illustrates some of the basic functionality of a set. In line (A), we include the header file for this container. Line (B) declares animals as a set of strings. Lines (C) through (F) illustrate how new elements can be inserted into a set. In line (G), we try to insert the object "cat" into the set a second time, but as the output of the print loop in line (I) shows, the set retains only one "cat". Line (J) illustrates the use of erase() to remove a set element. Lines (H) and (K) show the use of the size() function to determine the number of elements in a set. The iteration loops in lines (I) and (L) show that iterators work for a set the same way as for the other containers we have already seen.

```
//SetOps.cc

#include <string>
#include <set>                                                    //(A)
using namespace std;

int main()
{
    set<string> animals;                                          //(B)

    animals.insert( "cheetah" );                                  //(C)
    animals.insert( "lion" );                                     //(D)
    animals.insert( "cat" );                                      //(E)
    animals.insert( "elephant" );                                 //(F)
    animals.insert( "cat" );          //attempting a duplicate //(G)

    cout <<  animals.size() << endl;;    // 4                     //(H)

    typedef set<string>::const_iterator CI;
    for (CI iter = animals.begin();                               //(I)
            iter != animals.end();
            iter++)
        cout << *iter << " ";          // cat cheetah elephant lion

    animals.erase( "lion" );                                      //(J)
    cout <<  animals.size() << endl;;    // 3                     //(K)

    for ( CI iter = animals.begin();                              //(L)
          iter != animals.end();
          iter++ )
        cout << *iter << " ";          // cat cheetah elephant

    return 0;
}
```

5.1.9 Generic Algorithms

In addition to the containers, STL also provides us with algorithms that can be used with the container classes for searching, sorting, counting, merging, filling, comparing, swapping, deleting, partitioning, and much more.

The most significant thing to note about the algorithms is that they only require iterators for their arguments and that they do not need to know about the containers directly. As an example, suppose you initialize two iterators by having them point to two chosen locations in a container; if you supply those iterators to an STL sort algorithm, it would sort the elements between the two iterators. You would not need to tell the sort function directly about the container. This would work even if the container class was created by you, as long as it satisfied certain iterator requirements. For this reason, the STL algorithms are also known as *generic algorithms*. Whether or not a certain algorithm will work with a given container depends on whether or not the container supports the iterator types needed by the algorithm.

There are 60 different algorithms. Of these, 23 are *nonmutating* algorithms because they do not alter the contents of a container. The remaining 37 are *mutating*. Examples of nonmutating algorithms are `min_element`, which returns an iterator that points to the minimum element in a sequence; `find`, which returns an iterator that points to the first occurrence of a value in a sequence; `binary_search`, which performs a binary search for a given value in an ordered container, and so on. Examples of mutating algorithms are `fill` for assigning values to specified elements in a sequence; `sort` for in-place sorting of the elements within a specified range in a container, and so on.

With regard to the sorting algorithms provided by STL, although the reader has already seen examples of sorting in some of the example code we have shown in this section, Chapter 12 will present in greater detail how the contents of a C++ container can be sorted. For the sorting of class type objects, there are basically two approaches and they both require operator overloading:

- You can overload the '<' operator for the element type. By default, the generic `sort` algorithm uses the overloaded definition of this operator for ordering the elements. But, as we already mentioned earlier in this chapter, the default use of the '<' operator is not always appropriate for sorting.

- One can define what is known as a function object that is then supplied as an argument to the sorting algorithm. Through the overload definition supplied for the '()' operator, the function object tells the sorter how to compare two class type objects.

Chapter 12 will discuss these alternatives in detail.

5.2 CONTAINERS IN JAVA

Java containers are based on a hierarchy of abstract data types shown in Figure 5.3. Being Java interfaces, these data types only contain method declarations; in other words, they do not contain any implementation code for the methods. The interface `Collection` considers a container to be a group of objects, without any assumptions

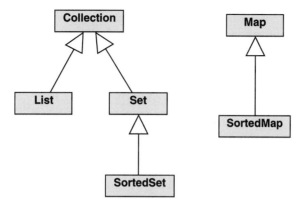

Fig. 5.3

about the uniqueness of the objects in the container. This interface declares methods common to all containers of types List and Set. These include such general-purpose methods like add to insert a new element into a container; clear to remove all the elements from a container; isEmpty to check whether a container is empty; iterator to return an iterator to a container; remove for removing a specific object from a container; removeAll for removing all the objects from a container that are specified via an argument container; and so on. A particularly noteworthy method declared in this interface is toArray. Since this method must be implemented by all containers of type Collection, it can be used to construct an array version of any of those containers.

A Set is a specialization of Collection in the sense that all the elements in a Set must be unique. Uniqueness of the elements is tested by the equals method defined for the element type. In other words, if e1 and e2 are any two elements in a Set, then e1.equals(e2) must return false. A SortedSet is a Set in which all the elements are kept in a sorted order, usually in the form of a height-balanced binary tree. For the comparison criterion needed for sorting, a SortedSet can use the compareTo method if defined for the element type[13] or a Comparator object supplied to a SortedSet constructor.

Compared to a Set, a List is a sequence container, in the same sense that vector, deque, and list are sequence containers in C++. Therefore, a List supports a next-element operation that can be used to traverse a List from the beginning to the end, one element at a time. Containers of type List give the user precise control over where in the list a new element is inserted. Unlike a Set, it is possible to place duplicate elements in a List.

---

[13]Recall from our Chapter 3 discussion on how class type objects are compared in Java that the compareTo method induces a *natural order* on a data type.

Going over to the interfaces shown on the right in Figure 5.3, a Map, like a C++ map, is a container that stores <key, value> pairs, with no duplicate keys allowed. While a C++ map always stores its <key, value> pairs in key-sorted order, Java provides a subtype SortedMap for that purpose.

As was mentioned previously, the types shown in Figure 5.3 are merely interfaces. They must be implemented by container classes that create physical storage for the data to be stored. Table 5.2 shows which interfaces are implemented by what classes. In addition to the recommended implementation classes like ArrayList and Linked-List for the interface List, we also show in Table 5.2 the older container classes Vector and Stack that have now been retrofitted to the List interface in order to make them a part of the Java Collections Framework. ArrayList is a modern replacement for Vector. Similarly, for the Map interface, we listed the recommended HashMap and TreeMap and also the historical HashTable.

Interface		*Implementation*		*Retrofitted Implementation*
Set		HashSet		
	SortedSet	TreeSet		
List		ArrayList	LinkedList	Vector Stack
Map		HashMap		HashTable
	SortedMap	TreeMap		

Table 5.2

The hierarchical organization of the container types shown in Figure 5.3 results in certain programming conveniences, such as easy copying over of the contents of one container into another container. This is a consequence of the fact that all container classes that implement any of the interface shown in the first column of Table 5.2 are required to have a constructor that takes an argument of type Collection. For example, the container class ArrayList is an implementation of the interface List and one of the three constructors for ArrayList is

```
ArrayList( Collection c )
```

What that implies is that an ArrayList container can be constructed from the elements stored in any container that is of type Collection. To see the benefits of that, let's say we have a Set of objects and that we would like to apply an operation to the objects that is defined for a List but not for a Set. Since a Set is a Collection, all we have to do is to copy over all the objects from the Set into an ArrayList by invoking the constructor shown above and apply the desired operation. After that, if so desired, we can copy the objects back to a Set type container using a constructor that again takes a Collection argument.

In the rest of this section, we will show example code for some of these implementation classes to give the reader a better sense of how they are actually used. However, before getting into the individual containers, we should mention at the outset that, whereas C++ containers can store the primitive types directly, Java containers only store items of type Object or its sub-types. With regard to the subtypes of Object in Java, note that int, float, char, and so on, — the *primitive types* — are not subtypes of Object (see Chapter 6). However, Java provides for each primitive type a corresponding *wrapper class* that is a subtype of Object. For example, the Character class is a wrapper class for the primitive type char; the Integer class a wrapper for the primitive type int, and so on.

5.2.1 List

Of the two implementations of the List interface, ArrayList of the java.util package is a modern version of the Java Vector class[14] and its properties are very much like those of the C++ vector and deque containers. The implementations Vector and Stack shown in Table 5.2 date back to the early releases of Java; more recently these classes have been retrofitted to implement the List interface to enable older Java code to run on the newer platforms.

The next program illustrates the following methods of a List:

```
add         :   for adding a new element at the back end

add         :   a two-argument vesion for adding a new element
                at a specified position

remove      :   for removing the first occurrence of an element
                that is the same (in content or value) as the
                argument to this method

remove      :   an integer argument version for removing an
                element from a specified position

addAll      :   for splicing one list into another
```

---

[14]This is important for multithreaded programs: while Vector is synchronized, an ArrayList is not. Therefore, ArrayList must be synchronized externally. Absence of synchronization is also true of the other containers shown under *Implementations* in Table 5.2. Thread synchronization is discussed in Chapter 18.

```
listIterator:    for iterating through a List using a ListIterator
                 object
```

The program also illustrates how `Collections.sort` can be used to sort a `List`.

The program starts in line (A) by declaring `animals` as an `ArrayList`. At this juncture, `animals` is an empty list. We could also have invoked a constructor that takes an integer argument, as in

```
List animals = new ArrayList(10);
```

The integer argument creates a `List` of a specified *initial capacity*, in this case 10 elements. Specifying an initial capacity can reduce the overhead associated with incremental reallocation of memory as new elements are added to a list.

In a block of lines starting at (B), the program then invokes a one-argument version of add to insert new elements into the list. Line (C) intentionally introduces a duplicate element into the list. Line (D) shows a one-argument version of `remove` to remove from the list a single element based on its value. The `remove` method compares its argument with each element using the `equals` predicate as it traverses the list. The first element for which `equals` returns true is removed from the list.

Next, in lines (E) and (F), the program shows the two-argument version of add for inserting a new element into a `List` at a specific position. This is followed in line (G) by the use an integer argument version of `remove` for removing an element from a specific position.

The list `animals` is then sorted by invoking `Collections.sort` in line (H). The sort algorithm yields a natural order for the elements since by default it uses the `compareTo` method defined for the element type. We could also have supplied a second argument to `sort`; the argument would be a `Comparator` object that tells `sort` how to compare two elements.

We then demonstrate how to splice one `List` into another. For that purpose, we create a second list, `pets`, in line (I). For the sake of variety, we make this list a `LinkedList`. By invoking `addAll` in line (K) the list `pets` is spliced into `animals` at a specific position that is the first argument to `addAll`.

Finally, we show in lines (L) through (N) how a `ListIterator` is used to iterate over a list. While an `Iterator` can only move in the forward direction, a `ListIterator` is bidirectional. With an `Iterator`, you can set up a `while` loop that yields successive elements by the invocation of `next` while testing for the end of the list via the predicate `hasNext()`. Being bidirectional, a `ListIterator` also supports `previous` and `hasPrevious` for a backwards traversal of a list, in addition to the usual `next` and `hasNext` for a forward traversal. The methods `previous` and `hasPrevious` are analogous to the methods `next` and `hasNext`.

```
//ListOps.java
```

```
import java.util.*;

class ListOps {
    public static void main( String[] args )
    {
        List animals = new ArrayList();                     //(A)
        animals.add( "cheetah" );                           //(B)
        animals.add( "lion" );
        animals.add( "cat" );
        animals.add( "fox" );
        animals.add( "cat" );           //duplicate cat      //(C)
        System.out.println( animals ); //cheetah, lion, cat, fox,
                                        //cat

        animals.remove( "lion" );                           //(D)
        System.out.println( animals ); //cheetah, cat, fox, cat

        animals.add( 0, "lion" );                           //(E)
        System.out.println( animals ); //lion, cheetah, cat, fox,
                                        //cat

        animals.add( 3, "racoon" );                         //(F)
        System.out.println( animals ); //lion, cheetah, cat,
                                        //racoon, fox, cat

        animals.remove(3);                                  //(G)
        System.out.println( animals ); //lion, cheetah, cat,
                                        //fox, cat

        Collections.sort( animals );                        //(H)
        System.out.println( animals ); //cat, cat, cheetah,
                                        //fox, lion

        List pets = new LinkedList();                       //(I)
        pets.add( "cat" );                                  //(J)
        pets.add( "dog" );
        pets.add( "bird" );
        System.out.println( pets );     //cat, dog, bird

        animals.addAll( 3, pets );                          //(K)
        System.out.println( animals ); //cat, cat, cheetah,
                                        //cat, dog, bird, fox,
                                        //lion

        ListIterator iter = animals.listIterator();         //(L)
        while ( iter.hasNext() ) {                          //(M)
            System.out.println( iter.next()  );             //(N)
        }
```

```
    }
}
```

An interesting difference between C++ iterators and Java iterators is the manner in which you must imagine their position in a container. A C++ iterator, like a C++ pointer, points directly at an element of a container. To illustrate this difference, let's say you declare and initialize an iterator to a vector in C++ as follows

```
vector<int> vec(4);
vector<int>::iterator iter = vec.begin();
```

With this initialization, `iter` is pointing directly at the first element of the vector, as shown in Figure 5.4.

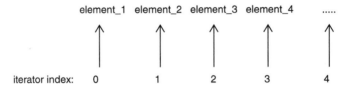

Fig. 5.4

On the other hand, in Java the operation of the `next` and the `hasNext` methods (and the `previous` and the `hasPrevious` methods) is best imagined by thinking of a Java iterator as pointing to imaginary gaps between the elements. Suppose we declare

```
List animals = new ArrayList( 4 );
animals.add();
...
...
ListIterator iter = animals.listIterator();
while ( iter.hasNext() ) {
    System.out.println( iter.next()  );
}
```

It is best to think of the successive positions of the iterator `iter` as shown in Figure 5.5. With this picture, the predicate `hasNext` tells us whether or not there exists a valid element immediately beyond the current position of the iterator and, if the element exists, the method `next` returns an object reference to the element. Similarly, for a position of the iterator of type `ListIterator`, the method `hasPrevious` will tell us whether or not there exists an element just before the current position of the iterator, and the method `previous` will return it. This mental picture of how an iterator traverses a container applies to all containers in the Java Collections Framework.

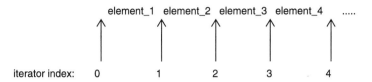

Fig. 5.5

While we are on the subject of iterators for Java containers, we should mention that the iterators returned by the `iterator` and `listIterator` methods are *fail-fast*.[15] What that means is that if you create an iterator and then proceed to structurally modify an `ArrayList` by the `ArrayList`'s add or remove operations as you are iterating through the list, a runtime exception of type `ConcurrentModificationException` will be thrown.[16] To illustrate this point, let us try to insert an add invocation inside the `while` loop in the lines (M) and (N) of the previous program. We will replace the lines (L), (M), and (N) of that program with the following code fragment

```java
ListIterator iter = animals.listIterator();
while ( iter.hasNext() ) {
    animals.add( "zebra" );              // ERROR
    System.out.println( iter.next()  );
}
```

If we compile and run the program with this modification, the runtime will throw a `ConcurrentModificationException`. If you must modify a container as you are scanning through it with an iterator, you are only allowed to use the add and remove methods defined directly for the iterator class. That makes sense because it is the `Iterator` object that knows where it is in the container as the container is being scanned. The container object itself would have no idea of that position.

The *fail–fast* property of iterators is a safety mechanism since modifying a container during an iteration loop will in general invalidate the initialization parameters of an iterator, as was also the case with C++ containers under similar conditions.[17]

---

[15]This actually applies to all of the containers in the Java Collections Framework. The iterators are always fail-fast.

[16]Since `ConcurrentModificationException` is a subtype of `RuntimeException`, it is an *unchecked exception*. As we will explain in greater detail in Chapter 10, methods that throw unchecked exceptions do not need to be called inside a `try–catch` block.

[17]This protection also helps out with multithreaded programs if one thread has initialized an iterator and is using it to iterate through a loop while another thread is trying to modify the container structurally. Multithreading is discussed in Chapter 18.

5.2.2   Set

HashSet implements the interface Set, whereas TreeSet implements the interface
SortedSet. The former uses a hashing function to store the elements, whereas the
latter keeps the elements in an ascending sorted order. If the hashing function used
is effective, the former will give constant-time performance for data access, but there
are no guarantees to that effect. On the other hand, the TreeSet implementation
carries a guarantee of $O(log(N))$ time cost.

The following program shows some of the common operations — such as add,
remove, size, and so on – one carries out on sets. The program starts by declaring
in line (A) a TreeSet by

```
Set animals = new TreeSet();
```

which creates an empty Set for us. If we had wanted to use a HashSet, we could
have used the following invocation:

```
Set animals = new HashSet(50);
```

where the integer argument to the constructor specifies the initial number of buckets
to be used for hashing. This is also referred to as the *initial capacity* of the HashSet.
The default value for the initial capacity is 101.[18]

Lines (B) through (E) show how the add method can be used to insert elements into
the set. Note the attempt to insert a duplicate element in line (F) — it simply replaces
the previous element of the same value. In other words, no duplicate elements can
exist simultaneously in this container. In line (G), we print out the contents of the
container, and in line (H) its size by invoking the size() method. In line (I), we show
how to remove an element of a set by value. Finally, in lines (K) through (M), we
show how to iterate over a set by constructing an Iterator object and then invoking
its hasNext() and next() methods. Here is the code:

```
//SetOps.java

import java.util.*;

class SetOps {

    public static void main( String[] args )
    {
        Set animals = new TreeSet();                        //(A)
```

---

[18]Further tuning of a HashSet can be achieved by specifying a *load factor* as a second argument to
the constructor. The load factor controls how full a hash-table based container is allowed to get before its
capacity is automatically increased.

```
animals.add( "cheetah" );                                    //(B)
animals.add( "lion" );                                       //(C)
animals.add( "cat" );                                        //(D)
animals.add( "elephant" );                                   //(E)
animals.add( "cat" );                        // duplicate cat //(F)
System.out.println( animals );                               //(G)
                        // cat cheetah elephant lion
System.out.println( animals.size() );  // 4                  //(H)

animals.remove( "lion" );                                    //(I}
System.out.println( animals );  // cat cheetah elephant      //(J)

Iterator iter = animals.iterator();                          //(K)
while ( iter.hasNext() )                                     //(L)
    System.out.println( iter.next() );                       //(M)
                        // cat cheetah elephant
    }
}
```

5.2.3 Map

The HashMap and the SortedMap implementations of the Map interface create, respectively, a hash-table based container and a binary-tree based container.

The Map container in Java acts much like the map container in C++: It stores a sequence of <key, value> pairs. However, there are important differences with regard to what can be stored as the keys and their values in a Java Map. Both the keys and the values must be class-type objects for a Java Map; both are stored as instances of the root class Object. To illustrate the consequences of this, suppose you wanted to create a Map of a telephone directory (with the implied constraint that no name would appear more than once in the directory). Unlike the map container class in C++, you will not be able to directly create a sequence of <String, int> pairs. Instead, you must now store a sequence of <String, Integer> pairs. In other words, the value part of a <key, value> pair for a given a key must be a class-type object and not a primitive. As mentioned before, the class-type objects for both the keys and the values are stored as instances of Object. Therefore, when you try to retrieve the value associated with a key, what you get back is of type Object, which you must then cast down to whatever type the value actually is. For the phone directory example, you will have to cast down the retrieved value from Object to Integer and to then invoke Integer.intValue() to actually get hold of the phone number associated with a name. This makes for code that is a bit longer compared to the case of a C++ map.

As the name implies, a HashMap is stored in the form of a hash table. This provides for fast constant-time access to the keys provided the hashing function used is effective for dispersing the keys uniformly over the buckets of the hash table. A TreeMap, on the other hand, is stored as a height-balanced binary tree (called the red-black tree), which guarantees a key-order storage for the <key, value> pairs. This makes for slower retrieval, but has the advantage of maintaining a key-order on the entries.

We will now show the Java version of the MapHist.cc program of Section 5.1.7 for constructing a word histogram for a text file. The C++ program used the STL container map for representing the histogram. The Java version of the same program shown here will give the reader a chance to compare a Java Map with a C++ map.

The program below starts out by declaring histogram as an empty TreeMap in line (A). The next order of business is to pull in all the words in the text file whose histogram is sought. Since Java input streams do not provide for word-by-word reading of an input text file, the program below achieves word-by-word reading by first reading all the characters in the input file into one large string (line B) and breaking the string down into the individual words by using the StringTokenizer class (lines C through E). If a string of delimiter characters is supplied as a second argument to the StringTokenizer constructor, it uses those characters as break points for constructing tokens.[19]   However, if this second argument is not supplied, white space characters are used as delimiters.

For each word supplied by the tokenizer in line (E), we seek its previously accumulated histogram count in line (F). If the word was not previously entered in the histogram, map.get(word) call in line (F) will return a null object. So in line (G), we first check the value returned for count. If null, we start counting for the word by depositing Integer(1) as its value in the histogram. Otherwise, we simply increment the previous value. In line (H), we invoke the size() method to print out the total number of <key, value> pairs stored in the container. Finally, in line (I) we print out the string representation of the container.

For a source file containing the following text

```
A hungry brown fox jumped over a lazy dog
but the lazy dog was not so lazy a dog
since the dog bit the hungry fox
```

the statement in line (I) causes the program to print out the following histogram:

```
Total number of DISTINCT words: 16

{A=1, a=2, bit=1, brown=1, but=1, dog=4, fox=2,
 hungry=2, jumped=1, lazy=3, not=1, over=1,
 since=1, so=1, the=3, was=1}
```

---

[19]A token is the maximal sequence of consecutive characters that are not delimiters.

with the second part all in one line. Here is the program:

```
//MapHist.java

import java.io.*;
import java.util.*;

class WordHistogram {

    public static void main (String args[]) throws IOException
    {
        Map histogram = new TreeMap();                          //(A)

        String allChars = getAllChars( args[0] );               //(B)
        StringTokenizer st = new StringTokenizer( allChars );   //(C)
        while ( st.hasMoreTokens() ) {                          //(D)
            String word = st.nextToken();                       //(E)
            Integer count = (Integer) histogram.get( word );    //(F)
            histogram.put( word, ( count==null ? new Integer(1)
                    : new Integer( count.intValue() + 1 ) ) );  //(G)
        }
        System.out.println( "Total number of DISTINCT words: "
                                + histogram.size() );           //(H)
        System.out.println( histogram );                        //(I)
    }

    static String getAllChars( String filename ) throws IOException {
        String str = "";
        int ch;
        Reader input = new FileReader( filename );
        while ( ( ch = input.read() ) != -1 )
            str += (char) ch;
            input.close();
            return str;
    }
}
```

Suppose we want this program to print out its output in the form of a table. This we can do by iterating over the <key, value> pairs of the Map and printing the keys in one column and the values in another column. Unfortunately, a Map container does not support an iterator directly. To iterate over a Map, we must first construct what is known as a Collection *view*. There are exactly three different ways, listed below, that a Map can be viewed as a Collection. The third choice below will print out the contents of a Map in the form of a table.

1. One can construct a Set of all the keys in a Map by invoking the keySet() method. One can then iterate over this set and display the keys, as in

```
for (Iterator i = histogram.keySet().iterator(); i.hasNext(); )
    System.out.println( i.next() );
```

The Set returned by keySet() is "backed" by the Map, in the sense that any changes made to this set will be reflected in the Map and vice-versa. So if a key were to be deleted in the Set view, the corresponding <key, value> would be removed from the Map.

2. One can construct a Collection of all the values in a Map in the same manner by invoking the values() method on the Map. The Collection returned is again backed by the Map.

3. One can construct a Set of all the <key, value> pairs contained in a Map by invoking the entrySet() method on the Map. Each element of the Set returned by the entrySet() method is an object of type Map.Entry, which is basically an encapsulation of a key and its corresponding value. The key and its value stored in a Map.Entry can be retrieved by the getKey() and the getValue() methods, as shown below:

```
for (Iterator i = histogram.entrySet().iterator(); i.hasNext(); ){
    Map.Entry pair = ( Map.Entry ) i.next();
    System.out.println( pair.getKey() + ":" + pair.getValue() );
}
```

This code fragment will print out in each separate row first the key and then the value of each <key, value> pair of the container.

5.2.4 Vector

As mentioned earlier, the Vector class dates back to the early releases of Java. It has now been retrofitted to implement the List interface to enable older Java code to run on the newer platforms. (We also mentioned earlier that the most commonly used modern replacement for Vector is ArrayList.) Obviously a Vector can be manipulated through all of the methods declared in the List interface. But a Vector also possesses additional methods that it had prior to its modernization. Some of the more commonly used of those methods are illustrated in the example code below.

The next program first illustrates, in lines (B), (C), and (D), the addElement method for inserting three Objects — in this case three Character objects corresponding to the letters 'c', 'a', and 't' — into a vector. As was mentioned in the introduction to Section 5.2, Java containers store items of type Object or its subtypes. So, if you wish to store primitives in a container, you have to use the wrapper classes to first convert them into class-type objects. The program then invokes the `size` method on the vector in line (E) to determine the number of elements stored in the vector.

The `elementAt` method is used in lines (F) through (I) to fill up an array of characters from the data stored in the vector.[20] Line (H) shows how this method can be invoked on a vector for array-like indexing to access the elements of a vector. Since, like all other Java containers, a `Vector` stores only class-type objects (each element as an `Object`), to retrieve the `Character` object stored, you have to cast the item returned by `elementAt` back to the `Character` type, as we do in line (H). The array thus filled is converted into a string in line (J) by invoking one of the constructors for the `String` class.

```
//VectorOps.java

import java.io.*;
import java.util.*;

class VectorOps {
    public static void main( String[] args )
    {
        Vector charVec = new Vector();                       //(A)

        charVec.addElement( new Character( 'c' ) );          //(B)
        charVec.addElement( new Character( 'a' ) );          //(C)
        charVec.addElement( new Character( 't' ) );          //(D)

        int n = charVec.size();              // 3            //(E)

        char[] charArray = new char[charVec.size()];         //(F)
        for ( int i=0; i<charVec.size(); i++ ) {             //(G)
            Character charac = (Character) charVec.elementAt(i); //(H)
            charArray[i] = charac.charValue();               //(I)
        }
        String str =  new String( charArray );               //(J)
        System.out.println( str );           // cat         //(K)
    }
}
```

---

[20]For converting a vector into an array, we could also have invoked the following shortcut:

```
Character[] characterArr = new Character[ charVec.size() ];
charVec.copyInto( CharacterArr );
```

But note that `characterArr` is an array of `Character`'s, whereas `charArray` used in the program is an array of the primitive `char`'s.

We will now illustrate how list operations are carried out on Java vectors. The functions used for such operations are

```
insertElementAt
removeElementAt
addElement
removeElement
```

The next program demonstrates these methods. In lines (A) through (D), the programs starts out in the same manner as the previous program — by constructing a vector containing three Character objects corresponding to the characters 'c', 'a', and 't'. Lines (E) through (H) then apply the above mentioned list operations to produce effects indicated by the commented out words shown. The rest of the program is the same as before.

```java
//VectorListOps.java

import java.io.*;
import java.util.*;

class VectorListOps {
    public static void main( String[] args )
    {
        Vector charVec = new Vector();                          //(A)

        charVec.addElement( new Character( 'c' ) );             //(B)
        charVec.addElement( new Character( 'a' ) );             //(C)
        charVec.addElement( new Character( 't' ) );             //(D)

        charVec.insertElementAt(new Character('h'), 1); // chat //(E)
        charVec.removeElementAt( 0 );                   // hat  //(F)
        charVec.addElement( new Character( 's' ) );     // hats //(G)
        charVec.removeElement( new Character( 't' ) );  // has  //(H)

        System.out.println( charVec.size() );           // 3

        char[] charArray = new char[charVec.size()];
        for ( int i=0; i<charVec.size(); i++ ) {
            Character Ch = (Character) charVec.elementAt(i);
            charArray[i] = Ch.charValue();
        }
        String str =  new String( charArray );
        System.out.println( str );                      // has

    }
}
```

A `Vector` declared with no arguments allocates by default sufficient memory for storing 10 elements. So the `charVec` vector in the program above has initial *capacity* of 10 elements. In order to reduce the overhead associated with growing a vector one element at a time, Java provides two other constructors for the `Vector` class:

```
Vector vec = new Vector( int initialCapacity );

Vector vec = new Vector(int initialCapacity, int capacityIncrement);
```

The first invocation can initially create a vector of arbitrary size as specified by the parameter `initialCapacity`. After this initial storage is filled up, the vector will grow one element at a time should we push further elements into it. To reduce the overhead associated with this one-at-a-time incremental growth, the second constructor shown above allows us to specify the minimum increments to be made to the storage allocated to the vector. If by chance you should allocate too much initial capacity to a vector and that you'd want to trim the size of the vector down to the actual number of elements stored, you can invoke the `trimToSize()` method on the vector.

5.2.5 Algorithms for Java Containers

The `java.util.Collections` class provides the same kind of algorithmic support for the Java containers that the generic algorithms provide for the C++ containers. In this section, we will first focus on the stable sorting property of the sorting algorithm of the `Collections` class and then mention some of its other useful methods.

In the example programs shown earlier, we have already shown invocations such as `Collections.sort( ... )` for sorting the elements of a container. This sorting algorithm is stable. Stated succinctly, *a sorting algorithm is stable if it does not reorder equal elements*. But what does that really mean? A goal of this section is to illustrate this concept.

Stability in sorting, or lack thereof, is best illustrated by comparing the sorted order obtained through the quick-sort algorithm with the sorted order obtained through the merge-sort algorithm. An optimized implementation of quick-sort is slightly faster than an optimized implementation of merge-sort but does not guarantee stability. On the other hand, merge-sort guarantees stability.

Stability in sorting becomes an issue for class-type objects with two or more data members. Class type objects are sorted on the basis of the values of one or more of their data members. Let's say we have multiple objects in a list whose values for the data member chosen for comparison are the same, but whose values for the other data members are different. A stable sorting algorithm will leave the original order of such objects untouched. To illustrate this notion, let us consider a class `Person`:

```
class Person {
    private String name;
    private int rank;
```

```
public Person( String nam, int r ) {
    name = new String( nam );
    rank = r;
}
public String getName() { return name; };
public String toString() { return name + "  " + rank; }
}
```

To sort `Person` objects, we may choose to do so on the basis of their names or on the basis of their rank (or perhaps some weighted combination of the two). We may even wish to first sort all the `Person` objects on the basis of their names, and next sort the resulting list on the basis of rank. In what follows, we will first sort a list of `Person`'s with the merge-sort algorithm of the `Collections` class and then sort the same list with the quick-sort algorithm of C++'s qsort.

For sorting by Java's `Collections.sort`, we will use the following `Comparator` class:

```
class PersonComparator implements Comparator {
    public int compare( Object o1, Object o2 ) {
        Person p1 = ( Person ) o1;
        Person p2 = ( Person ) o2;
        return p1.getName().compareTo( p2.getName() );
    }
}
```

The compare method of this class compares two `Person` objects on the basis of the name field. For the purpose of sorting, let's now construct a list of `Person` objects by

```
List perList = new ArrayList();

perList.add( new Person( "Zaphod", 0 ) );
perList.add( new Person( "Zaphod", 1 ) );
perList.add( new Person( "Zaphod", 2 ) );
perList.add( new Person( "Betelgeuse", 0 ) );
perList.add( new Person( "Betelgeuse", 1 ) );
perList.add( new Person( "Betelgeuse", 2 ) );
perList.add( new Person( "Trillion", 0 ) );
perList.add( new Person( "Trillion", 1 ) );
perList.add( new Person( "Trillion", 2 ) );
```

A stable sorting algorithm will reorder the names in the list, but for each name will leave untouched the order of appearance with respect to the rank. We can sort this list by

```
Collections.sort( perList, new PersonComparator() );
```

The sorted list is as follows:

```
Betelgeuse  0
Betelgeuse  1
Betelgeuse  2
Trillion    0
Trillion    1
Trillion    2
Zaphod      0
Zaphod      1
Zaphod      2
```

where the name is followed by the associated rank in each `Person` object.

On the other hand, if we sort the same original list with a quick-sort algorithm using again the `name` field for comparison, we get

```
Betelgeuse  0
Betelgeuse  2
Betelgeuse  1
Trillion    2
Trillion    0
Trillion    1
Zaphod      0
Zaphod      2
Zaphod      1
```

Notice that objects that are equal with respect to the `name` field are getting shuffled by the quick-sort algorithm.

The quick-sort results shown above were obtained with a C++ program that invoked the well-known `qsort` function with the following invocation

```
qsort( perList, 9, sizeof( Person* ), comparePersons );
```

where the list of `Person` objects was declared as

```
Person* perList[9];
```

with each element of the list instantiated by a statement like

```
perList[0] = new Person( "Zaphod", 0 );
perList[1] = new Person( "Zaphod", 1 );
...
...
```

The comparison function needed for the fourth argument of `qsort` was defined by

```
int comparePersons( const void* arg1, const void* arg2 ) {
    string str1 = (*( Person** )arg1)->name;
    string str2 = (*( Person** )arg2)->name;
    return ( str1 ).compare( str2 );
}
```

The other algorithms provided by the `Collections` class perform tasks such as searching, copying, filling, finding the max or the min in a container, reversing the contents of a container, shuffling the container contents, and so on. The `Collections` class also contains algorithms for creating singleton collections, read-only collections, synchronized collections, and so on.

A singleton `Set` is a set with a single element, a singleton `List` a list with a single element, and so on. That a singleton collection can play a useful role in a Java program should be evident from the following program fragment:

```
List list = new ArrayList();
list.add( "cat" );
list.add( "dog" );
list.add( "cat" );
....

list.removeAll( new Collections.singleton( "cat" ) );
```

This will eliminate all occurrences of "cat" from the container `list`. A singleton collection is immutable, meaning that once created, it cannot be modified.

Here is a program fragment that shows how to create a read-only version of a collection, in this case a `List`:

```
List list = new ArrayList();
list.add( "cat" );
list.add( "dog" );
list.add( "cat" );
....

List readOnlyList = new Collections.unmodifiableList( list );
```

and a program fragment that illustrates how to create a synchronized[21] version of a container, in this case a `List`:

```
List list = new ArrayList();
list.add( "cat" );
list.add( "dog" );
list.add( "cat" );
....

List syncList = new Collections.synchronizedlist( list );
```

While `list` by itself would not be safe for multithreaded programming, `syncList` will be. Thread safety is presented in Chapter 18.

---

[21] Synchronization is discussed in Chapter 18.

Since it is possible to construct an array version of any container of type `Collection` by invoking the `toArray` method on the container, it is also possible to use the algorithms defined for the `java.util.Array` class to manipulate the contents of any container of type `Collection`. The result obtained with this approach will usually be an array that, if so desired, can be converted back into, say, a `List` by invoking the method `Arrays.asList`.

5.3   CREDITS AND SUGGESTIONS FOR FURTHER READING

For a comprehensive presentation of the C++ container classes, see [42]. For a detailed discussion of the complexity and amortized complexity issues related to the C++ container classes, see Stroustrup [54, pp. 464-465]. For further insights into the Java Collections Framework, the reader is referred to the online tutorial at the Java Developer Connection [28]. For additional reading on the different sorting algorithms, such as the merge-sort and quick-sort mentioned in this chapter, the reader is referred to [46]. The material in Section 5.2.5 on stable sorting was first posted by the author at [44]. Regarding the `fail -- fast` property of the iterators in the Java Collections Framework, the reader may also like to see the note posted by the author at www.jguru.com [43].

5.4   HOMEWORK

1. With a C++ class Pet defined as

```
class Pet {
    string name;
    int age;
public:
    Pet( string n, int a ) : name( n ), age( a ) {}
};
```

three out of the nine `main`'s shown below do not compile. (The six others compile and run fine.) Identify the ones that do not compile and give reasons for why that is the case.

(a)   `int main() { Pet pets[3]; }`

(b)   `int main() { Pet* pets[3]; }`

(c)   `int main() { vector<Pet> pets; }`

(d)   `int main() { vector<Pet> pets(3); }`

(e)   `int main() { vector<Pet*> pets; }`

(f)   `int main() { vector<Pet*> pets(3); }`

   (g) `int main() { list<Pet> pets(3); }`

   (h) `int main() { list<Pet> pets; }`

   (i) `int main() { list<Pet*> pets; }`

Assume that all the needed library header files are included in the programs for the testing of the `main`'s shown.

2. The class X in the following program is supplied with a destructor in line (A). Whenever this destructor is invoked, it lets us know by printing out the message shown in the body of the destructor. In `main`, we first construct an empty vector in line (B) for holding objects of type X. We then construct three objects of type X in lines (C) through (E) and push them into the vector in lines (F) through (H). When this program is compiled and run, it produces the following output

```
Destructor invoked for X object with p = 1
Destructor invoked for X object with p = 1
Destructor invoked for X object with p = 2
Destructor invoked for X object with p = 3
Destructor invoked for X object with p = 2
Destructor invoked for X object with p = 1
Destructor invoked for X object with p = 1
Destructor invoked for X object with p = 2
Destructor invoked for X object with p = 3
```

Explain this output. Explain especially why for object x1 the destructor is invoked four times, for object x2 three times, and for object x3 only two times. Here is the program:

```
//VectorDest.cc

#include <iostream>
#include <vector>

class X {
    int p;
public:
    //constructor:
    X( int q ) { p = q; }
    //destructor:
    ~X() {                                              //(A)
        cout << "Destructor invoked for X object with p = "
            << p << endl; }
    };
```

```
int main()
{
    vector<X> vec;                              //(B)

    X x1( 1 );                                  //(C)
    X x2( 2 );                                  //(D)
    X x3( 3 );                                  //(E)

    vec.push_back( x1 );                        //(F)
    vec.push_back( x2 );                        //(G)
    vec.push_back( x3 );                        //(H)

    return 0;
}
```

3. The following program is a slight variation on the program of the previous problem. The class X is now supplied with an additional function, changeState() in line (A). In main we do the same thing as before, except that we also change the state of each of the three objects created before the program is allowed to run to completion. This program produces the following output:

```
Destructor invoked for X object with p = 1
Destructor invoked for X object with p = 1
Destructor invoked for X object with p = 2
Destructor invoked for X object with p = 300
Destructor invoked for X object with p = 200
Destructor invoked for X object with p = 100
Destructor invoked for X object with p = 1
Destructor invoked for X object with p = 2
Destructor invoked for X object with p = 3
```

Explain this output. Explain especially the order in which the three objects created in main, x1, x2, and x3, are destroyed and the order in which the copies of the objects held by the vector are destroyed.

```
//VectorDestOrder.cc

#include <iostream>
#include <vector>

class X {
    int p;
public:
```

```
        X( int q ) { p = q; }
        void changeState( int pp ) { p = pp; }                    //(A)
        ~X(){ cout << "Destructor invoked for X object with p = "
                << p << endl; }
};

int main()
{
    vector<X> vec;

    X x1( 1 );
    X x2( 2 );
    X x3( 3 );

    vec.push_back( x1 );
    vec.push_back( x2 );
    vec.push_back( x3 );

    x1.changeState(100);
    x2.changeState(200);
    x3.changeState(300);

    return 0;
}
```

4. What's wrong with the following program:

```
#include <iostream>
#include <vector>

int main()
{
    vector<string> wordVec;
    vector<string>::iterator p = wordVec.begin();
    wordVec.push_back("apples");
    wordVec.push_back("oranges");
    while ( p != wordVec.end() )
        cout << *p++ << endl;
}
```

5. The goal of this Java homework is to get you to appreciate the *fail-fast* property of the iterator defined for a List. Say you are scanning a list, item by item,

and as you do so you wish to remove some of the items from the list. Removal of items will cause structural modifications to the list. In general, such structural modifications to a list as it is being iterated through can cause the iterator to exhibit nondeterministic program behavior. To protect a program against such problems (which can also happen when one thread is iterating through a list while another thread is modifying the list), Java makes the list iterator fail-fast. What that means is that if a method detects that a list is being modified structurally as it is being iterated through, the method will throw a ConcurrentModificationException. This also applies to the other containers that support iterators in the Java Collections Framework.

Write a Java class PruneList that does the following:

(a) The class should require two command line arguments for its invocation. That is, the class would be invoked by a command line like

```
java PruneList filename  30
```

where the first argument, filename, is the name of the file containing an arbitrary number of integers in one or multiple lines. The second argument, in this case 30, is a threshold value to be used for pruning the integer data.

(b) Read the integers from the file named as described above into an ArrayList.

Suggestion: You could construct a BufferedReader stream and invoke its readLine() method to pull into your program each line of the data file at a time. You could then deploy the StringTokenizer class as shown below to extract the individual integers and stuff them into an ArrayList as shown below:

```
FileReader fr = new FileReader( args[0] );
BufferedReader br = new BufferedReader(fr);
ArrayList list = new ArrayList();
String line;
while((line = br.readLine()) != null){
    StringTokenizer st = new StringTokenizer(line);
    while(st.hasMoreTokens()){
        list.add(new Integer(st.nextToken()));
    }
}
```

(c) Sort the ArrayList container by invoking Collections.sort. (Sorting is not essential to the main goal of this homework. This step is included only because it makes it easier to see the result and to verify that the program is working correctly.)

(d) Iterate through the ArrayList and remove from the list all items whose value exceeds the threshold specified by the command line in (a) above.

(e) Print out the ArrayList before and after the removal of the items.

There are potentially two different ways of removing the items that meet the condition mentioned in (d) above. You could invoke the method remove(int index) defined directly for the ArrayList, or you could invoke the method remove() defined for the ListIterator class. However, the former will cause the ConcurrentModificationException to be thrown for reasons mentioned at the beginning of this homework problem. On the other hand, the latter approach will work just fine. Experiment with both approaches.

6. The goal of this homework[22] is to get you to understand some of the subtleties involved in the use of the generic library remove_if function for removing elements from a C++ sequence container. This function removes all elements for which a certain predicate is true, but not really. What it does is that all such elements are taken out of their existing locations, the remaining elements shuffled toward the beginning of the container, and then the "removed" elements placed at the end of the container, in the same order in which they existed originally in the container. So the overall size of the container remains unchanged. At the same time, the function returns the iterator pointing to the beginning of the section of the container where the "removed" elements were placed. If desired, this iterator value can be used to actually erase the "removed" elements, shrinking the size of the container.

Write a C++ program to do the following:

(a) Write a C++ program, PruneList.cc, that requires two command-line arguments, one for the file containing formatted integer data and the other for an integer value to be used as a threshold in the manner described below. There can be an arbitrary number of integers in the named data file, in an arbitrary number of lines.

(b) Establish an input file stream to read all the integers in the named file into a vector<int> container.

(c) Sort the vector using the generic library sort. (This step is not essential to the main goals of this homework. It is included merely because it makes it easier to see the results and to visually verify that the program is working correctly.)

(d) Display on your terminal the items in the vector by using the copy function from the generic library in the following manner:

```
copy( vec.begin(), vec.end(),
            ostream_iterator<int>( cout, " " ) );
```

---

[22]This homework is best done after the reader has gone through the material in Chapters 12 and 13 because it uses notions related to template classes and function objects that are presented in those chapters.

where vec is the vector<int> object into which you read all of the integers from the data file.

(e) Your program should use remove_if to eliminate each item from the vector vec whose value exceeds the threshold supplied as the second command-line argument in (a) above. This function takes three arguments, the first and the second being the beginning and the ending iterator values for that part of the container where the removal operations are to be conducted. In our case, these arguments can simply be vec.begin() and vec.end(). The third argument supplies the decision criterion for the removal of elements. The simplest possible call to remove_if will look like

```
remove_if( vec.begin(), vec.end(), 30 );
```

This will cause all elements that equal the value 30 to be moved to the end of the container. Obviously, this call will not work for us since we want all elements that are equal to or greater than a threshold to be removed. This can be done by supplying a function object for the third argument. Here is a possible definition for such a function object:

```
template<class Arg> struct ThresholdCheck
                        : public unary_function<Arg, bool>
{
    int threshold;
    //constructor:
    ThresholdCheck( int thresh ) : threshold( thresh ) {};
    bool operator() (const Arg& x) { return x >= threshold ?
                                             true : false; }
};
```

The class ThresholdCheck, defined as a templatized struct, is derived from the base class unary_function defined in the functional header file. The two template parameters supplied to the base class are for the argument type needed by the overloading of the '()' operator and for the result type returned by this operator. In our case, the overload definition for the '()' operator defines a predicate for comparing each vector element against the threshold.

(f) With the function object defined as above, you can now invoke remove_if in the following manner:

```
vector<int>::iterator result =
    remove_if( vec.begin(), vec.end(),
                    ThresholdCheck<int>( 50 ) );
```

if you want 50 to be the decision threshold for the removal of the vector elements.

(g) As mentioned before, remove_if does not actually remove the elements from the container; it just moves to the end of the container. To get rid of these elements altogether (and to thus shrink the size of the container) you must invoke the `erase()` function on the vector using the iterator returned by `remove_if`:

```
vec.erase( result, vec.end() );
```

(h) Display the resulting vector.

7. Section 5.1.7 showed a C++ program that used a `map` container to efficiently construct a word histogram for a text file. Implied in that program was the fact that the container kept the `<key, value>` pairs of the histogram in a sorted ascending order by using the '`<`' operator defined for the string type. This comparison operator carries out a character-by-character comparison of two strings using their ASCII codes. This causes the histogram to create separate counts for the same two words if one has upper case letters in it.

The goal[23] of this homework is to modify the earlier program to create a case-insensitive word histogram for a test file. This can be done by incorporating a user-defined comparison function object in the `map` declaration:

```
map<string, int, Nocase> hist;
```

where `Nocase` is a class that defines a user-defined comparison function for the keys through the overloading of the '`()`' operator.

8. Modify the Java class `WordHistogram` of Section 5.2.3 so that it displays the words in the decreasing order of the frequencies associated with the words.

9. This is a problem in the run-time resizing of C++ vectors. In what follows, we first provide the reader with an example from Stroustrup [54] that shows why you'd want to invoke the `resize` method on a vector at run time to increase its size (as opposed to just using the `push_back` operation to let the size grow one element at a time). This homework problem consists of writing code for the example presented.

Let's say we have a data source that is producing a stream of non-negative integers continuously. Our goal is to make a histogram of these integers and to keep this histogram continually updated as new integers arrive. To remind the reader about histogramming, suppose at some point in time the integers output by the stream were

---

[23][24]This homework is best done after you have gone through Chapter 12 and learned the concept of a function object presented there.

```
3   0   2   1   1   0   1   0   1   2   3   1
```

our histogram would need to contain four bins. If we used an array to represent the histogram, we could declare the array as

```
int hist[4] = {0};
```

For the integer stream shown above, the state of the histogram after that data was read would be

```
hist[0] = 3;
hist[1] = 5;
hist[2] = 2;
hist[3] = 2;
```

since we have three 0's, five 1's, two 2's, and two 3's in the stream. So if i is the next integer read from the data stream, all we would need to do to update the histogram would be

```
hist[i]++;
```

This array based approach would work fine as long as we knew the largest integer that we expected the data stream to produce. If we don't know the largest integer, a vector based approach would be more suitable. For the vector based approach, we could declare our histogram initially as

```
vector<int> hist(4);
```

When an integer i is read from the data stream, we'd update the histogram just as before, but after we compare the integer with the size of the histogram:

```
if ( i < hist.size() ) hist[i]++;
```

But if it turns out that the histogram does not have a bin for the latest integer because the integer is too large, we could do the following:

```
if ( i >= hist.size() ) {
  hist.resize( i + i );
  hist[i]++;
}
```

where the invocation of the function `resize` would increase the size of the vector to twice what's needed for including the integer i in the histogram. [Of course, we could also have said just `hist.resize( i + 1 )` or, for that matter, `hist.resize( 10 * i )`. The choice made with `hist.resize( i + i )` may, depending on the properties of a specific data source, be a happy medium between the absolute minimum needed to accommodate the new integer and some upper wild guess for accommodating future integers. The choice made would hopefully reduce the overhead associated with vector resizing, in terms of memory allocation/deallocation and element copying.]

Write a C++ program that implements the above notions and constructs a dynamically expandable histogram from a stream of integers of arbitrary values.

6

The Primitive Types and Their Input/Output

The primitives types are the variables that are declared to hold integer, character, floating-point, and boolean values. The first half of this chapter deals mainly with representational issues concerning the primitive types. But before getting into how the primitives types are represented, especially from the standpoint of differences between C++ and Java, we will address briefly the issue of what names can be used for variables in general.

The second half of this chapter discusses the input/output stream classes in C++ and Java. Although the focus will be primarily on the I/O of the primitive types, we will also discuss where appropriate the use of the C++ and Java streams for the input/output of the string type. The direct I/O for class-type objects will be discussed briefly as a part of the discussion in one of the homework problems.

6.1 TOKENS, IDENTIFIERS, AND VARIABLE NAMES

Tokens are the most basic syntactical constituents of source code. The set of all tokens can be visualized as shown in Figure 6.1. A token can be an operator, such as +, *, etc.; a keyword, such as main, #include, etc.; a string literal; a punctuation; an identifier; and so on. In both C++ and Java, tokens can be delimited by white

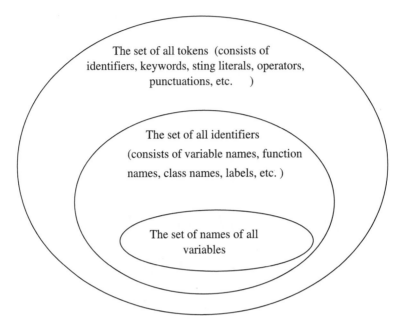

Fig. 6.1

space (meaning, spaces, tabs, newline characters, and form-feed characters)[1] and by operators, punctuation marks, and other symbols that are not permitted to be within identifiers, keywords, and so on. As illustration, the number of tokens in

```
cout<<"Height is: "  +  height << endl;
```

is 8. The first three and the last two tokens are NOT separated by white space.

Let's now talk about identifiers, since a variable name must be an identifier. Identifiers in both C++ and Java are used for naming constants, variables, labels, functions, objects, classes, and so on. In both C++ and Java, an identifier consists of a sequence of characters that must be letters or digits or the underscore character (_), with the stipulation that the first character is either a letter or the underscore. Some examples of identifiers in C++ are

```
x   y   i   j   hello var0 var1 var_x var_y ....
```

Identifiers in C++ are usually written using the 7-bit ASCII character set. As you know already from C, ASCII associates with each character a binary code word

---

[1]That white space is not always a delimiter of tokens should be clear from the fact that it can appear as the content of a character literal or as a part of a string literal:

```
char ch = ' ';
string str = "hi there";
```

whose decimal value is between 0 and 127 (that is, the binary code words range from 0000000 to 1111111). For example, the binary pattern associated with the letter A has a decimal value of 65. Some computers extend ASCII to 8 bits so that 256 characters can be represented.

An identifier in Java looks very much like an identifier in C++ except that the definition of a letter and a digit is now much broader because a 16-bit Unicode representation is used for characters in Java. This means Java can use a character set containing 65,536 characters. The first 256 characters of Unicode constitute the Latin-1 character set and the first 128 of these are equivalent to the 7-bit ASCII character set. The 16-bit representation for characters allows for letters and digits from many different geographical regions of the world to be included in a Java identifier. Current Java environments read ASCII or Latin-1 files, converting them to Unicode on the fly. Converting an ASCII character to a Unicode character means in most cases extending the bit pattern of an ASCII character with a byte of zeros.

6.2 PRIMITIVE TYPES IN C++ AND JAVA

Primitive types (also known as the fundamental types) common to both C++ and Java are:

1. A boolean type: `bool` in C++ and `boolean` in Java.

2. Character types: `char` in both C++ and Java. Additionally, `signed char` and `unsigned char` in C++.

3. Integer types: `short`, `int`, `long` in both C++ and Java. Additionally, `byte` in Java. Additionally, `signed int` and `unsigned int` in C++. The type `signed int` in C++ is synonymous with `int`.

4. Floating-point types: `float` and `double` in both C++ and Java. Additionally, `long double` in C++.

6.3 BOOLEAN TYPE

A Boolean type[2] is allowed to have only one of two values: `true` or `false`. A Boolean is used to express the result of logical operations. For example,

---

[2]Some of the older C++ compilers do not have `bool` as a built-in type. However, you can easily create the `bool` type with the following enumeration:

```
enum bool {false, true};
```

```
int x;
int y;
...
...
bool b = x == y;    in C++
boolean b = x==y;   in Java
```

For another example,

```
C++:     bool greater( int a, int b ) { return a > b; }
Java:    boolean greater( int a, int b ) { return a > b; }
```

In Java, casting to a `boolean` type from any other type or casting from a `boolean` type to any other type is not permitted. Note in particular that, unlike the `bool` type in C++, `boolean` values in Java are not integers.

6.4 CHARACTER TYPES

C++ gives you three different character types:

```
char
unsigned char
signed char
```

Almost universally, a C++ `char` is allocated one byte so that it can hold one of 256 values. The decimal value stored in such a byte can be interpreted to range from either -128 to 127, or from 0 to 255, depending on the implementation. But in either case, the bit patterns for values between 0 and 127 are almost always reserved for letters, digits, punctuations, and so on, according to the ASCII format. All printable characters belong to this set of 128 values. From the standpoint of writing portable code, note that some of the characters one usually sees in C++ source code may not be available in a particular character set available for C++ programming. For example, some European character sets do not provide for the characters {,},[,], and so on.

The decimal values of the bit patterns stored in a `signed char` are always interpreted as varying from -128 to 127, and those for a `unsigned char`[3] from 0 to 255. So, is a plain `char` in C++ an `unsigned char` or a `signed char`? That, as mentioned before, depends on the implementation.

Enumerations are discussed further in Chapter 7. Suffice it here to note that this declaration makes the symbols `false` and `true` as enumerators of the `bool` type, in the sense that they represent the complete set of values that objects of type `bool` are allowed to take.

[3]Unsigned chars of C and C++ are useful for image processing work. Most color cameras produce 8-bit values in each of the color channels, R, G, and B. You'd want to read these values into an `unsigned char`. If you read them into a `signed char`, unless care is taken the high values could get interpreted as negative numbers during downstream processing.

A char variable can be initialized by either an integer whose value falls within a certain range or by what's known as a *character literal*:

```
char ch = 98;        // ch is assigned the character 'b'
char x = 'b';
```

The quantity 'b' is referred to as a character literal or a character constant. A character literal is in reality a symbolic constant for the integer value of the character. In the code fragment

```
char y = '2';
int z = y + 8;           (works for both C++ and Java)
```

the value of z would be 58 because, under ASCII coding, the integer that corresponds to the bit pattern for the character '2' is 50.[4]

Like C, C++ also allows an individual character to be represented by an *escape sequence*, which is a backslash[5] followed by a sequence of characters that must be within a certain range. There are two kinds of escape sequences: *character escapes* and *numeric escapes*. Character escapes, such as \n, \t, and so on, represent ASCII's more commonly used control characters that when sent to an output device can be used to move the cursor to a new line, or to move the cursor to the next horizontal tab, etc. The character '\n' is frequently called the *newline character* and '\t' the *tab character*.

Since character escapes are few in number, a more general form of an escape sequence for representing an individual character is the numeric escape. A numeric escape comes in two forms: *hexadecimal* and *octal*. In the following declarations, all initializing x to the same value, the declaration in line (C) uses the hexadecimal form for the escape sequence shown, and the one in line (D) the octal form:

```
char x = 'b';        // decimal value of 'b' is  98           //(A)
char x = 98;                                                  //(B)
```

---

[4]The automatic type conversion involved here from char to int for y is known as *binary numeric promotion* in both C++ and Java. See the last paragraphs of Sections 6.7.1 and 6.7.2 for when such conversions can be carried out automatically in C++ and in Java, respectively.

[5]A second common use of backslash inside either a double-quoted string or between a pair of single quotes is that it tells the system to alter the usual meaning of the next character. For example, if you wanted to set the value of a character variable to a single quote that is ordinarily used as a character delimiter, you would not be able to say

```
char x = ''';        \\ERROR
```

Instead, you could use a backslash in the following manner

```
char x = '\'';
```

to suppress the character-delimiter meaning of the single quote that follows the backslash. Another illustration of this would be if you wanted to initialize a character variable to the backslash itself:

```
char x = '\\';
```

where the first backslash alters the usual meaning of the backslash that follows.

```
char x = '\x62';     // 62 is hex for 98                    //(C)
char x = '\142';     // 142 is octal for 98                 //(D)
```

In general, the hexadecimal (referred to frequently as just hex) form of a numeric escape in C++ must always be of the form

```
\xdddd....d
```

where every character after the letter 'x' is a hexadecimal digit (0 – 9 and a – f or A – F to represent the decimal values 0 – 15). C++ allows any arbitrary number of characters after the letter 'x' as long as each is a valid hexadecimal digit and with the additional stipulation that the decimal value of the hex number does not exceed 255 for 8-bit characters. The hexadecimal number x62 in line (C) represents the decimal 98, which is the ASCII code for the letter b. Similarly, the octal number 142 in line (D) also represents the decimal 98 and, therefore, corresponds again to the same letter, 'b'. Unlike octal numbers in general, an octal escape sequences does not have to begin with a 0. Also, a maximum of three digits is allowed in an octal escape sequence.

These properties of escape sequences require care when they are used as characters in string literals. This point is illustrated with the examples in the following program:

```
//CharEscapes.cc

#include <iostream>
#include <string>
using namespace std;

int main()
{
    string y1( "a\x62" );
    cout << y1 << endl;          // y1 is string "ab".
                                 // Printed output:  ab

    string y2( "a\x0a" );
    cout << y2 << endl;          // y2 is the string formed by
                                 // the character 'a' followed
                                 // by the newline character
                                 // Printed output:    a

    string y3( "a\nbcdef" );
    cout << y3 << endl;          // y3 is the string formed by
                                 // the character 'a' followed
                                 // by the newline character
                                 // represented by the character
                                 // escape '\n' followed by the
                                 // characters 'b', 'c', 'd', 'e',
```

```
                                   // and 'f'.
                                   // Printed output:    a
                                   //                    bcdef

    string y4( "a\x0awxyz" );
    cout << y4 << endl;            // y4 is the string formed by
                                   // character 'a' followed by the
                                   // newline character represented by
                                   // the numerical escape in hex, '\x0a',
                                   // followed by the characters 'w',
                                   // 'x', 'y', and 'z'.
                                   // Printed output:  a
                                   //                  wxyz

//  string y5( "a\x0abcdef" );    // ERROR
//  cout << y5 << endl;           // because the number whose hex
                                   // representation is '0abcdef' is
                                   // out of range for a char

    string y6( "a\xef" );
    cout << y6 << endl;           // Correct but the character after
                                   // 'a' may not be printable

    string w1( "a\142" );
    cout << w1 << endl;          // w1 is the string formed by
                                   // the character 'a' followed by
                                   // the character 'b'.
                                   // Printed output: ab

    string w2( "a\142c" );
    cout << w2 << endl;          // w2 is the string formed by the
                                   // character 'b' followed by the
                                   // character 'c'.
                                   // Printed output: abc
    string w3( "a\142142" );
    cout << w3 << endl;          // w3 is the string formed by the
                                   // character 'a' followed by the
                                   // character 'b' followed by the
                                   // characters '1', '4', and '2'.
                                   // Printed output: ab142

    string w4( "a\79" );
    cout << w4 << endl;          // w4 is the string formed by the
                                   // character 'a' followed by the
                                   // bell character, followed by
                                   // the character '9'. Printed
                                   // output: a9

    string w5( "\x00007p\x0007q\x0007r\x007s\x07t\x7u" );
```

```
    cout << w5 << endl;              // printed output: pqrstu

    return 0;
}
```

A Java `char` has 2 bytes. Any two contiguous bytes in the memory represent a legal Java `char`. Which 16-bit bit pattern corresponds to what character is determined by the Unicode representation. As was mentioned earlier, the integer values 0 through 255 in the Unicode representation correspond to Latin-1 characters and the first 128 of these are the same as the encodings for the 7-bit ASCII character set (except for an additional byte of zeros on the high side). A Java `char` is unsigned, meaning that its integer values go from 0 through 65,535.

In Java, all of the following four declarations are equivalent:

```
char x = 'b';          // value of 'b' is  98           //(E)
char x = 98;                                            //(F)
char x = '\u0062';     // 0062 is hex for  98           //(G)
char x = '\142';       // 142 is octal for 98           //(H)
```

As shown in line (G), the hex form of a numeric escape in Java begins with the letter 'u', as opposed to the letter 'x' for C++. In general, the hex form of a numeric escape in Java must always be of the form

```
    \udddd
```

where where each d is a hexadecimal digit. The declaration in line (H) above uses an escape sequence in its octal representation. In all four cases, the value of x will be the same, the letter 'b'. Comparing the numeric escapes in lines (E) through (H) for Java and in lines (A) through (D) for C++, we note that only the hex versions are different. The hex version for Java must consist of four hex digits, where C++ allows an arbitrary number of hex digits.

Suppose you are translating a C++ program into a Java program, is it always possible to substitute Java's \udddd escape for C++'s \xd...d escape of an identical decimal value (that is under 256)? Not so. For example, the declaration

```
    char ch = '\x000a';      // ok in C++                    //(I)
```

gives us a valid char in C++ consisting of the newline character. An equivalent Java declaration

```
    char ch = '\u000a';      // ERROR in Java                //(J)
```

is illegal. By the same token, the second string literal we used in the C++ program `CharEscapes.cc`

```
    string y2 = "a\x0a";     // ok in C++                    //(K)
```

is legal. However, a comparable declaration in Java

```
String s = "a\u000a";        // ERROR in Java              //(L)
```

is illegal for constructing a string literal. The reason for why the \udddd escapes shown in lines (J) and (L) cause errors in Java has to do with the fact that the very first thing a Java compiler does with a source file is to scan it for resolving on the fly all \udddd escapes. As each \udddd escape is encountered, it is replaced immediately by the corresponding 2-byte Unicode character. If a \udddd escape represents the newline character, as is the case with the escape sequence \u000a, a newline is inserted into the source file at that point immediately.[6] The same thing happens with the Unicode escape \u000d, which represents carriage return.

The above discussion should not be construed to imply that you cannot embed control characters such as the newline or the carriage-return characters in a character or a string literal. When, for example, a newline character is desired, one can always use the character escape '\n' for achieving the same effect.

Shown below is Java's version of the C++ program CharEscapes.cc presented earlier in this section. This program retains as many of the string literals of the C++ program as make sense in Java. We have also avoided the use of \u000a as a newline character in the string literals.

In the program shown below, note in particular that whereas the string y5 resulted in an error in C++, Java has no problems with it. Java forms a Unicode character out of the escape \u0abc, leaving the rest of the characters for the string literal. But since Java cannot find a print representation for the Unicode character, it outputs a question mark in its place when the print function is invoked on the string. The same is true for the print representation of the Unicode character formed from the escape sequence in y6. The string literals w1 - w4 use octal escapes in the same manner as we showed earlier for the C++ program.

```
//CharEscapes.java

class Test {
    public static void main( String[] args ) {

        String y1 = "a\u0062";
        print( "y1:\t" + y1 );          // Printed output:  ab

        String y2 = "a\n";
        print( "y2:\t" + y2 );          // Printed output:  a
```

---

[6]Java lexical grammar has the notion of a *LineTerminator*, which is not considered to be one of the *InputCharacter*s from which *Token*s are formed. When the Unicode escape \u000a is encountered during the initial scan of a source file, it is replaced by a *LineTerminator* [23].

```
        String y3 = "a\nbcdef";
        print( "y3:\t"+ y3 );           // Printed output:  a
                                        //                  bcdef
        String y4 = "a\nwxyz";
        print( "y4:\t" + y4 );          // Printed output:  a
                                        //                  wxyz
        String y5 = "a\u0abcdef";
        print( "y5:\t" + y5 );          // Printed output:  a?def

        String y6 = "a\u00ef";
        print( "y6:\t" + y6 );          // Correct, but the character
                                        // following 'a' may not have
                                        // a print representation

        String w1 = "a\142";
        print( "w1:\t" + w1 );          // Printed output:  ab

        String w2 = "a\142c";
        print( "w2:\t" + w2 );          // Printed output:  abc

        String w3 = "a\142142";
        print( "w3:\t" + w3 );          // Printed output:  ab142

        String w4 = "a\79";
        print( "w4:\t" + w4 );          // Printed output:  a9
    }

    static void print( String str ) { System.out.println( str ); }
}
```

6.5 INTEGER TYPES

C++ and Java have in common the following integer types:

```
short
int
long
```

In C++, typically a short has two bytes of memory, an int four bytes, and a long eight bytes. From the standpoint of portability of software, it is important to note that the C++ standard says nothing about the exact number of bytes to be used for each. All that is stipulated by the C++ standard is that the memory allocated to a short be at least as large as the memory assigned to a char, the memory assigned to an int be at least as large as the memory assigned to a short, and that the memory assigned to a long be at least as large as the memory assigned to an int.

By contrast, Java stipulates that a short have exactly two bytes, an int four, and a long eight. Java also supports one additional integer type:

    byte

which, as its name implies, gets one byte for its storage. As with the above three types, byte represents a signed integer and its value ranges from -128 to 127.

In addition to the three integer types mentioned previously, C++ also supports signed and unsigned types. A signed int is synonymous with a plain int. The unsigned integer types are ideal for uses that treat storage as a bit array.

Constant integer values are referred to as *integer literals*. For example, the integer 234 is an integer literal. For both C++ and Java, integer literals come in three forms:

    decimal
    octal
    hexadecimal

the most common being the decimal form. An integer literal starting with 0 followed by digits between 0 and 7 is an integer in octal form. An integer literal starting with 0x followed by hex digits is an integer in hexadecimal form. Here are some examples of integer literals:

decimal:	0	7	81	2345
octal:	00	07	0121	04451
hexadecimal:	0x0	0x7	0x51	0x929

Octal and hexadecimal notations are most useful for expressing and visualizing bit patterns. To illustrate, the int 81 is stored in the memory as the following 4-byte bit-pattern in the big-endian representation:

    00000000 00000000 00000000 01010001

The uppermost four bits of the last byte have a decimal value of 5 and the very last four bits have a decimal value of 1, leading to a hex representation of 0x51 for the 4-byte bit-pattern. One can much more readily visualize the bit-pattern associated with the hex 0x51 than with the equivalent decimal 81. For an even more difficult example, consider the int 2345 in the above table. It is difficult to visualize the bit pattern corresponding to the four bytes that will be occupied by this integer in the memory. However, dividing repeatedly by 16, we can quickly convert the integer into its hex representation — 0x929 — and write down the following bit pattern by concatenating the 4-bit patterns associated with each of the hex digits:

    00000000 00000000 00001001 00101001

Hex and octal representations are also useful for creating memory dumps. If you wanted to dump out the contents of a segment of memory in a byte-by-byte manner, you could read each byte as a char through a binary stream and print it out as a hexadecimal int. That way you could get a hardcopy map of what's in the memory.

An integer literal is of type long if it is suffixed with either the letter L or its lower-case version l.

6.6   FLOATING-POINT TYPES

C++ and Java have in common the floating-point types

```
float
double
```

C++ typically uses four bytes for a float and eight for a double. Although the C++ standard does not specify how many bytes exactly should be devoted to each type, it does stipulate that a double be allocated at least as many bytes as a float. On the other hand, Java stipulates that float will have exactly 4 bytes assigned to it and a double 8 bytes. In addition, C++ supports long double for extended precision which is usually allocated 16 bytes.

The exact meaning of float, double, and long double is implementation-defined in C++. That is, the number of bits reserved for the exponent and the fraction may vary from implementation to implementation. On the other hand, Java stipulates that the float and the double types conform to the IEEE 754 standard. Most modern implementations of C++ also conform to this standard.

Under the IEEE 754 standard, a floating-point number consists of three parts: a sign, an exponent, and a fraction (also known as the mantissa). The number of bits reserved for the exponent determines how large and small the overall magnitude of a number can be, while the number of bits reserved for the fraction determines its precision. For float, the exponent gets 8 bits, while the fraction gets 23. As a result, the smallest positive value of a float is 1.17×10^{-38}, its largest value 3.40×10^{38}, with a precision of 6 decimal digits. On the other hand, the smallest positive value of a double is 2.22×10^{-308}, its largest value 1.79×10^{308}, and its precision 15 decimal digits.

Additionally, under the IEEE 754 standard for floating-point numbers, a floating point number can overflow to infinity, which one could represent by a symbolic constant such as inf or underflow to zero (become too small for float or double). Furthermore, the result from an ambiguous arithmetic operation, such as adding a $+inf$ to a $-inf$, can be represented by another symbolic constant, which can be conveniently denoted NaN, for "Not a Number". Note again, the symbolic constant for infinity, inf, and the symbolic constant for an invalid number, NaN, only apply to floating-point numbers. Also useful to remember is the fact that it is possible for an arithmetic operation involving the inf symbolic constant to yield a regular number. For example, if x is a positive finite number, then x divided by $+inf$ will yield $+0.0$.

By default, a floating-point literal is of type `double` in both C++ and Java. However, when suffixed with either the letter F or the letter f, it will be stored as a `float` in both C++ and Java. If a floating-point literal needs to be stored as a `long double` in C++, it must be suffixed with the letter L.

Before ending this section, we would like to mention that in C++, the boolean, the character, and the integer types are collectively called the *integral types*, and the integral and the floating-point types are collectively called the *arithmetic types*.

On the other hand, in Java, only the character and the integer types are collective called the integral types, and the integral and the floating-point types are collectively called the *numeric types*.

For solving a majority of problems in C++, you are likely to use `bool` for logical values, `char` for characters, `int` for integer values, and `double` for floating-point values. You'd do the same in Java except that you'd use `boolean` for logical values.

6.7 TYPE CONVERSION FOR THE PRIMITIVE TYPES

Automatic type conversions are often carried out during initialization; assignment; matching of an argument with the corresponding parameter during a function invocation; conversion of the operands to a common type; and when the type of expression in a return statement does not match a function's return type. One can also force a type conversion by using the `cast` operator. Automatic type conversions are also referred to as *implicit* type conversions, whereas the type conversions brought about by the use of a `cast` operator are sometimes referred to as *explicit* type conversions.

Because Java is more strongly typed than C++, many *automatic* type conversions that are allowed in C++ are illegal in Java. As a case in point, while the following is acceptable to C++

```
int i = 98;
char c = i;              // initialization from an int
```

the second statement would NOT be acceptable to Java, although Java would be happy with the statement

```
char c = 98;             // initialization from an int literal
```

As we will explain in the rest of this section, automatic conversion from an `int` to a `char` is allowed only for initialization from literals in Java.

This section will discuss how one talks about the different kinds of type conversions for the primitive types in C++ and Java, which conversions are carried out automatically, and which can only be brought about through casting.

6.7.1   Implicit Type Conversions in C++

For automatic type-conversion for the primitive types, C++ makes a distinction between a *promotion* and a *standard conversion.* In a promotion, integral types stay integral and non-integral types stay non-integral. *In addition, there must not be a loss of information.* Examples of integral promotions include bool to int, char to int, short to int, and their unsigned counterparts; and examples of non-integral promotions include float to double, double to long double, and so on.[7]   The following program illustrates promotions in initialization, assignment, in function invocation, and in return from a function:

```
//Promo.cc

#include <iostream>
using namespace std;

void g1(short x) {cout << "short version invoked   x: " << x << endl;}
void g2(long x) { cout << "long version invoked   x: "<< x << endl; }
int  g3(short x) {
    cout << "promotion to match return type" << endl;
    return x;
}

int main()
{
    //promotion in initialization:
    char ch = 'a';
    int x = ch;

    //promotion in assignment:
    long j;
    j = x;
    cout << j << endl;        //output: 97                          //(A)

    //promote char into a short for function invocation:
    g1( ch );           //output: short version invoked x:97       //(B)
```

---

[7]In order to maintain backward compatibility with C, the integral type conversions to long and the non-integral type conversion to long double are not considered promotions. The original purpose of a promotion in C was to bring the operands to their "natural" sizes for arithmetic operations [54]. Integral conversions to long and non-integral conversions to long double are included in standard conversions.

```
    //promote int into a long for function invocation:
    g2( x );              //output: long version invoked x:97        //(C)

    short s = 16;

    //promotion inside g3 when matching returned value to return type:
    int w = g3( s );   //output: promotion to match return type    //(D)

    return 0;
}
```

The program output is shown in the commented out portions of the lines (A), (B), (C), and (D).

The other kind of automatic type conversion for the primitive types in C++ — the *standard conversion* — can entail loss of information. There are two ways to characterize this information loss: a loss of information regarding the overall value of a number, and a loss of precision. For example, when you convert an int to a short, the system would retain only the two lowest bytes of the int, which for a large enough int can cause its value to become completely meaningless. On the other hand, if an int is converted into a float, you don't lose information regarding the magnitude of the number since a float can hold much larger numbers than an int. What you can lose in this case is precision; as was mentioned earlier, the precision of a float is limited to only six significant digits. Therefore, if you convert a large int into a float and then re-convert the float back into an int, some of the least significant digits could be different between the two integers. This example is included in the program below.

Examples of standard conversions in C++ are int to double, double to int, int to float, float to int, and so on. Here is an example of a C++ program that illustrates some of the automatic standard conversions, and the loss of information entailed in some of them.

```
//StandardConvert.cc

#include <iostream>
using namespace std;

void g1(short x) {cout << "short version invoked   x: " << x << endl;}
void g2( int x ) { cout << "int version invoked   x: "<< x << endl; }
void g3( float x ) {cout << "float version invoked  x: "<< x << endl;}
float  g4( int x ) {
    cout << "standard conversion to match return type" << endl;
    return x;
}
```

```
int main()
{
    char ch = 'a';

    //standard conversion in initialization:
    float x = ch;

    long j;

    //standard conversion in assignment:
    j = x;

    cout << j << endl;      // output: 97                              //(A)

    int i = 1234567890;

    //standard conversion from int to float:
    float fi = i;

    //error in converting int to float:
    cout << i - (int) fi << endl;      // output: -46                 //(B)

    //value too large to fit into an int:
    float  y = 1e20f;

    //value too large to fit into a float:
    double z = 1e100;

    //standard-convert float into a short for function invocation:
    g1( y );     // output:  short version invoked   x: -32768    //(C)

    //standard-convert float into an int for function invocation:
    g2( y );     // output:  int version invoked x: -2147483648  //(D)

    //standard-convert double into a float for function invocation:
    g3( z );     // output:  float version invoked  x: inf       //(E)

    //standard-convert returned value to return type inside g4:
    float w = g4( i );
            // output: standard convert to match return type     //(F)

    //error in returned value:
    cout << i - (int) w << endl;  // output:  -46                 //(G)

    return 0;
}
```

This program output is shown in the commented out portions of the lines (A) through (G) above. The output in line (A) shows the result of automatic standard conversion during initialization from a `char` to a `float` and then from `float` to a `long`. There is obviously no loss of information here. The output in line (B) shows the loss of precision when a large `int`, in this case of value 1234567890, is converted to a `float`.

For the output shown in line (C), when the `float` value of 1*e*20 is converted into a `short` when matching the argument to the parameter type, the value becomes -32768 inside the function g1. This happens because the `float` is first converted into an `int` on the basis of IEEE 754 round-toward-zero mode and then from that is extracted the largest value that can be represented by a `short`. As the output in line (D) shows, the `int` that 1*e*20 is converted into is -2147483647. The output in line (E) shows what happens when we convert a `double` that is too large to be represented by a `float` into a `float` in a function call; the result is an overflow as represented by the symbolic constant inf. The output in line (G) shows what can happen as a result of the standard conversion performed when the type of the expression in a return statement does not match the return type of a function.

Converting a non-integral type to an integral type, as in lines (C) and (D) above, calls for a non-trivial and implementation dependent conversion. If the floating-point number is neither a NaN nor an inf, the floating value is typically rounded toward zero using the IEEE 754 standard round-toward-zero mode and its low-order bytes retained that can be accommodated in the target type. This means that a floating number such as 32.54 would be converted to the integer value 32 and a number like -32.54 to the integer value -32. Special cases deal with the symbolic values NaN and inf for the floating-point numbers.

Converting an integral type to a non-integral type is typically carried out using the IEEE 754 round-to-nearest mode, which means converting to the nearest representable non-integral type.[8]

So far we have talked about C++'s automatic type conversions during initializations, assignments, when matching arguments with parameters during function invocations, and when the type of the expression in a return statement does not match the return type of a function. Automatic type conversions in C++ are also carried out when arithmetic operations are performed if the operands are of different types. The strategy for these automatic type conversions, which are also known as *binary numeric promotions*, is to convert the operands to the "narrowest" type that will safely accommodate both operands. For example, if you are adding an `int` to a `float`, since the range of numbers that a `float` can accommodate is larger than the range that can be accommodated in an `int`, the narrowest type that would accommodate both would be `float`.

---

[8]The IEEE 754 standard defines four rounding modes for floating-point arithmetic: *round toward plus infinity*, *round toward minus infinity*, *round toward zero* (also called *truncate*), and *round to nearest*.

6.7.2   Implicit Type Conversions in Java

The automatic type conversions for the primitive types in Java fall into two categories: *widening conversions* and *narrowing conversions*. Widening primitive conversions include the promotions permitted in C++. Additional conversion in Java that are of the widening variety include integral to wider non-integral conversions, such as from int to float and double, etc.

Here are the 19 widening conversions permitted automatically in Java for initialization, assignment, for matching arguments with parameters during function invocation, and when the type of the returned value does not match the declared return type of a method:

- from byte to short, int, long, float, or double

- from short to int, long, float, or double

- from char to int, long, float, or double

- from int to long, float, or double

- from long to float or double

- from float to double

These do not entail any loss of information or precision when the conversions are from an integral type to another integral type, and from a non-integral type to another non-integral type. However, there may be a loss of precision (meaning that while the overall magnitude is preserved, some of the least significant bits may be lost) when converting from an integral type to a non-integral type, such as from long to float.[9]

Here is a program that illustrates some of the automatic widening type conversions:

```
//Widening.java

class Test {

    static void g1( short x ) {
        System.out.println( "short version invoked,  x = " + x );
    }
    static void g2( int x ) {
        System.out.println( "int version invoked,  x = " + x );
    }
```

---

[9]See the previous subsection for the distinction between the loss of information regarding the overall value of a number and the loss of precision.

```
static float g3( int x ) {
    System.out.println( "widening conversion on return" );
    return x;
}

public static void main( String[] args )
{
    byte b1 = 16;
    byte b2 = 24;
    // char c1 = b1;     // ERROR                          //(A)
    // c1 = b2;          // ERROR                          //(B)

    //widening from byte to short:
    short s = b1;
    System.out.println( s );     //  output: 16           //(C)

    //widening from char to int:
    char c = 'a';
    int i1 = c;
    System.out.println( i1 );    // output: 97            //(D)

    //widening from int to float:
    int i2 = 1234567890;
    float f1 = i2;
    System.out.println( i2 - (int) f1 );  // output: -46    //(E)

    //widening from float to double:
    float f2 = 1e20f;
    double d1 = f2;
    System.out.println(d1);   //output: 1.0000000200408773E20  //(F)

    //widening from byte to short in method invocation:
    g1( b1 );     // output: short version invoked,  x = 16   //(G)

    //widening from short to int in method invocation:
    g2( s );      // output: int version invoked,  x =  16   //(H)

    //widening from int to float in method invocation:
    float f3 = g3( i2 );
                  // output: widening conversion on return   //(I)

    //Error in widening conversion from int to float:
    System.out.println( i2 - (int) f3 );    // output: -46   //(J)
}
}
```

The output of the program is shown in the commented out portions of the lines (C) through (J).

As pointed out in lines (A) and (B), a widening conversion is not permitted from a byte to a char either for initialization or for assignment. This may seem like a curious omission since a char with its two bytes of storage is after all wider than a byte. The reason has to do with the fact that a byte is signed, whereas a char is unsigned. So if you were to convert a byte into a char, you could end up with an entirely meaningless value. Recall that the value of a byte can range from -128 to 127. Consider a value such as -128. It will be stored as a single byte using the two's complement representation, which in hex is 0x80.[10] If this were to be converted into a two-byte char using the usual rules for widening conversion from a signed integer type to an integral type, the system would simply sign-extend the two's complement representation, meaning that the wider format of the destination type would be filled with the sign bit. This would give us a hex of 0xFF80 for the two bytes of the char. The integer value of this bit pattern is $65,408$.

Line (C) shows the result of a widening conversion from a byte to a short. As expected, there is no loss of information or precision. Line (D) similarly shows a widening conversion from a char to an int. No loss of information or precision again. In both cases, integral types stayed integral. Line (E) shows the result of a widening conversion from a large int to a float and the consequent loss of precision. Line (F) demonstrates a widening conversion from a non-integral type to a non-integral type — in this case from a float to a double. The rest of the code in the program deals with automatic widening conversions performed when arguments are dispatched to functions and when a value is returned by a function. When the function g1 is called in line (G), the supplied argument is automatically converted from a byte to a short. The same thing happens in line (H), except that the conversion is from a short to an int. Line (J) demonstrates the error incurred when a function tries to return a large int after converting it to a float.

Compared to a widening conversion, a narrowing conversion in Java (like many of the standard conversions in C++) can entail loss of information besides loss of precision. A majority of the permissible narrowing conversions require an explicit use of the cast operator. Java allows very few narrowing conversions to take place automatically. The automatic narrowing conversions are limited to initializations that require conversions from an int *literal* to a byte, to a short, or to a char provided the value to be converted can be represented by the target types. For example, the following is legal syntax

```
byte b = 15;    // narrowing conversion from an int literal to byte
```

---

[10]We obtain this by taking the bit pattern of $+128$ (which is 10000000), reversing it to obtain 01111111, and adding 1 to the result. We get the bit pattern 10000000, whose hex representation is 0x80.

In particular, Java does not allow any narrowing conversions to take place automatically when matching arguments with parameters in function invocations. The error reports, all produced by the compiler, in the following program illustrate this fact. The output of the program is shown in the commented out portions of the lines (A), (B), and (C). If the program statements that are completely commented out are uncommented, the nature of the resulting compilation errors is shown in an abbreviated manner in the vicinity of the statements.

```java
//Narrowing.java

class Test {

    static void g1( short x ) {}
    static void g2( int x ) {}
    static void g3( float x ) {}

    public static void main( String[] args )
    {
        int i = 98;
        // char c = i;     // not allowed for initialization
        char c = 98;        // ok for initialization from literal
        System.out.println( c );    // output:  b                  //(A)

        byte b = 97;        // ok for initialization from literal
        System.out.println( b );    // output:  97                 //(B)

        // float y = 1e100;     // double to float not allowed

        double z = 1e100;
        // float y = z;         // double to float not allowed
        float y = (float) z;    // but ok with cast
        System.out.println( y );    // output: Infinity            //(C)

/*
        g1( y );    // ERROR:
                    //   cannot automatically convert float to short
        g2( y );    // ERROR:
                    //   cannot automatically convert float to int
        g3( z );    // ERROR:
                    //   cannot automatically convert double to float
*/
    }
}
```

In Java, automatic type conversions of the widening kind are also carried out when arithmetic, comparison, and logical operations are performed if the operands are of different types. The strategy for these automatic type conversions, which are also known as *binary numeric promotions*, is the same as in C++, that is to convert the operands to the "narrowest" type that will safely accommodate both operands, with the additional stipulation that the operands will never be narrower than an int. So if you add a long to an int, both operands will be converted to long. But if you add a short to an int, both operands will be converted to int.

6.7.3   Explicit Type Conversion in C++

A programmer can also force a type conversion between related types by using a cast operator. In the following program, the integer value of a character is printed out by using the C++'s cast operator static_cast. The program asks a user to type in a character and then returns the integer value of that character.

```
//ExplicitCast1.cc

#include <iostream.h>
using namespace std;

int main()
{
    char ch, ch_prev;

    while (1) {
        cout << "Enter a character: " ;
        cin >> ch;
        if ( ch == ch_prev ) break;                      //(A)
        ch_prev = ch;
        cout << "Integer value of the character is: "
             << static_cast<int>(ch) << endl;            //(B)
    }
    return 0;
}
```

The conversion from a character to its corresponding ASCII integer in this program is carried out by static_cast<int> in line (B). In general, the operation static_cast<T2>(T1) converts a value of type T1 to a value of type T2 *provided an implicit conversion exists from the former type to the latter type.* Recall from Section 6.7.1 that implicit (meaning automatic) type conversions in C++ include both the error-free promotions and the possibly error-producing standard conversions.

When casting to a narrower type, such as when converting an `int` into a `short`, or an `int` into a `char`, the upper bytes that cannot be accommodated in the narrower target type are discarded. Since the uppermost bit for a signed type is the sign bit, this can cause the sign to reverse for the target type, besides, of course, the magnitude getting changed. This is illustrated with the help of three examples in the following program:

```
//ExplicitCast2.cc

#include <iostream>

int main( )
{
    int i1 = 312;
    int i2 = -255;
    int i3 = 32768;

    cout << i1  << ": " << "cast to short is "
        << static_cast<short>(i1)  << ",  cast to char is "
        << static_cast<int>( static_cast<char>(i1) ) << endl;

    cout << i2  << ": " << "cast to short is "
        << static_cast<short>(i2)  << ",  cast to char is "
        << static_cast<short>( static_cast<char>(i2) ) << endl;

    cout << i3  << ": " << "cast to short is "
        << static_cast<short>(i3)  << ",  cast to char is "
        << static_cast<int>( static_cast<char>(i3) ) << endl;

    return 0;
}
```

The produces the following output:

```
312: cast to short is 312,   cast to char is 56
-255: cast to short is -255,   cast to char is 1
32768: cast to short is -32768,   cast to char is 0
```

To focus on the last output line above, the bit pattern for the number 32768 as an `int` is

```
00000000 00000000 10000000 00000000
```

When converted to a `short`, only the lower two bytes are retained, giving us

```
1000000 00000000
```

which is the two's complement representation of -32768.

When an integral type is cast explicitly to a wider integral type, the source type is sign-extended to fill the wider type. What that means is that if the uppermost bit (the sign bit) of the source type is a zero, the extra bits of the wider type are filled with zeroes. Otherwise, the extra bits are filled with 1's.

In the C++ code that was written before standardization, explicit type conversion was carried out by cast operators using the syntax

```
type( expression )
```

For backwards compatibility, it is still legal to use this form of casting. So line (B) of ExplicitCast1.cc could be replaced by

```
cout << "Integer value of the character is: " << int(ch) << endl;
```

One could also use the C-language cast, as in the following replacement for the above statement:

```
cout << "Integer value of the character is: " << (int) ch << endl;
```

But, in C++, it is safer to use the operator static_cast because it cannot cast away const.

C++ also provides three other cast operators for explicit type conversion: dynamic_cast for run-time type identification (RTTI), const_cast for removing the const qualifier, and reinterpret_cast for converting between unrelated types (as in converting an integer into a memory address). These cast operators are further discussed in Section 10 of Chapter 16.

In case the reader is puzzled by line (A) in the C++ program ExplicitCast1.cc we showed at the beginning of this section, it is to provide a way for program termination. As such, the job of the program is to supply you with the ASCII integer code for any character you enter through the keyboard as the program is executing the infinite while loop. You can terminate the program by asking the program to respond to the same character twice in a row.[11]

6.7.4   Explicit Type Conversion in Java

The Java program below uses a cast in line (A) to carry out a narrowing conversion from an int to a char. The program will try to print out as many characters as possible (depending on the print representations available to the program) for all integers between 0 and 10,000.

---

[11] In a Unix environment, you could also terminate that program by typing control-d, which would be trapped by the operating system, causing program termination.

```
//ExplicitCast1.java

import java.io.*;

class Test {
    public static void main( String[] args )
    {
        try {
            PrintWriter out = new PrintWriter(
                            new FileOutputStream( "out_file" ) );
            char ch_value;
            for (int i=0; i< 10000; i++) {
                ch_value = (char) i;                            //(A)
                out.println( "for i= " + i + " char is " + ch_value );
            }
            out.close();
        } catch( IOException e) { }
    }
}
```

When an explicit conversion is from an integral type to a narrower integral type, the upper bits of the source type that cannot be accommodated in the target type are discarded. Since the uppermost bit for signed types is the sign bit, casting to a narrower type can reverse the sign of a value, in addition to changing its magnitude. The following program shows examples of this.

```
//ExplicitCast2.java

class Test {
    public static void main( String[] args )
    {
        int i1 = 312;
        int i2 = -255;
        int i3 = 32768;

        System.out.println( i1 + ": " + "cast to short is " +
                    (short) i1 + ",  cast to byte is " + (byte) i1 );

        System.out.println( i2 + ": " + "cast to short is " +
                    (short) i2 + ",  cast to byte is " + (byte) i2 );

        System.out.println( i3 + ": " + "cast to short is " +
                    (short) i3 + ",  cast to byte is " + (byte) i3 );
    }
}
```

The output of this program is

```
312: cast to short is 312,  cast to byte is 56
-255: cast to short is -255,  cast to byte is 1
32768: cast to short is -32768,  cast to byte is 0
```

To explain the second line of the output above, using two's complement representation the number -255 as an int is stored as the bit pattern[12]

```
11111111 11111111 11111111 11111111 00000001
```

When this number is cast to a byte, only the lowest byte is retained

```
00000001
```

whose integer value is just 1. When the same number is cast to a short, the lowest two bytes are retained:

```
11111111 00000001
```

Since the uppermost bit (the sign bit) is set, the magnitude of the integer value represented by this bit pattern is obtained by reversing the pattern and adding 1, which gives us

```
00000000 11111111
```

which yields a magnitude value of 255, giving the short a value of -255.

The same thing happens for the other integral conversions of the narrowing kind. For example, when an int is cast to a char, the upper two bytes are discarded and only the bottom two bytes retained for the char.

When narrowing conversions take non-integral types into integral types, if the value of the floating-point number is valid and finite, the integer value is obtained by rounding toward zero the floating-point value using the IEEE 754 round-toward-zero mode. Special cases for when the floating-point value is too large, or too small, or NaN, and so on, are considered separately.

6.8 I/O STREAMS FOR C++

It is frequently the case in programming of any sort that you'd want to write data to a file, a socket, or memory. It is also frequently the case that you'd want to read data

---

[12]Which can be obtained by writing down the bit pattern for $+255$:

```
00000000 00000000 00000000 11111111
```

reversing the 0's and 1's in this pattern and then adding 1 to the result.

from such resources. In C++ and Java, data I/O is carried out with *streams*. You open a stream to the destination to which you want to write the data. You open a stream to the source from where you want to bring in the information. In this section, we will discuss how one sets up streams when the data consists of the primitive types and of type `string`, as is true in a vast majority of cases.

6.8.1 The C++ Stream Hierarchy

Shown in Figure 6.2 is the hierarchy of stream classes in C++, where the dashed arrows indicate that `ios` serves as a *virtual base*[13] for the derived classes `istream` and `ostream`. The solid arrows indicate regular class derivations.[14]

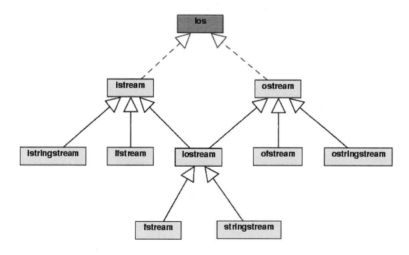

Fig. 6.2

Of the classes shown, input operations are supported by classes of type `istream` and output operations by classes of type `ostream`. The subclass `iostream`, which

---

[13]The concept of a virtual base is explained in Chapter 16.

[14]The hierarchy shown here is meant merely to convey the idea of the relationships between the different stream classes we will use in this book. In a standard implementation of C++, the class names `istream`, `ostream`, and the names that appear below those in the hierarchy, would actually be preceded by the prefix `basic_` and suffixed by the template parameter of the character type for the stream. Therefore, in a standard implementation of C++, the class `istream` would actually appear in the hierarchy as `basic_istream<T>` where the parameter T may be either `char` or `wchar_t`, the latter for holding character sets such as the 16-bit Unicode. In a standard C++ implementation, a stream class name such as `ifstream` would be a `typedef`:

```
typedef basic_ifstream<char> ifstream;
typedef basic_ifstream<wchar_t> wifstream;
```

The reader is referred to Chapter 21 of [54] for further details.

inherits from both `istream` and `ostream`, provides operations for both input and output.

6.8.2 Input–Output Operations for Character Streams

Let's say you want to open a file named *invoice.dat* for writing text into, you would create a stream object of type `ofstream` by

```
ofstream out("invoice.dat");
if ( !out ) print_error( "cannot open output file" );
```

where the identifier `out` is the name chosen for the output stream object and where `print_error` is your own print function for displaying error messages.

Using the system-provided overload definitions for the insertion operator '`<<`', our program could now contain statements like

```
int x = 1234;
out << x << "   "  << 56.78 << "   " << "apples" << '\n';
```

which would cause the character string

```
1234  56.78  apples
```

to be written out into the file *invoice.dat*. You must, of course, include the header `fstream` for this to work since the class `ofstream` is declared in that header file. When you construct an `ofstream` object in the manner shown, the file named as the argument will be created by default if it does not exist already. If the file existed previously, its contents would be overwritten starting at the beginning. If you wish to append to a file already in existence, you'd need to make the following invocation of the `ofstream` constructor:

```
ofstream out("invoice.dat", ios::app);
```

Now suppose you want to read the contents of the file *invoice.dat* back into a program. You'd need to create an input stream object, as in line (A) below, and to then use the extraction operator '`>>`' to read off the various items in the file into appropriate variables, as in lines (B), (C), and (D):

```
int x;  double y;  string z;

ifstream in( "invoice.dat" );                               //(A)
if ( !in ) error( "cannot open input file" );

in  >> x;                                                   //(B)
in  >> y;                                                   //(C)
in  >> z;                                                   //(D)

cout << x << "   "  << y << "   " << z << '\n';             //(E)
```

The input file stream object `in` will fetch information from the designated file and the extraction operator '`>>`' will do formatted extractions of the expected data types from this information. The system-supplied overload definition for the extraction operator will cause the statement in line (B) to extract an `int` from the input stream object and make that integer the value of the variable `x`. Since the first item in the file is the integer 1234 stored as a text string, this integer becomes the value of `x` in line (B). By the same token, the next item in the file, the floating-point number 56.78, will be "read into" the `double` variable `y` in line (C). And exactly the same mechanism will cause the third item in the file, the string "apples," to be read into the `string` variable `z`. The extraction operator will, by default, skip over the white spaces (blanks, tabs, newlines, and so on) between the different entries in the file. The header `fstream` would again have to be included in your program since that's where the class `ifstream` is declared.

As was mentioned earlier in Chapter 2, `cout` used in the above code fragment in line (E) is also a stream object, of type `ostream`, that represents the *standard output*. The output from `cout` would ordinarily be directed to a user's terminal. In the same vein, we have `cin`, a stream object of type `istream`, that represents the *standard input*; `cin` would ordinarily be directed to fetch information from a user's terminal. And we have `cerr`, a stream object of type `ostream`, for outputing a program's error messages. The object `cerr` represents the *standard error*; its output would also ordinarily be directed to a user's terminal. All three standard streams can be independently redirected by the operating system.

If you want a stream that can be used for both reading and writing, you need to construct an `fstream` object, again supplied by the header file `fstream`:[15]

```
fstream inout( "invoice.dat", ios::in | ios::out );
if ( !inout ) print_error( "file could not be opened" );
```

where we chose `inout` for the name of the stream object. It is the specification in the second argument, consisting of a disjunction, that indicates to the system that the designated file must be simultaneously opened in two modes, read and write. When using such streams, you have to pay careful attention to what is known as a *file position* or *file pointer*. Each open file has two positions associated with it:

---

[15]The second argument to the `fstream` constructor is of type `openmode`. The following "flags" or their disjunctions are of type `openmode`: `ios::in` for opening a file for reading; `ios::out` for opening a file for writing; `ios::ate` for opening a file with the file position at the end of the file; `ios::app` for opening a file in the append mode; `ios::trunc` for erasing the old contents of a file if it already exists; and `ios::binary` for opening a file in the binary mode. If the second argument is not supplied, the default mode used for the invocation of the `ifstream` constructor is `ios::in`; for the invocation of the `ofstream` constructor `ios::out | ios::trunc`; and for the invocation of the `fstream` constructor `ios::in | ios::out`.

1. The current file position for reading a byte. This is the index of the byte that will be read by the next call to a method such as get. When a byte is read, this file position, also referred to as the *get position*, moves past that byte.

2. The current file position for writing a byte. This is the index of the location where the next byte will be placed by a function such as put. When a byte is written into a file, this position, also referred to as *put position*, moves past that byte.

The get and the put positions should be independently variable. That is, either one should be able to point anywhere in a file. But a particular compiler implementation may or may not permit that. In general, the file positions can be controlled by invoking the seekp function for the put position and the seekg function for the get position. We get the current positions by invoking tellg() for the get position and tellp() for the put position.

Shown below is a demonstration program that shows the workings of the file-position-related functions mentioned above. Line (A) opens the designated file in read/write mode. Line (B) deposits a 20-character long string into the file. Subsequently, when we check the get and the put positions in lines (C) and (D), we get 21 for both with the compiler that was used (g++ version 2.96). We then reset the get position to the beginning of the file in line (E). Later, when we check the two positions in lines (F) and (G), we get the same answer — 0. Further proof of the fact that the get position is now at the beginning of the file is obtained by reading the contents of the file into the three variables x, y and z in lines (H) and (I). As verified by the output produced by line (J), we are indeed able to read all three values correctly.

```
//TestFilePosition.cc

#include <fstream>
#include <string>
using namespace std;

int main() {
    fstream inout( "invoice.dat", ios::in | ios::out );          //(A)

    //write to the file:
    inout << 1234 << "   "  << 56.78 << "  " << "apples" << '\n'; //(B)
    //current get position:
    cout << inout.tellg() << endl;            // 21            //(C)
    //current put position:
    cout << inout.tellp() << endl;            // 21            //(D)

    //reset get position to the beginning of the file:
    inout.seekg( ios::beg );                                   //(E)
    //new get position:
    cout << inout.tellg() << endl;            // 0             //(F)
```

```
//new put position:
cout << inout.tellp() << endl;                      // 0                //(G)

int x;
double y;
string z;

//read from file:
inout >> x >> y;                                                       //(H)
inout >> z;                                                            //(I)

cout << x << " " << y << " " << z << endl;                             //(J)
                             // 1234 56.78 apples
return 0;
}
```

Other useful stream functions dealing with file positions include the two-arg versions of `seekg` and `seekp` that allow the position of a stream to be set relative to some other position. The use of the two-arg version of `seek` is illustrated by the following version of the above program. The code shown in lines (K) through (Q) of the new version replaces the declarations of the variables x, y, and z and the lines (H)–(J) of the previous program. The previous program straightforwardly read the three items stored in the file into the three variables in lines (H) and (I). In the version below, after reading the first datum, we use the 2-argument version of `seekg` in line (O) to make the get position hop over the middle item in the file. In the two-arg version of `seek`, the first argument is the offset to be used with respect to the position specified in the second argument. The second argument can be either `ios::beg`, or `ios::cur`, or `ios::end`, for the beginning of the file, the current position in the file, and the end of the file, respectively. Whereas the `cout` statement in line (J) of `TestFilePosition1.cc` prints on the terminal

```
1234  56.78  apples
```

the same statement in line (Q) of the program below prints out

```
1234  0  apples
```

because we read into the variable z after the stream is moved 8 positions to the right in line (O), which causes it to skip over the floating-point datum in the middle.

```
//TestFilePosition2.cc

#include <fstream>
#include <string>
using namespace std;
```

```
int main() {
    fstream inout( "invoice.dat", ios::in | ios::out );

    //write to the file:
    inout << 1234 << "   "  << 56.78 << " " << "apples" << '\n';

    //current get position:
    cout << inout.tellg() << endl;              // 21
    //current put position:
    cout << inout.tellp() << endl;              // 21

    //reset:
    inout.seekg( 0 );
    //new get position:
    cout << inout.tellg() << endl;              // 0
    //new put position:
    cout << inout.tellp() << endl;              // 0

    int x = 0;                                              //(K)
    double y = 0.0;                                         //(L)
    string z = "";                                         //(M)

    //read first item from file:
    inout >> x;                                            //(N)

    //move the stream 8 positions to the right of the
    //current get position: (this will cause the stream
    //to skip over the number 56.78)
    inout.seekg( 8, ios::cur );                            //(O)

    //read next item from file:
    inout >> z;                                            //(P)

    cout << x << " " << y << " " << z << endl;             //(Q)
                            // 1234  0   apples
    return 0;
}
```

Note also that the program shown above used seekg(0) to reset the get position to the beginning of the file — it does the same thing as seekg(ios::beg) in the program TestFilePosition1.cc.

When provided with a negative offset, the seek function will move the file position towards the beginning of the file. An error condition is created by positioning before the beginning of the file or beyond the end of the file. When an error condition takes place, further processing of the stream is suspended. However, such error conditions can be cleared by invoking the clear() function.

The get() and put() functions for character I/O:

If it is desired to read from or write into an ASCII encoded text file one character at a time, it is convenient to use the istream member function get for reading and the ostream member function put for writing. The function get has been overloaded so that it can be invoked in the following three different ways, the last for retrieving multiple characters at a time:

1. The function is invoked through a call like

```
ifstream in( "dataFile" );
char ch;
while ( in.get( ch ) ) {
    . . .
```

The function get in this invocation returns the istream object on which it is invoked, unless the stream has reached the end of the file, in which case the function evaluates to false. Since in the example code fragment, the function is invoked on the object in, the same object is returned as long as the stream has not reached the end of the file (or entered some error state). Therefore, the while loop shown for reading one byte at a time makes sense. The loop will terminate automatically when the stream reaches the end of the file or enters an error state. To make certain that the while loop was terminated by the stream reaching the end-of-file condition as opposed to getting into an error state, we can invoke the following test after the above while loop:

```
if ( !in.eof() ) {
    // print error message and then
    exit( 1 );
}
```

where eof() is one of the four *condition functions* defined for testing the error state of a stream, the other three being bad(), fail(), and good(). The function eof() returns true if the stream has reached the end of the file. The function bad() returns true if the stream was asked to carry out an illegal operation, such as invoking a seek function that would cause the file position to be placed either before the beginning of the file or after the end. The function fail() returns true when either bad() returns true or when eof() evaluates to false. Finally, the function good() returns true as long as the stream has not transitioned into an error state. The invocations !fail() and good() are logically identical. As mentioned earlier, further operations are suspended on a stream when it enters an error state. The error state can be cleared up by invoking clear() on the stream object.

2. The function is invoked through a no-argument call, as in

```
fstream in( "dataFile" );
int ch;
while ( ch = in.get() && ch != EOF ) {
    ...
```

The function `get()` now actually returns the byte read from the input stream, as opposed to returning the `istream` object on which the function is invoked. Also note that the value returned by the function is placed in an `int`, as opposed to a `char`. This is to enable the detection of the end-of-file condition as represented by `get()` returning the EOF constant, which is often set to −1 in the `iostream` header file.

The reverse of the two `get` functions shown above is the `put` function defined for the `ostream` class. Its signature is

```
put( char )
```

It inserts a byte corresponding to its argument into the binary output stream on which the function is invoked and returns the output stream object. An example using a get-put pair to copy a binary file was presented in Chapter 2.

3. The third version of `get` has the following signature:

```
get( char* buffer, streamsize size, char deliminter='\n' )
```

Like the first form of `get`, the version shown here also returns the `istream` object on which the function is invoked. This `get` function reads the bytes up to the position where the delimiter character is found, but the number of bytes read will not exceed `size` − 1. The bytes thus read are stored in a character array starting at the address `buffer`. As shown by the signature, the default delimiter is the newline character. If the delimiter character is encountered, it is not actually extracted from the stream. So, unless care is taken, it will be encountered by the next invocation of `get`. So as not to corrupt the next invocation of `get`, the delimiter character when encountered can be gotten rid of by invoking `ignore()`.[16] After `get` has deposited all the bytes it can at the location `buffer`, it terminates the array with the null character. (That's the reason for why a maximum of only `size` − 1 bytes can be extracted from the stream at one time — the last place must be saved for the terminating null character.) The following program is a quick illustration of the use of this version of `get`. The program reads an executable file `a.out`. Some of the bytes will be construed to be newline characters. Try it and see what happens.

---

[16]We know that the delimiter character has been encountered if the number of characters read by `get` is strictly less than `size` − 1.

```
//GetThirdType.cc

#include <fstream>
using namespace std;

int main() {
    const int max_count = 256;
                // will read max of 255 bytes to
                // allow for null at the end

    char line[ max_count ];

    ifstream in( "a.out" );

    while ( in.get( line, max_count ) ) {                    //(A)
        int count = in.gcount();                             //(B)
        cout << "num of bytes read:" << count << '\n';
        if ( count < max_count - 1 ) in.ignore();            //(C)
    }
    return 0;
}
```

In order to figure out whether ignore() needs to be invoked to toss out the delimiter in the while loop in line (A), the program calls gcount() in line (B) to determine the number of bytes just read.[17] As mentioned already, if the number of bytes read is strictly less than max_count − 1, that means the newline character was encountered while trying to extract max_count − 1 bytes from the stream. When that happens, the program invokes ignore in line (C).

Since it would be easy to introduce a bug into a program by forgetting to remove the delimiter character when encountered, the iostream library also makes available another function getline that behaves in exactly the same manner as the 3-argument get, except that it automatically gets rid of the delimiter character. The signature of getline is the same as that of the 3-argument get:

```
getline( char* buffer, streamsize size, char deliminter='\n' )
```

The additional functions introduced here, getline, gcount() and ignore(), all return the istream object on which they are invoked.

---

[17]When called with an integer argument, the function ignore(int n) will skip over n bytes in the input stream. If also supplied with an optional second argument specifying the delimiter character, the function will skip at most the number of bytes corresponding to the first argument, but will not skip past the delimiter character in the input stream. The newline character is the default delimiter.

To end this subsection, we want to mention quickly the following additional functions that can be very useful for conditional retrieval of characters from an input stream. Before actually reading a character into our program, we may want to take a peek at the character that the next invocation of a function such as `get` would retrieve. The following functions are useful for that purpose:

putback(char c) for pushing the argument byte back into the stream.

unget() for resetting the file position to where it was at the time of the previous invocation of `get`.

peek() for its return value which is the next character that will be read by a call to `get`; this character will not be extracted from the stream.

6.8.3 Input–Output Operations for Byte Streams

The previous subsection showed how read/write operations can be implemented for character streams.[18] But what about byte streams (also called binary streams)? Suppose we wanted to read an image or a sound file, or copy the contents of an executable file, such as an `a.out` file output by a C++ compiler, into another file, how would one do that?

If it is desired to read and write an uninterrupted stream of bytes, the first thing to bear in mind is that the stream object created must be set to the binary mode. For example, to attach a binary write stream with a file, we say

```
ifstream in( "dataFile", ios::binary );
```

The second argument, `ios::binary`, supplied to the `ifstream` constructor causes the file to be opened in a binary mode. The reader might think that if you are reading only one byte at a time, it shouldn't matter whether you open the file in text mode or binary mode. But beware that if you use the text mode for reading a binary file, you may not see all the bytes if you are using one of the `get` functions to read the bytes. For example, on Windows platforms, when a binary file is opened in the text mode, the pair of characters corresponding to a newline, `<cr><lf>`, is read as a single character by the `get()` method. To illustrate, suppose your binary file contains the bytes for the following characters

```
hello <cr><lf>
```

Now suppose you open this file in the text mode and create its hex dump by retrieving the individual bytes from the file with the `get()` function discussed previously, what you get out of the file will look like

---

[18]It is possible to use the insertion and the extraction operators for binary streams also. See, for example, Stroustrup[54].

```
0x68 0x65 0x6c 0x6c 0x6f 0x20 0x0A
```

where 0x68, 0x65, 0x6c and 0x6f are the hex representations of the ASCII codes for the letters h, e, l, and o, and 0x20 is hex for the space that follows the word 'hello'. The remaining byte, 0x0A, representing the ASCII for linefeed, is the sole character that get() retrieves for the two characters <cr> and <lf>. In general, performing character based I/O on a binary file opened in the text mode may cause your operating system to carry out system-specific character translations on some of the bytes. Imagine sending an image file to an output stream attached to a printer. In the text mode, some of the bytes could end up being interpreted as form feed, and so on.

After you have created a binary stream object, the next problem is to decide how to read and write an uninterrupted stream of bytes. You, of course, have the choice of reading one byte at a time using the basic get function introduced in the previous subsection, and writing out one byte at a time with the basic put function, also introduced in the previous subsection. But it is more efficient to do binary I/O with the read and write functions, as demonstrated by the following program that copies one binary file into another. In line (A), the program reads the input file in chunks of 1000 bytes and writes each chunk out into the output file in line (B). Towards the end of the file, the last chunk read would encounter the end-of-file condition, which would cause in.read(buffer, N) in line (A) to evaluate to false. These last few bytes are written out separately to the output in line (E) after first invoking gcount in line (D) to figure out the number of bytes involved. In line (F), we check the condition of the input stream to make sure that the failure of the test in line (A) was caused by the end-of-file condition and not by the stream entering some error state.

```
//BinaryFileIO.cc

#include <fstream>
#include <cstdlib>
using namespace std;

const int N = 1000;

void print_error(const char* p1, const char* p2 = 0);

int main(int argc, char* argv[])
{
    char buffer[ N ];

    if (3 != argc)
        print_error("wrong number of arguments --- "
                "usage: function input_file output_file");

    ifstream in( argv[1], ios::binary);
    if (!in) print_error( "cannot open input file", argv[1] );
```

```
        ofstream out( argv[2], ios::binary);
        if (!out) print_error( "cannot open output file", argv[2] );

        while( in.read( buffer, N ) )                              //(A)
            out.write( buffer, N );                                //(B)

        if ( in.eof() ) {                                          //(C)
            int count = in.gcount();                               //(D)
            out.write( buffer, count );                            //(E)
        }

        if ( !in.eof() ) print_error("something strange happened");   //(F)

        in.close();
        out.close();
        return 0;
}

void print_error(const char* p1, const char* p2) {
    if ( p2 ) cerr << p1 << ' ' << p2 << endl;
    else cerr << p1 << endl;
    exit(1);
}
```

The above program carries out binary file I/O in blocks of N bytes, where N can be anything the programmer wants it to be. As we show in the next program, it is also possible to read all the bytes in one fell swoop by opening a file with the `ios::ate` option (line A of the program below) that puts the get-position pointer at the end of the file. Then by invoking the `tellg()` function (line B), we can figure out the size of the file in bytes. Once we have that information, we can allocate the memory needed in the program for the bytes to be read from the file (line C) and reset the get position to the beginning of the file (line D) so that the file can be read from the beginning. With the get position reset, we can invoke the `read` and the `write` functions as before, but this time read off all the bytes from the input file at one time and then write out all the bytes to the output file at one time, too, as we do on lines (F) and (G).

```
//BinaryFileIO2.cc

#include <fstream>
#include <cstdlib>
using namespace std;

void print_error(const char* p1, const char* p2 = 0);

int main(int argc, char* argv[])
```

```
{
    if (3 != argc)
        print_error("wrong number of arguments --- "
                "usage: function input_file output_file");

    //the ios::ate option below places the get-position pointer
    //at the end of the file, thus enabling tellg() to return
    //the size of the file:
    ifstream in( argv[1], ios::binary | ios::ate );         //(A)
    if (!in) print_error( "cannot open input file", argv[1] );

    //the size of the file in bytes:
    long N = in.tellg();                                    //(B)

    char buffer[N];                                         //(C)

    //reset get-position pointer:
    in.seekg( ios::beg );                                   //(D)

    ofstream out( argv[2], ios::binary);                    //(E)
    if (!out) print_error( "cannot open output file", argv[2] );

    //file copy in one fell swoop:
    in.read( buffer, N );                                   //(F)
    out.write( buffer, N );                                 //(G)

    if ( !in.good() ) {
        print_error("something strange happened");
        exit( 1 );
    }

    in.close();
    out.close();
    return 0;
}

void print_error(const char* p1, const char* p2) {
    if ( p2 ) cerr << p1 << ' ' << p2 << endl;
    else cerr << p1 << endl;
    exit(1);
}
```

Our previous two examples dealt with reading information from a binary input file and copying the same into a destination file. Let's now consider the case when we just want to write some data internal to a program into a file, but we wish for the output to be the binary representation of the data. Consider the following simple example in which we first create an int array of three numbers in line (A), with the intention of writing them out to a file in a binary form. Since each `int` occupies 4 bytes, we would want to write out 12 bytes, as is reflected by the second argument to the `write` function in line (B).

```
//WriteBinaryIntsToFile.cc

#include <fstream>
using namespace std;

int main() {
    ofstream out( "out.data", ios::binary);
    if (!out)
        cerr << "cannot open output file" << endl;

    int data[3] = {1, 2, 3};                    //(A)
    out.write( data, sizeof( data ) );          //(B)
    out.close();
    return 0;
}
```

If we execute this program on a Pentium machine and if we then examine the contents of the file `out.data`, in the hex representation they would be

```
01  00  00  00  02  00  00  00  03  00  00  00

<--- data[0] --->  <--- data[1] --->  <--- data[2] --->
```

where the first four bytes are the little-endian representation of the first integer in the array, the next four bytes of the next integer, and so on. However, if run the same program on a Sparc machine, we'll get

```
00  00  00  01  00  00  00  02  00  00  00  03

<--- data[0] --->  <--- data[1] --->  <--- data[2] --->
```

which is the big-endian representation of the three numbers.[19]

---

[19] Just imagine what would happen if you wrote out your binary data file on a Sparc machine but read it into your program on a Pentium machine, or vice versa. If you write out the integer 1 on a Sparc machine, its hex would be 00 00 00 01. But if you read this byte stream into an `int` on a Pentium machine, it would be read as the integer 16777216.

The following extension of the above program shows how you can read data from a binary file into a program. The first part of the program is the same as the program shown above. In lines (A) through (D), it opens an output file in the binary mode, writes out to the file in binary form the three integers of an int array, and then closes the output stream. The rest of the program then opens an input stream to the same file in line (E) in binary and ate modes. Assuming we only know that the file contains just int data and that we do not know how many integers are stored in the file, in line (F) the program figures out the total size of the file in bytes. By dividing the file size by 4, as in line (H), the program can then figure out the number of integers stored in the file. The program resets the get position in line (G) and reads off the data in the file into an array of int's in line (I). Finally, through line (J) we can see that the data from the binary file was correctly read.

```
//BinaryFileIO3.cc

#include <fstream>
using namespace std;

int main() {
    ofstream out( "out.data", ios::binary);              //(A)
    if (!out)
        cerr << "cannot open output file" << endl;

    int data[3] = {1, 2, 3};                              //(B)

    out.write( data, sizeof( data ) );                   //(C)
    out.close();                                         //(D)

    //the ios::ate option places the get-position
    //pointer at the end of the file, thus enabling
    //tellg() to return the size of the file:
    ifstream in( "out.data", ios::binary | ios::ate );   //(E)
    if (!in)
        cerr << "cannot open input file" << endl;

    //get size of the file in bytes:
    long size = in.tellg();                              //(F)

    //reset get-position pointer:
    in.seekg( ios::beg );                               //(G)

    int buffer[ size/4 ];                               //(H)

    in.read( buffer, size );                            //(I)

    cout << buffer[0] << " "
         << buffer[1] << " "
```

```
        << buffer[2] << endl;   //output:  1   2   3                //(J)

    in.close();
    return 0;
}
```

6.8.4 Controlling the Format

One often wants to output textual information according to a prescribed format. For example, you may want certain items of data to line up in the different rows of a tabular presentation and to be justified left or right; or you may want to display floating point numbers with a certain precision; or you may want to display integers using hexadecimal or octal bases; etc. All such, and many more, formatting decisions can be controlled by *stream functions* and *stream manipulators* in C++.

To explain the difference between a formatting stream function and a stream manipulator, let's say that we wish for our floating point values to be printed out using the fixed decimal notation with a precision of 10 (the default is 6). C++ gives us two choices for doing this: Either we can invoke the stream function precision:

```
    cout.precision( 10 );
    cout << sqrt( 2 );
```

or we can use the stream manipulator setprecision, as in

```
    cout << setprecision( 10 ) << sqrt( 2 );
```

In the first case, we invoke the function precision on the stream object, and, in the second, we insert the manipulator setprecision into the output stream. In both cases, the square root of 2 will be printed out with a precision of 10, meaning that 10 digits will be used to display the result (which is 1.414213562).[20]

Most of the stream member functions for formatting and the stream manipulators alter the *format state* of a stream. What that means in the context of the above example is that once the precision of an output stream is set to, say, 10 digits by either of the above methods, it will stay at 10 for all future insertions of floating point numbers into the stream. So if at a later point in the program, we said merely cout << sqrt(3), it will be printed out with a precision of 10.

---

[20]Invoking precision(), that is without an argument, on an output stream object returns the current value of the precision. Additionally, for any given precision, a floating point value is rounded and not truncated.

With regard to the output of integer values, the stream manipulators hex and oct can be used to display an integer in hexadecimal and octal notation, respectively. The default is the decimal notation, represented by the manipulator dec.

```
cout << 127 << oct << setw( 7 ) << 127
     << hex << setw( 5 ) << 127 << '\n';
```

will display on a terminal screen the following string

```
127    177    7f
```

where the decimal number 127 becomes 177 in the octal notation and 7f in the hexadecimal notion. If the cout statement shown above was followed by another statement like cout << 127, the displayed output would still be 7f because, with regard to the display of integer values, the most recent manipulator inserted into the stream was hex. The manipulator oct also alters the format state of a stream.

The above example also used the manipulator setw, which controls the width of the field used for the next output. So when the decimal number 127 is displayed in octal, a field of width 7 is used for display in which the result (consisting in this case of 3 digits) is shown right justified. By the same token, the hex value of 7f is shown, again right justified, inside a field of width 5. If a display field is wider than the number of digits needed for the value, the rest of the places are filled with a filler character, which by default is a blank space, but can be set to any character by using the manipulator setfill(char) or by invoking the ostream member function fill(char), as in the following example:

```
cout.fill( '#' );
cout << setw( 7 ) << 127 << oct << setw( 7 )
     << 127 << hex << setw( 7 ) << 127 << '\n';
```

This will produce the output

```
####127####177#####7f
```

If you wanted each integer value to appear left justified in its field, you'd need to insert the manipulator left into the output stream, or you could invoke the member function setf in the following fashion

```
cout.fill( '#' );
cout.setf( ios::left );
cout << setw( 7 ) << 127 << oct << setw( 7 )
     << 127 << hex << setw( 7 ) << 127 << '\n';
```

This produces the output

```
127####177####7f#####
```

As the reader might have noticed already, unlike the other manipulators setw does *not* alter the format state of a stream. So, in the above examples, we had to set the width of the field separately for each output value even when the field widths were the same for successive outputs.

When integer values are shown in different bases in the same output, it is helpful to use the prefix '0x' or '0X' for hexes and a leading '0' for octals. This can be accomplished either by inserting the manipulator `showbase` into the stream or by invoking `setf` as below:

```
cout.fill( '#' );
cout.setf( ios::left );
cout.setf( ios::showbase );
cout << setw( 7 ) << 127 << oct << setw( 7 )
     << 127 << hex << setw( 7 ) << 127 << '\n';
```

This would produce the output

```
127####0177###0x7f###
```

The manipulator `noshowbase` cancels the effect of `showbase`. Alternatively, one can invoke the member function `unsetf( ios::showbase )`.

By default, if a floating point number has a zero fractional part, the number is displayed without the decimal point. To force the display of the decimal point for such cases, use the manipulator `showpoint` or invoke the member function `setf` as in the following example. The code fragment shown

```
cout << 12.00 << '\n';
cout.precision( 10 );
cout << 12.00 << '\n';
cout.setf( ios::showpoint );
cout << 12.00 << '\n';
```

produces the following output:

```
12
12
12.00000000
```

The manipulator `noshowpoint` cancels the effect of `showpoint`. Alternatively, one can invoke the member function `unsetf( ios::showpoint )`. By default, a floating point value is displayed using the fixed decimal notation. But that can be changed by using the manipulator `scientific`, or by invoking the member function `setf`, as in the following example. The code fragment

```
cout << sqrt(200) << '\n';

cout.precision( 4 );
cout << sqrt(200) << '\n';

cout.setf( ios::scientific );
cout << sqrt(200) << '\n';
```

```
cout.precision( 8 );
cout << sqrt(200) << '\n';

cout.setf( ios::fixed );
cout << sqrt(200) << '\n';
```

produces the output:

```
14.1421
14.14
1.4142e+01
1.41421356e+01
14.142136
```

First the value is displayed with the default precision, which is 6. We then change the precision to 4. The next entry in the output is the rounded value printed out with the new precision. We next change the mode to scientific, which causes the third entry to be displayed — again with a precision of 4. The next entry corresponds to a precision of 8, while the stream is still in the scientific mode. Finally, we change the stream back to fixed, which results in the last entry — with a precision of 8.

For some of the other manipulators, the manipulator flush flushes the output stream buffer. The manipulator endl inserts a newline into the output stream and then flushes the output stream buffer. The manipulator ends inserts the null character and then flushes the output stream buffer.

So far we have only talked about manipulators for output streams. You can also have manipulators for an input stream. To illustrate, the default behavior of the input operator '>>' is to skip over the white space characters. (This can be very convenient in many applications, because you don't have to do anything special to ignore the tabs, the newlines, and so on, that may appear between the more useful data items in a file.) But, if for some reason, you don't want the white space characters to be ignored, you can insert the manipulator noskipws into the input stream. The effect of noskipws is canceled by the manipulator skipws. Alternatively, you can invoke the member functions unsetf(ios::skipws) and setf(ios::skipws) for the same effects. To illustrate, in the following program, the file *datafile* consists of the following entries:

```
a bc\td\ne\n
```

where there is a tab between the letters c and d and newlines after d and e. If we displayed the contents of this file on a terminal, they'd look like

```
a bc    d
e
```

The following program reads this file in two different modes. First it disables the default mode of skipping over white space characters in line (A) and then it restores the default in line (E). In the read loop in line (B), the white space characters will not be ignored, implying that *every* character in the file will be read into the variable ch. On the other hand, in the read loop in line (F), the tab and the newline characters will be ignored.

```
//Skipws.cc

#include <fstream>
using namespace std;

int main() {

    ifstream in("datafile");

    in.unsetf( ios::skipws );                          //(A)
    char ch;
    while ( in >> ch ) {                               //(B)
        cout << ch;                                    //(C)
    }
    cout << '\n';

    in.clear();
    in.seekg( ios::beg );                              //(D)

    in.setf( ios::skipws );                            //(E)

    while ( in >> ch ) {                               //(F)
        cout << ch;                                    //(G)
    }
    cout << '\n';

    return 0;
}
```

The output produced by the program is

```
a bc    d
e

abcde
```

The first two lines of the output are from the statement in line (C) and the last line from the statement in line (G).

You need to include the header iomanip if your program uses manipulators that take arguments, such as setw, setprecision, setfill, and so on.

6.8.5 String Streams

The iostream library also gives us string streams that allow read and write operations to be carried out with respect to string objects in the memory. Just as an ofstream object permits the use of the insertion operator '<<' to write information into a file, an ostringstream object permits the use of the same operator to write characters into a string. In the same vein, just as an ifstream object allows the extraction operator '>>' to be used to read information from a file, an istringstream object allows us to use the same operator to read the characters from a string. You must use the header file sstream for the string stream related functions shown in this section.[21]

One advantage of an ostringstream object is that you can use the formatting capabilities of the output operator '<<' to convert the numeric data types into their string representation. The following code fragment illustrates this.

```
int x = 100;
double y = sqrt(2);
string z = "Hello";
ostringstream os;
os << x << " " << y << " " << z;
```

To gain access to the string object to which the string stream ostringstream is attached, you invoke the str() function on the stream object. So, if the above code fragment was followed by

```
cout << os.str();
```

you'd see displayed on the terminal the following string:

```
100 1.41421 Hello
```

The following code fragment shows how we may construct a single string from the entire contents of a text file:

```
ostringstream os;
ofstream from( "textfile" );
char ch;
while ( os && from.get( ch ) )
    os.put( ch );
```

Note that the ostringstream object automatically takes care of appropriating the memory needed to grow as additional characters are inserted into it.

---

[21] It is possible that your C++ compiler still has the older version of the string streams that are defined in the header file strstream.h. If that's the case, you'd need to use ostrstream for the output string stream and istrstream for the input string stream. For one large difference between the older and the newer string streams, the constructor of the older ostrstream requires you to specify a block of memory of a fixed size into which it can then write characters. On the other hand, the newer ostringstream automatically appropriates the memory needed as characters are written into it.

An `istringstream` object can be used in a similar manner in conjunction with the '>>' operator (or the `get` function) to read values into variables.

The iostream library also provides a string stream class `stringstream` that combines the functionality of both an `ostringstream` and an `istringstream`.

Before ending this section, we want to mention that by default all C++ streams are buffered. The buffer associated with a stream is of type `streambuf`. Buffering implies that when we invoke a write operation to a file with a command such as `put`, the output byte will not in general be written immediately to the file. Instead, the byte will be transferred to a block of memory that serves as the buffer for the output stream. Every once in a while the buffer is *flushed*, which means that all of the data in the buffer is transferred to the file all at once. A buffer associated with an output stream is flushed (a) whenever it is full, (b) whenever the stream is closed, (c) explicitly by invoking `flush` or through the manipulator `endl`, or (d) whenever the stream member function `sync()` is invoked for immediate synchronization.

6.9 I/O STREAMS FOR JAVA

Here are some interesting differences between how I/O is set up in C++ and in Java:

- Whereas in C++ all the needed input/output functionality is packed into a relatively small number of stream classes, Java offers a separate class for practically every situation.[22] If you want to carry out byte stream I/O in its most basic form, Java offers classes designed just for that purpose. But if you are interested in the reading and writing of higher level primitive types, such as integers, floating point numbers, and so on, you use a different set of stream classes that you wrap around the streams for byte-level I/O. If you want to use buffering, you bring in yet additional classes. If your input/output happens to consist of Unicode character streams, there are stream classes that possess methods designed specially for that purpose. If you are interested in reading and writing with random access, Java gives you separate classes for that, too, and so on. Like C++, Java also gives you separate classes for reading from and writing into strings. Additionally, Java gives you classes for reading from and writing into arrays.

- While the C++ streams are buffered by default, the Java streams are unbuffered by default. However, you can incorporate buffering in a Java stream by invoking classes specified for that purpose.

---

[22]It is a matter of perspective whether you'd consider the number of stream classes in C++ to be "relatively small." The number of C++ stream classes begin to look not so small if (for a fair comparison with Java) you include the "w"prefixed versions of the classes shown in the previous section. C++ stream classes such as `wistream`, `wostream`, etc., are designed for dealing with 2-byte character representations.

- In Java, all integer and floating point numbers are output in the big-endian representation regardless of the underlying platform. This is different from C++, as we saw in the previous section. Therefore, data files produced by Java tend to be more portable.

- A typical C++ program uses ASCII-encoded bytes for the characters used either individually or in strings. When these characters are written out to an output device, they remain in their ASCII-encoded form. On the other hand, a character in a Java program is always represented by its 2-byte Unicode. However, if it is desired to write out these characters to an output device, a typical Java program will do so using the ASCII encodings. This is true of input also. A typical C++ program will expect the text based input to be ASCII encoded; the characters in such input will then remain ASCII-encoded inside the program. A typical Java program will also expect its text based input to be ASCII encoded, but will convert the characters into their Unicode representations on the fly as they are read into memory. We are only describing typical situations here. Java I/O provides the functionality needed for writing out character streams using Unicode and other representations and for reading character streams that are based on Unicode and other representations.

Shown in Figures 6.3 and 6.4 are the hierarchies of the Java stream classes. The classes that are particularly suitable for sequential bytestream I/O descend from the `OutputStream` and `InputStream` abstract classes. For character streams, the same is done by the classes that descend from `Reader` and `Writer`. Random access I/O capability is provided by the class `RandomAccessFile`:

The rest of this section is organized in a somewhat unconventional manner, the aim being to augment what the reader can glean easily from the on-line description for each of the classes. Toward that end, we will present some of the more commonly used functionality of the more frequently used classes as a whole, as opposed to in piecemeal. Of the classes whose use we will not illustrate in the programs shown here, `PipedOutputStream` and `PipedInputStream` will be taken up later in Chapter 18 on multithreading.

6.9.1 Writing Primitive Types

It is rather easy to get a feeling of being lost in the very large number of stream classes offered by Java, especially because one is often able to do the same thing by chaining different stream classes together in different ways. To illustrate the extent of choice available for all the primitive types, in this subsection we will show some of the different ways in which we can try to write an `int` into a file and examine what happens in each case. Although all our discussion here will be for the writing of `int`s, parallel arguments would hold for the other primitive types.

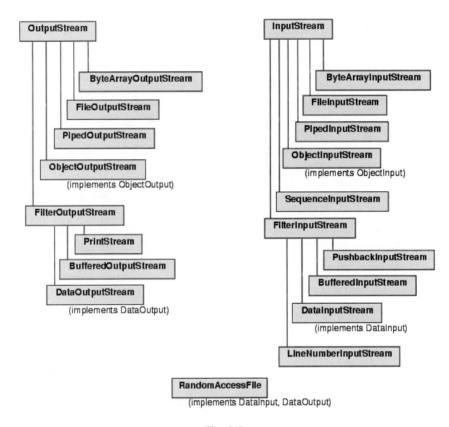

Fig. 6.3

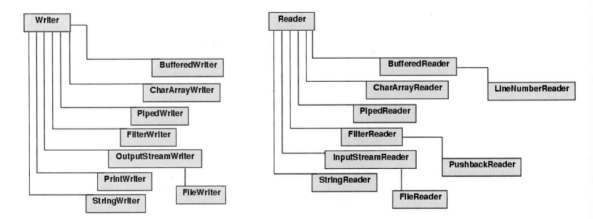

Fig. 6.4

With regard to the writing of an `int` to a file, realize (as we did for the case of C++ streams) that an `int` like 98 will be stored in the memory of the computer as a 4-byte entity whose bit pattern will correspond to the hex

```
00 00 00 62
```

in its big-endian representation, which as was mentioned before is the only representation Java understands for both integers and floating-point types. So when we talk about writing this integer to a file, the question becomes as to whether we want this bit pattern to be written out exactly as it is, or whether we want the characters 9 and 8 to be written out separately as two separate bytes. If we desire the character representation for the output, we then have to decide whether Java should output the 2-byte Unicode representation for the characters, or the 1-byte ASCII-based representation, or, perhaps, some other encoding that might be relevant in a particular context.

Shown below is a program that illustrates some of the many different ways in which an `int` can be written out to a disk file in Java. Not all of these attempts will produce the desired result, but the reader will nonetheless find it educational to see what happens to the output in each case.

```java
//WriteIntToFile.java

import java.io.*;

class WriteIntToFile {
    public static void main( String[] args ) throws Exception {

        int anInt = 98;                                         //(A)

        FileOutputStream fos = new FileOutputStream( "out.fos" ); //(B)
        fos.write( anInt );                                     //(C)
        fos.close();

        FileWriter fw = new FileWriter( "out.fw" );             //(D)
        fw.write( anInt );                                      //(E)
        fw.close();

        DataOutputStream dos = new DataOutputStream(
            new FileOutputStream( "out.dos" ) );                //(F)
        dos.writeInt( anInt );                                  //(G)
        dos.close();

        DataOutputStream dbos = new DataOutputStream(
                new BufferedOutputStream(
                    new FileOutputStream( "out.dbos" ) ) );     //(H)
        dbos.writeInt( anInt );                                 //(I)
        dbos.close();
```

```
        PrintStream ps = new PrintStream(
            new FileOutputStream( "out.ps" ) );              //(J)
        ps.print( anInt );                                   //(K)
        ps.close();

        PrintStream pbs = new PrintStream(
            new BufferedOutputStream(
                new FileOutputStream( "out.pbs" ) ) );       //(L)
        pbs.print( anInt );                                  //(M)
        pbs.close();

        PrintWriter pw = new PrintWriter(
            new FileOutputStream( "out.pw" ) );              //(N)
        pw.print( anInt );                                   //(O)
        pw.close();

        PrintWriter pbw = new PrintWriter(
            new BufferedOutputStream(
                new FileOutputStream( "out.pbw" ) ) );       //(P)
        pbw.print( anInt );                                  //(Q)
        pbw.close();

        PrintWriter pw2 = new PrintWriter(
            new FileWriter( "out.pw2" ) );                   //(R)
        pw2.print( anInt );                                  //(S)
        pw2.close();

        RandomAccessFile ra =
            new RandomAccessFile( "out.ra", "rw" );          //(T)
        ra.writeInt( anInt );                                //(U)
        ra.close();
    }
}
```

Table 6.1 shows how many bytes were output to the disk file in each case, the contents of each file in text and what the output looks like if read in text mode. The program starts with initializing an int inside (A). Our first attempt to write out this int, in lines (B) and (C) of the program, consists of the following code fragment:

```
    FileOutputStream fos = new FileOutputStream( "out.fos" );
    fos.write( anInt );
```

We attach a FileOutputStream object fos with a file named *out.fos* and invoke the method write(int) defined for the stream class to write out the integer. *This stream class only supports methods for writing a single byte or an array of bytes.*

filename	file size in bytes	file content in hex	output as displayed by 'cat filename' (cat reads in text mode)
out.fos	1	62	b
out.fw	1	62	b
out.dos	4	00 00 00 62	b
out.dbos	4	00 00 00 62	b
out.ps	2	39 38	98
out.pbs	2	39 38	98
out.pw	2	39 38	98
out.pbw	2	39 38	98
out.pw2	2	39 38	98
out.ra	4	00 00 00 62	b

Table 6.1

When its `write` method is supplied with an `int` argument, it takes the lowest byte of that `int` and writes that out into the file. As a consequence, only the byte whose hex is 62 is written into the file. This explains why the size of the output file `out.fos` in Table 6.1 is only one byte and why when this file is read in the text mode, the content of the file is the letter 'b'. `FileOutputStream` is an example of a byte stream in Java.

Our next attempt, in lines (D) and (E) of the program, consists of

```
FileWriter fw = new FileWriter( "out.fw" );
fw.write( anInt );
```

We attach a `FileWriter` stream with an output file called *out.fw* and invoke the method `write` defined for the stream class. *This stream accepts a character or an array of characters, and converts the 2-byte Unicode representation of each into a single byte according to the platform's default encoding scheme.* When the `write` method of this stream is invoked with an `int` argument, it puts out the character corresponding to the lowest 16 bits of the four bytes of the integer. In our example, the character put out will be the one corresponding to the hex 0062. That character is the letter 'b' and the one byte that will be written into the output file will be the hex 62. That explains why the size of the output file `out.fw` in Table 6.1 is only one byte and, when read in the text mode, the content of the file appears to be the letter 'b'. FileWriter is an example of a character output stream in Java.

Our next attempt, in lines (F) and (G) of the program, consists of

```
DataOutputStream dos = new DataOutputStream(
                        new FileOutputStream( "out.dos" ) );
dos.writeInt( anInt );
```

This is an example of a compound stream, a stream obtained by wrapping one stream, in our case a DataOutputStream, around another stream, FileOutputStream in the code shown. What do we achieve by wrapping one stream around another? Wrapping in the manner shown here allows you to use the "higher-level" functionality of the wrapper stream and the utility of the stream that is wrapped. Compared to just a byte or an array of bytes that a FileOutputStream can write, the class DataOutputStream supports methods for writing out higher level data types such as ints, floats, doubles, Strings, and so on, using methods with names like writeInt, writeFloat, writeDouble, writeChars, and so on. A DataOutputStream knows how to convert these higher level data types into byte streams, which can then be output by the FileOutputStream object. As a consequence, what will be written into the file out.dos will be the four bytes of hex 00 00 00 62 — the value of the variable anInt. This accounts for the size 4 for the file out.dos in Table 6.1. If this file is read in text mode, its only displayable character would correspond to the byte of hex 62 — the letter 'b'. DataOutputStream is also a byte stream, like the FileOutputStream.

The next attempt to write out an int, in lines (H) and (I) of the program, illustrates the syntax one uses for buffering a stream (although you'd, of course, have no need for buffering if all you want to do is to write out a single integer):

```
DataOutputStream dbos = new DataOutputStream(
        new BufferedOutputStream(new FileOutputStream("out.dbos")));
dbos.writeInt(anInt);
```

As mentioned already, unlike C++ streams Java streams do not provide buffering by default. Since the actual transfer of a data to and from a physical device such as a disk can be very slow in relation to the processing speeds, buffering can make a significant performance difference when doing I/O on long streams of data. A BufferedOutputStream accumulates the data to be written out in a section of the memory called the *buffer*. The actual transfer of the data to the physical device takes place only when the buffer is full or when it is explicitly flushed under program control. Like our previous attempt in lines (F) and (G), note that we are still attaching a DataOutputStream with the output file and we are still using the writeInt method of this stream to write out the integer. The only difference is that the byte stream produced by the DataOutputStream is being routed through a BufferedOutputStream. So, as shown by the entry for the output file out.dbos in Table 6.1, the overall effect in terms of what gets written into the output file and the size of the file remain the same as before. `BufferedOutputStream` is also a byte stream.

Our next attempt, in lines (J) and (K) of the program, consists of

```
PrintStream ps = new PrintStream(new FileOutputStream("out.ps"));
ps.print(anInt);
```

A `PrintStream` first creates a character representation for the data that is output and then puts out a byte stream, with one byte for each character. The character to byte translation takes place using the platform's default character coding — meaning ASCII in most cases. So for the integer 98, the `print` method invoked in line (K) will convert the 4-byte `int` into a two character sequence, the character 9 followed by the character 8. It will then put out two bytes, one for 9 and one for 8. This two-byte sequence will then be fed into the the `FileOutputStream` that is enclosed by the `PrintStream` object. The row for the output file `out.ps` in Table 6.1 corresponds to this case. The `print` or `println` methods defined for `PrintStream` take different types of arguments such as `int`, `double`, `String`, and so on. The `println` methods output a line separator character after the characters corresponding to the data. `PrintStream` is a byte stream, because in addition to putting out characters, it also supports `write` methods for outputting individual and array of bytes. The standard output stream `System.out` and the standard error stream `System.err` are `PrintStream` objects.

Our next attempt, in lines (L) and (M) of the program, consists of

```
PrintStream pbs = new PrintStream(
        new BufferedOutputStream(new FileOutputStream("out.pbs")));
pbs.print( anInt );
```

This produces exactly the same result as the previous example. In both cases, we attach a `PrintStream` with the output file, the difference here being that the output of the `PrintStream` is now routed through a `BufferedOutputStream`. The row for the output file `out.pbs` in Table 6.1 corresponds to this case.

Our next attempt, in lines (N) and (O), consists of

```
PrintWriter pw = new PrintWriter(new FileOutputStream("out.pw"));
pw.print( anInt );
```

The various `print` and `println` methods of `PrintWriter` class behave in a manner exactly similar to those for a `PrintStream`. So the integer 98 will first be converted into its print representation, that is a pair of characters consisting of 9 followed by 8. Subsequently, as shown by the entry for the output file `out.pw` in Table 6.1, a byte will be output for each character. `PrinterWriter` is an example of a character stream because, unlike `PrintStream`, it does not support any methods for the writing of individual bytes or arrays of bytes.

Our next attempt to write out an `int` to a disk file, in lines (P) and (Q) of the program, consists of

```
PrintWriter pbw = new PrintWriter(
    new BufferedOutputStream(new FileOutputStream("out.pbw")));
pbw.print( anInt );
pbw.close();
```

This is exactly the same case as in the lines (N) and (O), except that now we buffer the output of the `PrintWriter`. The output produced is shown in the row for the output file out.pbw in Table 6.1.

With regard to using compound streams, our next attempt in lines (R) and (S) of the program shows a departure from all the previous cases. Instead of having a `FileOutputStream` do the actual writing into the disk file, we now give that task to a `FileWriter`.

```
PrintWriter pw2 = new PrintWriter( new FileWriter( "out.pw2" ) );
pw2.print( anInt );
```

In this case, the `PrintWriter` object pw2 outputs the sequence of characters corresponding to the print representation of the argument `anInt` supplied to the `print` method. The `FileWriter` converts the sequence of characters into an array of bytes that it outputs to the file, as shown by the row for out.pw2 in Table 6.1.

All of the stream classes we have discussed so far give us *sequential* access to a disk file. With sequential access in the write mode, successive items of information are placed at the end of what's already there. But sometimes it is important to be able to read and write data anywhere in a file. Java gives us the `RandomAccessFile` stream class for that purpose. This class allows us to open a file in either just the read mode or the read/write mode. Since we want to write out an integer, in the code fragment shown below [these are lines (T) and (U) of the program], we have no choice but to open the file in the latter mode. This is done by supplying the string argument "rw" to the stream constructor.

```
RandomAccessFile ra = new RandomAccessFile( "out.ra", "rw" );
ra.writeInt( anInt );
ra.close();
```

A `RandomAccessFile` stream allows us to associate a *file pointer* with a file. An output operation writes bytes starting at the current position of the file pointer and advances the pointer until it is past the last byte written. (By the same token, input operations that we will talk about later start reading at the current location of the file pointer and the pointer is advanced until it is past the last byte read.) The methods `getFilePointer` and `seek` defined for the `RandomAccessFile` return the current position of the file pointer and allow us to set the position of the pointer under program control. In the example code shown above, we have invoked the `writeInt` method to write our integer into the output file. This is one of the many write methods defined for `RandomAccessFile`, one for each primitive type, and some additional ones for the string type. Each of these methods writes out a binary representation of the data. In our example, the four bytes of the integer will be written out, explaining in Table 6.1 the size of the output file `out.ra` and why the content of the file appears as the letter 'b' when read in the text mode.

The reader might have wondered why we had to designate a separate output file for each case separately. Why couldn't we have used a single output file and simply appended the output to the file for each case, perhaps in a separate line for clarity? Yes, we could have done so. Java allows the append file mode to be invoked for the two stream classes that we used for the physical transfer of bytes into the output files, `FileOutputStream` and `FileWriter`. To open a disk file in the append mode, the constructors for the two classes would have to follow the syntax

```
FileOutputStream( String fileName, boolean append )

FileWriter( String fileName, boolean append )
```

For the `RandomAccessFile` stream when used in the read/write mode, new information can be appended to what's already in a file by setting the file pointer to the end of the file:

```
RandomAccessFile ra = new RandomAccessFile( "out.ra", "rw" );
ra.seek( ra.length() );
```

Finally, note that Java's stream classes are in the package `java.io`, which you'd need to import into your program if it uses any of the stream classes shown here.

6.9.2 Writing Strings

We believe that the reader will gain additional insights into the Java stream classes if we repeat the exercise of the previous subsection for the case of writing a string to a disk file. Although no less illuminating, the discussion here will be shorter since the reader already knows about the basic properties of the stream classes that we will use. For example, the reader already knows that a `FileWriter` stream accepts a character or an array of characters, and converts the 2-byte Unicode representation of each into a single byte according to the platform's default encoding scheme.

Shown in the program below are ten of the many different ways of writing a string to a disk file. In some cases, the different ways correspond to the different write methods defined for the same stream class.

```
//WriteStringToFile.java

import java.io.*;

class WriteStringToFile {
```

```
public static void main( String[] args ) throws Exception {

    String aString = "hello";                               //(A)

    FileWriter fw = new FileWriter( "out.fw" );             //(B)
    fw.write( aString );                                    //(C)
    fw.close();

    DataOutputStream dos = new DataOutputStream(
                   new FileOutputStream( "out.dos" ) );     //(D)
    dos.writeBytes( aString );                              //(E)
    dos.close();

    DataOutputStream dos2 = new DataOutputStream(
        new FileOutputStream( "out.dos2" ) );               //(F)
    dos2.writeChars( aString );                             //(G)
    dos2.close();

    DataOutputStream dos3 = new DataOutputStream(
        new FileOutputStream( "out.dos3" ) );               //(H)
    dos3.writeUTF( aString );                               //(I)
    dos3.close();

    PrintStream ps =
        new PrintStream( new FileOutputStream( "out.ps" ) ); //(J)
    ps.print( aString );                                    //(K)
    ps.close();

    PrintWriter pw =
        new PrintWriter( new FileOutputStream( "out.pw" ) ); //(L)
    pw.print( aString );                                    //(M)
    pw.close();

    PrintWriter pw2 =
        new PrintWriter( new FileWriter( "out.pw2" ) );     //(N)
    pw2.print( aString );                                   //(O)
    pw2.close();

    RandomAccessFile ra =
        new RandomAccessFile( "out.ra", "rw" );             //(P)
    ra.writeBytes( aString );                               //(Q)
    ra.close();

    RandomAccessFile ra2 =
        new RandomAccessFile( "out.ra2", "rw" );            //(R)
    ra2.writeChars( aString );                              //(S)
    ra2.close();

    RandomAccessFile ra3 =
```

```
         new RandomAccessFile( "out.ra3", "rw" );          //(T)
     ra3.writeUTF( aString );                              //(U)
     ra3.close();
   }
}
```

Table 6.2 shows how many bytes were output to the disk file in each case, the actual contents of each file in hex, and what the contents of each file are according to a text reader.

filename	file size in bytes	file content in hex	output as displayed by 'cat filename' (cat reads in text mode)
out.fw	5	68 65 6c 6c 6f	hello
out.dos	5	68 65 6c 6c 6f	hello
out.dos2	10	00 68 00 65 00 6c 00 6c 00 6f	hello
out.dos3	7	00 05 68 65 6c 6c 6f	hello
out.ps	5	68 65 6c 6c 6f	hello
out.pw	5	68 65 6c 6c 6f	hello
out.pw2	5	68 65 6c 6c 6f	hello
out.ra	5	68 65 6c 6c 6f	hello
out.ra2	10	00 68 00 65 00 6c 00 6c 00 6f	hello
out.ra3	7	00 05 68 65 6c 6c 6f	hello

Table 6.2

To explain the output produced by the lines (B) and (C) of the program, the `write` method of the `FileWriter` stream class writes out the 5 ASCII bytes corresponding to the five letters of the string "hello". This is confirmed by the contents of the file `out.fw` shown in hex in the first row of Table 6.2.[23]

This behavior is also exhibited by the `writeBytes` method of the `DataOutput-Stream` class used in the lines (D) and (E) of the program, as shown by the size and the contents of the file `out.dos` in Table 6.2. The `writeBytes` method of

---

[23] In ASCII coding, the hex for the letter 'h' is 68, for the letter 'e' 65, for the letter 'l' 6c, and for the letter 'o' 6f.

DataOutputStream knows how to convert a string into an array of bytes, one for each character of the string. The byte array is then written out by the FileOutputStream object.

Contrast the previous two attempts with the code shown in lines (F) and (G) of the program. We now use the writeChars method of DataOutputStream to write out the string. This method outputs a character stream, meaning that for each character in the string it outputs the two bytes of the Unicode representation of the character. This byte array is then written out to the file by the FileOutputStream object. This explains the 10-byte size of the file out.dos2 in the third row of Table 6.2 and the hex content shown in the next column.

Lines (H) and (I) of the program again use a DataOutputStream, but this time we have used the method writeUTF. This method uses UTF-8 encoding[24] to convert the string "hello" into an array of 7 bytes, the first two of which represent an unsigned

---

[24]While the Unicode has the advantage that its 16 bits allow us to create bit patterns for almost all the characters used in the different languages of the world, it makes for inefficient storage and transmission of text that is in English and other closely related languages (whose characters can be well represented by the 7-bit ASCII code). To get around this problem, a variable-width encoding was invented — UTF-8 — that retains a single byte representation for the characters in the ASCII set, but has 2-byte and 3-byte representations for the other character sets. This is how Unicode is translated into UTF-8 bytes:

```
Characters in the range \u0001 to \u007f  encoded as a single byte
Characters in the range \u0080 to \u07ff  encoded as two bytes
Characters in the range \u0800 to \uffff  encoded as three bytes
```

In order to be able to distinguish between 1-byte, 2-byte, and 3-byte characters in a byte stream, a 1-byte character always begins with the high-order bit 0, a 2-byte character with the high-order bits 110, and a 3-byte character with the high-order bits 1110. The second byte of a 2-byte character and the second and the third bytes of a 3-byte character must always begin with 10 for the high-order bits. This is illustrated pictorially below, where 'x' represents a data bit:

```
1-byte character:    0xxx xxxx
2-byte character:    110x xxxx   10xx xxxx
3-byte character:    1110 xxxx   10xx xxxx   10xx xxxx
```

We therefore have 7 data bits for 1-byte characters, 11 for 2-byte characters, and 16 for 3-byte characters. Additionally, the first two bytes of the UTF-8 encoding of a string must represent the number of bytes needed for all the characters in the string. This 2-byte representation of the length must be in the *network byte order*, meaning that the first byte holds the largest part of the value. This is the agreed-upon byte order for transmitting integer and floating-point numbers over the internet. (Network byte order is the same as the big-endian byte order used by many processors for the representation of integers and floating-point values. The other byte order, used by the x86 family of processors, is the little-endian byte order in which the first byte is the least significant byte. As mentioned earlier in this chapter, Java uses the big-endian byte order for representing numbers regardless of the platform.) Here is a UTF-8 encoding of the string "hello":

```
00 05 68 65 6c 6c 6f
```

while its ASCII encoding would be

```
68 65 6c 6c 6f
```

Java uses UTF-8 with a slight modification: the character \u0000 is encoded using the two bytes 1100 0000 1000 0000, which follows the 2-byte rule shown previously. This eliminates the need for encoding this character with a byte of all zeros. The acronym UTF stands for UCS Transmission Format, where UCS stands for Universal Character Set.

integer whose value is the number of bytes needed for the characters of the string. Since the string "hello" consists entirely of ASCII characters and since in UTF-8 each such character is represented by a single byte consisting of the ASCII encoding itself, we have in the output file `out.dos3` what's shown Table 6.2.

The fifth row of the table corresponds to the lines (J) and (K) of the program. We now write out the string by invoking the `print` method of the `PrintStream` class. This method converts the string into an array of bytes, one for each character in the string using the platform's default encoding, which in most cases will be the ASCII encoding. As a result, the size of the output file `out.ps` is 5 and its contents just the ASCII codes for the five characters of "hello", as shown by the row for `out.ps` in Table 6.2. Exactly the same thing happens when we invoke the `print` of `PrintWriter` wrapped around `FileOutputStream`, as in lines (L) and (M), and `PrintWriter` wrapped around `FileWriter` as in lines (N) and (O). This is demonstrated by the rows for `out.pw` and `out.pw2` in Table 6.2.

The last three rows in Table 6.2 correspond to the output being written out by a `RandomAccessFile` stream: by using the `writeBytes` method in lines (P) and (Q); by using the `writeChars` method in lines (R) and (S); and, finally, by using the `writeUTF` method in lines (T) and (U). As you'd expect by now and as shown by the row for `out.ra` in Table 6.2, the `writeBytes` method writes out a single ASCII encoded byte for each character. On the other hand, the `writeChars` method writes out the two Unicode bytes for each character, as shown by the row for `out.ra2` in Table 6.2. Finally, the `writeUTF` method outputs the UTF-8 encoding for the entire string, as demonstrated by the row for `out.ra3` in Table 6.2.

6.9.3 Reading the Primitive Types

Compared to the options for writing the primitive types into a file, the options for reading the types are not as numerous. Basically, it boils down to this: If a primitive type is in its binary form, it can be read into a Java program by using one of the methods defined for either the `DataInputStream` or the `RandomAccessFile` stream classes. But if the primitive exists in its print representation (meaning as a sequence of characters), then you have to devise your own method for reading it in.

Shown below is a program that first writes out an integer in its binary representation into a disk file, `out.num`, in lines (A) and (B). So for the integer 123456, the four bytes of hex 00 01 e2 40 get written into the file. In lines (C) and (D), we then use the `readInt` method of the unbuffered `DataInputStream` to read the four bytes from the file into the local variable x. We do the same through a buffered version of `DataInputStream` in lines (E) and (F). Then the program does the same thing again by invoking the `readInt` method of the `RandomAccessFile` stream class in lines (G) and (H).

The output of the program is shown in the commented out portions of the lines containing calls to the `System.out.println` method.

```
//ReadIntFromFile.java

import java.io.*;

class ReadIntFromFile {
    public static void main( String[] args ) throws Exception {

        int anInt = 123456;

        int x;

        DataOutputStream dos = new DataOutputStream(
            new FileOutputStream( "out.num" ) );              //(A)
        dos.writeInt( anInt ); //writes hex 00 01 e2 40 to file   //(B)
        dos.close();

        // read int with DataInputStream
        DataInputStream dis = new DataInputStream(
            new FileInputStream( "out.num" ) );               //(C)
        x = dis.readInt();                                     //(D)
        System.out.println( x );     // 123456
        dis.close();


        // read int with buffered DataInputStream
        DataInputStream dbis = new DataInputStream(
            new BufferedInputStream(
                new FileInputStream("out.num")));              //(E)
        x = dbis.readInt();                                    //(F)
        System.out.println( x );     // 123456
        dbis.close();

        // read int with RandomAccessFile
        RandomAccessFile rai = new
            RandomAccessFile( "out.num", "r" );               //(G)
        x = rai.readInt();                                     //(H)
        System.out.println( x );     // 123456
        rai.close();
    }
}
```

One could write similar demonstration programs for the reading of the other primitive types, such as `longs`, `floats`, `doubles`, `bytes`, `chars`, and so on.

6.9.4 Reading Strings

The following two issues arise in the reading of strings from files, sockets, or any other source:

- Does a string have some overall encoding, such as a UTF-8 encoding, or is it represented by a fixed number of bytes for each character?

- If each character of a string is represented by the same number of bytes, is it one ASCII-encoded byte per character or is it two Unicode bytes per character?

Since a string can be composed of an arbitrary number of characters, in general it is not possible to devise a `readString` method that would work for strings the way the `readInt` of the `DataInputStream` class works for the reading of integers. For the case of reading integers in their binary representation, the `readInt` method can safely use the fact that every four bytes represent an integer, implying that it does not have to look for boundaries between consecutive integers. But any method that tries to read a string in one fell swoop would have no way to detect the end of one string and the beginning of another for the cases of ASCII or Unicode encodings. But that problem does not arise for UTF-8 encodings of strings for obvious reasons.

Shown below is a program that first writes two UTF-8 encoded strings consecutively into a file called `out.dos` in lines (C), (D), and (E). The strings were originally declared in lines (A) and (B). The hex for the bytes that are written into the file is shown commented out in the program. These byte patterns are in accord with our explanation of UTF-8 coding in the previous subsection. Subsequently, the program invokes the method `readUTF` of the `DataInputStream` in lines (F), (G), and (H) to read the two strings in the file. Finally, the program does the same with the help of the `RandomAccessFile` class in lines (I), (J), and (K).

```
//ReadStringFromFile.java

import java.io.*;

class ReadStringFromFile {
    public static void main( String[] args ) throws Exception {

        String aString = "hello";                             //(A)
        String bString = "there";                             //(B)
        String str;

        DataOutputStream dos = new DataOutputStream(
            new FileOutputStream( "out.dos" ) );              //(C)

        //hex output for "hello":  00 05 68 65 6c 6c 6f
        dos.writeUTF( aString );                              //(D)
```

```
            //hex output for "there":  00 05 74 68 65 72 65
            dos.writeUTF( bString );                          //(E)
            dos.close();

            DataInputStream dis = new DataInputStream(
                new FileInputStream( "out.dos" ) );          //(F)
            str = dis.readUTF();                              //(G)
            System.out.println( str );     // hello
            str = dis.readUTF();                              //(H)
            System.out.println( str );     // there
            dis.close();

            RandomAccessFile ra =
                new RandomAccessFile( "out.dos", "r" );       //(I)
            str = ra.readUTF();                               //(J)
            System.out.println( str );     // hello
            str = ra.readUTF();                               //(K)
            System.out.println( str );     // there
            ra.close();
    }
}
```

For reading strings that are ASCII encoded or in Unicode, you have to write your own routines that either read a file character by character and look for delimiter characters for the string boundaries, or that read the entire file into a single large string and then use a string tokenizer to recover the strings placed originally in the file.

6.10 SUGGESTIONS FOR FURTHER READING

The IEEE 754 Floating-Point Standard is available at [31]. A highly recommended reading on this topic is the article by Goldberg [22].

The reader is referred to [39] for further details on Unicode, See Chapter 5 of [23] for a more detailed discussion on conversions and promotions in Java. Chapter 4 of [54] does the same for C++.

Chapter 21 of Stroustrup [54] presents in great detail the implementation level details of the C++ stream classes.

Our discussion on the I/O streams focussed primarily on the input and the output of the primitive types since the I/O in most cases is geared toward those types. However, as shown in Figure 6.3, the java.io package also contains classes for direct object-level I/O. A Java class must implement the Serializable interface if it is to be subject to I/O using the object streams. The homework section of this chapter includes a problem on this topic. Direct object-level I/O in C++ can be carried out by suitably overloading the output and the input stream operators.

6.11   HOMEWORK

1. Is this code fragment legal in C++?

   ```
   int a[10] = {0};
   int i;
   int* p;
   p = &i;
   a = &i;
   ```

2. Using the vector data structure in C++, write and test the following functions:

   - readAllStrings()
   - readAllInts()
   - readAllDoubles()

   Each function should read all of the data items on a line of the user's terminal and return the items in the form of an array of the appropriate kind. You must also allow the user to put any number of spaces between the entries. Also, there could be an arbitrary number of spaces before the first entry and after the last entry.

3. Write a Java class `TerminalIO` with the following static methods for terminal IO:

   - readOneString()
   - readOneInt()
   - readOneDouble()
   - readAllStrings()
   - readAllInts()
   - readAllDoubles()

   Each method should read one or all, as the case may be, of the data items on a line of the user's terminal and, for multiple item entry, return the items in the form of an array of the appropriate kind. You must allow the user to enter an arbitrary number of spaces between the items, before the first item, and after the last item.

4. Write a Java class, `FileReaderData`, with the following static methods and their return types:

   - String[] readAllStrings()
   - int[] readAllInts()
   - double[] readAllDoubles()

5. As you well know, one cannot always display the content of a file. For example, if a file contains object code, you cannot display it on a screen by reading it as a text file. Yet, it is sometimes useful to peer into such files for diagnostic purposes. This you can do by reading the file one byte at a time and printing out the hex representation of the bytes.

   Write a Java program that creates a hex dump of a file regardless of whether it is an alphanumeric file, a binary file containing object code, or an image or a sound file of some kind. The program should read each byte from the file and print out its two-character hex representation into an output text file. Your program should take command line arguments for the input and the output file names. In other words, after compilation it should be possible to execute your Java program by using an invocation of the following type

   ```
   java class_name  in_file_name  out_file_name
   ```

   The file `out_file_name` will be the hex dump of the contents of the file `in_file_name`. The hex output in the output file should be formatted so as to show the hex characters for 20 bytes at a time. It should look like:

   ```
   7f 45 4c 46  1  2  1  0  0  0  0  0  0  0  0  0  0  2  0  2
    0  0  0  1  0  1 10 80  0  0  0 34  0  0 34 84  0  0  0  0
    0 34  0 20  0  5  0 28  0 19  0 17  0  0  0  6  0  0  0 34
         . . . . .
         . . . . .
   ```

   Suggestions:

   (a) Since the input can be a binary file, use an input stream of type `FileInputStream` for reading the file one byte at a time.

   (b) The output file will be a regular alphanumeric file (since it will contain the hex characters representing each byte of the input source file). Therefore, you might wish to use a text output stream to feed a binary output stream by invoking

```
PrintWriter out =
        new PrintWriter( new FileOutputStream( .... ) );
```

(c) Recall that main() is invoked with the parameter args of type String[].
What that means is that args[0] will be the input file name and the args[1]
the output file name. (Note the difference between the indexing of the
command-line arguments in C++ and Java.)

(d) Use the method int read() defined for FileInputStream to read one
byte at a time. This method returns −1 for denoting the end of a file.

(e) To create the hex representation of the value returned by read(), use the
method Integer.toHexString(int) .

6. Write a C++ program that creates a hex dump of a file regardless of the nature
of the file. Using the no-arg version of the get() function presented in Section
6.8.2,[25] the program should read each byte from the file, as in

```
ifstream in( "in_file", ios::binary );
....
int ch;
....
while ( ( ch = in.get() ) != EOF ) {
    ....
}
```

and print out its two-character hex representation into an output text file. Your
program should take command-line arguments for the input and the output file
names. In other words, you should be able to call the program in the following
manner:

```
a.out  in_file  out_file
```

The file out_file will be the hex dump of the contents of the otherwise un-
printable in_file. The hex output in the output file should be formatted in the
same manner as in the previous Java problem, that is it should show the hex
characters for 20 bytes at a time.

---

[25]While it is true that Section 6.8.2 deals with text file I/O, but, as was mentioned in Section 6.8.3,
the get() functions of Section 6.8.2 can also be used to read the bytes in a binary file provided the file is
opened in the binary mode.

7. Rework the previous problem by reading the input file with the `read()` function described in Section 6.8.3 for reading N bytes at a time, as in

```
const int N = 1000;
....
ifstream in( "in_file", ios::binary );
....
unsigned char buffer[N];                              //(A)
while ( in.read( buffer, N ) ) {
   //output the hex for each byte
}
```

Be sure to use `gcount()` to get any remaining bytes in the input stream when `read()` hits the end-of-file condition.

8. With the help of bit patterns, explain precisely why the following replacement for the declaration in line (A) of the program fragment of the previous problem does not work

```
char buffer[N];
```

With this change, you will see a two-character hex representation for most of the bytes in the input file. But every once in a while it will generate an 8-character hex sequence for a single byte of the input file. This longish looking hex sequence would seem like it was generated by a "negative integer." Why?

9. A text file with the following integer entries, one per row, is provided to the program shown below. The program tries to read the integers, but instead reads garbage, as shown by the output displayed after the program. Why?

```
//file: input.txt
12
12
12
12
12
23
```

The program is

```
import java.io.*;

class Test {
    public static void main( String[] args ) {
        try {
            FileInputStream fin = new FileInputStream("input.txt");
            DataInputStream din = new DataInputStream(fin);
            for (int i = 1; i <= 6; i++) {
                System.out.println( din.readInt() );
            }
            fin.close();
        } catch(IOException e) {System.out.println(e);}
    }
}
```

The program produces the following output (the output will vary depending on the underlying architecture of the machine):

```
825362993
839528754
170996234
825362994
java.io.EOFException
```

10. As mentioned in Section 6.10, the java.io package contains stream classes for direct object level I/O. These, as shown in Figure 6.3, are ObjectOutput-Stream and ObjectInputStream. A Java object can be output directly to an external resource if the class to which the object belongs has implemented the Serializable interface. An object is converted into a stream of bytes so that it can be output via an object stream to, say, a disk file. This process is known as *object serialization*. The opposite process, namely reading a stream of bytes through an input object stream and converting those those bytes back into an object is known as *object serialization*.. The byte stream produced for an object through serialization includes a 64-bit long *serial version UID* that is a secure hash of the full class name, its super-interfaces, its members. This unique identifier is used during object input to discover any incompatibilities with the existing classes in the Java Virtual Machine.

Shown below is a simple class User that is serializable because it implements the Serializable interface. Notice how the object streams are set up in lines (A) and (B) and how the writeObject() method of ObjectOutputStream

is invoked to write the objects out to a disk file and how the readObject()
method of ObjectInputStream is invoked to read the objects back from the
disk file.

```java
//ObjectIO.java

import java.io.*;

class User implements Serializable {
    private String name;
    private int age;

    public User( String nam, int yy ) { name = nam;  age = yy; }
    public String toString(){return "User: " + name + "  " + age;}

    public static void main( String[] args ) throws Exception {
        User user1 = new User( "Melinda", 33 );
        User user2 = new User( "Belinda", 43 );
        User user3 = new User( "Tralinda", 53 );

        FileOutputStream os = new FileOutputStream( "object.dat" );
        ObjectOutputStream out = new ObjectOutputStream( os );

        out.writeObject( user1 );
        out.writeObject( user2 );
        out.writeObject( user3 );

        out.flush();
        os.close();

        FileInputStream is = new FileInputStream( "object.dat" );
        ObjectInputStream in = new ObjectInputStream( is );

        User user4 = (User) in.readObject();
        User user5 = (User) in.readObject();
        User user6 = (User) in.readObject();

        is.close();

        System.out.println( user4 );
        System.out.println( user5 );
        System.out.println( user6 );
    }
}
```

The straightforward approach shown above works only for simple classes. For a more complex class, such as when the class User is provided with an array data member, this approach would not work. Now you would need to provide the class with two methods of the following exact signatures:

```
private void writeObject( ObjectOutputStream out )
           throws IOException

private void readObject( ObjectInputStream in )
           throws IOException, ClassNotFoundException
```

When a class is endowed with these functions, the ObjectOutputStream's writeObject will call the writeObject method defined as above for the serialization process. The same goes for the ObjectInputStream's readObject method vis-à-vis the readObject defined as above for the class in question.

The goal of this homework is to create a serializable version of the following class by providing implementation code for the methods writeObject and readObject in accordance with the signatures shown above. Your implementation of these methods would need to write out each data member of the class and each element of the array separately by using the writeInt and writeString (or writeUTF) methods of the ObjectOutputStream class. To deserialize the byte streams, you'd need to use the readInt and readString (or readUTF) of the ObjectInputStream class for each data member of the class and also for each element of the array.[26]

```
class User implements Serializable {
    private String name;
    private int age;
    transient private String[] children;
    private int numChildren;

    // constructor(s)

    // implementation code for writeObject()

    // implementation code for readObject()
}
```

---

[26]Note that we have marked the array data member children as *transient*. You declare a class data member *transient* if you do not want it to be serialized. So for the class shown we do not want the array reference to be serialized; however, you'd still want to serialize each element of the array. Your implementation code for the readObject method should then create a fresh array reference for children and then read off each element of the array from the byte stream into the array.

7

Declarations, Definitions, and Initializations

Before an identifier can be used, it must first be declared in both C++ and Java. Declaring an identifier is *not* the same thing as defining an identifier. *An identifier is not defined until an appropriate amount of memory is allocated for the identifier.* And then, when an identifier is the name of a variable, there is also the issue of whether or not the variable will get default-initialized when it is defined.

Initially focusing mostly on variables, this chapter starts with a discussion of when the declaration of a variable also constitutes its definition. This will be followed by the issue of default initialization of variables. The question we will answer there is: If you declare a variable and its declaration also constitutes its definition, is the variable given a default initialization?

Subsequently, we will talk about the scope of an identifier in a computer program. This will be followed by the issues of declaration, definition, and initialization of arrays in C++ and Java.

7.1 WHEN IS A DECLARATION ALSO A DEFINITION?

Whether or not a declaration also constitutes a definition is different for C++ and Java.

Most declarations in C++, such as

```
char ch;
```

```
string s;

int j;

int count = 1;
```

also constitute the definitions for the variables involved. In each case, an appropriate amount of memory will be put aside for the variable. For example, the first declaration will cause one byte of memory to be allocated to the variable ch, the second declaration 4 or 8 bytes (depending on the compiler), the third usually 4 bytes, and so on. The fact that most C++ declarations are also definitions holds true regardless of whether a variable is global, local, or a data member of a class type object. Therefore, in the code fragment:

```
int x;

class Book {
    double price;
    int yearPublished;
    //...

public:
    // constructors defined here

    double estimateResalePrice() {
        int estimatedDemand;
        //...
    }
};

int main()
{
    Book* b1 = new Book( .. constructor arguments .. );        //(A)
    Book* b2 = new Book( .. constructor arguments .. );        //(B)
}
```

the global variable x, and the data members price and yearPublished in each of the two objects created in lines (A) and (B) are also defined. While memory for the global variable x will be allocated at compile time, for the data members price and yearPublished the memory will be allocated at run time when the objects pointed to by b1 and b2 are created. The memory for the local variable estimatedDemand will be allocated when the function estimateResalePrice() is invoked. The memory allocation for the identifier Book will take place at compile time.

However, there are C++ declarations that do *not* constitute definitions. Here are some examples:

```
extern int error_num;
class Student;
double d( double );
```

As you know from C, the `extern` storage class for a variable enables several source files to share the same variable. The `extern` declaration above informs the compiler that `error_num` is an `int` variable, but doesn't cause it to allocate memory for the variable. The second declaration above

```
class Student;
```

is an incomplete definition of `Student` that is allowed in C++ to get around the problems caused by lack of look-ahead in compilation. The compiler will expect to see a complete definition elsewhere. Such declarations are needed when you have two or more interleaved classes in the same file, as is the case for the `Teacher` and `Student` classes below:

```
class Student;

class Teacher {
    Student* studentsSupervised;   // list of students supervised
};                                 // by teacher

class Student {
    Teacher* classTeachers;        // list of teachers for the
};                                 // classes taken this semester
```

When the compiler gets to the `Teacher` class, at the least it needs to have previously seen `Student` declared as a type. Obviously, the class `Student` cannot be defined fully before the class `Teacher` since the former has a data member of type `Teacher*`.

Finally, a declaration such as

```
double d( double );
```

is also not a definition. This declaration is a function prototype that says that `d` is a function that expects a `double` argument and that returns a `double`. Evidently, the compiler would look elsewhere for its definition.

In Java, whether or not a declaration also constitutes a definition depends on whether an identifier is local to a method or if it is a data member of a class. (Note that Java does not permit variables to be global in the sense permitted in C++.) In Java, the statement

```
int j;
```

constitutes only a declaration (and not a definition) if the statement is local to a method. This declaration will not cause any memory to be set aside for the variable `j`. To also define a local variable, you have to include an initializer, as in

```
int j = 0;
```

On the other hand, when a variable is a data member in a class type object in Java, its declaration does constitute its definition also. Therefore, in the program fragment

```
class Book {
    double price;
    int yearPublished;
    //...

    public double estimateResalePrice() {
        int estimatedDemand;
        //...
    }
}

class Test {
  public static void main( String[] args )
  {
      Book b1 = new Book( ... constructor arguments ... );    //(A)
      Book b2 = new Book( ... constructor arguments ... );    //(B)
  }
}
```

the declarations of the data members `price` and `yearPublished` will cause them to also get defined when the objects b1 and b2 are created in lines (A) and (B). But no memory will be set aside for the local variable `estimatedDemand` in the function `estimateResalePrice()` until this variable is also initialized.

7.2 ARE THE DEFINED VARIABLES IN C++ INITIALIZED BY DEFAULT?

Let's say a declaration defines a variable without an initializer. Now the question is, Will the compiler give such a variable a default initialization? The answer to this question is again different for C++ and Java. In C++, only the following kinds of variables are default initialized:

For Primitive Types: Only the global variables of the primitive types are default initialized.

For Class Types: Both local and global variables that are the names of class-type objects are default initialized provided the class has a no-arg constructor.

Table 7.1 summarizes the manner in which the global variables of the primitive types and all variables of class types are default initialized to zeros of the appropriate kind.

The following program is a small demonstration of the default initialization of a class type object. The program defines a class `User` in line (A) and supplies the class with a no-arg constructor in line (B).

Type	Initial Value
bool	false
char	'\0'
all integer types	0
all floating-point types	0.0
class type	depends on the no-arg constructor

Table 7.1

```
//DefaultInit.cc

#include <iostream>
#include <string>
using namespace std;

class User {                                               //(A)
public:
    string name;
    int age;
    User() { name = "John Doe";  age = 25; }               //(B)
};

int main()
{
    //object u defined and initialized :
    User u;                                                //(C)
    cout << u.name << "  "  << u.age << endl;   // John Doe  25

    //object *p defined and initialized:
    User*  p = new User();                                 //(D)
    cout << p->name << "  "  << p->age << endl;   // John Doe  25

    return 0;
}
```

The following declaration in line (C) of the program

```
    User u;
```

not only defines the object u, it also default initializes the object according to the code in the no-arg constructor of line (B), as borne out by the print-out statement that follows line (C). For the other User object in the above program, in line (D), you'd of course expect it to be constructed according to the no-arg constructor since the no-arg constructor is specifically invoked.

Here is a more elaborate example that illustrates that when an object is created through the mechanism of default-initialization, the class-type data members of the object are also default-initialized according to their own no-arg constructors. Line (D) shows the data member chief of the class UserGroup as an object of type User. The class User, defined in line (A), comes with a no-arg constructor in line (B). And the class UserGroup, defined in line (C), comes with its own no-arg constructor in line (F).

```
//DefaultInit2.cc

#include <iostream>
#include <string>
using namespace std;

class User {                                                  //(A)
public:
    string name;
    int age;
    User() { name = "John Doe";   age = 25; }                 //(B)
};

class UserGroup {                                             //(C)
public:
    User chief;                                               //(D)
    User* p;             // pointer to Users in the group     //(E)
    int priority;
    UserGroup() { p = 0;   priority = 10; }                   //(F)
};

int main()
{
    UserGroup ug;                                             //(G)

    cout << "chief's name: " << ug.chief.name << " "     // John Doe
         << "chief's age: " << ug.chief.age << " "       // 25
         << "pointer value: " << ug.p << " "             // 0
         << "priority level: "  << ug.priority << endl;  // 10

    return 0;
}
```

When a `UserGroup` object ug is constructed and default-initialized in line (G) by the no-arg constructor of `UserGroup`, the data member `chief` is default-initialized according to the no-arg constructor of `User`. This is borne out by the output shown in the commented out line endings. Note particularly that the no-arg constructor of `UserGroup` makes no mention of the initialization of the data member `chief`. This data member is nonetheless default-initialized according to `User`'s no-arg constructor.

7.2.1 What Happens When a No-arg Constructor Is Not Supplied?

Our previous discussion states that when a class type variable is declared without an explicit initializer, it is default-initialized according to the code in the no-arg constructor of the class. That raises the important issue of what happens if the programmer has not supplied a no-arg constructor for a class. There are two different situations to consider in this regard:

1. If the class has not been supplied with any constructors at all, the system will provide the class with a default no-arg constructor. Ideally, this system-supplied default no-arg constructor ought to initialize each data member of the class to a zero of the appropriate kind. But in practice what happens is implementation dependent and cannot be relied upon. It is entirely possible that the system-supplied default no-arg constructor will merely appropriate the memory and not initialize it at all.

2. The class has been provided with other constructors, but not a no-arg constructor. In this case, a no-arg constructor simply does not exist. As a result, the compiler will consider illegal a declaration without an explicit initializer.

To illustrate the first case, we have commented out in line (F) below the no-arg constructor for the `UserGroup` class. The rest of the program is the same as before. Now this class will possess no programmer-supplied constructors at all. The system will therefore provide the class with a default no-arg constructor.

```
//DefaultInit3.cc

#include <iostream>
#include <string>
using namespace std;

class User {                                            //(A)
public:
    string name;
    int age;
    User() { name = "John Doe";  age = 25; }            //(B)
};
```

```
class UserGroup {                                                //(C)
public:
    User chief;                                                  //(D)
    User* p;                // pointer to Users in the group     //(E)
    int priority;
    //    UserGroup() { p = 0;   priority = 10; }                //(F)
};

int main()
{
    UserGroup ug;                                                //(G)

    cout << "chief's name: " << ug.chief.name << " "    // John Doe
         << "chief's age: " << ug.chief.age << " "      // 25
         << "pointer value: " << ug.p << " "            // GARBAGE
         << "priority level: "  << ug.priority << endl;  // GARBAGE

    return 0;
}
```

The output of this program, as shown in the commented-out line endings in main, illustrates that the system-supplied no-arg constructor for UserGroup invokes the programmer-supplied no-arg constructor for the class User. As a result, chief's name and age get initialized to John Doe and 25, respectively. For the other two data members of UserGroup, while the memory is allocated, it is not properly initialized. So we end up with garbage bits for the data members p, and priority.

We said earlier that if a class has been provided with any constructors at all, but not with a no-arg constructor, then there does not exist a no-arg constructor for the class. That condition exists in the UserGroup class in the following program. Line (H)) of the program supplies the class UserGroup with a two-argument constructor; this class, therefore, cannot be provided with a system-supplied default no-arg constructor. As a result, the declaration of the variable ug in line (I) now elicits a compilation error.

```
//DefaultInit4.cc

#include <iostream>
#include <string>
using namespace std;

class User {
public:
    string name;
    int age;
```

```
    User() { name = "John Doe";   age = 25; }
};

class UserGroup {
public:
    User chief;
    User* p;              // pointer to Users in the group
    int priority;
    UserGroup( User u, User* q, int pr ) {}                     //(H)
};

int main()
{
    UserGroup ug;             // COMPILATION ERROR            //(I)
    return 0;
}
```

While we are on the subject of no-arg constructors, a class can also be provided with a programmer-defined no-arg constructor through the mechanism of assigning default values to all the parameters of a more regular constructor, as in

```
    User {
        string name;
        int age;
    public:
        User( string nam = "John Doe", int yy = 25 ) {         //(J)
            name = nam; age = yy;
        }
    };
```

Note the default values for the parameters nam and yy in line (J). With this definition of User, we can again construct objects of type User with declarations like

```
    User uobj;               // uobj.name = "John Doe"   uobj.age = 25
    User* p = new User();    // p->name  = "John Doe"    p->age = 25
```

and, using the same constructor, construct objects with specified values for the parameters, as in

```
    User uobj( "Jane Doe", 28 );
                    //uobj.name = "Jane Doe"   uobj.age = 28
```

Note that the following syntax is not acceptable for the invocation of a no-arg constructor:

```
    User uobj();          // Wrong for invocation of default constructor
```

Using this wrong syntax is not an infrequent error made by beginning C++ programmers. The main reason for this error should be obvious.[1]

7.2.2 Special Consideration for const and Reference Members

As already mentioned, a default no-arg constructor for a class is not supplied by the system if it has any constructors defined for it explicitly. The system also does not supply its own default no-arg constructor if a class contains uninitialized const or reference members.[2] For example,

```
class Y {
public:
  const int a;
  const char ch;
};

  Y y;                        // ERROR                          //(A)
```

Lacking a default no-arg constructor, the compiler refuses to accept the declaration in line (A). When a class has const or reference members, in most cases one has no choice but to also provide a programmer-defined no-arg constructor with special initialization syntax, as in

```
class Y {
public:
  const int a;
  const char ch;
  Y() : a(0), ch(0) {}                                          //(B)
};
```

---

[1]Let's consider a class with both a regular constructor with parameters and a programmer-defined no-argument constructor

```
User {
    string name;
    int age;
public:
    User() { name = "john doe"; age = 25; }
    User( string nam, int yy ) { name = nam; age = yy; }
};
```

An object of type User may now be created by

```
User u1( "zahphod", 112 );
```

So it seems natural that if we wanted to invoke the no-arg constructor, we could do so by

```
User u2();       // Wrong for invoking no-arg constructor
```

Unfortunately, this declaration is construed to be a declaration of a function of name u2 that takes void arguments and whose return type is User.

[2]Object *reference* in C++ is the subject of the next chapter.

where in line (B) we have used what is known as the *member initialization syntax* for the constructor. In case the reader is wondering why we couldn't do in-class initialization, as in

```
class X {
  const n = 100;        // WRONG
};
```

that is prohibited by the language. In-class initialization of the data members of a class, including those that are of type const, is not permitted unless the const members are also static. In other words, the in-class initialization is permitted in C++ for only those data members that are specifically of type static const.[3] As we will see in the next section, Java places no such constraints on in-class initialization of data members.

For another example that includes a reference member r of type int (as was mentioned earlier, object reference in C++ will be explained in detail in the next chapter), consider

```
class X {
public:
    int& r;
    const int n;
    int i;
    X(int s, int t, int u) : r(s), n(t) { i = u; }          //(C)
};

int main()
{
    X xobj(1, 2, 3);
    cout << xobj.r << endl;
}
```

Note the member initialization syntax in line (C) for the reference member r and the const member n.

7.3 ARE THE DEFINED VARIABLES IN JAVA INITIALIZED BY DEFAULT?

The basic rule to remember for Java is that whenever a variable is defined, as opposed to just being declared but not defined, it is always default-initialized to a zero of the appropriate kind according to the entries in Table 7.2.

---

[3]The notion of a static data member was introduced briefly in Chapter 3 and will be taken up in fuller detail in Chapter 11.

Type	Initial Value
boolean	false
char	\u0000
all integer types	0
float	0.0f
double	0.0
object reference	null

Table 7.2

Based on what we said in Section 7.1, the only time a variable is only declared but not defined in Java is when it makes a first-time appearance in a function without an initializer. For example, in the following program, the variable u1 is local to main; it has been declared without initialization. In Java, no memory will be allocated to such a variable until it is subsequently given a value somewhere in a program. Until that time, the variable remains undefined. It's for this reason that the commented out statement in line (B) after the declaration in line (A) elicits an error message from the compiler. By contrast, the variable u2 in line (C) is properly defined, resulting in the output shown in line (D).

```java
//DefaultInit.java

class User {
    private String name;
    private int age;
    public User() { name = "John Doe";   age = 25; }
    public String toString() { return name + "   " + age; }
}

class Test {
    public static void main( String[] args ) {

        //u1 declared but not defined:
        User u1;                                              //(A)
        // System.out.println( u1 );    // ERROR             //(B)

        //u2 defined and initialized:
        User u2 = new User();                                 //(C)
        System.out.println( u2 );      // John Doe   25       //(D)
    }
}
```

To show a more elaborate example that parallels the C++ example code in
`DefaultInit3.cc` of Section 7.2.1, the following program includes a programmer-
defined no-arg constructor for `User` in line (A), but such a constructor is not provided
for the class `UserGroup`. Nonetheless, the object ug of type `UserGroup` is constructed in line (D) by invoking its system-supplied default no-arg constructor (which
exists because we have not supplied the `UserGroup` class with any constructors at
all). According to Table 7.2, in the `UserGroup` object constructed the data member
`groupName` is default-initialized to `null`, the data member `chief` also to `null`, the
data member `priority` to 0, and the data member `members` also to `null`. (Why
the last data member, `members`, is set to `null` will be clear from our discussion on
arrays in Java at the end of this chapter.) That explains the output produced by the
print statement in line (E). Recall from Chapter 3 that the output shown in line (E)
is produced by the override definition of the `toString` method for the `UserGroup`
class in line (C).

```
//DefaultInit2.java

class User {
    public String name;
    public int age;
    public User() { name = "John Doe";  age = 25; }           //(A)
    public String toString() { return name + "  " + age; }    //(B)
}

class UserGroup {
    public String groupName;
    public User chief;
    public int priority;
    public User[] members;
    public String toString() {                                //(C)
        return groupName + " " + chief + "  "
                    + priority + "  " + members ;
    }
}

class Test {
    public static void main( String[] args ) {
        UserGroup ug = new UserGroup();                       //(D)
        System.out.println( ug );    // null null  0  null    //(E)
    }
}
```

Contrast this behavior with that of C++ where the no-arg constructor for a class is
happy to invoke on its own the no-arg constructors for class-type data members if
they need default-initialization. In Java, the default initialization for a class type data

member (and also for the primitive type data members) is strictly according to Table 7.2.

7.3.1   Is Default Initialization Affected by Default Values for Class Members?

The following program does not provide a constructor for the User class. So the system supplies its own no-arg constructor for the object u in line (C) of main. Ordinarily, this constructor would initialize each data member of the object according to Table 7.2. But if the programmer has supplied default values for the data members, as in the program below in lines (A) and (B), those are used in lieu of the entries in the table. This explains the output of the print statement in line (D).

```
//DefaultInit3.java

class User {
    public String name = "John Doe";                        //(A)
    public int age = 25;                                    //(B)

    public String toString() { return name + "  "  + age; }
}

class Test {
    public static void main( String[] args ) {
        User u = new User();                                //(C)
        System.out.println( u );      // John Doe  25        //(D)
    }
}
```

We mentioned earlier that C++ does not allow us to give default values to class members at class definition time (except for the special case of static const data members). On the other hand, such class definitions, as shown above, are not only legal in Java but also used frequently.

7.3.2   Is the Default Value of a Class Member Ignored If a Constructor Specifies a Value for the Member?

Our previous discussion makes it clear that a class data member possesses a default initialization according to the entries in Table 7.2, unless that value is overridden by a programmer-supplied default value as in the program DefaultInit3.java. The question now is whether this default value, either system-supplied according to Table

7.2, or programmer-supplied as in `DefaultInit3.java`, is ever used if a class has a regular constructor that assigns a value to a data member.

The answer to the question is, Yes. When a new object is constructed in Java with the `new` operator, the data members are set either to the values according to Table 7.2, or to the default values specified explicitly for the data members. It is only *after* the object is created in this fashion that the values of the data members are reset according to the code in the constructor.

Finally, since Java does not permit default values for the parameters of a function, the C++ method of defining a no-arg constructor by giving default values to the parameters of a regular constructor cannot be used in Java.

7.4   DECLARATION OF POINTER TYPES IN C++

One of the most notable differences between C++ and Java is that the former has pointers and the latter does not.[4]

For any type T in C++, T* is of the type *pointer to an object of type T*. A variable of type T* can hold the address of an object of type T. For example,

```
int i = 100;
int* p = &i;                                    //(A)
```

where & is the *address* operator. The declaration in line (A) makes p a pointer of type `int*`.

A fundamental operation on a pointer is *dereferencing*, that in effect retrieves the object pointed to by the pointer. The operation of dereferencing, also called *indirection*, is carried out by applying the operator * to a pointer. For example, we could dereference the pointer p defined above by

```
int a = *p;                                     //(B)
```

One must bear in mind the two different semantic roles played by the symbol * in the context of pointers. In a declaration of a pointer variable, as in line (A) above, the symbol * tells the compiler that the identifier p will be used to hold the address of an `int` variable. But, when used as in line (B) above, the symbol * is an operator that when applied to a pointer causes it to be dereferenced.

Pointers and, as we will be discussed in the next section, arrays of pointers play an extremely important role in C++ programming. While all of the usual reasons

---

[4]This statement sometimes elicits a retort from some programmers who say that an object reference in Java *is* a pointer. All we are saying here is that an object reference in Java is not directly a memory address that can be dereferenced and that you can do pointer arithmetic on.

for using pointers in C also apply to C++,[5] here are three more that are particularly relevant to C++:

Polymorphism: Object-oriented programming derives much of its power and utility from polymorphism, a concept presented briefly in Chapter 3 and explained more fully in Chapter 15. Polymorphism works in C++ only when objects are manipulated through pointers and references.

Interleaved Classes: Unlike Java, the order in which classes are presented to a C++ compiler is important. To explain, suppose class X has a data member of type W. When the compiler gets to that data member in X, it had better already have seen the class W. But what does one do when we have two classes, say, W and X, with W containing a data member of type X and X containing a data member of type W — a not uncommon situation on OO? To deal with such situations, C++ allows us to just declare a class name without having to provide its definition. So we could just declare X as a class name and not give its definition, then define class W, and then proceed to define X. But this can only be done if the reference to the incompletely defined X in W is via a pointer. This is explained in greater detail in Chapter 11.

The Need for a "null" Object: In OO programming there often arises a need to "null" out an object. To elaborate, let's say that a class type variable is holding a reference of some kind to an object. At a later point in the program, the program conditions may require that we "zero out" or "nullify" the value of the variable. In Java, this can be done conveniently by changing the value of the variable to the `null` object reference. The only way to achieve the same effect in C++ is by using the notion of the null pointer that is denoted by the symbol 0. In C++, when the value of a pointer variable pointing to a class type object is set to 0, we can be certain that it is not pointing to any particular location in the memory.

While the first two of the three reasons given above will be discussed in greater detail elsewhere in the book, in the rest of this section we will provide examples of what we mean by "nulling" an object and why pointers are useful for that purpose. Let's say we have created a `Person` class by

```
class Person {
    string name;
    string address;
    // many more
public:
```

---

[5] Such as getting around the limitations that are caused by the fact that a function can only return one value. By passing pointer arguments to a function and using side effects, a called function can be made to bring about multiple changes visible in the calling program even though the called function can return only one value.

```
    Person( string theName, string theAddress ) {
        name = theName;
        address = theAddress;
    }
};
```

Now suppose inside an object-oriented program we make a new `Person` as follows:

```
Person* ptr = new Person( "John Doe", "Main Street USA" );
```

If at some later place in the program, we wish to "zero out" or "nullify" this new person, all we have to do is to say

```
ptr = 0;
```

although in actuality we would say

```
delete ptr;
ptr = 0;
```

The `delete` operator would also free up the memory occupied by the object to which `ptr` was pointing.[6]

An alternative would be to create the object by

```
Person peson1( "John Doe",  "Main Street USA" );               //C)
```

which does not involve the use of pointers. Let's say that at some point we wish to "zero out" the object `person1`. We evidently cannot say

```
person1 = 0;          // WRONG
```

because that would make no sense to the compiler. We could destroy the object which is referred to by `person1` by invoking the same `delete` operator as before:

```
delete &person1;      // WRONG                                  //(D)
```

but that would not work because the `delete` operator can only free up that memory which is acquired by the `new` operator — that is, the memory allocated on the heap. When we construct a `Person` object in the manner shown in line (C), the memory for the object is allocated on the stack. Therefore, invoking the `delete` operator, in the manner shown in line (D), will in general elicit a memory-segmentation fault message from the system.

As another example, consider

```
string str( "hello" );
```

---

[6]Memory allocation and deallocation will be discussed in detail in Chapter 8.

If at a later time, we wanted to "zero out" the value of str, we are not allowed to say[7]

```
str = 0;       // WRONG
```

However, if we had said

```
string* ptr = new string( "hello" );
```

If so needed, we'd then be able to zero out the value of ptr by simply saying

```
ptr = 0;
```

although we should actually say

```
delete ptr;
ptr = 0;
```

in order to properly deallocate the memory before nullifying the pointer.

7.5 ARRAYS OF POINTERS IN C++

Here are a couple of examples of declarations of arrays of pointers in C++:

```
int* int_array[1000];    // an array of 1000 pointers
                         // each pointing to an int

string* names[100];      // an array of 100 pointers, each
                         // pointing to a string type
```

Arrays of pointers are extremely useful for C++ programming. To illustrate, let's say that we expect a maximum of 100 students to enroll in a class. To hold the names of these students we create an array by a declaration such as

```
const int MaxClassSize = 100;
string* names[ MaxClassSize ];
```

Before allowing the students to register for a class, we could initialize this array by

```
for ( int i = 0; i < MaxClassSize; i++ )
  names[ i ] = 0;
```

---

[7]This is a good time to mention that the often-used NULL pointer of C becomes the *symbol* 0 in C++. If your programming habits compel you to use NULL for a null pointer, you could use the following definition in your program:

```
const int NULL = 0;
```

or, using the array initialization syntax we discuss later in this chapter, even more simply by

```
string* names[100] = {0};
```

Now as a student enrolls, his or her name could be added to the list by a statement like

```
names[ i ]  =  new string( "Zaphod" );
```

And if, after registering, this student chooses to drop the course, we could take care of that situation by resetting

```
names[i] = 0;
```

If at some point during this registration process, we wanted to print out the list of all the names currently enrolled, we could use a loop like

```
for ( int i = 0; i < MaxClassSize; i++ )
  if ( names[ i ] != 0 )
    cout << *names[ i ] << endl;
```

The advantage of this approach is that the test on the ith pointer in the array

```
if ( names[ i ] != 0 ) ....
```

tells us right away whether or not the ith element in the array currently belongs to a registered student. If we did not use this test and simply used an ostensibly simpler loop like

```
for ( int i = 0; i < MaxClassSize; i++ )
    cout << *names[ i ];
```

you could get a hard-to-decipher run-time error because you could be trying to reach a memory location that was not yet appropriated, let alone properly initialized, or probably deallocated when a student dropped the course. Testing for whether or not we have a non-null pointer in an array of pointers *is a very convenient way to check whether or not an object has yet been created.*

An alternative to using a array of pointers would be to declare directly an array of strings, as opposed to an array of pointers to strings, by

```
string names[ MaxClassSize ];
```

Now suppose we try to print out the names of the students who have enrolled so far by

```
for ( int i = 0; i < MaxClassSize; i++ )
  cout << names[ i ] << endl;
```

This would work as expected if the entire array is full — that is, if all the 100 students in this example have registered. But if suppose the array is not yet full, this loop would give us a run-time error as we'd be trying to read memory locations that have not be yet been initialized. You see, we no longer have the luxury of using a test like

```
if ( names[ i ] != 0 ) .....              // WRONG NOW
```

because comparing a string to 0 makes no sense to the compiler, especially if that element of the array has not yet been created. Some readers might say that before allowing any students to register, why not initialize the entire array by using empty string literals:

```
for ( int i = 0; i < MaxClassSize; i++ )
  names[ i ] = "";
```

And then we could print out the entire array by using a construction similar to what was used for the pointer case:

```
for ( i = 0; i < MaxClassSize; i++ )
  if ( names[ i ] != "" )
    cout << rnames[ i ] << endl;
```

This would certainly work for the case of strings, because an empty string literal is something the compiler understands. But an empty something may not be defined for other class types. For example, for the class User that we have used in previous examples, it would be difficult to define the notion of an empty User.

7.6 DECLARING MULTIPLE NAMES

It is possible to declare several names in a single declaration. The declaration simply contains a list of comma-separated declarators:

```
int x, y, v[10];    in C++ or Java
```

is equivalent to

```
int x;
int y;
int v[10];
```

Similarly,

```
float[] x, y;    in Java
```

is equivalent to

```
float[] x;
float[] y;
```

Declaring several names in a single statement can sometimes lead to unreadable code. For example, you could say in C++

```
int* p, y;
```

If you have become accustomed to thinking of int* as a type specifier, you'd think that the above declaration is equivalent to

```
int* p;
int* y;
```

But that is wrong, because, syntactically speaking, the symbol * is a unary operator that is right associative. Therefore, when the compiler sees

```
int* p, y;
```

it actually reads

```
int *p, y;
```

which is how you'd write it in a C program anyway. But to quickly assimilate a program visually it is better to write a pointer declaration as "int* p;" as opposed to "int *p;," even though the two are completely equivalent. Thinking of int* as a pointer type, you immediately see p as a pointer to an integer variable. In any case, regardless of your preferences, in C++ it has now become common to declare a pointer in the fashion exemplified by "int* p;."

7.7 SCOPE OF AN IDENTIFIER IN C++

A declaration introduces an identifier into a scope, meaning that after the declaration the identifier can only be used in a specific part of the program. The five scopes of an identifier are

- namespace scope
- file scope
- block scope
- function scope
- function-prototype scope

We have already discussed in detail the namespace scope in Chapter 3. To quickly summarize the discussion in that chapter: (a) The identifiers that are the members of a namespace can be accessed outside the namespace through their namespace-qualified names. (b) Using-directives and using-declarations are available for convenience; with these a namespace member can be invoked without the use of the scope operator. (c) Namespaces can import other namespaces through the mechanism of using-directives and using-declarations. (d) Namespaces can be nested. (e) Unwieldy namespace names can be aliased to more convenient names. (f) Unnamed namespaces allow us to declare identifiers with internal linkage. And, (g) Koenig lookup allows an unqualified function name to be accessed if its argument type is defined in that namespace.

The scope of a global identifier — that is an identifier which is defined outside any function, class, or namespace — extends from the point of declaration to the end of the file in which its declaration occurs. Therefore, if you declare a function prototype at the beginning of a program file outside of any other function, the name of the function will be recognized everywhere from the point of the declaration and until the end of the file. Similarly, if you define a global variable, the name of the variable will be "known" until the end of the file. This is referred to as *file scope*.

The scope of a local identifier, which is an identifier declared inside a block, starts at the point of declaration and ends with the end of the block. Recall that a block is a section of code delimited by a {} pair. This is referred to as *block scope*. Local variables and function parameters have block scope. Note that an identifier can be declared at any point in a C++ program.

The fact that an identifier can be declared at any point in a C++ program leads naturally to the following question concerning nested blocks: What happens when an inner block contains an identifier declaration with the same name as one in the enclosing block? In such situations, the inner block declaration *hides*, or takes precedence over, the declaration in the enclosing block.[8] When an already declared identifier is redefined inside a block so as to refer to a different entity within the block, after exit from the block the identifier resumes its previous meaning. This is illustrated by the following example:

```
//HideScope.cc

int x;                  // global x

void f() {
    int x;              // local x hides global x
    x = 1;              // assigns to local x
    {
        int x;          // hides first local x
        x = 2;          // assigns to second local x
        ::x = 20;       // assigns to global x
    }
    x = 3;              // assigns to first local x
}
```

---

[8]By the same token, if an identifier inside a block has the same name as a global identifier, the former will hide the latter until the end of the block.

```
int main()
{
    int* p = &x;        // take address of global x
    return 0;
}
```

Although it may seem that hiding names is unavoidable when writing large programs, it is known to be a source of hard to locate bugs. That is because in a visual scan of a program it can often be difficult to determine as to which meaning of a variable one is referring to in such situations.

That brings us to the last two of the different types of scopes listed at the beginning of this section. The only identifiers with *function scope* are labels. Labels, recognized by the colon that follows them, are used mainly for marking the destination of goto statements. Another example consists of case labels used in switch structures. With regard to the *function-prototype scope*, as its name would suggest, the only identifiers that have this scope are the parameters used in function prototypes. As the reader should know from his or her C programming experience, it is not really necessary to name the parameters in a function prototype; only the types of the parameters need to be specified. However, it is common to include parameter names in function prototypes to make the code more readable by humans. The compiler ignores such names.

7.8 SCOPE OF AN IDENTIFIER IN JAVA

Java does not permit global identifiers with file scope; all identifiers must be local to classes in which they are declared. With regard to local identifiers, as in C++, they may be declared anywhere in a program. All local identifiers have block scope; that is, they are recognized from the point of their declaration to the end of the block containing the declaration. Java does not permit redeclaring an identifier in an inner block if it has already been declared in the enclosing block. For illustration, the following Java program does not compile because of the repeated declarations of the variable of the same name inside the nested block inside main.

```
class Test {                              // will NOT compile
    public static void main( String[] args )
    {
        int x;
        x = 1;
        {
            int x;
```

```
        x = 2;
    }
    x = 3;
}
}
```

However, there is no problem with the name of a variable inside a method being the same as the name of a data member. For example, in the following legal program we have a data member of name x and a local variable in main of name x:

```java
//ScopeTest.java

class Test {
    public int x = 100;

    public static void main(String[] args)
    {
        int x;          // local x hides data member x
        x = 3;          // assigns to the local x

        Test testObj = new Test();
        testObj.x = 200;
        System.out.println( "Local x: " + x );                  // 3
        System.out.println( "Data member x: " + testObj.x );   // 200
    }
}
```

Of course, if you want to access the data member x inside main, you have to do so through an object of type Test, as we have done via the object testObj.

7.9 ARRAYS AND THEIR INITIALIZATION IN C++

In C++ you can create an array with either of the following two kinds of declarations

```
    int d[10];
    int* dp = new int[10];
```

for arrays of integers. Similar declarations can be constructed for other types. With either declaration you can use array indexing to access the individual elements. So you could access, say, the fourth element by

```
    d[3]
```

in the first case, or by

    dp[3]

in the second case.

While it is true that an array name can be treated as a pointer, it is strictly speaking not a pointer, in the sense you cannot do certain kinds of pointer arithmetic on an array name. For example, you could get the value of the fifth element of the array by either of the following dereferencing operations:

    *(d + 4)

or

    *(dp + 4)

But, since you cannot assign to an array name, what does NOT work for an array name are the incrementing and decrementing operators. Therefore, the following does not work:

    *d++   // error

while the following is a common operation with a pointer to an array:

    *dp++

And, for the same reasons, while a pointer variable can be made to point to any other entity as long it is of the same type, an array name cannot be made to point to some some other array in the memory.

An array declaration is also a definition, since it reserves a block of memory for the array. But whether or not the memory allocated for an array is also default-initialized depends on whether we are dealing with an array of primitive types or class types, and whether the array is local or global in scope. Here is a summary of how default initialization works for arrays in C++:

- For arrays of primitive types, an array is default-initialized to a zero of the appropriate kind only if the array is in global scope. That means that a local array will not be default initialized.

- For arrays of class types, array declarations are illegal if the class does not possess a no-arg constructor.

- For arrays of class types, if the class is supplied with a programmer-defined no-arg constructor, both the local and the global arrays are default-initialized according to the no-arg constructor.

- For arrays of class types, if the class has to use a system-supplied default no-arg constructor, only the global arrays are default-initialized according to the no-arg constructor. In other words, in this case any local arrays of the class type will not be default-initialized.

Consider the following example that shows the difference between the default initialization for global and local arrays:

```
//DefaultInitPrimArray.cc

#include <iostream>
using namespace std;

int global[10];

int main()
{
    int local[10];
    cout << local[0] << endl;      // GARBAGE
    cout << local[1] << endl;      // GARBAGE

    cout << global[0] << endl;     // 0
    cout << global[1] << endl;     // 0

    return 0;
}
```

Obviously, the global array `global` is getting zeroed out, while the local array `local` just has random bits in its memory.

If you wish to initialize the array at the same time you are declaring it, you can use the following syntax:

```
int data[]  =  {3, 2, 4, 5, 9, 8, 7, 6, 1, 0};
```

When an array is initialized in this manner, it is common to omit the size from the declaration on the left; the compiler figures out the size from the initializer on the right. However, if you do include the size as in

```
char ch[3] = {'a', 'c', 'b'};
```

then you'd better make sure that the number of elements on the right does *not* exceed the size declared on the left. However, the number of elements in the initializer is allowed to be smaller than the declared size on the left. If the declared size is M and the number of elements supplied in the initializer is N with N < M, the first N elements of the array are set according to the initializer, and the rest to zeros of the appropriate kind. This is to allow the initialization of large arrays with simple statements like[9]

```
int data[10] = {0};
```

Regarding arrays of class types in C++, the following code fragment shows that when a class does not possess a no-arg constructor (because it has been supplied with one or more other constructors), it is not possible to declare arrays of that class type.

```
class User {
public:
    string name;
    int age;
    User( string nam, int yy ) { name = nam; age = yy; }
};

User uList[10];                          // ERROR

User* uptr[10];                          // OK
```

The following example shows the difference between the default initializations for local and global arrays of class type objects. Both classes in the example, `User` and `Date`, possess system-supplied no-arg constructors because they have not been explicitly provided with any constructors at all.

```
//DefaultInitClassArray.cc

#include <iostream>
using namespace std;

class Date {
public:
    int d, m, y;
};

class User {
public:
    int ID;
    int age;
    Date dateOfBirth;
};
```

---

[9]It is not uncommon for beginning programmers to assume that in the statement

```
int data[10] = {2};
```

all ten elements are getting initialized to the integer 2. But, as mentioned, that is obviously not the case. This declaration will cause only the first element of the array to be initialized to the number 2, the other nine elements would be set to 0.

```
User uGlobal[10];                      // global array

int main()
{
    User uLocal[10];                   // local array

    cout << uLocal[1].ID << endl;                          // GARBAGE
    cout << uLocal[1].age << endl;                         // GARBAGE
    cout << uLocal[1].dateOfBirth.y << endl;               // GARBAGE
    cout << uLocal[1].dateOfBirth.m << endl;               // GARBAGE

    cout << uGlobal[1].ID << endl;                         // 0
    cout << uGlobal[1].age << endl;                        // 0
    cout << uGlobal[1].dateOfBirth.y << endl;              // 0
    cout << uGlobal[1].dateOfBirth.m << endl;              // 0

    return 0;
}
```

Note that for `dateOfBirth`, the class type data member of the `User` class, is getting default initialized according to the system-supplied no-arg constructor for the class.

The following example shows that local and global arrays are treated the same with respect to default initialization when a class type is provided with a programmer-supplied no-arg constructor:

```
//DefaultInitClassArray2.cc

#include <iostream>
#include <string>
using namespace std;

class Date {
public:
    int d, m, y;
    Date() { d = 1; m = 1; y = 1970; }
};

class User {
public:
    string name;
    int age;
    Date dateOfBirth;
    User() { name = "Zaphod"; age = 10; }
};
```

```
User uGlobal[10];                // global array

int main()
{
    User uLocal[10];             // local array

    cout << uLocal[1].name << endl;              // Zaphod
    cout << uLocal[1].age << endl;               // 10
    cout << uLocal[1].dateOfBirth.y << endl;     // 1970
    cout << uLocal[1].dateOfBirth.m << endl;     // 1

    cout << uGlobal[1].name << endl;             // Zaphod
    cout << uGlobal[1].age << endl;              // 10
    cout << uGlobal[1].dateOfBirth.y << endl;    // 1970
    cout << uGlobal[1].dateOfBirth.m << endl;    // 1

    return 0;
}
```

One final point concerning C++ arrays: Ascertaining the memory address of the fictitious element just past the end of an array is permitted [54]. Consider the declarations:

```
int data[] = {3, 4, 6, 7};

int* p1 = data;

int* p2 = &data[0];

int* p3 = &data[4];
```

Whereas the pointers p1 and p2 point to exactly the same place in the memory — the first element of the array data — the pointer p3 points to a fictitious element just beyond the array. Many algorithms in the C++ Standard Template Library rely on p3 returning a valid address; its calculation is guaranteed to work by the C++ standard.

7.10 ARRAYS AND THEIR INITIALIZATION IN JAVA

An array in Java is created by a declaration such as:

```
int[] data = new int[3];
```

or by a statement that includes initialization:

```
int[] data = new int[ ] {2, 4, 7};
```

Here is an example of the latter declaration for the case of strings:

```
String[] str = new String[] {"Peter", "Paul", "Mary"};
```

When declaring Java arrays with initialization as shown above, you never explicitly specify the array dimension on the left. The compiler infers the dimension of the array from the number of elements inside the initializer. A shorter form of an array declaration with initialization is:

```
int[] data = {2, 4, 7};
```

The default-initialization issues related to C++ arrays simply do not arise for Java arrays. Recall that in C++ the default initialization of an array of a primitive type depends on whether the array is in file scope or in block scope, and, for arrays of class types, it depends additionally on the no-arg constructor of the class.

On the other hand, whenever you create a new array in Java by using new, the array elements get automatically initialized to the number 0 for int arrays, to the null character (\u0000) for arrays for chars, to 0.0f for floating point arrays, to 0.0 for arrays of doubles, to false for arrays of booleans, and, finally, to the null object reference for arrays of class type objects.

Note especially the last clause above: an array of class-type objects is always default-initialized so as to hold the null reference in each of its elements. So given a class

```
class User {
    String name;
    int age;
    public User( String nam, int yy ) {
        name = nam;
        age = yy;
    }
}
```

let's declare an array of User elements by, say,

```
User[] user_list = new User[10];
```

Each element of the user_list array will be default-initialized to hold the null reference.[10] After such an array is created, we are free to store in each element an object reference of type User, as in the following example for the i-th element of the array:

```
user_list[i] = new User( "Zaphod", 129 );
```

---

[10]A Java array of class type objects is analogous to a C++ array of pointers, especially when, at the time the array is created, each pointer in the array is initialized to 0, the null pointer.

The following example demonstrates the fact that when an array of class type objects is first created in Java, each element is default-initialized to a hold the null reference. The output produced by the print loop in `main` is just `null null null null` for the declared array of four `User` type objects. This fact is independent of whether or not the class possesses a no-arg constructor, or on the nature of the constructors actually provided for the class.

```
//ArrayBasic.java

class User {
    String name;
    int age;
    public User( String nam, int yy ) {
        name = nam;
        age = yy;
    }
}

class Test {
    public static void main( String[] args ) {
        User[] user_list = new User[ 4 ];
        for ( int i=0; i<user_list.length; i++ )
            System.out.print( user_list[ i ] + "  " );
                                    // null null null null

    }
}
```

7.10.1 A Java Array Is an Object

When you define a Java array by saying

```
class User { String name; int age; }

User[] userList =  new User[ 10 ];
```

you create a class type object of the user-defined type `User[]`. And suppose you extend the class `User` by defining two additional subclasses, `StudentUser` and `StaffUser`:

```
class StaffUser extends User {String staffStatus;}

class StudentUser extends User {String schoolEnrolled;}
```

and then define two new arrays for these new subclasses:

```
StaffUser[] staffList = new StaffUser[30];

StudentUser[] studentList = new StudentUser[200];
```

These definitions create the hierarchy of classes shown in Figure 7.1.

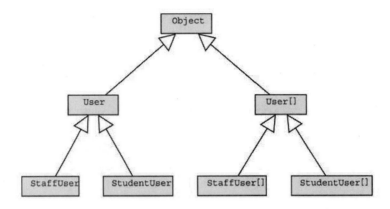

Fig. 7.1

Being class type objects, arrays exhibit polymorphism just like other class type objects in Java. (The concept of polymorphism, introduced earlier in Chapter 3, will be discussed more fully in Chapter 15.) What that implies is that an array reference can be used wherever an Object reference is called for. For example, an array of type StaffUser[] could be assigned to a variable of type Object and the value of that variable cast back to a variable of type StaffUser[]:

```
StaffUser[] staffList = new StaffUser[30];

Object ob = staffList;

StaffUser[] us = (StaffUser[]) ob;
```

Again, by virtue of being class type objects, one can associate data members with Java arrays. In fact, all Java arrays are supplied with the data member length that evaluates to the number of elements in the array. So with the above declarations,

```
int len = staffList.length;
```

would give a value of 30 to the variable len.

The discussion here should not be construed to imply that the arrays of only the user-defined types belong to the object hierarchy in Java. All arrays are objects in Java, including int[], double[], float[], and so on.

Unlike C and C++, a subscript used for indexing a Java array is range checked. An out-of-range access if attempted will throw an `IndexOutOfBoundsException` at run time.

7.10.2 java.lang.Arrays Class for Sorting, Searching, and so on

The `java.lang.Arrays` class has a number of very useful methods for array processing. The methods provided can be divided into the following four categories:

fill methods: These methods fill an entire array, or a portion thereof, with a given element value. Different overload definitions of `fill` are for arrays of different types; each primitive type has its own fill method. There are also fill methods for arrays of `Object` type. For the two-argument versions of these methods, the first argument is the array that needs to be filled, and the second argument the element value for the fill. For the four-argument versions, the first argument is the array to be filled, the second argument the beginning index where the filling is to start, the third argument one past the ending index, and the last argument the element value for the fill.

binary search methods: These methods search for a given element value in an array. Different overload definitions of the method `binarySearch` are for arrays of different types. Each primitive type has its own `binarySearch` methods; there are also `binarySearch` methods for arrays of `Object` type.

sort methods: These methods are for sorting arrays of different types. The sort methods for the arrays of primitive types are based on a tuned quicksort algorithm described by Bentley and McIlroy [3]. For an array of N elements, this algorithm sorts with a computational complexity of $O(Nlog(N))$ on most data sets on which a regular implementation of quicksort would work with N^2 performance. The sort methods for arrays of `Object` type are based on the mergesort algorithm. An important issue related to the sorting of arrays of class-type objects is whether the object that are deemed to be equal according to the comparison criterion used for sorting will maintain their respective positions in the sorted list. Algorithms that do not alter the relative positioning of equal elements are called `stable`.[11] Merge sort guarantees stability, with a guaranteed computational complexity of $O(Nlog(N))$.

In addition, `java.util.Arrays` class also comes with a special method, `asList`, that returns a `List` composed of the array elements. This method can be used as a bridge between array-based and collection-based methods. Any changes made to the `List` constructed in this manner are reflected in the underlying array.

---

[11]See Chapter 5 for further discussion on and for an example of stable sorting.

The following program illustrates the `fill` and the `binarySearch` methods. The example shows these methods for only a couple of the primitive types. But note that these two methods are available for all primitive types and for the `Object` type.

```java
//ArraysFill.java

import java.util.*;

class Test {
    public static void main( String[] args ) {

        int[] intArr = new int[4];
        Arrays.fill( intArr, 99 );                           //(A)
        for ( int i=0; i<intArr.length; i++ )
            System.out.print( intArr[ i ] + " " );   // 99 99 99 99
        System.out.println();

        double[] dbArr = new double[4];
        Arrays.fill( dbArr, 2, 3, 9.9 );                     //(B)
        for ( int i=0; i<dbArr.length; i++ )
            System.out.print( dbArr[ i ] + " " );    // 0.0 0.0 9.9 0.0
        System.out.println();

        int pos = Arrays.binarySearch( dbArr, 9.9 );         //(C)
        System.out.println( pos );                  // 2
    }
}
```

We first declare, `intArr`, an `int` array of four elements. This array will be default-initialized to the integer 0. We then use the two-argument version of `Arrays.fill` in line (A) to fill the array with the integer 99. Next, we construct `dbArr`, a `double` array of four elements. This array is default-initialized to the number 0.0. In line (B) we invoke a four-argument version of `fill` to only partially fill the array with the number 9.9. Finally, we show in line (C) how `Arrays.binarySearch` can be invoked to search for the number 9.9 in the array `dbArr`.

The next example shows how useful it can be to convert an array into a `List`. The class `List` comes with a method called `shuffle` that randomizes the elements of a list; each element of the list is moved to a randomly chosen position in the list. In the program below, we use the `shuffle` method of `List` to construct an array of random numbers. In lines (A) and (B), the program fills an `Integer` array with `Integer` objects for a consecutive set of integers from 0 through 9, both inclusive. Line (C) then converts this array into a `List` object, on which is invoked the `shuffle` method in line (D). We convert the `List` object back into an array in line (E) by invoking the `toArray` method on the list. We finally print out the contents of the array in line

(F). As the reader can see, we have an array of random numbers. Note that since `Arrays.asList` can only be invoked on arrays of type `Object`, we must use the wrapper class `Integer` as shown.

```
//ArraysShuffle.java

import java.util.*;

class Test {
    public static void main( String[] args ) {

        Integer[] intArr2 = new Integer[10];                    //(A)

        for ( int i=0; i<intArr2.length; i++ )                  //(B)
            intArr2[i] = new Integer(i);

        List list = Arrays.asList( intArr2 );                   //(C)

        Collections.shuffle( list );                            //(D)

        Integer[] intArr3 = (Integer[]) list.toArray();         //(E)

        for ( int i=0; i<intArr2.length; i++ )                  //(F)
            System.out.print( intArr3[ i ].intValue() + " " );
                    // 9 8 5 1 3 4 7 2 6 0  (different with each run)
        System.out.println();
    }
}
```

7.11 SYMBOLIC CONSTANTS

In programming, it is common for the values of some of the objects, after they are initialized, to remain unchanged throughout the execution of the program. In C++, it is best to add `const` to the declaration of such objects. A `const` object is a read-only object. Thus you eliminate any possibility that the value of such an object might get inadvertently modified through a bug in the program. In Java, the effect is achieved by the type modifier `final`. Here are some examples for C++ :[12]

---

[12]Regarding the third example shown, note that the elements of a C++ array that is declared to be const can only be accessed by a const pointer. By the same token, the elements of a const container can only be accessed by a const iterator.

```
const int N = 100;

const double PI = 3.141592653587932385;

const int a[] = {0, 1, 2, 3};
```

and some examples for Java:

```
final int N = 100;

final double PI = 3.141592653587932385;

final int[] a = new int[] {0, 1, 2, 3};
```

None of these objects can be modified within the scope of their declarations. It should be obvious that since a const object cannot be assigned to, it *must* be initialized when it is first declared.

Unlike C++, Java does not insist that a variable declared to be final be also initialized at the same time. In other words, Java lets you declare a variable final in one statement and to then initialize it separately in a later statement. You are therefore allowed to do the following in Java:

```
final int N;
// ...
N = 1000;        // N cannot be changed hereafter
```

In C++, the modifier const can also be used for pointer types, but its meaning has to be treated with care. For example, if you say

```
const T* p;                                              //(A)
```

this says that p is a pointer to an object of type const T. Therefore, the object that p points to cannot be changed, although p itself could be. If we wanted the pointer itself to be const, we would declare

```
T* const p = new T( ....constructor args.... );          //(B)
```

To infer the correct meaning of such declarations, it can be helpful to read them from right to left. In this manner, you'd read the declaration at (A) as p *is a pointer to T that must remain* const and the one at (B) as *p is a* const *pointer to T*.

To illustrate further the distinction between the declarations at (A) and (B) above, the following syntax would not be acceptable to a C++ compiler:

```
T* const p;
p = new T( ...constructor arguments ....);     // ERROR
```

because a const pointer cannot be assigned to; it can only be initialized. The following syntax is also illegal, but for a different reason

```
const T* p;
p = new T(  ...constructor args....  );
*p =  T(  .... constructor args ....  );        // ERROR
```

Since p is now a pointer to a const object, by assigning to *p, you are trying to change the contents of the memory where that object resides. But that memory was previously declared to be read-only memory.

However, the following piece of code is legal:

```
const T* p;
const T* q;
p = new T(  ...constructor args....  );
q = p;
p =  new T(  .... constructor args ....  );
```

These statements are legal because both p and q are modifiable pointers (although the objects they point to are not modifiable).

7.12 MACROS IN C++

Macros are ubiquitous in C, but used much less often in C++ programs. Macros are created by the preprocessor directive #define. Here is an example from C:

```
#define ARRAY_SIZE 1000
```

This definition would cause the C pre-processor to replace every occurrence of the name ARRAY_SIZE to be replaced by the number 1000. And if someday there was a need to change ARRAY_SIZE, one would need to edit only one line in the program, the line where the macro ARRAY_SIZE is defined.

Notwithstanding the obvious usefulness of macros for creating program *constants*, they tend to reduce the performance of C++ software tools such as debuggers, profilers, cross-reference tools, and so on, and their use is discouraged by Stroustrup [54]. In C++, a constant such as ARRAY_SIZE would be created by using the const modifier in a declaration, as in

```
const int ARRAY_SIZE = 1000;
```

7.13 THE ENUMERATION TYPE IN C++

To recap the basic idea behind an enumeration, suppose we wish to declare variables of type weight and suppose that these variables will only take one of a small number of values. We can then define an enumeration in the following manner:

```
enum weight {light, medium, heavy, very_heavy};                    //(A)
```

The symbolic constants `light`, `medium`, `heavy`, and `very_heavy` represent symbolically the small number of different values we wish for a variable of type `weight` to possess. Now we can declare a variable to be of type `weight` by[13]

```
weight w;                                                          //(B)
w = heavy;
cout << w;                                                         //(C)
```

As the reader knows from his or her experience with C, while such enumerations can make the source code clearer to read, the compiler actually replaces the symbolic constants by integral values, known as the *enumerators*. The enumerators must be integer constants. Ordinarily, the enumerators will start at 0 for the first symbolic constant, 1 for the next, and so on. So the statement in line (C) above will actually display 2 on a terminal.

The following example shows the different ways in which an `enumeration` type can be used in C++: globally, inside a class definition, inside a function, and so on. The definition of the class X starts with a declaration of two enumeration types, one in line (A) for `weight` and the other in line (B) for simply declaring two symbolic constants `d1` and `d2` of particular integer values. After that we declare two data members for the class, x of type `int` and wx of type `weight`. This is followed by a constructor in line (C). The scope of the enumerations shown in lines (A) and (B) ends with the class definition. The class definition is followed by two more enumerations in global scope in lines (D) and (E).

```
//Enum.cc

#include <iostream>
using namespace std;

class X {
public:
    enum weight {light, medium, heavy, very_heavy};               //(A)
    enum {d1 = 3, d2 = 5};                                        //(B)
    int x;
```

---

[13]Contrast this with C, where, with the `enum` definition of line (A), you would use the following syntax for the declaration in line (B):

```
enum weight w;
```

That's because `weight` is *not* a type name in C. However, in C we can use a `typedef` to make `weight` a type name by

```
typedef enum {light, medium, heavy, very_heavy} weight;
```

and then we can declare w to be of type `weight` by

```
weight w;
```

```
    weight wx;
    X( int i, int j ) {x = i + d1; wx = (weight) (j + medium) ;}  //(C)
};

enum {c1=17, c2 =19};              //global                    //(D)

enum height {tall, very_tall};     //global                    //(E)

int main()
{
    X obj1(100, 200);                                          //(F)
    cout << obj1.x  << "  "        // 103                       //(G)
         << obj1.wx << endl;       // 201                       //(H)

    //  X obj2(100, light);        // ERROR                     //(I)

    int y = c1;                                                //(J)
    cout << y << endl;             // 17                        //(K)

    height h;                                                  //(L)
    h = tall;                                                  //(M)
    cout << h << endl;             // 0                         //(N)

    return 0;
}
```

In main, we invoke X's constructor with two arguments, 100 and 200, in line (F). The interesting thing about the object thus constructed is that the value printed out for the data member wx is 201, as shown in line (H). But this value does not correspond to any of the enumerators for the small number of permissible symbolic constants declared for the weight type in line (A). In general, an enumeration type can acquire an integer value that may not be any of the enumerators listed in or implied by the enumeration definition.

The constructor invocation in the commented out line (I) results in a compile-time error since the symbolic constant light in not in scope in main(). As we mentioned before, the symbolic constants introduced via the two enumerations in lines (A) and (B) are not in scope outside the definition of the class.

On the other hand, the statements in lines (J) and (L) that involve the symbolic constants c1 and h are legal since these symbolic constants were introduced through the enumerations defined in global scope in lines (D) and (E).

We will now show how enumerations can prove useful in object-oriented programming. Let's say we want to define a class Student with data members for designating what department the student is enrolled in, and what the status of the student is (in the sense of a student being full-time, part-time, and so on). In other words, the Student class will have data members whose values will be symbolic. We can accomplish this by declaring the following enumerations:

```
enum Status { FullTime,
              PartTime,
              Exchange,
              StatusUnknown };

enum School { Engineering,
              Mathematics,
              Physics,
              Arts,
              Chemistry,
              SchoolUnknown };
```

This would allow us to endow the class `Student` with data members of type `Status` and `School`. It would also allow us to declare a variable of type `Status` and `School` by statements like

```
Status st = PartTime;
```

But note that the compiler will replace the symbolic constant `PartTime` by some integer, as mentioned previously. So if at some point later we said

```
cout << st;
```

we will see some integer printed out on the screen (1 in this case). What we'd really like to see is the symbolic value of the variable `st` printed out. This can be accomplished by defining a label array at the same time an enumeration is created:

```
enum Status { FullTime,
              PartTime,
              Exchange,
              StatusUnknown };

static const string statusLabels[] = { "full-time",
                                       "part-time",
                                       "exchange",
                                       "unknown" };
```

Now if we say

```
Status st = PartTime;
cout << statusLabels[ st ];
```

the output command will cause the symbol `part-time` to be printed out on the screen. If desired, we could have the string literals in the `statusLabels` array to correspond exactly to the identifiers used in the enumerations.

The following program shows the use of the enumeration types as data members of a class and how a declaration of an array of labels corresponding to the symbolic constants of an enumeration can be used for a user-friendly output.

```cpp
//EnumWithLabelArray.cc

#include <string>

enum Status { FullTime,
              PartTime,
              Exchange,
              StatusUnknown };

static const string statusLabels[] = { "full-time",
                                       "part-time",
                                       "exchange",
                                       "unknown"
};

enum School { Accounting,
              Business,
              Engineering,
              Mathematics,
              Physics,
              Arts,
              Chemistry,
              SchoolUnknown
};

static const string SchoolLabels[] = { "Accounting",
                                       "Business",
                                       "Engineering",
                                       "Mathematics",
                                       "Physics",
                                       "Arts",
                                       "Chemistry",
                                       "unknown"
};

class Student {
    string name;
    Status status;
    School school;
public:
    Student( string nam, Status st, School sch)
      : name( nam ), status( st ), school( sch ) {}
```

```
    string getName() const { return name; }

    void print() const {
        cout << getName()
            << " is a "
            << statusLabels[ (int) status ]
            << " student in the school of "
            << SchoolLabels[ (int) school ] << endl;
    }
};

int main()
{
    Student amy( "Amy", FullTime, Arts );
    amy.print();
    retrun 0;
}
```

This program produces the output:

```
Amy is a full-time student in the department of Arts
```

7.14 CREDITS AND SUGGESTIONS FOR FURTHER READING

The information in Section 7.10.2 regarding the computational efficiency of the Bentley and McIlroy [3] algorithm for sorting was taken from [33]. The example code shown in the program EnumWithLabelArray.cc was patterned after Dattatri's [16] examples of C++ code in his discussion on multiple inheritance in C++.

7.15 HOMEWORK

1. Why does this C++ program not compile?

```
class X {
    int i;
public:
    X( int ii ) { i = ii; }
};

int main() { X xarray[10]; }
```

2. Is this C++ program legal?

```
class X {
    int i;
 };

 int main() { X xarray[10]; }
```

3. The class X does not possess a no-arg constructor, either user-defined or system-supplied. Nonetheless, main declares a vector as shown. Will this C++ program compile?

```
#include <vector>
using namespace std;

class X {
    int i;
public:
    X( int ii ) { i = ii; }
};

int main() { vector<X> xvec; }
```

4. This C++ program does not compile. Why?

```
#include <vector>
using namespace std;

class X {
    int i;
public:
    X( int ii ) { i = ii; }
};

int main() { vector<X> xvec(100); }
```

5. Will C++ this program compile and execute?

```
#include <vector>
using namespace std;

class X { int i; };

int main() { vector<X> xvec; }
```

6. Will this C++ program compile? If it does compile, will it do what the programmer mostly likely wanted it to do?

```
#include <string>
using namespace std;

class User {
    string name;
};

class UserGroup {
    User chief;
    User uList[10];
};

int main() { UserGroup ug(); }
```

7. What is the output of this C++ program?

```
#include <iostream>
#include <string>
using namespace std;

class User {
public:
    string name;
};

class UserGroup {
public:
    User chief;
    User uList[10];
};

int main()
{
    UserGroup ug;
    cout << ug.chief.name;
    cout << ug.uList[0].name;
}
```

8. It was mentioned in Section 7.2 that when a programmer does not provide a class with any constructors, the class does not get a system-supplied default no-arg constructor if it has a const data member. In the following program,

the class Y has not been provided with any constructors at all and it has a const data member. Class X has been provided with a no-arg constructor as shown. The program compiles and runs without errors. Why?

```
#include <iostream>
using namespace std;

class Y {
public:
    const int yval;
};

class X {
public:
    Y y;
    int xval;
    X() {}
};

int main() {
    X x;
    cout<<x.y.yval<<endl;
    return 0;
}
```

8

Object Reference and Memory Allocation

If we had to choose one word on which we could bestow the honor of being the source of the greatest confusion between C++ and Java, that word would be "reference". An object reference in C++ does not at all mean the same thing as an object reference in Java. In C++, the following phrase makes sense: "A variable serves as a reference for a *previously* created object." On the other hand, the following phrase is more appropriate for Java: "A variable holds a reference for a class-type object." On the face of it, the two phrases sound about the same; yet they have very different meanings. When a variable in Java holds a reference to a newly created object, it's like a pointer in C++ holding the memory address of an object. And when a variable in C++ serves as a reference for a previously created object, the variable becomes an alias for that object. The goal of this chapter is to clarify these usages of the word "reference" in C++ and Java. This chapter will also address the issues of memory allocation and deallocation, and the definition of structures in C++.

8.1 OBJECT REFERENCE IN C++

An object reference in C++ is merely an alternative name for an object or a variable. In C++, the notation

```
T&
```

means a reference for an object of type T. For example, we could say

```
int i = 2;
int& r = i;
```

With the second declaration, the variable r is a reference for the variable i; r is simply another name for the variable i. So if we say

```
r = 3;
```

we are also causing the value of i to become 3. You might think of r as serving as an alias for i. If you apply the address operator '&' to r, you will get the address of i. That is,

```
int* q = &r;
```

will cause q to point to i. Now if we declare

```
int* p = &i;
```

the pointers p and q would both point to exactly the same location in the memory. And if we incremented r by

```
r++;
```

we would actually be incrementing i and achieving i++. Don't forget that, on the basis of the above discussion, if we want to obtain a pointer to an object that is referenced by the identifier r, all we have to do is to find[1]

```
&r;
```

The following declaration is an error:

```
int& r = 100;          // WRONG
```

That's because the initializer for a T& type must be an object of type T whose address can be ascertained. The constant 100 has no address associated with it. This constraint does not apply to a reference of const T& type. For example, it would be legal to say

```
const int& r = 100;
```

You *cannot* change the object of a reference. Here is an example:

```
int i = 3;
int j = 100;
int& r = i;
r++;                   // i is now 4
```

---

[1] Some beginning programmers might say that maybe an analogy could be drawn between a C++ object reference and a pointer. They might say r serves as some sort of a pointer to i. This analogy breaks down immediately when you realize that the ostensibly dereferencing operation *r is illegal because r is NOT a pointer.

```
r = j;                      // i is now 100
r++;                        // i is now 101
```

With these declarations, r remains a reference to i no matter what happens subsequently.

You can even have a reference for a pointer type, as the following example illustrates:

```
int i = 3;
int* p = &i;
int*& q = p;                // q serves as a reference for pointer p
cout << *q;                 // will output 3
*q = 100;                   // i is now 100
cout << *p;                 // will output 100
cout << i;                  // will output 100
```

While our discussion above used examples involving only the primitive types in C++, exactly the same considerations apply to class-type objects, as we demonstrate in the following C++ program:

```
//ReferenceClassType.cc

#include <iostream>
#include <string>
using namespace std;

class User {
public:
    string name;
    int age;
    User( string nam, int a ) { name = nam; age = a; }
};

int main()
{
    User  u1( "Melinda", 87 );                      //(A)
    User* u2 = new User( "Belinda", 129 );          //(B)
    User& u3 = u1;                                  //(C)
    const User& u4 = User( "Tralinda", 187 );       //(D)

    cout <<  u1.name << endl;        // Melinda      //(E)
    cout <<  u2->name << endl;       // Belinda
    cout <<  u3.name << endl;        // Melinda      //(F)
    cout <<  u4.name << endl;        // Tralinda

    User* p = &u1;                                  //(G)
    User* q = &u3;                                  //(H)
```

```
    cout << p->name << endl;                    // Melinda        //(I)
    cout << q->name << endl;                    // Melinda        //(J)

    return 0;
}
```

Lines (A) through (D) of the program define four different kinds of variables. The variable u1 gives us direct access to a new User whose name is Melinda. The variable u2 is a pointer to a new User of name Belinda. The variable u3 is a reference for the object u1. And, finally, u4 is a const reference to a User object with name Tralinda.[2] In accordance with our earlier discussion, u3 serves as an alias for u1. Therefore, the output statements in lines (E) and (F) yield the same answer — Melinda. Also, the two declarations for the pointers p and q in lines (G) and (H), respectively, yield the memory address of the same object — the User with name Melinda — as borne out by the output in lines (I) and (J).

8.2 OBJECT REFERENCE IN JAVA

While a class-type object in C++ can be accessed directly, or via a pointer, or via a reference, in Java there is only one mode of accessing non-primitive objects — by reference. But the concept "reference" in Java does not have the same meaning as "reference" in C++.

While a C++ reference is simply another name for an object that was created previously, a Java reference is really more like a pointer, albeit one that cannot be dereferenced and that cannot be subject to any pointer arithmetic.

Let's say that with a Java class User defined as

```
class User {
    private String name;
    private int age;
    public User( String nam, int a ) { name = nam; age = a; }
}
```

---

[2]Note that for u4 you would get either a compiler warning or a compiler error if you declared

```
    User& u4 = User( "Tralinda", 187 );
```

without the const. It's for the same reason that the declaration "int& r = 100;" is an error, as pointed out previously. The initializer for a variable that's to serve as a reference must be an object whose memory address can be ascertained. That the object on the right above is not something whose address can be ascertained is made clear by the fact that the following statement is unacceptable to the compiler

```
    User* p = &User( "Tralinda", 187 );   // WRONG
```

we declare a variable u as follows:

```
User u = new User( "Orpheus", 109 );
```

With a declaration and initialization such as this, in Java we say that u is *holding a reference* to an object of type User. The C++ analogy here would be

```
User* p = new User( "Orpheus", 109 );
```

which would cause p to *hold* a memory address that points to an object of type User.

8.3 MEMORY ALLOCATION IN C++

As mentioned previously, the operator new allocates memory on the heap in C++, as in the following statement:

```
string* str = new string( "hello" );
```

or in the following statement:

```
int* p = new int[500];
```

While visually the operator new looks the same in the two statements above, in the second case we are actually invoking the operator new[] since we are requesting memory for an array.[3] In both cases, though, you are requesting heap space for the objects constructed.

The operator new actually invokes the following special memory allocation *function*:

```
void* operator new( size_t size );                          //(A)
```

and the operator new[] the following function

```
void* operator new[](size_t size );                         //(B)
```

For the case of appropriating memory for a single object, the operator new does the following three things

1. The operator new first figures out the size of the object to be constructed and then supplies it as an argument to the memory allocation function of line (A).

---

[3]The commonly seen declaration for an array, as in

```
int data[500];
```

does not allocate memory on the heap, meaning that it does not allocate memory that can later be deallocated under program control. To allocate memory that a programmer can deallocate at will, you must use the operators new and new[].

2. The operator `new` then invokes the memory allocation function of line (A).

3. Lastly, the operator `new` casts the `void*` returned by the function of line (A) to the pointer type for the object constructed.

The operator `new[]` goes through the same three steps for the case of arrays, except that now the operator must figure out the memory needed by the entire array before invoking the memory allocation function of line (B).

Memory is deallocated by using the `delete` operator for the case of a single object and the `delete[]` operator for the case of arrays, as in the following examples:

```
string* str = new string(buffer);
delete str;

int* p = new int[1000];
delete[] p;
```

It is critical to bear in mind that after such memory deallocation, the pointers `str` and p are still pointing to the original locations in memory. If a pointer left in such a state is subsequently dereferenced, a program could crash.

The operators `delete` and `delete[]` actually invoke the following memory deallocation functions:

```
void operator delete( void* );

void operator delete[]( void* );
```

In the absence of any automatic garbage collection,[4] for every call to `new` there must exist somewhere in the code a call to `delete` and for every call to `new[]` there must exist somewhere later a call to `delete[]`. Unlike Java, C++ does not come with any guaranteed way for cleaning out unreferenced objects.

8.4   MEMORY ALLOCATION IN JAVA

All objects in Java, including arrays, are created by using the operator `new`. This operator constructs an object of a given class and returns a reference to it. For example, if we first define a `User` class by

```
class User {
    private String name;
    private int age;
```

---

[4]By using add-on libraries, it is possible to carry out automatic garbage collection in C++ also. See for example the references [4, 5].

```
    public User( String nam, int a ) { name = nam; age = a; }
}
```

we could then a create an object of type `User` by

```
User u = new User( ''Zygot'', 38 );
```

An array of, say, 100 `User`s would be created by[5]

```
User[] uAarr = new User[ 100 ];
```

and an array of a primitive type, say `int`s, would be created by

```
int[] arr = new int[ 100 ];
```

As was the case with C++, memory allocated for new objects created in this manner comes from a part of the system memory known as the heap.

Because of automatic garbage collection, Java does not need a `delete`-like operator to free up the memory occupied by objects that are no longer referenced. So in the following code fragment

```
User u = new User( ''Zygot'', 38 );              //(A)
u = null;                                         //(B)

User[] uAarr = new User[ 100 ];                   //(C)

//code for assigning User references
//to the individual elements of the
//array uArr

uArr = new User[500];                             //(D)
```

after the reference held by u is changed to `null` in line (B), there would not exist a variable holding a reference to the object created in (A). Similarly, after the assignment in line (D), there would not exist a variable holding a reference to the array object created in line (C). (We are assuming in both cases that no other variables in the rest of the program are holding references to the objects created in (A) and (C).) Such objects are automatically scooped up by the garbage collector and the memory occupied by them freed up. [6]

Garbage collection in Java was introduced briefly in Chapter 3; the topic is presented more fully in Chapter 11.

---

[5]Arrays in Java are discussed in greater detail in Chapter 7.

[6]Additionally, all of the `User` objects to which the array elements brought into existence in line (C) are holding references to will also become eligible for garbage collection, assuming that no other variables are holding references to those objects.

8.5   STRUCTURES IN C++

Simple structures in C++ look very much like structures in C. For example, we could declare User to be a C++ structure by

```
struct User {                                            //(A)
    string name;
    int age;
};
```

In C, the identifier User is called a structure tag that can be used to declare a variable, say, u1, to be of type struct User by

```
struct User u1;
```

However, in C++, User is a new type name directly. And we can say

```
User u1, u2;
```

if we wish to declare the variables u1 and u2 to be of type User.

A structure in C++ can be thought of as a light-weight C++ class. We can use the dot (.) or the member-access operator (->) to access the members of a structure, as in

```
void f() {                                               //(B)
    User u;
    u.name = "Orpheus";
    u.age = 89;

    User* p = new User();
    p->name = "Ophelia";
    p->age = 21;
}
```

This function first creates a new user, u, whose name is Orpheus and age 89, the rest of the members, if any, remaining uninitialized. Next, the function creates another User with the name and the age fields initialized to Ophelia and 21, respectively.

One can even embed functions inside the definition of a C++ structure. We could expand the definition of the User structure in line (A) above and include a print() function in it:

```
struct User {
    string name;
    int age;
    void print() {
        cout << "User " << name << " is of age " << age << endl;
    }
};
```

Now suppose u is a `User`. We can invoke its print method by

```
u.print();
```

We can even engage in data hiding by declaring private some of the members of a structure. The default access privilege of a structure member is public, which is the opposite of what it is for a class. In the following example, we have declared the two data members to be private. Of course, with private data members, we'd also need to provide the structure with a constructor, as in line (C) below:

```
struct User {
private:
    string name;
    int age;
public:
    //constructor:
    User( string s1, int yy ) { name = s1; age = yy; }          //(C)

    void print() {
        cout << "User " << name << " is of age " << age << endl;
    }
};
```

With a constructor provided in this manner, we can use the same syntax as with classes for constructing objects from a C++ structure:

```
User u( "Zaphod", 27 );

User* p = new User( "Beeblebrox", 16 );
```

The following example shows a particularly quick way to initialize a small array of structures.

```
//StructInit.cc

#include <iostream>
using namespace std;

struct User {
    char* name;
    int age;
    short rank;
};

void print( User*, int );

int main()
{
```

```
    User usr_list[] = {                                          //(A)
        "Bigshot, I. R.    ",     39,     1,
        "Allears, U. B,    ",     29,     100,
        "Moonstruck, H. I.",      58,     45
    };

    int size = sizeof( usr_list ) / sizeof( usr_list[0] );
    print( usr_list, size );

    return 0;
}


void print( User* up, int n ) {
    for ( int i=0; i < n; i++ )
        cout << up[i].name << '\t' << up[i].age
            << '\t' << up[i].rank << '\n';
}
```

The initializer provided to the array declaration in line (A) consists simply of a sequence of comma-separated values for each data member for all the elements of the array. The compiler automatically figures out the size of the array — in this case 3.

8.6 HOMEWORK

1. How many times will the destructor of class X be invoked as the variables go out of scope when the flow of execution hits the right brace of main in the following C++ program? Note that main consists of four groupings of statements: the 'A' grouping, the 'B' grouping, the 'C' grouping, and the 'D' grouping. In each grouping, the first statement constructs a new object, with the other statements creating references to the previously created objects or references. So you need to ask yourself that as the variables xobj1, xobj2, and xobj3 from the 'A' grouping go out of scope, how many times will X's destructor be invoked. And so on for the other three groupings.

```
//Reference.cc

#include <iostream>
using namespace std;

class X {
    int n;
public:
```

```
        X( int nn ) : n(nn) {}
        ~X() {
            cout << "destructor invoked for X obj with n= " << n
                << endl;
        }
    };


    int main() {
        X xobj1( 100 );                                    //(A1)
        X& xobj2 = xobj1;                                  //(A2)
        X& xobj3 = xobj2;                                  //(A3)

        const X& xobj4 = X(200);                           //(B1)
        const X& xobj5 = xobj4;                            //(B2)
        const X& xobj6 = xobj5;                            //(B3)

        X* p = new X(300);                                 //(C1)
        X*& q = p;                                         //(C2)
        X*& r = q;                                         //(C3)
        delete r;                                          //(C4)

        const X* s = new X(400);                           //(D1)
        const X*& t = s;                                   //(D2)
        const X*& u = t;                                   //(D3)
        delete u;                                          //(D4)

        return 0;
    }
```

2. Note carefully the difference between the `main` of the program in the previous problem and the `main` below. The statements that invoke the `delete` operator appear to be at odd locations — look at the statements in lines (C2) and (D2). The new `main` also includes in lines (E1) and (E2) additional statements involving a `const` pointer. Now answer the following questions:

   (a) Will this program compile?

   (b) Assuming this program compiles, are there any obvious memory leaks in the program? Is the destruction of the object constructed in line (E1) an issue from the standpoint of a memory leak?

   (c) Assuming that this program compiles and runs to completion, how many times will the destructor of the class X be invoked?

```
//Reference2.cc

#include <iostream>
using namespace std;

class X {
    int n;
public:
    X( int nn ) : n(nn) {}
    ~X() {
        cout << "destructor invoked for X obj with n= " << n
            << endl;
    }
};


int main() {
    X xobj1( 100 );                                 //(A1)
    X& xobj2 = xobj1;                               //(A2)
    X& xobj3 = xobj2;                               //(A3)

    const X& xobj5 = X(200);                        //(B1)
    const X& xobj6 = xobj5;                         //(B2)
    const X& xobj7 = xobj6;                         //(B3)

    X* p = new X(300);                              //(C1)
    delete p;                                       //(C2)
    X*& q = p;                                      //(C3)
    X*& r = q;                                      //(C4)

    const X* s = new X(400);                        //(D1)
    delete s;                                       //(D2)
    const X*& t = s;                                //(D3)
    const X*& u = t;                                //(D4)

    X* const w = new X(500);                        //(E1)
    *w = X(600);                                    //(E2)

    return 0;
}
```

3. Numerically intensive applications often require extensive memory allocation and deallocation. As an exercise that is somewhat numerically intensive, write a C++ program that extracts the numerical information contained in a JPEG image file. Note that this exercise is not about decoding a JPEG image, but about allocating (and, when so needed, deallocating) the memory needed for an array representation of the data generated by a publically available decoding function such as djpeg. With appropriate flags, a function such as djpeg can convert an encoded JPEG image into a PPM file in which each image pixel is represented by three consecutive bytes for the three RGB components of color at that pixel. Each byte represents the numerical value of a color component as an unsigned integer between 0 and 255. The djpeg function also deposits at the top of the PPM file a header that contains information about the height of the image, its width, and so on. More specifically, the format of a PPM file is as follows, where the specific numbers shown refer to a particular image

```
comment lines that start with the character #

the label P6 for color image and P5 for a
        black and white image

579 768 for specifying the image width and
        the height in pixels

255 for the number of quantization levels
        for each color

The rest of the data in the file consists of
        3 * width * height bytes.  Each pixel in
        the image is represented by three
        consecutive bytes, the first for Red,
        the second for Green, and the third for
        Blue.
```

Your program must read this header and determine whether the image is color or just black and white. Your program must then extract information about the height and the width of the image and the number of quantization levels for each color. Your program must also include a filter function that allows you do simple pixel manipulation (such as subtracting adjacent pixels to enhance edges). Finally, your program should invoke another publically available function, such as cpeg for converting the processed PPM file back into an output JPEG image.

Your program should be in the form of a class called JpegToData with the following data members:

```
int width

int height
```

```
int quantLevels

string colorLabel

int* pixelArray

int* resultArray
```

where `width` is the width of the image, `height` the height of the image, `quantLevels` the number of quantization levels for each of the colors, `pixelArray` the array of integers corresponding to the pixels of the JPEG image, and `resultArray` the array obtained by applying the filter to the contents of `pixelArray`. You need to provide the `JpegToData` class with at least the following methods:

```
void imageFilter()

void toJpeg()
```

The `imageFilter` method when applied to an object of type `JpegToData` numerically processes the `pixelArray` with some sort of a filter function and puts the result in `resultArray`. The `toJpeg` method creates a JPEG image out of the contents of `resultArray` by using the `cjpeg` function.

Suggestions:

For executing the "djpeg" and "cjpeg" commands in C++, you'd need to invoke the `system` command as in

```
system( command_string_as_a_C_style_string );
```

In addition, your C++ program will most likely use the `get()` or `get(ch)`, and `peek()` functions defined for the input stream objects (see Section 6.8 of Chapter 6) in order to extract the information from the PPM file, as in the following snippets of code:

```
ifstream in( "temp.ppm" );

// for getting rid of the comment block
if ( '#' == in.peek() )
    while( '\n' != in.get() )
        ;

in >> colorLabel;
in >> width;
....
....

int i = 0;
```

```
unsigned char pix;
while ( in.get( pix ) )
    pixelArray[ i++ ] = pix;

.....
```

and the put(ch) method defined for the file output stream for writing the pixels back into an output PPM file:

```
ofstream out( "temp_out.ppm" );
//....
int* ptr = resultArray;
for ( int i = 0; i < 3 * wideth * height; i++ )
    out.put( (unsigned char) *ptr++ );
// ...
```

4. Do the same as in the previous problem but for Java. (The reader should note that Java comes with a class java.awt.image.BufferedImage class that gives you access to the numerical data for the pixels in an image.)

9

Functions and Methods

The main goal of this chapter is to explain how arguments are passed to functions in C++ and Java. While C++ gives us three different options — pass by value, pass by pointer, and pass by reference — Java uses only pass by value.

But for class type arguments, *pass by value* in C++ does not mean the same thing as *pass by value* in Java. An important goal of this chapter is to explain the distinction between the two. To differentiate between the two "pass by value" modes, we say that in Java arguments are *passed by value of object reference*.

The other important topics discussed in this chapter include function overloading, overload resolution algorithms, function inlining in C++, const parameters in C++, final parameters in Java, and so on.

Recall from our earlier mention that when a function is defined as a member of a class, it is usually called a method, especially if polymorphism can be used with respect to that function. Strictly speaking, only *virtual* member functions in C++ should be called methods because only these functions exhibit polymorphic behavior. (Virtual member functions are discussed in Chapter 15.) In Java all functions are methods because functions cannot be defined outside the encapsulation provided by a class and because polymorphism works for all member functions.

In this chapter, we will use the term *function* generically, particularly in the context of C++. Whatever we say about a function in C++ will also apply to methods in C++. For Java, on the other hand, we will frequently use the term *method* when referring to functions.

9.1 FUNCTION DECLARATIONS

Because C++ compilers do not possess look-ahead capability, it is necessary to declare a function prior to its invocation. A C++ function may be declared either via its implementation code, or by just declaring its *prototype*. C++ function prototypes look like this:

```
double cos( double );
double cos( double x);
void f(int, int, int*);
void g();
```

A function prototype may contain parameter names for better program readability, as in the second example. However, the compiler simply ignores such names.

Java does not require that methods be declared prior to their invocation.

9.2 PASSING ARGUMENTS IN C++

When a function is called, each of its parameters is initialized with the corresponding argument in the function call, provided that their types agree after taking into account any allowable type conversions.[1]

There are three different ways to pass arguments to functions in C++:[2]

- pass by value
- pass by pointer
- pass by reference

To fully understand them — especially so from the standpoint of understanding the distinction between "pass by value" in C++ and "pass by value" in Java — it is best to consider the primitive types and the class types of arguments separately.

9.2.1 Passing a Primitive Type Argument by Value

The following example shows the case when an argument is passed by value in the function invocation in line (A). The called function, defined in line (B), makes a local

---

[1]Implicit type conversions for assignment of arguments to parameters in a function call are discussed in Chapter 7.

[2]Strictly speaking, the "pass by pointer" is just another version of "pass by value," the only difference being that the argument being passed is a memory address. Although that's technically true, it's still useful to make a distinction between the two modes of argument passing, because with "pass by pointer" a function can be made to do useful things to the argument object through side effects. On the other hand, "pass by value" does not allow for side effects to alter the state of the argument object.

copy of the argument object. Any changes to the local copy are not visible in the calling function, in this case `main`.

```
//PassPrimByValue.cc

#include <iostream>
using namespace std;

void g( int );

int main()
{
    int x = 100;
    g(x);                                       //(A)
    cout << x << endl;          // 100
    return 0;
}


void g( int y ) { y++; }                        //(B)
```

Therefore, the function `g(x)` cannot cause any change in the value of `x` in `main`. As a result, the value of `x` printed out by `cout` in `main` will remain 100.

9.2.2 Passing a Primitive Type Argument by Pointer

Passing arguments by pointer could be thought as merely a special case of passing arguments by value, since, after all, you are passing a copy of the memory address to the called function. However, through *side effect*, a called function can be made to bring about changes that are visible in the calling function.

Consider the following example that shows two called functions, `g( int* )` and `h( int* )`, one whose local changes are visible in `main` and one whose local changes are not.

```
//PassPrimByPointer.cc

#include <iostream>
using namespace std;

void g( int* );
void h( int* );

int main()
{
    int x = 100;
    int* p = &x;                                              //(A)
    g(p);                                                     //(B)
    cout << x << endl;      // 100                            //(C)
    h(p);                                                     //(D)
    cout << x << endl;      // 200 (changed by side effect)   //(E)
    return 0;
}

void g( int* q ) {                                           //(F)
    int y = 200;
    q = &y;                                                   //(G)
}

void h( int* q ) { *q = 200; }                              //(H)
```

When function g is called in line (B), the local variable q in line (F) is initialized to the same memory address that p is pointing to in line (A) of main. Inside g, we then change the value of q by making it point to another object in line (G). But that in no way changes what p is pointing to in main. It also does not change the contents of the memory location to which p is pointing. Therefore, the first cout in main in line (C) prints out the same value for x that was set earlier in the program.

On the other hand, the called function h in line (H) actually alters the contents of the memory location to which p is pointing in main. While the local variable q in line (H) is pointing to the same memory location as it was for the case of g, we are now actually altering the contents of that memory location. As a result, the second cout in main in line (E) will print out the new value for x — 200 — as set inside the function h. This is a classic example of a called function affecting change in the calling function through side effect.

9.2.3   Passing a Primitive Type Argument by Reference

In the following example, when the function g(int&) is called in line (A) of main, the local variable y in line (C) becomes a reference for the variable x in main. In other words, the object of the reference y in line (C) is the object x inside main. As the reader should know from our Chapter 8 discussion on the reference types in C++, this causes y to serve as merely another name — an alias — for x. So any changes made to y will be reflected in x.

```
//PassPrimByRef.cc

#include <iostream>
using namespace std;

void g( int& );

int main()
{
    int x = 100;
    g(x);                                                       //(A)
    cout << x << endl;          // 101                          //(B)
    return 0;
}

void g( int& y ) { y++; }                                       //(C)
```

Therefore, when g(x) is called in main, it brings about a change in the value of x itself through side effect. As a result, the cout in line (B) in main will print out 101.[3]

---

[3]It is interesting to realize that in this example we could not have written main as

```
    int main() { g( 100 ); }
```

With this main, the compiler will compile the program but only after warning of an anachronism. The compiler will complain about the following assignment involved in the matching of the argument with the parameter when g(int&) is called in main:

```
    int& y = 100;
```

As was mentioned in the previous chapter, such as assignment is an error. The initializer for a T& type must be an object of type T whose address can be ascertained. The constant 100 has no address associated with it. This constraint does not apply to a reference of const T& type. For example, it would be legal to say

```
    const int& y = 100;
```

So with the version of main shown in this footnote, we would need to rewrite g as

```
    void g( const int& y ) { y++; }
```

9.2.4 Passing a Class Type Argument by Value

Passing a class type argument by value works the same way as passing a primitive type argument. The called function makes a local copy of the argument elsewhere in the memory and any changes made to this local copy by the called function are not visible in the calling function.

In the following example, `main` first constructs a `User` object in line (A). The function call in line (B) passes the `User` object by value to the function in line (C). Because the argument is passed by value, what the local variable v in line (C) gets is a copy of the `User` object u of `main`.

```
//PassClassTypeByValue.cc

#include <iostream>
#include <string>
using namespace std;

class User {
public:
    string name;
    int age;
    User( string nam, int yy ) { name = nam; age = yy; }
};

void g( User );

int main()
{
    User u( "Xenon", 89 );                              //(A)
    g(u);                                               //(B)
    cout << u.name << "  " << u.age << endl;  // Xenon 89
    return 0;
}

void g( User v ) {                                      //(C)
    v.name = "Yukon";
    v.age = 200;
}
```

Therefore, the changes made inside the function g are confined to the copy of the User object it receives. The original object in `main` remains untouched. As a result, the `cout` statement in `main` prints out the `name` and the `age` fields as set when the object was first constructed.

9.2.5   Passing a Class Type Argument by Pointer

When an argument object is passed by pointer in a C++ program, any changes made to the object inside the called function can become visible in the calling function through side effect, as was the case with the primitive type in Section 9.2.2.

In the following example, we have two functions, g(User*) and h(User*); the former's changes are not visible inside main, whereas the latter's changes are.

```
//PassClassTypeByPointer.cc

#include <iostream>
#include <string>
using namespace std;

class User {
public:
    string name;
    int age;
    User( string nam, int yy ) { name = nam; age = yy; }
};

void g( User* );
void h( User* );

int main()
{
    User* p = new User( "Xeno", 89 );                        //(A)
    g( p );                                                  //(B)
    cout << p->name << " " << p->age << endl;    // Xeno 89
    h( p );                                                  //(C)
    cout << p->name << " " << p->age << endl;    // Yuki 200
    return 0;
}

void g( User* q ) {                                          //(D)
    q = new User( "Yuki", 200 );                             //(E)
}

void h( User* q ) {                                          //(F)
    q->name = "Yuki";                                        //(G)
    q->age = 200;                                            //(H)
}
```

The main first constructs a User object in line (A). When g is called in line (B), the address of the User object is passed to this function in line (D). But, inside g, the value of the local pointer q, set originally to point to the User object constructed in main, is redirected to point to a new User object in line (E). However, this redirection of q has no effect on where p is pointing in main. It also has no effect on the contents of the memory where p is pointing. Therefore, g cannot cause any change inside main. So the first cout statement in main prints out the originally set values of the data members of the User object.

By contrast, the function h(User*) called in line (C) of main changes through side effect the User object created previously in main. The local pointer q inside h in line (F) will point to the User object created in main. By altering in lines (G) and (H) the contents of the memory where q points, we change the object created in main. Therefore, the second cout statement in main prints out the new state of the object, as illustrated by the commented out portion of the line.

9.2.6 Passing a Class Type Argument by Reference

In the following example, the User object constructed in line (A) in main becomes the argument in the function call in line (B). The argument is passed by reference to the function in line (C). The local variable v in line (C) serves as a reference for the User object u in main. This makes the local variable v essentially an alias for the variable u in main. Therefore, the changes made to v in lines (D) and (E) are reflected in the state of the object u inside main.

```
//PassClassTypeByRef.cc

#include <iostream>
#include <string>
using namespace std;

class User {
public:
    string name;
    int age;
    User( string nam, int yy ) { name = nam; age = yy; }
};

void g( User& );

int main()
{
    User u( "Xenon", 89 );                                      //(A)
    g(u);                                                       //(B)
    cout << u.name << "   " << u.age << endl;  // Yukon 200
```

```
        return 0;
}

void g( User& v ) {                                          //(C)
    v.name = "Yukon";                                       //(D)
    v.age = 200;                                            //(E)
}
```

As a result, the `cout` statement in `main` will print out the state of the `User` object showing the changes made in the body of g.

9.3 PASSING ARGUMENTS IN JAVA

As was mentioned at the beginning of this chapter, Java gives you only one mode for passing arguments to methods — pass by value. For class type arguments, a more precise way to talk about this argument passing mode is to describe it as *pass by value of object reference*. To explain what that means, let's consider separately the two cases: passing primitive type arguments and passing class type arguments.

9.3.1 Passing a Primitive Type Argument by Value

The following example shows that there is no difference between how a primitive argument is passed by value in C++ and how it is passed (by value) in Java.

```
//PassPrimByValue.java

class Test {
    public static void main( String[] args )
    {
        int x = 100;                                       //(A)
        g(x);                                              //(B)
        System.out.println( x );       // outputs 100
    }

    static void g( int y ) { y++; }                        //(C)
}
```

As was true for the same case in C++, the change made to the local variable in line (C) in the body of the function g(int) is not visible in main. Therefore, the print statement in main will print out the value of x as set originally.

9.3.2 Passing a Class Type Argument by Value of Object Reference

As this example illustrates, passing a class type argument by value in Java is different from passing a class type argument by value in C++.

The example first creates a User object in line (A) of main of the Test class. The variable u, which holds a reference to the object constructed in line (A), is the argument of the function call in line (B).

```java
//PassClassTypeByValue.java

class User {
    String name;
    int age;
    User( String nam, int yy ) { name = nam; age = yy; }
};

class Test {
    public static void main( String[] args )
    {
        User u = new User( "Xeno", 89 );                    //(A)
        g(u);                                               //(B)
        System.out.println( u.name + "   " + u.age );    // Yuki 200
    }

    static void g( User v ) {                               //(C)
        v.name = "Yuki";                                    //(D)
        v.age = 200;                                        //(E)
    }
}
```

What the local variable v in line (C) gets is a *copy* of the object reference held by u in main. So we say that an argument is passed by value of object reference. Recall that a Java object reference can be thought of as a disguised pointer. So the situation here is similar to the case of passing a class type argument by pointer in C++.

For the example code shown above, since the object reference held by the local variable v inside g is a copy of the object reference held by u inside main, both u and v are pointing to the same block of memory that contains the User object created in line (A). Therefore, the changes made by g in lines (D) and (E) will alter the data members of the User object u of main. Hence, the print statement in main will display the state of the object as changed by g.

We said that the pass-argument-by-value-of-object-reference mode in Java is similar to the pass-argument-by-pointer mode in C++. However, a discerning reader might have also noticed a similarity between the above example for Java and the pass-argument-by-reference example for C++. In both cases, the changes brought about by the called function were visible in the calling function. So can we say the mode for argument passing in Java is similar to the pass-by-reference mode in C++? The answer is categorically a No.

We will now show that the argument passing mode in Java does not at all work like the pass-by-reference mode in C++. If the arguments were passed by reference in Java,[4] as opposed to by value, then the call to swap in line (C) of the Java program below would actually cause the object references held by the two arguments to get swapped. But that does not happen.

```java
//Swap.java

class User {
    String name;
    int age;
    User(String nm, int a) {name=nm; age=a;}
}

class Test {
    public static void main(String[] args)
    {
        User u1 = new User("Xeno", 95);             //(A)
        User u2 = new User("Yuki", 98);             //(B)
        swap( u1, u2 );                             //(C)
        System.out.println( u1.name );    // Xeno
        System.out.println( u2.name );    // Yuki
    }

    static void swap(User s, User t) {              //(D)
        User temp = s;
        s = t;
        t = temp;
    }
}
```

---

[4]In the manner that arguments are passed by reference in C++, that is by making a local variable in the called function an alias for the argument variable in the calling function.

This program simply does not swap the object references assigned to u1 and u2 in lines (A) and (B) above. The function call in line (C) passes the object references held by these two variables by value to the function in line (D). The local variable s acquires a copy of the object reference held by u1 and t gets a copy of the object reference held by u2. While it is true that the references held by s and t get locally swapped inside swap(), the object references held by u1 and u2 inside main() remain unchanged.

In contrast to this behavior of Java, let's consider a program in C++ where the arguments are passed by reference to a swap function:

```
//Swap.cc

#include <iostream>
#include <string>
using namespace std;

class User {
public:
    string name;
    int age;
    User(string nm, int a) {name=nm; age=a;}
};

void swap( User&, User& );

int main()
{
    User u1("Xeno", 95);                                //(A)
    User u2("Yuki", 98);                                //(B)
    swap( u1, u2 );                                     //(C)
    cout << u1.name  << endl;         // Yuki
    cout << u2.name  << endl;         // Xeno
    return 0;
}

void swap(User& s, User& t) {                           //(D)
    User temp = s;
    s = t;
    t = temp;
}
```

When the function swap() is called in line (C) above, the references s and t in line (D) become aliases for the objects u1 and u2 of main. When s and t get swapped in the function swap(), u1 and u2 will also get swapped. We should mention that the same result can also be achieved in C++ by passing pointer arguments if we dereference the pointers in the called function for a wholesale exchange of the contents of the memory pointed to by the pointers, as in lines (E), (F), and (G) in the program shown below:

```
//SwapWithPointer.cc

#include <iostream>
#include <string>
using namespace std;

class User {
public:
    string name;
    int age;
    User(string nm, int a) {name=nm; age=a;}
};

void swap( User*, User* );

int main()
{
    User u1("Xeno", 95);                            //(A)
    User u2("Yuki", 98);                            //(B)
    swap( &u1, &u2 );                               //(C)
    cout << u1.name  << endl;       // Yuki
    cout << u2.name  << endl;       // Xeno
    return 0;
}

void swap(User* s, User* t) {                       //(D)
    User temp = *s;                                 //(E)
    *s = *t;                                        //(F)
    *t = temp;                                      //(G)
}
```

To summarize the differences between C++ and Java with regard to the different argument passing modes for class-type arguments:

- To pass an argument by value in C++ means that the parameter of the called function is handed a copy of the argument object in the calling function.

- On the other hand, to pass an argument by value in Java means that the parameter of the called function is handed a copy of the object reference held by the argument.

- Said another way, in the pass-by-value mode in Java, the calling function hands the called function a copy of the object reference, but not a copy of the object itself. On the other hand, in the pass-by-value mode in C++, the calling function hands to the called function a copy of the object.

- To pass an argument by reference in C++ — not possible in Java — means that the reference parameter in the called function simply serves as an alias for the argument object in the calling function.

9.4 C++ FUNCTIONS RETURNING REFERENCE TYPES

This section addresses the following question: What exactly is returned by a function whose return has been specified as non-void? Is it a local object itself, or is it a *copy* of the local object? To illustrate this question with a simple example, suppose we have the situation depicted in the following program where main calls a function f in line (B), the function being defined in line (A):

```
//CopyOnReturn.cc

#include <iostream>
#include <string>
using namespace std;

class User {
public:
    string name;
    int age;
    User( string nam, int yy ) { name = nam; age = yy; }
};

User f( User usr ) { return usr; }                          //(A)

int main()
{
    User u( "Xino", 120 );
    User y = f( u );                                        //(B)
    cout << y.name << endl;          // Xino
    return 0;
}
```

The function f(User) in line (A) is passed an argument by value. Therefore, when this function is called by main in line (B), a copy of the object u will be constructed elsewhere in the memory and this copy will become the local object usr inside the function f. When f executes its return statement, we are faced with the question: Is f returning the local object usr or a copy of usr? Said another way, Is the User object y in `main` going to be the same as what was the local object `usr` inside `f` or a copy of that object?

In the code as written above, what the function `f` returns is a copy of the local object it is supposed to return. Therefore, the program will make a copy of the argument object when it invokes the function `f` and then another copy of that copy when it executes its return statement. That can amount to a lot of copying for large objects. We have already seen how this copying can be eliminated when passing an argument to a function — by using either a reference parameter or a pointer parameter. But what about "copy on return?" That copying can be eliminated by declaring the return type to be a reference, as we do in the following version of the above program:

```
//NoCopyOnReturn.cc

#include <iostream>
#include <string>
using namespace std;

class User {
public:
    string name;
    int age;
    User( string nam, int yy ) { name = nam; age = yy; }
};

User& f( User& usr ) { return usr; }                          //(A)

int main()
{
    User u( "Xino", 120 );
    User y = f( u );                                          //(B)
    cout << y.name << endl;          // Xino
    return 0;
}
```

In line (A), we have changed the parameter type and the return type to references. This suppresses the object copying involved in passing the argument to the function and in the function returning the object. When using a reference for a return type, *it is an error to return a reference to an object that is local to a function.* That should explain why we made the function parameter in line (A) a reference also.

In the program shown above, if we also wanted to guarantee that the object being passed to the function in line (A) would not get corrupted inside that function, we could use the following version of the program where the parameter in line (A) has now been declared to be a `const` reference. But, for reasons we will explain later, that makes it necessary for the return type to be a `const` reference also.

```
//ConstRefReturn.cc

#include <iostream>
#include <string>
using namespace std;

class User {
public:
    string name;
    int age;
    User( string nam, int yy ) { name = nam; age = yy; }
};

const User& f( const User& usr ) { return usr; }              //(A)

int main()
{
    User u( "Xino", 120 );
    User y = f( u );                                          //(B)
    cout  << y.name << endl;        // Xino
    return 0;
}
```

9.5 FUNCTION INLINING IN C++

Function inlining — an important part of the code optimization that can be carried out by modern compilers — involves replacing a function call with the body of the function in order to eliminate the overhead associated with the function call, with parameter passing, and with the passing of the return object. If so directed through appropriate command line options, a compiler will scan the source code for candidate functions suitable for inlining. These are usually small and frequently used functions with not too much branching.

In C++, all member functions that are defined within a class — as opposed to just being declared there through their prototypes — are by default assumed to be inline functions. And all member functions that are only declared inside a class definition but defined outside are by default assumed to be non-inline functions. However, if a programmer wishes for a member function that is defined outside a class to be considered as a candidate for inlining, the function must be explicitly declared to be *inline*.

In the following example, the function foo() is by default considered to be an inline function because it is defined inside the class definition.

```
class X {
    //
    void foo() {
        // body of function
    }
    void bar();
};
```

On the other hand, the function `bar()` is only declared inside the class definition. If we wanted this function to also be a candidate for inlining, its outside definition would have to include the keyword *inline*:

```
inline void X::bar() {
    // body of function
}
```

Member function declared inline must be included in the same file as the class definition for the inlining declaration to be effective.

Stand-alone functions can also be declared to be inline in the same manner. But note that the inline declaration, whether for class member functions or stand-alone functions, is only a recommendation to the compiler. Depending on its competence level, a compiler has the option of ignoring the recommendation, or implementing it only partially. To see how an inlining recommendation may be honored only partially, consider the case where a function `f1` calls a function `f2`, which in turn calls a function `f3`, all functions declared inline. A compiler may choose to only carry out inlining up to level 1, meaning that inside `f1` it will replace a call to `f2` by the body of `f2`, but inside `f2` it will leave the function call to `f3` unchanged.

9.6 STATIC VARIABLES IN C++

The word `static` has three meanings in C++, while it has only one meaning in Java.

One meaning of `static` refers to its use as a qualifier for the data members or the member functions of a class. When a data member or a member function is declared `static`, it becomes a *per class* member, as opposed to the more common *per object* member. This use of `static`, mentioned rather briefly in Chapter 3, will be discussed more fully in Chapter 11. This is also how `static` gets used in Java.

The second meaning of `static` in C++ concerns its use for limiting the scope of a global variable or a function to the file in which they are defined. A global identifier that is static has internal linkage only, meaning that it cannot be linked to from another file with an `extern` declaration. This use of `static`, more common in older C++ code, is now discouraged. In modern programming practice, nameless namespaces are used to achieve the same effect (see Chapter 3).

It is the third meaning of `static` in C++ that is the focus of this section — the storage duration of a local variable in a function. When a local variable in C++ is declared to be `static`, it is stored in memory that does *not* get deallocated between the different invocations of the function. Consider the following example:

```
//StaticStorage.cc

#include <iostream>
using namespace std;

void f() {
    static int m = 0;                                       //(A)
    int n = 0;
    cout << "m = " << m++ << ", and n = " << n++ << endl;   //(B)
}

int main()
{
    f();
    f();
    f();
    return 0;
}
```

This code produces the following output

```
m = 0, and n = 0
m = 1, and n = 0
m = 2, and n = 0
```

The function `f()` contains two variables, a `static` variable `m` and a regular variable `n`. Both these variables are initialized to 0 and, in line (B), both are incremented in the `cout` statement. However, since `m` is static, during each invocation of `f()` the variable `m` retains its value from the previous invocation. In other words, the variable `m` persists from invocation to invocation of the function `f()` even though it is not visible outside that function. This persistence of `m` is reflected in the output produced by the program. Note that the initialization statement in (A) is executed only during the first invocation of `f()`.

9.7 CONST **PARAMETER AND RETURN TYPE FOR C++ FUNCTIONS**

A function may be called either for its returned value or for its side effects. When a function is invoked for only its returned value, you want to make sure that the argument objects supplied to the function do not get inadvertently corrupted by the function through some unintended side effect. When an argument object is passed to a function by value, this is not a worry because what the function gets is a copy of the argument object. So in pass-argument-by-value, there is no way for a function to mess up the argument object.

But it is not always possible to use the pass-by-value mode for passing arguments to functions. For large objects, the copying entailed in pass-by-value may significantly degrade the performance of a program with respect to both time and space considerations.[5] So we must resort to the more efficient modes of passing arguments — pass by reference or pass by pointer. But now we must worry if the writer of a function will accidently corrupt the argument object. When a function is being used purely for its return value and when we cannot pass argument objects to such a function by value, we can use const to characterize the parameters corresponding to those argument objects.

Over the years, this use of const has emerged as a sort of programming convention that tells a human reader of the program that the corresponding argument in the function call will not be modified by the called function [54]. So while the following prototype carries no guarantees that the object for which the parameter will serve as a reference will not get modified by the function f,

```
User f( User& u ) {
    // code
    return u;
}
```

a guarantee to that effect is entailed by the following version of the function

```
User f( const User& u ) {
    // code
    return u;
}
```

The const object will be copied elsewhere in the memory when the return statement is executed. So it can be returned as a non-const object without problems.

If in the above example you also wanted to suppress the copying involved in constructing the returned object, you'd have to use the form

---

[5]Of course, in some cases we do not even have the option of passing an argument by value. For example, an array cannot be passed by value in C++.

```
const User& f( const User& u ) {
    // code
    return u;
}
```

If the function is simply returning a const object without copying it elsewhere in the memory, then the return type must also be const. For example, the following function will not compile

```
User& f( const User& u ) { return u; }        // WRONG
```

Because copying is prohibited when the return statement is executed in this example, the const qualifier cannot be stripped away. You need to declare const T& for the return type of a function if you want to suppress copying when returning an object of type const T.

Finally, when deciding whether or not to declare a parameter to be const, one needs to bear in mind that a const argument will not match a non-const reference parameter or a non-const pointer parameter. On the other hand, if a parameter is const, it can be used for both const and non-const arguments. For example, the following will code fragment is wrong:

```
void f( int& x ) {}              // non-const parameter

void g() {
    const int i = 100;
    f( i );                      // WRONG
}
```

whereas the following version of the function f works fine for both const and non-const arguments:

```
void f( const int& x ) {}        // const parameter

void g() {
    const int i = 100;
    f( i );                      // OK
    int j = 200;
    f( j );                      // OK
}
```

To construct a parallel example for pointer parameters, the following code fragment is wrong

```
void h( int* x ) {}              // non-const parameter

void g() {
    const int i = 100;
    const int* p = &i;
    h( p );                      // WRONG
}
```

whereas the following version of the function h works fine for both const and non-const pointers:

```
void h( const int* x ) {}           // const parameter

void g() {
    const int i = 100;
    const int* p = &i;
    h( p );                         // OK

    int j = 200;
    int* s = &j;
    h( s );                         // OK
}
```

9.8 FINAL **PARAMETERS FOR JAVA METHODS**

What const does for C++, final does for Java. But, for class type parameters, one has to exercise care and not push the analogy too far, as the following discussion shows.

When a parameter of a method in Java is declared to be final, its value cannot be changed inside the method. In the following example, it would be illegal to change the value of the variables x and u:

```
void g( final int x, final User u ) {
    x = 100;                        // WRONG
    u = new User();                 // WRONG
}
```

But for class type parameters there is a subtle but important difference between how the qualifier const works for a parameter in C++ and how final works in Java. While the following would be unacceptable in C++

```
void g( const User u ) {
    u.name = "Zodi";                // WRONG
}
```

Java would have no trouble with

```
void g( final User u ) {
    u.name = "Zodi";                // OK
}
```

The reason has to do with the fact that for C++, the variable u is the User object itself, which becomes immutable if u is const. On the other hand, for the Java case the variable u is holding an immutable reference to a User object, but the object itself remains mutable. So, if the variable u is final, the object reference held by u cannot be changed. But we are free to change the object itself.

The kinds of issues we raised in the previous section — issues arising from the fact that a const argument cannot be matched with a non-const reference or pointer parameter — do not arise in Java since all arguments are passed by value. When a function parameter in Java is final, it simply means that the value of that parameter cannot be changed inside the body of the function. But there is no problem with matching a non-final argument with a final parameter.

9.9 ARRAY ARGUMENTS

There is a big difference between C++ and Java in how array arguments are passed to functions. In C++, it is not possible to pass an array by value; an argument of type T[] is converted to a T* when passed to a function. Since only a pointer to the array is passed, the size of the array is not available to the called function. For C-style strings that is not a problem, since the size of the array of characters can be determined locally by looking for the null terminating character. For other arrays, however, it becomes necessary to use an additional argument for specifying the size of the array.

In Java, an array is passed to a function like any other object. As was mentioned earlier in Section 7.10, a Java array is a class type object.

9.10 FUNCTION OVERLOAD RESOLUTION IN C++

Stated simply, overloading a function name, a constructor name, or an operator symbol means being able to use the same name with a different number and/or types of arguments. In this section, we will discuss the overloading of function and constructor names in C++.

To see why overloading a constructor might be useful, suppose you define an Employee class with data members name, title, level, contactInfo, and so on, as shown below. For employees for whom the information is available for all the data members, you would want to provide a constructor that has parameters for all the data members. But if, say, the contact information was not currently available for a new employee, it would be convenient if you also provided a constructor that did not require this information. And, if most of the new employees are hired with the title "memberOfStaff", it would be a nice feature to make available a constructor that does not have a parameter for title for such employees. Considerations such as these could lead to a class design with multiple constructors as shown below:

```
class Employee {
    string name;
    string title;
    short level;
    string contactInfo;
public:
    //first constructor:
    Employee() {}

    //second constructor:
    Employee( string aName, string aTitle, short aLevel, string cInfo )
    {
        name = aName;
        title = aTitle;
        level = aLevel;
        contactInfo = cInfo;
    }

    //third constructor:
    Employee( string aName, string aTitle, short aLevel )
    {
        name = aName;
        title = aTitle;
        level = aLevel;
        contactInfo = "not available";
    }

    //fourth constructor:
    Employee( string aName, string aTitle )
    {
        name = aName;
        title = aTitle;
        level = 9;
        contactInfo = "not available";
    }

    //fifth constructor:
    Employee( string aName )
    {
        name = aName;
        title = "memberOfStaff";
        level = 9;
        contactInfo = "not available";
    }

    // more constructors if needed in the rest of the code
};
```

As an example illustrating the usefulness of overloading a function name, you could define a Student class with multiple versions of calculateTuition method, as shown below:

```
class Student {
  Name name;
  Date birthDate;
  bool inState;
  StudentStatus status;
  //.....
public:
  //....
  double calculateTuition( bool inStateStatus,
                           int numOfCourses,
                           StudentStatus aStatus);        //(A)
  double calculateTuition( bool inStateStatus,
                           StudentStatus aStatus);        //(B)
  double calculateTuition();                              //(C)
  // ....
};
```

The first function in line (A) could be used for part-time and temporary students whose fees are calculated on the basis of how many courses they register for, in addition to considerations such as their in-state residence status, and so on. The second version, in line (B), would be good for students carrying a full load where the number of courses is immaterial. And the last version, in line (C), would be useful for situations where someone wants to know the basic fee structure for attending a university during a given semester.

Having the compiler select the most appropriate constructor or the most appropriate function from amongst the choices available is straightforward when the number of parameters is different. But choosing the right constructor or the right function is not so straightforward if the different constructors and functions differ with respect to just the parameter types.

For example, let's say we have a set of math functions of the following prototypes, all functions calculating the same function but with different types of arguments:

```
int foo( int x, int y );              //(D)
double foo( double x, int y );        //(E)
int foo( int x, double y );           //(F)
```

Now let's say that we have the following function invocation in a computer program:

```
float u;
float v;
float w = foo( u, v );
```

Now it is not so straightforward to say which of the three choices in lines (D), (E), and (F) would be the right function to use for the invocation f(u,v). And, after we have specified a set of criteria for choosing the best applicable function, what if it turns out that we have more than one "best" function as a candidate, as seems to be the case with the above example? What should the compiler do then?

Given more than one function definition to choose from for a given function call, selecting the most appropriate function definition is called *overload resolution*. Overload resolution also refers to choosing the most applicable constructor if more than one choice is available.

Both C++ and Java compilers come equipped with algorithms for overload resolution. For overload resolution, a function is represented by its *signature*, which is the name of the function together with its parameter list specifying how many parameters and what type to expect for each parameter position. *It is important to bear in mind that the return type from a function or the type of exceptions thrown by a function do not contribute to the signature of a function and, therefore, do not play a role in overload resolution.*[6]

Overload resolution algorithms, in general, are based on the notion of the *specificity* of a match between the type of an argument in a function call and the type of the corresponding parameter in the function definition. When the two types are exactly the same, that is the most specific match one can hope to achieve. But when type conversions are required for matching, we can have matches at different levels of specificity. In the rest of this section, we will talk about these different levels of specificity in C++'s overload resolution.

Here are the different levels of specificity, reproduced from [54], with which the arguments in a function call can be matched with the corresponding parameters in a function definition in C++:

Specificity Level 1: In matching a single argument with the corresponding parameter, if the two types agree exactly or after trivial type conversion, we have the most specific match. Examples of trivial type conversions are array name to pointer, function name to pointer-to-function, and T to const T.

Specificity Level 2: If the type conversion between the argument type and the parameter type requires a *promotion*, we have a less specific match than the previous one. As defined in Section 6.7.1 of Chapter 6, a type conversion is a promotion if (a) the integral types stay integral; (b) the non-integral types stay non-integral; and (c) there is no loss of information.

Specificity Level 3: Matching takes place at a level of specificity lower than the previous one if it entails a *standard conversion*. As discussed earlier in Section

---

[6]That the return type of a function should play no role in overload resolution makes sense because functions are frequently invoked for just their side effect behavior and their return values ignored.

6.7.1 of Chapter 6, examples of standard conversions for the primitive types include int to double, double to int, and so on. For pointer types, standard conversion include T* to void*, int* to unsigned int*, and so on. And for class types in general, a conversion from Derived* to Base* is a standard conversion. The last conversion means that it is permissible to convert a pointer to an object of a derived class into a pointer of the base class type. The reader will recall that one special feature of object-oriented programming is polymorphism, which means that an object of a subclass type can always be considered to be an object of the superclass type (when manipulated through pointers and references in C++).

Specificity Level 4: A still lower level of specificity in matching takes place if it requires a user-defined type conversion. When a new class is defined, one can also specify what type conversions should be allowed to occur automatically for this class.[7]

Specificity Level 5: Match using the ellipsis ... in a function definition results in a least specific match. The reader will recall from C programming that an ellipsis at the end of the parameter list of a function allows an indefinite number of arguments to be matched to it.

Overload resolution chooses that function which supplies the most specific match. If more than one function is found to match at the highest possible level of specificity, an ambiguity is declared, resulting in a compile-time error.

Recall again that only the signature of a function is allowed to participate in the overload resolution algorithm. Since the return type and the types of exceptions thrown play no role in a signature, overload resolution does not depend on them. Overload resolution is also independent of the order in which the functions are declared.

Finally, functions declared in different scopes do not overload. Consider this adaptation of an example from [54] in which we have two functions of the same name, g(int) in line (C) and g(double) in line (D), with the prototype of the latter declared inside another function, f(), in line (A). Ordinarily, the function call in line (B) would cause the compiler to apply the overload resolution algorithm to the two definitions of g in lines (C) and (D). But since the version g(double) is declared inside the function f(), where it hides the function g(int) declared in the global scope, no overload resolution is needed. Of the two versions of g, g(double) is the only function in scope inside f().

---

[7]Automatic type conversions for user-defined classes is presented in Section 12.9 of Chapter 12.

```
//DiffScope.cc

#include<iostream>
using namespace std;

void f();
void g(int);

int main()
{
    f();
    return 0;
}

void f() {
    void g(double);  // function prototype declared inside f()    //(A)
    g( 1 );                                                       //(B)
}

void g( int x ) { cout << "g(int): x is " << x << endl; }         //(C)
void g( double x ) { cout << "g(double): x is " << x << endl; }   //(D)
```

The program produces the output:

```
from g(double): x is 1
```

9.11 FUNCTION OVERLOAD RESOLUTION IN JAVA

As in C++, overload resolution in Java is based on the notion of match specificity. If there is more than one method whose parameters match the arguments in a function call, the compiler selects that method which is maximally specific. If more than one method is found to be maximally specific, the compiler declares ambiguity and puts out a compile-time error message to that effect.

So while the overall approach remains the same as described in the last section for C++, the algorithmic details are different for the following reasons:

- As already mentioned in Section 6.7, Java is more strongly typed than C++; Java does not permit many of the type conversions that are allowed in C++. In fact, in function invocation, Java allows only the widening kind of type conversions discussed earlier in Chapter 6 for the primitive types and the widening kind of type conversions for the class types, these being from a derived class to a superclass or a superinterface. Allowing only widening kind of type conversions in function invocations eliminates one of the specificity levels in C++ — the one corresponding roughly to standard conversions.

- Since Java does not allow user-defined type conversions the way C++ does, that eliminates another level of specificity.

- Since there is no ellipsis in Java, that eliminates yet another level of specificity.

These reasons and the fact that, compared to C++, Java is more modern and has had the benefit of hindsight in its design, have led to the following three-step procedure for overload resolution in Java. There are reproduced here from [2].

1. For a given function call, find the set of all applicable methods on the basis that there must exist either an exact match or a widening type conversion from each argument in the function call to the corresponding parameter of the method being considered. If this set consists of only one method, select that method for invocation. Otherwise proceed to the next step.

2. If there exists either an exact match or a widening type conversion from each of the parameters of a method in the set to the corresponding parameters of another method, eliminate the latter method from the set. If you are left with only one method after pruning the set in this manner, select that method for invocation. Otherwise proceed to the next step.

3. Declare the source code invalid because there does not exist a single maximally specific method that can be invoked for the function call.

Consider the following example:

```java
//Overload.java

class Employee { String name; }
class Manager extends Employee { int level; }

class Test {
    static void foo( Employee e1, Employee e2 ) {   //first foo    //(A)
        System.out.println( "first foo" );
    }
    static void foo( Employee e, Manager m ) {      //second foo   //(B)
        System.out.println( "second foo" );
    }
    static void foo( Manager m, Employee e) {        //third foo    //(C)
        System.out.println( "third foo" );
    }
```

```
public static void main( String[] args )
{
    Employee emp = new Employee();
    Manager man = new Manager();

    foo( emp, man );      // will invoke the second foo      //(D)

    //foo( man, man );    // Error because it produces an    //(E)
                          // ambiguity in overload resolution
}
}
```

The argument types in the function call in line (D) match the parameter types in the first and the second definitions of foo in lines (A) and (B). So at the end of the first step of overload resolution, we have two candidate methods in the set. We therefore proceed to the second step and discover that both the parameters of the second definition of foo in line (B) can be matched via widening conversions with the corresponding parameters of the first definition of foo in line (A). This means that the second foo is more specific than the first foo. We therefore drop from the set the first foo. That leaves us with only one method in the set. The compiler selects this method.

Now consider that happens if we uncomment the call to foo in line (E). Its argument types match the parameter types for all three definitions of foo. So at the end of the first step of overload resolution, we have three candidates in the set. By the same reasoning as before, we now discover that the first definition of foo is less specific than the other two. So we delete it from the set. However, we also discover that it is not possible to delete either of the remaining two entries from the set, for the simple reason that an Employee type does not possess a widening type conversion to a Manager type. So we declare ambiguity and, therefore, compile time error results.

9.12 DEFAULT ARGUMENTS FOR C++ FUNCTIONS

If at the time of defining a C++ function it is known that a parameter of the function is likely to take on a certain value, then that value can be embedded in the function header itself using standard initialization syntax. For example, if for a function foo(int x, int y), the parameter y will in most cases be set to, say, 100, we could define the function in the following manner:

```
int foo( int x, int y = 100 ) {
    // function body
}
```

The value of 100 is a *default argument* for the parameter y of the function. With such a definition, we could make the following types of invocations of this function:

```
foo( 23 );          // x will be set to 23 and y to 100

foo( 34, 200 );     // x will be set to 34 and y to 200
```

Default arguments can only be supplied for the *trailing parameters* of a function. To explain this point, consider a function of three argument int bar(int x, int y, char* p). We could supply a default argument for the parameter p, as in the definition:

```
int bar( int x, int y, char* p = 0 ) {
    // body of function goes here
}
```

or we could supply default arguments for the last two parameters, y and p, as in

```
int bar( int x, int y = 37, char* p = 0 ) {
    // body of function goes here
}
```

or we could supply default arguments for all three parameters, as in

```
int bar( int x = 29, int y = 37, char* p = 0 ) {
    // body of function goes here
}
```

but, if we do not give a default argument to the last parameter p, we are not allowed to assign default arguments to either x or y. For example, the following definition would not be acceptable to the compiler

```
int bar( int x, int y = 37, char* p ) {          // WRONG
    // body of function goes here
}
```

The reason that only trailing parameters can be given default arguments is that the argument list in an invocation of such a function is *resolved by position*. If it were permissible to give a default argument to a non-trailing parameter, the compiler would not be able to figure out as to which argument to assign to what parameter.

9.13   POINTERS TO FUNCTIONS IN C++

Consider the following two declarations:

```
int print( char* );

int (* fp)(char*) = &print;                              //(A)
```

While the first declaration is a prototype of some function `print()`, the second declaration declares `fp` to be a variable that can serve as a pointer to a function that takes a `char*` argument and returns an `int`. The second declaration also initializes `fp` to point to the function `print()`. Since function names can also serve as pointers in some contexts, for the second declaration we could also have said

```
int (*fp)(char*) = print;                          //(B)
```

Let's further say that the definition of `print()` is as follows:

```
int print( char* str ) {
    cout << str << endl;
    return strlen( str );
}
```

We could now write a `main()` as follows:

```
int main()
{
    int n = fp( "hello this is a test" );
    cout << "Number of characters printed: " << n << endl;
}
```

Note that in this example in `main()`, the name `fp` is a global variable that can only be a pointer to a function. The function to which `fp` can point must meet the conditions laid out on the left hand side in the declaration at (A) above. The declarations in lines (A) and (B) also initialize `fp` to point to the function `print()`.

Pointers to functions are useful in programs in which a function name is a variable. A classic example of this is the `qsort` function defined in the C standard library header `<stdlib.h>` for sorting an array of whatever:

```
void qsort( void* base,
            size_t nmemb,
            size_t size,
            int (* compar) (const void*, const void*) );
```

where the last parameter, `compar`, can be bound to any function of two parameters, both of type `void*`, that returns an `int`. Using a variable for a function name allows `qsort()` to be written in a most general form, so general that it can be used to sort `ints`, `chars`, `strings`, or any other object type, provided that you are able to supply a suitable comparison function for the parameter `compar`. (See Section 4.3.3 of Chapter 4 for a more complete presentation of this function.)

We will next show an example that illustrates how you can use a `typedef` for a function pointer (and therefore for a function name). The following statement

```
typedef void (* FPT) ( double );
```

says that the identifier FPT will serve as a type definition for a pointer to a function that returns void and which has exactly one parameter of type double. Compare the syntax of this typedef with the more familiar one shown below:

```
typedef int Bool;
```

which tells the compiler that it should treat the type Bool as a synonym for the type int. By the same token, the previous definition says that wherever the compiler sees something declared as of type FPT, it should treat that as a function pointer (or as a function) which returns void and which takes exactly one argument of type double. Now we could say

```
void foo( double d ) { cout << ''hello from foo''; }
FPT goo = foo;
```

which first defines foo as a function that returns void and that takes one argument of type double. We then use this function to initialize goo which is of type FPT, meaning a function that returns void and that takes one argument of type double.

The following example illustrates the use of typedefs with pointers to function:

```
//Silly.cc

#include <iostream>
#include <string>

class huphalumpusdumpusgumpus {
public:
    string name;
    huphalumpusdumpusgumpus( string nam ) : name( nam ) {}
};

typedef huphalumpusdumpusgumpus SILLY;

void g( SILLY s ) { cout << "silly is as silly does, says "
                         << s.name << endl; }

void (* FP) ( SILLY ) = g;

typedef void (* FP_TYPE)( SILLY );

FP_TYPE h( SILLY s ) {
    cout << "silly, says function h" << endl;
    return g;
}

typedef void (* FPT) ( double );
```

```
void foo( double d ) { cout << "hello from foo"; }

FPT goo = foo;

int main()
{
    SILLY s( "Billy" );
    (*FP)( s );              // silly is as silly does, says Billy
    FP( s );                 // silly is as silly does, says Billy
    h( s );                  // silly, says function h
    goo( 3.0 );              // hello from foo
    return 0;
}
```

The output produced by the program is shown in the commented out line endings in `main`.

9.14 SUGGESTIONS FOR FURTHER READING

Chapter 7 of [54] and Chapter 7 of [50] are recommended further readings on the subject of functions in C++. For further reading on methods in Java, the reader is referred to [23, pp. 155–182] and [2, pp. 36–57].

9.15 HOMEWORK

1. In the following program, `main` calls a function `g()` in line (B) and passes the argument to this function by value. The function `g()` is defined in line (A). How many times will the destructor of class X be invoked as the program runs to completion.

```
//CountDestructorInvoc1.cc

#include <iostream>
using namespace std;

class X {
    int n;
public:
    X( int nn ) : n(nn) {}
```

```
    ~X() {
        cout << "destructor invoked for X obj with n= " << n
            << endl;
    }
};

void g( X x ) {}                                              //(A)

int main() {
    X xobj( 100 );
    g( xobj );                                               //(B)
    return 0;
}
```

2. The program below differs from the program of the previous problem in only
   one small respect: the function call in line (B) passes the argument to the function in line (A) by reference. How many times will the destructor of class X be
   invoked in this case as the program runs to completion?

```
//CountDestructorInvoc2.cc

#include <iostream>
using namespace std;

class X {
    int n;
public:
    X( int nn ) : n(nn) {}
    ~X() {
        cout << "destructor invoked for X obj with n= " << n
            << endl;
    }
};

void g( X& x ) {}                                            //(A)

int main() {
    X xobj( 100 );
    g( xobj );                                               //(B)
    return 0;
}
```

3. In a further variation on the programs shown in the previous two problems, the function g() in line (A) now takes an X argument by value and returns an object of type X. How many times will the destructor of X be invoked as the program runs to completion?

```
//CountDestructorInvoc3.cc

#include <iostream>
using namespace std;

class X {
    int n;
public:
    X( int nn ) : n(nn) {}
    ~X() {
        cout << "destructor invoked for X obj with n= " << n
            << endl;
    }
};

X g( X x ) { return x; }                                    //(A)

int main() {
    X xobj( 100 );
    g( xobj );                                              //(B)
    return 0;
}
```

4. In another variation on the programs shown in the previous homework problems, the function g() in line (A) below takes an argument of type X by reference and returns an object of type X. How many times will X's destructor be invoked as this program runs to completion?

```
//CountDestructorInvoc4.cc

#include <iostream>
using namespace std;

class X {
    int n;
public:
```

```
        X( int nn ) : n(nn) {}
        ~X() {
            cout << "destructor invoked for X obj with n= " << n
                << endl;
        }
};

X g( X& x ) { return x; }                                    //(A)

int main() {
    X xobj( 100 );
    g( xobj );                                               //(B)
    return 0;
}
```

5. In yet another variation on the previous programs, the function g() in line (A) now takes its X argument by reference and also returns an X object by reference. How many times will X's destructor be now invoked as the program runs to completion?

```
//CountDestructorInvoc5.cc

#include <iostream>
using namespace std;

class X {
    int n;
public:
    X( int nn ) : n(nn) {}
    ~X() {
        cout << "destructor invoked for X obj with n= " << n
            << endl;
    }
};

X& g( X& x ) { return x; }                                   //(A)

int main() {
    X xobj( 100 );
    g( xobj );                                               //(B)
    return 0;
}
```

6. In one last variation on the previous homework programs, the function g() in line (A) now takes its X argument by value. It then a returns a reference to the local variable x. Since, in general, returning a reference to a local variable is an error, will this program compile? If the program were to compile and it ran without problems, how many times would X's destructor be invoked?

```
//CountDestructorInvoc6.cc

#include <iostream>
using namespace std;

class X {
    int n;
public:
    X( int nn ) : n(nn) {}
    ~X() {
        cout << "destructor invoked for X obj with n= " << n
            << endl;
    }
};

X& g( X x ) { return x; }                           //(A)

int main() {
    X xobj( 100 );
    g( xobj );                                      //(B)
    return 0;
}
```

7. Provide implementations for the overloaded versions of the constructor, the member function setLastName(), and of the function modifyLastName() in the following code:

```
class User {
    string firstName;
    string lastName;
    int age;
public:
    User(string first, string last, int yy);            //(A)
    User(const string& first, const string& last, int yy);  //(B)
```

```
        void setLastName( string newLastName );
        void setLastName( string* newLastName );

        string getFirst(){ return firstName; }
        string getLast(){ return lastName; }
};

User modifyLastName( User u, const string newName );        //(C)

User& modifyLastName( User& u, const string& newName );     //(D)

User* modifyLastName( User* p, string* const ptr );         //(E)
```

By inserting print statements in the implementations for the two constructors and the three version of the modifyLastName() function, find out what function calls will invoke which versions. In particular, state what you'd need to do to your program so that the version of the constructor in line (B) and the version of the function modifyLastName in line (D) will be invoked by the calls you see in the following main:

```
    int main()
    {
        User u1( "joe", "schmo", 88 );
        User u2 = modifyLastName( u1, "sixpack" );
        User& u3 = u1;
        User u4 = modifyLastName( u3, "smith" );
        User& u5 = modifyLastName( u3, "hardhat" );
        cout << "First name: " << u4.getFirst()
             << " Last name: " << u4.getLast() << endl;
        return 0;
    }
```

8. The Java program shown below is a slight modification of the program Overload.java of Section 9.12. In the program of Section 9.12, the first call to foo in main invokes the second foo and, if we uncomment the commented out statement, the second call to foo results in a compile-time error. Now examine the code in the program shown below and answer the following question:

Will any of the calls to foo in the lines (A), (B), and (C) elicit a compile-time error? Also, of the three overload definitions of foo provided, which foo will be selected for each call to the function by Java's overload resolution algorithm?

```
//Overload2.java

class Employee { String name; }
class Manager extends Employee { int level; }

class Test {
    // first foo:
    static void foo( Employee e1,
                        Employee e2, double salary ) {
        System.out.println( "first foo" );
    }

    // second foo:
    static void foo( Employee e,
                            Manager m, int salary ) {
        System.out.println( "second foo" );
    }

    // third foo:
    static void foo( Manager m, Employee e, int salary ) {
        System.out.println( "third foo" );
    }

    public static void main( String[] args )
    {
        Employee emp = new Employee();
        Manager man = new Manager();

        foo( emp, man, 100.25 );                        //(A)
        foo( emp, emp, 100 );                           //(B)
        foo( man, man, 100.25 );                        //(C)
    }
}
```

10

Handling Exceptions

The following runtime situation exemplifies the need for exception handling in a computer program: Let's say that your program is trying to read data from a file that was accidently or otherwise deleted by some other program just moments earlier. Your program now has the following options: it could crash — with possibly disastrous consequences in real-world applications; or it could trap the error condition and take remedial measures of some sort, including seeking help from a human or some other program. Other similar situations that can lead to runtime error conditions include encountering wrong kind of data or incorrectly formated data in a file during read operations, trying to write to a file when the disk is full, trying to access an array index that is out of range, encountering excessive communication delays or disruptions in network programming, and so on.

A measure of protection against potentially error-condition producing statements in a program can be achieved by embedding such statements inside if blocks and making their execution conditional. This is commonly done in C for file I/O when we first make sure that the file pointer is not NULL before attempting any I/O operations, and when we test the error and the end-of-file indicators associated with the input and the output streams to make sure that it was not an error condition that terminated an I/O operation.

One shortcoming of error (or, in modern parlance, *exception*) handling by such if statements is that the decision to use them is left entirely to the discretion of a programmer. This approach to the handling of exceptions is also much too local to allow for a smooth transfer of control to a different function or even to an entirely different software module when an exception is thrown. While in C (and in C++)

it is possible to achieve nonlocal transfer of control with the `setjmp` and `longjmp` macros, they are not appropriate for object-oriented programming, as we will see in this chapter.

Since it is sometimes easier to appreciate the virtues of something by examining the lack thereof in the alternatives, in this chapter we will first quickly review the `setjmp`–`longjmp` mechanism of C for multilevel return and point out its shortcomings for OO. That will set us up to review the `try`–`catch` of C++ and Java for the right approach to exception handling.

10.1 SETJMP–LONGJMP **FOR MULTILEVEL RETURN IN C**

In C, transferring control to a different function for exception handling (called error handling in the jargon of C) is accomplished by the `setjmp` and `longjmp` macros from the `setjmp.h` header file. The specific place in source code where we want to handle an error is marked by the `setjmp` macro. The `longjmp` macro can then be used to affect a multilevel return to this place should there be an error in some other part of the code. This is demonstrated in the following example.

As we show in line (A) of the program below, first you define a global variable of type `jmp_buf` by[1]

```
static jmp_buf env;
```

where env is the name of the variable used — we could have used any name. An object of type `jmp_buf` can be used for storing environment variables and registers.

The calling program then establishes a point to which the control should return when `longjmp` is executed in one of the called functions. As shown in line (B), this point of control return is defined by using `setjmp()` as follows:

```
int ret = setjmp( env );
```

At runtime, when the thread of execution reaches this statement, `setjmp()` stores away the current "environment" — consisting of, for example, the function stack and the contents of the various registers — as an array in the `jmp_buf` variable that is its

---

[1]The type `jmp_buf` is defined in the C standard library header `setjmp.h`. If needed in a C++ program, this header file can be accessed through the name `csetjmp`. Any header file from the C standard library can be included in C++ by dropping the suffix ".h" and attaching the letter "c" at the beginning of the name of the file. (It is also permissible to use the ".h" header files from C directly in C++, but beware that a header `X.h` differs from the header `cX` in one important respect: Whereas the former defines names in the global namespace, the latter defines names in the `std` namespace.) To include a nonstandard header, it is best done inside an "extern "C"" directive to suppress the mangling of the function names in the C header file. Mangling is the process used by a C++ compiler to give a unique name to each function. After mangling, the names of the different overloaded versions of the same function name will be unique. Linkers expect function names to be unique regardless of overloading. See Meyers [51] for more information.

argument, env in this case. At this point, setjmp() returns 0. Subsequently, when and if the thread of execution reaches longjmp(), the environment is restored to the status stored in the global variable that is the first argument of longjmp. In the following program, this would happen when the thread of execution reaches line (D). If that were to happen, the control would shift back to the next statement after line (B) but with the value of ret variable set to the second argument of longjmp(). It is as if, in the restored environment, setjmp "returned" the value of longjmp()'s second argument.

In the following example of multilevel return, we have a function f(int j) that calls itself recursively. Each time the function calls itself, the argument j is first incremented by 1. When the value of the argument equals 3, longjmp is executed. When that happens, control is returned to just after the setjmp statement in main.

```
//MultiJmp.cc

#include <iostream>
#include <csetjmp>
#include <cstdlib>
using namespace std;

static jmp_buf env;                                          //(A)
void f(int);

int main()
{
    // setjmp() in the following statement returns 0 when first
    // called. If longjmp() causes the control to return to the
    // point defined by this statement, the value of ret is set
    // to the second argument of longjmp.
    int ret = setjmp( env );                                //(B)

    if (ret == 1) {                                         //(C)
        cout << "Maximum depth of recursion reached" << endl;
        exit(0);
    }
    f(0);

    return 0;
}

void f(int j) {
    cout << "function f called with j = " << j << endl;
    if (j == 3)
        longjmp( env, 1 );                                  //(D)
    f( ++j );
}
```

This program produces the following output:

```
function f called with j = 0
function f called with j = 1
function f called with j = 2
function f called with j = 3
Maximum depth of recursion reached
```

It is instructive to look at the function stack that is built up by the recursion and the thread of execution with respect to the stack. As shown in Figure 10.1, the call to

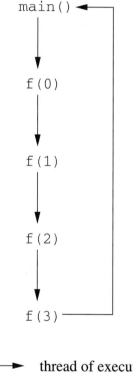

main()

f(0)

f(1)

f(2)

f(3)

────▶ thread of execution

Fig. 10.1

f(0) invokes f(1), which in turn invokes f(2), and so on, until the function f(3) is invoked, when the recursion terminates by transferring the control abruptly back to main().

Although we wrote MultiJmp.cc as a C++ program, its resemblance to C++ is limited to the use of cout for displaying the output. So MultiJmp.cc is basically a C program, especially because the use of setjmp–longjmp is discouraged in C++, having been replaced by the much superior try–catch–throw construct. There are two basic problems with the C's `setjmp-longjmp` approach to multilevel return that have been rectified in C++:

1. As mentioned earlier in Chapter 3 and as we will explain in greater detail in Chapter 11, when a class type object goes out of scope in C++, its destructor is automatically invoked. The destructor can free up the memory and other system resources if they were allocated during object construction. If used in a C++ program, a problem with the `setjmp-longjmp` mechanism is that a call to `longjmp()` will skip over the destructor calls. So any allocations made on the way down the function stack get abandoned when `longjmp()` is called in a C++ program. The `try-catch-throw` approach, to be presented next, works much better for C++ because, when an exception is thrown, it allows destructors to be called for the objects that were constructed along the way.

2. Another problem is that `setjmp()` is a very expensive call in terms of the computational effort required to save all the parameters that represent a snapshot of the environment at the instant `setjmp` is invoked. This can pose problems, especially when `setjmp-longjmp` is embedded in some sort of an iterative loop for error handling and you expect there to be no errors a vast majority of the times.[2]

In the next section, we present the `try-catch-throw` of C++ for exception handling. In this mechanism, a call to `try` has very little overhead, since all it does is to mark a point in the program to which the control should return, the point being the `catch` block. No environment variables or registers are saved in any sort of a global variable. *It is the job of* `throw` *to walk the function stack backwards to the point of the applicable* `catch` *and to "call" the applicable destructors during this process.* `longjmp()` isn't able to call destructors since all it does is to abandon the current stack and restore the old stack from what is in the `env` variable.

10.2   EXCEPTION HANDLING IN C++

Let's now consider the more truly C++ version of the program we showed in the previous section.

In line (A), we define an empty class `Err`. Objects of type `Err` will be used for throwing, as we do on line (D). There is nothing special about the name `Err`. The recursive invocation of `f()` is started by a call to `f(0)` in line (B). When the exception is thrown in line (D), it is caught by the *exception handler* defined by the catch block

---

[2]The reader could argue that `longjmp()` should require just as much computational effort as `setjmp()` since in terms of the work entailed one is opposite of the other. But note that, unlike `setjmp()`, `longjmp()` would only be executed in response to an error condition.

in line (C). The invocation of the `throw` clause in line (D) causes immediate exit from the function being executed.

```
//TryCatch.cc

#include <iostream>
#include <cstdlib>
using namespace std;

void f( int );

class Err {};                                                   //(A)

int main()
{
    try {                                                       //(B)
        f(0);                                                   //(C)
    } catch( Err ) {
        cout << "caught Err" << endl;
        exit(0);
    }

    return 0;
}

void f(int j) {
    cout << "function f invoked with j = " << j << endl;
    if (j == 3) throw Err();                                    //(D)
    f( ++j );
}
```

The above program produces the following output

```
function f invoked with j = 0
function f invoked with j = 1
function f invoked with j = 2
function f invoked with j = 3
caught Err
```

The function stack produced by the recursion in this program and the flow of execution looks as shown in Figure 10.2.

While the winding up of the recursion looks the same as before, what we have for the unwinding is now different. The unwinding, representing by the looping arrows going from bottom to the top in Figure 10.2, is similar to the unwinding in recursive function calls, except for one very important difference. The difference is that when the flow of control shifts back to the calling program, as from f(3) to f(2), it goes to the ending right brace of the calling program, as opposed to just past the point where the function invocation was made.[3] Therefore, from f(3) the control shifts back to the ending right brace of f(2), and from there back to the ending right brace of f(1), and so on.

As the reader would expect at this time, the main advantage of throw walking the function stack backwards is that now the destructors can be invoked for the objects going out of scope as the flow of control hits the right brace of each function block.

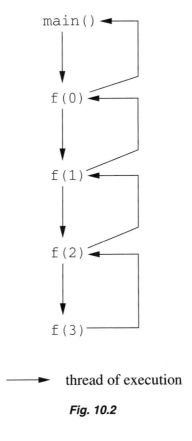

thread of execution

Fig. 10.2

10.3 SOME USAGE PATTERNS FOR EXCEPTION HANDLING IN C++

There is obviously something to be said for learning a new language construct by simply seeing a variety of the usage patterns for the construct. This section shows

---

[3]In other words, control returns directly to the exit point of the invoking function.

some of the different ways in which the try–catch mechanism can be made to work for handling exceptions in C++. Our list of the usage patterns is not exhaustive by any means, but should be good enough for starters.

Usage Pattern 1:

Here is what could perhaps be called the simplest possible example of using the try–catch mechanism in C++:

```
//ExceptionUsage1.cc

#include <iostream>
using namespace std;

void f() { throw 1; }                                           //(A)

int main()
{
    try {
        f();                                                    //(B)
    } catch( int ) { cout << "caught it"; }                     //(C)
    return 0;
}
```

The function f is written in line (A) to throw an int of value 1. This function is invoked in main in line (B) inside a try clause, followed by a catch clause where the object thrown is caught. Note that the parameter of the catch clause in line (C) only mentions the type of the object expected to be caught.

Usage Pattern 2:

While the previous example used a primitive type for the throw, this example, like the program TryCatch.cc presented earlier, shows the use of a class type for the same purpose.

```
//ExceptionUsage2.cc

#include <iostream>
using namespace std;

class MyException {};

void f() { throw MyException(); }                               //(A)
```

```
int main()
{
    try {
        f();                                            //(B)
    } catch( MyException ) {                            //(C)
        cout << "caught MyException";
    }

    return 0;
}
```

The function f is written so as to throw a class type exception. The object thrown is of type MyException. The syntax MyException() in line (A) is an invocation of the system-supplied default no-arg constructor for the MyException class. The system supplies a no-arg constructor since the programmer did not provide any constructors for this class. (No-arg constructors are discussed in Chapters 7 and 11.) As before, f is invoked inside a try clause in line (B). As for the previous example, note again that in line (C) we only show the type of the exception object to be caught.

Usage Pattern 3:

The usage example below is identical to the previous one, except for the header of the function f. By incorporating the clause throw(MyException), the header now declares explicitly the type of exception this function will throw. The throw clause in the header of the function is referred to as its *exception specification*. When a function is given an exception specification, it is a guarantee that if the function throws an exception, the exception will be of the type mentioned in the exception specification.[4] When a function header carries no exception specification, it means that the function can throw an exception of any arbitrary type. And when a function is given an empty exception specification with the clause throw(), the function is expected to throw no exceptions at all. It is recommended that the reader get into the habit of incorporating exception specifications in the headers of exception throwing functions.[5]

```
//ExceptionUsage3.cc

#include <iostream>
using namespace std;

class MyException {};
```

---

[4]However, in practice, a function may violate this guarantee by throwing an exception that is not listed in the exception specification. When that happens, the function std::unexpected() is invoked whose default behavior is to call std::terminate() that in turn calls abort().

[5]As we will later in this chapter, incorporating such declarations in exception throwing functions is mandatory in Java.

```
void f() throw( MyException ) { throw MyException(); }              //(A)

int main()
{
    try {
        f();
    } catch( MyException ) { cout << "caught MyException"; }
    return 0;
}
```

Usage Pattern 4:

It is possible for the same function to throw multiple exceptions in response to different conditions encountered during its execution. In the following usage pattern, the function f is written to throw two different exceptions, one of type MyException and the other of type Err. This fact is declared in the header of the function in line (A).

```
//ExceptionUsage4.cc

#include <iostream>
using namespace std;

class MyException {};
class Err {};

void f( int j ) throw( MyException, Err ) {                         //(A)
    if ( j == 1 ) throw MyException();
    if ( j == 2 ) throw Err();
}

int main()
{
    try {
        f( 1 );
    } catch( MyException ) {
        cout << "caught MyException -- arg must be 1" << endl;
    } catch( Err ) {
        cout << "caught Err -- arg must be 2" << endl;
    }

    try {
        f( 2 );
    } catch( MyException ) {
```

```
            cout << "caught MyException -- arg must be 1" << endl;
    } catch( Err ) {
            cout << "caught Err -- arg must be 2" << endl;
    }

    return 0;
}
```

Usage Pattern 5:

This usage pattern shows that a calling function can re-throw a caught exception. The exception re-thrown can be the same as the one that is caught, or it can be a different object.

In the following example, the function f is written in line (A) so as to throw an exception of type MyException. The function g of line (B) calls f and traps the MyException object thrown by f in line (C). In response to this trapping, g throws an exception of type Err in line (D).

```
//ExceptionUsage5.cc

#include <iostream>
using namespace std;

class MyException {};
class Err {};

void f() throw( MyException ) { throw MyException(); }          //(A)

void g() throw( Err ) {                                         //(B)
    try {
        f();
    } catch( MyException e ) {                                  //(C)
        cout << "oh my" << endl;
        throw Err();                                            //(D)
    }
}

int main()
{
    try {
        g();
    } catch( Err ) { cout << "caught Err" << endl; }
    return 0;
}
```

Usage Pattern 6:

The function that traps the exception does not have to be the one that invokes the exception-throwing function. The exception can be caught by some other function higher up in the function stack.

The following usage example is similar to the previous one except that the exception-throwing function g of line (B) is invoked by another function h of line (C) that does not care to trap the exception thrown by g. Despite the fact that h ignores the exception thrown by g, when h is invoked in line (D) of main, the exception thrown by g can still be trapped in main.

```
//ExceptionUsage6.cc

#include <iostream>
using namespace std;

class MyException {};
class Err {};

void f() throw( MyException ) { throw MyException(); }          //(A)

void g() throw( Err ) {                                          //(B)
    try {
        f();
    } catch( MyException e ) {
        cout << "oh my" << endl;
        throw Err();
    }
}

void h() { g(); }                                               //(C)

int main()
{
    try {
        h();                                                    //(D)
    } catch( Err ) { cout << "caught Err" << endl; }
    return 0;
}
```

Usage Pattern 7:

A function can carry an exception specification even if its implementation code does not explicitly contain a throw clause. To illustrate, if in the previous example we wanted to make explicit the fact that h will throw an exception of type Err if such an exception were to be generated by the implementation code for h(), we can state so explicitly in the header of h, as in line (A) of the following usage pattern:

```
//ExceptionUsage7.cc

#include <iostream>

class MyException {};
class Err {};

void f() throw( MyException ) { throw MyException(); }

void g() throw( Err ) {
    try {
        f();
    } catch( MyException e ) { cout << "oh my" << endl;  throw Err(); }
}

void h() throw( Err ) { g(); }                                        //(A)

int main()
{
    try {
        h();
    } catch( Err ) { cout << "caught Err" << endl; }
    return 0;
}
```

Usage Pattern 8:

The purpose of this pattern is to show that the *prototype* of an exception-throwing function must include a throw clause if such a clause is included in the header of the function definition, as shown in lines (A) and (B) below.

```
//ExceptionUsage8.cc

#include <iostream>

class MyException {};

void f() throw( MyException );                                       //(A)

int main()
{
```

```
    try {
        f();
    } catch( MyException ) { cout << "caught MyException"; }
    return 0;
}

void f() throw( MyException ) { throw MyException(); }              //(B)
```

Usage Pattern 9:

In the previous examples we threw empty objects for exceptions. But that obviously would not serve a very useful purpose in real programming. In practice, you'd want an object thrown to carry with it some useful message to the point where the exception is trapped. The following usage example illustrates this.

```
//ExceptionUsage9.cc

#include <iostream>
#include <string>

class MyException {                                                //(A)
    string message;                                                //(B)
public:
    MyException( string m ) { message = m; }                       //(C)
    string getMessage() { return message; }
};

void f() throw( MyException );


int main()
{
    try {
        f();
    } catch( MyException ex ) { cout << ex.getMessage(); }          //(D)
    return 0;
}

void f() throw( MyException ) {
    throw MyException( "hello there" );                            //(E)
}
```

The class MyException in line (A) now has a data member, message, shown in line (B), that can be set to the message that the exception object must carry with it when it is thrown. For this purpose, the class has been provided with a constructor, as shown in line (C). In line (E), when we construct the exception object, we provide it with a message as the argument to the constructor. This message is retrieved in line (D) when the exception is trapped.

10.4   DIFFERENCES BETWEEN C++ AND JAVA FOR EXCEPTION HANDLING

There are important differences between C++ and Java with regard to how exceptions are handled and processed.[6] These arise on account of the following:

1. While literally any type can be used for throwing in C++, that's not the case in Java. An object that's used for throwing in Java must of type that is a subclass of Throwable. By convention, however, user-defined exceptions are of type Exception, a subclass of Throwable. Therefore, if we wish to write a Java method that throws an exception of a user-defined type MyException, we must define MyException by extending Exception, as in

   ```
   class MyException extends Exception { ...... }
   ```

2. If a function is written so as to throw an exception, that fact must be declared in the header of the function. So if a function f() is written to throw an exception of type MyException, we have no choice but to include the throws MyException clause in the header of the function, as in

   ```
   void f(int j) throws MyException  {
       //.....
       throw new MyException( //..... );
   }
   ```

   Also note that, as the reader should expect by this time, the use of the keyword new for constructing an object of type MyException.

3. An exception-throwing function can only be invoked in one of the following modes:

   - It must be invoked inside a try–catch block and the exception must be caught; or
   - The calling function must re-throw that exception so that it can be caught elsewhere, possibly by the system-supplied default exception handler.

---

[6]The discussion in this and the next two sections applies only to what are known as *checked* exceptions in Java — the kind of exceptions you are most likely to incorporate in your own programs. The difference between Java's checked and unchecked exceptions is explained in Section 10.7.

- The calling function can do both of the above.

It goes without saying that the behavior of a program with regard to exception throwing and catching will be different depending on which mode is chosen.

4. Another important difference between the Java syntax and the C++ syntax is that a parameter must be explicitly specified for the catch block. In other words, one now has no choice but to say

```
catch( MyException e ) {   ....   }
```

and explicitly mention an identifier, in this case e of type MyException in the parameter list of catch() even if this parameter does not get used for anything inside the definition of the catch block.

We will now show the code for a Java implementation of the C++ example of Section 10.2.

```
//TryCatch.java

import java.io.*;

class Err extends Exception { }

class Test {
    public static void main( String[] args )
    {
        try {
            f(0);
        } catch( Err e ) {
            System.out.println( "Exception caught in main" );
        }
    }

    static void f(int j) throws Err {
        System.out.println( "function f invoked with j = " + j );
        if (j == 3) throw new Err();
        f( ++j );
    }
}
```

Note that the header of the function f includes the clause throws Err. The output produced by this program is

```
function f invoked with j = 0
function f invoked with j = 1
```

```
function f invoked with j = 2
function f invoked with j = 3
Exception caught in main
```

10.5 JAVA SYNTAX FOR EXCEPTION HANDLING

Here is the general syntax for exception handling in Java:

```
try {
     .....
     .....

} catch( exception_type_1 identifier_1 ) {
     .....
     .....

} catch( exception_type_2 identifier_2 ) {
     .....
     .....

} catch( exception_type_3 identifier_3 ) {
     .....
     .....

} finally {
     .....
     .....
}
```

where .... stands for statements. If all the statements in the body of the try block are executed successfully, the flow of control shifts directly from the try block to the finally block. However, as soon as an exception occurs during the execution of any of the try statements, the type of the exception is compared with the types declared for the parameter of each of the catch blocks in the order of appearance of the catch blocks. When a match is found, the statements in that catch block are executed. No further catch blocks are examined. After the end of processing in the invoked catch block, the flow of control shifts to the finally block if one is included. Therefore, the code in the finally clause is executed whether or not an exception is thrown. The finally clause is useful for affecting processing that must be carried out even when an exception is thrown. For example, suppose you open an input stream to a local file from which you read data incrementally, meaning one item at a time. Let's say an exception is thrown during this process, either because the data item could not be read because it was of the wrong kind, or for whatever other reason, you'd still want to close the input stream. The finally clause comes handy for that, as we will see in the next section.

10.6 SOME USAGE PATTERNS FOR EXCEPTION HANDLING IN JAVA

Usage Pattern 1:

The first usage pattern shown below is probably the most straightforward example of exception handling in Java. The class MyException is provided with two constructors in lines (B) and (C). The constructor in line (C) makes use of the base class's facility for storing a message that can be packed with the object of a throw. Since a class with any constructors at all is not provided with a system-supplied no-arg constructor, so we have defined one in (B) to construct a throw object without a message. In line (D), the function f is written so as to throw an exception of type MyException. This function is invoked in a try–catch block in line (E). The catch block traps the exception if it is thrown and, in line (F), recovers the message if one was packed with the object thrown.

```java
//ExceptionUsage1.java

class MyException extends Exception {                       //(A)
    public MyException() {                                  //(B)
        super();
    }
    public MyException( String s ) {                        //(C)
        super( s );
    }
}

class Test {
    static void f( ) throws MyException {                   //(D)
        throw new MyException( "Exception thrown by function f()" );
    }

    public static void main( String[] args )
    {
        try {
            f();                                            //(E)
        } catch( MyException e ) {
            System.out.println( e.getMessage() );           //(F)
        }
    }
}
```

Usage Pattern 2:

As this example shows, it is not necessary for a function that contains a throws clause in its header to actually throw that exception. Although there is no real reason for including the `throws` clause in the header of a function if it is not going to throw the exception, it is useful to know that Java gives you this freedom. The `throws` clause in the function header could be a part of the exception specification of a class as supplied by a vendor. A specific implementation of the function would dictate whether or not the function would actually throw that exception.

```java
//ExceptionUsage2.java

class MyException extends Exception {}

class Test {
    static void f( ) throws MyException {}

    public static void main( String[] args ) {
        try {
            f();
        } catch( MyException e ) {}
    }
}
```

Usage Pattern 3:

A function can be written as to throw multiple exceptions, as the following example demonstrates. The function `f` in line (A) has been defined to throw two different exceptions, in lines (B) and (C), in response to two different circumstances during program execution.

```java
//ExceptionUsage3.java

class MyException extends Exception {}
class Err extends Exception {}

class Test {
    static void f( int j ) throws MyException, Err {          //(A)
        if ( j == 1 ) throw new MyException();                //(B)
        if ( j == 2 ) throw new Err();                        //(C)
    }

    public static void main( String[] args )
    {
        try {
            f( 1 );
        } catch( MyException e ) {
            System.out.println("caught MyException -- arg must be 1");
```

```
        } catch( Err e ) {
            System.out.println("caught Err -- arg must be 2");
        }

        try {
            f( 2 );
        } catch( MyException e ) {
            System.out.println("caught MyException -- arg must be 1");
        } catch( Err e ) {
            System.out.println("caught Err -- arg must be 2");
        }
    }
}
```

Note that when a function is written as to throw multiple exceptions, they must all be mentioned in a comma separated list in the header of the function, as shown in line (A).

Usage Pattern 4:

The function h() in line (C) below invokes two separate functions, f and g, each capable of throwing a different exception, as shown by the code in lines (A) and (B). The function h must either trap these exceptions by invoking f and g inside try–catch blocks, or declare the exceptions in its header for re-throw. In the example code shown, we have chosen the latter option. Of course, we must trap the exceptions when h is called in line (D).

```
//ExceptionUsage4.java

class MyException extends Exception {}
class Err extends Exception {}

class Test {
    static void f() throws MyException {                      //(A)
        throw new MyException();
    }
    static void g() throws Err {                              //(B)
        throw new Err();
    }
    static void h() throws MyException, Err {                 //(C)
        f();
        g();
    }
```

```
    public static void main( String[] args ) {
        try {
            h();                                            //(D)
        } catch( MyException e ) {
            System.out.println( "caught MyException" );
        } catch( Err e ) {
            System.out.println( "caught Err" );
        }
    }
}
```

Usage Pattern 5:

We will now show the importance of the `finally` clause. As was mentioned earlier, the `finally` clause is used for executing those steps that must be carried out whether or not an exception is thrown. Ordinarily, the flow of execution inside a function halts at the point an exception is thrown and the control shifts to the right brace of the `try` block in the calling function. The exception thrown by the called function would presumably be caught or re-thrown by the calling function. In either case, we may want to execute some clean-up operations.

In the example code below, the following functions throw the exceptions shown:

```
    FileReader constructor    --        throws FileNotFoundException

    read()                    --        throws IOException

    close()                   --        throws IOException
```

In the code shown below, let's say that the statement in line (A) is executed successfully and the input stream object created. But now, let's assume that some exception-causing situation can arise in the `while` loop that starts at line (B). We have simulated such a problem by invoking `foo()` in line (C). The question now arises as to how to close the opened input stream. We could close the stream in an appropriate `catch` block. But that would not work if the exception is not thrown. You see, we wish for the opened stream to be closed in both cases — when an exception is thrown and when a problem function like `foo()` does not get invoked. We therefore stick the statement to close the stream in the `finally` clause. The code in that clause gets executed regardless of whether all of the code in the `try` block is executed successfully, or whether an exception is thrown in any of the statements.

```
//ExceptionUsage5.java

import java.io.*;

class Test {
```

```
static void foo() throws Exception { throw new Exception(); }

static void bar() throws Exception {
    FileReader input = null;
    try {
        input = new FileReader( "infile" );                       //(A)
        int ch;
        while ( ( ch = input.read() ) != -1 ) {                   //(B)
            if ( ch == 'A' ) {
                System.out.println( "found it" );
                foo();                                            //(C)
            }
        }
    } finally {
        if ( input != null ) {
            input.close();
            System.out.println("input stream closed successfully");
        }
    }
    System.out.println( "Exiting bar()" );                        //(D)
}

public static void main( String[] args ) {
    try {
        bar();
    } catch( Exception e ) {
        System.out.println( "caught exception in main" );
    }
}
}
```

Note that the statement in line (D) will not get executed if an exception is thrown in line (C). So we do not have the luxury of closing the input stream outside the try–finally construct shown.

This usage pattern also shows that a try block does not necessarily have to be followed by a catch block. A try block can be followed directly by a finally block, but then you must include a throws clause in the method header so that it can re-throw that exception.

Usage Pattern 6:

This example is a small variation over the examples shown earlier. The method g shown below catches and then re-throws the same exception — an exception of type MyException that is then eventually caught in main.

```
//ExceptionUsage6.java

class MyException extends Exception {}

class Test {

    static void f() throws MyException {
        throw new MyException();
    }

    static void g() throws MyException {
        try {
            f();
        } catch( MyException e ) {
            System.out.println( "catching and re-throwing in g" );
            throw new MyException();
        }
    }

    public static void main( String[] args )
    {
        try {
            g();
        } catch( MyException e ) {
            System.out.println( "caught MyException in main" );
        }
    }
}
```

Usage Pattern 7:

The purpose of this example is to draw a reader's attention to the fact that one can pack additional functionality in a programmer-defined exception class over and above what is provided by the base class. This one can do with the help of data members for the programmer-defined exception class, as we show in the following example. The code shown uses a data member of type String that can be used to pack a message with the thrown object. (The example merely demonstrates the notion of additional functionality in a programmer-defined exception class. If all you want to do is to send a simple string back with the thrown object, you can use the base class Exception's string data member for that purpose, as we showed in the first usage pattern in this section.) The class MyException now has a data member called message in line (A) and a constructor in line (B). The constructor allows us to set the value of the data member as desired when a MyException object is constructed, as we do in line (C) below.

```
//ExceptionUsage7.java

class MyException extends Exception {
    String message;                                          //(A)
    public MyException( String mess ) { message = mess; }    //(B)
}

class Test {
    static void f() throws MyException {
        throw new MyException( "Hello from f()" );           //(C)
    }

    public static void main( String[] args )
    {
        try {
            f();
        } catch( MyException e ) {
            System.out.println( e.message );
        }
    }
}
```

10.7   CHECKED AND UNCHECKED EXCEPTIONS IN JAVA

All of the Java exception handling examples we have shown so far deal with *checked exceptions.* For a checked exception, the compiler makes sure that your code makes provisions for either catching the exception or for re-throwing it.

Java also supports another kind of exceptions — *unchecked exceptions* — that are objects of type RuntimeException or of type Error. An unchecked exception is beyond the purview of the compiler, in the sense that the compiler will not insist that your program include exception handling code (meaning code to either catch the exception, or to re-throw the exception). However, if a method capable of throwing an unchecked exception actually ends up throwing the exception during program execution, the exception will be trapped by the runtime and will cause termination of the Java Virtual Machine unless, of course, your program catches the exception.

Unchecked exception of type Error usually indicate serious problems at run time; there is never a good reason for catching them. Here are some examples of system-defined exceptions that are of type Error: OutOfMemoryError, NoSuchMethod-Error, StackOverflowError, and so on.

Examples of system-defined exceptions of type `RuntimeException` include `ArithmeticException`, `ClassCastException`, `IllegalArgumentException`, `NullPointerException`, and so on.

Simply to illustrate that an exception of type `RuntimeException` does not have to be handled in the same manner as a checked exception, the following example shows a modified form of the code shown earlier in `ExceptionUsage1.java`:

```
//RuntimeExcep.java

class MyException extends RuntimeException {                          //(A)
    public MyException() {
        super();
    }
    public MyException( String s ) {
        super( s );
    }
}

class Test {
    static void f( ) throws MyException {
        throw new MyException( "Exception thrown by function f()" );
    }
    public static void main( String[] args ) {
            f();                                                       //(B)
    }
}
```

Comparing this program to the one in `ExceptionUsage1.java`, note that in line (A) we now extend `RuntimeException` as opposed to `Exception`. That allows us to call `f()` in line (B) without the `try-catch` block used in main of ExceptionUsage1.java. If we compile and execute this code, the function `f()` will throw the designated exception which will be trapped by the runtime that will bring the program to a halt.

10.8   SUGGESTIONS FOR FURTHER READING

Becoming familiar with Java's unchecked exceptions would allow a reader to make better sense of the error reports displayed on a terminal screen when a Java program crashes. The online Java platform documentation at [33] lists all of the system-defined unchecked exceptions as a part of the description for the `java.lang` package. A complete list of unchecked exceptions for an earlier version of Java appears in Appendix A of [2].

The discussion in this chapter on C's multilevel return with the setjmp–longjmp mechanism follows King's treatment of the subject [45].

10.9 HOMEWORK

1. Many methods defined for the Java I/O stream classes throw exceptions of type IOException. Therefore, in a large Java program with numerous I/O operations, it is sometimes difficult to pinpoint the statement that might be responsible for generating this type of an exception.[7] This homework exercise is about using a programmer-defined exception type that can be more helpful for localizing a problem in a designated set of I/O operations.

   Define a new exception by

   ```
   class FileIOException extends Exception {}
   ```

   to be used for a new Java class, FileIO with the static methods listed below. Each method should re-throw any exceptions of the form IOException as a FileIOException.

   ```
   public static String readOneString( String filename )
           throws File IOException

   public static int readOneInt( String filename )
           throws FileIOException

   public static double readOneDouble( String filename )
           throws FileIOException

   public static String[] readAllStrings( String filename )
           throws FileIOException

   public static int[] readAllInts( String filename )
           throws FileIOException

   public static double[] readAllDoubles( String filename )
           throws FileIOException

   public static void
           writeOneString( String data, String filename )
   ```

---

[7]Although this problem can be mitigated by invoking printStackTrace() on a caught exception and/or by printing out some features of the state of the environment when an exception is caught.

```
                    throws FileIOException

    public static void
        writeOneInt( int data, String filename )
            throws FileIOException

    public static void
        writeOneDouble( double data, String filename )
            throws FileIOException

    public static void
        writeAllStrings( String[] strArray, String filename )
            throws FileIOException

    public static void
        writeAllInts( int[] intArray, String filename )
            throws FileIOException

    public static void
        writeAllDoubles( doubles[] doubleArray,
                                    String filename )
            throws FileIOException
```

Note that the first three function headers listed above are for reading just one data item from a file; the next three are for reading all the data in a file and returning it in the form of an array of the appropriate type; the next three are for writing just one item into a file; and, finally, the last three are for writing arrays of different types into an output file. Each "read" method listed above should open a source file for reading data and then close it after the data are acquired. Similarly, each "write" method should open a destination file for writing and then close it after the writing is done.

2. The goal of this homework is to use C++ and Java exceptions to terminate search when you find a given word in a dictionary of words stored in the form of a binary tree. To keep matters simple, assume that all the words are stored in the leaf nodes of the tree and that the word stored at each internal node is the 'greater' of the words at the two child nodes according to ASCII-based lexicographic ordering of the words. You'd obviously need to first write C++ and Java programs that can construct binary-tree dictionaries from the words in a text file. And then write search programs in each language that search for a query word by descending down the dictionary tree. When there is a match between a query word and the word stored at a node, throw an exception to terminate the search.

3. Write a Java class WordFinder for locating a a word in a text file; the designated word could be a substring of a longer word. Your class should possess one method with the following prototype:

```
public static boolean searchFor( String file, String word )
```

The method should use the readAllStrings method of the FileIO class of Problem 1 to read all the words in the text file. Concatenate the words thus read into one long string and use the substr method of the String class to locate the desired word. Make sure your program has an appropriate handler for the FileIOException thrown by the methods of the FileIO class.

4. Write a C++ function that returns an input stream to a file. But if something were to go wrong, such as if the file was missing, the function should throw the following user-specified exception:

```
class IfstreamException {};
```

5. Why is the following *not* a good example for demonstrating the utility of the finally clause in a try–catch–finally structure? The program tries to locate the character 'A' in a text file. If it finds the character, the program prints out a message to that effect and terminates, but only after closing the input stream properly in the finally clause. If it does not find the character, a message to that effect is printed out and the input stream is closed as before in the finally clause.

```
import java.io.*;

class Test {

    public static void main( String[] args )
    {
        FileReader input = null;
        try {
            input = new FileReader( "infile" );
            int ch;
            while ( -1 != ( ch = input.read() ) ) {
                if ( ch == 'A' ) {
                    System.out.println( "found it" );
                    System.exit( 0 );
                }
            }
            System.out.println( "did not find it" );
```

```
        } catch( FileNotFoundException e ) {
            System.out.println( "file not located" );
        } catch( IOException e ) {
            System.out.println( "problems with I/O" );
        } finally {
            if ( input != null ) {
                try {
                    System.out.println( "closing input stream" );
                    input.close();
                } catch( IOException e ) {
                    System.out.println( "problems with close()" );
                }
            }
        }
    }
}
```

11

Classes, The Rest of the Story

Before reading this chapter, the reader should review the discussion in Chapter 3 on simple classes in C++ and Java. The reader would also benefit from a quick review of other class-related concepts we have already discussed in the earlier chapters.

In particular, we have already discussed the issues of declaration, definition, and initialization of class types in Chapter 7, where we also talked about the no-arg constructors for classes and the role such constructors play in the initialization of array and other container types in C++. The member initialization syntax that must be used for a constructor if a C++ class has `const` or reference data members was also covered in Chapter 7.

A review of Chapter 9 where we talk about class-type arguments for functions, overloading of member functions and constructors, and so on, for both C++ and Java would also prove helpful to the reader in understanding the material in this chapter.

11.1 ACCESS CONTROL OF CONSTRUCTORS

Constructors are not always placed in the public section of a class. Sometimes it is necessary to place one or more constructors in the private or the protected section. While this forbids certain forms of object creation, it makes possible other behaviors by a class.

In this section, we will show two examples that call for limiting the access to a constructor. In the first example, our goal will be to program up a class in such a way

415

that only a limited number of objects are allowed to be made from the class. Our second example, specific to C++, addresses situations when it is not possible to give meaningful initializations to the data members in the no-arg constructor of a class. As we will point out, it is best to place such a no-arg constructor in a nonpublic section of the class. (The issue addressed in the second example does not arise for the case of Java because a class-type data member in Java can always be default-initialized to the null object reference, as pointed out in Chapter 7.)

11.1.1 Limiting the Number of Objects

Shown below[1] is a Java class X whose sole constructor, in line (B), is private. Therefore, it is not possible to make instances of this class in the usual manner — that is, by invoking its constructor.

The class provides in line (C) a public method, makeInstanceOfX(), that returns the same unique instance of the class each time the method is invoked. As shown in line (D), this unique instance of the class is not created until the first request for an object of type X is received.[2] The class X as written only allows a single object of X to be made. With a slight modification, we could have the class allow a certain designated but fixed number of objects of type X to be made.

```
//Singleton.java

class X {
    private int n;
    private static X unique;                        //(A)
    private X( int m ){ n = m; }                    //(B)
    public static X makeInstanceOfX() {             //(C)
        if ( unique == null ) unique  = new X( 10 );  //(D)
        return unique;
    }
}

class Test {
    public static void main( String[] args )
    {
        X xobj_1 = X.makeInstanceOfX();
        X xobj_2 = X.makeInstanceOfX();
        System.out.println( xobj_1 == xobj_2 );     // true
```

---

[1]This section is best read after the reader has gone through the rest of this chapter and Chapter 12. This section, although important, stands on its own and is not crucial to understanding of the rest of this chapter.

[2]This is referred to as *lazy instantiation*.

```
        }
}
```

Shown below is a C++ version of the Java example. The constructor of this class is also in the private section in line (B); so it cannot be accessed by either a stand-alone function or other classes. Therefore, it is not possible to make instances of this class in the usual manner, that is, by invoking its constructor. The class provides in line (E) a public method, `makeInstanceOfX()`, that returns the same unique instance of the class each time the method is invoked.

Shown in lines (C) and (D) are the private placements of the *copy constructor* and the *copy assignment operator* of the class — notions that will be explained later in this chapter. By making them private, it becomes impossible to make a duplicate of the unique instance of X supplied by the `makeInstanceOfX()` method. In other words, we cannot use ploys shown in lines (H) and (I) for constructing duplicates of the unique instance of X.

The initialization in line (F) will make sense after you have gone through the material on static class members in the rest of this chapter. And the function in line (G) will make more sense after you have gone through Chapter 12. In the function defined in line (G), we overload the equality operator '==' to test whether or not two X objects are the same because they are located at the same place in the memory.

```
//Singleton.cc

#include <iostream>
using namespace std;

class X {
    int n;
    static X* unique;                                     //(A)

    X( int m ){ n = m; }                                  //(B)

    X( const X& );                                        //(C)
    X& operator=( const X& );                             //(D)
public:
    static X& makeInstanceOfX() {                         //(E)
        if ( unique == 0 ) unique  = new X( 10 );
        return *unique;
    }
};

X* X::unique = 0 ;                                        //(F)

bool operator==( const X& obj1, const X& obj2 ) {         //(G)
```

```
    return &obj1 == &obj2 ? true : false;
}

int main()
{
    X& xobj_1 = X::makeInstanceOfX();
    X& xobj_2 = X::makeInstanceOfX();

    cout << (xobj_1 == xobj_2) << endl;     // true

    // X xobj_3 = xobj_1                                          //(H)
    // xobj_2 = xobj_1;                                           //(I)

    return 0;
}
```

11.1.2 Limiting the Access to No-Arg Constructor in C++

A constructor that in certain situations is a good candidate for the private or the protected section of a C++ class is the no-arg constructor. Ideally, when a new object is constructed, no data member of the constructed object should remain uninitialized. This precept applies equally well to a no-arg constructor also. To fulfill this ideal, a no-arg constructor must obviously provide default initializations for the data members of a class. But a default initialization for a class-type data member may make no sense whatsoever in certain contexts. When that happens, a no-arg constructor may have to leave one or more of the data members uninitialized. Since constructors that leave data members uninitialized can be a source of hard-to-trace bugs, it may become necessary to place such a constructor in the private or the protected section of a class.

In this section, we will consider no-arg constructors in the context of the initializations needed for C++ arrays and other container types. As mentioned earlier in Chapters 5 and 7, it is not possible in C++ to construct an array or a container of class-type objects if the type does not support a no-arg constructor.

For example, in the program shown below, it is obviously not possible to construct an array or any other container type for storing objects of the class X shown below. Since the class has a programmer-supplied constructor, it does not possess a system-supplied no-arg constructor. But, memory allocation for arrays and the container classes requires the container elements to provide either a no-arg constructor explicitly, or no constructors at all, in which case the class would possess a system-supplied default no-arg constructor.[3]

```
//NoArgMissing.cc

#include <vector>

class X {
    int p;
public:
    X( int m ) : p(m) {}
};


int main() {
    X xob;                          // Error, no-arg constructor missing
    X arr[ 100 ];                   // Error, no-arg constructor missing
    vector<X> vec1( 100 );          // Error, no-arg constructor missing

    // OK, no-arg constructor not needed:
    vector<X> vec2;                                                 //(A)
    X xobj( 12 );
    vec2.push_back( xobj );
    return 0;
}
```

So, if you needed to make arrays and other container types of objects of class X, you could try to provide it explicitly with a no-arg constructor:

```
X(){}
```

or, more smartly,

```
X() : p( 0 ) {}
```

if the number 0 is an appropriate choice for the initialization of the data member p.

A do-nothing no-arg constructor, our first choice above, leaves the data members uninitialized, leading to possible sources of bugs for the case of large classes in complex programs. So, ideally, if you must specify a no-arg constructor you should also provide initializations for the data members, as we did in our second choice above. But, unfortunately, that is not always possible, especially when the data members of a class are other class-types whose design may not be under your control. Since a meaningless no-arg constructor in the public section of a class can be abused, a

---

[3]If we did not want to preallocate memory for a vector, which is the case in line (A) of the program, it is not necessary for X to possess a no-arg constructor in order to construct a vector for storing elements of type X.

solution to the dilemma may be to place a no-arg constructor in the private section of a class and to declare a container type to be a *friend* of the class,[4] as we show below:

```
//PrivateConstructor.cc

#include <vector>
using namespace std;

class X {
    friend class vector<X>;                              //(A)
    int p;
    X(){}                                                //(B)
public:
    X( int m ) : p(m) {}
};


int main()
{
    // X xob1;              // Error, no-arg constructor private
    // X arr[ 100 ];        // Error, no-arg constructor private

    vector<X> vec(100);     // OK now
    X xob2( 12 );
    vec[0] = xob2;
    return 0;
}
```

The *friend* declaration in line (A) makes the private data members of class X accessible to objects of type vector<X>. Thus the private no-arg constructor in line (B) will become accessible to vector<X>, but will remain inaccessible for more general construction of objects of type X.

But note that this solution — placing a constructor in the private section and declaring a container class to be a *friend* — can only be used for class type containers. It obviously will not work for array types since a C++ array is not a class.

While C++ containers, including arrays, can hold objects directly, Java containers only hold references to objects. So a Java container does not need access to a constructor to figure out how to allocate memory for each element in the container. So the C++'s requirement that a class possess an accessible no-arg constructor does not apply to Java.

---

[4]The C++ concept of a *friend* was introduced in Chapter 3.

In both C++ and Java, if a class has one or more constructors in its private section *but none in the public section*, then it would not be possible to construct individual objects of such a class. Possessing at least one constructor — even if it is in the private section — would prevent the system from supplying the class with a default public no-arg constructor.

11.2 CAN MULTIPLE CONSTRUCTORS HELP EACH OTHER?

When multiple constructors are defined for a class, can they help each other during the construction of an object of the class? The answer to this is yes in Java and no in ISO compatible C++.

In Java it is permissible for one constructor to call another constructor defined for the same class through the function this(). Here is an example:

```
//MultiConstructors.java

class X {
    private int x;
    private int y;

    public X() { x = 5; }                                //(A)

    public X( int m ) {                                  //(B)
        this();                                          //(C)
        y = m;
    }

    public static void main( String[] args )
    {
        X xobj = new X( 100 );
        System.out.println ( xobj.x + " " + xobj.y );    // 5 100
    }
}
```

We have two constructors for this class, in lines (A) and (B). The constructor of line (B) invokes the constructor of line (A) in line (C) by using the function call this(). In Java, the special function call

```
this( ....... )
```

can always be used to invoke any constructor inside any other constructor for the same class. The standard overload resolution, presented in Chapter 9, is used to decide which constructor to invoke in response to this(). So, evidently, the arguments supplied to this() play a principal role in determining which specific constructor is selected. When a constructor invokes another constructor in this manner, the statement this(....) must be the first executable statement. This is referred to as *explicit constructor invocation* in Java.

11.3 STATIC MEMBERS IN C++

As mentioned earlier in Chapter 3, a static member of a class is global to all objects of the class. Applications often require that all objects of a given type share a piece of information among themselves. Such information, whether in the form of a variable or in the form of a function, can be declared to be static. A data member or a member function of a class is declared static by using the static modifier in the declaration. A static data member is also sometimes called a *class variable*. A static member does not belong to any particular object of that class. There is exactly *one copy per class* of such a member, as opposed to *one copy per object* for nonstatic members.

In this section, we will illustrate different aspects of static class members via different examples.

Consider the following C++ class that has data members of type int, static int, and static const int. It has an in-class initialization for one of the two data members of type static const. Note that, in general, C++ does not permit in-class initialization of the data members of a class. As mentioned in Chapter 7, the only exception to this rule is for data members of type static const.

```
//Static1.cc

#include <iostream>
using namespace std;

class X {
public:
    int m;
    static int n;
    static const int p;
    static const int q = 51;
    X( int mm ) { m = mm; }
};

int X::n = 100;                                         //(A)

const int X::p = 101;                                  //(B)
```

```
int main()
{
    cout << X::n << endl;              // 100                          //(C)

    X xobj_1( 20 );
    cout << xobj_1.m << " " << xobj_1.n << endl;  // 20 100            //(D)

    X xobj_2( 40 );
    cout << xobj_2.m << " " << xobj_2.n << endl;  // 40 100

    X::n = 1000;                                                       //(E)

    cout << xobj_1.m << " " << xobj_1.n << endl;  // 20 1000
    cout << xobj_2.m << " " << xobj_2.n << endl;  // 40 1000

    return 0;
}
```

Note especially the syntax for the initialization of the static members n and p in lines (A) and (B). Even though the class definition declares that these variables are of type int and const int, those facts have to be reasserted in the initialization syntax in lines (A) and (B).

A common way to retrieve the value of a static data member that is public is through the *classname::static_data_member* syntax, as we show in line (C) above. However, a static data member may also be retrieved through the individual objects of the class, as in line (D) above.

From the output of this program shown in the commented out line endings, it is clear that changing the value of the static member n in line (E) changes the value of n as seen through the previously constructed objects xobj_1 and xobj_2. This should reinforce what we said at the beginning of this section: *There exists only one copy of a static data member for all the objects made from a class. If the value of the static member is changed, that change will become evident to all the objects of that class, even objects constructed prior to the change in the value of the static data member.*

The syntax *classname::static_data_member* for accessing a static data member evidently can only be used when the data member is in the public section of a class. How does one initialize and modify a static data member that is in the private section of a class? To consider this situation, the program below defines a class X with a static data member n in the private section of the class:

```
//Static2.cc

#include <iostream>
using namespace std;

class X {
    static int n;
public:
    int m;
    X( int mm ) { m = mm; }
    static int getn() { return n; }                    //(A)
    static void setn( int nn ) { n = nn;    }          //(B)
};

int X::n = 100;                                         //(C)

int main()
{
    cout << X::getn() << endl;              // 100       //(D)

    X xobj_1( 20 );
    cout << xobj_1.m << " " << xobj_1.getn() << endl;   // 20 100

    X xobj_2( 40 );
    cout << xobj_2.m << " " << xobj_2.getn() << endl;   // 40 100

    X::setn( 1000 );                                    //(E)

    cout << xobj_1.m << " " << xobj_1.getn() << endl;   // 20 1000 //(F)

    cout << xobj_2.m << " " << xobj_2.getn() << endl;   // 40 1000

    return 0;
}
```

Perhaps the most noteworthy feature of this program is that even though the static data member n is in the private section of the class, its initialization syntax remains unchanged, as shown in line (C) of the program.

The program also defines two public *static member functions*,[5] getn() and setn(), in lines (A) and (B) for retrieving and modifying the value of the private static data member. A static function can be called directly with respect to the class name using

---

[5]An important property of static member functions to remember for future is: A static member function is *not* allowed to access the nonstatic members of a class.

the scope operator. Therefore, as we show in line (E), to set the value of n to 1000, we can say

```
X::setn(1000);
```

Similarly, as we show in line (D), we can retrieve the value of n by

```
cout << X::getn();
```

What's interesting is that while the static property allows the functions getn() and setn() to be invoked directly on the class, these static functions can also be invoked on the objects of the class, as in line (F) above. That is, if xobj_1 is an object of type X, we can say:

```
cout << xobj_1.getn();
```

The simple class X used above, while serving as a convenient example to get across the basic idea of static members, is much too sterile to show some of the nuances associated with their use in more meaningful situations. In what follows, we will present two different examples to illustrate the different ways of initializing and updating static data members. Each example has a different problem description and the manner in which the static members are used is dictated by that description. Before we actually delve into the examples, here is what they are about:

- Our first example, from Stroustrup [54], involves a class Date. It would be convenient if all objects of type Date had access to a single object today. This would require that today be a static data member of the Date class.

- Our second example, patterned after a similar Java example from Arnold and Gosling [2], will deal with a robot factory. Suppose, in order to keep track of the robots manufactured by a factory, we define a class Robot with a data member idNumber whose value designates the serial number for each robot. We would need a way to keep track of the next available idNumber for the next robot to come off the manufacturing line. For that purpose, we may define a static member nextIdNumber that would reside in the class itself.

Example 1:

Here is an implementation of the Date class. Note the static data member today in line (A) and the static member functions setToday() and getToday() in lines (B) and (C).

```
//Date.cc

#include <iostream>
using namespace std;
```

```
class Date {
    int d, m, y;
    static Date today;                                      //(A)
public:
    Date( int dd = 0, int mm = 0, int yy = 0 );
    static void setToday(int, int, int);                    //(B)
    static Date getToday() { return today; };               //(C)
    void print() {
        cout << "day: " << d << " month: " << m
            << " year: " << y << endl;
    }
};

Date::Date( int dd, int mm, int yy ) {
    d = dd ? dd : today.d;
    m = mm ? mm : today.m;
    y = yy ? yy : today.y;
}

void Date::setToday( int dd, int mm, int yy ) {             //(D)
    today = Date(dd, mm, yy);
}

Date Date::today( 31, 10, 2001 );                           //(E)

int main()
{
    Date d1( 1, 1, 1970);
    d1.print();                 //day: 1  month: 1  year: 1970
    Date d2( 2 );
    d2.print();                 //day: 2  month: 10 year: 2001
    Date::setToday(3, 4, 2000);                             //(F)
    Date::getToday().print();   //day: 3  month: 4  year: 2000  //(G)
    Date d3( 7 );
    d3.print();                 //day: 7  month: 4  year: 2000
    Date d4 = Date();
    d4.print();                 //day: 3  month: 4  year: 2000
    return 0;
}
```

Note the initialization of the static member today outside the class definition in line (E). Despite the fact that the static member today is private, for the purpose of initialization (and only initialization) it is accessible outside the class in the same manner as a public static member, a point that was also made earlier with the help of class X.

In lines (F) and (G), the program shows the invocations of the static member functions getToday and setToday directly on the class.

Finally, note that in line (C) the data member today is of the same type as the class itself of which it is a member. In C++, you can do this for only static data members. In other words, if today were a nonstatic member, we could not have written

```
Date today;              (WRONG)
```

However, we would be able to write

```
Date* today_ptr;
```

C++ does not permit a nonstatic member of a class T to be of type T. However, it can be of type T*. Java makes no such distinction. In other words, a data member, static or nonstatic, of Java class can be of the same type as the enclosing class.

Example 2:

Lest the reader think that static data members can only be changed by static member functions, we will now show an example where that is not the case. The Robot class below has one static data member in line (A), but no static member functions at all. As we make Robot objects, we want to associate with each robot a serial number to be stored in the data member idNum. The static data member nextIdNum keeps track of the next available serial number for the robot that will be made next.

```
//Robot.cc

#include <iostream>
#include <string>
using namespace std;

class Robot {
    int idNum;
    static int nextIdNum;                                    //(A)
    string owner;
public:
    int getIdNum();
    int whatIsNextIdNum();                                   //(B)
    string getOwner();
    Robot( string ownername);
    void print() { cout << idNum << " " << owner << endl; }
};

int Robot::nextIdNum = 1;                                    //(C)

int Robot::whatIsNextIdNum() { return nextIdNum++; }
```

```
int Robot::getIdNum() { return idNum; }

string Robot::getOwner() { return owner; }

Robot::Robot( string name ) {
    idNum = whatIsNextIdNum();                          //(D)
    owner = name;
}

int main()
{
    Robot r1( "ariel" );
    r1.print();                          // 1  ariel
    Robot r2( "mauriel" );
    r2.print();                          // 2  mauriel
    Robot r3( "mercurial" );
    r3.print();                          // 3  mercurial
    return 0;
}
```

Note the following special feature of the static member nextIdNum: Every time we use its value for an object of type Robot, the value is automatically incremented for the next robot. This is accomplished by the nonstatic method whatIsNextIdNum(), declared at (B), and by the incorporation of this method in the main constructor at (D). The static member nextIdNum is set initially to 1 by the usual initialization syntax in line (C).

11.3.1   Initialization and Destruction of Static Objects in C++

One of the more interesting aspects of C++ is that there is usually more to the main of a program than meets the eye, especially if the program includes static class members and their initializations in global scope. Consider the following program:[6]

```
//StaticInit.cc

#include <iostream>
using namespace std;
```

---

[6]If the reader is not already familiar with the concept of a destructor in C++ from its earlier brief introduction in Chapter 3, this subsection is best read after the material in Section 11.8.

```
class X {
public:
    X() { cout << "X's constructor invoked" << endl; }
    ~X() { cout << "X's destructor invoked" << endl; }
};

class Y {
public:
    static X xobj;                                          //(A)
};

X Y::xobj;                                                  //(B)

int main()
{
    cout << "This is the first executable statement of main"   //(C)
        << endl;
    return 0;
}
```

As evident from line (C), all that the `main` of this program calls for is the printing out of the string

```
This is the first executable statement of main
```

But if you compile and run this program, it outputs the following three lines:

```
X's constructor invoked
This is the first executable statement of main
X's destructor invoked
```

Where did this additional output come from? From *static initialization* and *static destruction*, as we explain below.

When a program includes initialization of static class members in the global scope, as in line (B) above, the C++ compiler introduces additional code into `main`, before the first programmer-written executable statement, for the creation of the static objects. For the eventual destruction of objects created in this manner, the compiler introduces yet more code into `main` immediately after the last programmer-written statement. In the above program, X's constructor for the initialization in line (B) is invoked before the statement in line (C) and X's destructor after line (C), accounting for the output shown.

11.4   STATIC MEMBERS IN JAVA

We will start by writing a Java program that imitates the first C++ program, Static1.cc, we showed in the previous section. We have a class X whose data members are of type int, static int, and static final int.

For the initialization of the data member q in the C++ program, we used the fact that C++ allows in-class initialization if a data member is of type static const. But there we left a similar data member p uninitialized inside the class to show that even a static const data member can be initialized outside the class.

For the case of Java, a static final data member must be provided with an in-class initialization. So the C++ option of initializing a static const data member outside a class does not exist in Java.

The program below shows in lines (A) and (B) the two different ways of providing the required in-class initializations for the two static final data members of X. While we provide a value directly for the initialization in line (A), we invoke a static method init for the initialization in line (B). Invoking methods in this manner is allowed for the in-class initialization of all data members, static or nonstatic, in Java.

```
//Static1.java

class X {
    public int m;
    public static int n = 100;
    public static final int p = 50;                      //(A)
    public static final int q = init();                  //(B)

    public X( int mm ) { m = mm; }

    public static int init() { return 200; }
}

class Test {
    public static void main(String[] args)
    {
        System.out.println( X.n );        // 100              //(C)
        System.out.println( X.q );        // 200

        X xobj_1 = new X( 20 );                                //(D)
        System.out.println(xobj_1.m + " " + xobj_1.n);   //20 100

        X xobj_2 = new X( 40 );
        System.out.println(xobj_2.m + " " + xobj_2.n);   //40 100
```

```
        X.n = 1000;                                          //(E)

        System.out.println(xobj_1.m + " " + xobj_1.n);    //20 1000

        System.out.println(xobj_2.m + " " + xobj_2.n);    //40 1000

    }
}
```

As was the case for C++, the most common way to access a static data member in Java is through the class directly, as by the following invocation in line (C) above:

```
    X.n
```

However, a static data member can also be accessed through the objects of the class, as was also the case for C++. The following invocation in the statement after line (D) demonstrates this:

```
    xobj_1.n
```

Also note that when we change the value of the static member in line (E), this change is reflected in the value of n as seen through the objects xobj_1 and xobj_2 constructed prior to line (E). This is demonstrated by the output produced by the statements after line (E).

Let's now consider the case when a static data member is private and see what that entails as to how we would retrieve the static member and how we would change its value:

```
//Static2.java

class X {
    private static int n = 100;                          //(A)
    public int m;
    public X( int mm ) { m = mm; }
    public static int getn() {return n;}                 //(B)
    public static void setn( int nn ) { n = nn; }        //(C)
}

class Test {
    public static void main(String[] args)
    {
        System.out.println( X.getn() );        // 100        //(D)

        X xobj_1 = new X( 20 );
        System.out.println(xobj_1.m + " " + xobj_1.getn()); //20 100
```

```
        X xobj_2 = new X( 40 );
        System.out.println(xobj_2.m + " " + xobj_2.getn()); //40 100

        X.setn( 1000 );                                              //(E)

        System.out.println(xobj_1.m + " " + xobj_1.getn()); //20 1000

        System.out.println(xobj_2.m + " " + xobj_2.getn()); //40 1000
    }
}
```

Because the static member is private in line (A), we had to add to the class the getn and the setn methods, both static, in lines (B) and (C). Instead of accessing the static member n directly, we now do so through getn, which may be invoked directly on the class as shown in line (D), or on the objects made from the class, as in the two statements after line (D). Similarly, to change the value of the static member n, we invoke setn directly on the class, as in line (E). We could also invoke setn on the objects made from the class.

To illustrate the use of static members in more meaningful situations, we will now consider the same two examples — the Date class and the Robot class — we presented for the case of C++ in the previous section. For each, we will point out the similarities and differences between the Java and the C++ programs.

Example 1:

We will consider first the Date class. Here is a comparable Java definition of the Date class:

```
//Date.java

class Date {
    private int d, m, y;
    private static Date today = new Date( 31, 10, 2001 );        //(A)

    public Date( int dd, int mm, int yy ) {                      //(B)
        d = dd;
        m = mm;
        y = yy;
    }

    public Date( int dd, int mm ) {                              //(C)
        d = dd;
        m = mm;
        y = today.y;
```

```
    }

    public Date( int dd ) {                                          //(D)
        d = dd;
        m = today.m;
        y = today.y;
    }

    public Date() {                                                  //(E)
        d = today.d;
        m = today.m;
        y = today.y;
    }

    public static void setToday( int dd, int mm, int yy ) {          //(F)
        today = new Date(dd, mm, yy);
    }

    public void print() {
        System.out.println( "day: " + d + " month: " + m
                                      + " year: " + y );
    }

    public static void main( String[] args ) {
        Date d1 = new Date( 1, 1, 1970 );
        d1.print();                // day: 1  month: 1  year: 1970
        Date d2 = new Date( 2 );
        d2.print();                // day: 2  month: 10  year: 2001
        setToday(3, 4, 2000);                                        //(G)
        today.print();             // day: 3  month: 4  year: 2000
        Date d3 = new Date( 7 );
        d3.print();                // day: 7  month: 4  year: 2000
        Date d4 = new Date();
        d4.print();                // day: 3  month: 4  year: 2000
    }
}
```

Note how the static member today is declared and initialized at the same time at (A), something that cannot be done in C++. (A static data member must also be const for C++ to allow for its in-class initialization.)

Additionally, for the C++ implementation of the Date class in the Date.cc program of Section 11.3, we used the mechanism of default arguments in a single three-argument constructor to simulate a two-argument constructor, a one-argument constructor, and a no-argument constructor. Java does not permit default arguments for method parameters. So if we want these other constructors in addition to a three-argument constructor in line (B), we have to provide those explicitly. That's what has been done in lines (C), (D), and (E) of the program.

Line (F) of the program above defines a static method for resetting the value of the static data member today. Line (G) of main invokes this method directly on the class to change the value stored in today. The code that follows line (G) demonstrates the results achieved with the constructors that set the state of the object partly according to what is stored in today.

Example 2:

As was the case with the C++ program Robot.cc of the previous section, we will now show that a static data member can be modified by a nonstatic method to give a class useful functionality. The following program, with a static data member and no static methods at all (except, of course, for main), is the Java version of Robot.cc:

```java
//Robot.java

class Robot {
    public int idNum;
    public static int nextIdNum = 1;                        //(A)
    public String owner;

    public int getIdNum() { return idNum; }
    public String getOwner() { return owner; }

    public Robot() { idNum = nextIdNum++; };                //(B)
    public Robot( String name) { this(); owner = name; }    //(C)

    public void print() { System.out.println( idNum + " " + owner ); }

    public static void  main( String[] args )
    {
        Robot r1 = new Robot( "ariel" );
        r1.print();                             // 1 ariel
        Robot r2 = new Robot( "mauriel" );
        r2.print();                             // 2 maurial
        Robot r3 = new Robot( "mercurial" );
        r3.print();                             // 3 mercurial
    }
}
```

The static member nextIdNum is declared at (A) and also initialized right there. This class member will keep track of the next ID number available for the next robot. The purpose of the no-arg constructor at (B) is to assign a value to the idNum member of a new Robot and, at the same time, to increment the value of the static member nextIdNum. The regular constructor calls the no-arg constructor as its first executable statement.

11.5   CONST MEMBER FUNCTIONS IN C++

If the sole purpose of a member function in C++ is to retrieve data that may be in the private section of an object, it is best to declare such a function to be of type const, as in the example below:

```
class Date {
    int d, m, y;
public:
    int getDay() const { return d; }
    int getMonth() const { return m; }
    int getYear() const;
    // ....
};
```

By declaring the 'get' functions to be const, the compiler will make sure that the code written for these functions does not inadvertently alter the state of the object.

The tag const is also required in the headers of such member functions if they are defined outside the class. For example, the header of the getYear() function declared above must contain const as shown below:

```
int Date::getYear() const {
    return y;
}
```

11.6   SELF-REFERENCE IN C++

Sometimes it makes for more convenient code if a member function can access the object on which the function is invoked. Additionally, in some situations a constructor needs to directly access the object under construction. A member function accessing the object on which the function is invoked, or a constructor accessing the object under construction, is referred to as *self-reference*. Self-reference in both C++ and Java is achieved by using the keyword this.

As an example of self-reference in C++, let's say that for reasons of convenience we want to use the same identifier for a data member of a class as for a parameter in the definition of a constructor for the class. How can we distinguish between the two uses of the same identifier in the implementation code for the constructor? By using the keyword `this` to qualify the data member, as in the example below:

```
//SelfRef.cc

#include <iostream>
using namespace std;

class X {
public:
    int m;                                              //(A)
    X( int m ) { this->m = m; }                         //(B)
};

int main()
{
    X xobj( 20 );
    cout << "m: " << xobj.m << endl;        // m: 20
    return 0;
}
```

The name of the data member in line (A) is the same as the identifier used as a parameter in line (B). But this does not create a problem for the compiler since the syntax `'this->m'` makes clear as to which m is what in the body of the constructor in line (B). In general, the keyword `this` is a pointer to the object on which the method is invoked. For the case of a constructor, the keyword `this` points to the object under construction.

Self-reference also plays an important role in the definition of those functions whose multiple invocations we want to "chain together," as in the following call:

```
some_object.funct( arg_1 ).funct( arg_2 ).funct( arg_3 );
```

This statement calls for invoking `funct` on `some_object`. On the object returned by the operation `some_object.funct( arg_1 )`, we invoke `funct` again but with a different argument, and so on. Presumably, `funct` changes the state of `some_object` in some way. And presumably we want `some_object.funct( arg_1 )` to return this modified object so that `funct( arg_2 )` can be invoked on it. For `funct` to be able to return the modified `some_object`, it would need to access the object on which it is invoked.

The following example illustrates how multiple invocations of a function can be chained together if the function returns the object on which it is invoked. The program shown uses a class `SpecialInt`, which you may think of as a range-limited integer type for some application. The integer value held by a `SpecialInt` is not allowed to be outside the range $(-100, 100)$. This class comes with a `plus` function defined as:

```
    SpecialInt& SpecialInt::plus( SpecialInt sm ) {
        accumulator += sm.getI();
        if ( accumulator > 100 || accmulator < -100 ) throw Err();
        return *this;
    }
```

Note especially the return statement:

```
    return *this;
```

So when the function `plus` is invoked on a `SpecialInt` object, it modifies the `accumulator` in the object on which the function is invoked and returns a reference to this modified object. This allows the chaining together of the `plus` invocations on the same object. So if we say

```
    SpecialInt s1( 4 );
    SpecialInt s2( 5 );
    s1.plus( s2 );
```

the value of the accumulator in the `s1` object will become 9. And if we say

```
    SpecialInt s1( 4 );
    SpecialInt s2( 5 );
    SpecialInt s3( 6 );
    s1.plus( s2 ).plus( s3 );
```

the value of the accumulator in the `s1` object will now become 15. In this manner we could chain together as many invocations of `plus` as we wanted. Here is the complete code:

```
//SpecialInt.cc

#include <iostream>
using namespace std;

class Err {};

class SpecialInt {
    int i;
public:
    int accumulator;
    SpecialInt( int m ) {
        if ( m > 100 || m < -100 ) throw Err();
        i = m;
        accumulator = m;
    }

    int getI() { return i; }
```

```
    SpecialInt& plus( SpecialInt m );
};

SpecialInt& SpecialInt::plus( SpecialInt sm ) {                    //(A)
    accumulator += sm.getI();
    if ( accumulator > 100 || accumulator < -100 ) throw Err();
    return *this;
}

int main()
{
    SpecialInt s1( 4 );
    SpecialInt s2( 5 );
    SpecialInt s3( 6 );
    SpecialInt s4( 7 );
    s1.plus( s2 ).plus( s3 ).plus( s4 );
    cout << s1.accumulator << endl;         // prints out 22
    // SpecialInt s5( 101 );                // range violation
    return 0;
}
```

It is important to note that the following version of plus will not work, even though the only difference from the version shown previously in line (A) is in the return type. In the following version, we return a copy of the object, as opposed to a reference to the object on which plus is invoked.

```
    SpecialInt SpecialInt::plus( SpecialInt sm ) {                 //(B)
        accumulator += sm.getI();
        if ( accumulator > 100 || accmulator < -100 )
            throw Err();
        return *this;
    }
```

With this new version, the object returned by

```
    SpecialInt s1( 4 );
    SpecialInt s2( 5 );
    s1.plus( s2 );                                                 //(C)
```

s1.plus(s2) will actually be a copy of the s1 object constructed previously. While the statement in line (C) above will cause the accumulator data member of s1 to change to 9, a second invocation of plus, as in the statement in line (D) below

```
    SpecialInt s1( 4 );
    SpecialInt s2( 5 );
    SpecialInt s3( 6 );
    s1.plus( s2 ).plus( s3 );                                     //(D)
```

will now be invoked on the copy of s1 returned by s1.plus(s2), as opposed to on the original s1 itself. It is for this reason that, if we use the version of plus shown in line (B), the final value printed out in main above will be the erroneous number 9 as opposed to the correct answer 22.

11.7 SELF-REFERENCE IN JAVA

As mentioned already, Java also supports the keyword this for self-reference. As with C++, we can use this keyword to avoid name conflicts in the implementation code for a method or a constructor if convenience dictates that the identifier used for a data member have the same name as a parameter of the method or the constructor. The following example illustrates:

```
//SelfRef.java

class X {
    private int n;                                         //(A)
    public X( int n ) { this.n = n; }                      //(B)

    public static void main( String[] args ) {
        X xobj = new X( 20 );
        System.out.println( xobj.n );
    }
}
```

Note that the name of the parameter in the constructor in line (B) is the same as the name of the data member in line (A). Yet, because we have accessed the data member by this.n, the compiler has no trouble keeping track of which n is which in the body of the constructor.

As was the case with C++, self-reference also plays an important role in defining methods that must return the object on which the method is invoked. Shown below is the Java version of the C++ program SpecialInt.cc of the previous section. The plus method in the Java version is defined as follows:

```
SpecialInt plus( SpecialInt sm ) throws Exception {
    accumulator += sm.getI();
    if ( accumulator > 100 || accumulator < -100 )
        throw new Exception();
    return this;
}
```

The return statement of this method uses the keyword this to return a reference to the object on which the method is invoked. So given repeated invocations as in line (C) below

```
SpecialInt s1 = new SpecialInt( 4 );
SpecialInt s2 = new SpecialInt( 5 );
SpecialInt s3 = new SpecialInt( 6 );
SpecialInt s4 = new SpecialInt( 7 );

s1.plus( s2 ).plus( s3 ).plus( s4 );                        //(C)
```

the first invocation of plus in s1.plus(s2) returns a reference to the modified s1 object. The next invocation of plus is on this modified s1, and so on.

The complete program is shown below:

```
//SpecialInt.java

class SpecialInt {
    int i;
    int accumulator;

    SpecialInt( int m ) throws Exception {
        if ( m > 100 || m < -100 ) throw new Exception();
        i = m;
        accumulator = m;
    }

    int getI() { return i; }

    SpecialInt plus( SpecialInt sm ) throws Exception {
        accumulator += sm.getI();
        if ( accumulator > 100 || accumulator < -100 )
            throw new Exception();
        return this;
    }

    public static void main( String[] args ) throws Exception {
        SpecialInt s1 = new SpecialInt( 4 );
        SpecialInt s2 = new SpecialInt( 5 );
        SpecialInt s3 = new SpecialInt( 6 );
        SpecialInt s4 = new SpecialInt( 7 );
        s1.plus( s2 ).plus( s3 ).plus( s4 );
        System.out.println( s1.accumulator );        // 22
        //SpecialInt s5 = new SpecialInt( 101 );   // range violation
    }
}
```

11.8 DESTRUCTORS IN C++

As mentioned already in Chapter 3, when a newly created object goes out of scope, it is automatically destroyed in the memory by invoking its destructor. For example, consider the following program, in which we have first defined a class GameScore with two data members, homeTeamScore and otherTeamScore. We have also defined for this class a constructor and a destructor, the latter denoted ~GameScore(). The destructor is given the name of the class prefixed by a tilde. *It can neither return a value, nor can it take any parameters.*

Except for the message it prints out, the destructor provided in line (A) below is a do-nothing destructor. A trivial class like GameScore really does not need a programmer-defined destructor at all since it does not appropriate any system resources (such as memory) that would need to be freed up explicitly under program control prior to object destruction. Whatever memory is required for storing the two data members homeTeamScore and otherTeamScore would be automatically freed up when a GameScore object is destroyed. Nonetheless, the destructor shown in line (A) will help us shed light on some important properties of object destruction in C++.

```
//Destruct.cc

#include <iostream>
using namespace std;

class GameScore {
    int homeTeamScore;
    int otherTeamScore;
public:
    GameScore( int score1, int score2 ) {
        homeTeamScore = score1;
        otherTeamScore = score2;
    }
    ~GameScore() {                                        //(A)
        cout << "GameScore object destroyed    "
            <<  homeTeamScore << " vs. "
            <<  otherTeamScore << endl;
    }
};

int main()
{
    GameScore gs1( 28, 3 );
    GameScore gs2( 35, 7 );
    return 0;
}
```

When this program is executed, the objects gs1 and gs2 created in main() will go out of scope when the flow of control hits the right brace of main(). As the two objects go out of scope, their destructors will be invoked. The result will be that the following message will appear on the terminal:

```
GameScore object destroyed   35 vs. 7
GameScore object destroyed   28 vs. 3
```

Note that the destructors are invoked in an order that is reverse of the order in which the objects are created. That is, the last object created will be the first to be destroyed.

Now let's examine a small variation on the example above. In main of the program below, in addition to the GameScore objects gs1 and gs2 created directly by the invocation of the constructor, let's have another object, p, of type GameScore* that points to a GameScore object created by using the operator new:

```cpp
//Destruct2.cc

#include <iostream>
using namespace std;

class GameScore {
    int homeTeamScore;
    int otherTeamScore;
public:
    //constructor:
    GameScore( int score1, int score2 ) {
        homeTeamScore = score1;
        otherTeamScore = score2;
    }
    //destructor:
    ~GameScore() {
        cout << "GameScore Object destroyed "
             <<   homeTeamScore << " vs. "
             <<   otherTeamScore << endl;
    }
};

int main()
{
    GameScore gs1( 28, 3 );
    GameScore gs2( 35, 7 );
    GameScore* p = new GameScore( 29, 0 );            //(A)
    return 0;
}
```

When this program is executed, we still get the same two lines of output as before:

```
GameScore object destroyed    35 vs. 7
GameScore object destroyed    28 vs. 3
```

In other words, the GameScore object pointed to by p in line (A) above is not getting destroyed. The reason for this is not too hard to understand. As the thread of execution hits the right brace of main(), what goes out of scope are the variables gs1, gs2 and p. That frees up the memory occupied by these three objects. With regard to the third object, note that only the memory where p is stored is freed up. But what's stored at this memory location is just the address of the last GameScore object. The end result is that the last GameScore object itself is not destroyed.

Objects that are created with the operator new can only be destroyed by applying the operator delete to the pointer returned by new. *When either a reference or a pointer to a class type object goes out of scope, the object destructor is NOT automatically invoked.*

To also free up the memory to which the variable p points in line (A) in the above program, we would have to change main so as to be

```
int main()
{
    GameScore gs1( 28, 3 );
    GameScore gs2( 35, 7 );
    GameScore* p = new GameScore( 29, 0 );
    delete p;
    return 0;
}
```

When the program shown previously is run with main() modified as above, the following messages are output on the terminal:

```
GameScore object destroyed    35 vs. 7
GameScore object destroyed    28 vs. 3
GameScore object destroyed    29 vs. 0
```

Instead of using the operator delete, we could also have destroyed the object pointed to by p by invoking the destructor directly, as in this version of main():

```
int main()
{
    GameScore gs1( 28, 3 );
    GameScore gs2( 35, 7 );
    GameScore* p = new GameScore( 29, 0 );
    p->~GameScore();
    return 0;
}
```

This would produce exactly the same output as before.

The example we showed above is much too trivial, in the sense that the class GameScore as defined does not really need an explicitly defined destructor because the objects of this class do not appropriate any special resources, except for the memory needed for storing the values of the data members. The system-supplied default destructor for this class would work just fine in this case.

To consider a case when a programmer-supplied destructor is genuinely needed, here is an example in which the creation of an object entails appropriating a chunk of memory. All that is stored in a data member of the object is a pointer to this memory. Here is the code:

```
//DestructorNecessary.cc

#include <iostream>
using namespace std;

class X {
public:
    int* ptrToArray;
    int size;

    X( int* ptr, int sz ) : size(sz) {                          //(A)
        ptrToArray = new int[size];                             //(B)
        for ( int i = 0; i < size; i++ ) ptrToArray[i] = ptr[i]; //(C)
    }

    ~X() {                                                      //(D)
        cout << "hello from the destructor" << endl;
        delete [] ptrToArray;                                  //(E)
    }
};

int main()
{
    int freshData[100] = {0};
    X xobj( freshData, 100 );                                  //(F)
    X* p = new X( freshData, 100 );                            //(G)
    delete p;                                                  //(H)
    return 0;
}
```

The data member `ptrToArray` stores a pointer to the array for which memory is appropriated in the constructor in line (B). After acquiring the memory, the constructor copies over in line (C) its argument array into the freshly acquired memory pointed to by `ptrToArray`. The destructor, defined in line (D), invokes the `delete[]` operator in line (E) for releasing the memory that was appropriated by the constructor in line (B).

If you run this program, when the flow of execution hits the right brace of `main`, the destructor will be invoked for destroying the two X objects created in lines (F) and (G), for the latter through the invocation of `delete` in line (H). As a result, the following two messages will be printed out on the terminal:

```
hello from the destructor
hello from the destructor
```

In connection with explicit invocations of destructors, invoking a destructor when it should not be can lead to unpredictable behavior and often hard-to-locate bugs in computer programs. Consider the following program:

```
//DestructWhenNot.cc

class X {
public:
    int* ptrToArray;
    int size;
    X( int* ptr, int sz ) : size(sz) {
        ptrToArray = new int[size];
        for ( int i = 0; i < size; i++ ) ptrToArray[i] = ptr[i];
    }
    ~X() { delete [] ptrToArray; }
};

int main()
{
    int freshData[100] = {0};
    X* p1 = new X( freshData, 100 );
    X* p2 = new X( freshData, 100 );
    delete p1;                                                //(A)
    delete p1;                               // ERROR         //(B)
    return 0;
}
```

Here we have, presumably inadvertently, mistyped p2 as p1 in line (B) of `main()`. Inadvertently calling twice the destructor for p1 may or may not not be detected even at run time. But note that deleting an object twice is a serious error and can lead to unpredictable behavior, if not a memory segmentation fault. The second invocation of the destructor could delete the contents of some part of the memory that, after the first invocation in line (A), got put to use for something else.[7]

11.9 OBJECT DESTRUCTION IN JAVA

Unlike what's achieved by a destructor in C++, Java does not provide a way to destroy an object at will. While you are allowed to recommend to Java runtime that unreferenced objects (referred to as *garbage*) be destroyed and the memory occupied by them reclaimed, you cannot destroy a particular object at a specific moment during the execution of a Java program.

Memory occupied by unreferenced objects in Java is automatically reclaimed by a low-priority *garbage collection* thread that runs continuously in the background while your application program is being executed. However, before actually destroying an unreferenced object, the garbage collector invokes the class's `finalize` method for the object. Every class inherits a do-nothing `finalize` from the root class `Object`, but you can provide an override definition for your own class. An override definition is needed if an object appropriates non-Java resources, such as open files, I/O connections, and so on, that the object must either close or free up before the object is permanently discarded. When an object's `finalize` method is invoked, the object is said to be *finalized*.

The garbage collection process in Java carries no guarantees as to the order in which the unreferenced objects will be finalized and the memory occupied by them reclaimed. There are even no guarantees that the garbage collection will be invoked on all the unreferenced objects, or, for that matter, on any unreferenced objects at all. The application program may exit before the garbage collector can do its thing, which would cause the underlying system to free up all of the memory occupied by the application program anyway — but without the finalization of the objects destroyed without the benefit of the garbage collector. For most applications this will not cause a problem because, as the Java Virtual Machine exits, it will automatically close all open files and sockets.

The following program is a simple demonstration of the fact that the unreferenced objects may be finalized and destroyed in an order that cannot be predicted beforehand and that not all unreferenced objects may get finalized before the Java Virtual Machine exits.

---

[7]As our examples have shown, most commonly a destructor is invoked implicitly when a class-type variable goes out of scope, or explicitly through the invocation of either the `delete` or the `delete[]` operator on a *pointer* acquired through the `new` or the `new[]` operator, respectively. However, as mentioned in the C++ standard [41, clause 12.4], it is legal to invoke a destructor explicitly on a class-type variable. But such direct invocations are rarely needed in practice. The standard shows an example related to memory management where such a direct invocation of a destructor could be useful.

The class X in the program has a data member id that serves as a serial number for the object. The first object of type X will have a value of 1 for value of id, the second object a value of 2, and so on. In the main of Test, we construct an array of 10,000 objects of type X in line (C) through (E); their id numbers will range from 1 through 10,000. After creating the array, we suddenly set the array reference to null in line (F), causing the entire array object to become unreferenced. This causes all the objects whose references are held in the elements of the array to also become unreferenced, and to thus become candidates for garbage collection. We then *ask* the garbage collector in line (G) to *try* to reclaim the memory occupied by the unreferenced objects by invoking

```
System.gc();
```

If we did not explicitly request the garbage collector to make a fresh sweep of the allocated memory, it is possible that the application would exit before any of the objects is finalized. When control returns from a call to System.gc(), this means that the Java Virtual Machine has made a best effort to reclaim space from all unreferenced objects.

In the code below, note that the finalize method in line (A) prints out a message if the id of the object involved is a multiple of 1000.

```
//GC.java

class X {
    int id;
    static int nextId = 1;

    //constructor:
    public X() { id = nextId++; }

    protected void finalize() throws Throwable {              //(A)
        if ( id%1000 == 0 )
            System.out.println("Finalization of X object, id = " + id);
        super.finalize();                                     //(B)
    }
}

class Test {
    public static void main( String[] args ) {
        X[] xarray = new X[ 10000 ];                          //(C)
        for (int i = 0; i < 10000; i++ )                      //(D)
            xarray[i] = new X();                              //(E)
        xarray = null;                                        //(F)
        System.gc();                                          //(G)
    }
}
```

Shown below is the output from five different runs of the program. As is clear from the output, the unreferenced objects may be finalized and discarded in virtually any order.

First run:

```
Finalization of X object, id = 10000
Finalization of X object, id = 8000
Finalization of X object, id = 5000
Finalization of X object, id = 1000
Finalization of X object, id = 2000
Finalization of X object, id = 3000
Finalization of X object, id = 4000
```

Second run:

```
Finalization of X object, id = 3000
Finalization of X object, id = 1000
Finalization of X object, id = 2000
```

Third run:

```
Finalization of X object, id = 5000
Finalization of X object, id = 1000
Finalization of X object, id = 2000
Finalization of X object, id = 3000
Finalization of X object, id = 4000
```

Fourth run:

```
Finalization of X object, id = 8000
Finalization of X object, id = 9000
Finalization of X object, id = 1000
Finalization of X object, id = 2000
Finalization of X object, id = 3000
Finalization of X object, id = 4000
Finalization of X object, id = 5000
Finalization of X object, id = 6000
```

Fifth run:

```
Finalization of X object, id = 1000
Finalization of X object, id = 2000
Finalization of X object, id = 3000
Finalization of X object, id = 4000
```

```
Finalization of X object, id = 5000
Finalization of X object, id = 6000
Finalization of X object, id = 7000
```

Obviously, the garbage collector is not able to finalize all the objects before the Java Virtual Machine quits. For the second run, fewer than half of the 10,000 objects are getting finalized and garbage collected.

Note that the override definition of finalize in line (A) invokes super.finalize in line (B). As recommended by Arnold and Gosling [2, p. 49], it is a good practice to always remember to invoke super.finalize in the code for finalize. Failure to do so may result in the superclass part of the object to not get finalized.

As the following "pathological" variation on the above program shows, it is possible to resurrect an object that is being finalized. Even when there are no further references to an object (which causes the garbage collector to invoke its finalize), for obvious reasons the object has to be accessible inside its own finalize method. This fact can be used to resurrect the object, preventing its destruction — at least until what was resurrected becomes unreferenced or goes out of scope. In the following program, as each X object is being finalized, it is resurrected by

```
X resurrect = this;
```

in line (B) of the program. This step creates a new reference to the object, which is then put away in line (C) in a static array that was defined earlier in line (A). This causes the object in question to not get destroyed until the Java Virtual Machine exits. It is interesting to know that finalize will not be invoked again on resurrected objects. The garbage collector invokes finalize exactly once for each object.

```
//GC_Resurrect.java

class X {
    int id;
    static int nextId = 1;
    static X[] staticArr = new X[10000];                        //(A)

    //constructor:
    public X() { id = nextId++; }

    protected void finalize() throws Throwable {
        if ( id%1000 == 0 )
            System.out.println("Finalization of X object, id = " + id);
        super.finalize();
        X resurrect = this;                                     //(B)
        putItAway( resurrect );                                 //(C)
    }

    public void putItAway( X xobj ) { staticArr[ id ] = this; }
}
```

```
class Test {
    public static void main( String[] args ) {
        X[] xarray = new X[ 10000 ];
        for (int i = 0; i < 10000; i++ )
            xarray[i] = new X();
        xarray = null;
        System.gc();
    }
}
```

What if the finalize method for a class throws an exception? The exception is ignored and finalization of the object terminated.

It is also possible to call the gc method through the Runtime class by invoking

```
Runtime.getRuntime().gc()
```

This is equivalent to the System.gc() call.

11.10 COPY CONSTRUCTORS AND COPY ASSIGNMENT OPERATORS IN C++

Let's say we have a class without any pointer members:

```
class X {
    int n;
public:
    X( ..... ) { .........}
};
```

For a simple class such as this, the initializations and the assignment in the following statements have obvious meanings:

```
void f() {
    X x1;
    X x2 = x1;                                                    //(A)
    X x3;
    x3 = x2;                                                      //(B)
}
```

The *initialization* at (A) is to be interpreted as: Copy byte-by-byte the data members of object x1 into the memory locations reserved for the data members of object x2. The *assignment* at (B) says the same thing — to copy byte-by-byte the data members of object x2 into the memory locations reserved for the data members of object x3.

At the end of the function, when the variables x1, x2, and x3 go out of scope, all three will be deleted, even though all three are copies of the same object. This is not a problem because all three will occupy different places in the memory.

Now consider the case when one of the members is a pointer:

```
class X {
   int* ptr;
   int size;
public:
   X( ..... ) { .........}
   ~X() { delete[] ptr; }
};
```

The data member `ptr` is presumably a pointer to an array of `int`s. The second data member, `size`, will help us keep track of how many elements there are in the array. We will again define a function as before

```
void f() {
   X x1;
   X x2 = x1;                              //(C)
   X x3;
   x3 = x2;                                //(D)
}
```

Let's start by assuming that the initialization at (C) and the assignment at (D) have the same semantics as before — a memberwise copy of the object on the right into the memory locations for the members of the object on the left side of the '=' operator. A memberwise copy for the initialization at (C) would cause x2.ptr to be a copy of x1.ptr, both pointers pointing to the *same* chunk of memory. The effect is the same as in the following two declarations:

```
int* ptr = new int[5];
int* p = ptr;
```

The pointers p and `ptr` will point to the same location in the memory.

If we also assume a memberwise copy for the assignment operator at (D), then x3.ptr will also point to the same chunk of memory as x2.ptr, which is pointing to the same memory as x1.ptr.

Therefore, just before the objects x1, x2 and x3 go out of scope as the thread of execution hits the right brace of the function f shown above, they will each contain a pointer member pointing to the same chunk of memory. As they go out of scope, they will all be deleted via their destructors, which is the destructor for class X. *But this will cause triple deletion of the same chunk of memory pointed to by the data member* ptr *in each of the three objects.* What happens when a program tries to free up the same chunk of memory multiple times in this manner is undefined. It may cause the program to behave in an unpredictable manner or it might even cause the program to crash.

Such anomalies can be avoided by defining what it means to copy an object for the purpose of initialization and for the purpose of assignment. The definition of what it means to copy an object for initialization is called a *copy constructor*. And the definition of what it means to copy an object for the assignment operation is called a *copy assignment operator*, or just an *assignment operator*.

For type T, the prototype of the copy constructor is[8]

```
T( const T& );
```

and the prototype of the copy assignment operator is

```
T& operator=( const T& );
```

The following would be an acceptable definition for a copy constructor for the class X we talked about before:

```
//copy constructor:
X( const X& xobj ) {                              //(E)
    size = xobj.size;
    ptr = new int[ size ];                        //(F)
    for (int i=0; i<size; i++) {                  //(G)
        ptr[i] = xobj.ptr[i];
    }
}
```

This copy constructor's charge is to construct an object of type X whose members are set according to the composition of the specific object xobj that's supplied as an argument to the constructor in line (E). In line (F), the `ptr` member of the object under construction points to the freshly acquired memory for the array data member of the object under construction. And, then, in the `for` loop in line (G), we copy into this new memory the elements of the array from the argument object xobj.

In a similar manner, we can write a definition of the copy assignment operator for class X:

---

[8]The modifier const for the parameter in the headers of both the copy constructor and the assignment operator is not mandatory, but it makes for safer code and it permits both const and non-const objects to be duplicated. Making a duplicate without altering the original is not always desirable. For example, it is sometimes necessary to embed in a class the notion of ownership of an object that must not have more than one owner. Both the copy construction and assignment operations for such classes require transfer of ownership from the right-hand side to the left-hand side of the assignment operator. A smart pointer class, such as the auto_ptr class from the C++ Standard Library, represents this case. The prototype of a copy constructor for such a class would be

```
T( T& );
```

and the prototype of the assignment operator

```
T& operator=( T& );
```

Smart pointer classes are discussed in Chapter 12.

```
//copy assignment operator:
X& operator=( const X& xobj) {                                           //(H)
    if ( this != &xobj ) {                                              //(I)
        delete [] ptr;                                                  //(J)
        size = xobj.size;
        ptr = new int[ size ];                                          //(K)
        for (int i=0; i<size; i++) ptr[i] = xobj.ptr[i];               //(L)
    }
    return *this;                                                       //(M)
}
```

To fully appreciate this definition, recall that it will be called in the following sort of a situation

```
X xobj_1(...);
X xobj_2(...);
xobj_1 = xobj_2;              // need a copy assignment operator
```

The compiler reads the last line as

```
xobj_1.operator=( xobj_2 );
```

Therefore, the keyword this in line (I) refers in this example to object xobj_1. The members size and ptr in lines (J) and (K) also refer to the object xobj_1. To explain what is happening in lines (I) through (M): we first delete in line (J) the block of memory pointed to by the ptr member of the object on the left side of the assignment operator, xobj_1. In line (K), the same member is then made to point to freshly acquired memory. In line (L), we then copy from the array that's a part of the object on the right side of the operator to the object on the left side. The boolean expression in line (I)

```
if ( this != &xobj ) ....
```

is meant to take care of self-assignment, as in

```
X xobj( .. );
xobj = xobj;
```

In the event of such a self-assignment, the copy assignment operator does nothing, except returning a reference to the same object. And that brings us to line (M). The code shown above for the copy assignment operator would be perfectly legal even if it did not include line (M), with the proviso, of course, that we make the return type a void. What is being said here is that the operator function operator= does not need to return anything in order to do a correct job of the assignment. What we gain by including line (M) is that we can now chain together assignment operators like

```
X xobj_1(...);
X xobj_2(...);
X xobj_3(...);
```

```
    xobj_1 = xobj_2 = xobj_3;
```

With the copy assignment returning a reference to the object constructed, this chaining is equivalent to

```
    xobj_1.operator=( xobj_2.operator=( xobj_3 ) );
```

While it is rare to see chaining of the assignment operator like "xobj_1 = xobj_2 = xobj_3;" in computer programs, one has to allow for it since that is dictated by the language definition of the assignment operator.

Note the important difference between the copy constructor in line (E) and the copy assignment operator in line (H): the latter includes memory deallocation in line (J).

Shown below is a redefinition of class X with the copy constructor and the copy assignment operator included:

```
//CopyAssignX.cc

#include <iostream>
using namespace std;

class X {
    int* data;
    int size;
public:
    //constructor:
    X( int* ptr, int sz ) : size(sz) {
        data = new int[size];
        for ( int i = 0; i < size; i++ ) data[i] = ptr[i];
    }
    //copy constructor:
    X( const X& xobj ) {
        size = xobj.size;
        data = new int[ size ];
        for (int i=0; i<size; i++) data[i] = xobj.data[i];
    }
    //copy assignment operator:
    X& operator=( const X& xobj) {
        if ( this != &xobj ) {
            delete [] data;
            size = xobj.size;
            data = new int[ size ];
            for (int i=0; i<size; i++) data[i] = xobj.data[i];
        }
        return *this;
    }
```

```
    //destructor:
    ~X() { delete [] data; }
};

int main()
{
    int freshData[5] = {1, 2, 3, 4, 5};

    X x1( freshData, 5 );
    X x2 = x1;

    X x3( freshData, 5 );
    x3 = x2;

    return 0;
}
```

The examples we have shown so far regarding when a copy constructor is invoked have all been of the following kind:

```
    class X { /* .... */ };        // class X has copy constructor
    X xobj_1( /*  .... */ );       // construct X object xobj_1
    X xobj_2 = xobj_1;             // copy construct xobj_2          (N)
```

A copy constructor, if available, would also be invoked for the following kinds of situations:

```
    class X { /* ...   */ };
    X xobj( /* ...   */ };
    X* ptr = new X( xobj );        // copy constructor invoked       (O)
```

Note that the invocation X(xobj) on the right in line (O) matches the header X(const X&) of the copy constructor of class X. Comparing the statements in lines (N) and (O) above, the initialization syntax in (N) causes fresh memory to be acquired on the stack for the construction of a new X object. This memory is subsequently filled by copying over the contents of the object xobj_1 according to the copy constructor for X. On the other hand, in line (O) the operator new allocates fresh memory from the heap for constructing a new object of type X. The call X(xobj) then invokes the copy constructor of X for filling up this memory.

11.11 SEMANTICS OF THE ASSIGNMENT OPERATOR IN JAVA

Since there are no pointers in Java — at least not in the same sense as in C++ — there is no need to specify the copy constructors and copy assignment operators now. However, that does not mean that a simple assignment, whether for initialization or otherwise, has what intuition would ascribe to it at first thought. Consider the following code:

```
//AssignTest.java

class User {
    public String name;
    public int age;
    public User( String str, int n ) { name = str; age = n; }
}

class Test {
    public static void main( String[] args )
    {
        User u1 = new User( "ariel", 112 );
        System.out.println( u1.name );        // ariel
        User u2 = u1;                                          //(A)
        u2.name = "muriel";                                   //(B)
        System.out.println( u1.name );        // muriel
    }
}
```

One would want to know as to what meaning to give to the following statement in line (A) above

```
    User u2 = u1;
```

There is only one meaning that Java associates with this kind of an initialization: the variable u2 gets a copy of the same object reference that u1 is holding. In other words, after this initialization, both u1 and u2 have references to the same object, that is to the same chunk of memory. Any changes made to u2 will be reflected in u1. That's what the above program tries to show. When we change u2's name member to muriel in line (B), u1's name member undergoes the same change — because both u1 and u2 are pointing to exactly the same object in the memory.

But what if we wanted u2 to refer to a *copy* of the object to which u1 is holding a reference? We may need to do so because we anticipate modifying the copy without changing the original object. This can be done by invoking the clone() function that every object inherits from Object. In the next section, we discuss cloning in greater detail.

11.12 OBJECT CLONING IN JAVA

We will start with the simplest of examples and build up from there. Consider a simple class like

```
class X {
    int n;
    X() { n = 3; }
}
```

We can make an object of this class by

```
X xobj = new X();
```

Let's say that we want to clone such objects, in the sense defined at the end of the previous section. As it is, we will not be able to do so, even though the class is simple. For Java to clone an object, the class must implement the interface Cloneable.[9] To make X cloneable, we need to define X as

```
class X implements Cloneable {
   int n;
   X() { n = 3; }
}
```

By making X implement the Cloneable interface, X can use the byte-by-byte cloning function, clone(), that it inherits from the root class Object. Suppose we now construct an object of type X by

```
X xobj = new X();
```

its clone can then be constructed by

```
X xobj_clone = (X) xobj.clone();
```

The reason for casting down to X on the right side is that the Object cloning function deals with only Objects. Recall, on account of polymorphism, every object in Java is an Object (while the converse is of course not true). So the Object cloning function thinks of xobj as being of type Object and makes its byte-by-byte copy that is returned as an Object. The cast operator then casts it down to an object of type X.

The interface Cloneable is empty. It is simply a signal to the Object.clone() function that it is okay to clone objects of type X in our example here. If X did not state explicitly that *X implements Cloneable*, then the Object.clone() function would throw an exception of type CloneNotSupportedException. What this means is

---

[9]Interfaces in Java, introduced earlier in Chapter 3, are presented more fully in Chapter 15.

that if you did not want the objects of a certain class to be cloned, you would define that class without the *implements Cloneable* clause in its header.

Here is a working program for this simple case:

```
//ClonableX.java

class X implements Cloneable {
    public int n;
    public X() { n = 3; }

    public static void main( String[] args )
    {
        X xobj = new X();
        X xobj_clone = null;

        try {
            xobj_clone = (X) xobj.clone();                    //(A)
        } catch (CloneNotSupportedException e){}

        System.out.println( xobj.n );             // 3
        System.out.println( xobj_clone.n );       // 3

        xobj_clone.n = 3000;

        System.out.println( xobj.n );             // 3
        System.out.println( xobj_clone.n );       // 3000
    }
}
```

In the above example, we used Object's cloning method directly in line (A). Another approach to doing the same thing would be to write one's own cloning method that invokes Object's cloning method. Doing so serves as a stepping stone to writing cloning methods that are needed when a class possesses non-primitive data members. First, let's show how to write a cloning method that invokes Object's cloning method:

```
//CloneBasic.java

class X implements Cloneable {
    public int n;

    public X() { n = 3; }
```

```
    public Object clone() throws CloneNotSupportedException {     //(A)
        return super.clone();                                     //(B)
    }
}

class Test {
    public static void main( String[] args )
    {
        X xobj = new X();
        X xobj_clone = null;

        try {
            xobj_clone = (X) xobj.clone();
        }  catch (CloneNotSupportedException e){}

        System.out.println( xobj.n );                   // 3
        System.out.println( xobj_clone.n );             // 3

        xobj_clone.n = 3000;

        System.out.println( xobj.n );                   // 3
        System.out.println( xobj_clone.n );             // 3000
    }
}
```

The important thing here is that the class X has its own cloning method in line (A), even though it doesn't do much since all it does is to invokes the cloning method of the superclass in line (B), which is Object's cloning method.[10]

Also note that the clone() method we wrote for X has a return type of Object. That return type cannot be changed because clone() of X overrides clone() of Object. As mentioned in Chapter 15, a subclass method that overrides a method defined originally for a superclass is not allowed to change the return type of the overridden method.

While for the simple example above, we could have gotten away with not writing our own cloning method, that's not the case when a class possesses non-primitive data members. There is usually no alternative to writing your own clone() method when your class includes class-type objects for data members. A byte-by-byte copying carried out by Object.clone() may now result in bizarre and unexpected behavior.

---

[10]If X was extending another class, then the invocation super.clone() in line (B) would take care of the cloning of the data members of the superclass, including those that are private to the superclass.

In the following example, the class X has an array object as a member. The constructor fills this array with pseudorandom numbers between 0 and 9, both inclusive.[11]

```
//CloneArray.java

import java.util.*;                                    // for Random

class X implements Cloneable {

    public int[] arr = new int[5];

    public X() {
        Random ran = new Random();
        int i=0;
        while ( i < 5 )
            arr[i++] = (ran.nextInt() & 0xffff)%10;              //(A)
    }

    public Object clone() throws CloneNotSupportedException {     //(B)
        X xob = null;
        xob = (X) super.clone();
        //now clone the array separately:
        xob.arr = (int[]) arr.clone();                           //(C)
        return xob;
    }

    public String toString() {
        String printstring = "";
        for (int i=0; i<arr.length; i++) printstring += " " + arr[i];
        return printstring;
    }

    public static void main( String[] args ) throws Exception {
        X xobj = new X();
        X xobj_clone = (X) xobj.clone();                         //(D)
```

---

[11]The call `ran.nextInt()` in line (A) returns a uniformly distributed pseudorandom integer spanning the full range of the `int` type. The logical bit-wise AND with `0xffff` and then taking division modulo 10 yields non-negative integers between 0 and 9, both inclusive. Another way to generate a pseudorandom number within a specific range is to invoke `nextInt` with a specific argument. For example, the call

```
Random ran = new Random();
ran.nextInt( 10 );
```

yields a pseudorandom integer greater than or equal to 0 but less than 10. Pseudorandom numbers can also be generated in Java by calling the static method `Math.random()`, which returns a positive double greater than or equal to 0.0 and less than 1.0.

```
System.out.println( xobj );            // 0 4 5 2 5
System.out.println( xobj_clone );      // 0 4 5 2 5

xobj.arr[0] = 1000;                                      //(E)

System.out.println( xobj );            // 1000 4 5 2 5
System.out.println( xobj_clone );      // 0 4 5 2 5
    }
}
```

Compared to the previous program `CloneBasic.java`, the cloning method in line (B) now includes a statement for the cloning of the array object in line (C). Without this statement (that is, if we had opted for the byte-by-byte `Object.clone()`), the member `arr` of the cloned object would have acquired the same object reference as held by the member `arr` in the original object. In other words, `arr` in the cloned object would have pointed to exactly the same place in the memory as the `arr` array in the original X object.

By including in line (C) the extra statement for the cloning of the array object, the cloned X object gets a duplicate copy of the original array at a different place in the memory. Subsequently, if we change one of the array element in one of the objects, it would not affect the array in the other object. In the above program, this is demonstrated in `main()` by first creating in line (D) a clone and then changing the first element of the `arr` array in the original object in line (E). By printing out the arrays before and after this change, we can see that the change made to the original array did not affect the cloned array.

11.12.1 Cloning Arrays of Class-Type Objects

While the system is happy to clone arrays of primitive types for you (provided, of course, you invoke `clone()` on the array reference, as we did in line (C) of the previous program), you have to provide your own implementation code if you need to clone arrays (or other container types) of class-type objects. This is demonstrated by the following program in which the class Z has an array data member `yarr` of type Y[], with each Y element of the array containing a reference to an object of type X. If, for the cloning method of Z, you merely invoke

```
yarr.clone();
```

as we have in the commented out line (B) in the program below, the cloned Z object would have its `yarr` at a different location in the memory, but the X objects contained in the Y elements of the array would be the same as before. This is forestalled by providing our own implementation for the cloning of the array in the method in line (A). This implementation creates a new Y[] array in line (C) and fills this array in line (D) with clones of the elements in the Y[] array of the original Z object. The Y[]

array thus created is then assigned to the data member yarr of the cloned Z object in line (E).

```
//CloneClassTypeArr.java

class X implements Cloneable {
    public int p;
    public X( int q ) { p = q; }
    public Object clone() throws CloneNotSupportedException {
        return super.clone();
    }
    public String toString() { return p + ""; }
}

class Y implements Cloneable {
    public X x;
    public Y( X x ) { this.x = x; }
    public Object clone() throws CloneNotSupportedException {
        Y clone = (Y) super.clone();
        clone.x = (X) x.clone();
        return clone;
    }
    public String toString() { return x + ""; }
}

class Z implements Cloneable {
    public Y[] yarr;
    public Z( Y[] arr ) { this.yarr = arr; }
    public Object clone() throws CloneNotSupportedException {        //(A)
        Z zclone = (Z) super.clone();
        // zclone.yarr = ( Y[] ) yarr.clone();        // WRONG        //(B)
        Y[] yarrClone = new Y[ yarr.length ];                        //(C)
        for (int i=0; i < yarr.length; i++ )
            yarrClone[i] = (Y) yarr[i].clone();                      //(D)
        zclone.yarr = yarrClone;                                     //(E)
        return zclone;
    }
    public String toString() {
        String superString = "";
        for ( int i = 0; i < yarr.length; i++ ) {
            superString += yarr[i] + "   ";
        }
        return superString;
    }
}
```

```
class Test {
    public static void main( String[] args ) throws Exception
    {
        X xobj0 = new X( 5 );
        X xobj1 = new X( 7 );

        Y yobj0 = new Y( xobj0 );
        Y yobj1 = new Y( xobj1 );

        Y[] yarr = new Y[2];
        yarr[0] = yobj0;
        yarr[1] = yobj1;

        Z zobj = new Z( yarr );
        System.out.println( zobj );             // 5 7

        Z zclone = (Z) zobj.clone();
        System.out.println( zclone );           // 5 7

        zclone.yarr[0].x.p = 1000;

        System.out.println("\n\nComparing again zobj and its clone:");
        System.out.println( zobj );             // 5 7
        System.out.println( zclone );           // 1000 7

        if ( zobj.yarr == zclone.yarr )
            System.out.println(
                        "\n\nThere was no cloning of the Y array" );
        if ( zobj.yarr[0].x == zclone.yarr[0].x )
            System.out.println( "\n\nThe Y array was cloned, "
                    + "but its elements point to the same X objects" );
    }
}
```

11.13 POINTERS TO CLASS MEMBERS IN C++

Instead of using the designated names for accessing class members, it is also possible in C++ to use pointers that point *directly* to the data members and the member functions of a class. Different syntax is used for creating such pointers for static and nonstatic class members, and, within each category, for data members and member functions. Such pointers can be dereferenced with the operators

    .*   or   ->*

depending on whether we invoke the operator with respect to an object or with respect to a pointer to an object.

We will use the following example to illustrate how to set up pointers that point directly to class members:

```
//PointerDirectToMember.cc

#include <iostream>
#include <string>
using namespace std;

class Robot {
    int idNum;
    string owner;
    static int nextIdNum;
public:
    Robot( string ownername);
    int getIdNum();
    string getOwner();
    static int getNextIdNum();
};

Robot::Robot( string name ) {
    idNum = getNextIdNum();
    owner = name;
}

int Robot::getIdNum() {                                  //(A)
    int Robot::* ptr_idNum = &Robot::idNum;              //(B)
    return (*this).*ptr_idNum;                           //(C)
}

string Robot::getOwner() {                               //(D)
    string Robot::* ptr_owner = &Robot::owner;           //(E)
    return this->*ptr_owner;                             //(F)
}

//initialization of the static
//data member:
int Robot::nextIdNum = 1;

int Robot::getNextIdNum() {                              //(G)
    int* ptr_nextIdNum = &Robot::nextIdNum;              //(H)
    return (*ptr_nextIdNum)++;                           //(I)
}
```

```
int main()
{
    int (Robot::* pf_1)() = &Robot::getIdNum;                    //(J)
    string (Robot::* pf_2)() = &Robot::getOwner;                 //(K)
    int (* pf_3)() = &Robot::getNextIdNum;                       //(L)

    Robot r1( "ariel" );
    cout << (r1.*pf_1)() << "   " << (r1.*pf_2)();  // 1  ariel    //(M)
    cout << endl;

    Robot r2( "muriel" );
    cout << (r2.*pf_1)() << "   " << (r2.*pf_2)();  // 2  muriel
    cout << endl;

    Robot r3( "mercurial" );
    cout << (r3.*pf_1)() << "   " << (r3.*pf_2)();  // 3  mercurial
    cout << endl;

    cout << "Next available ID: " << (*pf_3)();     // 4          //(N)

    return 0;
}
```

Examine the implementation we wrote for the function getIdNum() in line (A). The left-hand side of the statement in line (B), reproduced here for convenience,

```
    int Robot::* ptr_idNum = &Robot::idNum;
```

declares the identifier ptr_idNum to be of type int Robot::*, that is a pointer to an int data member of class Robot. The right hand side makes this pointer point to the data member idNum. As mentioned earlier, the operators '.*' and '->*' can be used for dereferencing such a pointer depending on whether we invoke the operator with respect to an object or a pointer to the object. In the following statement in line (C) of the program

```
    return (*this).*ptr_idNum;
```

we used the .* operator with respect to the object *this on which the function getIdNum() will be invoked.

To illustrate the use of the operator '->*,' in the implementation code for the function getOwner() in line (D), in line (E) we have a declaration similar to what we showed earlier in line (B), but to access the owner data member, we now use the syntax

```
    this->*ptr_owner;
```

in line (F). Note that the pointer `ptr_owner` is of type `string Robot::*`.

The syntax for setting up a pointer to a static data member is shown in the implementation for the static member function `getNextIdNum()` in line (G). The pointer `ptr_nextIdNum` is now of the type `int*`, as opposed to `int Robot::*`, as made evident by the declaration in line (H). Also, as line (I) shows, dereferencing such a pointer is like dereferencing any pointer.

This takes us to the subject of setting up pointers to nonstatic and static member functions. At the beginning of `main()`, we declared three function pointers in lines (J), (K), and (L). The function pointer `pf_1` in line (J) is of type

```
int (Robot::*)()
```

which means that `pf_1` can be used for pointing to any `Robot` class member function that returns an `int` and that takes a void argument. The function pointer `pf_2` in line (K) is of type

```
string (Robot::*)()
```

This pointer can be used as a pointer for any `Robot` class member function that returns a `string` and that takes a void argument. Finally, the function pointer `pf_3` in line (L) is of type

```
int (*)()
```

which means that this pointer can be used for pointing to any function — in our context any static function — that returns an `int` and that takes a void argument.

Note how each of these function pointers is initialized. The first two, `pf_1` and `pf_2`, declared as pointers to nonstatic member functions, are initialized by the function names `Robot::getIdNum` and `Robot::getOwner`. The third, `pf_3`, declared as a pointer to a global function, is initialized by the static member function name `Robot::getNextIdNum`.

Also pay attention to the dereferencing of the function pointers in the rest of `main()`. The pointers to nonstatic member functions must be invoked on specific objects, as we show in line (M) of the program. On the other hand, pointers to static member function can be dereferenced as ordinary function pointers, as demonstrated by line (N).

11.14 INTERLEAVED CLASSES

Let's say that class X has a data member of type Y and class Y has a data member of type X. We can define these classes in the following manner:

```
//partial definition of X:
class X;
```

```
class Y {
    X* x;
    // ......
};

//complete definition of X:
class X  {
    Y* y;
    // ......
};
```

But you have to be careful about the following: In the definition of Y, you cannot call the constructors or the destructors or any other member functions of X because they have not yet been defined.

To get around this problem, you only declare function prototypes in Y, especially for those functions that need the functionality of X. You then supply implementations for these function prototypes after X is defined.

For example, the following is wrong because it calls the destructor of X in line (A) — before the X's destructor is defined.

```
//partial definition of X:
class X;

class Y {
    X* x;
public:
    //
    ~Y(){ delete x; }              // WRONG                    //(A)
};

// complete definition of X:
class X  {
    Y* y;
    // ......
};
```

But the following is correct:

```
//partial definition of X:
class X;

class Y {
    X* x;
    // ......
public:
    //only the prototype provided here for destructor:
    ~Y();
```

```
};

//complete definition of X:
class X  {
   Y* y;
   // ......
};

//complete def of Y's destructor provided separately:
Y::~Y(){ delete x; }
```

11.15 A C++ STUDY OF INTERLEAVED CLASSES OF MODERATE COMPLEXITY

So far in this chapter we have examined separately the many different aspects of C++ and Java classes. It's almost like six blind men trying to identify an elephant by feeling out its different parts. Pulling together this topic-by-topic level of understanding into a more integrated whole is not too difficult for Java, but can be challenging for the case of C++. To alleviate this problem, in this section we will present a mini case study of a moderately complex C++ class. The program shown here is an educational tool to help the reader with the following issues in the design of C++ programs:

- Class interleaving and how it impacts the design of code with regard to declarations and definitions.

- Testing for null pointers. A frequent source of bugs in C++ is that a pointer is not tested for null before it is dereferenced.

- No initialization (or improper initialization) of unused pointer fields in a constructor.

- When a data member is a pointer that points to an array of objects, not testing for whether the *argument* pointer in a constructor is non-null before proceeding to allocate memory for the array.

- Memory leaks caused by the absence of the delete or the delete[] operator in the destructor, or by using just delete where delete[] is needed.

- When using container classes, not taking advantage of the copy constructors, copy assignment operators, and so on, provided by STL for the container classes.

- and so on.

We'll consider an Employee class whose data members are of diverse type, each placing a different constraint on how the rest of the code is structured (we are talking about the code involving constructors, copy constructors, copy assignment operators, destructors, and so on):

```
class Employee {
    string firstName, lastName;
    Date dateOfBirth;
    Employee* friends;
    int numFriends;
    Auto* autos;
    int numAutos;
    Cat* kitty;
    vector<Dog> dogs;
    map<string, int> phoneList;
    // .......
};
```

About the data members of this class and the constraints each places on the design of the program:

- The first two data members, firstName and lastName, are straightforward, placing no special constraints on the rest of the code.

- The data member dateOfBirth is of class type. Because dateOfBirth is not a pointer, we'd need to define the Date class before the compiler sees the Employee class.

- The data member friends is a pointer to an array of Employee objects. Because this data member will point to dynamically allocated memory, we will have to make sure that the destructor of the Employee class invokes the delete[] operator to free up this memory. We will also have to make sure that the code for the constructors, the copy assignment operator, and so on, pays due regard to memory allocation and deallocation. Also, not be to underestimated is the importance of initialization of this pointer data member especially if it is not needed in the body of a constructor. *Without appropriate initialization, the destructor could try to delete segments of memory pointed to by the random bits contained in the pointer data member.*

- To keep track of how many friends a given Employee object has, we need the next data member, numFriends.

- The next data member, autos, is a pointer to an array of Auto objects. Since, as the reader will see shortly, the Auto class has a data member of type Employee, it cannot be defined before the Employee class. So we will assume that when the compiler sees the data member autos, it knows only that Auto is the name of a class. This means that the implementations of Employee constructors, destructors, and so on, that involve autos can only be provided after the class Auto is defined. The comments that were made earlier for the friends data member with regard to memory allocation, deallocation, and initialization, also apply here.

- The next data member, `numAutos`, is supposed to keep track of the number of `Auto` objects in the array `autos`.

- The next data member, `kitty`, is for illustrating that a pointer data member can also be used for an individual object. In this case, we have a choice of defining `Cat` either before or after the class `Employee`.

- The next data member, `dogs`, is a vector of `Dog` objects. As we will see, it is much easier to use STL containers for holding groups of objects than to use raw arrays. *With STL containers, you can use the copy constructor and the assignment operator supplied by the system.* That way all the memory allocation and deallocation headaches related to such data members disappear.

- The last data member, `phoneList`, is a map of `<string, int>` pairs. The comments we made about the `dogs` data member also apply here.

These constraints are reflected in the source code shown below. The reader should pay particular attention to the comments included. The reader should note especially the layout of the classes. For educational reasons, each definition has been placed the earliest it could be placed without the compiler complaining. For general C++ programming, it is commonly the case that the main class declarations would contain only the function prototypes. We have intentionally deviated from that practice to highlight the ramifications of the fact that a C++ compiler does not possess the look-ahead capability.

Our basic aim in the source code shown below is to be able to create `Employee` objects with the data members as discussed above. The constructors provided for this class take into the fact that the values for all of the data members may not be known in advance when a new `Employee` object is created. The source code also defines all the other support classes needed. Each class is provided with

- one or more constructors,

- a copy constructor,

- a copy assignment operator,

- a destructor,

- an overload definition for the output stream operator,

but only when necessary. If it is possible for a class to make do with the system supplied defaults for these constructors and operators, we do not gratuitously supply that class with our own definitions.

```
//Interleaved.cc

#include <string>
#include <iostream>
#include <vector>
#include <map>
using namespace std;


/////////////////// class Auto (declaration only) ///////////////////

class Auto;
// This class is intentionally only declared at this time, but
// not defined.  It cannot be defined because it needs a
// data member of type Employee that the compiler would not
// know about at this point.  However, we need to declare
// Auto as a class because it is needed in Employee.


/////////////////////////// class Date ///////////////////////////

// The following class is needed to add variety to the
// data members of Employee class.  The Employee data
// member of type Date will be referred to directly,
// as opposed to through a pointer, etc.
class Date {
    int month;
    int day;
    int year;
public:
    Date() : month(0), day(0), year(0) {}

    Date( int mm, int dd, int yy )
        : month( mm ), day( dd ), year( yy ) {}

    friend ostream& operator<<( ostream& os, const Date& date) {
        os << "Date of Birth: " << date.month
           << "--" << date.day << "--" << date.year;
        return os;
    }
};
// Note the absence of both a copy constructor and the copy
// assignment operator.  That's because we'll be content
// with the system-supplied default definitions here.
// The destructor is missing for the same reason.
// Also note that the friend function is defined right
// inside the class definition.  But this does NOT make
```

```
// that function a member function of class Date.


/////////////////////////// class Cat ////////////////////////////

// The following class is needed to add a different kind of
// variety to the data members of Employee.  An object of
// type Cat will be referred to via a pointer.  This class
// does not need a copy constructor or a copy assignment
// operator for the same reason as the Date class.

class Cat {
    string name;
    int age;
public:
    Cat(){};
    Cat( string nam, int a ) : name( nam ), age( a ) {}
    friend ostream& operator<<( ostream& os, const Cat* cat) {
        os << "Name: " << cat->name << "   Age: " << cat->age;
        return os;
    }
    // The way it is written, must check for null pointer for
    // the second argument in the calling program.  Otherwise,
    // core dump possible.  An alternative would consist of
    // incorporating the null pointer check right here.
};


/////////////////////////// class Dog ////////////////////////////

class Dog {
    string name;
    int age;
public:
    Dog(){}
    Dog( string nam, int a ) : name( nam ), age( a ) {}
    friend ostream& operator<<( ostream& os, const Dog dog) {
        os << "Name: " << dog.name << "   Age: " << dog.age;
        return os;
    }
};


/////////////////////////// class Employee ////////////////////////////

class Employee {
    string firstName, lastName;
    Date dateOfBirth;
    Employee* friends;
```

```
        int numFriends;
        Auto* autos;
        int numAutos;
        Cat* kitty;
        vector<Dog> dogs;
        map<string, int> phoneList;
public:
        // First constructor:
        Employee() : friends(0), numFriends(0), autos(0),
                     numAutos(0), kitty(0) {}
        // This is needed for memory allocation statements.  If you do not
        // initialize the pointers as shown, the destructor with its delete
        // and delete[] operators will try to delete segments of memory that
        // the random bits point to.  And that would lead to program crash.
        // Initialization of these leads to more foolproof code in the copy
        // assignment operator for Employee.  In general, all variables
        // should be initialized.  So good practice would demand that we
        // also initialize the other fields.

        // Second constructor:
        Employee( string first, string last )
           : firstName( first ), lastName( last ), friends(0),
             numFriends(0), autos(0), numAutos(0), kitty(0) {}
        // The pointers must be initialized for the same reasons
        // as for the no-arg constructor

        // Third constructor:
        Employee( string first, string last, Date dob )
           : firstName( first ), lastName( last ),
             dateOfBirth( dob ), friends(0), numFriends(0),
             autos(0), numAutos(0), kitty(0) {}

        // Fourth constructor:
        Employee( string first, string last, Date dob, Cat* kit )
           : firstName( first ), lastName( last ),
             dateOfBirth( dob ), friends(0), numFriends(0),
             autos(0), numAutos(0)
        {
            if ( kit == 0 ) kitty = 0;
            else kitty = new Cat( *kit );                        //(A)
        }
        // The statement at (A) will invoke the copy constructor
        // of Cat, which in this case will be the system supplied
        // default copy constructor.  A common mistake for
        // novice programmers is to use the initializer "kitty( kit )"
        // But that would be asking for trouble if the same Cat
        // object belonged to more than one Employee objects, since
        // when the different such Employee objects go out of scope,
        // they would all be trying to delete the same block of memory,
```

```
// with possibly disastruous results.

// Fifth constructor:
// This is for exercising the vector data member.
Employee( string first, string last, vector<Dog> dawgs )
    : firstName( first ), lastName( last ), dogs( dawgs ),
      friends(0), numFriends(0), autos(0), numAutos(0),
      kitty(0) { }
// Note how we invoke the system-supplied copy constructor
// for the class vector<Dog> to copy from dawgs to the
// data member dogs

// Sixth constructor:
// This is for exercising the map data member.
Employee( string first, string last, map<string, int> phList )
    : firstName( first ), lastName( last ), phoneList( phList ),
      friends(0), numFriends(0), autos(0),
      numAutos(0), kitty(0) {}

// Seventh constructor:
// In the following constructor, the unused pointers must
// be initialized for the same reasons as for the no-arg
// constructor.
Employee( string first, string last, Date dob,
      Employee* fnds, int n )
    : firstName( first ), lastName( last ), numFriends( n ),
      dateOfBirth( dob ), autos(0), numAutos(0), kitty(0)
{
    if ( fnds != 0 ) {
        friends = new Employee[ numFriends ];
        for (int i=0; i<numFriends; i++ )
            friends[i] = fnds[i];
    }
}

// Eighth constructor:
Employee( string first, string last, Date dob,
    Employee* fnds, int n, Auto* ats, int m, Cat* c );
// this constructor cannot be defined here because the
// the definition of the Auto class is not yet complete


Employee( const Employee& other );
// this copy constructor cannot be defined here because
// the definition of the Auto class is not yet complete

Employee& operator=( const Employee& other );
// this copy assignment operator cannot be defined here
// because the definition of the Auto class is not yet
```

```
    // complete

    ~Employee();
    // destructor cannot be defined here because the definition
    // of the Auto class is not yet complete

    friend ostream& operator<<( ostream& os, const Employee& e );
};


///////////////////////////// class Auto /////////////////////////////

class Auto {
    string autoBrand;
    Employee owner;
public:
    Auto() {}
    Auto( string brand ): autoBrand( brand ){}
    Auto( string brand, Employee e )
        : autoBrand( brand ), owner( e ){}
    friend ostream& operator<<( ostream& os, const Employee& e );
};
// Note that the friend declaration above makes no mention of
// Auto class. We need this declaration to be able to access
// the data members of Auto in the overload definition of the
// output stream operator for Employee.


////// Remaining definitions for Employee members    //////

// Eighth constructor:
Employee:: Employee( string first, string last, Date dob,
        Employee* fnds, int n, Auto* ats, int m, Cat* c )
    : firstName( first ), lastName( last ),
      dateOfBirth( dob ), numFriends( n ),
      numAutos( m )
{
    if ( fnds == 0 || numFriends == 0 ) friends = 0;
    else {
        friends = new Employee[ numFriends ];
        for (int i=0; i<numFriends; i++ )
            friends[i] = fnds[i];
    }

    if ( ats == 0 || numAutos == 0 ) autos = 0;
    else {
        autos = new Auto[ numAutos ];
        for (int j=0; j<numAutos; j++ )
            autos[j] = ats[j];
```

```
    }

    if ( c == 0 ) kitty = 0;          // special care needed for pointer
    else kitty = new Cat( *c );
}


// Copy constructor:
Employee::Employee( const Employee& other )
    : firstName( other.firstName ),
      lastName( other.lastName ),
      dateOfBirth( other.dateOfBirth ),
      numFriends( other.numFriends ),
      numAutos( other.numAutos ),
      dogs( other.dogs ),             // use vector copy constructor
      phoneList( other.phoneList )    // use map copy constructor
{
    if ( other.friends == 0 || numFriends == 0 ) friends = 0;
    else {
        friends = new Employee[ numFriends ];
        for (int i=0; i<numFriends; i++ )
            friends[i] = other.friends[i];
    }

    if ( other.autos == 0 || numAutos == 0 ) autos = 0;
    else {
        autos = new Auto[ numAutos ];
        for (int j=0; j<numAutos; j++ )
            autos[j] = other.autos[j];
    }

    if ( other.kitty != 0 )
        kitty = new Cat( *other.kitty );
    else kitty = 0;
}


// Copy assignment operator:
Employee& Employee::operator=( const Employee& other ) {
    if ( this == &other ) return *this;

    firstName = other.firstName;
    lastName = other.lastName;
    dateOfBirth = other.dateOfBirth;
    numFriends = other.numFriends;
    numAutos = other.numAutos;
    dogs = other.dogs;                // use vector assignment op
    phoneList = other.phoneList;      // use map assignment op

    if ( this->kitty != 0 )
        delete kitty;
```

```
        if ( other.kitty != 0 )
            kitty = new Cat( *other.kitty );
        else kitty = 0;

        if ( friends != 0 )
            delete[] friends;

        if ( other.friends == 0 || numFriends == 0 ) friends = 0;
        else {
            friends = new Employee[ numFriends ];
            for (int i=0; i<numFriends; i++ )
                friends[i] = other.friends[i];
        }

        if ( autos != 0 )
            delete[] autos;

        if ( other.autos == 0 || numAutos == 0 ) autos = 0;
        else {
            autos = new Auto[ numAutos ];
            for (int j=0; j<numAutos; j++ )
                autos[j] = other.autos[j];
        }

        return *this;
}

// Destructor:
Employee::~Employee() {
    if ( friends != 0 ) delete[] friends;
    if ( autos != 0 ) delete[] autos;
    if ( kitty != 0 ) delete kitty;
}

//overloading of << for Employee class
ostream& operator<<( ostream& os, const Employee& e ) {
    os << e.firstName << " " << e.lastName << endl;
    os << e.dateOfBirth;
    os << endl;

    if ( e.friends != 0 ) {
        os << "Friends: " ;
        for (int i=0; i<e.numFriends; i++)
            os << e.friends[i].firstName << " "
                << e.friends[i].lastName << "       ";
        os << endl;
    }

    if ( e.autos != 0 ) {
```

```
        os << "Automobiles: " ;
        for (int j=0; j<e.numAutos; j++)
            os << e.autos[j].autoBrand << "    " ;
    os << endl;
    }

    os << "Cat info:    ";
    if ( e.kitty == 0 ) os << "the cat ran away" ;
    else os << e.kitty;
    os << endl;

    if ( e.dogs.size() != 0 ) {
        os << "Dog info:  ";
        vector<Dog>::const_iterator p = e.dogs.begin();
        while ( p != e.dogs.end() )
            cout << *p++ << "      ";
        os << endl;
    }

    if ( e.phoneList.size() != 0 ) {
        os << "Phone Nums: ";
        map<string, int>::const_iterator q = e.phoneList.begin();
        while ( q != e.phoneList.end() ) {
            cout << q->first << ": " << q->second << "    ";
            q++;
        }
        os << endl;
    }

    return os;
}


/////////////////////////// main //////////////////////////////

int main()
{
    Employee e1( "Zoe", "Zaphod" );
    Employee e2( "YoYo", "Ma", Date( 2, 12, 2000 ) );

    Employee empList[2];
    empList[0] = e1;            // These statements need the
    empList[1] = e2;            // assignment op for Employee

    Auto autoList[2];
    Auto a1( "Chevrolet" );
    Auto a2( "Ford" );
    autoList[0] = a1;
    autoList[1] = a2;
```

```
Cat* purr = new Cat( "socks", 5 );

cout << "TEST 1:  " << endl;
Employee e3( "Bebe", "Ruth", Date(1, 2, 2000),
                    empList, 2, autoList, 2, purr );
Employee e4;
e4 = e3;
cout << e4;

cout << "\n\nTEST 2: " << endl;
// what if the kitty pointer is 0 ?
Employee e5( "Bebe", "Ruth", Date(1, 2, 2000),
                    empList, 2, autoList, 2, 0 );
cout << e5;

cout << "\n\nTEST 3: " << endl;
// what if autoList pointer is 0 ?
Employee e6( "Bebe", "Ruth", Date(1, 2, 2000),
                    empList, 2, 0, 0, 0 );
cout << e6;

cout << "\n\nTEST 4: " << endl;
// what if empList pointer is 0 ?
Employee e7( "Bebe", "Ruth", Date(1, 2, 2000),
                    0, 0, 0, 0, 0 );
cout << e7;

Employee e8 = e7;

cout << "\n\nTEST 5: " << endl;
// try the vector data member
Dog dog1( "fido", 3 );
Dog dog2( "spot", 4 );
vector<Dog> dawgs;
dawgs.push_back( dog1 );
dawgs.push_back( dog2 );
Employee e9( "Linda", "Ellerbee", dawgs );
cout << e9;

cout << "\n\nTEST 6: " << endl;
// try the map<string, int> data member
map<string, int> phList;
phList[ "Steve Martin" ] = 1234567;
phList[ "Bill Gates" ] = 100100100;
Employee e10( "Will", "Rogers", phList );
cout << e10;

cout << "\n\nTEST 7: " << endl;
```

```
    Employee e11 = e10;
    cout << e11;

    cout << "\n\nTEST 8: " << endl;
    e5 = e11;
    cout << e5;

    return 0;
}
```

This produces the following output:

```
TEST 1:
Bebe Ruth
Date of Birth: 1--2--2000
Friends: Zoe Zaphod     YoYo Ma
Automobiles: Chevrolet   Ford
Cat info:   Name: socks   Age: 5

TEST 2:
Bebe Ruth
Date of Birth: 1--2--2000
Friends: Zoe Zaphod     YoYo Ma
Automobiles: Chevrolet   Ford
Cat info:   the cat ran away

TEST 3:
Bebe Ruth
Date of Birth: 1--2--2000
Friends: Zoe Zaphod     YoYo Ma
Cat info:   the cat ran away

TEST 4:
Bebe Ruth
Date of Birth: 1--2--2000
Cat info:   the cat ran away

TEST 5:
Linda Ellerbee
Date of Birth: 0--0--0
Cat info:   the cat ran away
Dog info: Name: fido   Age: 3       Name: spot    Age: 4

TEST 6:
Will Rogers
Date of Birth: 0--0--0
Cat info:   the cat ran away
```

```
Phone Nums: Bill Gates: 100100100     Steve Martin: 1234567

TEST 7:
Will Rogers
Date of Birth: 0--0--0
Cat info:   the cat ran away
Phone Nums: Bill Gates: 100100100     Steve Martin: 1234567

TEST 8:
Will Rogers
Date of Birth: 0--0--0
Cat info:   the cat ran away
Phone Nums: Bill Gates: 100100100     Steve Martin: 1234567
```

11.16   A JAVA STUDY OF INTERLEAVED CLASSES OF MODERATE COMPLEXITY

Class interleaving is not an issue with Java because of the look-ahead capability of the Java compiler. Each Java class is self-contained and Java classes can appear in any order in a file. Although the recommended approach to code organization is for a file to contain a single class, it is not uncommon to bundle a large class with some related but small ancillary classes in the same file.

The purpose of this section is simply to draw a comparison with the code shown in the previous section and to point out the programming ease made possible by the absence of issues related to class interleaving, pointers, memory allocation and deallocation, and so on. It will not be necessary now to have copy constructors and copy assignment operators, although you may have to provide override definitions for clone so that duplicates of objects can be constructed. Also, since garbage collection in Java automatically deallocates the memory occupied by an object if there are no variables holding references to the object, you will also not need destructors any more. Here is the code:

```
//Interleaved.java

import java.util.*;

///////////////////////// class Date /////////////////////////

class Date implements Cloneable {
    int month;
    int day;
    int year;
    public Date( int mm, int dd, int yy ) {
```

```
            month = mm; day = dd; year = yy;
        }
    public String toString() {
            return month + " : " + day + " : " + year;
        }
    public Object clone()
        {
            Date date = null;
            try {
                date = ( Date ) super.clone();
            } catch( CloneNotSupportedException e ) {}
            return date;
        }
}


///////////////////////////// class Cat //////////////////////////////

class Cat implements Cloneable {
    String name;
    int age;
    public Cat( String nam, int a ) { name = nam ; age = a; }
    public String toString() { return "  Name: " + name
                                    + "    Age: " + age; }
    public Object clone() {
        Cat cat = null;
        try {
            cat = ( Cat ) super.clone();
        } catch( CloneNotSupportedException e ) {}
        return cat;
        }
}


///////////////////////////// class Dog //////////////////////////////

class Dog implements Cloneable {
    String name;
    int age;
    public Dog( String nam, int a ) { name = nam; age = a; }
    public String toString() { return "\nName: " + name
                                    + "    Age: " + age; }

    public String getName() { return name; }
    public int getAge() { return age; }

    public void print() {
        System.out.println( this );
    }
```

```java
    public Object clone() throws CloneNotSupportedException {
        Dog dog = null;
        try {
            dog = ( Dog ) super.clone();
        } catch( CloneNotSupportedException e ) {}
        return dog;
    }
}


////////////////////////// class Employee //////////////////////////

class Employee {                    // intentionally left uncloneable

    String firstName, lastName;
    Date dateOfBirth;
    Employee[] friends;
    Auto[] autos;
    Cat kitty;
    Vector dogs;
    Map phoneList;

    public Employee( String first, String last ) {
        firstName = first;  lastName = last;
    }

    public Employee( String first, String last, Date dob ) {
        firstName = first;  lastName = last;
        dateOfBirth = dob == null ? null : (Date) dob.clone();
    }

    public Employee( String first, String last, Date dob, Cat kit ) {
        firstName = first;  lastName = last;
        dateOfBirth = dob == null ? null : (Date) dob.clone();
        kitty = kit == null ? null : (Cat) kit.clone();
    }

    public Employee( String first, String last, Vector dogs ) {
        firstName = first;  lastName = last;
        this.dogs = dogs == null ? null : (Vector) dogs.clone();
    }

    Employee( String first, String last, Date dob, Employee[] fnds ) {
        firstName = first;  lastName = last;
        dateOfBirth = dob == null ? null : (Date) dob.clone();
        friends = fnds == null ? null : (Employee[]) fnds.clone();
    }
```

```
Employee( String first, String last, Map phoneList ) {
    firstName = first;  lastName = last;
    this.phoneList = phoneList == null ? null
      : new TreeMap( (TreeMap) phoneList );
}


Employee( String first, String last, Date dob, Employee[] fnds,
              Auto[] ats, Cat c )
{
    firstName = first;  lastName = last;
    dateOfBirth = dob == null ? null : (Date) dob.clone();
    friends = fnds == null ? null : (Employee[]) fnds.clone();
    autos = ats == null ? null : (Auto[]) ats.clone();
    kitty =  c == null ? null : (Cat) c.clone();
}


String getFirstName() { return firstName; }

String getLastName() { return lastName; }

public String toString() {
    String str = "";
    if ( dogs != null ) {
        str += "\nDOGS: ";
        for ( int i=0; i<dogs.size(); i++ ) {
            str += (Dog) dogs.elementAt(i);
        }
        str += "\n";
    }
    if ( autos != null ) {
        str += "\nAUTOS: ";
        for ( int i=0; i<autos.length - 1; i++ ) {
            str += " " + autos[i] + ",";
        }
        str += " " + autos[autos.length - 1];
        str += "\n";
    }
    if ( friends != null ) {
        str += "\nFRIENDS:";
        for ( int i=0; i<friends.length; i++ ) {
            str += "\n";
            str += friends[i].getFirstName();
            str += " " + friends[i].getLastName();
        }
        str += "\n";
    }
    if ( kitty != null ) {
        str += "\nCAT:";
        str += kitty;
```

```
        }
        if ( phoneList != null ) {
            str += "\nPhone List:";
            str += phoneList;
        }

        return "\nFirst Name: " + firstName
                    + "\nLast Name: " + lastName
                    + "\n" + str + "\n";
    }
}


/////////////////////////// class Auto ////////////////////////////

class Auto {
    String autoBrand;
    Employee owner;
    public Auto( String brand ) { autoBrand = brand; }
    public Auto( String brand, Employee e )
    {
        autoBrand = brand;
        owner = e;
    }
    public String toString()
    {
        return autoBrand;
    }
}


///////////////////////// class TestEmployee ////////////////////////

class TestEmployee {
    public static void main( String[] args )
    {
        Employee e1 = new Employee( "Zoe", "Zaphod" );
        Employee e2 = new Employee ( "YoYo", "Ma",
                                new Date( 2, 12, 2000 ) );

        Employee[] empList = new Employee[2];
        empList[0] = e1;
        empList[1] = e2;

        Auto[] autoList = new Auto[2];
        Auto a1 = new Auto( "Chevrolet" );
        Auto a2 = new Auto( "Ford" );
        autoList[0] = a1;
        autoList[1] = a2;
```

```
Cat purr = new Cat( "socks", 5 );

System.out.println( "TEST 1:  " );
Employee e3 = new Employee( "Bebe", "Ruth",
                new Date(1, 2, 2000),
                empList, autoList, purr );
System.out.println( e3 );


Employee e4;
e4 = e3;
System.out.println( e4 );


System.out.println( "\n\nTEST 2: " );

// what if the kitty reference is null ?
Employee e5 = new Employee( "Bebe", "Ruth",
                new Date(1, 2, 2000),
                empList, autoList, null );
System.out.println( e5 );


System.out.println( "\n\nTEST 3: " );

// what if autoList reference is null also ?
Employee e6 = new Employee( "Bebe", "Ruth",
                new Date(1, 2, 2000),
                empList, null, null );
System.out.println( e6 );


System.out.println( "\n\nTEST 4: " );

// what if empList reference for friends is null also ?
Employee e7 = new Employee( "Bebe", "Ruth",
                new Date(1, 2, 2000),
                null, null, null );
System.out.println( e7 );

Employee e8 = e7;


System.out.println( "\n\nTEST 5: " );

// try the vector data member
Dog dog1 = new Dog( "fido", 3 );
Dog dog2 = new Dog( "spot", 4 );
```

```
        Vector dawgs = new Vector();
        dawgs.addElement( dog1 );
        dawgs.addElement( dog2 );


        Employee e9 = new Employee( "Linda", "Ellerbee", dawgs );
        System.out.println( e9 );


        System.out.println( "\n\nTEST 6: " ) ;

        // try the map<string, int> data member
        Map phList = new TreeMap();
        phList.put( "Steve Martin", new Integer( 1234567 ) );
        phList.put( "Bill Gates", new Integer( 100100100 ) );

        Employee e10 = new Employee( "Will", "Rogers", phList );
        System.out.println( e10 );
    }
}
```

The output of this program is as follows:

```
TEST 1:
First Name: Bebe
Last Name: Ruth
AUTOS:  Chevrolet, Ford
FRIENDS:
Zoe Zaphod
YoYo Ma
CAT:  Name: socks    Age: 5

TEST 2:
First Name: Bebe
Last Name: Ruth
AUTOS:  Chevrolet, Ford
FRIENDS:
Zoe Zaphod
YoYo Ma

TEST 3:
First Name: Bebe
Last Name: Ruth
FRIENDS:
Zoe Zaphod
YoYo Ma
```

```
TEST 4:
First Name: Bebe
Last Name: Ruth

TEST 5:
First Name: Linda
Last Name: Ellerbee
DOGS:
Name: fido    Age: 3
Name: spot    Age: 4

TEST 6:
First Name: Will
Last Name: Rogers
Phone List: {Bill Gates=100100100, Steve Martin=1234567}
```

11.17 SUGGESTIONS FOR FURTHER READING

The programs Singleton.cc and Singleton.java we showed in Section 11.1 are examples of the Singleton design pattern. This is one of the 23 design patterns described in [21] that provide best-practice solutions for some of the more common problems in object-oriented design. Java implementations of the patterns are presented in [13]. Copy construction in C++ and cloning in Java play central roles in the Prototype design pattern. See [21, 13] for further details.

Static initialization and static destruction explained in Section 11.3.1 place important constraints on the mixing of C++ and C code. If part of your code is in C++ and part in C, you'd be faced with the question of whether to write main in C or in C++. As explained by Meyers [51], it is better to write the main in C++ so that any static data members are properly initialized and destroyed. Meyers also shows how to get around this difficulty if circumstances dictate that the main be written in C. (While we are on the topic of mixing C++ and C, Chapter 10 briefly alluded to the "extern "C" " directive that must wrap the C headers and the C functions to prevent C function names from getting mangled by the C++ compiler.)

11.18 HOMEWORK

1. Suppose we have three classes X, Y, and Z in a C++ program. Let's say each class depends on the other two. In what order will you declare/define each class in the source code?

2. Complete the following interleaved C++ classes by adding constructors (at least a no-arg and one other constructor for each class), copy constructors, assignment operators, and destructors.

```
class Course;

class Student {
public:
    string fn, ln;          // First name, Last name
    int s;                  // Semester
    Student* rm;            // Array of roommate students
    int numRm;              // How many roommates
    Course* c;              // Array of courses that this
                            //            student is taking
    int numC;               // How many courses
    .....
};

class Course {
public:
    string t;               // Title of the course
    int n;                  // Course number
    int maxS;               // Maximum number of students
                            //    allowed to take this course
    Student* s;             // Array of students taking the course
    int numS;               // Number of students taking the course
    .....
};
```

3. The following C++ program will compile and run without any problems. But it has a deadly flaw embedded in it? What is it? Also, what is the output of the program?

```
#include <iostream>
using namespace std;

class X {
public:
    X() { cout << "X's no-arg constructor invoked" << endl; }
 };

class Y  {
    X* x;
public:
    Y() {
        cout << "Y's no-arg constructor invoked" << endl;
        x = new X();
```

```
        }
    };

    int main()
    {
        Y arr[5];
        return 0;
    }
```

4. The following version of the program of the previous problem also has a deadly flaw in it. What is it? Will it create a compile-time problem or a run-time problem?

```
#include <iostream>
using namespace std;

class X {};

class Y  {
    X* x;
public:
    Y() { cout << "no-arg constructor invoked" << endl; }

    ~Y(){
        cout << "destructor invoked" << endl;
        delete x;
    }
};

int main()
{
    Y arr[5];
    return 0;
}
```

5. Does the following program fix all problems with the programs in the previous two questions? If so, what is the output of the program?

```
#include <iostream>
using namespace std;

class X {};

class Y  {
    X* x;
```

```
public:
    Y() {
        cout << "no-arg constructor invoked" << endl;
        x = 0;
    }

    ~Y() {
        cout << "destructor invoked" << endl;
        if ( x != 0 ) delete x;
    }
};

int main()
{
    Y arr[5];
    return 0;
}
```

6. If the intent in the following C++ program is for `ptr` to be a pointer to an array of X objects, is there anything wrong with the program? (Of course, the compiler has no way of knowing directly if you intended for `ptr` to be a pointer to a single X object or a pointer to an array of X objects. But a human can, by looking at the implementation of the destructor. How is that possible?)

```
#include <iostream>
using namespace std;

class X {};

class Y {
    X* ptr;
    int n;
public:
    Y() {
        cout << "no-arg constructor invoked" << endl;
        ptr = 0;
    }
    ~Y(){
        cout << "destructor invoked" << endl;
        delete ptr;
    }
};

int main()
{
    Y y;
    return 0;
}
```

7. What is the output of the following C++ program? Note that it does not use pointers anywhere.

```
#include <iostream>
using namespace std;

class X {
public:
    X() { cout << "X's no-arg constructor invoked" << endl; }
    ~X() { cout << "X's destructor invoked" << endl; }
};

class Y {
    X x;
public:
    Y() { cout << "Y's no-arg constructor invoked" << endl; }
    ~Y() { cout << "Y's destructor invoked" << endl;  }
};

int main()
{
    Y arr[5];
    return 0;
}
```

8. In the C++ code shown here, we have gratuitously supplied the class Dog with a copy constructor. If this program is run, how many times will the print statement in the copy constructor be executed?

```
#include <string>
#include <iostream>
using namespace std;

class Dog {
    string name;
    int age;
public:
    Dog( string nam, int a ) : name( nam ), age( a ) {}
    Dog( const Dog& dog ) : name( dog.name ), age( dog.age ) {
        cout << "invoking Dog copy constructor" << endl;
    }
};

class Person {
    string name;
    Dog dog;
public:
```

```
        Person( string nam, Dog d ) : name( nam ), dog( d ) {}
};

int main()
{
    Dog dog( "Fido", 4 );
    Person p1( "Zaphod", dog );
    Person p2 = p1;
    return 0;
}
```

9. In the code of the previous question, is there any way to reduce the number of times the copy constructor of Dog is invoked?

10. What would happen if we did not overload the output operator '<<' for the Dog class in the following C++ example code?

```
#include<iostream>
#include<string>
using namespace std;

class Dog {
    string name;
    int age;
public:
    Dog( string nam, int a ) : name( nam ), age( a ) {}
    friend ostream& operator<<( ostream& os, const Dog dog) {
        os << "Dog's Name: " << dog.name
            << "  Dog's Age: " << dog.age;
        return os;
    }
};

class Person {
    string name;
    Dog dog;
public:
    Person( string nam, Dog& d ) : name( nam ), dog( d ) {}
    friend ostream& operator<<( ostream& os, const Person per) {
        os << "Name: " << per.name << "   Dog:     " << per.dog;
        return os;
    }
};

int main()
```

```
{
    Dog dog( "Fido", 4 );
    Person p( "Zaphod", dog );
    cout << p << endl;
    return 0;
}
```

11. In the program of the previous question, is there any way for the overload definition of the output operator '<<' for Person to print out its Dog's information without overloading the same operator for the Dog class? The Dog's data members must remain private.

12. Is Person p1's dog the same object as Person p2's dog in line (A) of the C++ code shown below? If we change person p1's dog, as in line (B), will person p2's dog also change?

```
#include<iostream>
#include<string>
using namespace std;

class Dog {
    string name;
    int age;
public:
    Dog( string nam, int a ) : name( nam ), age( a ) {}
    friend ostream& operator<<( ostream& os, const Dog dog) {
        os << "Dog's Name: " << dog.name
            << "  Dog's Age: " << dog.age;
        return os;
    }
};

class Person {
    string name;
    Dog dog;
public:
    Person( string nam, Dog& d ) : name( nam ), dog( d ) {}
    void changeDog( Dog newDog ) { dog = newDog; }
    friend ostream& operator<<(ostream& os, const Person per){
        os << "Name: " << per.name << "   Dog:    " << per.dog;
        return os;
    }
};

int main()
```

```
{
    Dog dog1( "Fido", 4 );
    Dog dog2( "Zoro", 8 );

    Person p1( "Zaphod", dog1 );
    cout << p1 << endl;

    Person p2 = p1;                              //(A)
    cout << p2 << endl;

    p1.changeDog( dog2 );                        //(B)

    cout << p1 << endl;
    cout << p2 << endl;

    return 0;
}
```

13. The class Person in the following C++ program has a vector data member, but is not provided with a copy constructor of its own. When we say

    ```
    Person p2 = p1;
    ```

    The system has no choice but to use the default copy constructor for Person. Is the vector data member of p2 the same as that of p1, or is it a copy?

    ```
    #include <string>
    #include <vector>
    using namespace std;

    class Dog {
        string name;
        int age;
    public:
        Dog( string nam, int a ) : name( nam ), age( a ) {}
        friend ostream& operator<<( ostream& os, const Dog dog) {
            os << "Dog's Name: " << dog.name
               << "  Dog's Age: " << dog.age;
            return os;
        }
    };

    class Person {
        string name;
        vector<Dog> dogs;
    public:
        Person( string nam, vector<Dog> dv )
    ```

```cpp
                              : name( nam ), dogs( dv ) {}

    void getNewDog( Dog newDog ) {
        dogs.pop_back();
        dogs.push_back( newDog );
    }

    friend ostream& operator<<(ostream& os, const Person per){
        os << "Name: " << per.name << "   Dogs:    " << endl;
        printDogs( os, per );
        return os;
    }

    friend void printDogs( ostream& os, const Person& per  );
};

void printDogs( ostream& os, const Person& per  ) {
    vector<Dog>::const_iterator p = per.dogs.begin();
    while ( p != per.dogs.end() )
        os << *p++ << endl;    // needs overloaded '<<' for Dog
    os << endl << endl;
}

int main()
{
    Dog dog1( "Fido", 4 );
    Dog dog2( "Zoro", 8 );
    Dog dog3( "Ninja", 10 );

    vector<Dog> dogvec;
    dogvec.push_back( dog1 );
    dogvec.push_back( dog2 );

    Person p1( "Zaphod", dogvec );

    cout << p1 << endl;

    Person p2 = p1;        // uses system-supplied copy const.
    cout << p2 << endl;

    p1.getNewDog( dog3 );

    cout << p1 << endl;
    cout << p2 << endl;

    return 0;
}
```

12
Overloading Operators in C++

You have already seen numerous examples of overloaded operators in C++ and Java. For example, when you say in Java

```
String str = "hello" + "there";
```

or in C++

```
string str = "hello" + "there";
```

you are using the overloaded definition of the '+' operator. Generically, the operator '+' is intended for adding numbers, but here we are using it to join together two strings. We are able to do so because the class definition for the string type usually includes an appropriate overload definition for the operator '+' that makes it possible to join together two strings.

While you will find overloaded operators in both C++ and Java, you are not allowed to create your own operator overloadings in Java.

Here is a list, reproduced from [54], of key points to remember about operator overloading in C++.

- When an operator is overloaded in C++, at least one of its operands must be of class type or enumeration type.
- At least one of the operands in an operator overload definition must not be a built-in type.
- The predefined precedence of an operator cannot be altered by an overload definition.

- An overload definition also cannot alter the predefined arity of an operator, meaning that an operator that is designated to be only unary (for example, the logical NOT operator '!') cannot be turned into a binary operator by overloading. For operators that can be used for both unary and binary operations (these being the four operators '+' '−' '*' and '&'), both arities can be overloaded.
- Arguments can be passed to the parameters in the overload definitions either by value or by reference, but not by pointer.
- Default arguments for overloaded operators are illegal, except for the operator '()'.
- Finally, the following operators cannot be overloaded:

```
::   .*   .   ?:
```

12.1   OPERATOR TOKENS AND OPERATOR FUNCTIONS

You have seen many instances of the usual operator tokens in C++:

```
+   -   *   /   =   ->   &&   new   new[]   delete   delete[]   etc.
```

When the arguments supplied to any of these and other operators are of class type, what the compiler actually invokes is an *operator function* that is associated with the operator token. For example, for the case of class type arguments, associated with the operator token '+' is the following operator function

```
operator+
```

Similarly, associated with the operator token, or operator for short, '=' is the operator function

```
operator=
```

and with the operator '<<,' the operator function

```
operator<<
```

Overload definitions for operator functions come in two forms: Definitions that are global and definitions that are member functions for a class. When it is possible to provide overload definitions both ways, the overloaded operator works the same with either implementation.

12.2   GLOBAL OVERLOAD DEFINITIONS FOR OPERATORS

Let's consider the following example class as a candidate for operator overloading:

```
class MyComplex {
    double re, im;
public:
    MyComplex( double r, double i ) : re(r), im(i) {}
    double getReal() { return re; }
    double getImag() { return im; }
};
```

This class is supposed to represent a complex number by keeping together its real and imaginary parts. In the arithmetic of complex numbers, one wants to be able to carry out the same operations as in the arithmetic of, say, integers and floating point types. So given two complex numbers as

```
MyComplex c1( 3, 5 );
MyComplex c2( 1, 4 );
```

it would be convenient if we could say

```
MyComplex sum = c1 + c2;
MyComplex diff = c1 - c2;
...
...
```

To be able to do this, we need to overload the binary operators such as '+,' '-,' and so on, for the MyComplex class. This overloading can be accomplished by providing global overload definitions such as

```
MyComplex operator+( MyComplex arg1, MyComplex arg2 ) {
    double d1 = arg1.getReal() + arg2.getReal();
    double d2 = arg1.getImag() + arg2.getImag();
    return MyComplex( d1, d2 );
}

MyComplex operator-( MyComplex arg1, MyComplex arg2 ) {
    double d1 = arg1.getReal() - arg2.getReal();
    double d2 = arg1.getImag() - arg2.getImag();
    return MyComplex( d1, d2 );
}
```

and so on for the other arithmetic operators such as '*' for multiplication, '/' for division, and so on. Since we would also need to display the results of complex number arithmetic, we would also want to overload the output operator '<<':

```
ostream& operator<< ( ostream& os, const MyComplex& arg ) {
    double d1 = arg.getReal();
    double d2 = arg.getImag();
    os << "(" << d1 << ", " << d2 << ")" << endl;
    return os;
}
```

The function operator<< needs to return the ostream object that is its first argument so that we can chain these operators together in the following manner:

```
cout << expr1 << exp2 << exp3  ..
```

Shown below is a working program that includes the above overload definitions. In the code shown below, we have declared the access member functions getReal() and getImag() to be of type const (see Chapter 11 as to why).

```
//OverloadBinaryGlobal.cc

#include <iostream>
using namespace std;

class MyComplex {
    double re, im;
public:
    MyComplex( double r, double i ) : re(r), im(i) {}
    double getReal() const { return re; }
    double getImag() const { return im; }
};

MyComplex operator+( const MyComplex arg1,
                            const MyComplex arg2 ) {            //(A)
    double d1 = arg1.getReal() + arg2.getReal();               //(B)
    double d2 = arg1.getImag() + arg2.getImag();               //(C)
    return MyComplex( d1, d2 );
}

MyComplex operator-( MyComplex arg1, MyComplex arg2 ) {        //(D)
    double d1 = arg1.getReal() - arg2.getReal();
    double d2 = arg1.getImag() - arg2.getImag();
    return MyComplex( d1, d2 );
}

ostream& operator<< ( ostream& os, const MyComplex& arg ) {    //(E)
    double d1 = arg.getReal();
    double d2 = arg.getImag();
    os << "(" << d1 << ", " << d2 << ")" << endl;
    return os;
}

int main()
{
    MyComplex first(3, 4);
    MyComplex second(2, 9);
```

```
    cout << first;                    // (3, 4)
    cout << second;                   // (2, 9)
    cout << first + second;           // (5, 13)
    cout << first - second;           // (1, -5)
    return 0;
}
```

12.3 MEMBER-FUNCTION OVERLOAD DEFINITIONS FOR OPERATORS

In the following implementation of `MyComplex`, we have provided member function overload definitions for the same operators as in the previous section, *except for the output operator* '<<'. The reason for why the output operator cannot be overloaded as a member function of `MyComplex` is very important and crucial to understanding the difference between global overload definitions and member-function overload definitions.

```
//OverloadBinaryMemb.cc

#include <iostream>
using namespace std;

class MyComplex {
    double re, im;
public:
    MyComplex( double r, double i ) : re(r), im(i) {}
    MyComplex operator+( MyComplex) const;
    MyComplex operator-( MyComplex) const;
    //  ostream& operator<< ( const MyComplex& );            // WRONG
    friend ostream& operator<< ( ostream&, const MyComplex& );    //(A)
};

MyComplex MyComplex::operator+( const MyComplex arg ) const {    //(B)
    double d1 = re + arg.re;                                     //(C)
    double d2 = im + arg.im;                                     //(D)
    return MyComplex( d1, d2 );
}

MyComplex MyComplex::operator-( const MyComplex arg ) const {    //(E)
    double d1 = re - arg.re;
    double d2 = im - arg.im;
    return MyComplex( d1, d2 );
}
```

```
ostream& operator<< ( ostream& os, const MyComplex& c ) {          //(F)
    os << "(" << c.re << ", " << c.im << ")" << endl;
    return os;
}

int main()
{
    MyComplex first(3, 4);
    MyComplex second(2, 9);

    cout << first;                    // (3, 4)
    cout << second;                   // (2, 9)
    cout << first + second;           // (5, 13)
    cout << first - second;           // (1, -5)
    return 0;
}
```

Comparing the global overload definition for '+' in line (A) of the program in the previous section with the member-function overload definition in line (B) of the above program, note that while the global overload definition has two arguments, the member-function definition has only one. Given two MyComplex objects c1 and c2, a statement such as

```
c1 + c2;
```

will be translated by the compiler into the following invocation of the operator function for '+':

```
c1.operator+( c2 );
```

provided that there exists a member-function overload definition for the function operator+. Such an invocation supplies one argument — c1 here — implicitly and the other argument — c2 here — explicitly to the function operator+. In the member-function definition for operator+, the directly-accessed variables re and im in lines (B) and (C) of the program above are the data members of the implicitly supplied argument c1.

In general, when an operator χ is overloaded with a member-function definition, a construct such as

```
object1  χ  object2
```

is interpreted by the compiler as

```
object1.operator χ ( object2 )
```

For this mode of operator use, we can talk about `object1` as the *invoking object* for the operator χ and `object2` the *argument object*. On the other hand, if the operator χ was overloaded with a global definition, the construct

```
object1  χ  object2
```

would be interpreted by the compiler as

```
operatorχ ( object1, object2 )
```

Now both `object1` and `object2` become explicitly-supplied argument objects.

It should now be obvious why the global overload definition for the output operator in line (E) of the program in the previous section cannot be replaced by something like

```
ostream& MyComplex::operator<< ( const MyComplex c ) {    // WRONG
    os << "Real part: " << c.re
       << "  Imag part: " << c.im << endl;
    return os;
}
```

This implementation would be wrong for the simple reason that the manner of usage of the output operator, as in

```
cout << expression;
```

would be interpreted by the compiler as

```
cout.operator<<( expression );
```

if there were a member-function based overload definition available for '<<' for the output stream class `basic_ostream` of which `cout` is an object. But we are not at liberty to define new member functions for the output stream classes. Therefore, we have no choice but to use the global overload definition for the output operator. However, we can still can come close to the nature of a member function by declaring the global overload definition for `operator<<` to be a *friend* of `MyComplex` with the following declaration inside `MyComplex`:

```
friend ostream& operator<<( ostream&, const MyComplex& );
```

as we have done in line (A) of the program in this section. As mentioned in Chapter 3, the *friend* declaration, which can be in any of the private, public, or protected sections of a class, allows the global overload definition supplied in line (F) of the program to directly access the private data members of the `MyComplex` argument object.

12.4 GLOBAL OVERLOAD DEFINITIONS FOR UNARY OPERATORS

As with binary operators, if the *arity* of an operator is unary with respect to the built-in types, then such an operator can be overloaded and made to behave like a unary operator for the user-defined types. As before, this overloading may be accomplished either by supplying a global overload definition or a member-function overload definition.

Consider again the case of the MyComplex class, but with just the unary operator '–' defined this time for changing the sign of a complex number, and the previously presented overloaded binary operator '<<' so that we can see the results of applying the unary operator to a MyComplex object:

```
//OverloadUnaryGlobal.cc

#include <iostream>
using namespace std;

class MyComplex {
    double re, im;
public:
    MyComplex( double r, double i ) : re(r), im(i) {}
    double getReal() const { return re; }
    double getImag() const { return im; }
};

// global overload definition for "-" as a unary operator
MyComplex operator-( const MyComplex arg ) {
    return MyComplex( -arg.getReal(), -arg.getImag() );
}

// global overload definition for "<<" as a binary operator
ostream& operator<< ( ostream& os, const MyComplex& arg ) {
    double d1 = arg.getReal();
    double d2 = arg.getImag();
    os << "(" << arg.getReal() << ", " << arg.getImag() << ")" << endl;
    return os;
}

int main()
{
    MyComplex c(3, 4);
    cout << c;              // (3, 4)
    cout << -c;             // (-3, -4)
    return 0;
}
```

The global overload definition shown here for `operator-` as a unary operator function parallels the global overload definition for `operator-` shown in Section 12.2 as a binary operator function.

12.5 MEMBER-FUNCTION OVERLOAD DEFINITIONS FOR UNARY OPERATORS

Paralleling our discussion for binary operators in Section 12.3, the following example shows a member-function overload definition for '−' as a unary operator.

```
//OverloadUnaryMemb.cc

#include <iostream>
using namespace std;

class MyComplex {
    double re, im;
public:
    MyComplex( double r, double i ) : re(r), im(i) {}
    MyComplex operator-() const;
    friend ostream& operator<< ( ostream&, MyComplex& );
};

//Member-function overload definition for "-"
MyComplex MyComplex::operator-() const {                        //(A)
    return MyComplex( -re, -im );
}

//This overload definition has to stay global
ostream& operator<< ( ostream& os, const MyComplex& c ) {
    os << "(" << c.re << ", " << c.im << ")" << endl;
    return os;
}

int main()
{
    MyComplex c(3, 4);
    MyComplex z = -c;                                           //(B)
    cout << z << endl;                  // (-3, -4)
    return 0;
}
```

Note that the following statement in line (B) of the program

```
MyComplex z = -c;
```

is translated by the compiler into

```
MyComplex z = c.operator-();
```

which makes c the invoking object. Thus the values of re and im available inside the definition of the operator- function in line (A) would then correspond to the MyComplex number c.

12.6   A CASE STUDY IN OPERATOR OVERLOADING

We will now consider a user-defined class and take the reader through the various operators we would want to define for this class. This user-defined type will be our own MyString class, to be thought of as a poor man's substitute for the highly optimized system-supplied string class in the string header file. Some type of a string class is a frequently used pedagogical tool in the teaching of operator overloading in C++. That is because it is straightforward to specify the meaning that one would want to associate with the various operators for strings.

An important property of our MyString class will be that it will check for any violations of array bounds if a program tries to access a character outside of those included specifically in a MyString. In the event of such a violation, our MyString will throw an exception. Here is a partial definition of MyString, with an ancillary class Err included inside to serve as the exception type:[1]

```
class MyString {
    char* charArr;
    int length;
    class Err {};
public:
    //...
};
```

The string will be stored in the form of a null-terminated array of characters starting at the address charArr. The actual number of characters in the string will be stored in the data member length. The fact that MyString will store the characters in the form of a C-style string will allow us to use C's well-known string processing functions in the overload definitions of the various operators for MyString.

In the rest of this section, we will add incrementally to the above partial definition of the MyString class, starting with the main constructor below:

---

[1]See Chapter 3 for how nested classes behave vis-à-vis enclosing classes.

THE MAIN CONSTRUCTOR:

This constructor will help us construct a `MyString` object from a string literal. The constructor should first appropriate the required amount of memory and then copy over the string literal into this memory:

```
MyString( const char* ch ) {
    length = strlen( ch );
    charArr = new char[ length + 1];
    strcpy( charArr, ch );
}
```

where `strlen` returns the actual number of characters in the string literal (not including the null terminator) and `strcpy` copies over the characters from the literal into the freshly acquired memory for the `charArr` data member of the `MyString` object under construction.[2] With this constructor in place, we can construct a new `MyString` from a string literal by

```
MyString str("hello");
```

NO-ARG CONSTRUCTOR:

We'll need a no-arg constructor for declarations like

```
MyString s;
MyString words[100];
vector<MyString> vec(100);
```

Recall that C++ arrays and various container types (if they need preallocated memory at the time of declaration) cannot be declared unless there exists, by specification or by default, a no-arg constructor for the element type. The following definition could serve as a no-arg constructor for our string class:

```
MyString() {charArr = 0; length = 0;}
```

THE DESTRUCTOR:

In order to avoid memory leaks, we also need a destructor that would free up the memory when a `MyString` variable goes out of scope:

```
~MyString() { delete[] charArr; }
```

THE COPY CONSTRUCTOR:

Every user-defined type appropriating system resources needs a copy constructor so that declarations of the following kind can be made:

---

[2]See Chapter 4 for a brief review of the C's string functions used in this section.

```
MyString s1( "hello" );
MyString s2 = s1;
```

A copy constructor will also help us pass a MyString argument by value during a function call and help with copy-on-return if a function returns a MyString object by value. Here is a copy constructor that follows the format discussed in Chapter 11:

```
MyString( const MyString& str ) {
    length=str.length;                        //(A)
    charArr = new char[length+1];             //(B)
    strcpy( charArr, str.charArr );
}
```

For a declaration such as

```
MyString s2 = s1;
```

the members `length` and `charArr` that are accessed directly in lines (A) and (B) belong to the invoking MyString, which in this case is s2. The copy constructor first declares the length of s2 to be equal to the length of s1. Next it allocates memory for the array of characters in the new string s2. Finally, it copies over the contents of the `charArr` member of s1 into the `charArr` member of s2.

THE COPY ASSIGNMENT OPERATOR:

The copy constructor is usually followed by the closely related copy assignment operator needed for statements like

```
MyString s1 = "hello";
MyString s2 = "jello";
s1 = s2;
```

The assignment of s2 to s1 here requires an appropriate definition for the function `operator=`:

```
MyString& operator=( const MyString& str ) {
    if (str.charArr == 0) {                   //(A)
        delete[] charArr;
        charArr = 0;
        length = 0;
        return *this;
    }
    if (this != &str) {                       //(B)
        delete[] charArr;
        charArr = new char[str.length + 1];
        strcpy(charArr, str.charArr );
        length = str.length;
    }
    return *this;                             //(C)
}
```

where the first `if` block in line (A) is supposed to take care of assignments like

```
MyString s1("hello");
MyString s2;
s1 = s2;
```

where the string s2 gets initialized by the no-arg constructor of `MyString`. Evidently, the assignment s1=s2 above should cause s1's members to be the same as if s1 were initialized by the no-arg constructor also.

The reason for the test

```
if (this != &str) {
    ....
```

in line (B) is to protect the assignment operator from self-assignments of the kind

```
MyString s("hello");
s = s;
```

Barring self-assignment, in the second `if` block starting in line (B) we first free up the memory occupied by the characters in the invoking string. The `charArr` pointer of the invoking `MyString` is then made to point to freshly appropriated memory whose size is determined by the size of the argument string. The characters from the argument string are then copied over into the fresh memory just appropriated for the string on the left side of the assignment operator.

Regarding the return statement in line (C), one could say that after we have set the `length` and the `charArr` members of the invoking `MyString`, no purpose is served by returning anything. But, as mentioned in Chapter 11 in the section on self-reference, the purpose served by returning `*this` is that we can now chain the assignment operator as in

```
MyString s1("hello");
MyString s2("othello");
MyString s3("byebye");
s1 = s2 = s3;
```

Since '=' is right associative, the last statement would be interpreted by the compiler as

```
s1 = ( s2 = s3 );
```

Therefore, whatever is returned by the assignment s2=s3 will be assigned to s1.

The reader is probably wondering whether it is really necessary for the header of the assignment operator function to be

```
MyString& MyString::operator=( const MyString& str ) {        //(D)
    // see previous implementation
}
```

More specifically, could we have defined the function without the const preceding the typename of the parameter? Also, how important is it for the parameter to be of reference type? Let's consider what happens when the header is

```
MyString& MyString::operator=( MyString& str ) {          //(E)
    //  same as before
}
```

Let's say we invoke this operator function with the following call:

```
MyString s1( "hello" );
MyString s2( "mello" );
s1 = s2;                                                  //(F)
```

For this case the header in line (E) would work. However, now you'll run into a problem if you try to assign a const string, as in

```
MyString s3( "jello" );
const MyString s4( "cello" );
s3 = s4;                                                  //(G)
```

Since a const object cannot be assigned to a non-const variable, the compiler will refuse to initialize the parameter str in line (E) with the string object s4. A second problem with the header in (E) arises when the string to be assigned is the result of an operator action, as in

```
MyString s1( "hello" );
MyString s2( "mello" );
MyString s3( "jello" );
s3 = s1 + s2;                                             //(H)
```

Now if we use the assignment operator with the header as in line (E) above, the compiler will complain because it will not be able to assign the MyString object returned by the '+' operator to the MyString& parameter in the header in line (E). That's because the '+' operator for the MyString class returns a MyString object whose address cannot be ascertained. You will recall from our discussion in Chapter 8 that an object reference, unless it is of type const, can only be initialized with an object whose address can be ascertained.

THE '[]' OPERATOR:

Let's now discuss how we may provide access to the individual characters in a MyString string. If we create a MyString object str by

```
MyString str("hello");
```

we want to access each character in str by str[i], i = 0, 1, ... This we can do by providing MyString with the '[]' operator. If we do not provide this operator, the compiler simply would not know how to interpret a construct such as str[i]. However, when we do provide such an operator, it is incumbent upon us to make sure that the index does not violate the subscript bounds for the array. In fact, it is this safety feature that makes a MyString string an attractive alternative to a C-style char* string. Here is an overload definition for the '[]' operator, along with a definition for check(), the function for range-checking the index used for accessing the individual characters in a string:

```
bool MyString::check( int i ) const {                      //(A)
    return ( i >= 0 && i <= length ) ? true: false;
}

char MyString::operator[]( int i ) const {                 //(B)
    if ( check(i) )                                        //(C)
        return charArr[ i ];                               //(D)
    else throw Err();                                      //(E)
}
```

The subscript function operator[] in line (B) first makes sure that the index i does not violate any array bounds by invoking in line (C) the check() function defined in line (A). If there is not a violation, then the requested character is returned in line (D). Otherwise, an exception is thrown in line (E). This definition assumes that the class Err was previously defined for throwing exceptions.

THE WRITE FUNCTION:

Now that we have a subscript operator for our MyString, what about a write function that would permit us to alter an individual character. This is how we can include this functionality in the MyString class:

```
void MyString::write( int k, char ch ) {
    if ( check(k) )
        charArr[k] = ch;
    else throw Err();
}
```

The write() function makes sure that the index corresponding to the array element falls within the array. The check() function is the same as defined earlier for the overloading of the '[]' operator.

THE '+' OPERATOR:

This operator will be invoked when the compiler is processing statements like s3 = s1 + s2 in the following program segment:

```
MyString s1("hello");
MyString s2("there");
MyString s3("hi");
s3 = s1 + s2;
```

Here is a member-function overload definition for the '+' operator:

```
MyString operator+( const MyString str ) const {
    int temp = length + str.length + 1;                    //(A)
    char* ptr = new char[temp];                            //(B)
    strcpy( ptr, charArr);                                 //(C)
    strcat(ptr, str.charArr);                              //(D)
    MyString s( ptr );                                     //(E)
    delete[] ptr;                                          //(F)
    return s;                                              //(G)
}
```

The statement in line (A) calculates the size of the memory that is needed to hold the MyString resulting from the joining of the two operand strings. The extra '1' is for the null terminator. In line (B), an appropriate amount of memory to hold the new string is procured. In line (C), the character array of the invoking MyString is copied into the new memory, followed in line (D) by the copying over of the character array of the argument MyString. The strcat() function automatically places the terminating null at the end of the copying in (D). In line (E), a MyString object is formed from the char* string resulting from the step in line (D). In line (F), the memory occupied by the char* string is freed since it is no longer needed. Finally, in line (G), we return the new MyString.

THE '+=' OPERATOR:

This compound assignment operator will be invoked for calls as in

```
MyString s1("hello");
MyString s2("kitty");
s1 += s2;                               // hellokitty
```

An overload definition of the compound assignment operator '+=' as a member function of the MyString could be:

```
MyString& operator+=( const MyString str ) {
    *this = *this + str;
    return *this;
}
```

It is important to realize that we could *not* have simplified the definition of this function to

```
MyString& MyString::operator+=( MyString str ) {
    return *this + str;                 // WRONG
}
```

because the '+' operator, by its very meaning, does not modify the first operand. In a compound assignment implied by s1 += s2, we want the first operand to get modified by the second operand.

Also note that the overload definition returns a reference to suppress copy on return. We obviously want to return the same object to which the argument is appended.

EQUALITY OPERATORS:

To test whether or not two MyString strings have the same content, meaning that they are made up of the same characters, we can use the following overload definitions for the equality operators '==' and '!=':

```
bool operator==( const MyString str ) const {
    return strcmp( charArr, str.charArr ) == 0;
}

bool operator!=( const MyString str ) const {
    return !( *this == str );
}
```

RELATIONAL OPERATORS:

If we wish to know whether the character string in one MyString object is "greater" than the character string in another MyString object on the basis of lexicographic ordering implied by ASCII codes, we can use the following overload definition for the '>' operator. Similarly for the other relational operators.

```
bool operator>( const MyString str ) const {
    return strcmp( charArr, str.charArr ) > 0;
}

bool operator<( const MyString str ) const {
    return strcmp( charArr, str.charArr ) < 0;
}

bool operator<=( const MyString str ) const {
    return strcmp( charArr, str.charArr ) <= 0;
}

bool operator>=( const MyString str ) const {
    return strcmp( charArr, str.charArr ) >= 0;
}
```

OUTPUT and INPUT OPERATORS:

Even for a minimally functional MyString type, we would need to display the strings we create on a terminal or output them into a file, or read strings from a terminal or from a file. The following global overload definitions for the output operator and the input operators do those jobs:

```
ostream& operator<< ( ostream& os, const MyString& str ) {
    os << str.charArr;
```

```
        return os;
    }

    istream& operator>> ( istream& is, MyString& str ) {
        char* ptr = new char[100];                          //(A)
        is >> ptr;                                          //(B)
        str = MyString( ptr );                              //(C)
        delete ptr;
        return is;
    }
```

The implementation for the input operator assumes that the number of characters in an input string will not exceed 99.[3] Also note that the system-supplied overload definition of the input operator for the `char*` argument in line (B) writes out a null terminator after the characters fetched from the input stream. Thus, the size of the `MyString` object constructed in line (C) corresponds to the string that is actually input and not to the size of the memory allocated in line (A).

Since the two overload definitions shown above are global, we need to also include the following "friend" declarations inside the definition of the `MyString` class:

```
    friend ostream& operator<<( ostream&, const MyString& );
    friend istream& operator>>( istream&, MyString& );
```

In the following code, we have brought all these overload definitions together in one place. The following code also includes `getSize()` and `getCharArray()` functions that we will find useful in a later section.

```
//MyString.cc

#include <cstring>
#include <vector>
#include <iostream>
using namespace std;

class MyString;
typedef vector<MyString>::iterator Iter;
int split( Iter, int low, int high );
void quicksort( Iter, int low, int high );

class MyString {
    char* charArr;
    int length;
    class Err {};
```

---

[3]A more sophisticated overloading for the input operator will not have this limitation. It will use dynamic memory allocation to read in a string no matter how long.

```
public:
    MyString() {charArr = 0; length = 0;}

    MyString( const char* ch ) {
        length = strlen( ch );
        charArr = new char[ length + 1];
        strcpy( charArr, ch );
    }

    MyString( const char ch ) {
        length = 1;
        charArr = new char[2];
        *charArr = ch;
        *(charArr + 1) = '\0';
    }

    ~MyString() { delete[] charArr; }

    MyString( const MyString& str ) {
        length=str.length;
        charArr = new char[length+1];
        strcpy( charArr, str.charArr );
    }

    MyString& operator=( const MyString& str ) {
        if (str.charArr == 0) {
            delete[] charArr;
            charArr = 0;
            length = 0;
            return *this;
        }
        if (this != &str) {
            delete[] charArr;
            charArr = new char[str.length + 1];
            strcpy(charArr, str.charArr );
            length = str.length;
        }
        return *this;
    }

    bool check( int i ) const {
        return ( i >= 0 && i <= length ) ? true : false;
    }

    char operator[]( int i ) const {
        if (check(i))
            return charArr[ i ];
        else throw Err();
    }
```

```
void write( int k, char ch ) {
    if (check(k))
        charArr[k] = ch;
    else throw Err();
}

MyString operator+( const MyString str ) const {
    int temp = length + str.length + 1;
    char* ptr = new char[temp];
    strcpy( ptr, charArr);
    strcat(ptr, str.charArr);
    MyString s( ptr );
    delete[] ptr;
    return s;
}

MyString& operator+=( const MyString str ) {
    *this = *this + str;
    return *this;
}

MyString& operator+=( const char ch ) {
    *this = *this + MyString( ch );
    return *this;
}

bool operator==( const MyString str ) const {
    return strcmp( charArr, str.charArr ) == 0;
}

bool operator!=( const MyString str ) const {
    return !( *this == str );
}

bool operator>( const MyString str ) const {
    return strcmp( charArr, str.charArr ) > 0;
}

bool operator<( const MyString str ) const {
    return strcmp( charArr, str.charArr ) < 0;
}

bool operator<=( const MyString str ) const {
    return strcmp( charArr, str.charArr ) <= 0;
}

bool operator>=( const MyString str ) const {
    return strcmp( charArr, str.charArr ) >= 0;
```

```
    }

    int getSize() const { return length; }

    int size() const { return length; }

    char* getCharArray() const { return charArr; }

    char* c_str() { return charArr; }

    int find( char* substring ) {
        char* p = strstr( charArr, substring );
        return p - charArr;
    }

    int compare( const MyString& str ) {
        char* p = getCharArray();
        char* q = str.getCharArray();
        if( p == 0 && q == 0 ) return 0;
        else if( p != 0 && q == 0 ) return 1;
        else if( p == 0 && q != 0 ) return -1;
        return strcmp( p, q );
    }

    friend ostream& operator<<( ostream&, const MyString& );
    friend istream& operator>>( istream&, MyString& );
};

ostream& operator<< ( ostream& os, const MyString& str ) {
    os << str.charArr;
    return os;
}

istream& operator>> ( istream& is, MyString& str ) {
    char* ptr = new char[100];
    is >> ptr;
    str = MyString( ptr );
    delete ptr;
    return is;
}

void sort( Iter first, Iter last ) {
    quicksort( first, 0, last - first -1 );
}

void quicksort( Iter first, int low, int high ) {
    int middle;
    if ( low >= high ) return;
    middle = split( first, low, high );
```

```
        quicksort( first, low, middle - 1 );
        quicksort( first, middle + 1, high );
}

int split( Iter first, int low, int high ) {
    MyString partition_str = *( first + low );

    for(;;) {
        while ( low < high  &&  partition_str <= *( first + high ) )
          high--;
        if ( low >= high ) break;
        *( first + low++ ) = *( first + high );

        while ( low < high  &&  *( first + low ) <= partition_str )
            low++;
            if ( low >= high ) break;
        *( first + high-- ) = *( first + low );
    }

    *(first + high ) = partition_str;
    return high;
}

int main()
{
    MyString s0;
    MyString s1( "hello" );
    cout << s1.getSize() << endl;          // 5
    cout <<  s1 << endl;                    // hello
    MyString s2 = s1;
    cout << s2.getSize() << endl;          // 5
    cout <<  s2 << endl;                    // hello
    s1.write(0, 'j');
    cout << s1 << endl;                     // jello
    MyString s3 = s1 + s2;
    cout << s3 << endl;                     // jellohello
    s3 += s3;
    cout <<  s3 << endl;                    // jellohellojellohello

    if ( s2.compare( s1 ) < 0 )
        cout << "s2 is \"less than\" s1"
            << endl;                        // s2 is "less than" s1

    MyString s4 = "jello";
    if (s1 == s4)
        cout << "the operator == works" << endl;
    if (s3 > s1)
        cout << "the operator > works" << endl;
```

```
MyString s5("yellow");
s1 = s2 = s5;
cout << s1 << endl;                    // yellow
cout << s2 << endl;                    // yellow
MyString s6;
s1 = s6;
cout << s1 << endl;                    // null

MyString str[] = { "jello", "green", "jolly", "trolley", "abba" };
int size = sizeof(str)/sizeof(str[0]);
vector<MyString> vec(str, &str[size]);
cout << "Initial list:    ";
for (Iter p = vec.begin(); p != vec.end(); p++ )
    cout << *p << " ";
                                // jello green jolly trolly abba
cout << endl;

sort( vec.begin(), vec.end() );

cout << "Sorted list:     ";
for ( Iter p = vec.begin(); p != vec.end(); p++ )
    cout << *p << " ";
                                // abba green jello jolly trolly
cout << endl << endl;

return 0;
}
```

The code shown includes a `quicksort()` function that allows a vector of the `MyString` strings to be sorted with the following call

```
vector<MyString> vec;
sort( vec.begin(), vec.end() );
```

12.7 SMART POINTERS: OVERLOADING OF DEREFERENCING OPERATORS

We will now show how by overloading the dereferencing operators '->' and the '*', you can program up a smart pointer class whose objects can serve as smart proxies for regular pointers.[4] But first a few comments about the shortcomings of regular pointers are in order.

Given a class X

```
class X {
// ...
};
```

we can construct an object of this class by invoking its constructor via the new operator

```
X* p = new X( ... );
```

We can dereference the pointer by calling *p, which retrieves the object for us, or we can dereference the pointer by p->some_member, which first retrieves the object and then gives us access to the member some_member of class X.

From the standpoint of memory management, there is a major shortcoming to using a pointer as a handle to a new object in the manner shown above. When the pointer goes out of scope, only the memory assigned to the pointer variable — usually four bytes — is freed up. The memory occupied by the object to which the pointer is pointing is not freed up unless you invoke the operator delete on the pointer before it goes out of scope.

What this means is that you just have to remember to invoke delete somewhere for every new (and delete[] somewhere for every new[]). In a majority of situations, this programming rule of thumb works just fine to prevent memory leaks. But there can be special circumstances where this rule of thumb cannot be applied so easily. Consider the following example:

```
//PretendGiant.cc

class Giant{};;

class Big {};

class MyClass {
    Giant* giant;
    Big* big;
public:
    MyClass()
        : giant( new Giant() ),                          //(A)
          big( new Big() )                                //(B)
    {}
```

---

[4]The dereferencing operator -> is also known as the member access operator.

```
        ~MyClass() { delete giant; delete big; }
};

int main()
{
        MyClass myobject;                                              //(C)
        return 0;
}
```

When `myobject` in `main` goes out of scope, its destructor will be invoked, which would free up the memory occupied by the objects pointed to by the pointer data members `giant` and `big`.

Now let's pretend that objects of type `Giant` and `Big` occupy huge amounts of memory and that after the execution of the statement in line (A), there is not enough memory left over for the construction in line (B). This could cause an exception to be thrown, which would halt any further construction of the object in line (C). In the following version of the program, we have simulated this condition by causing the constructor of `Big` to explicitly throw an exception in line (D):

```
//ConstructorLeak.cc

class Err{};

class Giant{};

class Big {
public:
        Big() throw( Err ) { throw Err(); }                            //(D)
};

class MyClass {
        Giant* giant;
        Big* big;
public:
        MyClass() : giant( new Giant() ), big( new Big() ) {}          //(E)
        ~MyClass() { delete giant; delete big; }
};

int main()
{
        try {
                MyClass myobject;                                      //(F)
        } catch( Err ) {}
        return 0;
}
```

Now the destructor of `myobject` will never be invoked when this object goes out of scope at the end of the `try` block in `main`. But note that the exception was thrown during the construction of the `Big` object in line (E) — but that was *after* the `Giant` object was already constructed. Since the destructor of `MyClass` is never invoked in this program, the memory occupied by the `Giant` object would never get released — causing a "giant" memory leak in the program.

One way to eliminate such potential memory leaks is by using a smart pointer instead of a regular pointer. When a smart pointer goes out of scope, it takes care of cleaning up after itself — in the sense that its destructor is invoked to free up the memory occupied by the object to which the pointer points.

Here is a rudimentary version of a smart pointer class, `SmartPtr`, whose objects can serve as smart pointers to objects of type `X`. We overload the dereferencing operators to make an object of type `SmartPtr` behave like a regular pointer.

```
class SmartPtr {
    X* ptr;
public:
    //constructor
    SmartPtr( X* p ) : ptr( p ) {};

    // overloading of *
    X& operator*() { return *ptr; }                         //(G)

    // overloading of ->
    X* operator->() { return ptr; }                         //(H)
    //....
};
```

An object of type `SmartPtr` is simply a wrapper around an object of type `X*`. The overload definitions for the '`*`' and the '`->`' operators in lines (G) and (H) give an object of type `SmartPtr` the same functionality as possessed by a regular pointer. To explain, consider the following example. Let's say we have

```
X* s = new X( .... );
```

We can now construct a `SmartPtr` for the newly created object by

```
SmartPtr smart_p( s );
```

Due to the overloading defined in the `SmartPtr` class for the member access operator '`->`,' we may now access a member of the `X` object constructed by

```
smart_p->some_member;                                       //(I)
```

When the compiler sees this construct, it first checks whether `smart_p` is a pointer to an object of some class (as that is the usual situation with an identifier on the left of the member-access arrow operator). In our case, that is not true. The compiler then checks whether the identifier on the left of the arrow is an object of some class for which the member access operator is overloaded. For the statement in line (I), that is indeed the case. The compiler then examines the overload definition for the '->' operator in line (H) above. If the return type specified in this definition is a pointer to a class type, the semantics for the built-in member access operator are then applied to the returned value.[5] For the example at hand, the compiler will extract from the overload definition of '->' the object returned by

```
smart_p->
```

which is the value stored in the data member `ptr` of the `smart_p` object. That turns out to be a regular pointer to the X object to which s points. The compiler now applies the same semantics to the pointer thus obtained and whatever is on right side of the member-access arrow operator in line (I) above as it does to the regular usage of this operator.

With regard to the overload definitions, both '*' and '->' are unary operators. Additionally, while the former is right-associative, the latter is left-associative. It is for this reason that the compiler tries to interpret

```
smart_p->
```

in line (H) before examining the object on the right of the arrow.

The overload definition for * in line (G) permits a `SmartPtr` object to be dereferenced in exactly the same manner as a regular pointer:

```
X* p = new X( .... );
SmartPtr s( p );
cout << *s;
```

The call *s returns *p and, if the output stream operator is overloaded for class X, the last statement would print out the X object constructed.

So far we have discussed how we may define a smart pointer, but we have not put any smarts into the example we showed above. We will now make the class `SmartPtr` "smart" by giving it the following functionality: Every time a pointer of type `SmartPtr` goes out of scope, we want the object pointed by its data member `ptr` to be deleted automatically. This can be achieved by defining the following destructor for `SmartPtr`:

```
SmartPtr::~SmartPtr() { delete ptr; }
```

Pulling together the definitions shown above, we can write the following program that is our first demonstration of the working of a smart pointer:

---

[5]See Lippman and Lajoie [50, p. 757] for a more thorough discussion concerning this point.

```
//SmartPtrInitial.cc

#include <iostream>
using namespace std;

class X {};

class SmartPtr {
    X* ptr;
public:
    SmartPtr( X* p ) : ptr( p ) {};
    X& operator*() { return *ptr; }
    X* operator->() { return ptr; }

    ~SmartPtr() {
        delete ptr;
        cout << "Memory pointed to by ptr freed up" << endl;
    }
};

int main()
{
    X* xp = new X();
    SmartPtr s( xp );

    return 0;
}
```

The SmartPtr class shown above is only minimally functional as a replacement for pointers of type X*. Used as such, it could inject dangerous bugs into a program. Suppose we initialize a new SmartPtr object with an existing SmartPtr object:

```
int main()
{
    X* xp = new X();
    SmartPtr s1( xp );
    SmartPtr s2 = s1;
}
```

With no copy constructor provided, the system will use the default definition of copy construction for initializing the object s2 from the object s1. This will cause ptr of s2 to point to the same X object as the ptr of s1. So when s1 and s2 go out of scope, their destructors will try to delete the same X object — with unpredictable results, possibly a system crash. So we must provide SmartPtr with an appropriate copy constructor. Very similar reasoning will also convince us that we must provide SmartPtr with a copy assignment operator.

Defining a copy constructor and a copy assignment operator for a smart pointer class is not as straightforward as it seems — because of the special nature of this class. You see, we never want more than one SmartPtr object to serve as a smart pointer to a given X object. So we do not want copy construction and copy assignment operation to result in two different SmartPtr objects pointing to the same X object. We therefore need to embed in our class definition for SmartPtr the notion of owning a given X object and the notion of transferring this ownership if copy construction or copy assignment is called for. This notion can be enforced by defining a release() member function for the SmartPtr class:

```
X* release() {
    X* oldPtr = ptr;
    ptr = 0;
    return oldPtr;
}
```

which simply releases a smart pointer's ownership of an X object by setting its ptr data member to 0. The function returns the old value of this pointer so that it can be handed over to some other smart pointer. In order to bring about this hand-over, we also need some sort of a reset member function for changing the X object owned by a smart pointer:

```
void reset( X* newPtr ) {
    if ( ptr != newPtr ) {
        delete ptr;
        ptr = newPtr;
    }
}
```

We can now write the following definitions for the copy constructor and the copy assignment operator:

```
//copy constructor:
SmartPtr( SmartPtr& other ) : ptr( other.release() ) {}


//copy assignment operator:
SmartPtr operator=( SmartPtr& other ) {
    if ( this != &other )
        reset( other.release() );
    return *this;
}
```

Pulling all of these definitions together gives us a more complete smart pointer class for objects of type X:

```
//SmartPtrWithOwnership.cc

class X {};

class SmartPtr {
    X* ptr;
public:
    explicit SmartPtr( X* p = 0 ) : ptr( p ) {};                    //(A)
    X& operator*() { return *ptr; }
    X* operator->() { return ptr; }

    SmartPtr( SmartPtr& other ) : ptr( other.release() ) {}

    SmartPtr operator=( SmartPtr& other ) {
        if ( this != &other )
            reset( other.release() );
        return *this;
    }

    ~SmartPtr() { delete ptr; }

    X* release() {
        X* oldPtr = ptr;
        ptr = 0;
        return oldPtr;
    }

    void reset( X* newPtr ) {
        if ( ptr != newPtr ) {
            delete ptr;
            ptr = newPtr;
        }
    }
}; // end of SmartPtr class

int main()
{
    X* xp = new X();
    SmartPtr s1( xp );
    SmartPtr s2 = s1;          // test copy const (s2 now owns X object)
    SmartPtr s3;               // use no-arg constructor
    s3 = s2;                   // test copy assign (s3 now owns X object)
    return 0;
}
```

where we have also included a no-arg constructor for SmartPtr by giving a default value of 0 to the pointer argument of the one-arg constructor in line (A). The keyword explicit that qualifies the constructor is to prevent the use of this constructor for implicit type conversion, as explained in Section 12.9.

The SmartPtr class still has one operational deficiency associated with it — it is custom designed for holding objects of type X. Going back to the MyClass example in the ConstructorLeak.cc program at the beginning of this section, this would imply creating separate smart pointer classes for Giant and Big. Fortunately, the notion of a template class that we will discuss in some detail in Chapter 13 makes that unnecessary. A templatized version of the SmartPtr class would be along the following lines:

```
//SmartPtr.h

template<class T> class SmartPtr {
    T* ptr;
public:
    explicit SmartPtr( T* p = 0 ) : ptr( p ) {}
    T& operator*() const { return *ptr; }
    T* operator->() const { return ptr; }

    SmartPtr( SmartPtr<T>& other ) : ptr( other.release() ) {}

    SmartPtr operator=( SmartPtr<T>& other ) {
        if ( this != &other )
            reset( other.release() );
        return *this;
    }

    ~SmartPtr() { delete ptr; }

    T* release() {
        T* oldPtr = ptr;
        ptr = 0;
        return oldPtr;
    }

    void reset( T* newPtr ) {
        if ( ptr != newPtr ) {
            delete ptr;
            ptr = newPtr;
        }
    }
};
```

Now we can reprogram the ConstructorLeak.cc program shown earlier in the manner shown below using the template class through the header SmartPtr.h. The smart-pointer based implementation shown below does not suffer from the resource leak that was present in the earlier implementation.

```
//ConstructorLeakPlugged.cc

#include "SmartPtr.h"
#include <iostream>
using namespace std;

class Err{};

class Giant {
public:
    ~Giant() {cout << "Giant's destructor invoked" << endl;}
};

class Big {
public:
    Big() throw( Err ) { throw Err(); }

    ~Big() {cout << "Big's destructor invoked" << endl;}
};

class MyClass {
    SmartPtr<Giant> giant;
    SmartPtr<Big> big;
public:
    MyClass() : giant( 0 ), big( 0 ) {
        giant.reset( new Giant() );
        big.reset( new Big() );
    }

    ~MyClass() {}                    // no destructor needed anymore
};

int main()
{
    try {
        MyClass myclass;
    } catch( Err ) {}

    return 0;
}
```

Fortunately for the programmer, the C++ Standard Library comes equipped comes with a smart pointer class, auto_ptr, in the header file <memory> that has all the smarts we talked about in this section. The reader is referred to p. 368 of Stroustrup [54] and pp. 291-294 of Meyers [51] for the definition of the auto_ptr class.

12.8 OVERLOADING INCREMENT AND DECREMENT OPERATORS

The goal of this section is to demonstrate the overloading of the increment operator '++' and the decrement operator '--', and to also dwell on the interesting problem posed by the fact these operators can be both prefix and postfix.

We will illustrate these with the help of a class SmallInt that should behave like a regular int as long as the numbers are between 0 and 255, inclusive of both ends of the range. If an attempt is made to alter the value held by a SmallInt so that it would violate the range constraint, we want an exception to be thrown. We endow the class with a function rangeCheck() to check for range violations:

```
class SmallInt {
    int value;                 // integer value held here
    class Err {};              // nested class for exceptions

    int rangeCheck( int i ) throw( Err ) {
        if ( i < 0 || i > 255 )
        throw Err();
        return i;
    }
public:
    // constructor:
    SmallInt( int ival = 0 ) {
        try {
            value = rangeCheck( ival );
        } catch (Err) {
            cerr << "Error: Range of SmallInt violated" << endl;
            exit( 1 );
        }
    }
    // ....
};
```

Since we want a SmallInt to behave very much like a regular integer, it would be nice if we could overload the increment and the decrement operators for SmallInt. The problem here is how to make a distinction between the overload definitions for the prefix and the postfix versions of the operators. As the following definitions for the increment operator show, this distinction is intimated to the compiler by including the int parameter type in the argument of the postfix version of the overload function, as shown in line (B) below. The compiler passes 0 as the value of the argument when the postfix function is invoked.

```
// overload for the prefix increment operator:
inline SmallInt& SmallInt::operator++() {                            //(A)
    try {
        rangeCheck( ++value );              // increment
    } catch(Err) {
        cerr << "Error: Range of SmallInt violated" << endl;
        exit( 1 );
    }
    return *this;                           // fetch
}

// overload for the postfix increment operator:
inline const SmallInt SmallInt::operator++( int ) {                  //(B)
    SmallInt oldValue = *this;              // fetch
    ++(*this);                              // increment
    return oldValue;
}
```

Note from line (B) above that the postfix increment operator returns a const object. This is to prevent[6] a double application of the postfix increment operator, as in

```
SmallInt si( .. );
si++++;
```

The first application of the increment operator will return a const object that will not allow the second application of the same operator to be invoked on it. A non-const member function cannot be invoked on a const object. (Note that the postfix operator is a non-const member function.) On the other hand, there are no such problems with a double application of the prefix increment operator. The following invocation is legal and will increment si twice:

```
SmallInt si( .. );
++++si;
```

Exactly the same considerations apply to the prefix and the postfix versions of the decrement operator.

---

[6]As Meyers [51, p. 33] has so well explained, a double application of the postfix increment operator does not do what a programmer would like to think it does. So it is best prohibited by a suitable definition of the operator overload function.

The code below shows a working example of SmallInt with overloaded increment and decrement operators. The reason for the use of the explicit modifier for the constructor in line (A), the comment "unsafe implicit conversion" with regard to the statement in line (B), and the "dangers of implicit conversion" comment after the statement in line (C) will be clear from the discussion in the next section.

```
//SmallIntWithIncrDecr.cc

#include <iostream>
#include <cstdlib>
using namespace std;

class SmallInt {
    int value;
    class Err {};
    int rangeCheck( int i ) throw( Err );
public:
    explicit SmallInt( int ival = 0 );                      //(A)
    SmallInt( const SmallInt& other );
    SmallInt& operator=( const SmallInt& other );
    SmallInt& operator=( const int i );
    //unsafe implicit conversion:
    operator int() const { return value; }                  //(B)
    SmallInt& operator++();
    SmallInt& operator--();
    const SmallInt operator++(int);
    const SmallInt  operator--(int);
    friend ostream& operator<<( ostream& os, const SmallInt& s );
};

//constructor:
inline SmallInt::SmallInt( int ival ) {
    try {
        value = rangeCheck( ival );
    } catch (Err) {
        cerr << "Error: Range of SmallInt violated" << endl;
        exit( 1 );
    }
}

//copy constructor:
inline SmallInt::SmallInt( const SmallInt& other ) {
    value = other.value;
}

//copy assignment operator:
inline SmallInt& SmallInt::operator=( const SmallInt& other ) {
```

```cpp
    if ( this != &other )
        value = other.value;
    return *this;
}


//assignment from an int:
inline SmallInt& SmallInt::operator=( const int i ) {
    try {
        value = rangeCheck( i );
    } catch(Err) {
        cerr << "Error: Range of SmallInt violated" << endl;
        exit( 1 );
    }
    return *this;
}


//prefix increment operator:
inline SmallInt& SmallInt::operator++() {
    try {
        rangeCheck( ++value );
    } catch(Err) {
        cerr << "Error: Range of SmallInt violated" << endl;
        exit( 1 );
    }
    return *this;
}


//prefix decrement operator:
inline SmallInt& SmallInt::operator--() {
    try {
        rangeCheck( --value );
    } catch(Err) {
        cerr << "Error: Range of SmallInt violated" << endl;
        exit( 1 );
    }
    return *this;
}


//postfix increment operator:
inline const SmallInt SmallInt::operator++(int) {
    SmallInt oldValue = *this;
    ++(*this);
    return oldValue;
}


//postfix decrement operator:
inline const SmallInt SmallInt::operator--(int) {
    SmallInt oldValue = *this;
    --(*this);
```

```
      return oldValue;
}

//range check function:
inline int SmallInt::rangeCheck( int i ) throw( Err ) {
    if ( i < 0 || i > 255 )
        throw Err();
    return i;
}

//overload for the output stream operator:
ostream& operator<<( ostream& os, const SmallInt& s ) {
    os << s.value;
    return os;
}

int main()
{
    SmallInt si( 3 );
    cout << si + 3.14159 << endl;    // 6.14159
    cout << ++si << endl;            // 4
    cout << si++ << endl;            // 4
    cout << si << endl;              // 5
    cout << --si << endl;            // 4
    cout << si << endl;              // 4
    cout << si-- << endl;            // 4
    cout << si << endl;              // 3

    si = 255;
    cout << si << endl;
    //  si++;                // range violated, exception thrown
    //  si = 300;            // range violated, exception thrown

    cout <<  si + 400 << endl;                               //(C)
                            // 655   (shows the dangers of
                            // implicit conversion)
    return 0;
}
```

12.9 USER-DEFINED CONVERSIONS

Chapter 6 talked about implicit type conversions for the primitive types in C++. As mentioned there, implicit type conversions are applied automatically by the compiler.

It is possible to give the compiler the freedom to carry out implicit type conversions for class-type objects also. This is done by embedding in the class definition a member function with specially designated syntax.

To illustrate this syntax, consider the classes Point3D and Point2D in the example code below, the former for designated a point in 3D xyz space, and the latter a point in the xy plane of the 3D space. It is not difficult to imagine an application which could require a 2D point to be processed as a 3D point for some geometrical calculation. To make that happen automatically, in the code shown below we endow the class Point2D with a special member function in line (A). The prototype of this member function is:

```
operator Point3D()
```

Its implementation shown below is presented in line (B) of the program:

```
operator Point3D() { return Point3D( x, y, 0 ); }
```

That's all we have to do to enable the compiler to automatically convert a Point2D object into a Point3D object.

To demonstrate the auto-conversion of a Point2D object into a Point3D object, in main we create a Point2D object point2D in line (C). To print out this object, we call in line (D):

```
cout << point2D << endl;
```

But note that we have not overloaded the output operator for the class Point2D; *it is overloaded for only the* Point3D *class.* However, the compiler does not complain. It silently converts our Point2D object into a Point3D object and prints that out.

```
//UserConv.cc

#include <iostream>
using namespace std;

class Point3D;

class Point2D {
    int x;
    int y;
public:
    Point2D( int p, int q ) : x(p), y(q) {}
    operator Point3D();                                    //(A)
};

class Point3D {
    int x;
    int y;
```

```
    int z;
public:
    Point3D( int p, int q, int r ) : x(p), y(q), z(r) {}
    friend ostream& operator<<( ostream& os, const Point3D& point );
};

ostream& operator<<( ostream& os, const Point3D& point )
{
    os << "(" << point.x <<", " << point.y << ", " << point.z << ")";
    return os;
}

inline Point2D::operator Point3D() { return Point3D( x, y, 0 ); } //(B)

int main()
{
    Point2D point2D( 3, 4 );                                  //(C)
    cout << point2D << endl;                                  //(D)
                        // (3, 4, 0) using Point3D's operator<<
    return 0;
}
```

To summarize, a user-defined conversion function takes the general form

```
    operator type();
```

where 'type' is replaced by a built-in type, a class type, or a typedef name. Also, a conversion function *must* be a member function. Its declaration must not specify a return type. Nor can a parameter list be specified.

Unless prevented from doing so by the `explicit` keyword, a compiler will also try to carry out implicit type conversion of class-type objects by using a *one-argument* constructor if such a constructor is available. In the following version of the above example, we do NOT provide the class `Point2D` with a type conversion operator. Instead, in line (E) we have equipped the class `Point3D` with a 1-arg constructor that takes a `Point2D` argument. In `main`, we construct an object of type `Point2D` and ask the output operator to print it out. The compiler has no problem with this. The compiler notices that it is allowed to construct a `Point3D` object from a `Point2D` object and that the former carries an overload definition for `operator<<`. So the compiler goes ahead and makes use of the 1-arg constructor of `Point3D` to do the job in `main`.

```
//UserConvConstructor.cc

#include <iostream>
using namespace std;
```

```
class Point3D;

class Point2D {
    int x;
    int y;
public:
    Point2D( int p, int q ) : x(p), y(q) {}
    friend Point3D;
};

class Point3D {
    int x;
    int y;
    int z;
public:
    Point3D( int p, int q, int r ) : x(p), y(q), z(r) {}
    Point3D( Point2D point2D ) :                               //(E)
               x( point2D.x ), y( point2D.y ), z( 0 ) {}
    friend ostream& operator<<( ostream& os, const Point3D& point );
};

ostream& operator<<( ostream& os, const Point3D& point ) {
    os << "(" << point.x <<", " << point.y << ", " << point.z << ")";
    return os;
}

int main()
{
    Point2D point2D( 3, 4 );
    cout << point2D << endl;
                    // (3, 4, 0) using Point3D's 1-arg constructor
    return 0;
}
```

If a class is equipped with a 1-arg constructor, the fact that the compiler has the license to use it for implicit type conversion can sometimes have unintended and dangerous consequences. What if you did not want a Point2D to be converted into a Point3D without your permission? What if you were involved in calculations concerning 2D points not in the xy plane, but in some other plane of the 3D space? Now the particular conversion embodied in the 1-arg constructor of Point3D would be inappropriate. Fortunately, C++ gives us a mechanism to prevent such unauthorized type conversions by using the keyword explicit, as in line (F) of the example below. If the header of a 1-arg constructor is preceded by explicit, it can be used for type conversion only with the help of explicitly invoked cast operator, as we show in line (G) of the program below.

```
//UserConvExplicit.cc

#include <iostream>
using namespace std;

class Point3D;

class Point2D {
    int x;
    int y;
public:
    Point2D( int p, int q ) : x(p), y(q) {}
    friend Point3D;
};

class Point3D {
    int x;
    int y;
    int z;
public:
    Point3D( int p, int q, int r ) : x(p), y(q), z(r) {}
    explicit Point3D( Point2D point2D )                        //(F)
            : x( point2D.x ), y( point2D.y ), z( 0 ) {}
    friend ostream& operator<<( ostream& os, const Point3D& point );
};

ostream& operator<<( ostream& os, const Point3D& point ) {
    os << "(" << point.x <<", " << point.y << ", " << point.z << ")";
    return os;
}

int main()
{
    Point2D point2D( 3, 4 );
    //  cout << point2D << endl;    // will not work now

    // note explicit cast:
    cout << static_cast<Point3D>( point2D );                   //(G)

    return 0;
}
```

As stated earlier, implicit type conversions can be dangerous, since the compiler could invoke them when that was the last thing you wanted to see happen. Such conversions can therefore result in difficult to locate problems in large and complex programs. The solution obviously lies in not including type conversion operators in a class and declaring 1-arg constructors where the class appears as an argument as explicit.

12.10   OVERLOADING OF THE '()' OPERATOR

It is also possible to overload the function call operator '()'. Overloading this operator allows an object to be used as a *function object*. A function object, also known as a *functor*, can serve a role akin to that of a function pointer when supplied as an argument to another function. In other words, if you overload the function call '()' for a class, an object of that type can act like a function. When such an object is invoked like a function, it is the code that is in the overload definition of '()' that gets executed. One of the primary advantages of a functor over a regular function is that the data members of the former can be deployed to advantage in the operations carried out by the code in the overloading of '()'.[7]

To illustrate the concept of a function object, let's say we want to sort by age a list of Cat objects made from the following class:

```
class Cat {
public:
    string name;
    int age;
    Cat( string nam, int yy) : name(nam), age( yy ) {}
};
```

The Cat objects will be the elements of a list of type list<Cat>:

```
list<Cat> kittyList;
```

To sort the cats by age, we have to tell the generic STL algorithm sort how to compare two Cat objects by their age fields. For that purpose we define a comparator class as follows:

```
class Cat_Comparator {
public:
    bool operator() ( const Cat&, const Cat& ) const;
};
```

and provide the following overload definition for the '()' operator:

```
bool Cat_Comparator::operator()( const Cat& x1,
                                 const Cat& x2 ) const {
    return x1.age < x2.age;
}
```

---

[7]As an example of how a data member can prove useful to a function object, see the class ThresholdCheck defined in Problem 4 in the homework section of Chapter 5.

With operator() overloaded for the Cat_Comparator class, an object of type Cat_Comparator can be made to act like a function. This is demonstrated by the following code in lines (A) and (B) of the program SortWithFunctor.cc below:

```
Cat_Comparator comp;
kittyList.sort( comp );
```

Note that the argument to sort in line (B) is an object. Its role is very much like that of the function pointer argument in the call to qsort in Chapter 4. What is invoked where comp is called in the body of sort is the code in the overloading of the '()' operator. The return type when an object is invoked like a function is the return type for the overloading of the operator '().'

Here is the code for SortWithFunctor.cc:

```
//SortWithFunctor.cc

#include <string>
#include <list>
using namespace std;

class Cat {
public:
    string name;
    int age;
    Cat( string nam, int yy) : name(nam), age( yy ) {}
};

class Cat_Comparator {
public:
    bool operator()(const Cat&, const Cat&) const;
};

bool Cat_Comparator::operator()(const Cat& x1, const Cat& x2) const {
    return x1.age < x2.age;
}

template<class T> void print( list<T> );

int main()
{
    Cat kitty1( "socks", 6 );
    Cat kitty2( "cuddles", 3 );
    Cat kitty3( "tabby", 8 );

    list<Cat> kittyList;

    kittyList.push_back( kitty1 );
```

```
    kittyList.push_back( kitty2 );
    kittyList.push_back( kitty3 );

    Cat_Comparator comp;                                        //(A)
    kittyList.sort( comp );                                     //(B)

    print( kittyList );        // cuddles 3    socks 6    tabby 6

    return 0;
}

template<class T> void print( list<T> li ) {
    typedef list<T>::const_iterator CI;
    for ( CI iter = li.begin(); iter != li.end(); iter++ )
        cout << iter->name << " " << iter->age << "   ";
    cout << endl << endl;
}
```

To shed further light on the parallels between a regular function and a function object, we obviously cannot compare two Cat object, kitty1 and kitty2, by making the following call

```
    Cat_Comparator( kitty1, kitty2 );          // WRONG
```

since that would try to invoke a two-parameter constructor for Cat_Comparator, if such a constructor were to exist, and not the comparison code in the overloading of the function call operator. If we wanted to, we could make a direct invocation of the function-call overloading by the following calls:

```
    Cat_Comparator cat_comp;
    bool test = cat_comp.operator()( kitty1, kitty2 );
    cout << ''value of test is: '' << test << endl;
```

12.11   SORTING CLASS-TYPE OBJECTS BY OVERLOADING THE '<' OPERATOR

In the previous section, we showed how we can use a function object to tell a sorting routine how to compare two class type objects. An alternative approach consists of overloading the '<' operator as we show in this section.

Shown below is an example where we have defined a Cat class and then provided a global overload definition for the operator '<' for this class in line (A) of the program. With the operator overload definition in place, a call to the usual sort for a list<Cat> will automatically sort the Cat objects.

```
//SortWithLessThan.cc

#include <string>
#include <list>
using namespace std;

class Cat {
    string name;
    int age;
public:
    Cat( string nam, int yy) : name(nam), age( yy ) {}
    string getName() const { return name; }
    int getAge() const { return age; }
    friend bool operator<( const Cat& x1, const Cat& x2 );
};

bool operator<( const Cat& x1, const Cat& x2 ) {                    //(A)
    return x1.age < x2.age;
}

template<class T> void print( list<T> );

int main()
{
    Cat kitty1( "socks", 6 );
    Cat kitty2( "cuddles", 3 );
    Cat kitty3( "tabby", 8 );

    list<Cat> kittyList;

    kittyList.push_back( kitty1 );
    kittyList.push_back( kitty2 );
    kittyList.push_back( kitty3 );


    kittyList.sort();
    print( kittyList );

    return 0;
}

template<class T> void print( list<T> li ) {
    typedef list<T>::const_iterator CI;
    for ( CI iter = li.begin(); iter != li.end(); iter++ )
        cout << iter->getName() << " " << iter->getAge() << endl;
    cout << endl << endl;
}
```

Sorting class-type objects by overloading the '<' operator will not work on a container of pointers to user-defined types. Suppose, instead of storing Cat objects in a container of type vector<Cat>, we store Cat* pointers in a vector<Cat*> container. Now we could try to overload the '<' operator in the following manner:

```
bool operator<( const Cat* x1, const Cat* x2 ) {        // WRONG
    return x1->age < x2->age;
}
```

and declare this definition to be a friend of Cat by

```
friend bool operator<( const Cat* x1, const Cat* x2 );  // WRONG
```

This does not work because the compiler will insist that the arguments to the overloading of '<' be class-type objects and not pointers to class type objects. This is in accord with the constraints on operator overloading listed in the introduction to this chapter.

So how does one sort a container of pointers to user-defined class-type objects? By going back to the functor based approach of the previous section. Shown below is an example that illustrates this. Note that for the sake of variety this implementation uses the vector container class and the generic library sort, since, unlike list, the class vector does not come equipped with a sort function of its own. Additionally, we have defined Cat_Comparator as a nested class.

```
//SortPointerTypes.cc

#include <string>
#include <vector>
#include <algorithm>
using namespace std;

class Cat {
    string name;
    int age;
public:
    class Cat_Comparator {
    public:
        bool operator() ( const Cat* x1, const Cat* x2 ) const {
            return x1->age < x2->age;
        }
    };
    Cat( string nam, int yy) : name(nam), age( yy ) {}
    string getName() const { return name; }
    int getAge() const { return age; }
    friend bool Cat_Comparator::operator()( const Cat* x1,
                                            const Cat* x2 ) const;
};
```

```
template<class T> void print( vector<T> );


int main()
{
    Cat* kitty1 = new Cat( "cuddles", 3 );
    Cat* kitty2 = new Cat( "tabby", 8 );
    Cat* kitty3 = new Cat( "socks", 6 );

    vector<Cat*> kittyVec;

    kittyVec.push_back( kitty1 );
    kittyVec.push_back( kitty2 );
    kittyVec.push_back( kitty3 );

    sort( kittyVec.begin(), kittyVec.end(), Cat::Cat_Comparator() );
    print( kittyVec );                    // cuddles 3   socks 6   tabby 8
}

template<class T> void print( vector<T> li ) {
    typedef vector<T>::const_iterator CI;
    for ( CI iter = li.begin(); iter != li.end(); iter++ )
        cout << (*iter)->getName() << " " << (*iter)->getAge() << "   ";
    cout << endl << endl;
}
```

12.12 CREDITS AND SUGGESTIONS FOR FURTHER READING

The book by Meyers [51] is a "must read" for anyone seriously interested in operator overloading in C++. Many ideas presented in this chapter were much influenced by what Meyers has to say.

The operator overload definitions we showed for the MyString class create separate string objects in the memory even when the strings are identical in value. See [54, 51] on how to create a more efficient reference-counted string class. With reference counting, all strings of the same value will be represented by a single string object in the memory.

Certain operators should not be overloaded, even when so allowed by the language. See the book by Meyers [51] for why the logical operators '&&' and '||' and the comma operator ',' should not be overloaded. To summarize Meyers, C++ language specifies that the logical operators '&&' and '||' carry out a *short-circuit evaluation* of their operands, which causes the right operand to not be evaluated if the truth value of the logical expression can be ascertained from the left operand. Overloading the logical operators causes their short-circuit semantics to change to function-call semantics, entailing the evaluation of both operands. The comma operator should not be overloaded because the left-to-right evaluation of the operands cannot be guaranteed in the overloaded definition.

For additional reading on smart pointers, the reader is referred to [50] and [51].

12.13   HOMEWORK

1. The following program elicits an "undefined symbol problem" message from the linker. What's the problem with this program? How can the problem be fixed?

```
#include <iostream>
using namespace std;

class X {
    friend ostream& operator<<( ostream&, X& );
};

ostream& operator<<( ostream& os, const X& xobj ) {
    os << "message from an X object" << endl;
}

int main()
{
    X xob;
    cout << xob;
    return 0;
}
```

2. The following program has a flaw similar to the one you saw in the program of the previous problem, but it results in a different error message from the compiler. Why?

```
#include <iostream>
using namespace std;

class X {
    int n;
public:
    X() : n(10) {}
    friend ostream& operator<<( ostream&, X& );
};
```

```
ostream& operator<<( ostream& os, const X& xobj ) {
    os << "n: " << xobj.n << endl;
}

int main()
{
    X xob;
    cout << xob;
    return 0;
}
```

3. Define a function object that would allow a vector of strings to be sorted in a case-insensitive manner.

4. Modify the program for the sorting example of Section 12.10 for the case when the object to be sorted has private data members.

5. Modify the program of the previous problem to sort a vector of user-defined class-type objects.

6. The program of Section 12.11 shows how a list of class-type objects can be sorted by merely supplying an overload definition for the operator '<'. Modify that code for the case of a vector of class-type objects.

7. Pretending that a programmer would not need a copy constructor or a copy assignment operator and as an exercise in giving additional smarts to a smart pointer, write a smart pointer class for your own string type, for example for the MyString type presented in Section 12.6. In addition to the usual smarts of automatic freeing up of the memory occupied by the string owned by a smart pointer, also give it the following smarts: Whenever a string goes out of scope, it should get dumped into a string archive.

8. Generalize the smart pointer of the previous question so that it can be used to point to either a single object or to an array of objects. Overload the increment and the decrement operators so that an array can be stepped through in the same

manner as with a regular pointer. Make sure that you range check the pointer as it is incremented or decremented so that there is no range violation.

13

Generics and Templates

Templates (also known as generics) allow code to be written in such a way that the same program can be used for different data types. Consider for example a C linked-list program that is written to hold a list of integers. If you wanted to store a list of, say, floating point types, you'd need to create a new program for that. And if you wanted to store a list of strings, you'd need to create yet another version of the same program. All of these different versions of the linked-list program would have a great deal in common, since, after all, all linked lists possess the same fundamental structure: you have a list of linked nodes, and, at the least, each node must hold one element and, at the same time, point to the next node.

Ordinarily, this problem also exists with C++ programs. If you were to create, say, a linked-list program in C++ for storing integers, you would not be able to use the same program for storing strings. Java, on the other hand, stands at the other extreme: You could easily write a Java linked-list program that would be able hold items of any type. In fact, within the same linked list, you could have the first node hold an integer, the second node hold a string, and so on. That's because what would actually be stored in a node would be a reference to an `Object`, the root class of all objects in Java, and each such reference could point to a data item of a different type. But, unfortunately, as the reader will see from the examples in this chapter, this behavior of Java comes at a price: *When you want to extract an item from a container, you have to remember to cast it back to the type that was actually stored in the container.* Forgetting to cast or using an incorrect cast can result in run-time errors.

Modern thinking is that both these extremes of language behavior — container classes that work for only one data type or that work for all data types — lead to programming inefficiencies. The former because you have to create a new container class for each separate data type and the latter because of the casts that are needed for the retrieval of the correct data type.

To get around these limitations, we have templates in C++ and generics in Java. A templatized program (or a generic program) can be a class or a method that is parameterized by a variable that can be instantiated to different types. For example, an ordinary linked-list program in C++ may look like

```
class LinkedList {
    struct Node {
        Node* next;
        int val;
    };
    Node* head;
public:
    // public interface of the class
    ....
    ....
};
```

The individual nodes of the linked list will be instances of the nested class, a `struct` named Node. Note that since the data member `val` of the struct Node is defined to be of type `int`, this linked list will only be able to hold integers. Now compare this with the following templatized version:

```
template<class T> class LinkedList {
    struct Node {
        Node* next;
        T val;
    };
    Node* head;
public:
    // public interface of the class
    ....
    ....
};
```

Note how the header of the class has been parameterized by incorporating the variable T and how the type of the data member `val` inside the nested class Node has been declared to be of type T. With this new definition, `LinkedList<int>` would do exactly the same as our previous `LinkedList` class. But now we can use the same program to create a `LinkedList<double>` class for storing a list of doubles, a `LinkedList<string>` class for storing a list of strings, and so on.

Let's now consider Java. An ordinary linked list class in Java may have its header and the beginning section look like this:

```
class LinkedList {
    class Node {
        Object element;
        Node next;
    }
    Node head;
    // the public interface of the class
    ...
    ...
}
```

The individual nodes of the linked list will be of type Node, which is a nested class above. Each node will store an item of the list in the data member element. Since this data member is of type Object, we have the freedom to store any class-type object in the different nodes of the list. But, as mentioned earlier, the price to pay for this flexibility is that we must remember to cast the item down to its correct type when it is retrieved from the list. Alternatively, we can use the parameterized version of this class shown below that lets us use the same program for linked lists of different data types and, at the same time, does away with the need for casting at the time of retrieval:

```
class LinkedList<T> {
    class Node {
        T element;
        Node next;
    }
    Node head;
    // the public interface of the class
    ....
    ....
}
```

With the parameterization[1] of the class header, now the list items stored in the individual nodes will be of type T. This new parameterized class could now be used as LinkedList<Integer> to store items of type Integer, LinkedList<String> to store items of type String, and so on.

In the rest of this chapter, we will first present the class and function parameterization in C++. Class and function parameterizations are integral parts of the C++ language. In fact, as a programming language, C++ derives much of its power from such parameterizations.

Next, we will show how to write parameterized classes and methods in Java. Although such parameterizations are not yet features of the language as officially released (and therefore should not be used for writing portable Java code at this time),

---

[1]The words *templatization* and *parameterization* will be used interchangeably in this chapter. Same with the words *templatized* and *parameterized*.

there is much educational value in seeing that Java can be endowed with the same sort of parameterizations that one finds in C++.

13.1 TEMPLATIZED CLASSES AND FUNCTIONS IN C++

We will use the prototypical example of a linked list to illustrate the concepts and the syntax of class and function parameterization in C++. We will first see how one might structure a regular (meaning, a non-parameterized) C++ program for a linked-list of ints. We will then "templatize" (or "parameterize") the program so that the same program can be used for different data types.

13.1.1 A C++ Implementation of a Linked-List Program

We evidently need some kind of a data structure to serve as a node in a linked list. We could use the following structure:

```
struct Node {
    Node* previous;
    Node* next;
    int item;
    // ....
};
```

In this node, the data member item can be used to store one item in a list of integers and the data members previous and next tell us how to get to the previous node and to the next node in a linked list.[2]

To be able to create a node, we also need a constructor for a Node:

```
struct Node {
    Node* previous;
    Node* next;
    int item;
    //node constructor:
    Node(Node* p, Node* n, int i) : previous(p), next(n), item(i){}
};
```

We can now create a new Node by

```
int i = 10;
Node* newNode = new Node(0, 0, i);
```

---

[2]A minimalist implementation of a linked list would only use one of the linking pointers, either a pointer to the next node or a pointer to the previous node.

and then link it to previousNode, a previously constructed node, by

```
previousNode->next = newNode;
newNode->previous = previousNode;
```

The entire chain of nodes created in this manner can be encapsulated in an object of type LinkedList, defined below, so as to hide the details of the implementation from a user of the linked list:

```
class LinkedList {

    struct Node {                                       //(A)
        Node* previous;
        Node* next;
        int item;

        Node( Node* p, Node* n, int i)
                : previous(p), next(n), item(i) {}
    };

    Node* head;                                         //(B)

public:

    // code for constructors, destructor,
    // copy constructor, copy assignment
    // operator, add and remove functions
    // for the nodes, and so on.

};
```

Note how the struct Node in line (A), together with its constructor, belongs to the private section of LinkedList. That's because the users of a LinkedList do not need to know how exactly the members of a LinkedList are stored and constructed. Also private to the class LinkedList is the data member head in line (B), which will serve as a pointer to the first node of a linked list.

What follows is a working partial implementation for the LinkedList class. We have provided implementation code for a no-arg constructor; a constructor for the first item inserted in the list; a destructor; an addToList() function; a removeFromList() function; and a print function. However, we have left the implementations of the copy constructor and the copy assignment operator as exercises for the reader.

```
//LinkedList.cc

#include <iostream>
using namespace std;

class LinkedList {

    struct Node {
        Node* previous;
        Node* next;
        int item;
        Node( Node* p, Node* n, int i)
                : previous(p), next(n), item(i) {}
    };

    Node* head;
public:
    //no-arg constructor:
    LinkedList();                                           //(C)
    //constructor:
    LinkedList( int x );                                    //(D)
    //copy constructor (exercise for the reader):
    LinkedList( const LinkedList& ll );                     //(E)
    //copy assignment operator (exercise for the reader):
    LinkedList& operator=( const LinkedList& ll );          //(F)
    //destructor:
    ~LinkedList();                                          //(G)

    void addToList( int );                                  //(H)
    void removeFromList( int );                             //(I)
    void printAll();                                        //(J)
};   //end of class definition


LinkedList:: LinkedList() : head(0) {}                      //(K)

LinkedList::LinkedList( int x )  : head( new Node(0, 0, x) ) {}   //(L)

//always add at the end of the list
void LinkedList::addToList( int m ) {                       //(M)
    Node* p = head;
    //check if the list was created previously.  If not
    //start the list:
    if ( p == 0 ) {
        head = new Node( 0, 0, m );
        return;
    }
```

```
    //find the end of the list:
    while (p->next)
        p = p->next;
    //now add a new node at the end:
    p->next = new Node(0, 0, m);
    p->next->previous = p;
}


//removes the first occurrence only
void LinkedList::removeFromList( int m ) {                          //(N)
    Node* p = head;
    //trying to remove from an empty list:
    if ( p == 0 ) return;
    //search for the item to be removed:
    while (p->item != m) {
        //end of list reached without finding the item:
        if (p->next == 0) return;
        p = p->next;
    }
    //if item was found in the first node:
    if (p == head) {
        head = head->next;
        head->previous = 0;
        delete p;
        return;
    }
    //link the previous node to the next node so that
    //the current node containing the item can be deleted:
    p->previous->next = p->next;
    //unless the item to be deleted is at the end of the list,
    //link the next node back to the previous node:
    if (p->next != 0) p->next->previous = p->previous;
    //now delete the node containing the item:
    delete p;
}

void LinkedList::printAll() {                                       //(O)
    for ( Node* p = head; p; p = p->next ) cout << p->item << ' ';
    cout << endl;
}

LinkedList::~LinkedList() {                                         //(P)
    Node* p = head;
    while ( p != 0 ) {
        Node* temp = p;
        p = p->next;
        delete temp;
    }
}
```

```
int main() {
    LinkedList alist(3);          // 3
    alist.addToList(5);           // 3 5
    alist.addToList(7);           // 3 5 7
    alist.addToList(9);           // 3 5 7 9
    alist.addToList(11);          // 3 5 7 9 11
    alist.printAll();             // 3  5  7  9 11

    alist.removeFromList(7);
    alist.printAll();             // 3 5 9 11

    alist.removeFromList(3);      // 5 9 11
    alist.printAll();

    alist.removeFromList( 11 );
    alist.printAll();             // 5 9
}
```

The no-arg constructor, declared in line (C) and defined in line (K), sets the data member head to the null pointer, an appropriate thing to do for an empty list. We then declare in line (D) and define at (L) what it means for a LinkedList to contain a single integer. For this case, we have a LinkedList of just one node, pointed to by the data member head, whose previous and next pointers are both null and for which the item data member is set equal to the int to be stored.

Lines (E) and (F) carry declarations for the copy constructor and the copy assignment operator. Implementations of these are left as exercises for the reader. (Obviously, the code in main does not invoke either the copy constructor or the copy assignment operator.)

The destructor is declared in line (G) and its implementation provided in line (L). As you'd expect, the destructor hops from node to node and frees up the memory occupied by each.

A linked list would not be very useful if it was not possible to add to it new items and to delete from it existing item. The functions addToList() and removeFromList(), declared in lines (H) and (I) and with implementations provided in lines (M) and (N), provide the class with this basic functionality.

Finally, we have also provided the class with a print function declared in line (J), with its implementation in line (O).

13.1.2 A Parameterized Linked-List Program

The program we showed in the previous section can only be used for storing a list of ints, or for storing other data types that the compiler is allowed to convert to int. We could write a similar program for storing a list of chars, strings, and so on. All of these programs would have a great deal in common, as was mentioned before, but would not be interchangeable functionally.

We will now create a parameterized version of the linked-list program of the previous section. We will then be able to use this more general program directly for creating linked lists of different data types.

Here is a parameterized version of the class LinkedList, with only the prototypes shown for four out of six functions in the public section of the class. This class definition does not include a copy constructor and a copy assignment operator for the class, whose implementations are left as exercises for the reader.

```
template <class T> class LinkedList {                              //(A)

    struct Node {
        Node* previous;
        Node* next;
        const T& item;                                            //(B)
        Node( Node* p, Node* n, const T& t)                       //(C)
                 : previous(p), next(n), item(t) {}
    };

    Node* head;                                                   //(D)
public:
    LinkedList() : head() {}                                      //(E)
    LinkedList( const T& t )  : head( new Node(0, 0, t)) {}       //(F)
    ~LinkedList();                                                //(G)
    void addToList( const T& );                                   //(H)
    void removeFromList( const T& );                              //(I)
    void printAll();                                              //(J)
};
```

Note the prefix

```
template<class T>
```

in the header of the class definition in line (A). This prefix specifies that a templatized (or parameterized) class is being declared, with the identifier T serving as a type parameter (or the template parameter). What we have created above is a class template, as opposed to a function template that we will talk about shortly. The name of this class template is LinkedList. The scope of the type parameter T extends to the end of the block that follows the header in line (A).

A templatized class can be used like any other class in C++ after a previously defined type is substituted for the template parameter. For example, the above templatized class could be used as the following classes:

```
LinkedList<int>
LinkedList<double>
LinedList<float>
LinkedList<string>
```

or, even,

```
LinkedList<LinkedList>
```

provided the operators used in the function definitions are defined for this type.

A templatized class will, in general, contain constructors and functions that utilize the type parameters used for the parameterization of the class. For example, the constructor shown in line (F) utilizes the type parameter T. When such constructors and functions are given in-class definitions, the implementation code looks much like that for a non-templatized class. However, when it is desired to provide the implementation code outside the body of a class, the headers of the the definitions need to be expressed in a particular way.

Consider, for example, the function addToList(T item) whose prototype is included in line (H) in the definition of the LinkedList class above. To provide a definition for this function outside the class, its syntax would be something like this:

```
template <class T> void LinkedList<T>::addToList( const T& item ) {
    Node* p = head;
    //check if the list was created previously.  If not
    //start the list:
    if ( p == 0 ) {
        head = new Node( 0, 0, item );
        return;
    }
    //find the end of the list:
    while (p->next)
        p = p->next;
    //now add a new node at the end:
    p->next = new Node(0, 0, item);
    p->next->previous = p;
}
```

Note how the implementation of the function carries the prefix template<class T> in its header. Then comes the return type of the function, in this case void. This is followed by the name of the class template for which the function is being defined, the name here being `LinkedList<T>`. Next comes the scope operator `::`, followed by actual name of the function, `addToList`. The parameter list that comes next also contains the type parameter `T` in the example here. Such a function definition may be referred to as a *function template*, although that name is used more frequently for templatized versions of stand-alone functions.

Here is the code for a templatized version of the linked list program. Note again that it is only a partial working implementation of the class, partial in the sense that we have not provided the class with a copy constructor and a copy assignment operator, and so on, whose implementations are left to the reader as exercises.

```
//LinkedListGeneric.cc

#include <iostream>
#include <string>
using namespace std;

template <class T> class LinkedList {                       //(A)

    struct Node {
        Node* previous;
        Node* next;
        const T& item;                                      //(B)
        Node( Node* p, Node* n, const T& t)                 //(C)
                : previous(p), next(n), item(t) {}
    };

    Node* head;                                             //(D)
public:
    LinkedList() : head() {}                                //(E)
    LinkedList( const T& t )  : head( new Node(0, 0, t)) {} //(F)
    ~LinkedList();                                          //(G)
    void addToList( const T& );                             //(H)
    void removeFromList( const T& );                        //(I)
    void printAll();                                        //(J)
};


template<class T> LinkedList<T>::~LinkedList() {
    Node* p = head;
    while ( p != 0 ) {
        Node* temp = p;
        p = p->next;
        delete temp;
    }
}
```

```
template <class T> void LinkedList<T>::addToList( const T& item ) {
    Node* p = head;
    //check if the list was created previously.  If not
    //start the list:
    if ( p == 0 ) {
        head = new Node( 0, 0, item );
        return;
    }
    //find the end of the list:
    while (p->next)
        p = p->next;
    //now add a new node at the end:
    p->next = new Node(0, 0, item);
    p->next->previous = p;
}

template<class T> void LinkedList<T>::removeFromList( const T& item ) {
    Node* p = head;
    for (; p->item != item; p = p->next)                              //(K)
        if (p->next == 0) return;   // item not in list
    if (p == head) {                      // item in the first node
        head = head->next;
        head->previous = 0;
        delete( p );
        return;
    }
    p->previous->next = p->next;
    if (p->next != 0)        // item to be deleted is at the end of list
      p->next->previous = p->previous;
    delete( p );
}

template<class T> void LinkedList<T>::printAll() {
    for (Node* p = head; p; p = p->next )
        cout << p->item << ' ';
}

//a class for testing the linked-list program for user-defined types:
class X {                                                        //(L)
    int n;
public:
    X( int nn ) : n(nn) {}
    bool operator==( const X& xobj ) const { return n == xobj.n; }
    bool operator!=( const X& xobj ) const { return n != xobj.n; }
    friend ostream& operator<<( ostream& os, const X& xobj ) {
        os << xobj.n << " ";
    }
    ~X(){}
};
```

```cpp
int main() {

    //a linked-list of ints:
    int i = 1;                                              //(M)
    LinkedList<int>* numlist = new LinkedList<int>(i);
    numlist->addToList( 5 );
    numlist->addToList( 6 );
    numlist->printAll();                    // 1 5 6
    cout << endl;
    numlist->removeFromList( 6 );
    numlist->printAll();                    // 1 5
    cout << endl;
    delete numlist;

    //a linked-list of chars:
    char x = 'c';                                          //(N)
    LinkedList<char>* charlist = new LinkedList<char>(x);
    charlist->addToList( 'a' );
    charlist->addToList( 't' );
    charlist->printAll();                   // c a t
    cout << endl;
    charlist->removeFromList( 'c' );
    charlist->printAll();                   // a t
    cout << endl;
    delete charlist;

    //a linked-list of string types:
    string str1( "high" );                                 //(O)
    string str2( "sierras" );
    string str3( "green" );
    string str4( "tiaras" );
    LinkedList<string>* stringList = new LinkedList<string>( str1 );
    stringList->addToList( str2 );
    stringList->addToList( str3 );
    stringList->addToList( str4 );
    stringList->printAll();            // high sierras green tiaras
    cout << endl;
    stringList->removeFromList( str1 );
    stringList->printAll();            // sierras green tiaras
    cout << endl;
    delete stringList;

    //a linked-list of user-defined class types:
    X xobj1( 300 );                                        //(P)
    X xobj2( 400 );
    X xobj3( 500 );
    LinkedList<X>* listptr = new LinkedList<X>( xobj1 );
```

```
        listptr->addToList( xobj2 );
        listptr->addToList( xobj3 );
        listptr->printAll();                    // 300 400 500
        cout << endl;
        listptr->removeFromList( xobj1 );
        listptr->printAll();                    // 400 500
        cout << endl;
        delete listptr;

        return 0;
}
```

The code shown in `main` above tests the templatized linked-list by constructing a list of integers in the code section starting in line (M); a list of characters in the code section beginning in line (N); a list of strings in the code section starting in line (O) ; and, finally, a list of objects of type X, a programmer-defined class defined in line (L) of the program. The last linked-list is in the code section beginning in line (P).

With regard to using the above program for a linked-list of class type objects, the list only stores `const` references to the objects created in `main`. (On the other hand, the STL list stores copies of the objects.) This should be clear from the type of the data member `item` in line (B). As shown in line (C), the node constructor is passed the object to be stored as a `const` reference. The same is the case with the functions for adding new objects to the list and removing objects from the list. This implies that there is only one copy of each class type object created in `main`. This can be verified by placing a print statement in the destructor for class X. As the reader will see, X's destructor will be invoked only once for each of the X objects created in `main`.

13.1.3 Template Specialization

It is not always possible to write a C++ template class that would work universally for every data type. In such cases, it could become necessary to provide alternative definitions for the same template and let the compiler choose the most applicable one.

For example, the previously defined class template for a linked list would not work for those types for which the overload definitions of the operators '`==`' and '`!=`' (needed, for instance, in line (K) of the code for `removeFromList()` above) are not provided.

To illustrate this point, let's say we would like to use the previously defined class template for C-style strings — that is, for the type `char*`. In other words, we wish to create objects of type

```
LinkedList<char*>
```

But that obviously will not work because C-style strings are traditionally compared using the `strcmp()` function from the `string.h` library and not by using the '==' and '!=' operators. So, in such cases, we may wish to provide an alternative definition of the template, as we do below.

Shown below is a specialization of the `LinkedList<T>` class for the case of `char*`. Note that the program pulls in the template class of the previous program, `LinkedListGeneric.cc`, through the header file `LinkedListGeneric.h`. So, now, when we try to make a linked-list of integers in `main`, the compiler automatically chooses the original template class defined in `LinkedListGeneric.cc`. On the other hand, when we try to make a linked-list of C-style strings, the compiler uses the specialization provided here.

```
//LinkedListSpecialized.cc

#include<iostream>
#include "LinkedListGeneric.h"    // This is the same as the program
                                  // LinkedListGeneric.cc but without
                                  // its main()
class LinkedList<char*> {                                         //(A)

    struct Node {
        Node* pre;
        Node* next;
        char* item;
        Node( Node* p, Node* n, char* c )
                : pre(p), next(n), item(c) {}
    };
    Node* head;
public:
    LinkedList() : head( 0 ) {}
    LinkedList( char* t )  : head( new Node(0, 0, t)) {}
    ~LinkedList() {
        Node* p = head;
        while ( p != 0 ) {
            Node* temp = p;
            p = p->next;
            delete temp;
        }
    }
    void printAll() {
        for (Node* p = head; p; p = p->next )
            cout << p->item << ' ';
    }
    void addToList( char* );
    void removeFromList( char* );
};
```

```
void LinkedList<char*>::addToList( char* item ) {                    //(B)
    Node* newNode = new Node(0, head, item);
    head = newNode;
    newNode->next->pre = head;
}
void LinkedList<char*>::removeFromList( char* item ) {
    Node* p = head;
    for (; 0 != strcmp(p->item, item); p = p->next)
        if (p->next == 0) return;        // string not in list
    if (p == head) {                      // string in the first node
        head = head->next;
        head->pre = 0;
        delete p;
        return;
    }
    p->pre->next = p->next;
    if (p->next != 0) p->next->pre = p->pre;
    delete p;
}

int main() {
    // use the template class from LinkedListGeneric.h for storing ints
    int i = 1;
    LinkedList<int>* numlist = new LinkedList<int>(i);
    numlist->addToList( 5 );
    numlist->addToList( 6 );
    numlist->printAll();                         // 6 5 1
    cout << endl;
    numlist->removeFromList( 6 );
    numlist->printAll();                         // 5 1
    cout << endl;

    // use the specialized template class defined here
    // for a list of C-style strings
    char* cstr = "high";
    LinkedList<char*>* cstringList = new LinkedList<char*>( cstr );
    cstringList->addToList( "sierras" );
    cstringList->addToList( "green" );
    cstringList->addToList( "tiaras" );
    cstringList->printAll();            // tiaras green sierras high
    cout << endl;
    cstringList->removeFromList( "high" );
    cstringList->printAll();             // tiaras green sierras
    cout << endl;
    return 0;
}
```

As shown in line (A) of the template specialization provided above, the prefix `template <class T>` is now missing from the header of the class definition. However, if we so wanted, we could have used the prefix `template <>` and defined the specialization as

```
template <> class LinkedList<char*> {
    // same as before
};
```

Although we do not need the prefix any more, the compiler knows that this specialization is an alternative to the `LinkedList` template defined previously in `LinkedList-Generic.cc`. So when we try to make objects of type `LinkedList<char*>`, it will automatically choose the specialization rather than the original implementation.

For the same reason we did not need the prefix `template<class T>` for the class template, we do not need it for the functions whose implementation code is provided outside the class, as shown by the function header in line (B) above.

In some cases, it might be possible to provide a single specialization for all pointer types. In fact, Stroustrup recommends defining a specialization for `void*` that'd work for all pointer types [54]. But it may not always be possible to do so. For example, we could not have defined a `LinkedList<void*>` specialization in the same manner we defined `LinkedList<char*>` because the function `strcmp()` in `removeFromList()` must have `char*` arguments.

13.1.4 General Syntax of a Template Declaration

Now that the reader has an idea of what C++ templates are, it is time to introduce the full syntax of a template declaration for a templatized class:

```
template< ---- template parameter list ---- > class nameOfClass {
    // implementation
};
```

What follows the keyword `template` inside the tokens '`<`' and '`>`' is called the *template parameter list*. In this list, a parameter can be either a *type parameter* or a *nontype parameter* representing a constant expression.

A type parameter consists of the keyword `class` or the keyword `typename` followed by an identifier.[3] A nontype parameter consists of an ordinary parameter declaration.

Let's first consider the case in which the template parameter list consists of only type parameters:

---

[3]The keyword `typename` may not be supported in some of the current compilers. The reason for why we need the keyword `typename` is explained in Section 2.2.1 of Josuttis [42].

```
template < class T1, class T2, class T3 > class className {
    // ...
};
```

Here the parameters T1, T2, and T3 can be any built-in or user-defined types.

Now let's consider the case, taken from Stroustrup [54], in which a template parameter list has both a type parameter and a nontype parameter:

```
template< class T, int i > class Buffer {
    T v[ i ];
    int sz;
public:
    Buffer() : sz( i ) {}
    //
};
```

Here i is a nontype parameter in the parameter list of the template. So nontype parameters in a template parameter list are ordinary parameter declarations. You can think of a nontype parameter as representing a constant in a template definition. In the above definition, the parameter i determines the size of the buffer. So a declaration like

```
Buffer<char, 128> cbuf;
```

declares cbuf to be a char Buffer of size 128.

The parameters in a template parameter list are allowed to have default values. These work just like the default values for function parameters. As was the case with function parameters, the parameters are default initialized from the right of the parameter list, meaning that a default-initialized parameter cannot be to the left of an uninitialized parameter. For example, the above definition for the template class Buffer could have been written in the following manner:

```
template< class T, int i = 128 > class Buffer {
    T v[ i ];
    int sz;
public:
    Buffer() : sz( i ) {}
    //
};
```

which specifies a default value of 128 for the nontype parameter i, or, in the following manner:

```
template< class T = string, int i = 128 > class Buffer {
    T v[ i ];
    int sz;
public:
    Buffer() : sz( i ) {}
    //
};
```

where we have default choices for both the type parameter and the nontype parameter. The second choice for defining our templatized `Buffer` class allows us to declare different kinds of buffers of different sizes as in the examples below:

```
Buffer<> buf1;                  // a string buffer of size 128
Buffer<string, 512> buff2;      // a string buffer of size 512
Buffer<int> buff3;              // an int buffer of size 128
Buffer<int, 512> buff4;         // an int buffer of size 512
```

13.2 ITERATORS REVISITED

In Chapter 5, we provided a usage perspective on the primary container classes of the C++ Standard Library. The goal of this section is to provide further insights into the iterators used for STL containers. Iterators are supported by all the sequence and associative container classes.

As was mentioned earlier, iterators are a generalization of pointers. An iterator is to a container class what a pointer is to an array. However, there is one important respect in which an iterator is different from a pointer: An iterator cannot be given null initialization. In other words, an iterator cannot be set to, say, 0 in order to point to nothing. All container classes that support iterators also support special functions `begin()`, `end()`, `rbegin()`, and `rend()` that can be invoked for initializing an iterator and for testing its value against the beginning or the end of a sequence.

As the reader already knows from Chapter 5, one of the useful features of the Standard Template Library is the availability of the generic algorithms for all kinds of processing associated with the container elements. These algorithms are generic in the sense that they can be invoked in a container-independent manner. The algorithms take iterator arguments and they don't care what specific container an iterator is defined for.

13.2.1 Iterator Categories for Generic Algorithms

Again as mentioned already in Chapter 5, the different algorithms of the generic library run the gamut from performing simple tasks like searching for a specific element in a container to more complex tasks like sorting, merging, and so on. It obviously makes sense that if the algorithms are defined solely in terms of operations on iterators (and the data pointed to by iterators), then each algorithm should be specific about the minimum iterator functionality that it needs. For example, an algorithm that searches for a specific element — such as the generic algorithm `find()` — only needs an iterator that can step through the elements, one at a time, and make a comparison. Here is a possible implementation of `find()` that shows how a generic algorithm can make explicit the minimum-functionality iterator it needs:

```
template <class InputIterator, class T>
InputIterator find( InputIterator first,
                       InputIterator last,   const T& value )
{
    for ( ; first != last; ++first )
        if ( value == *first )
            return first;
    return last;
}
```

What this says is that find() needs just the minimum functionality encased in an InputIterator. But, of course, it would be just as happy with other iterator types if they can do what a InputIterator does.

There is then obviously a need to create a categorization of the different iterator capabilities. For this purpose, the designers of the generic library have defined five different categories of iterators:

InputIterator

OutputIterator

ForwardIterator

BidirectionalIterator

RandomAccessIterator

An InputIterator is a forward incrementing iterator that can be used to read the elements of a container. It supports both the prefix and the postfix versions of the increment operator ++. The algorithm find() is an example of the generic library algorithms requiring just this level of support. An OutputIterator — also a forward incrementing iterator — can be used to write into the elements of a container. The algorithm copy(), whose prototype is shown below, is an example of a generic algorithm that takes an OutputIterator as the third argument to mark the position where writing should begin.

```
template <class InputIterator, class OutputIterator>
OutputIterator copy( InputIterator first,
                     InputIterator last,
                     OutputIterator destination );
```

Starting with the position first and ending with the position one before last, this algorithm copies all the elements over to the positions starting with destination. The algorithm can copy elements from one container to another, or from one section of a container to another non-overlapping section of the same container. The function returns the iterator position that points to one past the last value written out.[4]

As its name implies, a `ForwardIterator` is also a forward incrementing iterator. It can be used to both read from and write into the elements of a container. In that sense, it combines the functionalities of the `InputIterator` and the `OutputIterator`. The generic algorithms `adjacent_find()`, `replace()`, and so on, need just this level of functionality.

A `BidirectionalIterator` can step through a container in both directions and read from and write into the elements. A `BidirectionalIterator` can always be substituted where a `ForwardIterator` is needed. An example of a generic library algorithm that needs just this level of support is `reverse()`.

Finally, a `RandomAccessIterator`, in addition to supporting all the functionality of a `BidirectionalIterator`, provides an array-like constant-time access to any element of a container. Let's say p is the current value of a random-access iterator. Obviously, *p yields the container element to which p points. Now suppose we invoke the dereferencing operation *(p + i) for some value of an integer i that will not take us outside the container. Since p was assumed to be a random-access iterator, *(p + i) will retrieve directly in constant time the sequence element pointed to by (p + i). To get to this position, an iterator that is only bidirectional could wend its way through by repeated invocations of the '++' operator, but that would obviously be inefficient. The algorithms `sort` and `sort_heap()` are examples of the generic algorithms that need the level of iterator support provided by a random-access iterator.

It should be evident from the above discussion that only those containers can support random-access iterators that store the elements in consecutive memory segments, in the same manner in which arrays are stored. This is indeed the case with the container classes `vector` and `deque`. On the other hand, since container classes such as `list`, `map`, and so on, do not store their elements in consecutive memory blocks, but in forms resembling linked lists, they can only support bidirectional iterators.

13.2.2   How to Declare an Iterator

An identifier is declared to be an iterator by the following declaration:

```
container< type >::iterator  iter;
```

---

[4] `copy` naturally assumes that the destination container has (`last - first`) number of positions available for writing into. However, if the `OutputIterator` supplied as the third argument in a call to `copy` also happens to be an *inserter*, the destination container will be expanded to accommodate any additional elements. An inserter is an *iterator adapter*. Iterator adapters are meant to give specialized behaviors to iterators. There are two other iterator adapters, one that allows an algorithm to operate on a container in reverse and one for working with streams.

where 'container' is one of the sequence or associative containers; 'type' the data type of elements in the container; 'iter' the identifier being declared as an iterator; and 'iterator' one of the following names:

```
iterator
reverse_iterator
const_iterator              // cannot modify elements
const_reverse_iterator      // cannot modify elements
```

As one would expect from the iterator names that have "reverse" in them, the increment operator '++' and the decrement operator '--' have opposite meanings for `reverse_iterator` and for `const_reverse_iterator`. What that means is that if p is a reverse iterator, then ++p points to the preceding element, as opposed to the next element. As with `const` pointers, `const_iterator` and `const_reverse_iterator` do not permit any modifications to the element they point to.

Here are some examples of iterator declarations, some taken from our examples in the earlier chapters of this book:

```
vector<Shape*>::iterator p;
list<string>::iterator iter;
list<int>::reverse_iterator r;
list<string>::const_iterator iter;
map<string, int>::iterator mit;
```

While all sequenced and associative container classes support `iterator`, `reverse_iterator`, `const_iterator`, and `const_reverse_iterator`, the nature of these iterators is different for different container classes and that affects the computational efficiency of the various operations we may wish to carry out with the help of the iterators. For example, all four of these iterators for the `vector` container class are of type `RandomAccessIterator`, whereas all four of these iterators for the `list` container class are of type `BidirectionalIterator`. The iterators will be of random access variety for a container class only if it can store the elements of a data sequence in continuous segments of memory. If elements have to be stored in disjoint segments, as in a linked list, then the container class is more likely to support a bidirectional iterator.

13.3 PARAMETERIZED CLASSES IN JAVA

As was mentioned in the introduction, Java container classes typically store all items as `Object` references. Although this keeps the language simple, it does create an extra burden on the programmer who has to remember to cast an item back to its correct type when it is extracted from the container. Forgetting to do so or using an incorrect cast can result in a run-time error caused by the throwing of a `ClassCastExeption`.

To get around this limitation of Java, an extension to Java has been put forward by Bracha, Odersky, Stoutamire, and Wadler [8, 9]. This extension, known as GJ (for Generic Java), presently comes with its own compiler that can be invoked through two different aliases, `gjc` and `gjcr`, the former for the compilation of the user-defined parameterized types and the latter if you also wish to use the GJ version of the `java.util` package. By invoking `gjcr`, you can use the generic versions of the Java container classes as opposed to their standard versions. The letter 'r' in `gjcr` stands for "retrofitted", since the container classes in the GJ-supplied `java.util` package can be thought of as the retrofitted versions of the standard containers.

In what follows, we will first show a simple Java program in which a `List` is used to store various items. We will show that if the cast used at the time of extracting these items from the list is incorrect, you will get a run-time error. Here is the program:

```
//ListMixedType.java

import java.util.*;

class ListMixedType {
    public static void main( String[] args ) {
        List list = new ArrayList();
        list.add( "one" );
        list.add( "two" );
        list.add( "three" );
        //   list.add( new Integer( 4 ) );                      //(A)

        ListIterator iter = list.listIterator();
        while ( iter.hasNext() )
            System.out.println( (String) iter.next() );         //(B)
    }
}
```

As you'd expect, this program compiles and runs fine. But if you uncomment the commented out statement in line (A), the program would still compile fine, but now you'd get a run-time error. The source of the error would be the statement in line (B) where we are casting each extracted list item to the `String` type. The run-time will throw a `ClassCastException` when it tries to cast an `Integer` type to a `String` type for the last item in the list.

Let's now consider the GJ version of this program. In the program shown below, the type `List` of the previous program becomes the type `List<String>` in line (C), and the type `ArrayList` becomes `ArrayList<String>` in the same line:

```
//ListGeneric.java

import java.util.*;

class ListGeneric {
    public static void main( String[] args ) {
        List<String> list = new ArrayList<String>();              //(C)
        list.add( "one" );
        list.add( "two" );
        list.add( "three" );
        //   list.add( new Integer( 4 ) );                        //(D)

        ListIterator iter = list.listIterator();

        while ( iter.hasNext() )
            System.out.println( iter.next() );                    //(E)
    }
}
```

There are two most important observations to be made about this program: (1) Now
we do not have to use a cast when we extract items from the list in line (E); compare
line (E) of this program with line (B) of the earlier program. And, (2) If we uncomment
the commented out statement in line (D), the error will be trapped at compile time.
Both of these are steps in the right direction for writing good code.

The GJ program shown above will not compile with the usual javac compiler,
since that compiler knows nothing about parameterized types such as List<String>.
You compile this program with the gjcr compiler command. As instructed in the
installation documents for the GJ software, the compile command gjcr has to be set
up as an alias for executing the class gjc.Main. On the author's Linux machine, the
command gjcr is aliased in the following manner:

```
alias gjcr 'java -cp ".:/home/kak/gj/classes" gjc.Main      \
    -bootclasspath "/home/kak/gj/classes:                   \
      /opt/jdk1.3/jdk1.3/jre/lib/rt.jar:                    \
      /opt/jdk1.3/jdk1.3/jre/lib/i18n.jar"'
```

where all the four lines shown are actually a single line of text in a .cshrc file. As the
reader can see, the compilation with gjcr consists of invoking the java application
launcher on gjc.Main. Note that in order to find the class Main, you have to supply
the classpath, which in the case above, consists of /home/kak/gj/classes, as specified.[5]

----

[5]To help the reader better understand the example syntax shown for aliasing the command gjcr, the
downloaded GJ software sits in the directory /home/kak/gj of the author's Linux machine. The directory

The reader should also take note of the *bootclasspath* specified in the alias for gjcr. This is needed because you want the system to load the GJ version of the java.util package, as opposed to the version that comes with the standard Java platform. Since the GJ version of this package is in the directory */home/kak/gj/classes/java*, the combination of the string */home/kak/gj/classes* in the bootclasspath and the package name java.util will ensure that the system will access and load the right thing. The other two pathnames in the bootclasspath are for the JAR files containing the standard Java platform.

13.3.1 Creating Your Own Parameterized Types in Java

To show how you can create your own parameterized types in Java, we will take the reader through the linked list example again. We will first show a LinkedList class; this will be a minimalist version of its implementation in the java.collections package. We will then show its generic version by parameterizing the class header and its implementation. All of the code we show in this section is from a tutorial by Bracha, Odersky, Stoutamire and Wadler [8].

The program shown below first declares two interfaces, Collection and Iterator, in lines (A) and (B), respectively. The former declares the public interface of the LinkedList class and the latter a means to walk though a linked list. The class LinkedList provides implementations for the methods of the interface Collection. The method iterator() of this interface is implemented by creating in line (G) an anonymous class of type Iterator; the anonymous class provides implementations for the methods declared in the interface Iterator. An object whose type is the same as that of the anonymous class is then returned by the method iterator() in line (F).

LinkedList uses the nested class Node for the individual nodes of a linked list. As explained in Chapter 3, if we had to refer to the nested class outside the class LinkedList, we would need to use its full name, which is LinkedList.Node.

Here is the code for the LinkedList class:

```
//LinkedList.java
// code by Bracha, Odersky, Stoutamire, and Wadler

interface Collection {                                          //(A)
    public void add( Object x );
    public Iterator iterator();
}
```

---

consists of the following subdirectories: *classes, doc,* and *src.* The directory *classes* consists of the subdirectories *com, gj, gjc,* and *java.* The class Main that is supplied to java in the above invocation is in the directory gjc. So the combination of the supplied classpath and the class name gjc.Main helps the system to figure out what exactly to execute by invoking the java command.

```
interface Iterator {                                         //(B)
    public Object next();
    public boolean hasNext();
}

class NoSuchElementException extends RuntimeException {}      //(C)

class LinkedList implements Collection {                      //(D)

    protected class Node {                                    //(E)
        Object item;
        Node next = null;
        Node( Object item ) { this.item = item; }
    }

    protected Node head = null, tail = null;

    public LinkedList() {}

    public void add( Object item ) {
        if ( head == null ) {
            head = new Node( item );
            tail = head;
        }
        else {
            tail.next = new Node( item );
            tail = tail.next;
        }
    }

    public Iterator iterator() {                              //(F)
        return new Iterator() {                               //(G)
                protected Node ptr = head;
                public boolean hasNext() { return ptr != null; }
                public Object next() {
                    if ( ptr != null ) {
                        Object item = ptr.item;
                        ptr = ptr.next;
                        return item;
                    } else throw new NoSuchElementException();
                }
            };
    }
}  // end of class LinkedList
```

```
class Test {
    public static void main( String[] args ) {

        String str = "";

        //int list
        LinkedList intList = new LinkedList();
        intList.add( new Integer( 0 ) );
        intList.add( new Integer( 1 ) );
        intList.add( new Integer( 2 ) );
        Iterator int_it = intList.iterator();
        while ( int_it.hasNext() )
            str += ( (Integer) int_it.next() ).intValue() + "  "; //(H)
        System.out.println( str );                  // 0  1  2

        //string list
        LinkedList stringList = new LinkedList();
        stringList.add( "zero" );
        stringList.add( "one" );
        stringList.add( "two" );
        str = "";
        Iterator string_it = stringList.iterator();
        while ( string_it.hasNext() )
            str += (String) string_it.next() + "  ";            //(I)
        System.out.println( str );          // zero one two

        // string list treated as int list
        // gives rise to run-time exception
        // Integer w = ( Integer ) stringList.iterator().next();  //(J)
    }
}
```

You can compile and run this program in the usual manner — that is, by using javac for compilation and java for execution. As was the case in the previous subsection when we used the ArrayList container, if you uncomment the last statement in line (J) above, you'll still be able to compile the program, but you'll get a run-time error.

Shown below is a version of the program that uses parameterized types. It first declares the parameterized interfaces Collection<T> and Iterator<T> in lines (A) and (B), respectively, and then goes on to provide an implementation for the parameterized class LinkedList<T> in line (D). The flow of logic in the program is exactly the same as in the unparameterized version shown before, except that now we do not use casts when extracting items from the list in lines (H) and (I). For a parameterized class, the scope of the parameter is the entire class, excluding static members and static initializers.[6] So even though the nested class for the nodes of a linked list is named just Node, it inherits the type parameter T from the scope. The full name of the nested class is LinkedList<T>.Node.

```java
//LinkedListGeneric.java
// code by Bracha, Odersky, Stoutamire, and Wadler

interface Collection<T> {                                    //(A)
    public void add( T x );
    public Iterator<T> iterator();
}

interface Iterator<T> {                                      //(B)
    public T next();
    public boolean hasNext();
}

class NoSuchElementException extends RuntimeException {}      //(C)

class LinkedList<T> implements Collection<T> {               //(D)
    protected class Node {                                    //(E)
        T item;
        Node next = null;
        Node( T item ) { this.item = item; }
    }
    protected Node head = null, tail = null;
    public LinkedList() {}
    public void add( T item ) {
        if ( head == null ) {
            head = new Node( item );
            tail = head;
        }
        else {
            tail.next = new Node( item );
            tail = tail.next;
        }
    }
    public Iterator<T> iterator() {                           //(F)
        return new Iterator<T>() {                            //(G)
                protected Node ptr = head;

                public boolean hasNext() { return ptr != null; }
```

---

[6]This is necessitated by the fact that the different instances of a class may use different values for the type parameters. The syntax for accessing a static member, therefore, remains the same as before; that is, you do not mention the parameter when accessing a static member of an otherwise parameterized class.

```
                public T next() {
                    if ( ptr != null ) {
                        T item = ptr.item;
                        ptr = ptr.next;
                        return item;
                    } else throw new NoSuchElementException();
                }
            };
    }
}

class Test {
    public static void main( String[] args ) {

        String str = "";

        //int list
        LinkedList<Integer> intList = new LinkedList<Integer>();
        intList.add( new Integer( 0 ) );
        intList.add( new Integer( 1 ) );
        intList.add( new Integer( 2 ) );
        Iterator<Integer> int_it = intList.iterator();
        while ( int_it.hasNext() )
            str += int_it.next().intValue() + " ";              //(H)
        System.out.println( str );            // 0  1  2

        //string list
        LinkedList<String> stringList = new LinkedList<String>();
        stringList.add( "zero" );
        stringList.add( "one" );
        stringList.add( "two" );
        str = "";
        Iterator<String> string_it = stringList.iterator();
        while ( string_it.hasNext() )
            str += string_it.next() + " ";                      //(I)
        System.out.println( str );            // zero  one  two

        // string list treated as int list
        // gives rise to compile-time error
        // Integer w = stringList.iterator().next();             //(J)
    }
}
```

Note also that the commented out statement in line (J), if uncommented, will now cause a compile-time error, where the same would have caused a run-time error in the previous version of the program.

You can use the `gjcr` alias to compile this program, as in the previous subsection. However, since you will not be using any of retrofitted classes in the GJ version of the `java.util` package, you do not need to specify a bootclasspath. So, you can also use the `gjc` compiler, which on the author's Linux machine is defined as an alias as follows:

```
alias gjc 'java -cp ".:/home/kak/gj/classes" gjc.Main'
```

13.3.2 Parameterization of Methods

Continuing with the examples provided by Bracha et al. [8], we will now show how a Java method can be parameterized. This we will do by first showing a `max` method written using standard Java for determining the maximum value held by a container. Next we will show a GJ version of the same method. Reflecting the organization of the Java collection library, the `max` method will be defined as a static method for a `Collections` class for both cases. The method `max` would obviously need to scan the container, comparing the current item with the previously known maximum value. So we'd need to make available to `max` a comparison mechanism, which, in the spirit of the Java collection library, could consist of a `Comparator` object:

```
//CollectionMax.java
// code by Bracha, Odersky, Stoutamire, and Wadler
// with inconsequential changes by the author

interface Comparator {
    public int compare( Object x, Object y );
}

class IntComparator implements Comparator {
    public int compare( Object x, Object y ) {
        return ( (Integer) x ).intValue() - ( (Integer) y ).intValue();
    }
}

class Collections {
    public static Object max( Collection xs, Comparator comp ) {  //(A)
        Iterator it = xs.iterator();
        Object max = it.next();
        while ( it.hasNext() ) {
            Object next = it.next();
            if ( comp.compare( max, next ) < 0 )  max = next;
        }
        return max;
    }
}
```

```
class Test {
    public static void main( String[] args ) {
        // int list with int comparator:
        LinkedList intList = new LinkedList();                    //(B)
        intList.add( new Integer( 0 ) );
        intList.add( new Integer( 10 ) );
        Integer max =
            (Integer) Collections.max( intList, new IntComparator() );
        System.out.println( "Max value: " + max.intValue() );

        // string list with int comparator:
        LinkedList stringList = new LinkedList();
        stringList.add( "zero" );
        stringList.add( "one" );
        // the following will give runtime exception
        // String str =
        // (String) Collections.max( stringList, new IntComparator() );
    }
}
```

If this program is in the same directory as a compiled version of the previous Linked-List.java file, you can compile the program with javac and run it with the java tool. If not, you'd need to import java.util package so that the program would have access to the Collection interface required in line (A) and the LinkedList class required in line (B).

We will now show a GJ version of the above code. The program below first declares a parameterized interface Comparator. This is followed by the class IntComparator that implements the interface. Of particular interest to us here is the parameterized method max in the class Collections. Note how the method is parameterized by the incorporation of a type parameter, through <T>, just before the name of the method in line (C).

```
//CollectionMaxGeneric.java
// code by Bracha, Odersky, Stoutamire, and Wadler
// with inconsequential changes by the author

interface Comparator<T> {
    public int compare( Object x, Object y );                     //(A)
}
class IntComparator implements Comparator<Integer> {             //(B)
    public int compare( Object x, Object y ) {
        return ( (Integer) x ).intValue() - ( (Integer) y ).intValue();
    }
}
```

```
class Collections {
    public static <T> T
            max( Collection<T> coll, Comparator<T> comp ) {        //(C)
        Iterator<T> it = coll.iterator();
        T max = it.next();

        while ( it.hasNext() ) {
            T next = it.next();
            if ( comp.compare( max, next ) < 0 )   max = next;
        }
        return max;
    }
}

class Test {
    public static void main( String[] args ) {

        // int list with int comparator
        LinkedList<Integer> intList = new LinkedList<Integer>();
        intList.add( new Integer( 0 ) );
        intList.add( new Integer( 1 ) );
        Integer m =
          Collections.max( intList, new IntComparator() );
        System.out.println( "Max value: " + m );              // 1

        // string list with int comparator
        LinkedList<String> stringList = new LinkedList<String>();
        stringList.add( "zero" );
        stringList.add( "one" );
        // the following will give compile time error
        // String str =
        // Collections.max( stringList, new IntComparator() );
    }
}
```

An important question concerning parameterized methods is regarding what specific type should be assigned to the type parameter. That this is an issue becomes evident if you compare the header of the method

```
public static <T> T max( Collection<T> coll, Comparator<T> comp )
```

with the call to the method in the main of Test:

```
Integer x = Collections.max( stringList, new IntComparator() );
```

Unlike C++ invocation of parameterized methods, there does not appear to be a direct mechanism for T to get instantiated to a specific type by the pattern matching of the method header and the function call. For Java, the type parameters in a parameterized method are set by inference to the smallest type parameter that yields a valid call. To illustrate, the first argument in the invocation of max is a Collection<String> and the second argument a Comparator<Integer>, then, obviously, since there is no type that is a common ancestor of the types String and Integer, the inference will fail, resulting in a compile-time error. On the other hand, if the first argument in the invocation was of type Collection<Integer> and the second of type Comparator<Float>, then the smallest type that is consistent with both would be Number;[7] the type parameter for the method max would then be set to this value. In other words, the method actually invoked by such a call would have the following signature:

```
Number max( Collection<Number> arg1, Comparator<Number> arg2 )
```

This inferencing mechanism obviously will not work for methods that take no arguments or that are intentionally called with null arguments. The reader is referred to [8] for modifications to the inferencing algorithm to account for such situations.

13.3.3 Constraining the Parameters

Sometimes it becomes necessary to place a constraint on the types that can be bound to a type parameter. Following Bracha et al. [8], we will show an example to illustrate this. The example code consists of first showing an alternative implementation of the Collections.max method for computing the maximum value held by a container. Instead of using a Comparator object, this new implementation depends on the container elements to be of type Comparable.[8] The example then shows a GJ version of this implementation in which it is necessary to place a constraint on the type parameter in the header of max. We start with an abbreviated implementation of the Integer class and have it implement the Comparable interface.

```
//Integer.java
// code by Bracha, Odersky, Stoutamire, and Wadler
// with inconsequential changes by the author

import java.util.*;

interface Comparable {
    public int compareTo( Object that );                          //(A)
}
```

---

[7]The abstract class Number, defined in the java.lang package, is the superclass of the classes Byte, Double, Float, Integer, Long, and Short.

[8]The reader will recall from Chapters 4 and 5 that when a type implements the Comparable interface by providing an implementation for the compareTo method of the interface, we say the type possesses a natural order.

```java
class Integer implements Comparable {
    private int value;

    public Integer( int value ) { this.value = value; }

    public int intValue() { return value; }

    public int compareTo( Integer that ) {                          //(B)
        return this.value - that.value;
    }

    public int compareTo( Object that ) {                           //(C)
        return this.compareTo( ( Integer ) that );
    }

    public String toString() { return "" + value; }
}

class Collections {
    public static Comparable max( Collection coll ) {
        Iterator it = coll.iterator();
        Comparable max = ( Comparable ) it.next();
        while ( it.hasNext() ) {
            Comparable next = ( Comparable ) it.next();
            if ( max.compareTo( next ) < 0 ) max = next;
        }
        return max;
    }
}

class Test {
    public static void main( String[] args ) {

        // int collection
        LinkedList intList = new LinkedList();
        intList.add( new Integer( 0 ) );
        intList.add( new Integer( 1 ) );
        Integer maxVal = ( Integer ) Collections.max( intList );
        System.out.println( "Max value: " + maxVal );       // 1
    }
}
```

Note that the implementation had to provide two definitions for the compareTo method: the first in line (B) that actually carries out the comparison between two Integer objects, and the second in line (C) that conforms to the syntax dictated by the Comparable interface in line (A), *but actually calls the first definition for comparison.*

Shown below is the GJ version of this implementation. Note the syntax in the header of the Collections.max method in line (C). The type parameter is now expressed in the following constrained form:

```
<T implements Comparable<T> >
```

implying that the method can only be invoked if the inferencing algorithm we mentioned in the previous subsection yields a binding for T that is of type Comparable<T>. Here is the code:

```
//IntegerGeneric.java
// code by Bracha, Odersky, Stoutamire, and Wadler
// with inconsequential changes by the author

interface Comparable<T> {
    public int compareTo( T that );                            //(A)
}

class Integer implements Comparable<Integer> {
    private int value;

    public Integer( int value ) { this.value = value; }

    public int intValue() { return value; }

    public int compareTo( Integer that ) {                     //(B)
        return this.value - that.value;
    }

    public String toString() { return "" + value; }
}

class Collections {
    public static <T implements Comparable<T>> T
                              max( Collection<T> coll ) {       //(C)
        Iterator<T> it = coll.iterator();
        T max = it.next();
        while ( it.hasNext() ) {
            T next =  it.next();
            if ( max.compareTo( next ) < 0 ) max = next;
        }
        return max;
    }
}
```

```
class Test {
    public static void main( String[] args ) {
        // Integer collection
        LinkedList<Integer> list = new LinkedList<Integer>();
        list.add( new Integer( 0 ) );
        list.add( new Integer( 1 ) );
        Integer x = Collections.max( list );

        // boolean collection
        LinkedList<Boolean> listBool = new LinkedList<Boolean>();
        listBool.add( new Boolean( false ) );
        listBool.add( new Boolean( true ) );
        // Boolean b = Collections.max( listBook );
                                    // run-time exception
    }
}
```

Note that unlike the standard version of this program shown before, the new `Integer` class needs only one implementation for the `compareTo` method shown in line (B); the header of the implementation for this method corresponds to the header in the `Comparable<T>` interface in line (A). In order to be consistent with the standard version of `Integer`, you'd still need a version of `compareTo` that takes an `Object` argument. This version, known as the *bridge method*, is automatically created by the GJ compiler. The program shown above can be compiled with the `gjc` compilation command.

13.4 CREDITS AND SUGGESTIONS FOR FURTHER READING

As mentioned earlier in the chapter, all of the code we showed in Sections 13.3.1 and 13.3.2 is from the tutorial by Bracha, Odersky, Stoutamire, and Wadler [8]. The Generic Java compiler can be downloaded from the GJ home page at *http://www.cs.bell-labs.com/who/wadler/pizza/gj/index.html*. The downloaded code also includes the GJ version of the `java.util` package. The GJ tutorial from which we showed code examples in Section 13.3 is also available at the same URL.

There are other issues related to the use of generic types in Java that we have not addressed here. These issues pertain to subtyping, creation of arrays, and so on. The reader is referred to Bracha et al. [8] for a fuller discussion.

13.5 HOMEWORK

1. Provide implementations for a copy constructor and a copy assignment operator for the `LinkedList` class of Section 13.1.1.

2. Provide implementations for a copy constructor and a copy assignment operator for the parameterized `LinkedList` class of Section 13.1.2.

3. Create a parameterized Java class `Buffer<T>` that could be used as a buffer for different types of data. At the least, your class should implement the following interface:

```
interface BufferInterface<T> {
    public void addElement(T data);
    public void addElementAt(T data, int index);
    public T removeElementAt(int index);
    public int getSize();
}
```

4. Write a parameterized lookup table class, Lookup<T1, T2>, in Java for storing `<key, value>` pairs where T1 is the type parameter for `key` and T2 the type parameter for `value`. The class Lookup should support at least the following methods:

boolean addEntry(T1 key, T2 value) — to add an entry into the table. This method should return true if the operation is successful, and false otherwise. Only one `value` entry is allowed for a key. If `<key, value>` is inserted a second time for the same key, the new `value` should replace the old.

boolean removeEntry(T1 key) — to remove an entry from the table for a given key. It should return true if operation is successful, and false otherwise.

T1 retrieveKey(T2 value) — to retrieve the key associated with a given value.

T2 retrieveValue(T1 key) — to return the value associated with the specified key.

boolean hasValue(T2 value) — to test whether a particular is stored in the table.

boolean hasKey(T1 key) — to test whether the specified key is stored in the table.

`boolean expandTable( int size )` — to increase the capacity of the table so that it can hold the specified number of `<key, value>` pairs. Must return false if the table cannot be expanded.

`boolean isFull()` — returns true if the table is full, false otherwise.

`void printTable()` — to display the table in a two-column format, with the first column for the keys and the second for the corresponding values.

The user needs to specify the size of the table when it is first constructed.

5. Write a parameterized C++ version of the Java class of the previous homework problem. As for the Java homework, the C++ class will have two template parameters, T1 for key type and T2 for value type. Assume that the types used for T1 and T2 have preexisting overload definitions for the operators '==' and '!='. No need to write separate template specializations for the pointer types for T1 and T2.

6. Write a C++ template class that can serve as a dynamic FIFO queue for an arbitrary data type with support for at least the following methods. `T` is the template parameter for the element type in the queue.

`void enqueue( const T& item )` — for adding a new element at the end of the queue.

`T& dequeue()` — for removing the element at the front of the queue. The method must throw an exception if the element does not exist.

`int size()` — for returning the number of elements currently in the queue.

`T elementAt(int i)` — for ascertaining the element (without removing it) at the specified location.

`void printQueue()` — for displaying the contents of the queue.

7. Define a parameterized Java class `MyQueue<T>` to serve as a dynamic FIFO queue for elements of arbitrary data type. The class `MyQueue<T>` should implement the following interface

```
interface QueueInterface<T> {
    public void enqueue (T item);
    public T dequeue ();
    public Iterator<T> getIterator();

    class NoSuchElementException extends RuntimeException {}
}
```

where Iterator<T> is a parameterized interface defined as

```
interface Iterator<T> {
    public boolean hasNext();
    public T next();
    public boolean getNext();
}
```

with all methods possessing the usual semantics for the queue container and for Java iterators.

8. Augment your solution for the previous problem by providing the implementation code for the following methods:

(a) A parameterized Java method that returns an int for the number of elements in the queue.

(b) A parameterized Java method that returns the ith element in the queue.

Both these methods should work on any implementation of the QueueInterface defined in the previous problem.

14

Modeling Diagrams for OO Programs

So far in this book, for the most part we have focused on OO syntax at the level of a single class. We are now ready to dig into more advanced topics such as class derivation, multiple inheritance, multithreading, graphics programming, and so on. But before we get into these subjects, it would be useful to review the tools for creating visual representations of object-oriented programs that show the classes and their interactions in different ways. Obviously, if you are extending a class, it is because you believe that your program needs a concept that is an *extension* of a previously codified concept. Given multiple such concepts that are related to one another either through inheritance or otherwise, it can be difficult to keep in one's mental perspective a top-level view of all the interclass relationships. Visual representations can be of great help in such cases.

Making visual representations of classes can also aid the process of giving object orientation to a new problem domain — a process that is often more difficult than it appears at first sight. Object orientation of a nontrivial problem domain is usually a result of analytical thinking if you are yourself a domain expert, or analytical discourse with the domain experts. But analytical thinking does not result in the conceptualization of all the needed classes and their interrelationships in one fell swoop. Rather, one proceeds in an incremental and iterative fashion in which one starts with a set of classes that one believes would deliver the basic functionality expected of the software and then adds or subtracts from this set as one's understanding of the problem domain deepens. Visual representations of this evolving set of classes are evidently of great help for maintaining a mental perspective on the software, its evolution, and its dissemination to others.

Over the years, various tools have been proposed for creating visual representations of classes and their behaviors. More recently, many of these tools have been pulled together by the Object Management Group, a not-for-profit organization founded by the leading software corporations of the world for the standardization of object-based software development tools. One of the principal tools that has resulted from this activity is the Unified Modeling Language (UML). UML can be used to enhance one's productivity in literally every phase of OO software development — from the recording of initial thoughts about the central concepts in a new problem domain (using class and activity diagrams), to organizing one's communication with the domain expert (with the help of use cases), to graphical documentation of the final software product, and so on.

This chapter provides a quick review of the different types of UML-based modeling diagrams that are possible for object-oriented programs. The different types of diagrams portray different aspects of a program. For example, a *class diagram* is commonly used to display the main concepts of an OO program and their relationships. On the other hand, if you need to portray the functionality of an OO program, you would use a *use-case diagram*. To get a better understanding of the time-dependencies of the interaction between classes as they collaborate to achieve a certain functionality, you would use an *interaction diagram*. If you need a visual representation to show the different states of a particular object and how the object transitions from state to state, you would use a *statechart diagram*. You would use an *activity diagram* to highlight those portions of program execution that can be carried out in parallel and those that must be carried out sequentially. And, finally, if you modularize your software — as you invariably would if the software is large — you would use a *package diagram* to show the dependencies between the different modules.

14.1 USE CASE DIAGRAM

In the context of OO design, a *use case* represents a single interaction between a human and the software system. It can also represent an interaction between another software package and the software under development. The set of all use cases describes the overall functionality of a software system. Since software is written to serve some purpose (or a set of related purposes), one of the first things you do in OO design is to list as many of the use cases as can be envisioned and to then represent them diagrammatically with UML. Discovery of the different use cases is facilitated by first listing all the different roles that the users (or other systems) can play with respect to the software under development. Each interaction with the system that is engaged in by each role is given a name — the name of the use case.

Figure 14.1 could be a first attempt at a use-case diagram for an internet auction system. This diagram shows three *roles* — Seller, Buyer, and Auction Server — each played by an *actor*. The use cases carried out by the actors through their

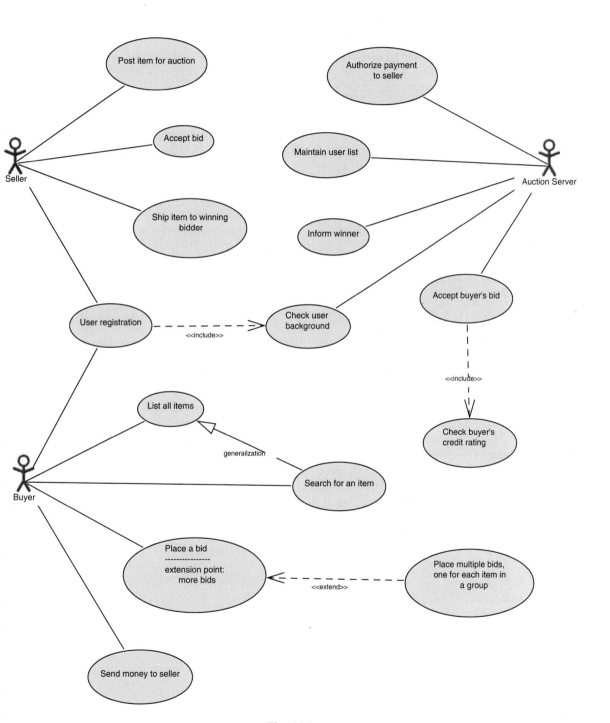

Fig. 14.1

designated roles are shown in ovals. Note that actors don't need to be human. In fact, one of the actors shown in the figure — Auction Server — is a software system. The link between an actor and a use case is referred to as a *communication association*, or just *communication*.

Use cases can have relationships between them. Figure 14.1 shows *extend*, *include*, and *generalization* relationships between the use cases. The extend relationship, shown with an arrowed, dashed line labeled <<extend>>, tells us that the use case at the tail of the line is a variation on the use case at its head. For example, the process of placing multiple bids simultaneously for a group of items offered by the same seller is a variation on the process of placing a single bid on a single item. The use case being extended can also display *extension points* to make explicit the condition under which the variant use case is to be invoked. The include relationship, shown with an arrowed, dashed line that is labeled <<include>>, tells us that the use case at the tail of the line needs to call on the use case at the head of the line for meeting its functional specification. For example, before a bid from a buyer can be accepted, a credit check must be run on the buyer. The generalization relationship, shown as a solid line with a closed triangle for an arrowhead, tells us that the use case at the head of the line is a more general case than the use case at the tail of the line, implying that the use case at the tail of the line only needs to implement some more specialized logic to meet its functional requirements.

14.2   CLASS DIAGRAM

Use cases and use case diagrams must at some point be translated into classes for eventual implementation. In UML, a class is represented by a rectangular box which in its most detailed representation is divided into three parts vertically. The name of the class is written in the uppermost partition of the box, followed by the class data members (called attributes in the parlance of UML) in the middle partition, followed by its member functions or methods (called operations in UML) in the lowest partition. The name of the class is shown in bold for a concrete class, and in italics for an abstract class. Figure 14.2 shows an example of this representation for a class Employee.

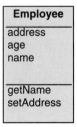

Fig. 14.2

In its most common usage, a class diagram shows two relationships between different classes: *generalization* and *association*. A class C1 is a generalization of a class C2 if the former is a superclass of the latter. For example, the class diagram of Figure 14.3 shows with an arrowed solid line the class Employee as a superclass, and therefore a generalization, of the class Manager. Note that the generalization arrow, a closed triangle arrowhead, points to the superclass. An association, on the other hand, is depicted with a solid line between two classes, as between Employee and Corporation in the figure. You show an association link between two classes if the objects of one class must know about the objects of the other class in order to do their job.

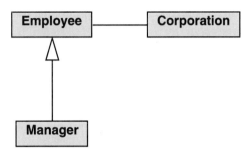

Fig. 14.3

Other types of relationships between classes that can be depicted in a class diagram are *aggregation* and *composition*. The next two subsections discuss in greater detail the depiction of associations, aggregations, and generalizations in class diagrams.

In the OO literature, one also commonly sees mention of IsA and HasA relationships between classes. The former, as was mentioned in Chapter 3, represents a generalization-specialization sort of a relationship and the latter an association, an aggregation, or a composition. The name IsA is supposed to capture relationships such as

```
A Manager IsAn Employee
A CorporateCustomer IsA Customer
```

In each such statement, what comes after IsA is a generalization or a super-type of what comes before (see Chapter 3 also). On the other hand, a statement like

```
An Order HasA Customer
An Orchestra HasA Player
A Window HasA Slider
```

expresses a containment, in the form of an association, an aggregation, or a composition.

We placed only the names of the classes in the boxes in the class diagram of Figure 14.3. How much detail one shows for a class depends on the perspective used in drawing the diagram. A class diagram may be drawn using three different perspectives: (i) *conceptual*, (ii) *specification*, and (iii) *implementation*

At the conceptual level, for each class you include only the bare minimum information needed to get an overall sense of the main concepts of a problem domain. This will most frequently be the diagram you would draw when you are just getting started with the design of an OO program. However, even after you have fully developed an OO system, a conceptual level diagram can be useful for communicating to others a coarse-level description of the system. At the specification level, you want to show the interfaces of each class. At this level you'd want to make explicit the class responsibilities, as embodied in the public operations for each class. At the implementation level, you want to show more precisely how a class was (or needs to be) implemented in code. Now you'd include the private and the protected attributes and operations as well.

14.2.1 Association as a Relationship Between Classes

The class diagram of Figure 14.3 showed an association to display the conceptual link between an object of type `Employee` and an object of type `Corporation`. An example of a more elaborate representation of such an association is shown in Figure 14.4. In the example depicted, an `Employee` has a data member called `employedBy` of type `Corporation`; this data member is shown as a label at the head of the arrowed association link from `Employee` to `Corporation`. We can talk about the label `employedBy` as the *role* played by a `Corporation` in an object of type `Employee`. The arrowhead on the association link from `Employee` to `Corporation` is referred to as the *navigability* arrow. The arrow tells us as to which of the two objects implements the association. In the example shown, the association with the rolename `employedBy` is implemented in the `Employee` class and therefore "belongs" to objects of type `Employee`. The label '0..1' at the `Corporation` end of the association is referred to as the *multiplicity* of the association, which specifies *how many* objects of type `Corporation` in role `employedBy` may associate with a single object of type `Employee`. The multiplicity of '0..1' means that an `Employee` is employed by no more than one `Corporation`.

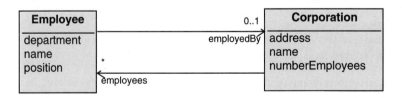

Fig. 14.4

We can make similar remarks about the association link that goes from Corporation to Employee in Figure 14.4. The navigability arrow points towards the latter and the rolename label is employees with the multiplicity symbol '*'. This could be construed to mean that Corporation has a data member called employees of type Employee[]. The multiplicity of '*' means that any number of employees, including zero, is allowed in an object of type Corporation. If there were a legal requirement that a corporation possess at least one employee, with no constraints on the upper limit, the multiplicity label associated with the rolename employees would change to '1..*'. So the symbol '*' in a multiplicity label means *an indefinite number.*

The two association links in Figure 14.4 can also be shown as a single line between the two classes. If we were to do so for our example, the line would show navigability arrows, rolenames, and multiplicity symbols at both ends. An association with no navigability arrows is considered bidirectional.

The association that was shown above is a binary association connecting two different classes. A binary association is also allowed to connect the same class to itself. Such an association link may connect two different objects from the same class, or one object to itself. In the latter case, the association would be called reflexive. Shown in Figure 14.5 is an example of an association that connects two different objects of the same class. This association would represent an Employee being

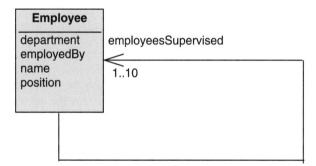

Fig. 14.5

allowed to supervise between 1 and 10 other employees.

14.2.2 Aggregation and Composition as Relationships Between Classes

The objects participating in an association will often have independent, and, in some sense, equal existences of their own. But that is not true of all interclass relationships. In other relationships, especially those that relate a "whole" to its "parts," there can be lifetime dependencies between the whole and its parts. When the whole ceases to exist, the parts may get destroyed at the same time. A composition represents such a tight linkage between a whole and its parts.

Consider the example shown in Figure 14.6 where we have used filled diamonds to show compositions. Obviously, the "parts" that form the compositions, such as sliders, scrollbars, and so on, will cease to exist when a Window ceases to exist:

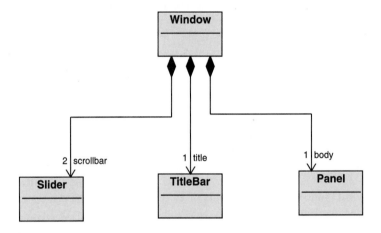

Fig. 14.6

When you have a whole–part relationship in which the parts can have lifetimes independent of the whole, you have an aggregation. In the aggregation depicted in Figure 14.7, the performers would continue to exist even after the Orchestra object ceased to exist. As shown, a hollow diamond is attached to the class that is an aggregate. While, of course, this type of a relationship could also be captured by a straightforward association with appropriate multiplicities, the concept of an aggregation is supposed to capture the fact that an orchestra is the sum total of its performers and has no existence but for the conjoint existence of its performers.

Fig. 14.7

14.2.3 Representing Attributes

As mentioned before, the class data members — known as attributes in UML — are shown in a separate partition below the classname partition of the class box. The UML convention for displaying an attribute is:

```
visibility  name [N] : type =  initialValue {property-string}
            ---------------
```

where the visibility is one of

+ for public visibility

\# for protected visibility

- for private visibility

although the keywords *public, protected*, and *private* can also be used. The absence of a visibility marker indicates that the visibility is not shown (not that it is undefined or public). In the notation shown above, the name of the attribute is the string name. The symbol N inside square brackets denotes the multiplicity allowed for the attribute. A language-dependent specification of the implementation type of the attribute is denoted by type. The string initialValue is a language-dependent expression for the default value of the attribute for a newly created instance of the class, and property-string a string for expressing those traits of the attribute that are not captured by the rest of the syntax. For example, for an attribute that is read-only (such as a const in C++ or a final in Java), the property-string would be set to frozen. The convention for expressing multiplicity is the same as for an association. For example, if an attribute is allowed to take two or more values, the multiplicity symbol N would be replaced by '2..*'. The absence of multiplicity designation means that exactly one value is allowed for the attribute.

The underscore, shown under name and type, if used, signifies that the attribute has class scope, which means the same thing that it is static or one per-class, as opposed to one per object. Except for the name, all other elements of the syntax specification are optional.

14.2.4 Representing Operations

The third partition from the top, when it exists, of a class box shows its operations, meaning the member functions of the class. When a class is drawn at the specification level, only the public operations of the class are displayed. However, at the implementation level, you'd also want to show the private and the protected operations. The full UML syntax for an operation is

```
visibility name (parameter-list) : return-type {property-string}
             ------------------------------------
```

where *visibility* and *name* mean the same as for the case of attributes. The *parameter-list* is a comma-separated list of formal parameters, each specified using the syntax

```
kind name : type = defaultValue
```

where `kind` can be *in, out,* or *inout*, where *in* is for a parameter that passes a value to the operation, *out* for a parameter that fetches a value from the operation, and *inout* for a parameter that can play both roles. The symbols `name`, `type`, and `defaultValue` serve their usual roles.

Back to the syntax for an operation, the symbol `return-type` is an implementation dependent language type of the value returned by the operation. The `property-string` can be used to express such traits as to whether an operation is abstract, which is the case when only the header is defined for the class and no implementation code is provided. Finally, operations that have class scope are underlined as shown above.

It is useful to make a distinction between two types of operations: `query` and `modifier`. A query operation simply tries to get the value of some class attribute without changing the state of the object. On the other hand, a modifier operation will change the state of the object.

14.2.5 Stereotypes

UML also allows a `stereotype` to be specified for a class just above the class name. The stereotype indicates what 'kind' of a class it is. The stereotype is enclosed in guillemots or the pair '<< >>,' as in Figure 14.8. The diagram of Figure 14.8 tells

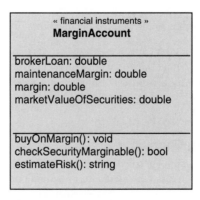

Fig. 14.8

us that the class `MarginAccount` is a class that belongs to the category `financial instruments`.

An *abstract class* is represented in the same way as the class shown above, except that the name of the class is in bold italics.

If it is necessary to show specific objects pictorially, the notation used is the same as for a class, except that now the object name is followed by the class name after a colon, the whole construct underlined, as shown in Figure 14.9.

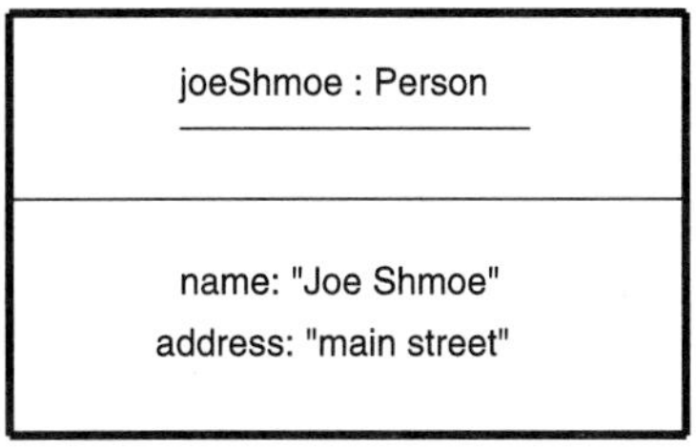

```
┌──────────────────────────────┐
│                              │
│      joeShmoe : Person       │
│      ─────────────────       │
├──────────────────────────────┤
│                              │
│     name: "Joe Shmoe"        │
│     address: "main street"   │
│                              │
└──────────────────────────────┘
```

Fig. 14.9

14.3 INTERACTION DIAGRAM

An interaction diagram shows how objects collaborate in achieving a use case or a small set of related use cases. Interaction diagrams are drawn at an early stage in a design process as they shed further light on the role of each class and give a more concrete focus to the responsibilities of each class. Since in an interaction diagram you make explicit how a class interacts with other classes, you get a better sense of what methods to endow a class with. There are two types of interaction diagrams: *sequence diagrams* and *collaboration diagrams*. Modern OO design software can switch automatically between the two. So you need to explicitly draw only one of the two. In what follows in this section, we will first discuss sequence diagrams and then collaboration diagrams.

14.3.1 Sequence Diagram

A sequence diagram shows in a time-sequenced manner the collaboration carried out by a group of objects to achieve a use case or a small set of related use cases. Each object is assigned a *lifeline* that hangs below it in the diagram. The time sequencing of the activities related to an object is made evident by placing the activities at different points on the lifeline. Time increases downwards along a lifeline.

In a sequence diagram, an object interacts with other objects by either sending messages to them or by receiving messages from them, as depicted in Figure 14.10. A C++ or Java implementation of these interactions will most commonly consist of one object invoking a method on another object — the argument object — for either eliciting some behavior from the argument object, or for ascertaining the value or status of a data member of the argument object. The purpose of the labels "synchronous" and "asynchronous" on the message arrows shown in the figure will become clear later in this section.

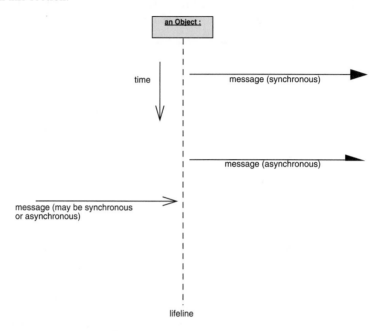

Fig. 14.10

The various components of a sequence diagram are:

1. Object icons

2. Lifelines

3. Arrowed lines for interaction messages between two different objects

4. Activation icons

5. Message to self lines

Our examples will make clear the function served by each of these components. But first we must present the rules of syntax to which the different kinds of interaction messages must conform. A message can be one of the following six different kinds:

1. Status message, like the value of a boolean variable, that an object transmits to another object.

2. Name of a method; this is the method that one object invokes on another object.

3. **[iteration basis] method*, where '*' is the iteration marker; the named method is invoked on multiple instances of the target object; as to which instances specifically is controlled by the expression inside the square brackets.

4. *flag := method*, where flag is set to TRUE or FALSE depending on the outcome of the specified method that is invoked on the receiver of the message.

5. *[condition] method*, where the specified method is executed on the receiver object only when the given condition is satisfied.

6. The special symbol *new*, which means to create a new instance of the receiver object.

To illustrate the various components of a sequence diagram and the different types of messages in such diagrams, consider the following closely related set of use cases for the internet auction example:

> The buyer first examines the max bid posted so far on all the items of interest to him/her. The buyer selects one item and posts his/her bid on that item. If the newly posted bid equals or exceeds the seller's minimum acceptable bid, the seller is notified. If seller is satisfied with the bid, he/she so notifies the auction site and prepares a sales document for the buyer.

We can implement this set of use cases with the following objects:

```
A Buyer object

An AuctionList object, this is simply a list
of all the items available for aution

An AuctionItem object (this object constantly
compares the latest highest posted bid with the
minimum highest bid acceptable to the seller)

A Seller object

A SalesDocument object
```

Figure 14.3.1 presents a sequence diagram for the use cases described above. The first message shown in this diagram is of the form

```
*[ iteration-basis ] method
```

As mentioned earlier, the presence of the iteration marker symbol '*' means that the method is to be applied to multiple instances of the target object; as to which target objects exactly, that is controlled by the expression inside the brackets. In this case, we wish to apply the method `getCurrentMaxBid()` to all the `AuctionItem` objects in the `AuctionList` object.

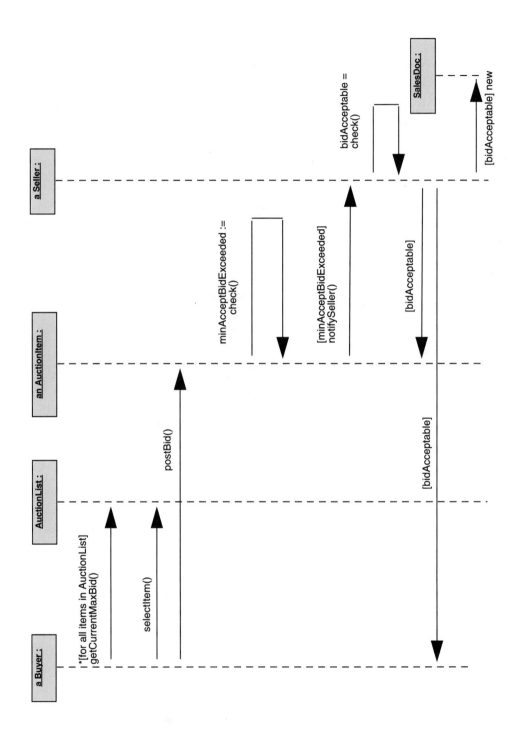

Fig. 14.11

600

The second and the third messages from the top are straightforward invocations of the designated methods on the target objects.

In the fourth from the top message, of form

```
flag := method
```

we want to execute the method check() in order to set the boolean value of the flag minAcceptBidExceeded.

Going down the lifelines, the next message, of form

```
[condition] method
```

is executed only after the boolean variable minAcceptBidAccepted is set to TRUE. The next message seeks to set the value of the boolean variable bidAcceptable by running a method check() on self, in this case a Seller object. The next two messages are merely notification messages. Finally, for the last message, notice how when the bidAcceptable variable checks out to be TRUE, the seller object creates a new object of type SalesDoc.

In the previous diagram, the time order in which the various interactions take place is strict, in the sense that a given interaction between any two objects takes place after some other known interaction and before some other interaction, also known. And even more importantly, each method invocation is synchronous, meaning that after an object invokes a method, it waits for the method to return. We can also say that the method call *blocks* until the method has finished execution.

But many OO programs are written today using multi-processing and/or multi-threading. In such programs, when an object invokes a method in a separate process or a separate thread, it does not necessarily have to wait for the method to finish execution. Such method invocation is called *asynchronous*. We will now see how an interaction diagram can represent a use case that calls for asynchronous interactions.

Consider the following set of related use cases for a robot engaged in autonomous navigation using its cameras to identify directions to landmarks in its environment:

> When desiring to navigate from its current location to a target location, the navigator module must first get a precise fix on its current location. This it must do by locating a certain minimum number of landmarks in its environment and then by triangulating its position from the directions to those landmarks.

As shown in the sequence diagram in Figure 14.12, the MobileRobot asks its Navigator module to get a fix on its current location, which in turn creates a number (in our figure, two, but it could be any number) of LandmarkLocator objects, each of which is responsible for a locating a particular landmark from a list of landmarks known to the robot. Since the computational difficulty associated with the extraction and identification of a particular landmark would vary widely from landmark to landmark, it would be best to spawn the landmark identification processes asynchronously. That would also make it easy to add additional landmark identification processes if necessary.

The concurrent processes here correspond to the different LandmarkSeeker threads. And by these threads running asynchronously is meant that they do not block the caller, in this case the method of the Navigator object that spawns the threads.

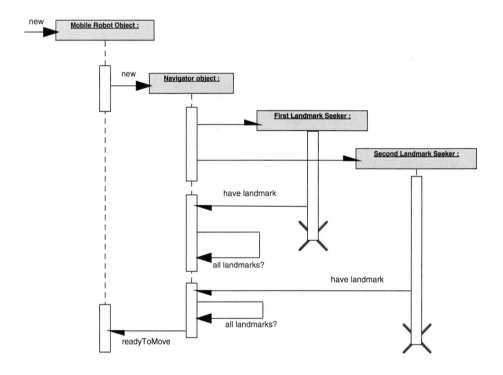

Fig. 14.12

Regarding the new notation here:

1. The half-arrowhead messages are asynchronous. When such methods are invoked, the caller does not block. Ordinarily, as mentioned before, when a method A invokes method B, A waits for B to return. But when B is launched asynchronously, A does not wait and continues doing what comes next after having launched B.

2. The thin vertical rectangles below the object boxes are called *activations* or *Focus of Control* (FOC). To explain this notation, notice the three activations below

the box for the `Navigator` object. The first activation says that the object stays in operation as it is spawning asynchronously the different `LandmarkSeeker` objects. The second activation takes effect when the return "have landmarks" is received from the first `LandmarkSeeker` object. During this activation, the `Navigator` object also checks whether a certain minimum number of the other `LandmarkSeeker` objects have returned "have landmark." The third activation does the same for the second `LandmarkSeeker` object.

3. The X below each activation for asynchronously created objects means that the thread is supposed to get destroyed after it has finished its task.

14.3.2 Collaboration Diagram

A collaboration diagram is another way of showing the interaction between objects. In this diagram, you do away with the lifelines of the sequence diagrams. Messages go directly from object icons to object icons. The temporal sequencing of the messages is displayed by assigning a sequence number to each message.

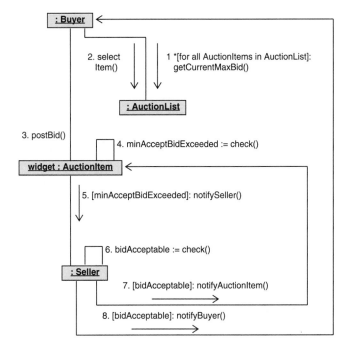

Fig. 14.13

The collaboration diagram for the internet auction example looks like what is shown in Figure 14.13. Note the syntax used for objects:

```
objectName : className
```

where either the object name or the class name may be omitted. But if you omit the object name, you must retain the colon to make it clear that you are using a class name.

Interaction diagrams are not so good at delineating the overall behavior of an object across several use cases. If it is important to show that, you should use statechart diagrams.

14.4 PACKAGE DIAGRAM

When the number of classes becomes large, it is best to organize the classes into *packages* on the basis of some useful criterion. The word "package" in UML means the same thing as it does in Java.

If you have organized your classes into packages, you may want to draw a *package diagram* to show the dependencies between packages. One package depends on another package if any class in the former depends on any class in the latter. Such interpackage dependencies come into existence any time a class in one package has either an IsA or a HasA relationship with a class in another package.

A package is denoted by a rectangular box with a "tab" at the left end of its top. The name of a package appears in the middle of the box. But sometimes it is desirable to list the names of the more prominent classes in the package or some other package-specific information inside the box. In that event, the name of the package is placed inside the tab. Both the tab and the main box are allowed to also list inside pairs of braces any additional information that characterizes a package. For example, if a package consists solely of interfaces in Java, it could be called an abstract package and the word "abstract" placed inside braces beside the name of the package.

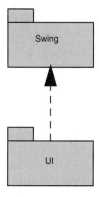

Fig. 14.14

If a package A is dependent on package B, in the package diagram that is shown by an arrow going from A to B. For example, if you extend one of Java's Swing classes to create a user interface in a package named UI, you'd show the resulting dependency by the package diagram of Figure 14.14. Package dependencies are shown by dashed lines with solid arrowheads. If all other packages in a system are dependent on one common package — because it contains some of the more basic types used by the other packages — instead of drawing arrows, you can simply place the characterization {global} beside the package name in a package diagram.

Continuing with the above example, let's say that there is another more application-oriented package, ProcessOrder, that depends on the UI package as shown in Figure 14.15. The important thing to bear in mind here is that the chained dependencies in

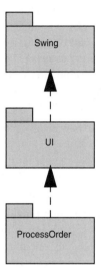

Fig. 14.15

a package diagram are not transitive. Meaning that while the UI package depends on the Swing package, and the ProcessOrder package depends on the UI package, the ProcessOrder package does not automatically become dependent on the Swing package. This corresponds to the property of the import command in Java programs. But it does not correspond to the #include compiler directive in C++. In C++ if A *includes* B and B *includes* C, then A will *include* C. So we can say that the interpackage dependencies in Java, as given rise to by the import command, correspond exactly to the semantics of the the arrow in the package diagrams of UML. On the other hand, the interpackage dependencies given rise to by #include in C++ do not correspond strictly to the meaning of the arrow in a UML package diagram.

The nontransitivity of interpackage dependency makes software maintenance easier. In the above example, this means that any changes to the Swing package would have no direct influence on the ProcessOrder package. So if the Swing package is changed, we would need to look at only the UI package to see if anything there would need to be changed. (Of course, if we make any changes to the UI package, we would then need to also look at the ProcessOrder package for possible changes.) On the other hand, with a transitive dependency, especially after our memory of how the program was implemented had faded, we would be less sure that a data type of Swing was not used directly in the ProcessOrder package.

14.5 STATECHART DIAGRAM

Statechart diagrams are best for displaying the different states that an object can get into across several use cases. In that sense, they help to give a better understanding of the lifetime behavior of a single object in an OO program. Shown in Figure 14.16 is a statechart diagram for the Buyer object in our internet auction example. The rounded rectangles show the different states of the Buyer object. The name of the state is shown as the topmost entry in bold in a rounded rectangle. If there is additional information inside the rectangle, it is separated from the name by a line. An entry preceded by "do/" denotes an *activity* in that state.

The paths with arrowheads show how an object transitions from state to state. The syntax of the state transition labels is

    Event[Guard]/Action

all three parts of which are optional. What this syntax means is that the occurrence of the Event will cause this state transition provided the Guard condition evaluates to TRUE. However, before the actual transition to the new state takes place, Action must be executed. Since at any time only one transition can be taken out of a state, the guards on all the outgoing transition paths from a given state must be mutually exclusive.

When a Buyer object is first created, it is in the Registration state attached to the Start state at the top.[1] From that state it has only one transition, labeled

    registered

to the Browse state. Evidently, this transition label only has the event part specified. Once in the Browse state, the object engages in the activity "examine all items in AuctionList." As the Buyer object goes through each item, the event itemChecked takes place, which causes the guard condition on the transition-to-self arc to be evaluated. As long as the Buyer does not select an item for actual bidding, the Buyer object will

---

[1]The Start state itself, shown as a filled black circle, is a dummy state that gets the action started. The final or the end state, represented by a filled black circle inside another circle, is also a dummy state. The statechart diagram of Figure 14.19 includes a couple of end states.

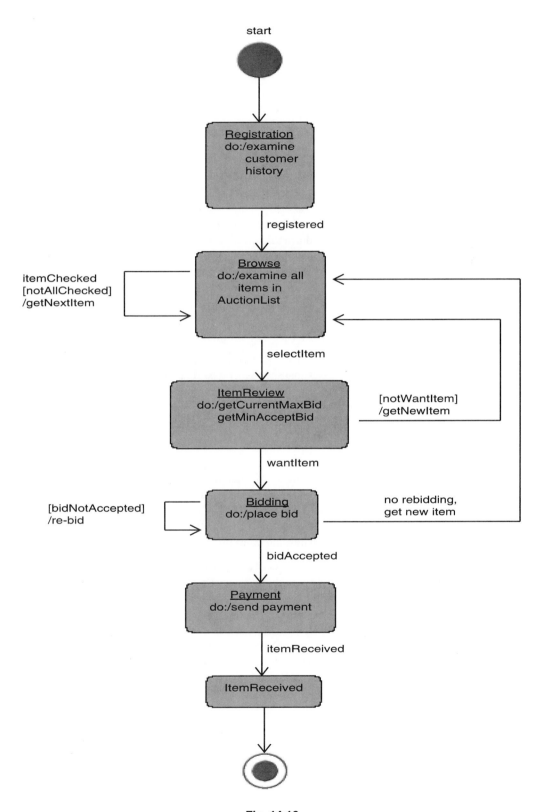

Fig. 14.16

continue to stay in the Browse state. However, when the event selectItem takes place, the Buyer object will transition to ItemReview state.

In the ItemReview state, the Buyer object examines the currentMaxBid placed on the item by some other buyer and the minAcceptBid specified by the Seller object. Depending on what it would take to place a meaningful bid on the item, the Buyer object could transition to the Bidding state or back to the Browse state. The rest of the statechart diagram should be self explanatory.

Each state shown in the figure, except the ItemReceived state, actually has one more outgoing transition that is not shown — this would be a transition to a state called TerminateSession. Since it should be possible to terminate the interaction with the auction server at any time during the lifetime of the Buyer object, from all the other states there should be a transition arc to a state called TerminateSession triggered by an event that could be called "terminateSession." Since such transition arcs are likely to visually clutter up a statechart diagram, an alternative consists of grouping all the states together that have a transition to a common target state. The grouped states can be called a superstate; one can then have a single transition from the superstate to the target state, as shown in Figure 14.17.

The statechart diagram of Figure 14.17 shows the various states of a Buyer object for a closely related set of use cases that the object would be involved in. A Buyer object would also be involved in use cases that deal with a check of his/her past record as an auction site participant, his/her creditworthiness, and so on, before the acceptance of the bid. One could conceive of the statechart diagram of Figure 14.18 that would show these other activities related to a Buyer object.

In a modern implementation, it is likely that the computations represented by the two previous statechart diagrams would be executed in two separate threads. In this way, the background check and credit authorization could proceed in parallel with the Buyer's interaction for placing a bid. This would, of course, imply that a Buyer object may simultaneously be in two states, one from the statechart diagram of Figure 14.17 and the other from the statechart diagram of Figure 14.18.

If we want to show the combined behavior of a Buyer object that would correspond to these two separate but concurrently running statechart diagrams, we can combine the two diagrams into what's called a *concurrent statechart diagram*, shown at a coarse level in Figure 14.19. The concurrent section of the statechart diagram is shown inside the large box with two partitions, one corresponding to each thread. As mentioned before, a Buyer object will be able to be simultaneously in two states, one from each partition. Outside the concurrent section, the Buyer object will be allowed to be in only one state at any one time. For our example, that means that the Buyer object could be simultaneously in, say, the ItemReview and the BackgroundCheck states. But at any one time it can only be either the SessionTerminated state, or the ItemReceived state, or the RejectionNotification state.

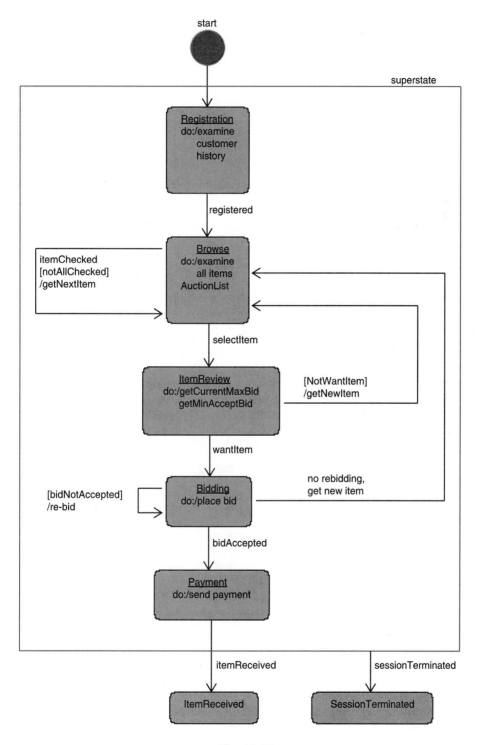

Fig. 14.17

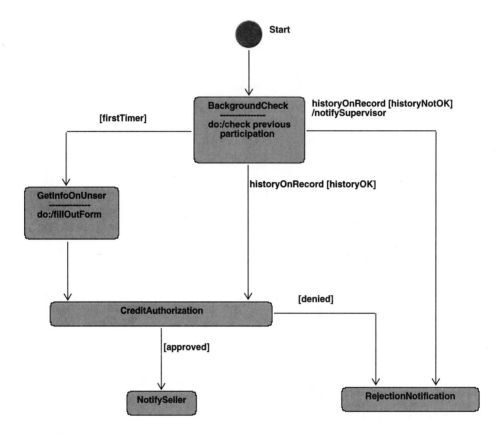

Fig. 14.18

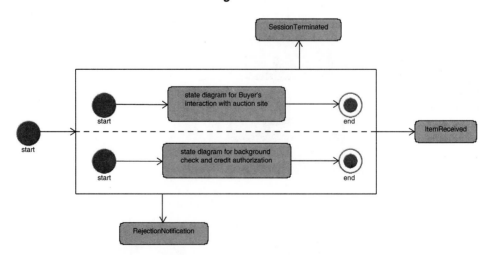

Fig. 14.19

14.6 ACTIVITY DIAGRAM

An activity diagram tells us how a desired end result can be achieved by a group of activities working together. An important issue in the construction of an activity diagram is the identification of those sub-activities that can be executed simultaneously, through either multiprocessing or multithreading, and those that must be executed serially. Toward that end, an activity diagram gives us a representational tool called the *synchronization bar*. In Figure 14.20, a synchronization bar is shown by a double line with activities flowing into it and flowing out of it. (Official UML notation for this bar is a thick solid line) The figure shows a synchronization bar with multiple

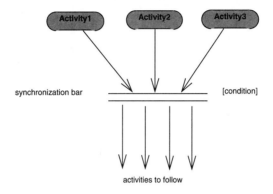

Fig. 14.20

incoming and outgoing activities and with a condition *[condition]* attached. The meaning of the synchronization bar with respect to the incoming and the outgoing activities is different. All multiple incoming activities must be executed successfully before control is allowed to proceed beyond the synchronization bar. The successful completion of all the incoming activities is subject to the condition attached to the bar. In that sense, a synchronization bar is *conjunctive* with respect to the incoming activities. With regard to the outgoing activities, a synchronization bar tells us that the activities are allowed to be executed in parallel and independently of one another.

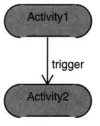

Fig. 14.21

As shown in Figure 14.20, activities are represented by ovals in an activity diagram. The arrows coming into an activity and emanating outwards from an activity are referred to as `triggers`. If an activity has a single incoming trigger, the activity is enabled upon the receipt of that trigger, which in most cases would be the successful completion of the previous activity that is the source of that trigger. In Figure 14.21, successful completion of Activity1 would send a trigger out along the path shown that would then enable Activity2.

An activity is *disjunctive* with respect to multiple incoming triggers. What that means that if a trigger is received from any one of the incoming paths, the target activity would be enabled. In Figure 14.22, `SpecialActivity` would be enabled provided at least one of `Activity1`, `Activity2`, ..., `ActivityN` is completed successfully. An activity diagram makes a special provision for representing a purely

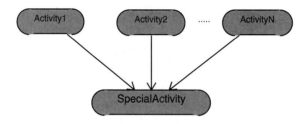

Fig. 14.22

decision activity, which in most cases will consist of testing the value of a boolean variable. This type of activity is represented by a diamond, as shown in Figure 14.23.

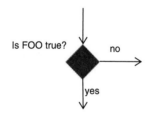

Fig. 14.23

The rest of this section shows an activity diagram for the internet auction example. This diagram represents the flow of activities for the process with the following textual description:

> When a buyer checks in, we must ascertain whether or not he/she is an already registered user of the system. If not, we ask the buyer to fill out a form and supply the information needed. The buyer proceeds to browse through the list of items that he/she is interested in. The buyer is given the option of either bidding

on the items individually, or bidding on groups of items together (what if the buyer wants two works of art together or none, or four Louis IV chairs together or none). When the buyer begins to start selecting items to bid on, we want to start the process of running a credit check on the buyer. If the bids placed by the buyer and the credit check are okay, we want to proceed to payment authorization before instructing the seller(s) to ship the item(s) to the buyer.

The activity diagram that is shown in Figure 14.24 identifies those activities that can be carried out concurrently. The concurrently implementable activities emanate from the two synchronization bars labeled "fork" in the figure. The synchronization bar labeled "merge" is used to denote the condition that the multiple activities incident on the bar must simultaneously conclude successfully before the flow of control can proceed forward. Note in particular the activity segment from P to Q. The condition label associated with the synchronization bar at P is

```
*[for each item in group]
```

The symbol '*' here means *multiple triggers*, in the sense that it designates that the displayed thread of activity from P to Q actually consists of a parallel bundle of threads, each consisting of the activity shown. Therefore, the number of concurrent paths emanating from the synchronization bar at P equals the number of items in the group of items the buyer is interested in.

14.7 CREDITS AND SUGGESTIONS FOR FURTHER READING

The latest information regarding UML can be accessed through Object Management Group's web site www.omg.org. Another useful website for object-modeling related issues is www.rational.com. This one belongs to the Rational Software Corporation that has played a leading role in the standardization of tools for designing object based systems. This is also the homesite of the Rational Unified Process for the development of OO software. You also need to know about three people who have played a central role in the creation of UML and now RUP: Grady Booch, Jim Rumbaugh, and Ivar Jacobson. All three are with Rational Software Corporation.

This chapter presented only the more prominent diagrams used today for the modeling of object-oriented systems. UML defines a total of the 12 diagrams. Besides the seven presented in this chapter, UML defines the following additional diagrams: Object Diagram, Component Diagram, Deployment Diagram, Subsystems Diagram, and Models Diagram. The reader is referred to the official OMG site for information on these additional diagrams.

At the level of concepts, much of what was said in this chapter is a paraphrase of the book by Fowler and Scott [20]. The reader is referred to that book for more detailed presentations of the notions presented here. Another recommended on-line source of information is the UML tutorial at www.togethersoft.com.

The UML diagrams shown in this chapter, and also in the rest of the book, were made with the JVISION modeling tool available from www.object-insight.com.

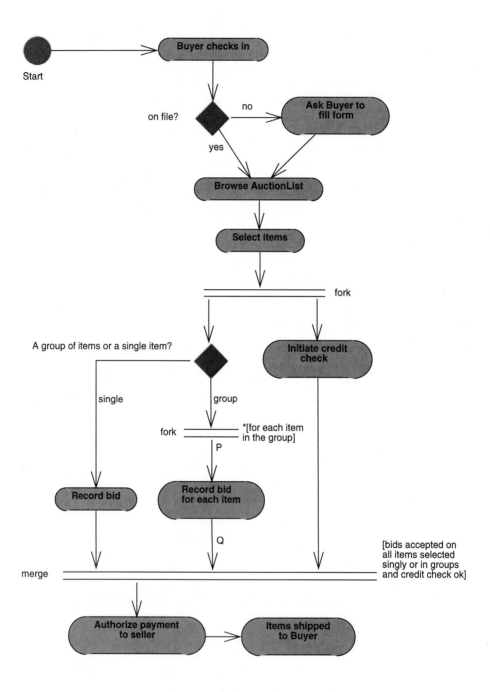

Fig. 14.24

14.8 HOMEWORK

1. Construct a use case diagram that portrays the following actors and use cases:

   (a) An actor named `Student`

   (b) An actor named `College`

   (c) The following use cases specific to the actor `Student`: "List All Courses," "Pay Fees," "Registration," and "Search for a Course". The use case "Search for a Course," meant to help a student decide which courses to sign up for, should extend the use case "List All Courses."

   (d) The following uses specific to the actor `College`: "Maintain a Database of Students," "Registration," "Administer Examinations," "Check Student Qualifications." The use case "Registration" is the same as for the actor `Student`.

2. Draw a sequence diagram showing the time progression of the interaction between the various objects needed for the following closely related set of use cases for an online course registration system for a college:

   > The student first logs into the online course registration system. The student browses through the courses being offered next semester and selects what he/she needs. The online registration system makes sure that the student has the prerequisites for the courses selected and there is space available in those courses. The course selection is automatically forwarded to a faculty advisor. Upon approval from the advisor, a fee statement is sent to the student. If the faculty advisor disapproves, the student is notified. The student is considered registered when the fee is received. At that point, the student is sent his/her class schedule.

   You may first want to list the individual use cases needed for the interaction described above, then identify the classes required for the use cases, and, finally, construct an interaction diagram. Also show a collaboration diagram.

3. Draw a statechart diagram that shows the different states of a `Student` object in the uses cases of the previous problem.

4. Construct an activity diagram for the interactions of Problem 2.

15

Extending Classes

Creating subclasses is central to object oriented programming. Chapter 3 showed the basic syntax for defining a subclass. This chapter will present in greater detail the various aspects of how to create subclasses and how to provide them with the needed functionality.

More specifically, this chapter talks about the constraints that must be observed by a subclass constructor in relation to the base class constructor for C++ and Java. We also discuss for C++ the special syntax of a subclass copy constructor, a subclass copy assignment operator; upcasting in operator overload definitions for a subclass; and destructors for derived classes. The chapter also presents the notion of a *virtual* function in C++; these are functions that exhibit polymorphic behavior. For both C++ and Java, this chapter goes into the concept of an abstract class, and for the case of Java, the concept of an interface. The last part of the chapter is devoted to case-study programs in C++ and Java that involve small but moderately complex class hierarchies.

15.1 PUBLIC DERIVATION OF A SUBCLASS IN C++

As already mentioned in Chapter 3, when we say

```
class Y : public X { /* ..... */ };
```

we declare X to be a public base of Y. The other options would be to declare X to be either a protected or a private base of Y. We will get to those later in this chapter.

A *public* derivation of a subclass in C++ buys us two things:

- An object of a derived-class type can at any time be treated as an object of base-class type without explicit type conversion, *provided both are manipulated through pointers or references*. Therefore, Y* can be substituted anywhere X* is needed. For the Animal example shown at the beginning of Chapter 3, the following is therefore legal:

```
Cat* cpr = new Cat( ... );
FourLegged* fpr = cpr;
```

But suppose we say

```
FourLegged* fpr = new FourLegged(....);
```

Now we cannot say

```
Cat* cpr = fpr;      // WRONG
```

because not every FourLegged is a Cat. If so needed, we are allowed to say

```
Cat* cpr = new Cat( ... );
FourLegged* fpr = cpr;
Cat* cpr_2 = static_cast<Cat*>( fpr );
```

This works because the system can figure out at run time that Cat is the true type of the object to which fpr points.

- With a public derivation, all of the public and protected data members and member functions of the base class become available in the derived class. It's as if they were declared in the derived class itself. Suppose we have

```
class FourLegged {                      // BASE
    double weight;
    //...
public:
    double getWeight();
    //...
};

class Cat : public FourLegged {        // DERIVED
    int numClaws;
    //...
public:
    void print() { cout << getWeight() << endl; }      //(A)
    //...
};
```

We are able to use the `getWeight()` function in the derived class in line (A) as if this function were defined locally in the derived class directly.

Although public and protected data members and member functions of a base class are directly visible in a derived class, the names used for them can be used again in a derived class. Therefore, as we show below, a public `print()` member function in the base class does not prevent us from defining a `print()` function again in the derived class. What about the resulting name conflict?

Name conflicts of this nature are avoided by using the rule that the derived class definition of a name hides all base class definitions of the same name.[1] If the base class definition of a name (that is also defined in a derived class) is needed in the derived class, it can be accessed via the scope operator ':: '.

Speaking of function names in particular, the derived-class definition of a function hides *all* base-class functions of the *same name*, even when their signatures are different from that of the derived-class function. Such hidden base-class function definitions can always be accessed in the derived class via the scope operator.

We show below a base class and a derived class, with both possessing a member function `print()`, the function being public in the base class. Notice how in line (C) of the derived class we use the scope operator to access the base class version of `print()`:

```
class FourLegged {                    // BASE
    double weight;
    //...
public:
    void print() { cout << weight << endl; }
};

class Cat : public FourLegged {       // DERIVED
    int numClaws;
    //...
public:
    int getNumClaws();
    void print() {                                            //(B)
        FourLegged::print();                                  //(C)
        cout << getNumClaws() << endl;
    }
    //....
};
```

The derived class's `print` in line (B) invokes the base class's `print` in line (C) by calling `FourLegged::print()`. You'd end up with infinite recursion if you replaced

---

[1] The process of determining as to which definition to use for a name is called *name lookup*. According to the C++ standard [41, clause 10.2], name lookup takes place *before* access control.

FourLegged::print() by just print() in line (C), because then the print() function in the derived class would be calling itself.

Since the private members of a base class are not visible in a derived class, one would naturally expect to be able to use those identifiers in a derived class. That is indeed the case. In the following example, we use the same two identifiers for the private data members in the base class and in the derived class, although the meanings ascribed to them in the two cases are different.

```
//DerivedNameConflict.cc

#include <iostream>
#include <string>
using namespace std;

class User {                        //BASE
    string name;                    // given name
    int age;                        // actual age
public:
    User( string nam, int yy) : name( nam ), age( yy ) {}
    string getName() { return name; }
};

class StudentUser : public User {   //DERIVED
    string name;                    // nickname used at school
    int age;                        // assumed age for partying
public:
    StudentUser( string str1, int yy1, string str2, int yy2 )
        : User( str1, yy1 ), name( str2 ), age( yy2 ) {}
    string getName() { return name; }
};

int main()
{
    StudentUser student( "maryjo", 19, "jojo", 21 );
    cout << student.getName() << endl;          // jojo         (D)
    cout << student.User::getName() << endl;    // maryjo       (E)
    return 0;
}
```

Note that when getName() is invoked on the derived-class object student in line (D) in main, it is the derived-class definition of this function that gets invoked. But when we make the following call in line (E) of main:

```
    student.User::getName()
```

it is the base-class definition of getName() that gets invoked.

15.2 CONSTRUCTORS FOR DERIVED CLASSES IN C++

A derived-class constructor must call a base-class constructor before it does anything else. If the base class constructor is not called explicitly in a derived-class constructor, the system will try to invoke the base-class's no-arg constructor. But, remember, a base class will have a no-arg constructor only if you provide one, or, by default, if you have defined no constructors at all for the base class. In what follows, we will first use the User class example to illustrate the more common case, which is that of a derived-class constructor making an explicit call to a base-class constructor.

```cpp
//DerivedConstructor.cc

#include <iostream>
#include <string>
using namespace std;

class User {                            // BASE
    string name;
    int age;
public:
    User( string nm, int a ) { name = nm; age = a;}
    void print(){cout << "Name: " << name << "   Age: " << age;}
};

class StudentUser : public User {       // DERIVED
    string schoolEnrolled;
public:
    StudentUser( string nam, int y, string school )
                : User( nam, y ) {                               //(A)
        schoolEnrolled = school;
    }
    void print() {
        User::print();
        cout << "   School Enrolled:  " << schoolEnrolled << endl;
    }
};

int main()
{
    StudentUser student( "Maura", 20, "ece" );
    student.print();
        // Name: Maura  Age: 20  School Enrolled: ece
    return 0;
}
```

Through the initialization syntax in line (A), the constructor of the derived-class object explicitly calls the base-class constructor to construct the base-class portion of the derived class object. After that, the derived class constructor proceeds to bring into existence what is defined explicitly for the derived class. A derived class object thus built is best shown pictorially as in Figure 15.1.

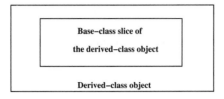

Fig. 15.1

As was mentioned at the beginning of this section, if a base-class constructor is not invoked explicitly in a derived-class constructor, the system tries to invoke the no-arg constructor of the base class for initializing the base-class subobject. In the following program, the derived-class constructor in line (D) makes no mention of a base-class constructor. The base-class has been provided with an explicitly defined no-arg constructor in line (A) and a 1-arg constructor in line (C):

```
//DerivedConstWithBaseNoArg.cc

#include<iostream>
using namespace std;

class X {                           // BASE
    int m;
public:
    // no-arg constructor:
    X() : m(10) {                                              //(A)
        cout << "inside X's no-arg constructor" << endl;       //(B)
    }
    // 1-arg constructor:
    X(int mm): m(mm){}                                         //(C)
    int getm() { return m; }
};

class Y : public X {                // DERIVED
    int n;
public:
    // constructor:
    Y(int nn) : n(nn) {}                                       //(D)
    int getn() { return n; }
};
```

```
int main()
{
    Y yobj( 100 );                                          //(E)
    cout << yobj.getm() << " "                              //(F)
        << yobj.getn() << endl;                             //(G)
}
```

Even though the derived-class constructor in the program above makes no explicit call to any base-class constructors, the system nonetheless has a need for initializing the base-class subobject inside the derived-class object yobj whose construction is called for in line (E) of main. So it proceeds to use the no-arg constructor defined for the base class in line (A). This is clear from the output of this program produced by the statements in lines (B), (F), and (G):

```
inside X's no-arg constructor
10  100
```

A derived class may be extended further and the process continued to any depth. For example, we could have

```
class X { /*   */ };

class Y : public X { /*   */ };

class Z : public Y { /*   */ };
```

If we invoke a constructor for class Z, the resulting object will have inside it a subobject corresponding to its immediate base Y, and that subobject will in turn have inside it a sub-subobject of type X, as we show in Figure 15.2.

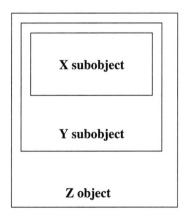

Fig. 15.2

15.3 COPY CONSTRUCTORS FOR DERIVED CLASSES IN C++

Since every object corresponding to a derived class has residing inside it a subobject corresponding to the base class, it stands to reason that when we copy a derived-class object we would want to ensure that the base-class subobject is also copied in a consistent fashion. This requires that the copy constructor of the base class be called inside the copy constructor of a derived class.

Here is an example that illustrates the point[2] :

```
//DerivedCopyConstruct.cc

#include <iostream>
using namespace std;

class X {                          // BASE
    int m;
public:
    //base class constructor:
    X( int mm ) : m( mm ) {}
    //base class copy constructor:
    X( const X& other ) : m( other.m ) {}                    //(A)
    void print() { cout << "m of X obj: " << m << endl; }
};

class Y : public X {              // DERIVED
    int n;
public:
    //derived class constructor:
    Y( int mm, int nn ) : X( mm ), n( nn ) {}
    //derived class copy constructor:
    Y( const Y& other ) : X( other ), n( other.n ) {}        //(B)
    void print() {
        X::print();
        cout << "n of Y obj: " << n << endl;
    }
};

int main()
{
    X* xptr1 = new X( 5 );
    xptr1->print();                // m of X object: 5
    cout << endl;
```

---

[2]At this point, the reader may wish to review the copy constructor syntax presented in Chapter 11.

```
    Y y1( 2, 3 );
    y1.print();                    // m of X subobject: 2
                                   // n of Y object: 3

    cout << endl;

    Y y2 = y1;                     // invokes copy constructor for Y
    y2.print();                    // m of X subobject: 2
                                   // n of Y object: 3

    return 0;
}
```

In this example, class Y is derived from X. While the copy constructor of the base class in line (A) above is

```
    X( const X& other ) : m( other.m ) {}
```

the copy constructor of the derived class in line (B) is

```
    Y( const Y& other ) : X( other ), n( other.n ) {}
```

Note the invocation of the base-class copy constructor by X(other) in the copy constructor for the derived class. This invocation causes the X slice of the Y object other to be copied over.

If a derived class has multiple bases, then the copy constructor for the derived class must include proper copying over of the subobjects corresponding to all those bases. Suppose we have

```
    class Y : public X1, public X2 {
      int n;
      //
    };
```

The copy constructor of this class will, in general, look like

```
    Y( const Y& other )
         : X1( other ), X2( other ), n( other.n )  { .... }
```

The example we showed above really did not need a copy constructor in either the base class or the derived class, since the system-supplied default copy constructor that does byte by byte copying would have sufficed in both cases. You can check that out by commenting out either or both of the copy constructor definitions in lines (A) and (B) of the above program. However, this example illustrates the basic syntax to be followed for incorporating the base-class copy constructor in a derived-class copy constructor.

15.4   ASSIGNMENT OPERATORS FOR DERIVED CLASSES IN C++

As was the case for the copy constructor of a derived class, the assignment operator of
a derived class must also invoke the assignment operator of the base class. Including
the assignment operators in the definitions of the base class X and the derived class Y
of the previous example, we get[3]

```
//DerivedAssignOp.cc

#include <iostream>
using namespace std;

class X {                                    // BASE
    int m;
public:
    //constructor:
    X( int mm ) : m( mm ) {}
    //copy constructor:
    X( const X& other ) : m( other.m ) {}
    //assignment op:
    X& operator=( const X& other ) {                            //(A)
        if ( this == &other ) return *this;
        m = other.m;
        return *this;
    }
    void print() {
        cout << "m of X obj: " << m << endl;
    }
};

class Y : public X {                      // DERIVED
    int n;
public:
    //constructor:
    Y( int mm, int nn ) : X( mm ), n( nn ) {}
    //copy constructor:
    Y( const Y& other ) : X( other ), n( other.n ) {}
    //assignment op:
    Y& operator=( const Y& other ) {                            //(B)
        if ( this == &other ) return *this;
        X::operator=( other );
        n = other.n;
        return *this;
    }
```

---

[3]Before looking at this example code, the reader may wish to review the material on copy assignment
operators in Chapter 11.

```
    void print() {
        X::print();
        cout << "n of Y obj: " << n << endl; }
};

int main()
{
    X xobj_1( 5 );                  // X's constructor
    X xobj_2 = xobj_1;              // X's copy constructor

    X xobj_3( 10 );
    xobj_3 = xobj_2;               // X's assignment op
    xobj_3.print();                // m of X obj: 5
    cout << endl;

    Y yobj_1( 100, 110 );          // Y's constructor
    Y yobj_2 = yobj_1;             // Y's copy constructor

    Y yobj_3( 200, 220 );
    yobj_3 = yobj_2;               // Y's assignment op
    yobj_3.print();                // m of X obj: 100
                                   // n of Y obj: 110
    cout << endl;
}
```

The assignment operator for the base class is defined as follows in line (A) above:

```
    X& operator=( const X& other ) {
        if ( this == &other ) return *this;
        m = other.m;
        return *this;
    }
```

And the assignment operator for the derived class is defined in line (B) above by

```
    Y& operator=( const Y& other ) {
        if ( this == &other ) return *this;
        X::operator=( other );                              //(C)
        n = other.n;
        return *this;
    }
```

Note the invocation in line (C):

```
    X::operator=( other );
```

This applies the base-class assignment operator to the base-class slice of the derived-class object.

These constructs for the assignment operation can be generalized to the case of a derived class inheriting from multiple bases. Suppose, we have

```
class Y : public X1, public X2 {
    int n;
    //
};
```

The assignment operator for this class will look like

```
Y& operator=( const Y& other ) {
    if ( this == &other ) return *this;
    X1::operator=( other );                              //(D)
    X2::operator=( other );                              //(E)
    n = other.n;
    return *this;
}
```

Note how the subobjects corresponding to the two bases are assigned over in lines (D) and (E).

It is important to note that the classes X and Y in the above program really do not need programmer-defined assignment operators, since the system-supplied default meaning of the assignment operator would suffice for these simple classes. You can check that out by commenting out either or both of the definitions of the copy assignment operators in lines (A) and (B) of the program. However, the example does illustrate the basic syntax to be used when incorporating the assignment operator of the base class in the assignment operator of a derived class.

15.5 OVERLOADING OPERATORS FOR DERIVED CLASSES IN C++

Operator overloading in C++ was discussed earlier in Chapter 12. The question that we will address in this section is whether anything different needs to be done in the overload definition of an operator for a derived class if the same operator has been overloaded for the base class. As you will see in this section, if you want the derived-class overload definition to use the base-class overload definition for doing part of the work, then you may have to use what is known as *upcasting*.

As an example of operator overloading for derived classes, in this section we will consider the specific case of overloading the output operator '<<' for a derived class. The same discussion extends to other operator overloadings. Let's consider the three-class hierarchy of Figure 15.3. For each class we will define a constructor, a copy constructor, and a copy assignment operator and will declare the function operator<< to be a friend. To appreciate this example, focus on the global overload definition of the output operator '<<' and see how this definition changes when we go from the base-class `Person` to the derived-class `Employee` and then to the further derived-class `Manager`.

Fig. 15.3

In the program shown below, for the base-class `Person`, the overload definition for the output operator in line (D) is

```
ostream& operator<<( ostream& os, const Person& p ) {
    os << p.name;
    return os;
}
```

which is straightforward and in accord with such examples shown earlier in Chapter 12. However, for the derived-class `Employee`, the overload definition as shown in line (E) is

```
ostream& operator<<( ostream& os, const Employee& e ) {
    Person* ptr = &e;                                       //(A)
    os << *ptr;                                             //(B)
    os << " " << e.department << " " << e.salary;           //(C)
    return os;
}
```

Note how in line (A) above, we first *upcast* the `Employee` object and obtain a pointer of type `Person` pointing to the same object. When the output operator is invoked in line (B) on the resulting `Person` object, it will print out the `Person` slice of the `Employee` object. We then output the rest of the `Employee` object in line (C). In the program below, as shown in line (F), we do the same thing in the `Manager` class vis-à-vis its base-class `Employee`.

```
//DerivedOverloadOp.cc

#include <iostream>
#include <string>
using namespace std;

/////////////////////////// class Person ///////////////////////////
class Person {
    string name;
public:
    Person( string nom ) : name( nom ) {}
    Person( const Person& p ) : name( p.name ) {}
    Person& operator=( const Person& p ) {
        if ( this != &p ) name = p.name;
        return *this;
    }
    virtual ~Person() {}
    friend ostream& operator<<( ostream& os, const Person& p );
};

//overload << for base class Person:
ostream& operator<<( ostream& os, const Person& p ) {               //(D)
    os << p.name;
    return os;
}

/////////////////////////// class Employee ///////////////////////////
class Employee: public Person {
    string department;
    double salary;
public:
    Employee( string name, string dept, double s )
        : Person( name ), department( dept ), salary( s ) {}
    Employee( const Employee& e )
        : Person( e ), department( e.department ),
          salary( e.salary ) {}
    Employee& operator=( const Employee& e ) {
        if ( this != &e ) {
            Person::operator=( e );
            department = e.department;
            salary = e.salary;
        }
        return *this;
    }
    ~Employee() {}
    friend ostream& operator<<( ostream& os, const Employee& p );
};
```

```cpp
//overload << for derived class Employee:
ostream& operator<<( ostream& os, const Employee& e ) {          //(E)
    const Person* ptr = &e;          //upcast
    os << *ptr;
    os << " " << e.department << " " << e.salary;
    return os;
}

////////////////////////////// class Manager //////////////////////////////
class Manager: public Employee {
    string title;
public:
    Manager( string name, string dept, double salary, string atitle )
            : Employee( name, dept, salary),
              title( atitle ) {}
    Manager( const Manager& m ) : Employee( m ), title( m.title ) {}
    Manager& operator=( const Manager& m ){
        if ( this != &m ) {
            Employee::operator=( m );
            title = m.title;
        }
        return *this;
    }
    ~Manager() {}
    friend ostream& operator<<( ostream& os, const Manager& m );
};

//overload << for derived class Manager:
ostream& operator<<( ostream& os, const Manager& m ) {          //(F)
    const Employee* ptr = &m;          //upcast
    os << *ptr;
    os << " " << m.title;
    return os;
}

////////////////////////////// main //////////////////////////////
int main()
{
    Manager m1( "Zahpod", "assembly", 100, "director" );
    Manager m2( m1 );                    // invokes copy construct
    cout << m2 << endl;                  // Zaphod assembly 100 director
    Manager m3( "Trillion", "sales", 200, "vice_pres" );
    m2 = m3;                             // invokes assignment oper
    cout << m2 << endl;                  // Trillion sales 200 vice_pres
    return 0;
}
```

15.6   DESTRUCTORS FOR DERIVED CLASSES IN C++

A destructor defined in a base class cannot be inherited by a derived class. However, the base class destructor can be overridden in a derived class. The usefulness of overriding a base class destructor in a derived class is discussed separately in Section 15.10.

If resources are appropriated in a derived class in C++, then a destructor must be explicitly defined for the derived class in order to free up those resources when an object made from the derived class goes out of scope or is explicitly deleted from the heap.

To illustrate the importance of defining a destructor explicitly for a derived class, let's consider a class X and a class Y derived from X, as shown in Figure 15.4. We will

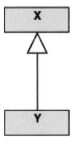

Fig. 15.4

assume that the base X possesses a pointer data member that is meant to point to a block of freshly allocated memory in each object of type X. We will also assume that X is provided with a destructor to free up this memory. With regard to the derived Y, we will consider the following three cases:

- The derived class Y does not appropriate any resources and is not provided with a destructor.

- The derived class Y also has a pointer data member that is meant to point to a block of freshly allocated memory in each object of type Y, but is *not* provided with a destructor.

- The derived class Y has a pointer data member as mentioned above and is also provided with an appropriate destructor.

Case 1:

This case can be depicted as in Figure 15.5.
The following program is an implementation of this case. The derived class Y does not appropriate any resources and is not provided with a destructor. Therefore, for class Y, we are dependent on the system-supplied default destructor, which suffices.

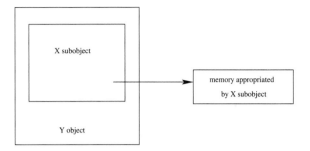

Fig. 15.5

When the system tries to destroy a derived-class object (either because it is going out of scope or because the `delete` operator was invoked on a pointer to the object) as in line (F), the default definition of the destructor works fine. The default destructor for Y invokes the user-supplied destructor in line (B) for the parent class X to free up the memory allocated in the X subobject of the Y object.

```
//DerivedDestructCase1.cc

#include <iostream>
using namespace std;

class X {                               // BASE
public:
    int* x_data;
    int x_size;
    //constructor:
    X( int* ptr, int sz ) : x_size(sz) {
        cout << "X's constructor invoked" << endl;          //(A)
        x_data = new int[ x_size ];
        int i=0;
        int* temp = x_data;
        while (i++<x_size) *temp++ = *ptr++;
    }
    //destructor:
    ~X() {                                                  //(B)
        cout << "X's destructor invoked" << endl;           //(C)
        delete [] x_data;
    }
};

//class Y is NOT supplied with a programmer-defined destructor:
class Y : public X {                    // DERIVED
    int y;
public:
```

```
    Y( int* xptr, int xsz, int yy) : X( xptr, xsz ), y( yy ) {
        cout << "Y's constructor invoked" << endl;                    //(D)
    }
};

int main()
{
    int freshData[100] = {0};
    Y* yptr = new Y( freshData, 100, 1000 );                          //(E)
    delete yptr;                                                      //(F)
    return 0;
}
```

We first construct a Y object in line (E). Then, in line (F) the `delete` operator invokes the system-supplied default destructor for the Y object. This default destructor invokes the user-supplied X's destructor of line (B) for that portion of the Y object that is X. So the output of this program, as produced by lines (A), (C), and (D), is

```
X's constructor invoked
Y's constructor invoked
X's destructor invoked
```

This output also demonstrates that an object of a derived-class type is constructed base up, meaning that first its base subobject is constructed and then the rest of the derived-class object is created.

Case 2:

Let's now consider the case when objects of derived-class type also acquire freshly allocated memory on the heap, as depicted in Figure 15.6. Now we must provide a destructor for Y also. The job of Y's destructor would be to free up the memory appropriated during the construction of a Y object as the Y object goes out of scope (or as the `delete` operator is applied to a pointer of type Y*). But just to see what happens, let's consider the following program, deliberately flawed, that does not provide a destructor for Y:

```
//DerivedDestructCase2.cc

#include <iostream>
using namespace std;

class X {                               // BASE
public:
    int* x_data;
    int x_size;
```

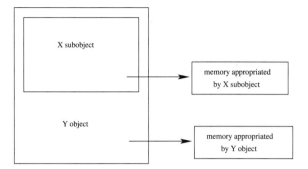

Fig. 15.6

```
    //constructor:
    X( int* ptr, int sz ) : x_size(sz) {
        cout << "X's constructor invoked" << endl;
        x_data = new int[ x_size ];
        int i=0;
        int* temp = x_data;
        while (i++<x_size)
          *temp++ = *ptr++;
    }
    //destructor:
    ~X() {                                                      //(G)
        cout << "X's destructor invoked" << endl;
        delete [] x_data;
    }
};

//class Y has NOT been supplied with a
//programmer-defined destructor even
//though it needs one:
class Y : public X {                      // DERIVED
    int* y_data;
    int y_size;
public:
    //constructor:
    Y( int* xptr, int xsz, int* yptr, int yz)
        : X( xptr, xsz ), y_size( yz ) {
        cout << "Y's constructor invoked" << endl;
        y_data = new int[ y_size ];                            //(H)
        int i=0;
        int* temp = y_data;
        while (i++<x_size)
            *temp++ = *yptr++;
    }
};
```

```
int main()
{
    int freshData[100] = {0};
    int moreFreshData[ 1000 ] = {1};
    Y* yptr = new Y( freshData, 100, moreFreshData, 1000 );        //(I)
    delete yptr;                                                    //(J)
    return 0;
}
```

Note that we have not defined a destructor for the derived class Y even though we are appropriating memory for its pointer data member in line (H). We again construct a Y object in line (I) and then call for its destruction in line (J) of main().

Since Y is not provided with a destructor, the statement in line (J) invokes the system-supplied default destructor for Y, which, frees up the eight bytes of memory occupied by the two data members of the Y object and invokes the base's destructor in line (G) for destroying the X subobject inside the Y object. As a result, the memory that was appropriated specially for the Y object through line (H) is never deallocated.

Therefore, this program has a memory leak with respect to the memory to which the pointer y_data points. The program produces the following output:

```
X's constructor invoked
Y's constructor invoked
X's destructor invoked
```

which is the same as for Case 1.

Case 3:

This case is the same as the previous one, except that now we show a correct program, in the sense that the derived class is now provided with a destructor of its own.

```
//DerivedDestructCase3.cc

#include <iostream>
using namespace std;

class X {                              // BASE
public:
    int* x_data;
    int x_size;
    //constructor:
```

```cpp
        X( int* ptr, int sz ) : x_size(sz) {
            cout << "X's constructor invoked" << endl;
            x_data = new int[ x_size ];
            int i=0;
            int* temp = x_data;
            while (i++<x_size)
                *temp++ = *ptr++;
        }
        //destructor:
        ~X() {
            cout << "X's destructor invoked" << endl;
            delete [] x_data;
        }
};

class Y : public X {                      // DERIVED
    int* y_data;
    int y_size;
public:
    //constructor:
    Y( int* xptr, int xsz, int* yptr, int yz)
        : X( xptr, xsz ), y_size( yz ) {
        cout << "Y's constructor invoked" << endl;
        y_data = new int[ y_size ];
        int i=0;
        int* temp = y_data;
        while (i++<x_size)
            *temp++ = *yptr++;
    }
    //destructor:
    ~Y() {
        cout << "Y's destructor invoked" << endl;
        delete [] y_data;
    }
};

int main()
{
    int freshData[100] = {0};
    int moreFreshData[ 1000 ] = {1};
    Y* yptr = new Y( freshData, 100, moreFreshData, 1000 );
    delete yptr;
    return 0;
}
```

When this program is run, the following messages are printed out:

```
X's constructor invoked
Y's constructor invoked
Y's destructor invoked
X's destructor invoked
```

Now the memory leak in Y is plugged. So the upshot is that if a destructor is not defined for a derived class, the system goes ahead and uses the base class destructor for destroying the base-class subobject inside the derived-class object. Not telling the system how to destroy the rest of a derived-class object can result in memory leaks if the derived-class object appropriates system resources apart from the system resources appropriated by any base-class subobjects contained therein.

The program output shown above demonstrates again that while a derived-class object is constructed base up, the destruction takes place in the reverse order. That is, the derived-class subobject is destroyed before the base-class subobject.

15.7   VIRTUAL MEMBER FUNCTIONS IN C++

In Chapter 3, we mentioned that in Java every member function defined for a class exhibits polymorphic behavior.[4] But, in C++, a member function must be declared virtual in order for it to behave polymorphically. So a C++ class can have member functions that are just that — *functions* — and member functions that behave polymorphically and are therefore methods.[5] When a C++ member function is declared virtual in a base class, and then when it is subsequently invoked on an object of a derived class, the system automatically chooses that definition of the function that is most applicable to the object provided the objects are manipulated through pointers or references. A virtual member function defined in a base class stays virtual in a derived class even if it is not explicitly declared virtual in the derived class.

To demonstrate the polymorphism achieved by declaring a member function virtual, we will consider a base class Employee and a derived class Manager, as in Figure 15.7. We will consider the following two situations for this two-class hierarchy:

- An Employee base class with a print() member function, and a Manager derived class with a print() member function of its own.

- Same as above, except that we will now declare the base-class print() member function virtual.

We will show that the print() function will not behave polymorphically in the first case, whereas it will in the second case. In the first case, when we invoke print() on

---

[4]We also mentioned in Chapter 3 that a member function must behave polymorphically in order to be called a method. Therefore, all member functions in Java are methods.

[5]However, as we mentioned earlier, this usage distinction between the words *function* and *method* is not followed strictly in the literature. It is common to refer to both functions and methods as just functions.

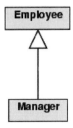

Fig. 15.7

a collection of Employee objects some of whom may actually be Manager objects, the print() function used will be the one for the Employee class. By contrast, when we do the same in the second case, the system will automatically figure out at run time the true identity of each Employee object and, when the object is actually a Manager, invoke the print() defined for the Manager class.

Case 1:

We show an Employee base class and a Manager derived class, each with its own print() member function in lines (A) and (B), respectively:

```
class Employee {                         // BASE
    string firstName, lastName;
    //.....
public:
    Employee( string fnam, string lnam ) {
        firstName = fnam; lastName = lnam;
    }
    void print() const {                                //(A)
        cout << firstName << " " << lastName << " ";
    }
};

class Manager : public Employee {      // DERIVED
    short level;
    //..
public:
    Manager( string fnam, string lnam, short lvl )
            : Employee( fnam, lnam ), level( lvl ) {}
    void print() const {                                //(B)
        Employee::print();
        cout << " works at level: " << level << endl;
    }
}
```

Now consider the following declaration that constructs a vector of pointers to `Employee` objects:

```
vector<Employee*> empList;
```

and let's say we have the following Employees in an organization:

```
Employee* e1 = new Employee( "john", "doe" );
Employee* e2 = new Employee( "jane", "doe" );
Manager* e3 = new Manager( "mister", "bigshot", 2);
Manager* e4 = new Manager( "ms", "importante", 10);
```

Note that for the last two employees, we could also have said [6]

```
Employee* e3 = new Manager( "mister", "bigshot", 2);
Employee* e4 = new Manager( "ms", "importante", 3);
```

We will now insert the four employees into the vector declared earlier:

```
empList.push_back( e1 );
empList.push_back( e2 );
empList.push_back( e3 );
empList.push_back( e4 );
```

Note that regardless of whether we declare e3 and e4 as `Manager*` or `Employee*`, these will be stored in the vector `empList` as `Employee*` because we declared `empList` to be a vector whose elements are of type `Employee*`. Keeping in mind that all items in `empList` will be stored as `Employee*`, we now want to be able to write a print loop like

```
vector<Employee*>::iterator p = empList.begin();          //(C)
while ( p < empList.end() )
  (*p++)->print();                                        //(D)
```

and, in line (D), we want that `print()` function to be invoked for each item in the vector which is most applicable to the item. So for e1 and e2, we want the function `Employee::print()` to be used, whereas for e3 and e4 we want the system to use `Manager::print()` automatically.

As things stand now, that is not what's going to happen. As the system goes through each item in the vector, it will apply the `Employee::print()` to each item. As a result, the output on the terminal will look like

```
john doe
jane doe
mister bigshot
ms importante
```

---

[6]This works because we declared `Employee` to be a public base of `Manager`, meaning that a `Manager*` can be assigned to an `Employee*` without explicit type conversion.

Case 2:

If we want the system to automatically use `Manager::print()` for items of type `Manager*`, we have to declare the function `print()` as a virtual function in the base class. So the definition of the base class will have to change to look like

```
class Employee {
    string firstName, lastName;
    //.....
public:
    Employee( string fnam, string lnam ) {
        firstName = fnam;
        lastName = lnam;
    }
    virtual void print() const {                              //(E)
        cout << firstName << " " << lastName << " ";
    }
};
```

Pay attention to the keyword *virtual* that appears in the header of the base class function `print()` in line (E).[7] Declaring `print()` virtual in the base class causes the print loop of line (C) to output

```
john doe
jane joe
mister bigshot  works at level: 2
ms importante  works at level: 3
```

A virtual function in a base class acts like an interface to the corresponding functions defined for the derived classes. If there exists in the derived class a definition for the same function, the runtime will ensure that the correct definition of the function is used for each object.

Here is the source code for this example:

```
//VirtualPrint1.cc

#include <iostream>
#include <string>
#include <vector>
using namespace std;

class Employee {                          // BASE
    string firstName, lastName;
public:
```

---

[7]We could also have written this function as `void virtual print(){ ...... }`.

```
    Employee( string fnam, string lnam ) {
        firstName = fnam;
        lastName = lnam;
    }
    virtual void print() const {                          //(F)
        cout << firstName << " " << lastName << " ";
    }
    virtual ~Employee(){}                                 //(G)
};

class Manager : public Employee {         // DERIVED
    short level;
public:
    Manager( string fnam, string lnam, short lvl )
        : Employee( fnam, lnam ), level( lvl ) {}
    void print() const {                                  //(H)
        Employee::print();
        cout << " works at level: " << level;
    }
    ~Manager(){}
};

int main()
{
    vector<Employee*> empList;

    Employee* e1 = new Employee( "john", "doe" );
    Employee* e2 = new Employee( "jane", "joe" );
    Employee* e3 = new Manager( "mister", "bigshot", 2 );
    Employee* e4 = new Manager( "ms", "importante", 3);

    empList.push_back( e1 );
    empList.push_back( e2 );
    empList.push_back( e3 );
    empList.push_back( e4 );

    vector<Employee*>::iterator p = empList.begin();
    while ( p < empList.end() ) {
        (*p++)->print();
        cout << endl;
    }

    delete e1;
    delete e2;
    delete e3;
    delete e4;
    return 0;
}
```

Line (F) of the program above defines a virtual `print()` function in the base class `Employee`. This function is overridden in the derived class `Manager` in line (H).

The reason for why the base class destructor in line (G) has been declared virtual will be made clear in Section 15.10.

15.7.1 Restrictions on Virtual Function Declarations

A requirement on a virtual function is that such a function must be defined for the class in which it is first declared, unless it is declared to be a pure virtual function (a concept defined in Section 15.12).

Additionally, although a virtual function will typically be in the protected or the public sections of a class, since only those members are visible in a derived class, *it is legal and sometimes very useful to define a virtual function in the private section of a class.* Later in Section 15.9 we will show an example of a private virtual function.

15.7.2 Virtual Functions in Multilevel Hierarchies

Consider the 3-level hierarchy of Figure 15.8. Suppose we define a `print()` function

Fig. 15.8

to be virtual in class `Person` and then provide override definitions for this function in `Employee` and `Manager` classes. Now suppose we create a vector of `Employee` objects by

```
vector<Employee*> empList;

Employee* e1 = new Employee( "mister", "bigshot", 2 );
Employee* e2 = new Employee( "ms", "importante", 3);
Manager* m3  = new Manager( "mister", "biggun", 5, 2 );
Manager* m4  = new Manager( "ms", "shiningstar", 5, 2 );
```

```
empList.push_back( e1 );
empList.push_back( e2 );
empList.push_back( m3 );
empList.push_back( m4 );
```

Will the print() function exhibit polymorphic behavior on this list of Employee objects even though the virtual declaration was made for the Person class?

The answer is yes. Once a function is declared virtual at any depth in a hierarchy, it will exhibit polymorphic behavior with respect to all classes at and below that level in the hierarchy. The following source code can be used to exercise this idea:

```
//VirtualPrint2.cc

#include <iostream>
#include <string>
#include <vector>
using namespace std;

class Person {                             // BASE
    string firstName, lastName;
public:
    Person( string fnam, string lnam )
            : firstName( fnam ), lastName( lnam ) {}
    virtual void print() const { cout << firstName          //(A)
                        << " " << lastName << " "; }
    virtual ~Person(){}                                      //(B)
};

class Employee : public Person {
    string companyName;
public:
    Employee( string fnam, string lnam, string cnam )
        : Person( fnam, lnam ), companyName( cnam ) {}
    void print() const {
        Person::print();
        cout << companyName << " ";
    }
    ~Employee(){}                                           //(C)
};


class Manager : public Employee {          // DERIVED
    short level;
public:
    Manager( string fnam, string lnam, string cnam, short lvl )
        : Employee( fnam, lnam, cnam ), level( lvl ) {}
```

```
      void print() const {
        Employee::print();
        cout << level;
      }
      ~Manager(){}                                          //(D)
};

int main()
{
      vector<Employee*> empList;

      Employee* e1 = new Employee( "mister", "bigshot", "megaCorp" );
      Employee* e2 = new Employee( "ms", "importante", "devourCorp" );
      Employee* m3 = new Manager("mister", "biggun", "plunderCorp" , 2);
      Employee* m4 = new Manager("ms", "shiningstar", "globalCorp", 2);

      empList.push_back( e1 );
      empList.push_back( e2 );
      empList.push_back( m3 );
      empList.push_back( m4 );

      vector<Employee*>::iterator p = empList.begin();
      while ( p < empList.end() ) {                         //(E)
          (*p++)->print();                                  //(F)
          cout << endl;
      }

      delete e1;
      delete e2;
      delete m3;
      delete m4;

      return 0;
}
```

This program produces the following output:

```
mister bigshot megaCorp
ms importante devourCorp
mister biggun plunderCorp 2
ms shiningstar globalCorp 2
```

With regard to the destructor statements in lines (B), (C), (D), especially with regard to the need for the virtual destructor in line (B), see the discussion in Section 15.10.

15.7.3 Can Operators Be Made to Behave Polymorphically?

While C++ functions can be made to behave polymorphically by declaring them virtual, what about the operators? Suppose we provide overload definitions for the output operator '<<' (as was shown in Section 15.5) for both the Employee class and the Manager class in the Employee–Manager example at the beginning of this section. Now suppose we include the following statements in main():

```
Employee* e_ptr = new Manager( "ms", "importante", 3);
cout << *e_ptr;            // Employee def for '<<' invoked
```

In light of our previous discussions on polymorphism, the true identity of the object pointed to by e_ptr is not known at compile time. It could either be an Employee object or it could be a Manager object. So which definition of the '<<' operator will be invoked for the above cout statement?

The answer is: The definition of the '<<' operator for the base Employee class. *Polymorphism cannot be exhibited with respect to operators.* All that is known at compile time is that e_ptr is of type Employee* and therefore the compiler will decide to use that definition of the output operator that applies to Employee objects. The only way to invoke the Manager definition is by using a cast operator, as below:

```
Employee* e_ptr = new Manager( "ms", "importante", 3);
Manager* m_ptr = static_cast<Manager*>( e_ptr );
cout << *m_ptr;            // Manager def for '<<' invoked
```

15.7.4 Polymorphic Types

A class that declares or inherits at least one virtual function defines a *polymorphic type*. If for some reason no other functions can be declared virtual, you can still create a polymorphic type by making the destructor virtual.[8] The reason for why you may want to declare a polymorphic type even when the mainstream functions are not polymorphic has to do with Run-Time Type Identification (RTTI) that we will discuss in the next chapter. RTTI works only for polymorphic types.

15.8 STATIC VERSUS DYNAMIC BINDING FOR FUNCTIONS IN C++

Ordinarily, a compiler is able to figure out which function definition to bind to a given function call. If function names are overloaded, the compiler may have to resort to overload resolution (as discussed in Chapter 9), but it will know which one of the

---

[8]As we will see in Section 15.10, there can be other important reasons for declaring a destructor to be virtual. A nonvirtual destructor can become a source of memory leaks for polymorphic types.

overload definitions to use. When the exact function definition to be invoked can be determined at compile time, we refer to that as the *static binding* of a function definition to a function call. In the following example, the constructor definition at (P) is statically bound to the constructor invocation at (R). Similarly, the constructor definition at (Q) is statically bound to the constructor invocation at (S).

```
//StaticBinding.cc

class UserProfile {
    string name;
    int age;
    // ...
public:
    UserProfile( string str, int yy )
            : name(str), age( yy ) {}                      //(P)
    UserProfile( string str )
            : name( str ) { age = averageAge(); }          //(Q)
    int averageAge(){ return 48; }
    // ...
};

int main()
{
    UserProfile user1( "Zaphod", 112 );                    //(R)
    UserProfile user2( "Trillion" );                       //(S)
    //...
    return 0;
}
```

Now let's consider the print loop in line (E) of the `main()` of `VirtualPrint2.cc` program of the previous section. A `print()` function cannot be statically bound to the invocation in the print loop because the true identity of the object pointed to by the iterator in line (F) of that program cannot be figured out at compilation time. The compiler only knows that an overridable function — overridable because `print()` was declared virtual in the base class in line (A) of `VirtualPrint2.cc` — is being invoked on an iterator that is pointing to an object of type `Employee`, but, within the `Employee` hierarchy, the more precise identity of the object pointed to is not known to the compiler. The true identity of this object can only be ascertained at run time.

Therefore, which particular version of `print()` to use for each invocation of this function in the print loop in line (F) of `VirtualPrint2.cc` can only be determined at run time. This is referred to as *dynamic binding*. When we declare a function virtual in the base class and thus make possible a run-time invocation of the correct form of the function for each derived class, we make it possible for that function to become dynamically bound.

Since for virtual functions, the choice of which specific function to invoke can only be made at run time through dynamic binding, one might wonder as to what costs are associated with dynamic binding and how these costs depend on the complexity of a class (in terms of, say, the number of virtual functions defined for a class). The rest of the discussion in this section should give the reader a sense of these costs. For most programming, these costs are completely insignificant and can safely be ignored.

virtual table for class X	
f1	pointer to the implementation code for f1
f2	pointer to the implementation code for f2

Table 15.1

Each class that either has its own virtual functions or that inherits virtual functions from a superclass is provided with a *virtual table*, commonly referred to as vtbl, that contains pointers to the implementations of the virtual functions for that class. So given a class X and its subclass Y as

```
class X {                          // BASE
    // ....
public:
    X();
    virtual void f1();
    virtual void f2();
    void f3();
    ~X();
};

class Y : public X {               // DERIVED
    //...
public:
    void f4();
    virtual f5();
};
```

the class X would have associated with it the virtual table shown in Table 15.1, and the class Y the virtual table shown in Table 15.2.

The virtual table of a class is stored somewhere in the memory outside the class and the class is given a pointer to the table. This pointer is called a *virtual table*

virtual table for class Y	
f1	pointer to the implementation code for f1
f2	pointer to the implementation code for f2
f5	pointer to the implementation code for f5

Table 15.2

pointer, commonly referred to by the symbol `vtpr`. A `vtpr` pointer is a hidden data member in every class that has at least one virtual function that may either be defined directly in the class or that may be inherited from a superclass.

To actually see the object enlargement caused by the concealed `vtpr` data member, consider the following test program in which the destructor has been declared to be virtual in order to make the class a polymorphic type:

```
//VtprConcealed.cc

#include <iostream>
using namespace std;

class X {
    int n;
public:
    X( int nn ) : n( nn ) {}
    virtual ~X(){}
};

int main(){
    cout << sizeof( X ) << endl;         // 8

    X xobj( 10 );                        // 8
    cout << sizeof( xobj ) << endl;
}
```

This small program prints out 8 bytes for the size of X, which is 4 bytes for the int data member n and additional 4 bytes for the concealed pointer data member `vtpr`. If you made the destructor nonvirtual and ran the same program, you'll only get 4 for the size of X. The additional concealed data member is stored on a per object basis since the `sizeof` operator when applied to a class type only returns the memory needed on a per-object basis.

Now let's see how a virtual table is actually used to appreciate what performance issues may arise if our program was suffused with a very large number of calls to functions that required dynamic binding. When the compiler sees the function call in line (T) of `main` in the program shown below

```
//VirtualFunctionCost.cc

class X {                           // BASE
    // ...
public:
    virtual void foo();
};

class Y : public X {                // DERIVED
    // ...
public:
    void foo();
};

int main() {
    X* p;
    // ....
    //   p could be made to point to either
    //   an X object or a Y object
    // ...
    p->foo();                                                       //(T)
    // ...
}
```

it has no way to know (at compile time) the true identity of the object to which p in main points. So all it does is to replace the call p->foo() by a piece of code that says to (i) first ascertain the true identity of the object to which the pointer p is pointing; (ii) then reach into the virtual table of the class corresponding to that object through the `vtpr` pointer data member in the object; and, finally, (iii) invoke the implementation of `foo` reached though the table. So, obviously, the invocation of a polymorphic function through dynamic binding takes a few more steps than is the case for statically bound functions. To the extent that there will be a few cpu cycles consumed by these extra steps, there is a slight performance penalty associated with polymorphic invocation of functions.

Calls to virtual functions also extract another performance penalty: interference with compiler optimizations through function inlining. As we mentioned in Chapter 9, when a compiler is allowed to inline a function, it replaces a call to that function with the body of the function. But a call to a virtual function that requires dynamic binding obviously does not allow for such code replacement, since the compiler would not know which version of the function to use at compilation time.

15.9 RESTRICTIONS ON OVERRIDING FUNCTIONS IN C++

When a function is declared virtual in a base class, it can be overridden by a function of the same signature in a derived class. The overriding function definition in the derived class must not violate certain restrictions[9] :

1. When the values returned are of primitive types, the return type of the overriding function in a derived class must be the same as the return type of the overridden function in the base class. Consider the following example:

   ```
   class X {                          // BASE
   public:
       virtual float foo( double m ) { return m; }
   };

   class Y : public X {               // DERIVED
   public:
       double foo( double n ) { return n; }       // Error
   };
   ```

   The compiler would not accept this. By using in the derived class a function of the same signature as a *virtual* function in the base class, you have told the compiler that you want to provide an overriding function in the derived class for the virtual function in the base class.[10] The compiler would now insist that the return types for both versions of `foo()` be identical. Of course, if we were to change the *parameter type* of the derived-class `foo` to, say, `float`, the compiler would not complain. The derived-class `foo` would now be considered to be a different function, not meant for overriding the base-class `foo`.

2. When the returned values are pointers or references to class types, the return type of an overriding function is allowed to be a subclass of the type returned by the base-class virtual function. In the following program, note the return type

---

[9]There are marked differences between C++ and Java with regard to the restrictions on overriding functions. The reader might wish to compare on an item-by-item basis the contents of this section with a similarly titled section later for Java.

[10]Recall from Chapter 9 that by a function signature we mean the function name, followed by an ordered list of its parameter types.

of the overriding bar() in line (B) vis-à-vis the return type of the overridden bar() in line (A).

```
//OverrideReturnRestrict.cc

#include <iostream>
using namespace std;

class X {};                          // BASE
class Y : public X {};               // DERIVED

class Base {                         // BASE
public:
    virtual X* bar() {                                          //(A)
        cout << "Base's bar invoked" << endl;
        return new X();
    }
    virtual ~Base(){}
};

class Derived : public Base {        // DERIVED
public:
    Y* bar() {                                                  //(B)
        cout << "Derived's bar invoked" << endl;
        return new Y();
    }
    ~Derived(){}
};

int main() {
    Base* b = new Derived();
    b->bar();    // program's output: Derived's bar invoked
    delete b;
    return 0;
}
```

In main of the program above, we invoke the function bar on a base-class pointer b that is actually pointing to a derived-class object. The output of the program, shown commented out in main, reveals that Derived's bar is correctly chosen for invocation at run time. (Section 15.10 explains why the destructor in the above program was declared to be virtual for the class Base.)

3. The access restriction on the base class virtual function plays no role in the legality of an override definition in a derived class. Obviously, if the base-class virtual function is in the public section, the derived class's override definition can be in either the private, or the protected, or the public section. But the same is true if the base-class virtual function is either private or protected. This

is illustrated by the following example in which the virtual function foo(), defined in line (C), is in the private section of Base. This function is invoked by the public function bar() defined in line (D). In main(), we construct a derived-class object but assign its address to a base-class pointer in line (G). When we invoke bar() on the base-class pointer in line (H), it is the derived-class version of foo(), defined in line (F), that gets executed.

```
//PrivateVirtual.cc

#include <iostream>
using namespace std;

class Base {                              // BASE
    int m;
    virtual void foo(){cout <<"Base's foo invoked"<< endl;}  //(C)
public:
    Base( int mm ) : m( mm ) {}
    void bar() { foo(); }                                    //(D)
    virtual ~Base(){}                                        //(E)
};

class Derived : public Base {          // DERIVED
    int n;
    void foo() { cout << "Derived's foo invoked" << endl; }  //(F)
public:
    Derived( int mm, int nn ) : Base( mm ), n( nn ) {}
    ~Derived(){}
};

int main() {
    Base* p = new Derived( 10, 20 );                         //(G)
    p->bar();                 //output: Derived's foo invoked  //(H)
    delete p;
    return 0;
}
```

See Section 15.10 as to why the base class destructor in line (E) has been declared virtual.

4. An overriding function in a derived class is not allowed to throw an exception that is excluded by the exception specification of the overridden function in the base class. In the following example, the virtual function foo() in line (I) in the class Base is allowed to throw an exception of type E1. The overriding foo() in Derived_1 throws an exception of type E2, a subtype of E1. Since an object of type E2 is also an object of type E1, that is permissible. However, what is shown in line (K) is not permissible. Here, the overriding foo() of Derived_2 throws an exception of type E3 that is not of type E1. So the com-

piler will not except the code in line (K).

```
//OverrideExceptionRestrict.cc

#include <iostream>
using namespace std;

class E1 {};                        // BASE exception type
class E2 : public E1 {};            // DERIVED exception type
class E3 {};

class Base {                        // BASE
    int m;
public:
    Base( int mm ) : m( mm ) {}
    virtual void foo() throw( E1 ) {                        //(I)
        cout << "Base's foo" << endl;  throw E1();
    }
    virtual ~Base() {}
};

class Derived_1 : public Base {     // DERIVED
    int n;
public:
    Derived_1( int mm, int nn ) : Base( mm ), n( nn ) {}
    void foo() throw( E2 ) {                                //(J)
        cout << "Derived_1's foo" << endl;  throw E2();
    }
    ~Derived_1() {}
};

class Derived_2 : public Base {     // DERIVED
    int p;
public:
    Derived_2( int mm, int pp ) : Base( mm ), p( pp ) {}
    // void foo() throw (E3) {}         //ERROR          //(K)
    ~Derived_2() {}
};

int main() {
    Base* p = new Derived_1( 10, 20 );
    try {
        p->foo();                                          //(L)
    } catch( E1 e ) { cout << "caught E1" << endl; }
    delete p;  return 0;
}
```

The output of the program is

```
Derived_1's foo
caught E1
```

indicating that even though we invoked foo on a base-class pointer in line (L) of main, it was the Derived_1's definition of foo that was used.

15.10 VIRTUAL DESTRUCTORS IN C++

The previous section showed three programs, OverrideReturnRestrict.cc, PrivateVirtual.cc and OverrideExceptionRestrict.cc, in which we declared the base class destructors to be virtual. Each of these programs would have a memory leak if the base class destructor was not declared virtual. The main in these programs invokes delete on a base-class pointer that is actually pointing to a derived-class object. If the base class destructor is not virtual, invoking delete on a base-class pointer will only delete the base-class subobject inside the derived class object. What's interesting here is that, in and of themselves, the base classes in each of the three programs do not need programmer-supplied destructors since the default meaning of object destruction for these simple classes would suffice. But when we derive classes from these base classes and we want object destruction to occur polymorphically on base-class pointers, we have to explicitly supply the base classes with destructors even though they have empty bodies.

For another example, consider the case of a vector of pointers to the base-class type, where some of the pointers are actually pointing to objects of a derived-class type. Let's say that you now set up a loop in which you invoke the delete operator on each of the pointers, with the hope that the destructor invoked for each object would be the one defined specifically for it. In other words, you'd want the destructor invocation to behave polymorphically. This will only happen if you declare the destructor to be virtual in the base class.

As a simple demonstration of a virtual destructor in action, consider the following program in which the base-class X extends into the derived-class Y, which in turn extends into a further derived-class Z. The base-class X is provided with a virtual destructor, declared in line (A) and defined in line (B). As we will demonstrate, this declaration causes the destructor invocations in the 3-layer class hierarchy to behave polymorphically.

```
//VirtualDestructor.cc

#include <iostream>
using namespace std;

class X {                        // BASE
public:
    virtual ~X();                                        //(A)
};
```

```
X::~X(){ cout << "X's destructor" << endl; }                          //(B)

class Y : public X {                    // DERIVED
public:
    ~Y() { cout << "Y's destructor" << endl; }
};

class Z : public Y {                    // DERIVED
public:
    ~Z() { cout << "Z's destructor" << endl; }
};

int main() {
    X* p = new Z();                                                   //(C)
    delete p;                                                         //(D)
    return 0;
}
```

In `main` of the above program, we construct an object of type Z and assign it to a base-class pointer of type X* in line (C). When we invoke `delete` on this pointer in line (D), we get the following output from the program:

```
Z's destructor
Y's destructor
X's destructor
```

implying that the runtime correctly identified the true identity of the object — it being of type Z — pointed to by p and thus invoked the destructor for Z. The Z destructor called Y's destructor to destroy the Y slice of the Z object. And, Y's destructor called the X's destructor for destroying the X slice inside the Y subobject. That accounts for the 3-line output of the program. The program would display the same correct behavior even if replace the statements in lines (C) and (D) of `main` by

```
Y* q = new Z();                                                      //(E)
delete q;                                                            //(F)
```

Knowing that object destruction is to behave polymorphically in all classes derived from X, the runtime will seek out the true identity of the object pointed to by q and then invoke the destructor for that object. So, as before, Z's destructor will be invoked again and the same 3-line ouput produced.

If the keyword `virtual` was dropped in line (A) of the program, the output of the `VirtualDestructor.cc` program would be

```
X's destructor
```

implying that only the X slice of the Z object of line (C) was getting destroyed. If the statements in lines (C) and (D) are replaced by those in lines (E) and (F), then without the virtual destructor, only the Y slice of the Z object of line (E) will be destroyed, producing the output

```
Y's destructor
X's destructor
```

15.11 CONSTRUCTOR ORDER DEPENDENCIES IN C++

Order dependencies in a derived-class constructor refers to the order in which the base-class subobjects are constructed inside a derived-class object; the order in which the specified initializations for the data members of the derived class are carried out; and so on.

To give the reader a sense of what is meant by these order dependencies, consider first the case of the Base class below:

```
//ConstructorOrder.cc

#include <iostream>
using namespace std;

class X {
public:
    X() { cout << "X object under construction" << endl; }
};

class Y {
public:
    Y() { cout << "Y object under construction" << endl; }
};

class Base {
    X xobj;                                                 //(A)
    Y yobj;                                                 //(B)
public:
    Base() : xobj( X() ), yobj( Y() ) {}                    //(C)
};

int main() {
    Base b;                                                 //(D)
    return 0;
}
```

When this program is executed, object construction in line (D) will call for the initializations of the data members `xobj` and `yobj` according to the code in line (C). The two initializations in line (C) will cause the following output to be produced:

```
X object under construction
Y object under construction
```

That is, in line (C) the data member `xobj` is initialized before the data member `yobj`. But if you were to switch the lines (A) and (B) in the program, but leave the code in line (C) unchanged, the following output will be produced:

```
Y object under construction
X object under construction
```

This example illustrates that if a constructor includes member initialization code for the data members of the class, the data members will be initialized in the order in which they are defined for the class. This order may not be the same order as indicated by the programmer in the member initialization syntax.

This order dependency of a constructor carries over to derived-class constructors. However, now we also have to worry about the order in which the base-class subobjects are constructed in the derived-class object. As we will show in the next chapter, C++ allows for multiple inheritance, meaning that a derived class can have multiple bases.

The official rules for the order in which the code for a derived-class constructor is executed are:

1. When a derived-class constructor is invoked, first the memory needed for constructing the derived-class object is appropriated.

2. Next, the constructor of the base class is called to construct the base-class slice of the derived-class object. (If the derived class has multiple bases, the base-class constructor for each base is invoked in the order in which the bases are declared in the header of the derived class, and regardless of the order used by the programmer in his/her coding of the derived-class constructor.)

3. If the derived-class constructor uses the member initialization syntax for the data member of the derived class, the initializers are invoked in the order in which the data members are declared in the class definition, and regardless of the order they are shown in the member initialization syntax by the programmer.

4. Finally, the code in the body of the derived-class constructor is executed.

Let's see what the second rule above implies when we try to construct an object of type `Manager` in the three-class inheritance chain of Figure 15.8. The construction of a `Manager` object begins with a call to an `Employee` constructor. But the `Employee` constructor will in turn call the `Person` constructor. During this process, the `Manager` object under construction will change its type identity as each direct or indirect base class constructor is successfully called.[11]

The fact that the type identity of an object under construction changes has an important bearing on which virtual function gets chosen for invocation if the base constructor code invokes such a function. To illustrate this point, both the base class and the derived class in the following example possess a virtual function named foo(). This function is invoked in line (A) during the construction of a base-class object using the no-arg constructor. This no-arg constructor will be called upon to construct the base-class slice of the derived-class object d in line (E). The question now is, Which foo() would be invoked, the base-class's foo() or the derived-class's foo()? On the basis of the explanation provided in the previous paragraph, it is Base's foo().[12]

```
//ConstructorOrderFoo.cc

#include <iostream>
using namespace std;

class Base {
public:
    Base() { foo(); }                                       //(A)
    virtual void foo() {                                    //(B)
        cout << "Base's foo invoked" << endl;
    }
};

class Derived : public Base {
public:
    Derived() {}                                            //(C)
    void foo() {                                            //(D)
        cout << "Derived's foo invoked" << endl;
    }
};

int main() {
    Derived d;              // invokes Base's foo()         //(E)
    return 0;
}
```

---

[11]The source of this insight is an explanation provided by James Kuyper Jr. in response to a query posted by the author on the comp.std.c++ newsgroup.

[12]As we will see later, Java will select Derived's foo() in a similar situation.

15.12 ABSTRACT CLASSES IN C++

In Chapter 3, we pointed out the importance of abstract classes in object-oriented programming. This section expands on that discussion for the case of C++. As a follow-up to the earlier discussion, consider the class hierarchy of Figure 15.9 in which the class Shape is abstract. We will use the base class Shape to lend organization to the shape hierarchy; this we will accomplish by making Shape a repository of all things common to all the concrete shape classes.

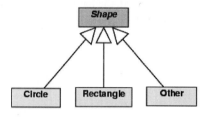

Fig. 15.9

Let's say that we want each of the concrete shapes to have the following two functions.

```
double area( );
double circumference();
```

and that we wish for the hierarchy to exhibit polymorphic behavior with respect to these two functions. We'll therefore "deposit" these functions in Shape and, to achieve polymorphism with respect to these functions, declare them virtual:

```
class Shape {
public:
  virtual double area( );
  virtual double circumference();
  //....
};
```

But now we run into a problem: C++ syntax demands that a function be defined in the class in which it is declared virtual (see Section 15.7.1). However, it makes no sense to define these two functions for Shape. While we need Shape to tie together all the other classes in the shape hierarchy, this class by itself is a purely abstract concept. We'd never make objects of type Shape. (That's the reason the class does not even need a constructor.)

C++ gives us a way out of this dilemma: declare the functions area() and circumference() to be *pure* virtual functions in the Shape class. A virtual function is "made pure" by the initializer '=0' shown below:

```
class Shape {
public:
  virtual double area( ) = 0;
  virtual double circumference() = 0;
  //....
};
```

Now the functions `area()` and `circumference()` will again be able to act as interfaces to the functions of the same names in the derived classes even though these functions are not defined for the base class Shape. Therefore, now we can write code like

```
Shape* shapes[ 3 ];
shapes[0] = new Circle( ... );
shapes[1] = new Rectangle( ..... );
shapes[2] = new Rectangle( ..... );

double total_area = 0;
for (int i=0; i < 3; i++ )
  total_area += shapes[i]->area();                       //(A)
```

Note polymorphism in action in line (A). At run time, the system will be able to figure out which `area()` function to invoke for what Shape object. For the shape object `shapes[0]`, the `area()` defined for the Circle class will be invoked. For the other two Shape objects, the `area()` function defined for the Rectangle class will be invoked. The following source code shows this example more fully:

```
//AbstractShape.cc

#include <iostream>
using namespace std;

class Shape {
public:
    virtual double area() = 0;
    virtual double circumference() = 0;
};

class Circle : public Shape {
protected:
    double r;
    static double PI;
public:
    Circle() { r = 1.0; }
    Circle( double r ) { this->r = r; }
    double area() { return PI*r*r; }
    double circumference() { return 2 * PI * r; }
    double getRadius() {return r;}
};
```

```
double Circle::PI = 3.14159265358979323846;

class Rectangle : public Shape {
    double w, h;
public:
    Rectangle() { w=0.0; h = 0.0; }
    Rectangle( double w, double h ) { this->w = w; this->h = h; }
    double area() { return w * h; }
    double circumference() { return 2 * (w + h); }
    double getWidth() { return w; }
    double getHeight() { return h; }
};

int main()
{
    Shape* shapes[ 3 ];
    shapes[0] = new Circle( 2.0 );
    shapes[1] = new Rectangle( 1.0, 3.0 );
    shapes[2] = new Rectangle( 4.0, 2.0 );
    double total_area = 0;
    for (int i=0; i < 3; i++ )
        total_area += shapes[i]->area();
    cout << "Total area = " << total_area << endl;
    return 0;
}
```

A C++ class is abstract if it has at least one virtual function that is pure. A pure virtual function is also called an *abstract method* or an *abstract function*

A pure virtual function that is not defined in a derived class remains a pure virtual function. So, in such a case, the derived class is also an abstract class. This, as was pointed out in Chapter 3, allows us to build an implementation in stages. To illustrate, consider the hierarchy of Figure 15.10. The source code shown below is a partial implementation of this hierarchy. We now include an abstract class Polygon, which is abstract because Polygon is derived from the abstract class Shape and because it does not provide implementations for the abstract methods of Shape. The class Polygon includes two data members, numVertices and starShaped, that are inherited by the classes derived from Polygon. We now also include a class CurvedShape, again abstract for the same reasons that Polygon is abstract, and for the additional reason that it includes a pure virtual function polygonalApprox(). In computer graphics, curved shapes often have associated with them polygonal approximations. The method polygonalApprox() is supposed to return a polygonal approximation to a curved shape.

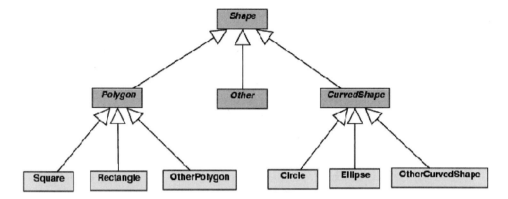

Fig. 15.10

```
//AbstractShapeIncremental.cc

#include <iostream>
using namespace std;

class Shape {
public:
    virtual double area() = 0;
    virtual double circumference() = 0;
};

class Polygon : public Shape {
protected:
    int numVertices;
    bool starShaped;
};

class CurvedShape : public Shape {
public:
    virtual void polygonalApprox() = 0;
};

class Circle : public CurvedShape {
protected:
    double r;
    static double PI;
public:
    Circle() { r = 1.0; }
    Circle( double r ) { this->r = r; }
    double area() { return PI*r*r; }
    double circumference() { return 2 * PI * r; }
```

```
        double getRadius() {return r;}
        void polygonalApprox() {
            cout << "polygonal approximation code goes here" << endl;
        }
};

double Circle::PI = 3.14159265358979323846;

class Rectangle : public Polygon {
        double w, h;
public:
    Rectangle() { w=0.0; h = 0.0; numVertices = 0; starShaped = true; }
    Rectangle( double w, double h ) {
            this->w = w;
            this->h = h;
            numVertices = 4;
            starShaped = true;
    }
    double area() { return w * h; }
    double circumference() { return 2 * (w + h); }
    double getWidth() { return w; }
    double getHeight() { return h; }
};

int main()
{
    Shape* shapes[ 3 ];
    shapes[0] = new Circle( 2.0 );
    shapes[1] = new Rectangle( 1.0, 3.0 );
    shapes[2] = new Rectangle( 4.0, 2.0 );

    double total_area = 0;
    for (int i=0; i < 3; i++ )
      total_area += shapes[i]->area();
    cout << "Total area = " << total_area << endl;
    return 0;
}
```

15.13 PROTECTED AND PRIVATE DERIVED CLASSES IN C++

In all the example of C++ derived classes we have shown so far, the base class was
extended through a *public* derivation, as in

```
    class Derived_class :  public Base_class {
      //...
    };
```

All of the discussion we have had so far about inheritance and how polymorphism works applies to this situation. This type of inheritance is also referred to as *type inheritance*. This is the kind of inheritance that is needed for defining subtypes of a type.

There are two other kinds of class derivations that are permissible in C++: *private* and *protected*. A private derivation, created by syntax of the form

```
class Derived_class :  private Base_class {
  //...
};
```

results in what's referred to as *implementation inheritance*. This name reflects the fact that this kind of derivation is good primarily for using locally the public and the protected interface of the base class, but not for making this inherited interface available to other classes, or even to further derived classes. A special case of the implementation inheritance is the *protected inheritance* obtained by a protected derivation, as in

```
class Derived_class :  protected Base_class {
  //...
};
```

Now the public and the protected interface inherited from the base class is made available for inheritance to the subclasses of the `Derived_class`.

Before we show an example of implementation inheritance, it needs to be emphasized that when you do not carry out a public derivation, you can no longer assign a `Derived*` to a `Base*` without explicit conversion. For example, in our `Employee–Manager` example, if we had derived `Manager` using the following syntax

```
class Manager :  protected Employee {
  // same as before
};
```

we would no longer be allowed to say

```
Employee* e3 = new Manager( "ms", "importante" );
```

because a `Manager` is no longer automatically an `Employee`. Now if we wish to make a single list, in the form of a vector, of `Employee*` types, we must first use explicit conversion as in

```
Employee* e3 = (Employee*) new Manager( "ms", "importante" );
```

But then, if a `Manager` was meant to be an `Employee`, it would be an error to carry out a protected or a private derivation of `Manager` from `Employee`.

Let's now try to gain a deeper understanding of what is meant by private and protected class derivations. In the following example, `Manager` is a subtype of `Employee`, and `Director` is a subtype of `Manager`. At the same time, `Manager` has a private

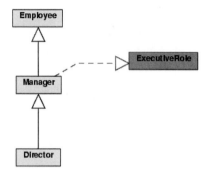

inheritance from the class ExecutiveRole. We can visualize the hierarchy in the manner shown in Figure 15.11 where solid lines indicate public derivations (and therefore type inheritance) and the dashed line a private inheritance (and therefore an implementation inheritance). The following rather trivial definition of the class ExecutiveRole will suffice for our example:

```
class ExecutiveRole {
public:
    void sayExecutiveHello() {
        cout << "Hello from Executive ranks" << endl;
    }
};
```

The private inheritance allows the Manager class to treat the public interface of ExecutiveRole as a private interface. In other words, the class Manager has full access to the nonprivate section of ExecutiveRole, but Manager treats this inheritance as if it belonged to its private section. What that implies is that this interface inherited from ExecutiveRole is not made available to any other classes, including any derived from Manager.

That should explain the reason why the following program does *not* compile if we use the commented out line for the header of the class definition of Manager — that is, if it says 'private' in the derivation of Manager from ExecutiveRole. The reason for not compiling in that case is the function sayExecutiveHello() that is invoked in the Director class in line (B). Note that there is no problem accessing sayExecutiveHello() in the Manager class itself in line (A), but the function is not inherited by the Director class if Manager has a private derivation from ExecutiveRole.

On the other hand, the program runs fine as shown — that is, when Manager has a protected derivation from the ExecutiveRole class. In a protected derivation, the public interface of a base class is made available to other classes that may be derived from the class in question. In our example, when Manager has a protected derivation from ExecutiveRole, the function sayExecutiveHello() becomes visible in the Director class.

```
//ImplementationInherit.cc

#include <iostream>
#include <string>
#include <vector>
using namespace std;

class Employee {
    string firstName, lastName;
    int age, yearsInService;
public:
    Employee( string fnam, string lnam )
        : firstName( fnam ), lastName( lnam ) {}
    virtual void print() const {
        cout << firstName << " " << lastName << endl;
    }
    void sayEmployeeHello() {
        cout << "hello from Employee class" << endl;
    }
};

class ExecutiveRole {
public:
    void sayExecutiveHello(){
        cout << "Hello from Executive ranks" << endl;
    }
};

//class Manager
//        : public Employee, private ExecutiveRole { // WILL NOT COMPILE
class Manager
        : public Employee, protected ExecutiveRole {  // WORKS FINE
    short level;
public:
    Manager( string fnam, string lnam, short lvl )
        : Employee( fnam, lnam ), level( lvl ) {
        cout<< "In Manager constructor: ";
        sayEmployeeHello();
        sayExecutiveHello();                                    //(A)
    }
    void print() const {
        Employee::print();
        cout << "level: " << level << endl;
    }
};
```

```
class Director : public Manager {
    short grade;
public:
    Director( string fnam, string lnam, short lvl, short gd )
            : Manager( fnam, lnam, lvl ), grade( gd ) {
        cout << "In Director constructor: ";
        sayEmployeeHello();
        sayExecutiveHello();                                    //(B)
    }
    void print() const {
        Manager::print();
        cout << "grade: " << grade << endl << endl;
    }
};

int main() {
    vector<Employee*> empList;

    Employee* e1 = new Employee( "joe", "schmoe" );
    Employee* e2 = (Employee*) new Manager( "ms", "importante", 2 );
    Employee* e3 =
            (Employee*) new Director("mister", "bigshot", 3, 4);    //(C)

    empList.push_back( e1 );
    empList.push_back( e2 );
    empList.push_back( e3 );

    vector<Employee*>::iterator p = empList.begin();
    while ( p < empList.end() ) (*p++)->print();

    Manager* m = new Manager( "jane", "doe", 2 );
    m->sayEmployeeHello();

    Director* d = new Director( "john", "doe", 3, 4 );
    d->sayEmployeeHello();
    return 0;
}
```

As we will discuss in the next chapter, a C++ class can have multiple superclasses. A C++ class is allowed to have different derivation types with respect to each of its base classes. That is, a class may have public derivation with respect to some of its base classes, private derivation with respect to some others, and a protected derivation with respect to the rest.

15.14 EXTENDING CLASSES IN JAVA

What is accomplished by making a public derivation from a class in C++ (see Section 15.1) is achieved by using the "extends" clause in Java, as in the following Employee–Manager example:

```
class Employee {                           // BASE
    private String firstName, lastName;
    public Employee( String fnam, String lnam ) {
        firstName = fnam;
        lastName = lnam;
    }
    public void print() {
        System.out.print( firstName + " " + lastName );
    }
}


class Manager extends Employee {           // DERIVED
    private short level;
    public Manager( String fnam, String lnam, short lvl ) {
        super( fnam, lnam );                              //(A)
        level = lvl;
    }
    public void print() {
        super.print();                                   //(B)
        System.out.println( "level: " + level );
    }
}
```

Note how the constructor for Manager calls the constructor of the base class by invoking super(fnam, lnam) in line (A). As was pointed out earlier in Chapter 3, invocation of a base constructor has to be the first line in a derived class constructor. In common with C++, if the base constructor is not invoked explicitly in a derived class constructor, the system will automatically try to invoke the no-arg constructor for the base class. But, recall that the base class will possess a no-arg constructor either because you provided it with one, or because it has no constructors at all, in which case the system will supply the class with a default no-arg constructor.

Object construction in Java has one feature that is not shared by object construction in C++: Instead of invoking, explicitly or implicitly, a base-class constructor, a derived-class constructor is allowed to invoke another one of the constructors for the derived class by using the this invocation.

We demonstrate the above with the following version of the Manager class. In this version, we have a 2-arg constructor besides the regular 3-arg constructor. Note how the 2-arg constructor invokes in line (C) the 3-arg constructor using the `this()` construct.

```java
class Manager extends Employee {
    private short level;
    public Manager( String fnam, String lnam, short lvl ) {
        super( fnam, lnam );
        level = lvl;
    }
    public Manager( String fnam, String lnam ) {
        this( fnam, lnam, 10 );                              //(C)
    }
    public void print() {
        super.print();                                      //(D)
        System.out.println( "level: " + level );
    }
}
```

As with C++, when you extend a class in Java to create a derived class, all the protected and public data members of the base class become directly available in the derived class. Also directly visible in the derived class are those protected and public methods of the base class that are are not overridden in the derived class. In the example above, the `print()` function in the `Manager` class overrides the `print()` function in the `Employee` class. Nonetheless, the base-class `print` can still be invoked in the derived class using the keyword `super`, as we show in lines (B) and (D).

As already mentioned, one great difference between C++ and Java is that while only those functions that are declared virtual behave polymorphically in C++, in Java all member functions are polymorphic. (And, that's why, as we have mentioned before, all member functions in Java are *methods*.)

With regard to the base-class functions that are available in a derived class, another very important difference between C++ and Java is as follows: As mentioned in Section 15.1, in C++ a derived-class function of a given name hides *all* base-class functions of the same name, regardless of their signatures; the hidden names can only be accessed through the scope operator in the derived class. That is not the case in Java. This is illustrated with the help of the following two programs that are meant to do exactly the same thing. The first program shown below, in Java, compiles and runs fine with the output shown in the commented out portions of the code in `Test.main`, but the C++ program shown after that does not even compile.

In the program below, the class `Base` possesses three overloaded definitions of the function name `foo`: a no-arg `foo` in line (A), a one-arg `foo` in line (B), and a two-arg `foo` in line (C). The class `Derived` possesses its own `foo` — a no-arg version in line (D). Line (E) of `Test.main` invokes a no-arg `foo` on an object of type `Derived`. As the output shown in the same line indicates, the function definition used for this call is the one defined for `Derived`. But when we invoke a one-arg `foo` on the same `Derived` object in line (F) and a two-arg `foo` in line (G), the definitions used are those for Base. What this establishes is that the use the function name foo in Derived does *not* hide *all* functions of name foo in Base — contrary to what happens in C++.

```
//NameLookup.java

class Base {
    public void foo() {                                          //(A)
        System.out.println( "Base's foo() invoked" );
    }
    public void foo( int i ) {                                   //(B)
        System.out.println( "Base's foo( int ) invoked" );
    }
    public void foo( int i, int j ) {                            //(C)
        System.out.println( "Base's foo( int, int ) invoked" );
    }
}

class Derived extends Base {
    public void foo() {                                          //(D)
        System.out.println( "Derived's foo() invoked" );
    }
}

public class Test {
    public static void main( String[] args )
    {
        Derived d = new Derived();
        d.foo();               // Derived's foo() invoked        //(E)
        d.foo( 3 );            // Base's foo( int ) invoked      //(F)
        d.foo( 3, 4 );         // Base's foo( int, int ) invoked //(G)
    }
}
```

Now compare the above Java program with its C++ version shown below. The C++ version does not even compile. The error message returned by the compiler is

```
in function 'int main()':
    no matching function for call to 'Derived::foo (int)'
    candidates are: void Derived::foo()
    no matching function for call to 'Derived::foo(int, int)'
    candidates are: void Derived::foo()
```

which shows the function foo() defined in Derived in line (D) below hides all versions of foo defined in Base. So Base's foo(int) and foo(int,int) defined in lines (B) and (C) below are simply not available in Derived — at least not available for unqualified access — even though they are not being overridden.

```
//NameLookup.cc                         // WILL NOT COMPILE

#include <iostream>
using namespace std;

class Base {
public:
    void foo() {                                        //(A)
        cout << "Base's foo() invoked" << endl;
    }
    void foo( int i ) {                                 //(B)
        cout << "Base's foo( int ) invoked" << endl;
    }
    void foo( int i, int j ) {                          //(C)
        cout << "Base's foo( int, int ) invoked" << endl;
    }
};

class Derived : public Base {
public:
    void foo() { cout << "Derived's foo() invoked"  << endl; }    //(D)
};

int main()
{
    Derived d;
    d.foo();                                            //(E)
    d.foo( 3 );                                         //(F)
    d.foo( 3, 4 );                                      //(G)
}
```

To capture in C++ the name lookup behavior of Java that we showed in the program
NameLookup.java, we would need to change the code in main above to:

```
    int main()
    {
        Derived d;
        d.foo();
        d.Base::foo(3);
        d.Base::foo(3,4);
    }
```

where we used the scope operator to access the hidden function names of Base.

15.15   RESTRICTIONS ON OVERRIDING METHODS IN JAVA

The definition of an overriding method in a derived class must not violate the following restrictions:[13]

1. The return type of an overriding method in a derived class must be the same as the return type of the overridden method in the base class. Consider the following example:

```
class X {                                        // BASE
    public float foo( double m ) { return m; }
}

class Y extends public X {                       // DERIVED
    public double foo( double n ) { return n; }      // Error
}
```

The compiler would not accept this. By using in the derived class a method of the same signature as a method in the base class, you have told the compiler that you want to provide an overriding method in the derived class for the method foo in the base class. The compiler would now insist that the return types for both versions of foo() be identical. Of course, if we were to change the parameter type of the derived-class foo to, say, float, the compiler would not complain. The derived-class foo would now be considered to be a different function, not meant for overriding the base-class foo. In contrast with C++, this restriction on the return type of an overriding method applies regardless of whether the return type is a primitive or a class-type object. Recall that for C++, for class type returns, the overriding function is allowed to have a return type that is a subtype of the value returned by the overridden function.

2. The access restriction for an overriding method can be no tighter than the restriction on the base-class overridden method. So if the access restriction on the base-class method is, say, protected, the overriding method in the derived class can either be protected or public, but not private. Unlike with C++, a method declared in the private section of a class cannot be overridden. To illustrate this difference between C++ and Java, the following program is the Java version of the C++ program PrivateVirtual.cc shown earlier in Section 15.9. As with the C++ program, the classes Base and Derived each define a private method foo() in lines (A) and (C), respectively. Contrary to what happened in the C++ program, the Derived's foo() does *not* override Base's foo() here. This is made evident by our constructing a Derived object and assigning it to a variable p of type Base in line (G). Invoking Base's bar() on p in line (H) only invokes Base's foo(). In other words, the foo() of Base does not

---

[13]The reader is urged to carry out a point-by-point comparison of the restrictions listed here with those for C++ in Section 15.9.

behave polymorphically.

```
//OverrideAccessRestrict.java

class Base {
    private int m;
    private void foo(){                                          //(A)
        System.out.println("Base's foo invoked" );
    }
    public Base( int mm ) { m = mm; }
    public void bar() { foo(); }                                 //(B)
}

class Derived extends Base {
    private int n;
    private void foo() {                                         //(C)
        System.out.println( "Derived's foo invoked" );
    }
    public Derived( int mm, int nn ) {                           //(D)
        super( mm );   n = nn;
    }
}

class Test {
    public static void main( String[] args ) {
        Base p = new Derived( 10, 20 );                          //(G)
        p.bar();              //output: Base's foo invoked       //(H)
    }
}
```

---

3. The exception specification for an overriding function in a derived class must be a subset of the exception specification on the overridden base-class method. For illustration, the following example code will elicit a compiler error. The compiler will take notice of the fact that foo() in the derived class Y has the same signature as foo() in the base class X. Therefore, the compiler will assume that the derived class foo() is meant to override the base class foo(). But the compiler will refuse to accept the provided override definition because the exception specification for Y's foo() in line (B) below is not a subset of the exception specification for X's foo() in line (A).

```
class Exception_1 extends Exception {}

class Exception_2 extends Exception {}

class X {                                      // BASE
    private int m;
    public  X( int mm ) { m = mm; }
    public void foo() throws Exception_1  {              //(A)
        System.out.println( "X's foo invoked" );
        throw new Exception_1();
    }
}


class Y extends X {                            // DERIVED
    private int n;
    public Y( int mm, int nn ) { super( mm ); n = nn; }
    public void foo() throws Exception_2  {              //(B)
        System.out.println( "Y's foo invoked" );
        throw new Exception_2();
    }
}
```

The reader will recall that C++ places a similar restriction on the exception specifications for overriding functions.

In the above example, it would be perfectly okay to have the overriding foo() of Y to throw no exceptions at all, since a null set is a subset of every set. So, in the following code fragment, Y's foo() is a legal overriding method for X's foo().

```
class Exception_1 extends Exception {}

class Exception_2 extends Exception {}

class X {
    private int m;
    public  X( int mm ) { m = mm; }
    public void foo() throws Exception_1  {
        System.out.println( "X's foo invoked" );
        throw new Exception_1();
    }
}
```

```
class Y extends X {
    private int n;
    public Y( int mm, int nn ) { super( mm ); n = nn; }
    public void foo()  {
        System.out.println( "Y's foo invoked" );
    }
}
```

15.16 CONSTRUCTOR ORDER DEPENDENCIES IN JAVA

The order in which constructors are invoked and the data members initialized for a derived-class object in Java is given by the following:

1. Invoke the constructor of the derived class by appropriating the required amount of memory and set all the data members in this memory to their default values (zero for all numeric types, `false` for boolean, '\u0000' for `char`, and `null` for object reference).

2. Invoke the base-class constructor.

3. Execute the initialization code attached to any of the data members in the base class and initialize those data members accordingly.

4. Execute the code in the body of the base-class constructor. This base-class constructor could be a no-arg constructor.

5. Execute the initialization code attached to any of the data members of the derived class and initialize those data members accordingly.

6. Execute the code in the body of the derived-class constructor.

Paralleling our C++ discussion of Section 15.11, now consider classes `Base` and `Derived` as shown below, each with its own version of a method named `foo()`, this method being invoked in only the base-class constructor. The question is whether the base-class constructor will invoke the base-class `foo()` or the derived-class `foo()` when we construct an object of type `Derived`. We saw that for the C++ case, it was the base-class `foo()`. However, as can be seen from the example shown below, for the Java case it is the derived-class `foo()` that is invoked.

```
//ConstructorOrderFoo.java

class Base {
    public void foo(){ System.out.println( "Base's foo invoked" ); }
    public Base() { foo(); }
}
```

```
class Derived extends Base {
    public void foo(){ System.out.println( "Derived's foo invoked" ); }
    public Derived() {}
}

class Test {
    public static void main( String[] args )
    {
        Derived d = new Derived();              //Derived's foo() invoked
    }
}
```

What this example teaches us is that one should be careful with using overridable methods in constructors. Any method that is neither private, nor static, nor final is overridable.

15.17 ABSTRACT CLASSES IN JAVA

Chapter 3 presented the reasons for why abstract classes are important in object-oriented programming. And, Section 15.12 of this chapter discussed how abstract classes are represented in C++.

As mentioned in Section 15.12, a C++ class is abstract if it possesses at least one pure virtual function. As the reader will recall, a member function in C++ must be declared virtual if it is to behave polymorphically. If a virtual member function is also pure, then that function is an abstract function — meaning that no implementation code is provided with the function declaration. The compiler expects to see the implementation code for such a function in a derived class.

In Java, on the other hand, polymorphic behavior is guaranteed for all member functions. So no special virtual-like designation is needed to get a member function to behave polymorphically in Java. However, we still need in Java a declaration that would correspond to the designation of a function as "pure virtual" in C++. Java's term for doing the same is *abstract*. When a function header includes the keyword abstract, that means an abstract function is being declared, without implementation code. The compiler would expect to see the implementation code for such a function later in a derived class. A Java class with at least one abstract function is abstract.

In Java, abstract classes must be declared so explicitly. (Contrast this with C++ where for a class to be considered abstract, although it must possess at least one function that is pure virtual, no explicit declaration of 'abstractness' is required in the class header.) Therefore, our definition of the Shape class of Section 15.12 would now be written as

```
abstract class Shape {
    abstract public double area( );
    abstract public double draw();
    //....
}
```

If a class has at least one abstract method, the compiler thinks of that class as abstract and demands that the keyword abstract appear in the header of the class. However, a class can be abstract even without possessing any abstract methods (another point of difference from C++). We will show an example of such a class at the end of this section.

Note we used the access modifier "public" for the two abstract methods in the above example. As far as the Java compiler is considered, the only restriction on the access modifier is that it cannot be "private" because that would make no sense for an abstract method, since it has to be inherited by a derived class where its implementation code is provided.

As was the case with C++, if a class derived from an abstract base class does not provide implementations for all of the abstract methods of the base class, the derived class is also considered to be abstract. Java demands that such a derived class be declared abstract in the class header. The following source code, which is the Java version of the C++ implementation shown in Section 15.12, illustrates this. We have declared the classes Polygon and CurvedShape as abstract as they both are derived from the abstract class Shape and they both do not provide implementations for the abstract methods of Shape.

```
//AbstractShapeIncremental.java

abstract class Shape {
    abstract protected double area();
    abstract protected double circumference();
}

abstract class Polygon extends Shape {
    protected int numVertices;
    protected boolean starShaped;
}

abstract class curvedShape extends Shape {
    abstract public void polygonalApprox();
}

class Circle extends curvedShape {
    protected double r;
    protected static double PI = 3.14159;
```

```java
    public Circle() { r = 1.0; }
    public Circle( double r ) { this.r = r; }
    public double area() { return PI*r*r; }
    public double circumference() { return 2 * PI * r; }
    public double getRadius() {return r;}
    public void polygonalApprox() {
        System.out.println(
            "polygonal approximation code goes here");
    }
}

class Rectangle extends Polygon {
    double w, h;
    public Rectangle() {
        w=0.0; h = 0.0; numVertices = 0; starShaped = true;
    }
    public Rectangle( double w, double h ) {
        this.w = w;
        this.h = h;
        numVertices = 4;
        starShaped = true;
    }
    public double area() { return w * h; }
    public double circumference() { return 2 * (w + h); }
    public double getWidth() { return w; }
    public double getHeight() { return h; }
}

class Test {
    public static void main( String[] args )
    {
        Shape[] shapes = new Shape[ 3 ];
        shapes[0] = new Circle( 2.0 );
        shapes[1] = new Rectangle( 1.0, 3.0 );
        shapes[2] = new Rectangle( 4.0, 2.0 );

        double total_area = 0;
        for (int i=0; i < shapes.length; i++ )
          total_area += shapes[i].area();
        System.out.println("Total area = " + total_area);
    }
}
```

The class diagram shown in Section 15.12 also applies to the code shown above.

As already mentioned, a Java class can be abstract even if it does not have any abstract methods, provided that the class is declared to be abstract. An example of such a class is the adapter[14] class `WindowAdapter` that we will present in Chapter 17 on graphics programming in Java. Its implementation is

```
public abstract class WindowAdapter implements WindowListener {
    public void windowActivated( WindowEvent e ) {};
    public void windowClosed( WindowEvent e ) {};
    public void windowClosing( WindowEvent e ) {};
    public void windowDeactivated( WindowEvent e ) {};
    public void windowDeiconified( WindowEvent e ) {};
    public void windowIconified( WindowEvent e ) {};
    public void windowOpened( WindowEvent e ) {};
}
```

Note that every method has a do-nothing implementation. Also note that since the class is abstract, it does not need a constructor and therefore none is defined.

With regard to abstract methods, Java has one feature not possessed by C++: In a class hierarchy, any method inherited from any of the superclasses can be declared to be abstract, making that particular class in the hierarchy an abstract class. This can be useful when it is necessary to block the inherited definition of a method to one or more derived classes in a class hierarchy. Blocking inheritance in this manner was presented earlier in Chapter 3.

15.18   INTERFACES IN JAVA

While a C++ class can have more than one superclass, a Java class can have exactly one superclass. As we will discuss in the next chapter, multiple superclasses can be a powerful tool in the hands of experienced programmers. But, they can also be a source of a lot of programming difficulties for the unwary.

While the "exactly one superclass" rule of Java does avoid the pitfalls associated with multiple inheritance, it can be excessively restrictive. Java gets around this limitation by using *interfaces. An interface is a class that consists solely of abstract methods.* Since an interface is not allowed to contain any implementation code, any implementation code inherited by a derived Java class can only come from its sole superclass. This is referred to as *Java has a single inheritance of implementation.* On the other hand, a Java class can implement an arbitrary number of interfaces. This is referred to as *a Java class has multiple inheritance for interfaces.*

---

[14]As presented in Chapter 17, an adapter class in Java is a trivial implementation of an interface, trivial in the sense that all of the methods declared in the interface are given do-nothing implementations. Adapter classes are defined for purely programming convenience. Java interfaces, introduced earlier in Chapter 3, are presented more fully in the next section.

To illustrate the idea of interfaces, we will provide the Shape hierarchy of the previous section with an interface so that the shapes can be drawn on a terminal screen. If we did not have to observe the "exactly one superclass" rule of Java, we could create a new abstract class Drawable where we could place the headers of all the methods that would be needed for drawing a shape in a window on a screen. We could then define a DrawableRectangle class that could inherit from the Rectangle and the Drawable classes, with the idea that the objects of type DrawableRectangle would know how to draw themselves (upon the invocation of a suitable "draw" method) on the screen. We can do this in C++, but not in Java on account of the "only one superclass" rule.

So in Java, we resort to declaring an interface Drawable by [15]

```
interface Drawable {
    public void setColor( Color c );
    public void setPosition( double x, double y );
    public void draw( DrawWindow dw );
}
```

All the methods declared in an interface are implicitly abstract. We have omitted the keyword abstract in this example, but it would be legal to use it to make explicit the abstract nature of these method declarations. We can now define a class DrawableRectangle in the following manner:

```
class DrawableRectangle extends Rectangle implements Drawable {
    private Color c;
    private double x, y;
    public DrawableRectangle(double w, double h) { super( w, h ); }
    //here are the implementations of the methods
    //inherited from the interface Drawable:
    public void setColor( Color c ) { this.c = c; }
    public void setPosition( double x, double y ) {
        this.x = x; this.y = y;
    }
    public void draw( DrawWindow dw ) {
        dw.drawRect( x, y, w, h, c );
    }
}
```

We can define a class DrawableCircle in a similar manner. The resulting class hierarchy will look like what's shown in Figure 15.12 where the inheritance from classes is shown by solid lines and that from interfaces by dashed lines.

What's interesting is that DrawableRectangle objects are not only instances of the class Shape, but also instances of the interface Drawable. In other words,

---

[15]The parameter names, such as c, x, y, and so on, in the example shown must be specified even though they do not serve any real purpose except for making the code more readable.

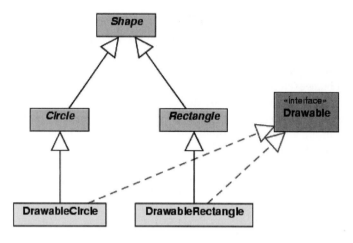

Fig. 15.12

a DrawableRectangle IsA Shape object, and, at the same time, IsA Drawable object. This implies that the hierarchy shown will display polymorphic behavior not only with respect to the methods declared in the Shape class, but also the methods declared in the Drawable interface. To illustrate this notion, let's now declare two arrays, one of type Shape and other of type Drawable:

```
Shape[] shapes = new Shape[3];
Drawable[] drawables = new Drawable[3];
```

and then let's create the following three objects

```
DrawableCircle dc = new DrawableCircle( 1.1 );
DrawableRectangle ds = new DrawableRectangle( 2.5, 3.2 );
DrawableRectangle dr = new DrawableRectangle( 2.3, 4.5 );
```

These objects can be assigned to either of the two arrays simply because each of the objects is of the two types declared for the array elements:

```
shapes[0] = dc;
shapes[1] = ds;
shapes[2] = dr;

drawables[0] = dc;
drawables[1] = ds;
drawables[2] = dr;
```

Polymorphism with respect to the methods of both the Shape class and the Drawable interface may now be demonstrated by a code fragment like the following:

```
double total_area = 0;
for (int i = 0; i < shapes.length; i++ ) {
```

```
        total_area += shapes[i].area();
        drawables[i].setPosition( i*10.0, i*10.0 );
        drawables[i].draw( draw_window );
    }
```

The above example shows that an interface defines a new type in Java, just as a class does, and that when a class implements an interface, instances of that class can be assigned to variables of the interface type. The following source code illustrates the these concepts:

```java
//MultiPolymorphism.java

abstract class Shape {
    abstract protected double area();
    abstract protected double circumference();
}

class Circle extends Shape {
    protected double r;
    protected static double PI = 3.14159;

    public Circle( double r ) { this.r = r; }
    public double area() { return PI*r*r; }
    public double circumference() { return 2 * PI * r; }
}

class Rectangle extends Shape {
    double w, h;
    public Rectangle( double w, double h ) {
        this.w = w;
        this.h = h;
    }
    public double area() { return w * h; }
    public double circumference() { return 2 * (w + h); }
}

interface Drawable {
    public void setColor( Color c );
    public void setPosition( double x, double y );
    public void draw( DrawWindow dw );
}

class DrawableRectangle extends Rectangle implements Drawable {
    private Color c;
    private double x, y;
    public DrawableRectangle( double w, double h ) { super( w, h ); }
    // Implementations of the methods inherited from the interface:
    public void setColor( Color c ) { this.c = c; }
```

```
    public void setPosition( double x, double y ) {
        this.x = x; this.y = y;
    }
    public void draw( DrawWindow dw ) { dw.drawRect( x, y, w, h, c ); }
}

class DrawableCircle extends Circle implements Drawable {
    private Color c;
    private double x, y;
    public DrawableCircle( double rad ) { super( rad ); }
    public void setColor( Color c ) { this.c = c; }
    public void setPosition( double x, double y ) {
        this.x = x; this.y = y;
    }
    public void draw( DrawWindow dw ) { dw.drawCircle( x, y, r, c ); }
}

class Color { int R, G, B; }

class DrawWindow {
    public DrawWindow() {};
    public void drawRect( double x, double y,
                double width, double height, Color col ) {
        System.out.println(
            "Code for drawing a rect needs to be invoked" );        //(A)
    }
    public void drawCircle( double x, double y,
                                double radius, Color col ) {
        System.out.println(
            "Code for drawing a circle needs to be invoked" );      //(B)
    }
}

class Test {
    public static void main( String[] args )
    {
        Shape[] shapes = new Shape[3];
        Drawable[] drawables = new Drawable[3];

        DrawableCircle dc = new DrawableCircle( 1.1 );
        DrawableRectangle dr1 = new DrawableRectangle( 2.5, 3.5 );
        DrawableRectangle dr2 = new DrawableRectangle( 2.3, 4.5 );

        shapes[0] = dc;
        shapes[1] = dr1;
        shapes[2] = dr2;

        drawables[0] = dc;
        drawables[1] = dr1;
```

```
        drawables[2] = dr2;

        int total_area = 0;
        DrawWindow dw = new DrawWindow();
        for (int i = 0; i < shapes.length; i++ ) {
            total_area += shapes[i].area();
            drawables[i].setPosition( i*10.0, i*10.0 );        //(C)
            drawables[i].draw( dw );                           //(D)
        }
        System.out.println("Total area = " + total_area);      //(E)
    }
}
```

The output produced by the statements in lines (A), (B), and (E) of this program is:

```
Code for drawing a circle needs to be invoked
Code for drawing a rect needs to be invoked
Code for drawing a rect needs to be invoked
Total area = 21
```

15.18.1 Implementing Multiple Interfaces in Java

As mentioned earlier, a class can implement more than one interface. Continuing with the Shape example, suppose we also want to scale the shapes to make them larger or smaller prior to drawing them. We could construct another interface, `Scalable`, for representing this specialized behavior:

```
interface Scalable {
    public Shape scaleTransform();
}
```

We could now define a class `DrawScalableRectangle` by extending `Rectangle` and implementing the `Drawable` and `Scalable` interfaces:

```
class DrawableScalableRectangle
        extends Rectangle
        implements Drawable, Scalable  {
    // the methods of the Drawable and Scalable interfaces
    // must be implemented here
}
```

When a class implements more than one interface, it must provide implementations for all the abstract methods declared in all of its interfaces.

15.18.2 Extending Interfaces in Java

Just as a class can extend another class, an interface can also extend another interface. In the Shape hierarchy example we presented earlier, we could extend the Drawable interface in the following manner:

```
interface Drawable {
    public void setColor( Color c );
    public void setPosition( double x, double y );
    public void draw( DrawWindow dw );
}

interface DrawScalable extends Drawable {
    public void drawScaledShape( int scaleFactor, DrawWindow dw );
}
```

Now we can create a class DrawScalableRectangle by

```
class DrawScalableRectangle
        extends Rectangle implements DrawScalable {
    private Color c;
    private double x, y;
    public DrawScalableRectangle( double w, double h ) {
        super( w, h );
    }
    // Implementations of the methods inherited
    // from the interface:
    public void setColor( Color c ) {
        this.c = c;
    }
    public void setPosition( double x, double y ) {
        this.x = x; this.y = y;
    }
    public void draw(DrawWindow dw) {dw.drawRect( x, y, w, h, c );}

    public void drawScaledShape( int scaleFactor, DrawWindow dw ){
        dw.drawScaledRect( x, y, w, h, c, scaleFactor );
    }
}
```

This class must evidently implement all the abstracts methods of DrawScalable, some of which will be the inherited abstract methods of Drawable. In the following source code, we have shown this example more fully:

```
//ExtendedInterface.java

abstract class Shape {
    abstract protected double area();
    abstract protected double circumference();
}

class Circle extends Shape {
    protected double r;
    protected static double PI = 3.14159;
    public Circle( double r ) { this.r = r; }
    public double area() { return PI*r*r; }
    public double circumference() { return 2 * PI * r; }
}

class Rectangle extends Shape {
    double w, h;
    public Rectangle( double w, double h ) {
        this.w = w;
        this.h = h;
    }
    public double area() { return w * h; }
    public double circumference() { return 2 * (w + h); }
}

interface Drawable {
    public void setColor( Color c );
    public void setPosition( double x, double y );
    public void draw( DrawWindow dw );
}

interface DrawScalable extends Drawable {
    public void drawScaledShape( int scaleFactor, DrawWindow dw );
}

class DrawScalableRectangle extends Rectangle implements DrawScalable {
    private Color c;
    private double x, y;
    public DrawScalableRectangle(double w, double h) { super( w, h ); }
    //Implementations of the methods inherited from the interface:
    public void setColor( Color c ) { this.c = c; }
    public void setPosition( double x, double y ) {
        this.x = x; this.y = y;
    }
    public void draw( DrawWindow dw ) {
        dw.drawRect( x, y, w, h, c );
    }
```

```java
    public void drawScaledShape( int scaleFactor,
                       DrawWindow dw ) {
       dw.drawScaledRect( x, y, w, h, c, scaleFactor );
    }
}

class DrawScalableCircle extends Circle implements DrawScalable {
    private Color c;
    private double x, y;
    public DrawScalableCircle( double rad ) { super( rad ); }
    public void setColor( Color c ) { this.c = c; }
    public void setPosition( double x, double y ) {
       this.x = x; this.y = y;
    }
    public void draw( DrawWindow dw ) { dw.drawCircle( x, y, r, c ); }
    public void drawScaledShape( int scaleFactor,
           DrawWindow dw ) {
       dw.drawScaledCircle( x, y, r, c, scaleFactor );
    }
}

class Color { int R, G, B; }

class DrawWindow {
    public DrawWindow() {};
    public void drawRect( double x, double y,
                double width, double height, Color col ) {
       System.out.println(                                      //(A)
         "Code for drawing a rect needs to be invoked" );
    }
    public void drawScaledRect( double x, double y, double width,
            double height, Color col, int scale ){
       System.out.println(                                      //(B)
         "Code for drawing a scaled rect needs to be invoked" );
    }
    public void drawCircle( double x, double y,
                                double radius, Color col ) {
       System.out.println(                                      //(C)
         "Code for drawing a circle needs to be invoked" );
    }
    public void drawScaledCircle( double x, double y, double radius,
                                Color col, int scale ){
       System.out.println(                                      //(D)
         "Code for drawing a scaled circle needs to be invoked" );
    }
}
```

```
class Test {
    public static void main( String[] args )
    {
        Shape[] shapes = new Shape[3];
        DrawScalable[] drawScalables = new DrawScalable[3];

        DrawScalableCircle dc = new DrawScalableCircle( 1.1 );
        DrawScalableRectangle dr1 =
                new DrawScalableRectangle( 2.5, 3.5 );
        DrawScalableRectangle dr2 =
                new DrawScalableRectangle( 2.3, 4.5 );

        shapes[0] = dc;
        shapes[1] = dr1;
        shapes[2] = dr2;

        drawScalables[0] = dc;
        drawScalables[1] = dr1;
        drawScalables[2] = dr2;

        int total_area = 0;
        DrawWindow dw = new DrawWindow();
        for (int i = 0; i < shapes.length; i++ ) {
            total_area += shapes[i].area();
            drawScalables[i].setPosition( i*10.0, i*10.0 );
            drawScalables[i].drawScaledShape( 2, dw );
        }
        System.out.println("Total area = " + total_area);        //(E)
    }
}
```

The output of this program, produced by the statements in lines (B), (D), and (E), is

```
Code for drawing a scaled circle needs to be invoked
Code for drawing a scaled rect needs to be invoked
Code for drawing a scaled rect needs to be invoked
Total area = 21
```

15.18.3 Constants in Interfaces

It is not infrequently the case that a program needs a set of constants for its execution. Java allows for convenient packaging of related constants in interfaces. When a class implements such an interface, the constants become locally available in that class, as if they were defined right there. Constants being constants must be declared "static final." Declaring them "static" makes them available to all the objects of that type and declaring them "final" causes them to be read only.

Instead of placing constants in interfaces, we could also place them inside classes, but then we would have to use the name of that class as a prefix to access the constants. For example, we could package the constant PI inside a class by saying:

```
class A { public static final double PI = 3.14159; }
```

In order to access this constant inside another class, we would have to use the class name A as a prefix as in

```
class Test {
    //....
    void foo() {
        double x = A.PI;
        //....
    }
}
```

On the other hand, if we packaged the constant in an interface as shown below:

```
interface A { public static final double PI = 3.14159; }
```

now a class that implements A can treat the constant PI as if it is locally defined:

```
class Test implements A {
    //....
    void foo() {
        double x = PI;
        //....
    }
}
```

15.19 A C++ STUDY OF A SMALL CLASS HIERARCHY WITH MODERATELY COMPLEX BEHAVIOR

In Chapter 11 (Section 11.15), we presented a C++ study of interleaved classes of moderate complexity. The purpose of that study was to demonstrate how much care one has to exercise in C++ programming with regard to memory allocation and deallocation, the interaction between classes, inadvertently accessing a null pointer, applying the `delete` operator where `delete[]` is actually needed, and so on.

In this section, we will expand on that example and present a case study that pulls together the following features of C++

- Run-time type checking.

- Employing polymorphism in operations such as the sorting of containers of base-class pointers using a criterion that depends on values stored in derived-class objects.

- Getting around the limitations caused by the fact that polymorphism does not work for operators through the invocation of overridable functions that call the locally defined operators.

These issues will be demonstrated with the help of the two interdependent class hierarchies shown in Figure 15.13. The hierarchies will be interdependent in the sense

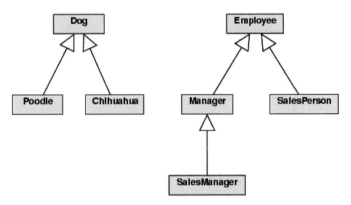

Fig. 15.13

that Dog has a data member of type Employee and Employee has a data member of type vector<Dog*>, and so on.

The actual implementation code shown in this section does not include definitions for the derived classes SalesManager and SalesPerson. This was done to keep an already long program from occupying even more space in a book. The reader is, however, urged to program up those extensions as an exercise.

We want the twin class hierarchies shown in Figure 15.13 to exhibit the following properties:

- Each derived class is to be provided, *but only when necessary*, with its own copy constructor, copy assignment operator, destructor, overload definition for the output operator, and so on.

- The Manager class should inherit from Employee a data member dogs declared as:
  ```
  vector<Dog*> dogs;
  ```

  While an Employee is allowed to own any ordinary dog, those owned by a Manager should only be Poodles or Chihuahuas. This means that when we assign a container of dogs to a Manager, we must perform runtime type checking to make sure that only `Poodles` and `Chihuahuas` are accepted into the dogs data member of the `Manager` object. The same goes for a `SalesManager`.

- A `Manager`'s dogs must always stay sorted by the weight of the dogs. What makes the implementation somewhat complicated is that the `weight` data member is not defined for the base class `Dog`, but only for the derived classes `Poodle` and `Chihuahua`.

- The `Manager` class should possess the following data members for representing an array of employees:

      Employee* workersSupervised;
      int numWorkersSupervised;

- The `SalesManager` class should possess the following data members:

      list<SalesPerson> listOfSalesPersons;
      int salesTarget;

  The data member `listOfSalesPersons` represents the list of sales persons supervised by a `SalesManager`. We will make sure that the list of `SalesPerson` objects in this data member always stays sorted by the last names. (The implementation of the `SalesManager` class and incorporation of this feature is left as an exercise for the reader.)

To bring about the functionality listed above, we will first need to make some small changes to the code presented in Section 11.15. For example, in order to store the `Poodle` and `Chihuahua` objects in the dogs data member of the parent `Employee` class, the first change we need to make is to replace the type `vector<Dog>` by `vector<Dog*>` for the dogs data member, as shown in line (C) of the header file below. Without this change, we'd only be storing the `Dog` slices of the `Poodle` and `Chihuahua` objects in the dogs data member.

Regarding the matter of keeping sorted by weight the `Poodle` and the `Chihuahua` entries in the dogs data member inherited by a `Manager`, the issue here is how to invoke a sort function on `vector<Dog*>` if the sorting parameter — `weight` — exists in only the derived classes of `Dog`, namely, `Poodle` and `Chihuahua` (see lines (K) and (M) of the program `Manager.cc` that follows the header file `Employee.h`. We need to somehow scoop up the derived class parameter `weight` into the base class `Dog` before invoking sort. To bring about this behavior, in line (A) of the program below we define in the base class `Dog` the following virtual function

      virtual double getDogCompareParameter() { return 0.0; }

It has a trivial definition in the base class `Dog`, but has the following definition in the derived `Poodle` and `Chihuahua` classes

      double getDogCompareParameter() { return weight; }

as shown in lines (L) and (N) of the program `Manager.cc` shown after the header file `Employee.h`. Through this mechanism, which depends entirely on polymorphic behavior of the function `getDogCompareParameter()`, we can "pull" the data member weight from the derived classes into the base class Dog. With that problem solved, we just have to define an appropriate functor for the Dog class for the purpose of sorting:

```
class Dog_Comparator {
public:
    bool operator() ( Dog* x1, Dog* x2 ) const {
        return x1->getDogCompareParameter()
                        < x2->getDogCompareParameter();
    }
};
```

Because of polymorphism, this functor will automatically extract the weight of a Dog when the dog is either a Poodle or a Chihuahua object. This functor makes its appearance in line (B) of the header file below.

Another modification that needs to be made to the code of Section 11.15 concerns the overloading of the '<<' operator for the Employee class. Now that we are going to be extending the Dog class, we must ensure that when we output the elements of the vector<Dog*> data member dogs of an Employee, we print out all of the fields of the Poodle and Chihuahua objects. This again requires us to use polymorphism.[16] Since polymorphism does not work on operators, we need to define a print() function for the base class Dog and supply its override definitions for the derived classes Poodle and Chihuahua. In the overload definition for the '<<' operator for Employee, we can then implement the following loop to output the dog information:

```
vector<Dog*>::const_iterator p = employee.dogs.begin();
while ( p != employee.dogs.end() ) {
    (*p++)->print();
    cout << "     ";
}
```

Now, through polymorphism, we would be sure that for a Poodle* pointer in the dogs data member the print() for a Poodle would be invoked, and for a Chihuahua* pointer the print() for a Chihuahua would be invoked. For this to work, we obviously need to declare print() in Dog to be virtual. This change is shown in the while loop in line (E) of the header file below.

The other change that needs to be made to the code of Section 11.15 is the inclusion of the following function in the Employee class:

```
void addDogToDogs( Dog* newDog ) {
    dogs.push_back( newDog );
    sort( dogs.begin(), dogs.end(), Dog::Dog_Comparator() );
}
```

---

[16]In the overloading of the '<<' operator for Employee in Section 11.15, we invoked the operator '<<' operator directly on the Dog members stored in the dogs data members. But that approach in the current context would only output the Dog slice of a Poodle or a Chihuahua.

This function is shown in line (D) of the header file below. Note that a function such as this can be a big trap for extremely difficult to locate bugs in a large C++ program. Since we are pushing pointers into a vector, we must make sure that the pointers point to some freshly acquired memory.

In what follows, first the modified version of the code of Section 11.15 will be shown here.[17] This version, which includes all the changes mentioned above, will be stored in a header file named Employee.h. After that we will show the extensions of the base classes in Employee.h for achieving the behavior mentioned at the beginning of this section. The extended classes will be in a file named Manager.cc to be presented after Employee.h.

```
//Employee.h

/***********************************************************************
 * Modified Version of the code of Section 11.15 of Chapter 11.
 * The modifications, discussed in this section, are necesary so
 * that the class hierarchies (to be obtained by extending the
 * classes in this file) have the specified behavior.
 *
 * This file is #included in the file Manager.cc.
 *
 * For some detailed and useful comments attached to the various
 * class and function declarations and definitions shown here, see
 * the implementation of Employee.cc in Section 11.15 of Chapter 11.
 ***********************************************************************/

#include <string>
#include <iostream>
#include <vector>
#include <map>
#include <algorithm>
using namespace std;

/////////////////// class Auto (declaration only)  ///////////////////
class Auto;

///////////////////////////// class Date  /////////////////////////////
class Date {
    int month;
    int day;
```

---

[17]For the specific demonstrations we'll be making in the Manager.cc program shown next in this section, we could have used a much smaller version of this header file. But we have chosen to keep the code of Section 11.15 intact in the header file shown here (except for the modifications mentioned) so that the reader can extend the Manager.cc program along the lines suggested earlier in this section and experiment with the varied data members of the Employee class in its derived classes.

```
        int year;
public:
    Date() : month(0), day(0), year(0) {}

    Date( int mm, int dd, int yy )
        : month( mm ), day( dd ), year( yy ) {}
    friend ostream& operator<<( ostream& os, const Date& date) {
        os << "Date of Birth: " << date.month
            << "--" << date.day << "--" << date.year;
        return os;
    }
};


/////////////////////////// class Cat ///////////////////////////
class Cat {
    string name;
    int age;
public:
    Cat(){};
    Cat( string nam, int a ) : name( nam ), age( a ) {}
    friend ostream& operator<<( ostream& os, const Cat* cat) {
        os << "Name: " << cat->name << "   Age: " << cat->age;
        return os;
    }
};


/////////////////////////// class Dog ///////////////////////////
class Dog {
    string name;
    int age;
public:
    Dog(){}
    Dog( string nam, int a ) : name( nam ), age( a ) {}
    friend ostream& operator<<( ostream& os, const Dog dog) {
        os << "\nName: " << dog.name << "   Age: " << dog.age;
        return os;
    }
    virtual void print() {
        cout << *this;
    }
    virtual double getDogCompareParameter() { return 0.0; }        //(A)
    class Dog_Comparator {                                         //(B)
    public:
        bool operator() ( Dog* x1, Dog* x2 ) const {
          return x1->getDogCompareParameter()
                                < x2->getDogCompareParameter();
        }
    };
    virtual ~Dog(){};
```

```
    friend bool Dog_Comparator::operator() ( Dog* x1,  Dog* x2 ) const;
};


/////////////////////////// class Employee ///////////////////////////
class Employee {
    string firstName, lastName;
    Date dateOfBirth;
    Employee* friends;
    int numFriends;
    Auto* autos;
    int numAutos;
    Cat* kitty;
    vector<Dog*> dogs;                                      //(C)
    map<string, int> phoneList;
public:
    // First constructor:
    Employee() : friends(0), numFriends(0), autos(0),
                numAutos(0), kitty(0) {}
    // Second constructor:
    Employee( string first, string last )
        : firstName( first ), lastName( last ), friends(0),
          numFriends(0), autos(0), numAutos(0), kitty(0) {}
    // Third constructor:
    Employee( string first, string last, Date dob )
        : firstName( first ), lastName( last ),
          dateOfBirth( dob ), friends(0), numFriends(0),
          autos(0), numAutos(0), kitty(0) {}
    // Fourth constructor:
    Employee( string first, string last, Date dob, Cat* kit )
        : firstName( first ), lastName( last ),
          dateOfBirth( dob ), friends(0), numFriends(0),
          autos(0), numAutos(0)
    {
        if ( kit == 0 ) kitty = 0;
        else
          kitty = new Cat( *kit );
    }
    // Fifth constructor:
    Employee( string first, string last, vector<Dog*> dogs )
        : firstName( first ), lastName( last ),
          friends(0), numFriends(0), autos(0), numAutos(0),
          kitty(0)
    {
        vector<Dog*>::iterator iter = dogs.begin();
        while ( iter != dogs.end() ) {
            Dog* p = new Dog( **iter++ );
            this->dogs.push_back( p );
        }
```

```
    }
    // Sixth constructor:
    Employee( string first, string last, map<string, int> phList )
        : firstName( first ), lastName( last ),
          friends(0), numFriends(0), autos(0),
          numAutos(0), kitty(0)
    {
        map<string, int>::iterator iter = phList.begin();
        while ( iter != phList.end() ) {
            phoneList[ iter->first ] = iter->second;
            iter++;
        }
    }
    // Seventh constructor:
    Employee( string first, string last, Date dob,
        Employee* fnds, int n )
        : firstName( first ), lastName( last ), numFriends( n ),
          dateOfBirth( dob ), autos(0), numAutos(0), kitty(0)
    {
        if ( fnds != 0 ) {
            friends = new Employee[ numFriends ];
            for (int i=0; i<numFriends; i++ )
                friends[i] = fnds[i];
        }
    }
    // Eighth constructor:
    Employee( string first, string last, Date dob,
        Employee* fnds, int n, Auto* ats, int m, Cat* c );

    Employee( const Employee& other );
    Employee& operator=( const Employee& other );

    void addDogToDogs( Dog* newDog ) {                          //(D)
        dogs.push_back( newDog );
        sort( dogs.begin(), dogs.end(), Dog::Dog_Comparator() );
    }

    virtual ~Employee();
    friend ostream& operator<<( ostream& os, const Employee& e );
};


////////////////////////// class Auto //////////////////////////
class Auto {
    string autoBrand;
    Employee owner;
public:
    Auto() {}
    Auto( string brand ): autoBrand( brand ){}
```

```
    Auto( string brand, Employee e )
        : autoBrand( brand ), owner( e ){}
    friend ostream& operator<<( ostream& os, const Employee& e );
};


//////////// Remaining definitions for Employee members  ////////////

// Eighth constructor:
Employee:: Employee( string first, string last, Date dob,
        Employee* fnds, int n, Auto* ats, int m, Cat* c )
    : firstName( first ), lastName( last ),
      dateOfBirth( dob ), numFriends( n ),
      numAutos( m )
{
    if ( fnds == 0 || numFriends == 0 ) friends = 0;
    else {
        friends = new Employee[ numFriends ];
        for (int i=0; i<numFriends; i++ )
            friends[i] = fnds[i];
    }
    if ( ats == 0 || numAutos == 0 ) autos = 0;
    else {
        autos = new Auto[ numAutos ];
        for (int j=0; j<numAutos; j++ )
            autos[j] = ats[j];
    }
    if ( c == 0 ) kitty = 0;            // special care needed for pointer
    else kitty = new Cat( *c );
}

// Copy constructor:
Employee::Employee( const Employee& other )
    : firstName( other.firstName ),
      lastName( other.lastName ),
      dateOfBirth( other.dateOfBirth ),
      numFriends( other.numFriends ),
      numAutos( other.numAutos ),
      dogs( other.dogs ),              // use vector copy constructor
      phoneList( other.phoneList )     // use map copy constructor
{
    if ( other.friends == 0 || numFriends == 0 ) friends = 0;
    else {
        friends = new Employee[ numFriends ];
        for (int i=0; i<numFriends; i++ )
            friends[i] = other.friends[i];
    }
    if ( other.autos == 0 || numAutos == 0 ) autos = 0;
    else {
```

```cpp
        autos = new Auto[ numAutos ];
        for (int j=0; j<numAutos; j++ )
            autos[j] = other.autos[j];
    }
    if ( other.kitty != 0 )
        kitty = new Cat( *other.kitty );
    else kitty = 0;
}

// Copy assignment operator:
Employee& Employee::operator=( const Employee& other ) {
    if ( this == &other ) return *this;
    firstName = other.firstName;
    lastName = other.lastName;
    dateOfBirth = other.dateOfBirth;
    numFriends = other.numFriends;
    numAutos = other.numAutos;
    dogs = other.dogs;              // use vector assignment op
    phoneList = other.phoneList;    // use map assignment op
    if ( other.kitty != 0 ) kitty = new Cat( *other.kitty );
    else kitty = 0;
    if ( friends != 0 ) delete[] friends;
    if ( other.friends == 0 || numFriends == 0 ) friends = 0;
    else {
        friends = new Employee[ numFriends ];
        for (int i=0; i<numFriends; i++ )
            friends[i] = other.friends[i];
    }
    if ( autos != 0 )
        delete[] autos;
    if ( other.autos == 0 || numAutos == 0 ) autos = 0;
    else {
        autos = new Auto[ numAutos ];
        for (int j=0; j<numAutos; j++ )
            autos[j] = other.autos[j];
    }
    return *this;
}

// Destructor:
Employee::~Employee() {
    delete[] friends;
    delete[] autos;
    delete kitty;
}

//overloading of << for Employee class
ostream& operator<<( ostream& os, const Employee& e ) {
    os << e.firstName << " " << e.lastName << endl;
```

```
os << e.dateOfBirth;
os << endl;
if ( e.friends != 0 ) {
    os << "Friends: " ;
    for (int i=0; i<e.numFriends; i++)
        os << e.friends[i].firstName << " "
            << e.friends[i].lastName << "      ";
os << endl;
}
if ( e.autos != 0 ) {
    os << "Automobiles: " ;
    for (int j=0; j<e.numAutos; j++)
        os << e.autos[j].autoBrand << "    " ;
os << endl;
}
os << "Cat info:    ";
if ( e.kitty == 0 ) os << "the cat died" ; //necessary for no cat
else os << e.kitty;
os << endl;
if ( e.dogs.size() != 0 ) {
    os << "Dog info:\n";
    vector<Dog*>::const_iterator p = e.dogs.begin();
    while ( p != e.dogs.end() ) {                           //(E)
        (*p++)->print();
        cout << "      ";
    }
    os << endl;
}
if ( e.phoneList.size() != 0 ) {
    os << "Phone Nums: ";
    map<string, int>::const_iterator q = e.phoneList.begin();
    while ( q != e.phoneList.end() ) {
        cout << q->first << ": " << q->second << "      ";
        q++;
    }
    os << endl;
}
return os;
}
```

We will now show how the classes defined so far can be extended for the desired program behavior described at the beginning of this section. In particular, we mentioned that we wanted to demonstrate runtime type checking for enforcing the condition that the dogs assigned to a Manager be only Poodles and Chihuahuas. The next program, Manager.cc, shows how this is done in Manager's constructor in line (O). The part of the constructor that does runtime type identification (RTTI) to figure out if a Dog* is a Poodle* or a Chihuahua* or none of these two is reproduced below:

```
vector<Dog*>::iterator iter = dogs.begin();                    //(F)
while ( iter < dogs.end() ) {
    Poodle* p = dynamic_cast<Poodle*>( *iter );    //RTTI  //(G)
    if ( p != 0 )
        addDogToDogs( new Poodle( *p ) );                     //(H)
    Chihuahua* c = dynamic_cast<Chihuahua*>( *iter ); //RTTI //(I)
    if ( c != 0 )
        addDogToDogs( new Chihuahua( *c ) );                  //(J)
    iter++;
}
```

where dogs in line (F) is a vector container of type vector<Dog*>. Note how the cast operator dynamic_cast[18] is used in line (G) to ascertain the true runtime identity of the object pointed to by the iterator. If the pointer returned in line (G) is non-null, then we know for sure that the true identity of the object pointed to by the iterator is Poodle. The same applies in line (I) for testing for a Chihuahua. The function addDogToDogs used in lines (H) and (J) above is defined in line (D) of the header Employee.h. This function is in charge of adding new dogs to the dogs data member that is stored in the Employee slice of a Manager object.

The program behavior specification at the beginning of this section also said that we wanted a Manager's dogs to always stay sorted according to their weights. The implementation of addDogToDogs in line (D) of the header Employee.h guarantees that. Any time we add a new dog to the list of dogs by invoking this function, the function calls on the generic library sort to re-sort the list of dogs. Note how the sort function calls the functor Dog_Comparator defined in line (B) of the Dog class.

Shown below is the source code for Manager.cc. As was mentioned at the very beginning of this section, the code shown here does not include the implementations of the SalesManager and SalesPerson classes. Those are left as exercises for the reader.

```
//Manager.cc

#include "Employee.h"
using namespace std;

//////////////////////////// class Poodle  ////////////////////////////
class Poodle : public Dog {
    Employee owner;
```

[18]The use of dynamic_cast for runtime type identification (RTTI) is discussed in greater detail in the next chapter.

```cpp
        double weight;                                               //(K)
        double height;
public:
    Poodle() : owner( Employee() ), weight( 0.0 ), height( 0.0 ) {};
    Poodle( Employee owner, string name,
                int age, double weight, double height )
        : Dog( name, age )  {
        this->owner = owner;
        this->weight = weight;
        this->height = height;
    }
    friend ostream& operator<<( ostream& os, const Poodle& poodle ) {
        cout << (Dog) poodle;
        cout << "\nPedigree: Poodle"
            << "  Weight: " << poodle.weight
            << "  Height: " << poodle.height << endl;
        return os;
    }
    void print() { cout << *this; }
    double getDogCompareParameter() { return weight; }              //(L)
};

//////////////////////////// class Chihuahua ////////////////////////////
class Chihuahua : public Dog {
        Employee owner;
        double weight;                                               //(M)
        double height;
public:
    Chihuahua() : owner( Employee() ), weight( 0.0 ), height( 0.0 ) {};
    Chihuahua( Employee owner, string name,
                    int age, double weight, double height )
        : Dog( name, age )  {
        this->owner = owner;
        this->weight = weight;
        this->height = height;
    }
    friend ostream& operator<<(ostream& os, const Chihuahua& huahua) {
        cout << (Dog) huahua;
        cout << "\nPedigree: Chihuahua"
            << "  Weight: " << huahua.weight
            << "  Height: " << huahua.height << endl;
        return os;
    }
    void print() { cout << *this; }
    double getDogCompareParameter() { return weight; }              //(N)
};

//////////////////////////// class Manager ////////////////////////////
class Manager : public Employee {
```

```
        Employee* workersSupervised;
        int numWorkersSupervised;
public:
    Manager() : workersSupervised(0), numWorkersSupervised( 0 ) {}
    Manager( Employee e, vector<Dog*> dogs ) : Employee( e ) {     //(O)
        vector<Dog*>::iterator iter = dogs.begin();
        while ( iter < dogs.end() ) {
            Poodle* p = dynamic_cast<Poodle*>( *iter );
            if ( p != 0 )
                addDogToDogs( new Poodle( *p ) );
            Chihuahua* c = dynamic_cast<Chihuahua*>( *iter );
            if ( c != 0 )
                addDogToDogs( new Chihuahua( *c ) );
            iter++;
        }
    }
    friend ostream& operator<<( ostream& os, const Manager& m );
};


ostream& operator<<( ostream& os, const Manager& m ) {
    os << (Employee) m;
    return os;
}


///////////////////////////// main //////////////////////////////////
int main()
{
    Employee e1( "Zoe", "Zaphod" );

//                name        age
    Dog dog1(    "fido",       3 );
    Dog dog2(    "spot",       4 );
    Dog dog3(    "bruno",      2 );
    Dog dog4(    "darth",      1 );

//                Employee    name     age    weight    height
    Poodle dog5(    e1,      "pooch",   4,    15.8,     2.1 );
    Poodle dog6(    e1,      "doggy",   3,    12.9,     3.4 );
    Poodle dog7(    e1,      "lola",    3,    12.9,     3.4 );
    Chihuahua dog8( e1,      "bitsy",   5,     3.2,     0.3 );
    Chihuahua dog9( e1,      "bookam",  5,     7.2,     0.9 );
    Chihuahua dog10( e1,     "pie",     5,     4.8,     0.7 );

    vector<Dog*> dawgs;
    dawgs.push_back( &dog1 );
    dawgs.push_back( &dog2 );
    dawgs.push_back( &dog5 );
    dawgs.push_back( &dog6 );
    dawgs.push_back( &dog3 );
```

```
        dawgs.push_back( &dog4 );
        dawgs.push_back( &dog10 );
        dawgs.push_back( &dog7 );
        dawgs.push_back( &dog8 );
        dawgs.push_back( &dog9 );

        Manager m1( e1, dawgs );
        cout << m1;
        return 0;
}
```

The output of the program is

```
Zoe Zaphod
Date of Birth: 0--0--0
Cat info:   the cat died
Dog info:

Name: bitsy   Age: 5
Pedigree: Chihuahua  Weight: 3.2  Height: 0.3

Name: pie   Age: 5
Pedigree: Chihuahua  Weight: 4.8  Height: 0.7

Name: bookam   Age: 5
Pedigree: Chihuahua  Weight: 7.2  Height: 0.9

Name: doggy   Age: 3
Pedigree: Poodle  Weight: 12.9  Height: 3.4

Name: lola   Age: 3
Pedigree: Poodle  Weight: 12.9  Height: 3.4

Name: pooch   Age: 4
Pedigree: Poodle  Weight: 15.8  Height: 2.1
```

As the reader can see, the Poodles and the Chihuahuas are stored in sorted order according to their weights.

15.20   A JAVA STUDY OF A SMALL CLASS HIERARCHY EXHIBITING MODERATELY COMPLEX BEHAVIOR

While programming a Java class hierarchy is much easier than programming a similar C++ class hierarchy, one still has to make design decisions regarding what containers to use, how to take advantage of polymorphism to bring about a certain behavior, when to copy objects through cloning and when to be content with just passing object references around, and so on.

While, relative to C++, you now don't have to worry about explicit memory allocation and deallocation, the writing of copy constructors and copy assignment operators, the writing of destructors, and so on, it does not mean that you can throw caution to the wind when programming in Java. You still have to worry about making sure that you are not trying to access a null reference, that you are not passing the same object reference around in a program while your intent was to create duplicates of an object since you did not want changes in one section of the program to affect program behavior elsewhere, and so on. So you have to make conscious program design decisions about when to clone and when not to clone, and so on.

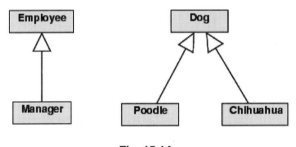

Fig. 15.14

We will use the classes of Figure 15.14 for the code in this section.[19] We want this twin hierarchy of classes to exhibit the same behavior as before. While an Employee can have any dog, a Manager can only have Poodles and Chihuahuas. So if a Manager constructor is presented with a container full of dogs, it should only select Poodles and Chihuahuas from the container. For the C++ case, we used RTTI for this check in the Manager constructor in line (O) of Manager.cc. (Also see the lines labeled (F) through (I) of the code in the previous section and the associated explanations.)

---

[19]The actual C++ code shown in the previous section also corresponds to the hierarchy of Figure 15.14 since we left the implementation of the classes SalesManager and SalesPerson in the class diagram of Figure 15.13 as exercises for the reader. The reader is urged to add the SalesManager and SalesPerson classes of Figure 15.13 to the code shown in this section also and to provide Java implementation of the SalesManager – SalesPerson feature mentioned at the beginning of the previous section.

The question now is, how can the same sort of runtime type checking be carried out in Java? In Java, not knowing whether a reference stored in the list dogs is to a Poodle object or to a Chihuahua object, or to neither, we can go ahead and try to cast it to one of these objects. If the cast is not valid, a ClassCastException will be thrown. So catching of the exception can be used to figure out whether or not a Dog reference is a Poodle or a Chihuahua reference, as in the loop below:

```
//dogs is a list of all dogs presented to Manager constructor
ListIterator iter = dogs.listIterator();
while ( iter.hasNext() ) {
    Object object = iter.next();
    try {
        Poodle p = (Poodle) object;                           //(A)
        addDogToDogs( (Dog) p.clone() );                      //(B)
    } catch( ClassCastException badpoodlecast ) {             //(C)
        try {
            Chihuahua c = (Chihuahua) object;                 //(D)
            addDogToDogs( (Dog) c.clone() );                  //(E)
        } catch( ClassCastException badhuahuacast ) {}        //(F)
    }
}
```

where the lines (A) and (C) help us figure out at runtime whether a Dog reference is actually a Poodle reference, and the lines (D) and (F) do the same vis-à-vis a Chihuahua reference. The calls to addDogToDogs in lines (B) and (E) add a new dog to those already assigned to a Manager object. Following the same implementation design as in the previous section, a part of the contract of this method is to make sure that the dogs always stay sorted according to their weight, which takes us to the issue discussed next. The runtime type checking shown above is incorporated in the Manager constructor in line (O) of the program below.

As was the case in the previous section, besides runtime type checking, what makes the current study moderately complex is that the Poodles and Chihuahuas that are owned by a Manager are to be stored in a sorted order, the sorting based on an attribute — weight — that is not defined for the parent class Dog, but only for the derived classes Poodle and Chihuahua (see lines (K) and (M) of the program below). The sorted list is to be kept in the Employee slice of a Manager object.

If the sorted list of Dogs for a Manager object is to be kept in the Employee slice of the Manager, we need to provide the Employee class with a function that can add new dogs to the list and make sure that function is available in the Manager class. And if this list of Dogs is to be sorted by using a parameter that exists only for Poodles and Chihuahuas, we need to define for Dog a method that would return the appropriate sorting criterion for each subclass of Dog. That way, when we are sorting a list of Dogs (that in actuality are Poodles and Chihuahuas), we can use polymorphism to scoop up the correct sorting parameter. In the code shown below, line (G) provides the base class Dog with the following method with a trivial implementation

```
public double getDogCompareParameter(){ return 0; }
```

and then, in lines (L) and (N), we supply the derived classes `Poodle` and `Chihuahua` with the following override definition:

```
public double getDogCompareParameter(){ return weight; }
```

This method is called in the `compare` method of the `Dog_Comparator` class in line (H) of the program below:

```
public static class Dog_Comparator implements Comparator {
    public int compare( Object o1, Object o2 ) {
        Dog d1 = (Dog) o1;
        Dog d2 = (Dog) o2;
        if ( d1.getDogCompareParameter()
                        == d2.getDogCompareParameter() )
            return 0;
        return ( d1.getDogCompareParameter()
                    < d2.getDogCompareParameter() ) ? -1 : 1;
    }
}
```

The `Dog_Comparator` class is an inner class of `Dog`.[20] A `Dog_Comparator` object is supplied to the `Collections.sort` routine in the following definition of addDogToDogs method of the `Employee` class:

```
public void addDogToDogs( Dog newDog ) {
    if ( dogs == null ) dogs = new ArrayList();
    dogs.add( newDog );
    Collections.sort( dogs, new Dog.Dog_Comparator() );
}
```

This method is provided to the `Employee` class in line (I) of the code shown below.

The program shown below is an extension of the Java case study presented in Section 11.16 of Chapter 11. The program starts out by presenting the same classes as in the earlier Java study. This part of the code consists of the main class `Employee` and the ancillary classes `Date`, `Dog`, `Cat`, and `Auto`. The ancillary classes are used for the different data members in the main class `Employee`. Subsequently, the program defines the derived ancillary classes `Poodle` and `Chihuahua` and the derived main class `Manager`.

```
//Manager.java

import java.util.*;              // for Comparator, Collections, etc
```

---

[20]See Chapter 3 on the behavior of nested and inner classes vis-à-vis the enclosing classes.

```
//////////////////////////// class Date ////////////////////////////
class Date implements Cloneable {
    private int month;
    private int day;
    private int year;
    public Date( int mm, int dd, int yy ) {
        month = mm; day = dd; year = yy;
    }
    public String toString() {
        return month + " : " + day + " : " + year;
    }
    public Object clone() {
        Date date = null;
        try {
            date = ( Date ) super.clone();
        } catch( CloneNotSupportedException e ) {}
        return date;
    }
}

//////////////////////////// class Cat ////////////////////////////
class Cat implements Cloneable {
    private String name;
    private int age;
    public Cat( String nam, int a ) { name = nam ; age = a; }
    public String toString() { return "  Name: "
                                    + name + "   Age: " + age; }
    public Object clone() {
        Cat cat = null;
        try {
            cat = ( Cat ) super.clone();
        } catch( CloneNotSupportedException e ) {}
        return cat;
    }
}

//////////////////////////// class Dog ////////////////////////////
class Dog implements Cloneable {
    private String name;
    private int age;
    public Dog( String nam, int a ) { name = nam; age = a; }
    public String toString() {
        return "\nName: " + name + "   Age: " + age;
    }
    public String getName() { return name; }
    public int getAge() { return age; }
    public void print() {
        System.out.println( this );
```

```java
    }
    public Object clone() {
        Dog dog = null;
        try {
            dog = ( Dog ) super.clone();
        } catch( CloneNotSupportedException e ) {}
        return dog;
    }
    public double getDogCompareParameter(){ return 0; }          //(G)
    public static class Dog_Comparator implements Comparator {    //(H)
        public int compare( Object o1, Object o2 ) {
            Dog d1 = (Dog) o1;
            Dog d2 = (Dog) o2;
            if ( d1.getDogCompareParameter()
                            == d2.getDogCompareParameter() )
                return 0;
            return ( d1.getDogCompareParameter()
                        < d2.getDogCompareParameter() ) ? -1 : 1;
        }
    }
}


/////////////////////////// class Employee ///////////////////////////
class Employee {                // intentionally left uncloneable
    String firstName, lastName;
    Date dateOfBirth;
    Employee[] friends;
    Auto[] autos;
    Cat kitty;
    ArrayList dogs;
    Map phoneList;
    public Employee( String first, String last ) {
        firstName = first;  lastName = last;
    }
    public Employee( String first, String last, Date dob ) {
        firstName = first;  lastName = last;
        dateOfBirth = dob == null ? null : (Date) dob.clone();
    }
    public Employee( String first, String last, Date dob, Cat kit ) {
        firstName = first;  lastName = last;
        dateOfBirth = dob == null ? null : (Date) dob.clone();
        kitty = kit == null ? null : (Cat) kit.clone();
    }
    public Employee( String first, String last, ArrayList dogs ) {
        firstName = first;  lastName = last;
        this.dogs = dogs == null ? null : (ArrayList) dogs.clone();
    }
    Employee( String first, String last, Date dob, Employee[] fnds ) {
        firstName = first;  lastName = last;
```

```
        dateOfBirth = dob == null ? null : (Date) dob.clone();
        friends = fnds == null ? null : (Employee[]) fnds.clone();
    }
    Employee( String first, String last, Map phoneList ) {
        firstName = first;  lastName = last;
        this.phoneList = phoneList == null
            ? null : new TreeMap( (TreeMap) phoneList );
        // creates the same mappings
    }
    Employee( String first, String last, Date dob, Employee[] fnds,
                Auto[] ats, Cat c )
    {
        firstName = first;  lastName = last;
        dateOfBirth = dob == null ? null : (Date) dob.clone();
        friends = fnds == null ? null : (Employee[]) fnds.clone();
        autos = ats == null ? null : (Auto[]) ats.clone();
        kitty =  c == null ? null : (Cat) c.clone();
    }
    Employee( Employee e ) {
        firstName = e.firstName;  lastName = e.lastName;
        dateOfBirth = e.dateOfBirth == null
            ? null : (Date) e.dateOfBirth.clone();
        friends = e.friends == null
            ? null : (Employee[]) e.friends.clone();
        autos = e.autos == null
            ? null : (Auto[]) e.autos.clone();
        kitty = e.kitty == null
            ? null : (Cat) e.kitty.clone();
        phoneList = e.phoneList == null
            ? null : new TreeMap( (TreeMap) e.phoneList );
    }
    public String getFirstName() { return firstName; }
    public String getLastName() { return lastName; }
    public void addDogToDogs( Dog newDog ) {                    //(I)
        if ( dogs == null ) dogs = new ArrayList();
        dogs.add( newDog );
        Collections.sort( dogs, new Dog.Dog_Comparator() );     //(J)
    }
    public String toString() {
        String str = "";
        if ( dogs != null ) {
            str += "\nDOGS: ";
            ListIterator iter = dogs.listIterator();
            while ( iter.hasNext() )
                str += (Dog) iter.next();
            str += "\n";
        }
        if ( autos != null ) {
            str += "\nAUTOS: ";
```

```java
            for ( int i=0; i<autos.length - 1; i++ ) {
                str += " " + autos[i] + ",";
            }
            str += " " + autos[autos.length - 1];
            str += "\n";
        }
        if ( friends != null ) {
            str += "\nFRIENDS:";
            for ( int i=0; i<friends.length; i++ ) {
                str += "\n";
                str += friends[i].getFirstName();
                str += " " + friends[i].getLastName();
            }
            str += "\n";
        }
        if ( kitty != null ) {
            str += "\nCAT:";
            str += kitty;
        }
        if ( phoneList != null ) {
            str += "\nPhone List:";
            str += phoneList;
        }
        return "\nFirst Name: " + firstName + "\nLast Name: "
          + lastName  + "\n" + str + "\n";
    }
}


////////////////////////////// class Auto //////////////////////////////
class Auto {
    String autoBrand;
    Employee owner;
    public Auto( String brand ) { autoBrand = brand; }
    public Auto( String brand, Employee e )
    {
        autoBrand = brand;
        owner = e;
    }
    public String toString()
    {
        return autoBrand;
    }
}


////////////////////////////// class Poodle //////////////////////////////
class Poodle extends Dog {
    private Employee owner;
    private double weight;                                      //(K)
    private double height;
```

```
    public Poodle( Employee owner, String name, int age,
                   double weight, double height )
    {
        super( name, age );
        this.owner = owner;
        this.weight = weight;
        this.height = height;
     }
    public Object clone() {
        Poodle poo = null;
        poo = ( Poodle ) super.clone();
        return poo;
    }
    public String toString() {
        return super.toString() + "   Pedigree: " + "Poodle "
               + "  Weight: " + weight + "   Height: " + height ;
    }
    public double getDogCompareParameter(){ return weight; }      //(L)
}

////////////////////////// class Chihuahua //////////////////////////////
class Chihuahua extends Dog {
    private Employee owner;
    private double weight;                                         //(M)
    private double height;
    public Chihuahua( Employee owner, String name, int age,
                      double weight, double height )
    {
        super( name, age );
        this.owner = owner;
        this.weight = weight;
        this.height = height;
    }
    public Object clone() {
        Chihuahua huahua = null;
        huahua = ( Chihuahua ) super.clone();
        return huahua;
    }
    public String toString() {
        return super.toString() + "   Pedigree: " + "Chihuahua "
               + "   Weight: " + weight + "   Height: " + height ;
    }
    public double getDogCompareParameter(){ return weight; }     //(N)
}

////////////////////////// class Manager //////////////////////////////
class Manager extends Employee {
    private Employee[] workersSupervised;
    public Manager( Employee e, ArrayList dogs ) {               //(O)
```

```java
        super( e );
        ListIterator iter = dogs.listIterator();
        while ( iter.hasNext() ) {
            Object object = iter.next();
            try {
                Poodle p = (Poodle) object;
                addDogToDogs( (Dog) p.clone() );
            } catch( ClassCastException badpoodlecast ) {
                try {
                    Chihuahua c = (Chihuahua) object;
                    addDogToDogs( (Dog) c.clone() );
                } catch( ClassCastException badhuahuacast ) {}
            }
        }
    }
}


/////////////////////////  class TestManager  /////////////////////////
class TestManager {
    public static void main( String[] args )
    {
        Employee e1 = new Employee( "Zoe", "Zaphod" );

        //                         name        age
        Dog dog1  =  new Dog(    "fido",       3 );
        Dog dog2  =  new Dog(    "spot",       4 );
        Dog dog3  =  new Dog(    "bruno",      2 );
        Dog dog4  =  new Dog(    "darth",      1 );

        //                         emp  name   age  weight  height
        Poodle dog5 = new Poodle(     e1, "pooch",  4,   15.8,  2.1 );
        Poodle dog6 = new Poodle(     e1, "doggy",  3,   12.9,  3.4 );
        Poodle dog7 = new Poodle(     e1, "lola",   3,   12.9,  3.4 );
        Chihuahua dog8 =new Chihuahua(e1, "bitsy",  5,    3.2,  0.3 );
        Chihuahua dog9 =new Chihuahua(e1, "bookum", 5,    7.2,  0.9 );
        Chihuahua dog10=new Chihuahua(e1, "pie",    5,    4.8,  0.7 );

        ArrayList dawgs = new ArrayList();
        dawgs.add( dog1 );
        dawgs.add( dog2 );
        dawgs.add( dog5 );
        dawgs.add( dog6 );
        dawgs.add( dog3 );
        dawgs.add( dog4 );
        dawgs.add( dog10 );
        dawgs.add( dog7 );
        dawgs.add( dog8 );
        dawgs.add( dog9 );
```

```
        Manager m1 = new Manager( e1, dawgs );
        Employee e = (Employee) m1;
        System.out.println( e );    // will invoke Employee's toString
    }
}
```

Executing the TestManager class produces the following output:

```
First Name: Zoe
Last Name: Zaphod

DOGS:
Name: bitsy   Age: 5   Pedigree: Chihuahua    Weight: 3.2    Height: 0.3
Name: pie     Age: 5   Pedigree: Chihuahua    Weight: 4.8    Height: 0.7
Name: bookum  Age: 5   Pedigree: Chihuahua    Weight: 7.2    Height: 0.9
Name: doggy   Age: 3   Pedigree: Poodle       Weight: 12.9   Height: 3.4
Name: lola    Age: 3   Pedigree: Poodle       Weight: 12.9   Height: 3.4
Name: pooch   Age: 4   Pedigree: Poodle       Weight: 15.8   Height: 2.1
```

As is clear from the output, the manager Zoe Zaphod only has poodles and chihuahuas for dogs and that these dogs are kept sorted according to their weights.

The test code in the TestManager class used only one ancillary class, Dog. The reader is encouraged to form more complex instances of Manager using the other ancillary classes shown and then forming scenarios of ownership and transfer of objects of different types among employees and managers.

15.21 CREDITS AND SUGGESTIONS FOR FURTHER READING

For a detailed discussion on the C++ topics of runtime type identification and static binding versus dynamic binding of function calls to function definitions, the book by Dattatri [16] is highly recommended.

The material in this chapter on virtual tables and the computational costs associated with dynamic bindings in C++ is based on the treatment of these topics by Meyers [51].

The Shape hierarchy code shown in Sections 15.12 and 15.17, and 15.18 is based on example programs by Flanagan [19] in his discussion on abstract classes and interfaces in Java.

15.22 HOMEWORK

1. Identify and correct the error in the derived-class constructor syntax in this Java code.

```
class Employee {
    private String fName, lName;
    public Employee(String f, String l) {
        fName = f;
        lName = l;
    }
}

class Manager extends Employee {
    private short level;
    public Manager(String f, String l, short lvl) {
        Employee(f, l);
        level = lvl;
    }
    public Manager(String f, String l) {
        this(f, l, 10);
    }
}
```

State what the data members of the following object will be set to after the following line is executed:

```
Employee e = new Manager ( "John",  "Doe" );
```

2. Is the following C++ syntax legal? Note that the base class X and the derived class Y use the same identifiers m and foo for class members. Pay careful attention to the syntax used for the function calls in main. If the code is legal, what's its output?

```
class X {
public:
    int m;
    X( int mm ) : m( mm ) {}
    void foo() { cout << "X's foo invoked" << endl; }
};

class Y : public X {
public:
    int m;
    Y( int a, int b ) : X(a), m( b ) {}
    void foo() { cout << "Y's foo invoked" << endl; }
};
```

```
int main() {
    X xobj( 10 );
    xobj.foo();

    Y yobj( 10, 20 );
    yobj.foo();

    yobj.X::foo();

    return 0;
}
```

3. If the goal was to write correctly the copy constructor for a derived class in C++, is the following example correct? If not, how will you fix it?

```
class X {
    int m;
public:
    X( int mm ) : m( mm ) {}
    X( const X& other ) : m( other.m ) {}
};

class Y : public X {
    int n;
public:
    Y( int mm, int nn ) : X( mm ), n( nn ) {}
    Y( const Y& other ) : n( other.n ) {}
};
```

4. The following C++ program compiles without any problems. When run, it even prints out the "hello" called for in line (B) of main. But subsequently the program aborts with a memory segmentation fault. Why? (Hint: If you comment out the assignment statement in line (A), the program runs flawlessly.)

```
//MysteryBug.cc

#include <iostream>
using namespace std;

class X {
    int* p;
    int size;
```

```
public:
    X() { p = 0; size = 0; }
    X( int* ptr, int sz ) : size( sz ) {
        p = new int[ size ];
        for ( int i=0; i<size; i++ ) p[i] = ptr[i];
    }
    ~X() { delete[] p; }
};

class Y : public X {
    int n;
public:
    Y() {};
    Y( int* ptr, int sz, int nn ) : X( ptr, sz ), n( nn ) {}
    Y( const Y& other ) : X( other ), n( other.n ) {}
    Y& operator=( const Y& other ) {
        if ( this == &other ) return *this;
        X::operator=( other );
        n = other.n;
        return *this;
    }
};

int main() {
    int data[ 3 ] = {3, 2, 1};
    Y y1( data, 3, 10 );
    Y y2;
    y2 = y1;                                       //(A)
    cout << "hello" << endl;                       //(B)
    return 0;
}
```

5. While the following C++ program compiles fine

```
#include <iostream>
using namespace std;

class X {
public:
    void foo();
    X() { }
};

class Y : public X {
public:
    void foo(){ cout << "Y's foo invoked" << endl; }
```

```
        Y() {}
};

int main() {}
```

the following program does not compile and reports a problem from the linker. Why?

```
#include <iostream>
#include <vector>
using namespace std;

class X {
public:
    virtual void foo();
    X() { }
};

class Y : public X {
public:
    void foo(){ cout << "Y's foo invoked" << endl; }
    Y() {}
};

int main() {}
```

6. Will the following C++ program compile?

```
class X {
public:
    virtual void f();
};

class Y : public X { };

int main() { Y yobj; }
```

7. Will the following version of the previous program compile?

```
class X {
public:
    virtual void f() = 0;
};

class Y : public X { };
```

```
int main() { Y yobj; }
```

8. Will the following version of the previous program compile and run?

```
class X {
public:
    virtual void f() = 0;
};

class Y : public X { void f() {}; };

int main() { Y yobj; }
```

9. With regard to exception specifications for overriding functions in Java, is the following code legal?

```
class MyException extends Exception {}

class X {
    public void foo() throws MyException  {
        throw new MyException();
    }
}

class Y extends X {
    public void foo()  {
        System.out.println( "Y's foo invoked" );
    }
}
```

10. Do you see any problems with the following Java code? Note that both the interfaces X and Y possess a function of the same signature. Will this code fragment compile?

```
interface X { public int foo( int m ); }

interface Y { public int foo( int n ); }

class W implements X, Y {
    public int foo( int x ) { return x; }
}
```

11. Vis-à-vis the code in the previous problem, the Java code shown here shows two interfaces possessing function foo of the same name but different signatures. Do you see any problems with this code? Will it compile?

```
interface X { public int foo( int m ); }

interface Y { public int foo( int n, int p ); }

class W implements X, Y {
    public int foo( int x ) { return x; }
}
```

12. Will the following Java program compile?

```
interface X { public int foo( int m ); }

class X { public int foo( int q ) { return q; } }

class W implements X {
    public int foo( int x ) { return x; }
}
```

16

Multiple Inheritance in C++

C++ allows a class to inherit implementation code from multiple superclasses. This is referred to as multiple inheritance (MI). This chapter has four goals: (1) to present programming scenarios that might justify MI; (2) to describe the programming issues that arise when a class inherits from the same base through multiple paths; (3) to present modifications to the syntax for constructors, copy constructors, and so on, when a class inherits from the same base through different paths; and (4) to present the notions of *mixin class* and *role-playing class* for getting around the complications introduced by MI.

Some programmers like multiple inheritance because real-world entities (such as yourself) do inherit traits from multiple sources. In that sense, MI allows for direct modeling of real-world problem domains. But there are also many programmers who shun MI because it can introduce deeply hidden bugs into a large program and can make it more daunting to extend a class hierarchy. In any case, it is good to know that any design that uses multiple inheritance can be converted into one in which a class inherits implementation code from only one superclass.

Java does not allow a class to inherit implementation code from multiple superclasses. However, as was shown in the previous chapter, Java does allow a class to inherit behaviors from multiple interfaces. As we showed there, this allows a Java object to behave polymorphically with respect to different types.

16.1 SOME EXAMPLES FOR MI

We will now illustrate some example problem domains in which multiple inheritance seems natural. However, beware that there are ways of "re-engineering" these problems so that they can be solved without the complications that could arise from a straightforward implementation of multiple inheritance. For example, one can use role-playing classes, as we will explain later in this chapter; one can limit the inheritance of implementation code to a single superclass while allowing behaviors to be inherited from multiple interfaces (as done in Java); and so on.

For our first example, let's say we wish to use classes to represent the following roles in an educational system:

```
Student
Teacher
TeachingAssistant
```

While the roles Student and Teacher are obviously distinct, the role Teaching-Assistant combines the two. So instead of duplicating the data members and the functions of the Student and the Teacher classes in TeachingAssistant class, it would make more sense if we had the class hierarchy shown in Figure 16.1.

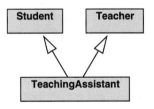

Fig. 16.1

For our next example, consider the class hierarchy of Figure 16.2 in which we mix a class GenericVehicle with specialized "trait" classes to create different kinds of vehicles. In a hierarchy such as this, the basic passenger safety norms and regulations, presumably different from those for freight carriers, would be stored in the class PeopleHaulerTraits, while those for carrying freight will be stored in FreightHaulerTraits. Regulations specific to vehicles meant for personal and light commercial use could be kept in the class PersonalTransporterTraits, while those intended for heavy-duty commercial use in CommercialTransporter-Traits.

While the above two examples lend themselves straightforwardly to multiple inheritance, let's now consider an example where the decision to use multiple inheritance may be dictated by some basic tenet of object-oriented programming, *such as keeping different data abstractions as loosely coupled as possible.*

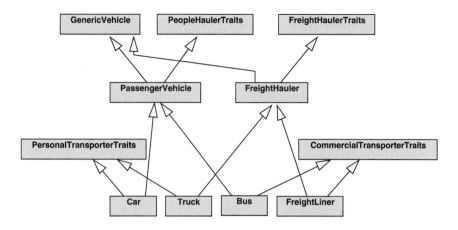

Fig. 16.2

Let's say we want to model the various ways in which a set of mechanical widgets can be assembled in a factory. (We may want to do so to carry out a cost–benefit analysis of the different methods for assembly.) The assembly operations may be carried out robotically, manually, or semiautomatically using different systems. If parts are assembled from random initial positions in a work area, automatic and semiautomatic assembly would need some sort of a computer vision module for localizing the parts before they can be assembled. After the parts are localized, the computer would also have to calculate the motion trajectories to use for mating one part with another part. For that, it would need to know the initial and the final pose of each part. We will assume that the computer has available to it full 3D geometric models of the parts for such path planning calculations.

We obviously have the following three issues to deal with here and, for program organization, it is best to think of them separately:

1. Specifying the assembly operations at a purely abstract level.

2. The choice of the agent that would actually carry out the assembly — again at an abstract level. The agent could be a robot, a human, or some semiautomatic system.

3. A geometry engine for computing the motion trajectories to be used for mating one part with another part when assembly is carried out robotically. Such motion trajectories may also be needed for some types of semiautomatic assembly. For manual assembly, the calculated motion trajectories may help us determine the level of dexterity expected of a human worker.

The first issue — capturing at an abstract level the assembly operations needed — could be addressed by defining an `Assemble` class as we do below. This class uses two ancillary classes: `Part` for representing the parts to be assembled, and `Pose` to represent the location and the orientation of each part in space. The class `Part` presumably has at least a data member that points to a geometric model of the part. Such models would be needed by a geometry engine to figure out the collision-free trajectories for assembling one part with another. Here is what `Assemble` could look like:

```
class Assemble {
protected:
    Part* part1;                 // part1 to be assembled with part2
    Part* part2;                 // part2 assumed fixtured
    Pose* part1_initial_pose;
    Pose* part1_final_pose;
    Pose* pose_part2;
    bool done;
public:
    Assemble( Part1* p1, Part* p2,
              Pose* s1_init, Pose* s1_final,
              Pose* s2, done = false );
    virtual void graspPart() {}
    virtual void orientPart() {}
    virtual void pickupPart() {}
    virtual void insert() {}
    virtual bool isAssemblyDone() { return done; }
    // the rest of the class
    virtual ~Assemble();
};
```

The names of the member functions speak for themselves. As a data abstraction, the class `Assemble` stands on its own, independent of the physical mechanism used for assembly. The simplistic implementations provided for the functions are supposed to take care of the requirement that when a function is declared to be virtual, it must be defined at the same time (see Chapter 15). Obviously, their override definitions in the subclasses of `Assemble` would be more useful.

For addressing the second of the three issues outlined above, we can now extend the `Assemble` class and provide more meaningful implementations for its various member functions depending on the specific assembly agent used:

```
class AssembleWithRobot  : public Assemble {
    // stuff related to robot calibration
    // and the coordinate transformation from
    // the world frame into a robot end-effector
    // based coordinate frame
public:
    AssembleWithRobot( Part1* part1, Part* part2,
                       Pose* part1_init_pose,
                       Pose* part1_final_pose,
                       Pose* s2, done = false );
    void graspPart();
```

```
        void orientPart();
        void pickupPart();
        void insert();
        // the rest of the class
    };

    class AssembleSemiAutomatically
            : public Assemble { /* ........ */ };

    class AssembleManually
            : public Assemble { /* ........ */ };
    ....
```

The functions such as graspPart(), orientPart(), and so on, for the robotic and semiautomatic assembly would take into account the kinematic and dynamic constraints of the machines involved, but again at a purely abstract level.

Now we can write a function that, through polymorphism, could be used to perform assemblies:

```
    void assemble( Assemble* agent ) {
        agent->graspPart();            // grasp part1
        agent->insert();               // insert part1 into part2
        //...
        if ( agent->done() ) {
            // assembly finished, start next step
        }
        else {
            // ...
        }
        // ...
    }
```

The important thing to note here is that the assemble() function is independent of the kind of Assemble object that we may actually be using. Polymorphism would guarantee us that, inside assemble(), the correct function is invoked for each Assemble.

This brings us to the issue of how to actually do geometry calculations for figuring out the motion trajectories needed for taking part1 from its initial pose, as given by the value of the data member part1_initial_pose of the class Assemble, to its final pose, as given by the data member part1_final_pose. The function insert() defined for Assemble would simply not work unless it has access to some kind of a geometry engine for path planning. The question now is: "How do we incorporate the path planning facilities offered by a vendor-supplied geometry engine in the Assemble class hierarchy?"

One option is to declare the GeometryEngine class as a base for the Assemble class:

```
class Assemble : public GeometryEngine {
protected:
    Part* part1;
    Part* part2;
    Pose* part1_initial_pose;
    Pose* part1_final_pose;
    Pose* pose_part2;
    bool done;
public:
    Assemble( Part1* p1, Part* p2,
              Pose* s1_init, Pose* s1_final,
              Pose* s2, done = false );
    virtual void graspPart();
    virtual void orientPart();
    virtual void pickupPart();
    virtual void insert();
    virtual bool isAssemblyDone() { return done; }
    // the rest of the class
    virtual ~Assemble();
};
```

The path planning functions inherited from the GeometryEngine class would be overridden in each subclass of Assemble class to take into account the special constraints of the assembly agent corresponding to that class. Graphically, our class hierarchy for Assemble and its extensions would look like what is shown in Figure 16.3. While this design could be made to serve its intended function, it violates a basic

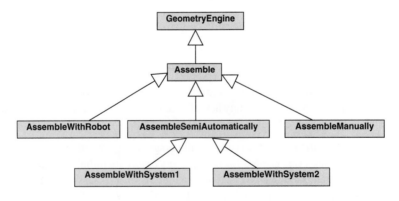

Fig. 16.3

tenet of good OO programming: *Data abstractions that are conceptually separate and distinct should be kept as uncoupled as possible.* As originally conceived, the data abstraction represented by the class Assemble was complete unto itself and distinct from the path planning implementation code packaged in the GeometryEngine class. But, by making Assemble a subclass of GeometryEngine, we have destroyed the separate identity of Assemble.

Now we will show a different design in which we do not violate the separateness of the abstractions. In this new design, we will specify `Assemble` as a pure interface, meaning an abstract class with no implementation code:

```
class Assemble {
public:
    virtual void graspPart() = 0;
    virtual void orientPart() = 0;
    virtual void pickupPart() = 0;
    virtual void insert() = 0;
    virtual bool isAssemblyDone() = 0;
    // the rest of the class
    virtual ~Assemble() {}
};
```

Now that all the functions of `Assemble` are pure virtual, we do not have to provide them with the simplistic implementations that we had to in our previous design. Being an abstract class, our new `Assemble` class does not need a constructor. We have also included a virtual destructor that can be used for cleaning up the data to be defined in the derived classes.

Now the definition of `AssembleWithRobot` might look like:

```
class AssembleWithRobot
    : public Assemble, protected GeometryEngine {
    Part* part1;
    Part* part2;
    Pose* part1_initial_pose;
    Pose* part1_final_pose;
    Pose* pose_part2;
    bool done;
protected:
    // code for overriding any virtual functions of
    // GeometryEngine class
public:
    AssembleWithRobot( Part1* p1, Part* p2,
                       Pose* s1_init, Pose* s1_final,
                       Pose* s2, done = false );
    virtual void graspPart();
    virtual void orientPart();
    virtual void pickupPart();
    virtual void insert();
    virtual bool isAssemblyDone();
    ~ AssembleWithRobot();
};
```

Here we have multiple inheritance. In this particular implementation of MI, the nature of inheritance from the two bases of `AssembleWithRobot` is different. The public derivation from the base class `Assemble` will allow us to use polymorphism with respect to the virtual functions declared in that base class. On the other hand, the protected derivation from `GeometryEngine` will allow `AssembleWithRobot` and its subclasses to inherit the path planning implementation code in that base. With this construction, we are evidently making a design decision that we do not need polymorphism with respect to the path planning functions in `GeometryEngine`. It goes without saying that `AssembleWithRobot` class is required to provide implementations for all the abstract functions declared in the base `Assemble`.

The other derived classes in the `Assemble` hierarchy can now be defined as follows:

```
class AssembleSemiAutomatically
    : public Assemble, protected GeometryEngine
{ /*....... */ };

class AssembleManually
        : public Assemble, protected GeometryEngine
{ /*........*/ };

....
```

Graphically, the entire hierarchy can be shown as in Figure 16.4.

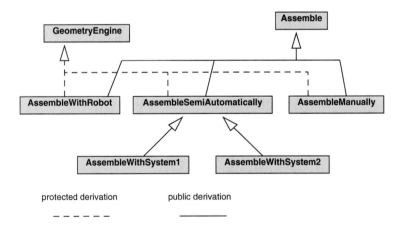

Fig. 16.4

The two approaches to the design we have presented are not the only ones available. Another possibility would be to use `GeometryEngine*` as a data member inside `Assemble`. That could be made to work, provided that `GeometryEngine` has no virtual member functions that would need to be overridden in `Assemble` and its subclasses. In any case, the MI-based design appears more natural and more logical to the situation at hand, and it meets a design criterion that it is best to keep distinct abstractions separate. Nonetheless, it is worthwhile to point out that the implementation code at the level of concrete classes such as `AssembleWithRobot` will remain substantially the same no matter which approach is used.

16.2   ISSUES THAT ARISE WITH REPEATED INHERITANCE

The most complicating issues that arise with MI have to do with what is known as *repeated inheritance*. Repeated inheritance takes place when a derived class inherits the same members of some base class through two different paths in a class hierarchy. To bring these issues into focus, consider the class hierarchy of Figure 16.5. The

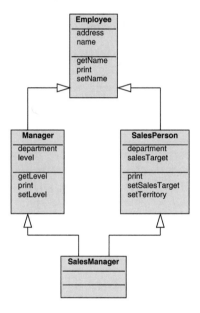

Fig. 16.5

classes `Manager` and `SalesPerson` are both derived from the base class `Employee`. And the class `SalesManager` is derived from both `Manager` and `SalesPerson`. We have intentionally left unspecified the data members and the member functions in the final derived-class `SalesManager`, as the following discussion bears directly on their specification.

When a derived class can inherit members through multiple paths and when the different paths have an upstream class in common, the following issues become immediately relevant:

1. *The Problem of Duplicate Construction of Common-Base Subobject:*
   Recall from Chapter 15 that when the constructor of a derived class is invoked, the derived-class object so constructed has built inside it a base-class subobject.

This is represented by Figure 16.6, which was also shown earlier in Chapter 15. That implies that, unless precautions are taken, when a constructor for

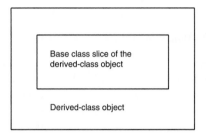

Fig. 16.6

SalesManager is invoked, we would end up with two different versions of the Employee slice in the constructed object, as illustrated by Figure 16.7. But that's not what we want. How do we prevent the formation of duplicate common-base subobjects in a derived-class object?

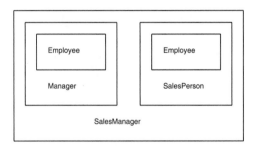

Fig. 16.7

2. *The Name-Conflict Problem for Member Functions:*

   Suppose two member functions of the same signature but different implementations are inherited by the SalesManager class from the two different inheritance paths shown. If these member functions are not overridden in the SalesManager class, we can end up with an ill-formed program. This could, for example, be the case with the print() member function that is listed originally as a member of the class Employee. Let's say this function is modified by each class between Employee and SalesManager. If for some reason, this modified function is not overridden in SalesManager but yet invoked on an object of type SalesManager, you would have a compile-time ambiguity.

3. *The Name-Conflict Problem for Data Members:*

   The class SalesManager inherits two different data members with the same name — department — one each from the two superclasses Manager and

SalesPerson. These two data members, although possessing the same name, possess different meanings for the derived class SalesManager because a SalesManager could conceivably have two different 'department' attributes associated with him or her. Such an individual could belong to a particular department of the corporation and, at the same time, be in charge of a particular unit of the sales organization which could also be referred to as a department. So how does one make sure that despite the same name — department — each data member gets the correct value when we construct an object of type SalesManager?

The next three sections will address each of the three problems listed above.

16.3 VIRTUAL BASES FOR MULTIPLE INHERITANCE

By declaring a common base to be virtual, we eliminate the problem of duplicate construction of subobjects of the common-base type.

For the purpose of explaining the concept of a virtual base, consider the hierarchy shown in Figure 16.8. Let's say we construct this hierarchy by using the following

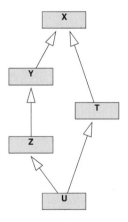

Fig. 16.8

class derivations:

```
class Y : public X { ........... }
class T : public X { ........... }
class Z : public Y { ........... }
class U : public Z, public T { ........}
```

Now if we construct an object of type U, we will have the subobjects shown in Figure 16.9 residing inside this object — clearly an undesirable situation. To forestall the

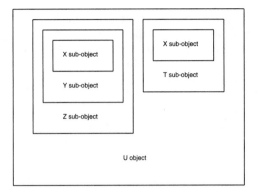

Fig. 16.9

duplication of subobjects of type X inside an object of type U, C++ requires us to declare X to be a virtual base of its immediate descendents, Y and T:

```
class Y : virtual public X {
//....
};

class T : virtual public X {
//....
};
```

Declaring X to be a virtual base would cause the X subobject to be shared by the Y and the T subobjects, resulting in the pictorial depiction shown in Figure 16.10. While declaring X as a virtual base of Y and T does result in the sharing of the X subobject, it requires that the constructor for X be now invoked explicitly in all the descendents of X. Ordinarily, a derived class constructor cannot invoke the constructor of its "indirect" base classes. (A base class is an indirect base if it is not an immediate base class.) So, ordinarily, the constructor for, say, the Z class is not allowed to invoke the constructor for the class X. But, with X as the virtual base, we must now explicitly call the constructor of X in the constructors of Y, Z, U, and T.

The program shown below constitutes an implementation of the hierarchy of Figure 16.8. Lines (A) and (B) declare X to be a virtual base of the classes Y and T. Note how that fact affects the syntax of the constructors in the lines (C) and (D) for the classes Z and U, respectively.

```
//VirtualBase.cc

#include <iostream>
using namespace std;
```

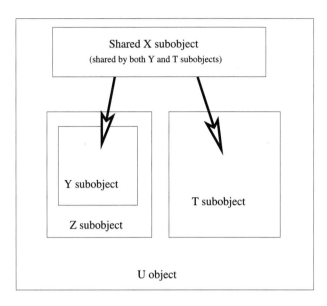

Fig. 16.10

```
class X {
    int x;
public:
    X( int xx ) : x(xx) {}
    virtual void print() {
        cout << "printing value of x of X subobject: " << x << endl;
    }
};

class Y : virtual public X {                              //(A)
    int y;
public:
    Y( int xx, int yy ) : X( xx ), y( yy ) {}
    void print() {
        X::print();
        cout << "printing value of y of Y subobject: " << y << endl;
    }
};

class T : virtual public X {                              //(B)
    int t;
public:
    T( int xx, int tt ) : X( xx ), t( tt ) {}
    void print(){
        X::print();
```

```cpp
            cout << "printing value of t of T subobject: " << t << endl;
    }
};

class Z : public Y {
    int z;
public:
    Z( int xx, int yy, int zz ) : Y( xx, yy ), X(xx), z( zz ) {}   //(C)
    void print() {
        Y::print();
        cout << "printing value of z of Z subobject: " << z << endl;
    }
};

class U : public Z, public T {
    int u;
public:
    U( int xx, int yy, int zz, int tt, int uu )
        : Z( xx, yy, zz ), T( xx, tt ), X( xx ), u( uu ) {}         //(D)
    void print() {
        Z::print();
        T::print();
        cout << "printing value of u of U subobject: " << u << endl;
    }
};

int main()
{
    cout << "X object coming up: " << endl;
    X xobj( 1 );
    xobj.print();                                          //(E)
    cout << endl;

    cout << "Y object coming up: " << endl;
    Y yobj( 11, 12 );
    yobj.print();                                          //(F)
    cout << endl;

    cout << "Z object coming up: " << endl;
    Z zobj( 110, 120, 130 );
    zobj.print();                                          //(G)
    cout << endl;

    cout << "T object coming up: " << endl;
    T tobj( 21, 22 );
    tobj.print();                                          //(H)
    cout << endl;

    cout << "U object coming up: " << endl;
```

```
    U uobj(9100, 9200, 9300, 9400, 9500 );                          //(I)
    uobj.print();
    cout << endl;

    return 0;
}
```

If X were not a virtual base in the hierarchy of Figure 16.8, the constructor for U in line (D) would look like

```
    U( int xx, int yy, int zz, int tt, int uu )
        : Z( xx, yy, zz ), T( xx, tt ), u( uu ) {}
```

But, because X is a virtual base, the constructor for U must include a direct invocation of the virtual base constructor:

```
    U( int xx, int yy, int zz, int tt, int uu )
        : Z( xx, yy, zz ), T( xx, tt ), X( xx ), u( uu ) {}
```

Note the appearance of X(xx) in the member initialization syntax. As shown in line (C), a similar modification has to be made to the constructor for Z.

The program produces the following output:

```
X object coming up:                         // output of line (E)
printing value of x of X subobject: 1

Y object coming up:                         // output of line (F)
printing value of x of X subobject: 11
printing value of y of Y subobject: 12

Z object coming up:                         // output of line (G)
printing value of x of X subobject: 110
printing value of y of Y subobject: 120
printing value of z of Z subobject: 130

T object coming up:                         // output of line (H)
printing value of x of X subobject: 21
printing value of t of T subobject: 22

U object coming up:                         // output of line (I)
printing value of x of X subobject: 9100
printing value of y of Y subobject: 9200
printing value of z of Z subobject: 9300
printing value of x of X subobject: 9100
printing value of t of T subobject: 9400
printing value of u of U subobject: 9500
```

This bring us to an important question about the program shown above: Considering that every descendent of X has a direct call to the constructor for X, whose job is it to create the the shared X subobject? The answer to this question is supplied by the following specification in the C++ language: *It is the job of the "most-derived" object to construct a virtual-base subobject.*

So, when we construct an object of type U, the job of constructing the shared X subobject falls on U's constructor's call to the X's constructor. To verify this fact, suppose we change the definition of the U class in the previous program to

```
class U : public Z, public T {
    int u;
public:
    U ( int xx, int yy, int zz, int tt, int uu )
      : W(4444, yy, zz), T(5555, tt), X( 6666 ), u( uu ){}      //(J)
    void print() {
        W::print();
        T::print();
        cout << "printing value of u of U subobject:" << u << endl;
    }
};
```

Note how we supply different arguments for the different calls to the X's constructor in line (J). For the direct invocation of X's constructor, we supply a value of 6666 for the data member of the X subobject. But, for the calls to the X's constructor through W, we supply a value of 4444 for the data-member of the X subobject, and so on.

When the above code is substituted for the definition of class U in the program VirtualBase.cc, we get the following output:

```
X object coming up:                          // output of line (E)
printing value of x of X subobject: 1

Y object coming up:                          // output of line (F)
printing value of x of X subobject: 11
printing value of y of Y subobject: 12

Z object coming up:                          // output of line (G)
printing value of x of X subobject: 110
printing value of y of Y subobject: 120
printing value of z of Z subobject: 130

T object coming up:                          // output of line (H)
printing value of x of X subobject: 21
printing value of t of T subobject: 22

U object coming up:                          // output of line (I)
printing value of x of X subobject: 6666                    //(K)
printing value of y of Y subobject: 9200                    //(L)
```

```
printing value of z of Z subobject: 9300                        //(M)
printing value of x of X subobject: 6666                        //(N)
printing value of t of T subobject: 9400                        //(O)
printing value of u of U subobject: 9500                        //(P)
```

The printout for the U object constructed by the statement in line (I) of main(), via the
new constructor shown in line (J) of the modified definition of the U class, is shown
in lines (K) through (P) above. As is clear from the output lines (K) and (N), the X
subobject corresponds to the constructor invocation

```
    X( 6666 )
```

in line (J) of the modified U class above. This invocation is U's attempt at direct
creation of the X subobject.

The "most-derived" rule for the construction of the common-base subobject applies
even to classes that are on single inheritance paths in a hierarchy with a virtual base.
For example, when we construct an object of type Z — even though Z is on a single
inheritance path, but it is a path that has a virtual base in it — the job of creating the
X subobject falls on Z's constructor making a direct call to the X's constructor.

16.4 VIRTUAL BASES AND COPY CONSTRUCTORS

Since the presence of a virtual base caused the downstream constructor definitions
to be modified, an obvious next question is, What about the implementation of the
downstream copy constructors? Yes, the downstream copy constructors also must
now make direct calls to the copy constructor of the common base.

In the following extension of the program of the previous section, note the syntax
of the copy constructors in line (D) and (E). Now there is direct invocation of the copy
constructor for the indirect base X.

```
//VirtualBaseCopyConstruct.cc

#include <iostream>
using namespace std;

class X {
    int x;
public:
    X( int xx ) : x(xx) {}
    //copy constructor:
    X( const X& other ) : x( other.x ) {}                       //(A)
    virtual void print() {
        cout << "printing value of x of X subobject: " << x << endl;
    }
};
```

```
class Y : virtual public X {
    int y;
public:
    Y( int xx, int yy ) : X( xx ), y( yy ) {}
    //copy constructor:
    Y( const Y& other ) : X( other ), y( other.y ) {}              //(B)
    void print() {
        X::print();
        cout << "printing value of y of Y subobject: " << y << endl;
    }
};

class T : virtual public X {
    int t;
public:
    T( int xx, int tt ) : X( xx ), t( tt ) {}
    //copy constructor:
    T( const T& other ) : X( other ), t( other.t ) {}              //(C)
    void print() {
        X::print();
        cout << "printing value of t of T subobject: " << t << endl;
    }
};

class Z : public Y {
    int z;
public:
    Z( int xx, int yy, int zz ) : Y( xx, yy ), X(xx), z( zz ) {}
    //copy constructor:
    Z( const Z& other ): Y( other ), X( other ), z( other.z ) {}  //(D)
    void print() {
        Y::print();
        cout << "printing value of z of Z subobject: " << z << endl;
    }
};

class U : public Z, public T {
    int u;
public:
    U ( int xx, int yy, int zz, int tt, int uu )
        : Z( xx, yy, zz ), T( xx, tt ), X( xx ), u( uu ) {}
    U( const U& other )          // copy constructor
      : Z( other ), T( other ), X( other ), u( other.u ) {}       //(E)
    void print() {
        Z::print();  T::print();
        cout << "printing value of u of U subobject: " << u << endl;
    }
};
```

```
int main()
{
    cout << "Z object coming up: " << endl;
    Z z_obj_1( 1110, 1120, 1130 );
    z_obj_1.print();                                      //(F)
    cout << endl;

    cout << "Z's duplicate object coming up: " << endl;
    Z z_obj_2 = z_obj_1;
    z_obj_2.print();                                      //(G)
    cout << endl;

    cout << "U object coming up: " << endl;
    U u_obj_1(9100, 9200, 9300, 9400, 9500 );
    u_obj_1.print();                                      //(H)
    cout << endl;

    //call U's copy constructor:
    cout << "U's duplicate object coming up: " << endl;
    U u_obj_2 = u_obj_1;
    u_obj_2.print();                                      //(I)
    cout << endl;

    return 0;
}
```

This program produces the following output:

```
Z object coming up:                      // output of line (F)
printing value of x of X subobject: 1110
printing value of y of Y subobject: 1120
printing value of z of Z subobject: 1130

Z's duplicate object coming up:          // output of line (G)
printing value of x of X subobject: 1110
printing value of y of Y subobject: 1120
printing value of z of Z subobject: 1130

U object coming up:                      // output of line (H)
printing value of x of X subobject: 9100
printing value of y of Y subobject: 9200
printing value of z of Z subobject: 9300
printing value of x of X subobject: 9100
printing value of t of T subobject: 9400
printing value of u of U subobject: 9500
```

```
U's duplicate object coming up:              // output of line (I)
printing value of x of X subobject: 9100
printing value of y of Y subobject: 9200
printing value of z of Z subobject: 9300
printing value of x of X subobject: 9100
printing value of t of T subobject: 9400
printing value of u of U subobject: 9500
```

16.5   VIRTUAL BASES AND ASSIGNMENT OPERATORS

Given that a virtual base requires modifying the syntax of the copy constructors for the downstream classes in a class hierarchy, what about the assignment operator definitions for the downstream classes? As it turns out, the syntax of the assignment operator function remains the same whether or not a base is virtual.

With that good news out of the way, we will use the rest of this section to give the reader a visual proof of the presence of duplicate base-class subobjects inside a derived-class object if the common-base is not declared virtual. Using the X, Y, Z, T, U hierarchy of Figure 16.8, our goal is to demonstrate visually that if X is not a virtual base, an object of type U will have sitting inside it two subobjects of type X. This we will do by playing with the assignment-operator overload definition for class U. Our demonstration will consist of showing to the reader two programs, one a correct implementation of the hierarchy of Figure 16.8 and another that is deliberately incorrect. Here is a top-level view of what is in the rest of this section:

1. We will first show the program `VirtualBaseCopyConstruct.cc` of the previous section with the assignment operator implementations added. The new program will be called `VirtualBaseAssign.cc`.

2. Next, in order to make a graphic demonstration of the presence of duplicate subobjects when a common base is not virtual, we will drop the "virtual" declaration of the common base in the program `VirtualBaseAssign.cc` and make appropriate changes to the rest of the program to make it consistent with a nonvirtual base. This new program will be called `DuplicateBase.cc`.

3. Finally, we will do something deliberately subversive in the program `DuplicateBase.cc`. In the assignment-operator definition for U, we will suppress the assignments along the right inheritance path in the hierarchy of Figure 16.8. So, when we assign a U object u2 to another U object u1, the latter will retain its own subobjects that correspond to the right inheritance path in the hierarchy. So if the X subobjects inside u1 and u2 are different, we should see them both in the new u1 after the assignment.

Here is the program of the previous section with the assignment operator included for each of the classes.

```
//VirtualBaseAssign.cc

#include <iostream>
using namespace std;

class X {
    int x;
public:
    X( int xx ) : x(xx) {}
    X( const X& other ) : x( other.x ) {}
    //assignment op:
    X& operator=( const X& other ) {
        if ( this == &other ) return *this;
        x = other.x;
        return *this;
    }
    virtual void print() {
        cout << "printing value of x of X subobject: " << x << endl;
    }
};

class Y : virtual public X {
    int y;
public:
    Y( int xx, int yy ) : X( xx ), y( yy ) {}
    Y( const Y& other ) : X( other ), y( other.y ) {}
    //assignment op:
    Y& operator=( const Y& other ) {
        if ( this == &other ) return *this;
        X::operator=( other );
        y = other.y;
        return *this;
    }
    void print() {
        X::print();
        cout << "printing value of y of Y subobject: " << y << endl;
    }
};

class T : virtual public X {
    int t;
public:
    T( int xx, int tt ) : X( xx ), t( tt ) {}
    T( const T& other ) : X( other ), t( other.t ) {}
    // assignment op:
    T& operator=( const T& other ) {
        if ( this == &other ) return *this;
```

```cpp
            X::operator=( other );
            t = other.t;
            return *this;
        }
        void print() {
            X::print();
            cout << "printing value of t of T subobject: " << t << endl;
        }
};

class Z : public Y {
    int z;
public:
    Z( int xx, int yy, int zz ) : Y( xx, yy ), X(xx), z( zz ) {}
    Z( const Z& other ) : Y( other ), X( other ), z( other.z ) {}
    // assignment op:
    Z& operator=( const Z& other ) {
        if ( this == &other ) return *this;
        Y::operator=( other );
        z = other.z;
        return *this;
    }
    void print() {
        Y::print();
        cout << "printing value of z of Z subobject: " << z << endl;
    }
};

class U : public Z, public T {
    int u;
public:
    U ( int xx, int yy, int zz, int tt, int uu )
        : Z( xx, yy, zz ), T( xx, tt ), X( xx ), u( uu ) {}
    U( const U& other )
      : Z( other ), T( other ), X( other ), u( other.u ) {}
    // assignment op:
    U& operator=( const U& other ) {
        if ( this == &other ) return *this;
        Z::operator=( other );                          //(A)
        T::operator=( other );                          //(B)
        u = other.u;
        return *this;
    }
    void print() {
        Z::print();
        T::print();
        cout << "printing value of u of U subobject: " << u << endl;
    }
};
```

```
int main()
{
    cout << "U object coming up: " << endl;
    U u_obj_1(9100, 9200, 9300, 9400, 9500 );
    u_obj_1.print();                                        //(C)
    cout << endl;

    U u_obj_2(7100, 7200, 7300, 7400, 7500 );

    u_obj_2 = u_obj_1;                                      //(D)

    cout << "U object after assignment: " << endl;
    u_obj_2.print();                                        //(E)
    return 0;
}
```

The above program produces the following output:

```
U object coming up:
printing value of x of X subobject: 9100    //output of line (C)
printing value of y of Y subobject: 9200
printing value of z of Z subobject: 9300
printing value of x of X subobject: 9100
printing value of t of T subobject: 9400
printing value of u of U subobject: 9500


The U object after assignment to another U object:

printing value of x of X subobject: 9100    //output of line (E)
printing value of y of Y subobject: 9200
printing value of z of Z subobject: 9300
printing value of x of X subobject: 9100
printing value of t of T subobject: 9400
printing value of u of U subobject: 9500
```

The program shown above, VirtualBaseAssign.cc, is a correct implementation of the class hierarchy of Figure 16.8. Shown below is a deliberately incorrect implementation of this hierarchy — we declare in lines (F) and (G) the common-base X to be nonvirtual and make other changes to the previous program to make it consistent with a nonvirtual X. The commented out lines indicate the changes that were made to VirtualBaseAssign.cc to obtain the new program. The changes made to the constructor and copy constructor for class Z are shown in lines (H) and (I), and those made to the the constructor and the copy constructor for class (U) are shown in lines (J) and (K).

```
//DuplicateBase.cc

#include <iostream.h>
using namespace std;

class X {
    int x;
public:
    X( int xx ) : x(xx) {}
    X( const X& other ) : x( other.x ) {}
    X& operator=( const X& other ) {
        if ( this == &other ) return *this;
        x = other.x;
        return *this;
    }
    virtual void print() {
        cout << "printing value of x of X subobject: " << x << endl;
    }
};

//class Y : virtual public X {
class Y : public X {                    // base is now nonvirtual      //(F)
    int y;
public:
    Y( int xx, int yy ) : X( xx ), y( yy ) {}
    Y( const Y& other ) : X( other ), y( other.y ) {}
    Y& operator=( const Y& other ) {
        if ( this == &other ) return *this;
        X::operator=( other );
        y = other.y;
        return *this;
    }
    void print() {
        X::print();
        cout << "printing value of y of Y subobject: " << y << endl;
    }
};

//class T : virtual public X {
class T : public X {                    // base is now nonvirtual      //(G)
    int t;
public:
    T( int xx, int tt ) : X( xx ), t( tt ) {}
    T( const T& other ) : X( other ), t( other.t ) {}
    T& operator=( const T& other ) {
        if ( this == &other ) return *this;
        X::operator=( other );
```

```
            t = other.t;
            return *this;
        }
        void print() {
            X::print();
            cout << "printing value of t of T subobject: " << t << endl;
        }
};

class Z : public Y {
    int z;
public:
    // Z( int xx, int yy, int zz ) : Y(xx, yy), X(xx), z(zz) {}
    Z( int xx, int yy, int zz ) : Y( xx, yy ), z( zz ) {}              //(H)
    //  Z( const Z& other ) : Y(other), X(other), z( other.z ) {}
    Z( const Z& other ) : Y( other ), z( other.z ) {}                 //(I)
    Z& operator=( const Z& other ) {
        if ( this == &other ) return *this;
        Y::operator=( other );
        z = other.z;
        return *this;
    }
    void print() {
        Y::print();
        cout << "printing value of z of Z subobject: " << z << endl;
    }
};

class U : public Z, public T {
    int u;
public:
    U ( int xx, int yy, int zz, int tt, int uu )
        //      : Z( xx, yy, zz ), T( xx, tt ), X(xx), u(uu) {}
                : Z( xx, yy, zz ), T( xx, tt ), u( uu ) {}             //(J)
    U( const U& other )
        //      : Z( other ), T( other ), X( other ), u(other.u) {}
                : Z( other ), T( other ), u( other.u ) {}             //(K)
    U& operator=( const U& other ) {
        if ( this == &other ) return *this;
        Z::operator=( other );                                        //(L)
        T::operator=( other );                                        //(M)
        u = other.u;
        return *this;
    }
    void print() {
        Z::print();  T::print();
        cout << "printing value of u of U subobject: " << u << endl;
    }
};
```

```
int main()
{
    cout << "U object coming up: " << endl;
    U u_obj_1(9100, 9200, 9300, 9400, 9500 );
    u_obj_1.print();                                            //(N)
    cout << endl;

    U u_obj_2(7100, 7200, 7300, 7400, 7500 );

    u_obj_2 = u_obj_1;

    cout << "The U object after assignment from another U object: "
        << endl;
    u_obj_2.print();                                            //(O)
    cout << endl;
    return 0;
}
```

The program produces the following output:

```
U object coming up:

printing value of x of X subobject: 9100    // output of line (N)
printing value of y of Y subobject: 9200
printing value of z of Z subobject: 9300
printing value of x of X subobject: 9100
printing value of t of T subobject: 9400
printing value of u of U subobject: 9500

The U object after assignment from another U object:

printing value of x of X subobject: 9100    // output of line (O)
printing value of y of Y subobject: 9200
printing value of z of Z subobject: 9300
printing value of x of X subobject: 9100
printing value of t of T subobject: 9400
printing value of u of U subobject: 9500
```

Now if we comment out line (M) in U's assignment operator function and run the same program again, we get the following output:

```
U object coming up:

printing value of x of X subobject: 9100    // output of line (N)
printing value of y of Y subobject: 9200
printing value of z of Z subobject: 9300
printing value of x of X subobject: 9100
```

```
printing value of t of T subobject: 9400
printing value of u of U subobject: 9500

The U object after assignment from another U object:

printing value of x of X subobject: 9100     // output of line (0)  //(P)
printing value of y of Y subobject: 9200
printing value of z of Z subobject: 9300
printing value of x of X subobject: 7100                            //(Q)
printing value of t of T subobject: 7400
printing value of u of U subobject: 9500
```

Note that in the copied over U object, the two X subobjects have two different values. The X subobject corresponding to the left inheritance path in the class diagram of Figure 16.8 has a value of 9100, as shown at (P), and the X subobject corresponding to the right inheritance path has the a value of 7100, as shown at (Q). This constitutes a direct visual proof of the existence of multiple subobjects of the common base type when we do not use virtual bases.

16.6 AVOIDING NAME CONFLICTS FOR MEMBER FUNCTIONS

Let's consider the hierarchy shown in Figure 16.11 in which we have a member function foo() defined originally for the common base X, and defined also for the derived classes Y, T, and U, with the implementation code as shown in the following program.

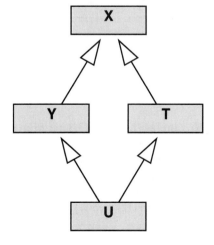

Fig. 16.11

```
//NameConflictMemFunc.cc

#include <iostream>
using namespace std;

class X {
public:
    void foo() { cout << "X's foo invoked" << endl; }
};

class Y : virtual public X {
public:
    void foo() { cout << "Y's foo invoked" << endl; }
};

class T : virtual public X {
public:
    void foo() {cout << "T's foo invoked" << endl;}          //(A)
};

class U : public Y, public T {
public:
    void foo() {cout << "U's foo invoked" << endl;}          //(B)
};

int main()
{
    U u;
    u.foo();            // U's foo invoked                   //(C)
    u.X::foo();         // X's foo invoked
    u.Y::foo();         // Y's foo invoked
    u.T::foo();         // T's foo invoked
    return 0;
}
```

Even though U inherits two different version of foo() from the different inheritance paths, it does not cause any problems in the function call u.foo() in line (C) of main. That is because U has its own definition for foo() that hides all other inherited definitions of the same function name. But if we were to comment out U's definition of foo() in line (B), the statement in line (C) will give rise to a compilation error because of the name conflict between the two versions of foo() inherited by U.

What's interesting is that if we comment out both the U's definition for foo() and the definition in one of the two inheritance paths converging at U, the program will again work fine. That is, suppose we also comment out the definition of foo() in

T in line (A), in addition to commenting out the definition in line (B), there will no problem with the compilation or the running of the program even though there is still a name conflict between the definition of foo() as inherited from Y and the definition of foo() as inherited from X through T. In this case, U will use the "most recent" definition of foo(), the one in Y in this case.

So we can always be sure that as long as a class where two or more inheritance paths converge has its own definition for member functions of the same signature that it inherits from the different paths, there is no name conflict problem. When such a class does not provide its own definition, then there can potentially be a name conflict. This name conflict will only be discovered if the member function in question is invoked on an object of that class or on objects of its derived classes. Therefore, name conflict problems for member functions can remain potentially hidden and may surface only at a later time when you or someone else tries to invoke those functions. To ward off such difficulties, it is best to be aware of such functions and to provide them with definitions in classes where inheritance paths converge.

The main of the program presented above also demonstrates that we can always access a superclass member function that is hidden in a derived class — even if the derived class is at the junction of converging inheritance paths — by invoking the scope operator on the superclass containing the desired function definition.

16.7 DEALING WITH NAME CONFLICTS FOR DATA MEMBERS

Let's consider the hierarchy shown in Figure 16.12 in which all the data members have the same name, called name. This data member has a different meaning in each class. In the class Alien, it stands for an Alien's name. In the class CatLovingAlien, it stands for a cat's name. In the class DogLovingAlien, it stands for a dog's name. Given that PetLovingAlien inherits the name fields of the same name from two

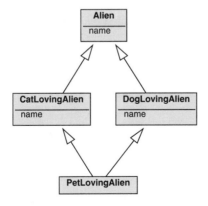

Fig. 16.12

different paths, each carrying a different meaning, we are faced with the problem of how to assign proper values to these fields in a `PetLovingAlien` constructor. This problem looks more difficult that it actually is. All we have to do is to ship off the different arguments in the `PetLovingAlien` constructor to the different superclass constructors, as shown below:

```
PetLovingAlien( string catName, string dogName, string ownerName )
    : CatLovingAlien( catName, ownerName ),
      DogLovingAlien( dogName, ownerName ),
      Alien( ownerName ) {}
```

Each superclass constructor will make sure that its own name data member gets the value that is assigned to it.

The other problem with data-member name conflicts is how to access such data members in the class where the name conflicts occur. Let's say we need access to both the cat's name and the dog's name, in addition to possibly the owner's name, in an object of type `PetLovingAlien`. This is easily taken care of by using the ':::' operator, as shown in lines (A), (B), and (C) of the example below.

```
//NameConflictDataMem.cc

#include <iostream>
#include <string>
using namespace std;

class Alien {
protected:
    string name;
public:
    Alien( string nam ) : name( nam ) {}
};

class CatLovingAlien : virtual public Alien  {
protected:
    string name;                    // Cat's name
public:
    CatLovingAlien( string catName, string ownerName )
        : Alien( ownerName),  name ( catName ) {}
};

class DogLovingAlien : virtual public Alien {
protected:
    string name;                    // Dog's name
public:
    DogLovingAlien( string dogName, string ownerName )
        : Alien( ownerName ), name( dogName ) {}
};
```

```
class PetLovingAlien : public CatLovingAlien, public DogLovingAlien {
public:
    PetLovingAlien( string catName, string dogName, string ownerName )
        : CatLovingAlien( catName, ownerName ),
          DogLovingAlien( dogName, ownerName ),
          Alien( ownerName ) {}
    void print() {
        cout << CatLovingAlien::name << " "                    //(A)
             << DogLovingAlien::name << " "                    //(B)
             << Alien::name << endl;                           //(C)
    }
};

int main()
{
    PetLovingAlien alien( "Tabby", "Pluto", "Zaphod" );
    alien.print();     // Tabby Pluto Zaphod
    return 0;
}
```

16.8 IMPLEMENTATION OF AN EXAMPLE IN REPEATED INHERITANCE

For an example in repeated inheritance, let's consider the hierarchy of Figure 16.13.

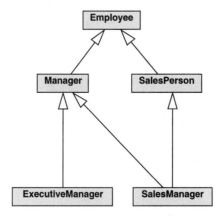

Fig. 16.13

Let's say that our overall goal is to figure out whether or not an employee is ready for a promotion. Let's assume that the following considerations enter into the promotion criteria:

- Assuming that a `Manager` is in charge of one department, his/her performance will be judged on the basis of the following three criteria: (a) the year-to-year gain in the productivity of his/her department; (b) the satisfaction level of the employees in his/her department; and (c) the number of years in rank. (This obviously means that we will also need a `Department` class to keep track of the yearly productivity numbers.)

- An `ExecutiveManager` will be assumed to supervise multiple departments. His/her performance will be measured by computing productivity gain numbers for all the departments under his/her supervision.

- A `SalesPerson`'s performance will be measured by the year-to-year change in the volume of sales and the number of years in rank.

For implementing the class hierarchy of Figure 16.13, the common base, `Employee`, will obviously have to be declared virtual. This fact will have to be reflected in all the downstream constructors and copy constructors, in accordance with the discussion in Sections 16.3 and 16.4 of this chapter.

We will now show a partial implementation of this hierarchy and leave it to the reader to complete it. However, before the implementation, we will show a header file containing some ancillary types that are used in the implementation. The header file contains the `Department` class and the enumerations needed for those data members of our classes that have specifically designated symbolic values.[1]   Note that the data members of type `Department` will carry different meanings in different classes, and sometimes different meanings within the same class. An `Employee`'s job will be in one specific `Department` (although it would be easy to change the structure of our classes so that an `Employee` could work in multiple departments at the same time). A `Manager` will be in charge of one `Department`. An `ExecutiveManager` will be in charge of multiple `Departments`. While a `Manager` will also work in the department of which he/she is in charge, a `ExecutiveManager` may not work in any of the departments that he/she is in charge of. Here is the header file:

```
//MI_Utilities.h

#ifndef MI_UTILITIES_H
#define MI_UTILITIES_H
```

---

[1] Placing this information in a separate header will allow us to use the same header in the next two sections of this chapter.

```cpp
#include <iostream>
#include <string>
#include <vector>
using namespace std;


//////////////////////// global constant ////////////////////////
//min number of years at job before promotion:
const int MinYearsForPromotion = 4;

//////////////////////// enumerations ////////////////////////
enum EducationLevel { HighSchool,
                      TradeSchool,
                      College,
                      CollegePlus,
                      eUnknown
};

static const string EducationLevels[] = { "highschool",
                                          "tradeschool",
                                          "college",
                                          "college plus",
                                          "unknown"
};

enum PeopleSkill { Loner,
                   Reserved,
                   Friendly,
                   ReachesOut,
                   Empathizer,
                   pUnknown
};

static const string PeopleSkills[] = { "loner",
                                       "reserved",
                                       "friendly",
                                       "reaches out",
                                       "empathizer",
                                       "unknown"
};

enum Leadership { CanLeadLargeGroups,
                  CanLeadSmallGroups,
                  NotLeader,
                  lUnknown
};
```

```
static const string LeaderQualities[] = {
                    "can lead large groups",
                    "can lead only small groups",
                    "unable to lead",
                    "unknown"
};




/////////////////////  utility class Department  /////////////////////

class Department {
    string name;
    int productionLastYear;     // Last year's production
    int productionPreviousYear; // Previous year's production
                                // (previous means two years back)
public:
    Department() {}
    Department( string nam ) : name( nam ) {}
    void setProductionLastYear( int dd ){
        productionLastYear = dd;
    }
    void setProductionPreviousYear( int dd ) {
        productionPreviousYear = dd;
    }
    int getProductionLastYear() {
        return productionLastYear;
    }
    int getProductionPreviousYear(){
        return productionPreviousYear;
    }
    string getName() { return name; }
    void print() {
        cout << "Department name: " << name << endl;
    }
};
#endif
```

Shown below is a partial implementation of the inheritance hierarchy of Figure 16.13. Each class is provided with a general-purpose constructor that initializes all the data members of a class. The Employee and Manager classes are also provided with one additional constructor for dealing with the situation of an ExecutiveManager or a SalesManager not belonging to any particular department.

In lines (A) and (F) of the program shown below, we declare Employee to be a virtual base of the classes Manager and SalesPerson, respectively. This creates a need for direct calls to the Employee constructor in the constructors of ExecutiveManager and SalesManager, as shown in lines (C), (D) and (H). The classes Manager, SalesPerson, and SalesManager are each provided with their own implementations for the virtual function productivityGainYtoY in lines (B), (E), and (G), respectively.. Since this function is virtual, it will work polymorphically for the manager types.

```
//RepeatInherit.cc

#include "MI_Utilities.h"

//////////////////////////// class Employee ////////////////////////////
class Employee {
protected:
    string name;
    string address;
    EducationLevel education;
    int yearsExperience;      // years on job
    Department dept;
    PeopleSkill pSkill;       // needed for sales positions
    Leadership leadership;    // needed for management
public:
    Employee( string nam,
              string add,
              EducationLevel edLevel,
              Department depart )
        :     name( nam ),
              address( add ),
              education( edLevel ),
              yearsExperience( 0 ),
              dept( depart ),
              pSkill( pUnknown ),
              leadership( lUnknown ) {}
    // since senior level managers do not belong to any particular
    // department, the next constructor is for such employees:
    Employee( string nam,
              string add,
              EducationLevel edLevel )
        :     name( nam ),
              address( add ),
              education( edLevel ),
              yearsExperience( 0 ),
              pSkill( pUnknown ),
              leadership( lUnknown ) {}
    void setYearsExperience( int yy ) { yearsExperience = yy; }
    void setPeopleSkill( PeopleSkill skill ){ pSkill = skill; }
    string getName() const { return name; }
    string getAddress() const { return address; }
```

```
        EducationLevel getEducationLevel() const { return education; }
        virtual void print() {
            cout << name << endl;
            cout << address << endl;
            cout << EducationLevels[ education ] << endl;
            cout << "Years in job: " << yearsExperience << endl;
            cout << "People skill: " << PeopleSkills[ (int) pSkill ]
                 << endl;
            cout << "Leadership quality: "
                 << LeaderQualities[ (int) leadership ]  << endl;
        }
        virtual ~Employee(){}
};

//////////////////////////  class Manager  //////////////////////////
class Manager : virtual public Employee {                        //(A)
    Department dept;      // note same name as dept in Employee
                          // but different meaning.  Here it is dept
                          // supervised and not department worked in
protected:
    bool employeeSatisfaction;
    int yearsInManagement;
public:
    Manager( string name,
             string address,
             EducationLevel education,
             Department aDept )
        :    Employee( name, address, education ),
             dept( aDept ),
             yearsInManagement( 0 ),
             employeeSatisfaction( false ) {}
    // Since senior-level managers do not belong to any particular
    // department, the next constructor is actually for them
    Manager( string name,
             string address,
             EducationLevel education )
        :    Employee( name, address, education ) {}
    virtual double productivityGainYtoY() {                      //(B)
        int lastProd = dept.getProductionLastYear();
        int prevProd = dept.getProductionPreviousYear();
        return 100 * ( lastProd - prevProd ) / (double) prevProd;
    }
    void setDepartment( Department dept ){ this->dept = dept; }
    int getYearsInManagement() { return yearsInManagement; }
    void setYearsInManagement( int y ) { yearsInManagement = y; }
    bool getEmployeeSatisfaction() { return employeeSatisfaction; }
    void setEmployeeSatisfaction( bool satis ) {
        employeeSatisfaction = satis;
    }
```

```
    virtual bool readyForPromotion(){
        return ( ( yearsInManagement
                        >= MinYearsForPromotion ) ? true : false )
                && ( productivityGainYtoY() > 10 )
                && employeeSatisfaction;
    }
    void print() { Employee::print(); dept.print(); }
    ~Manager(){}
};


/////////////////////// class ExecutiveManager ///////////////////////////
// An ExecutiveManager supervises more than one department
class ExecutiveManager : public Manager {
    short level;
    vector<Department> departments;     // depts in charge of
public:
    // no-arg const. needed in the second example for type conversion
    // from Manager to ExecutiveManager:
    ExecutiveManager()
        :       Manager( "", "", eUnknown ),
                Employee( "", "", eUnknown ),                    //(C)
                level( 0 ) {}
    ExecutiveManager( string name,
                      string address,
                      EducationLevel education,
                      short level )
            :       Manager( name, address, education ),
                    Employee( name, address, education ),       //(D)
                    level( level )
    {
        departments = vector<Department>();
    }
    void addDepartment(Department dept){departments.push_back( dept );}
    void setLevel( int lvl ) { level = lvl; }
    // overrides Manager's productivityGainYtoY():
    double productivityGainYtoY() {                              //(E)
        double gain = 0.0;
        vector<Department>::iterator iter = departments.begin();
        while ( iter != departments.end() ) {
            int lastProd = iter->getProductionLastYear();
            int prevProd = iter->getProductionPreviousYear();
            gain += ( lastProd - prevProd ) / prevProd;
        }
        return gain/departments.size();
    }
    void print() {
        Employee::print();
        cout << "Departments supervised: " << endl;
        vector<Department>::iterator iter = departments.begin();
```

```cpp
        while ( iter != departments.end() )
            iter++->print();
    }
    ~ExecutiveManager(){}
};


//////////////////////////  class SalesPerson  //////////////////////////
class SalesPerson : virtual public Employee {              //(F)
    int salesLastYear;
    int salesPreviousYear;
protected:
    int yearsInSales;
public:
    SalesPerson( string name,
                 string address,
                 EducationLevel education )
        :          Employee( name,
                             address,
                             education,
                             Department( "Sales" )),
                 salesLastYear( 0 ),
                 salesPreviousYear( 0 ),
               . yearsInSales( 0 ) {}
    int getSalesLastYear() {
        return salesLastYear;
    }
    void setSalesLastYear( int sales ) {
        salesLastYear = sales;
    }
    int getSalesPreviousYear() {
        return salesPreviousYear;
    }
    void setSalesPreviousYear( int sales ) {
        salesPreviousYear = sales;
    }
    int getYearsInSales() { return yearsInSales; }
    void setYearsInSales( int y ) { yearsInSales = y; }
    virtual double productivityGainYtoY() {                //(G)
        return 100 * ( salesLastYear
            - salesPreviousYear ) / (double) salesPreviousYear;
    }
    virtual bool readyForPromotion(){
        return ( ( yearsInSales
                        >= MinYearsForPromotion ) ? true : false )
                && ( productivityGainYtoY() > 10 );
    }
    ~SalesPerson(){}
};
```

```
/////////////////////// class SalesManager ///////////////////////////
class SalesManager : public SalesPerson, public Manager {
    int yearInSalesManagement;
    vector<SalesPerson> sellersSupervised;
public:
    SalesManager( string name,
                  string address,
                  EducationLevel education )
            :     Manager( name, address, education ),
                  SalesPerson( name, address, education ),
                  Employee( name, address, education ) {}          //(H)

    double productivityGainYtoY(){
        return 0;   // left for the reader to complete
    }
    ~SalesManager(){}
};

///////////////////////////// main ////////////////////////////////////
int main()
{
    Department d1( "Design" );
    d1.setProductionLastYear( 110001 );        // for last year
    d1.setProductionPreviousYear( 100000 );    // for two years back

    Manager manager1("Miz Importante", "UptownUSA", College, d1); //(I)
    manager1.setYearsInManagement( 8 );
    manager1.setEmployeeSatisfaction( true );

    if ( manager1.readyForPromotion() ) {
        cout << manager1.getName() << " "
             << "is ready for promotion." << endl;
    } else {
        cout << manager1.getName() << " "
             << "is not ready for promotion."
             << endl << endl;
    }

    Department d2( "Manufacturing" );
    Department d3( "Development" );

    SalesPerson salesman("Joe Seller", "DowntownUSA", College);   //(J)
    salesman.setYearsInSales( 5 );
    salesman.setSalesPreviousYear( 100 );
    salesman.setSalesLastYear( 100 );
    if ( salesman.readyForPromotion() ) {
        cout << salesman.getName() << " "
             << "is ready for promotion." << endl;
    } else {
```

```
        cout << salesman.getName() << " "
             << "is not ready for promotion." << endl;
    }

    ExecutiveManager bigshot( "Zushock Zinger",                    //(K)
                            "MainstreetUSA", CollegePlus, 4 );
    bigshot.addDepartment( d1 );
    bigshot.addDepartment( d2 );
    bigshot.addDepartment( d3 );
    bigshot.print();                                              //(L)

    return 0;
}
```

Line (I) of main defines a Manager whose name is Miz Importante and line (J) defines an SalesPerson of name Joe Seller. With regard to whether or not these individuals are ready for promotion, the program produces the output shown below. The output also shows the state of the bigshot object created in line (K).

```
Miz Importante is ready for promotion.

Joe Seller is not ready for promotion.

Zushock Zinger              // output produced by line (L)
MainstreetUSA
college plus
Years in job: 0
People skill: unknown
Leadership quality: unknown
Departments supervised:
Department name: Design
Department name: Manufacturing
Department name: Development
```

16.9 USING MIXIN CLASSES

As should be clear from the discussion so far, repeated inheritance complicates a C++ program and can make its extension particularly troublesome. Let's say you wish to extend a previously written program that did not have repeated inheritance and that your extension creates an inheritance loop because you bring together a couple of what seemed like disparate classes into a new derived class. For the new program to work correctly, you will have to go back into the old program and re-engineer it by declaring the common base to be virtual, by changing all the downstream constructors and copy constructors, and so on. These problems can often be avoided by using what are known in C++ as *mixin* classes. Ideally, a mixin class in C++ is very much like an interface in Java — an abstract class that only consists of pure virtual functions.

To illustrate the idea of mixin classes, let's first quickly review the inheritance hierarchy of the previous section. Recall, our program there kept a record of what departments were supervised by which manager. A Manager supervised only one department, while an ExecutiveManager could supervise an arbitrary number of departments. Each department kept a record of its productivity for the previous two years and the managers were promoted only after a certain minimum number of years on the job and only if their productivity was above a certain threshold. The same was true of SalesPersons and SalesManagers, although their productivity was measured taking into account the sales-related numbers.

We will now present an alternative design for achieving the same overall functionality as that described in the previous section. Our new design will use the more extendible hierarchy of Figure 16.14 which uses mixin classes and has no inheritance loops for the implementation code.

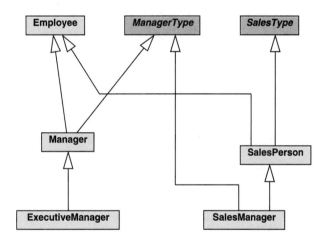

Fig. 16.14

In this new design, the classes ManagerType and SalesType are abstract — no objects will ever be made of these two classes. The responsibility of these classes is to impart some additional behavior to other classes. So when the behavior represented by the ManagerType class is combined with the behavior of the Employee class, we get the Manager class. On the other hand, when we impart the behavior represented by the ManagerType class to the SalesPerson class, we get the SalesManager class. By the same token, when we impart the behavior represented by the SalesType abstract class to the Employee class, we get the SalesPerson class. Classes such as ManagerType and SalesType are the mixin classes.

For our example here, we will assign the following behaviors to the mixin classes:

```
class ManagerType {
protected:
    virtual double productivityGainYtoY() = 0;
    virtual int getYearsInManagement() = 0;
    virtual bool getEmployeeSatisfaction() = 0;
};

class SalesType {
protected:
    virtual int getYearsInSales() = 0;
    virtual double salesGainYtoY() = 0;
};
```

Based on the discussion in the last section, these behaviors make sense. As was said earlier, managers will be judged by the year-to-year productivity gains in the departments they head, by the job satisfaction experienced by the employees in those departments, and by the number of years in rank. So calculating these measures of performance represents important behaviors for a program that keeps track of managers. Similarly, for the `SalesType` mixin class.

The code that follows pulls in the header file `MI_Utilities.h` we created in the previous section for the enumerations and the `Department` class needed here. As was the case with the implementation in the previous section, it is also true here that the data members of type `Department` will carry different meanings in different classes, and sometimes different meanings within the same class.

It is interesting to note that much of the code that was written for the repeated-inheritance based implementation of the previous section remains unchanged in the program shown below. To highlight this point, the implementation of important functions like `ProductivityGainYtoY()` for the various classes remains exactly the same as before, as can be seen by the functions in lines (A), (B), and (C). The source code follows:

```
//Mixin.cc

#include "MI_Utilities.h"

///////////////////////// class Employee /////////////////////////
class Employee {
protected:
    string name;
    string address;
    EducationLevel education;
    int yearsExperience;        // years on job
    Department dept;
    PeopleSkill pSkill;         // needed for sales positions
    Leadership leadership;      // needed for management
```

```cpp
public:
    Employee( string nam,
              string add,
              EducationLevel edLevel,
              Department depart )
        :     name( nam ),
              address( add ),
              education( edLevel ),
              yearsExperience( 0 ),
              dept( depart ),
              pSkill( pUnknown ),
              leadership( lUnknown ) {}
    // since senior level managers do not belong to
    // any particular department, the next constructor
    // is for such employees
    Employee( string nam,
              string add,
              EducationLevel edLevel )
        :     name( nam ),
              address( add ),
              education( edLevel ),
              yearsExperience( 0 ),
              pSkill( pUnknown ),
              leadership( lUnknown ) {}
    void setYearsExperience( int yy ) {
        yearsExperience = yy;
    }
    void setPeopleSkill( PeopleSkill skill ) {
        pSkill = skill;
    }
    string getName() const { return name; }
    string getAddress() const { return address; }
    EducationLevel getEducationLevel() const {
        return education;
    }
    virtual void print(){
        cout << name << endl;
        cout << address << endl;
        cout << EducationLevels[ education ] << endl;
        cout << "Years in job: " << yearsExperience << endl;
        cout << "People skill: "
             << PeopleSkills[ (int) pSkill ] << endl;
        cout << "Leadership quality: "
             << LeaderQualities[ (int) leadership ];
        cout  << endl;
    }
    virtual ~Employee() {}
};
```

```
///////////////////// mixin class ManagerType /////////////////////
class ManagerType {
protected:
    virtual double productivityGainYtoY() = 0;
    virtual int getYearsInManagement() = 0;
    virtual bool getEmployeeSatisfaction() = 0;
};


/////////////////////////// class Manager ///////////////////////////
class Manager : public Employee, public ManagerType {
    Department dept;   // note same name as dept in Employee
                       // but different meaning.  Here it is
                       // dept supervised and not
                       // department worked in
protected:
    int yearsInManagement;
    bool employeeSatisfaction;
public:
    Manager( string name,
             string address,
             EducationLevel education,
             Department aDept )
        :    Employee( name, address, education ),
             dept( aDept ),
             yearsInManagement( 0 ),
             employeeSatisfaction( false ) {}
    // Since senior-level managers do not belong to any particular
    // department, the next constructor is actually for them
    Manager( string name,
             string address,
             EducationLevel education )
        :    Employee( name, address, education ) {}
    double productivityGainYtoY() {                             //(A)
        int lastProd = dept.getProductionLastYear();
        int prevProd = dept.getProductionPreviousYear();
        return 100 * ( lastProd - prevProd ) / (double) prevProd;
    }
    void setDepartment( Department dept ){ this->dept = dept; }
    int getYearsInManagement() { return yearsInManagement; }
    void setYearsInManagement( int y ) { yearsInManagement = y; }
    bool getEmployeeSatisfaction() { return employeeSatisfaction; }
    void setEmployeeSatisfaction( bool satis ) {
        employeeSatisfaction = satis;
    }
    virtual bool readyForPromotion(){
        return ( ( yearsInManagement
                        >= MinYearsForPromotion ) ? true : false )
                && ( productivityGainYtoY() > 10 )
                && employeeSatisfaction;
```

```
    }
    void print() { Employee::print(); dept.print(); }
    ~Manager() {}
};


/////////////////////// class ExecutiveManager ///////////////////////
// An ExecutiveManager supervises more than one department
class ExecutiveManager : public Manager {
    short level;
    vector<Department> departments;
public:
    // Needed in the second example for type conversion
    // from Manager to ExecutiveManager
    ExecutiveManager()
        :         Manager( "", "", eUnknown ), level( 0 ) {}
    ExecutiveManager( string name,
                      string address,
                      EducationLevel education,
                      short level )
            :         Manager( name,
                              address,
                              education ), level( level ) {
        departments = vector<Department>();
    }
    void addDepartment( Department dept ) {
        departments.push_back( dept );
    }
    void setLevel( int lvl ) { level = lvl; }
    // overrides Manager's productivityGainYtoY():
    double productivityGainYtoY(){                              //(B)
        double gain = 0.0;
        vector<Department>::iterator iter = departments.begin();
        while ( iter != departments.end() ) {
            int lastProd = iter->getProductionLastYear();
            int prevProd = iter->getProductionPreviousYear();
            gain += ( lastProd - prevProd ) / prevProd;
        }
        return gain/departments.size();
    }
    void print() {
        Employee::print();
        cout << "Departments supervised: " << endl;
        vector<Department>::iterator iter = departments.begin();
        while ( iter != departments.end() )
            iter++->print();
    }
    ~ExecutiveManager(){}
};
```

```
///////////////////////// mixin class SalesType /////////////////////////
class SalesType {
protected:
    virtual int getYearsInSales() = 0;
    virtual double productivityGainYtoY() = 0;
};


///////////////////////// class SalesPerson /////////////////////////
class SalesPerson : public Employee, public SalesType {
    int salesLastYear;
    int salesPreviousYear;
protected:
    int yearsInSales;
public:
    SalesPerson( string name,
                 string address,
                 EducationLevel education )
        :           Employee( name,
                              address,
                              education,
                              Department( "Sales" )),
                 salesLastYear( 0 ),
                 salesPreviousYear( 0 ),
                 yearsInSales( 0 ) {}
    int getSalesLastYear() {
        return salesLastYear;
    }
    void setSalesLastYear( int sales ) {
        salesLastYear = sales;
    }
    int getSalesPreviousYear() {
        return salesPreviousYear;
    }
    void setSalesPreviousYear( int sales ) {
        salesPreviousYear = sales;
    }
    int getYearsInSales() { return yearsInSales; }
    void setYearsInSales( int y ) { yearsInSales = y; }
    double productivityGainYtoY() {                            //(C)
        return 100 * ( salesLastYear
            - salesPreviousYear ) / (double) salesPreviousYear;
    }
    virtual bool readyForPromotion(){
        return ( ( yearsInSales
                    >= MinYearsForPromotion ) ? true : false )
            && ( productivityGainYtoY() > 10 );
    }
    ~SalesPerson() {}
};
```

```
//////////////////////// class SalesManager ////////////////////////
class SalesManager : public SalesPerson, public ManagerType {
    int yearInSalesManagement;
    Employee* sellersSupervised;
public:
    SalesManager( string name,
                  string address,
                  EducationLevel education )
            :     SalesPerson( name, address, education ) {}
    double productivityGainYtoY(){
        return 0;   // left for the reader to complete
    }
};

//////////////////////////// main ////////////////////////////
int main()
{
    Department d1( "Design" );
    d1.setProductionLastYear( 110001 );        // for last year
    d1.setProductionPreviousYear( 100000 );    // for two years back

    Manager manager1("Miz Importante", "UptownUSA", College, d1); //(D)
    manager1.setYearsInManagement( 8 );
    manager1.setEmployeeSatisfaction( true );

    if ( manager1.readyForPromotion() ) {
        cout << manager1.getName() << " "
             << "is ready for promotion." << endl;
    } else {
        cout << manager1.getName() << " "
             << "is not ready for promotion." << endl;
    }

    Department d2( "Manufacturing" );
    Department d3( "Development" );

    SalesPerson salesman("Joe Seller", "Downtown, USA", College); //(E)
    salesman.setYearsInSales( 5 );
    salesman.setSalesPreviousYear( 100 );
    salesman.setSalesLastYear( 100 );
    if ( salesman.readyForPromotion() ) {
        cout << salesman.getName() << " "
             << "is ready for promotion."
             << endl << endl;
    } else {
        cout << salesman.getName() << " "
             << "is not ready for promotion." << endl;
    }
```

```
        ExecutiveManager bigshot( "Zushock Zinger",
                                  "MainstreetUSA", CollegePlus, 4 );
        bigshot.addDepartment( d1 );
        bigshot.addDepartment( d2 );
        bigshot.addDepartment( d3 );
        bigshot.print();
        return 0;
}
```

The test code shown in `main` above is again the same as in the implementation of the previous section. We construct a `Manager` and a `SalesPerson` objects in lines (D) and (E) and test whether or not they are ready for promotion. We also construct an `ExecutiveManager` object in line (F). The output produced for all these three objects remains the same as shown at the end of the previous section.

16.10   USING ROLE-PLAYING CLASSES

The approaches to OO design laid out so far — the one using repeated inheritance and the one based on mixin classes — will work for domains that lend themselves to mutually exclusive categorization. By mutually exclusive categorization we mean apples versus oranges kind of categorization — a fruit cannot be an apple and an orange at the same time. In both the repeated-inheritance and the mixin-classes examples of the previous two sections, an `Employee` can only be a `Manager`, or a `Salesperson`, or a `SalesManager`, and so on. Those programs will not allow for an `Employee` to be a `Manager` *and* a `SalesPerson` at the same time. This situation can be described by saying that each `Employee` in those programs is locked into one role. Yes, we could extend the class hierarchies in those examples to create further combination roles, but at some point we would run into combinatorial issues, not to speak of the inheritance loops that we might create in the process.

But there exist important domains that do not allow for mutually exclusive categorization. Even in the simple employee "domain" we have been considering, it is indeed possible for an `Employee` to be a `Manager` and a `SalesPerson` at the same time. We will now show how one can base OO design on role-playing classes that allow objects to play multiple roles simultaneously. In the particular employee-domain example of a role-based hierarchy we will present in this section, the same individual will be allowed to acquire multiple roles, but at any given time only one role will be active.[2]

---

[2]It would be easy to modify the program so that at any given time a *set* of roles would be active, as opposed to just one role.

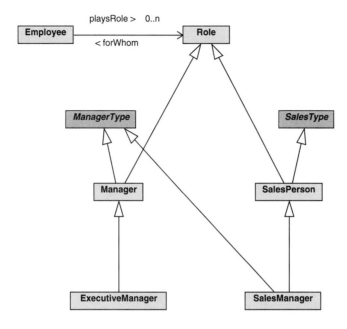

Fig. 16.15

Shown in Figure 16.15 is a role-based class hierarchy for achieving the same functionality as in the previous two sections. The hierarchy of role-playing classes hangs from the root class Role. So, as shown in the figure, a Manager IsA Role, a SalesPerson IsA Role, an ExecutiveManager IsA Role, and a SalesManager IsA Role. Whereas the links shown in the hierarchy that hang from Role are those of generalization/ specialization, the link between Employee and Role is an association. An Employee can have an arbitrary number of roles, including no roles. The purpose of the Role class vis-à-vis the Employee class is made clear by the following partial definition of the latter:

```
class Employee {
protected:
    string name;
    string address;
    EducationLevel education;
    PeopleSkill pSkill;
    Leadership leadership;
    vector<Role*> allRoles;
    Role* activeRole;
    //........
};
```

Note the new data members, allRoles and activeRole. The data member allRoles is supposed to store a list of all the roles that an employee is qualified to play. So if an `Employee` is qualified to serve both as a `Manager` and as a `SalesPerson`, both these roles would be in the vector `allRoles`. With a slight modification of the system, we could even store in this vector the different types of managerial obligations that an `Employee` could fulfill. For example, the vector could contain more detailed items such as "Manager of Design Department," "Manager of Development Department," and so on. The data member `activeRole` is supposed to capture the notion that an `Employee` can only be active in one role at one time.

The functionality of the `Employee` class with respect to the various roles is described by the following functions:

```
class Employee {
    //.....
public:
    // .....
    Role* setActiveRole( Role* role );
    Role* getActiveRole() const;
    void addToRoles( Role* newRole );
    void removeRole( Role* role );
    //.....
};
```

Obviously, now it will be possible for an employee to be, say, a manager at one time and then to be a salesperson at another time.

In our example, the class `Role` that sits at the root of the hierarchy of the role playing classes contains code that we want inherited by all the concrete roles in the hierarchy. We have defined it in the following manner:

```
class Role {
protected:
    string roleName;
    int roleExperience;             // in years
public:
    Role() {}
    Role( string arole, int experience );
    Role( const Role& other );
    string getRoleName() const;
    void setRoleName( string name );
    int getRoleExperience() const;
    void setRoleExperience( int yy );
    virtual bool operator==( const Role& role );
    void printRoleExperience() const;
    virtual void print() const;
    virtual ~Role();
};
```

Using the same definition for the mixin class `ManagerType` as shown in the last section, we can now define the `Manager` role class as follows:

```
class ManagerType {
protected:
    virtual double productivityGainYtoY() = 0;
    virtual bool computeEmployeeSatisfaction() = 0;
};

class Manager : public Role, public ManagerType {
    Department dept;
public:
    Manager();
    Manager( string roleName );
    Manager( Department aDept );
    double productivityGainYtoY();
    bool computeEmployeeSatisfaction();
    void print();
    ~Manager();
};
```

where the data member `dept` of `Manager` is private because it will have no meaning for the subclass `ExecutiveManager` since an `ExecutiveManager` supervises
multiple departments and, we will assume, does not belong to any one of them.
We have provided the class with a no-arg constructor because we need it in the
`ExecutiveManager` class. Remember, when a superclass constructor is not invoked
explicitly, the system implicitly invokes its no-arg constructor. It goes without saying that `Manager` must provide implementations for the pure virtual functions of
`ManagerType`. This class can then be extended in the following manner:

```
class ExecutiveManager : public Manager {
    short level;
    vector<Department> departments;
public:
    ExecutiveManager( short lvl );
    void addDepartment( Department dept );
    void setLevel( int lvl );
    double productivityGainYtoY();
    void print();
    ~ExecutiveManager();
};
```

Since an `ExecutiveManager` supervises multiple departments, the `productivityGainYtoY()`
function for such an individual will be different from this function for a `Manager`. So
its new definition here will override the definition in `Manager`.

The rest of the hierarchy, consisting of the role classes `SalesPerson` and `SalesManager`,
is set up in a similar manner. Shown below is the code for this example:

```
//RolePlayers.cc

#include "MI_Utilities.h"

/////////////////// incomplete def of class Role ///////////////////
class Role;

//////////////////////// class Employee ////////////////////////
class Employee {
protected:
    string name;
    string address;
    EducationLevel education;
    PeopleSkill pSkill;
    Leadership leadership;
    vector<Role*> allRoles;
    Role* activeRole;
public:
    Employee( string nam,
              string add,
              EducationLevel edLevel )
        :     name( nam ),
              address( add ),
              education( edLevel ),
              pSkill( pUnknown ),
              leadership( lUnknown ),
              allRoles( vector<Role*>() ),
              activeRole( 0 )
    {}
    Employee( const Employee& other );
    void setActiveRole( Role* role );
    Role* getActiveRole() const { return activeRole; }
    void addToRoles( Role* newRole );
    void removeRole( Role* role );
    void removeAllRoles();
    void setPeopleSkill( PeopleSkill skill ) { pSkill = skill; }
    string getName() const { return name; }
    string getAddress() const { return address; }
    void setEducationLevel(EducationLevel eduLvl) {education = eduLvl;}
    EducationLevel getEducationLevel() const { return education; }
    Leadership getLeadership() const { return leadership; }
    void setLeadership( Leadership lead ) { leadership = lead; }
    void print();           // needs role definitions
    ~Employee() {}          // see text for why this is do-nothing    //(A)
};
```

```
////////////////////////////  class Role  ////////////////////////////
class Role {
protected:
    string roleName;
    int roleExperience;              // in years
public:
    Role() {}
    Role( string arole, int experience )
        :  roleName( arole ),
           roleExperience( experience )
        {}
    Role( const Role& other )
        :  roleName( other.roleName ),
           roleExperience( other.roleExperience )
        {}
    string getRoleName() const { return roleName; }
    void setRoleName( string name ) { roleName = name; }
    int getRoleExperience() const { return roleExperience; }
    void setRoleExperience( int yy ) { roleExperience = yy; }
    virtual bool operator==( const Role& role ) {
        return ( roleName == role.roleName ) ? true : false;
    }
    void printRoleExperience() const {
        cout << "Years in this role: " << roleExperience << endl;
    }
    virtual void print() const {}
    virtual ~Role() {}
};


////////////  Employee member functions that need Role defs ////////////
Employee::Employee( const Employee& other )
    : name( other.name ),
      address( other.address ),
      education( other.education ),
      pSkill( other.pSkill ),
      leadership( other.leadership ),
      allRoles( other.allRoles ),
      activeRole( other.activeRole )
{}
void Employee::addToRoles(Role* newRole){allRoles.push_back(newRole);}
void Employee::removeRole( Role* role ) {
    vector<Role*>::iterator iter = allRoles.begin();
    while ( iter != allRoles.end() ) {
        if ( *iter == role ) {
            allRoles.erase( iter );
        }
        iter++;
    }
}
```

```cpp
void Employee::removeAllRoles() { allRoles = vector<Role*>(); }
void Employee::setActiveRole( Role* role ) { activeRole = role; }
void Employee::print() {
    cout << name << endl;
    cout << address << endl;
    cout << EducationLevels[ education ] << endl;
    cout << "People skill: " << PeopleSkills[ (int) pSkill ] << endl;
    cout << "Leadership quality:" << LeaderQualities[(int) leadership];
    cout << endl;
    if ( activeRole != 0 )
        cout << "ACTIVE ROLE: " << activeRole->getRoleName() << endl;
    if ( allRoles.size() != 0 ) {
        cout << "LIST OF ALL ALLOWABLE ROLES: " << endl;
        vector<Role*>::iterator iter = allRoles.begin();
        while ( iter != allRoles.end() ) {
            cout << (*iter)->getRoleName() << endl;
            (*iter++)->printRoleExperience();
        }
    }
}


/////////////// mixin class ManagerType (abstract) ///////////////
class ManagerType {
protected:
    virtual double productivityGainYtoY() = 0;
    virtual bool computeEmployeeSatisfaction() = 0;
};


//////////////////// class Manager (IsA Role) ////////////////////
class Manager : public Role, public ManagerType {
    Department dept;
public:
    Manager() {}           // Needed by the ExecutiveManager constructor
    Manager( string roleName ) : Role( roleName, 0 ) {}
    Manager( Department aDept )
        : Role( "Manager of " + aDept.getName(), 0 ), dept( aDept ) {}
    double productivityGainYtoY() {
        int lastProd = dept.getProductionLastYear();
        int prevProd = dept.getProductionPreviousYear();
        return 100 * ( lastProd - prevProd ) / (double) prevProd;
    }
    bool computeEmployeeSatisfaction() { return true; }
    void print() {
        printRoleExperience();
        dept.print();
    }
    ~Manager() {}
};
```

```
/////////////////// class ExecutiveManager ////////////////////
// An ExecutiveManager supervises more than one department
class ExecutiveManager : public Manager {
    short level;
    vector<Department> departments;
public:
    ExecutiveManager( short lvl )
        : Manager( "Executive Manager" ),
          level( lvl ) { departments = vector<Department>(); }
    void addDepartment(Department dept){departments.push_back( dept );}
    void setLevel( int lvl ) { level = lvl; }
    // overrides Manager's productivityGainYtoY():
    double productivityGainYtoY() {
        double gain = 0.0;
        vector<Department>::iterator iter = departments.begin();
        while ( iter != departments.end() ) {
            int lastProd = iter->getProductionLastYear();
            int prevProd = iter->getProductionPreviousYear();
            gain += ( lastProd - prevProd ) / (double) prevProd;
        }
        return gain/departments.size();
    }
    void print() {
        printRoleExperience();
        if ( departments.size() != 0 ) {
            cout << "Departments supervised: " << endl;
            vector<Department>::iterator iter = departments.begin();
            while ( iter != departments.end() )
                iter++->print();
        }
    }
    ~ExecutiveManager() {}
};


////////////////// mixin class SalesType (abstract) /////////////////
class SalesType {
protected:
    virtual double salesVolume() = 0;
    virtual double productivityGainYtoY() = 0;
};


////////////////////////// class SalesPerson /////////////////////////////
class SalesPerson : public Role, public SalesType {
    double salesVolLastYear;
    double salesVolPrevYear;
public:
    SalesPerson( string rolename ) : Role( rolename, 0 ) {}
    SalesPerson() : Role( "Sales Person", 0 ), salesVolLastYear( 0 ),
        salesVolPrevYear( 0 ) {}
```

```
        void setSalesVolLastYear(double sales){ salesVolLastYear = sales; }
        void setSalesVolPrevYear(double sales){ salesVolPrevYear = sales; }
        double salesVolume() { return salesVolLastYear; }
        double productivityGainYtoY() {
            return 100 * (salesVolLastYear
                    - salesVolPrevYear) / salesVolPrevYear;
        }
        void print() {
            cout << "Sales Department" << endl;
            printRoleExperience();
        }
        ~SalesPerson() {}
    };


//////////////////////////// class SalesManager ////////////////////////////
class SalesManager : public SalesPerson, public ManagerType {
        vector<SalesPerson*> sellersSupervised;
public:
        SalesManager()
            : SalesPerson( "Sales Manager" ),
              sellersSupervised( vector<SalesPerson*>() )
            {}
        // overrides SalesPerson's productivityGainYtoY():
        double productivityGainYtoY(){
            double gain = 0.0;
            vector<SalesPerson*>::iterator iter
                        = sellersSupervised.begin();
            while ( iter != sellersSupervised.end() ) {
                gain += (*iter++)->productivityGainYtoY();
            }
            return gain/sellersSupervised.size();
        }
        void print() {
            printRoleExperience();
            if ( sellersSupervised.size() != 0 ) {
                cout << "Sales Persons supervised: " << endl;
                vector<SalesPerson*>::iterator iter
                            = sellersSupervised.begin();
                while ( iter != sellersSupervised.end() )
                    (*iter++)->print();
            }
        }
        ~SalesManager() {}
    };


////////////////// special function that uses RTTI //////////////////
bool checkReadyForPromotion( Employee* e ) {                         //(B)
        Role* r = e->getActiveRole();
        Manager* m = dynamic_cast<Manager*>( r );
```

```
      if ( m != 0 ) {
          // add additional promotion criteria to the following test
          // as necessary (left as an exercise to the reader)
          if ( m->getRoleExperience() >= MinYearsForPromotion ) {
              cout << "yes, ready for promotion in the active role\n";
              return true;
          }
          else {
              cout << "Not ready for promotion in the active role\n";
              return false;
          }
      }
      SalesPerson* s = dynamic_cast<SalesPerson*>( r );
      if ( s != 0 ) {
          if ( s->productivityGainYtoY() > 50 ) {
              cout << "yes, ready for promotion in the active role\n";
              return true;
          }
          else {
              cout << "Not ready for promotion in the active role\n";
              return false;
          }
      }
      else {
          cout << "Unable to determine if ready for promotion\n";
          return false;
      }
}

/*****
class bad_cast {}                                            //(C)

bool checkReadyForPromotion( Employee* e ) {
  Role& role_ref = *( e->getActiveRole() );

  try {
    Manager& m_ref = dynamic_cast<Manager&>( role_ref );
    if ( m_ref.getRoleExperience() >= MinYearsForPromotion ) {
      cout << "yes, ready for promotion in the active role\n"
      return true;
    }
    else
        cout << "No, not ready for promotion in the active role\n";
  } catch( bad_cast& b ) {
    cout << "Unable to determine if ready for promotion" << endl;
    return false;
  }
}
*****/
```

```
///////////////////////////// main /////////////////////////////
int main()
{
    Department d1( "Design" );
    Department d2( "Manufacturing" );
    Department d3( "Development" );

    cout << "TEST 1: " << endl;                              //(D)

    Employee* emp1 = new Employee("Zippy Zester","Zeetown",HighSchool);

    Role* role1 = new Manager( d1 );
    Role* role2 = new Manager( d2 );

    role1->setRoleExperience( 2 );
    role2->setRoleExperience( 12 );

    emp1->addToRoles( role1 );
    emp1->addToRoles( role2 );
    emp1->setActiveRole( role2 );
    emp1->print();                                          //(E)

    checkReadyForPromotion( emp1 );                         //(F)
    cout << endl << endl;


    cout << "TEST 2: " << endl;                             //(G)

    Employee* emp2 = new Employee("Deny Deamon","Deensville",College);
    emp2->setPeopleSkill( Friendly );
    emp2->setLeadership( CanLeadLargeGroups );
    Role* role3 = new Manager( d1 );
    Role* role4 = new Manager( d2 );
    role3->setRoleExperience( 23 );
    role4->setRoleExperience( 7 );

    emp2->addToRoles( role3 );
    emp2->addToRoles( role4 );

    Role* role5 = new SalesPerson();
    role5->setRoleExperience(18);
    SalesPerson* sp = static_cast<SalesPerson*>( role5 );
    sp->setSalesVolLastYear( 200 );
    sp->setSalesVolPrevYear( 100 );
    emp2->addToRoles( role5 );
    emp2->setActiveRole( role5 );
    emp2->print();                                          //(H)
```

```
checkReadyForPromotion( emp2 );                              //(I)

    delete emp1;
    delete emp2;

    delete role1;
    delete role2;
    delete role3;
    delete role4;
    delete role5;

    return 0;
}
```

The reader is probably curious as to why the destructor for `Employee` in line (A) has a do-nothing body considering that this class has a pointer data member, `activeRole`, and a data member that is a vector of pointers, each element of the vector pointing to an object of type `Role`. The reason is that we have chosen to pass around pointer to unique `Role` objects; in other words, we do not copy the `Role` objects themselves. So when a new role is added to an employee's vector of roles, it is just a pointer to a previously constructed `Role` object. (An alternative design choice would have been to duplicate the `Role` object and store the pointers to the duplicates in both the `activeRole` and the `allRoles` data members of the `Employee` class.) So all the `Role` objects are created and destroyed at only one place — in `main`.

The `main` of the above program constructs two test cases. The first test case, beginning in line (D), is for an `Employee` who can play multiple managerial roles, the active role in the test case being "Manager of Manufacturing." The second test case, beginning in line (G), is for an employee whose active role is as a salesperson. The output of the program, produced by the statements in lines (E), (F), (H), and (I), is displayed below

```
TEST 1:
Zippy Zester
Zeetown
highschool
People skill: unknown
Leadership quality: unknown
ACTIVE ROLE: Manager of Manufacturing
LIST OF ALL ALLOWABLE ROLES:
Manager of Design
Years in this role: 2
Manager of Manufacturing
Years in this role: 12
yes, ready for promotion in the active role
```

```
TEST 2:
Deny Deamon
Deensville
college
People skill: friendly
Leadership quality: can lead large groups
ACTIVE ROLE: Sales Person
LIST OF ALL ALLOWABLE ROLES:
Manager of Design
Years in this role: 23
Manager of Manufacturing
Years in this role: 7
Sales Person
Years in this role: 18
yes, ready for promotion in the active role
```

The code shown in the program `RolePlayers.cc` also includes a function `checkReadyForPromotion()` in line (B). This function and the commented out code that follows are subjects of the next section.

16.11   RUN-TIME TYPE IDENTIFICATION IN C++

We will now answer the following question in the context of the role playing classes example of the previous section: Given an `Employee` object and given the fact that the active role of an employee is stored as a `Role*` pointer, how does one figure out the exact identity of the active role at run time? Or, for that matter, how does one figure out the "true" identities of the roles stored in the `allRoles` data member of the `Employee` class.

One approach would be to examine the value returned by the `getRoleName()` function when it is invoked on the role pointed to by the `activeRole` data member. However, C++ also makes available a couple of other approaches that come handy when we do not have a data member like `roleName` defined for a class such as `Role`. The first of these is based on *Run-Time Type Identification (RTTI)*. If we wanted to check whether a given `Role*` is of type, say, `Manager*`, we can use the `dynamic_cast` operator made available by C++'s RTTI in the following manner

```
Manager* m =  dynamic_cast<Manager*>( role );
```

where `role` is of type `Role*`. If `role`'s true identity is not `Manager*`, then `dynamic_cast` returns the null pointer. So in order to ascertain whether or not a role associated with an `Employee` is of type `Manager*`, all we have to do is to test whether or not m is a null pointer. Converting a base class pointer to a derived class pointer in this fashion is called *downcasting*. Using downcasting, we can write the kind of code that is shown for `checkReadyForPromotion()` in line (B) of the `RolePlayers.cc` program.

But note that dynamic casts work only for polymorphic type. As was mentioned in Chapter 15, a class is a polymorphic type if the class contains at least one virtual function. In the absence of any other virtual functions, we can always declare the destructor to be virtual.

In the function `checkReadyForPromotion()` in line (B) of the `RolePlayers.cc` program, we showed dynamic cast working through pointer variables. It can also work with object references, but then the operator `dynamic_cast` can only be invoked inside a `try-catch` block. This is demonstrated by the commented out code that starts in line (C) of the same program. The idea now is that if the `dynamic_cast` operator does not succeed, it would throw an exception. So in the `catch` block of the function we put the code that corresponds to the case when the true identity of the active role is not `Manager`. Note that now we are downcasting to `Manager&` and not to `Manager*`, hence the operator invocation with `dynamic_cast<Manager&>`. Also, the argument supplied to the casting operator is `Role&` and not `Role*`.

The RTTI feature of C++ also supports the `static_cast` operator that the reader has already seen for compile-time casts in earlier chapters. As was mentioned earlier, the operation `static_cast<T>(e)` converts a value e to type T *provided an implicit conversion exists from the type of* e *to the type* T. While, of course, a `Derived*` type can always be assigned directly to a `Base*` type, we could also do the conversion by using `static_cast`. The safety feature of `static_cast` is that it cannot cast away `const`. Yet another casting operator supported by RTTI is `reinterpret_cast` that is used primarily for converting an `int` into a memory address. Yet another cast operator is `const_cast`. The invocation `const_cast<T>(e)` removes the constness of e.

We have already pointed out that RTTI works only for the polymorphic types and, for a class to be of polymorphic type, at least one of its member functions must be virtual. *A class derived from a polymorphic class is also polymorphic.* Therefore, given a polymorphic class C at some level in a multilevel class hierarchy, all the direct and indirect subclasses of C will also act polymorphically.

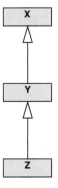

Fig. 16.16

We will illustrate this idea with a simple example shown in Figure 16.16. We will make X polymorphic by declaring its destructor virtual. The rest of the class hierarchy will be a straightforward derivation of Y from X and Z from Y:

```
//PolymorphicTypes.cc

#include <iostream>
using namespace std;

class X { public: virtual ~X(){}; };
class Y : public X {};
class Z : public Y {};

int main()
{
    Y* p = new Z();
    Z* q = dynamic_cast<Z*>( p );
    if ( q != 0 ) cout << "p was actually Z*" << endl;
    return 0;
}
```

For `dynamic_cast<Z*>` to return a non-null pointer in `main()`, the class Y has to act polymorphically, which it does on account of the fact that the Y's parent class X was made polymorphic by declaring its destructor to be virtual. So the output of the program is "p was actually Z*".

16.12 CREDITS AND SUGGESTIONS FOR FURTHER READING

The discussion in Sections 16.8 through 16.11 was much influenced by Dattatri's [16] treatment of the topic of multiple inheritance in C++. Dattatri's book is good reading for a lot of practical advice related to controlling complexity in large C++ programs.

16.13 HOMEWORK

1. In the following program, X is a virtual base for Y, which in turn is a regular base for Z. The constructors for both Y and Z invoke X's constructor. Notice that Z's constructor in line (B) invokes its two superclass constructors with two different arguments, 22 and 11. While the argument of 11 gets passed on to X constructor directly in line (B), the argument 22 gets passed on to X constructor

in line (A). What will be printed out in line (C) for the data member x inherited by Z? Will it be 11 or 22?

```
#include <iostream>
using namespace std;

class X {
public:
    int x;
    X( int xx ) : x( xx ) {}
};

class Y : virtual public X {
public:
    Y( int xx ) : X( xx ) {}                        //(A)
};

class Z : public Y {
public:
    Z() : Y( 22 ), X( 11 ) {}                       //(B)
};

int main()
{
    Z zobj;
    cout  << zobj.x << endl;                        //(C)
    return 0;
}
```

2. In the following program, even though the derived class Z does not make a direct invocation of the constructor of the virtual base X, the program compiles fine. Why?

```
#include <iostream>
using namespace std;

class X {
    int x;
public:
    X() {}
    X( int xx ) : x( xx ) {}
};

class Y : virtual public X {
public:
    Y( int xx ) : X( xx ) {}
};
```

```
class Z : public Y {
public:
    Z( int xx ) : Y( xx ) {}
};

int main() {}
```

3. In the following program, X is a virtual base for Y, which in turn is a regular
   base for Z. The compiler outputs the following error message for this program:

   No matching function for call to X::X()

Why?

```
#include <iostream>
using namespace std;

class X {
    int x;
public:
    X( int xx ) : x( xx ) {}
};

class Y : virtual public X {
public:
    Y( int xx ) : X( xx ) {}
};

class Z : public Y {
public:
    Z( int xx ) : Y( xx ) {}
};

int main() {}
```

4. In the following program, X is a virtual base for Y, which in turn is a regular
   base for Z. The output statement in line (A) causes the number -4261484 (or
   some other equally unexpected and bizarre looking number) to be printed out
   on the terminal. Why?

```
#include <iostream>
using namespace std;

class X {
    int x;
```

```
public:
    X() {}
    X( int xx ) : x( xx ) {}
    int getx() const { return x; }
};

class Y : virtual public X {
public:
    Y( int xx ) : X( xx ) {}
};

class Z : public Y {
public:
    Z( int xx ) : Y( xx ) {}
};

int main()
{
    Z zobj( 100 );
    cout << zobj.getx() << endl;                    //(A)
    return 0;
}
```

5. The following program has a diamond hierarchy of classes. X is a public base of Y and T. And, the classes Y and T are both superclasses of U. Note that X at the apex of the hierarchy is not a virtual base. This program does not compile. Why?

```
#include <iostream>
using namespace std;

class X {
public:
    int x;
    X( int xx ) : x( xx ) {}
};

class Y : public X {
public:
    Y( int xx ) : X( xx ) {}
};

class T : public X {
public:
    T( int xx ) : X( xx ) {}
};
```

```
class U : public Y, public T {
public:
    U( int xx ) : Y( xx ), T( xx ) {}
};

int main()
{
    U uobj( 100 );
    cout  << uobj.x << endl;
    return 0;
}
```

6. Write a Java version of the mixin classes example of Section 16.9. Use Java interfaces for serving the same purpose as the mixin classes of that section.

7. Write a Java version of the role playing classes of Section 16.10. Use Java interfaces for the abstract role types, `SalesType` and `ManagerType`, of that section.

8. C++ also makes available a function `typeid()` that can be used to ascertain the class identity of an object. Using this function, the implementation of the `checkReadyForPromotion()` function in Section 16.10 would become

```
bool checkReadyForPromotion( Employee* e ) {
    Role* r = e->getActiveRole();
    if ( typeid( *r ) == typeid( Manager ) ) {
        if ( r->getRoleExperience() >= MinYearsForPromotion ) {
            cout << "yes, ready for promotion in the active role"
                << endl;
            return true;
        }
        else {
            cout << "No, not yet ready for promotion "
                << "in the active role" << endl;
            return false;
        }
    }
    else if ( typeid( *r ) == typeed( SalesPerson ) ) {
        if ( s->productivityGainYtoY() > 50 ) {
            cout << "yes, ready for promotion in the active role"
                << endl;
            return true;
        }
```

```
        else {
            cout << "Not ready for promotion in the active role"
                << endl;
            return false;
        }
    }
    else {
        cout << "Unable to determine if ready for promotion"
            << endl;
        return false;
    }
}
```

Incorporate this version of checkReadyForPromotion() in the source code in Section 16.10.

17

OO for Graphical User Interfaces, A Tour of Three Toolkits

Graphical user interface (GUI) programming is probably the most fertile application of object-oriented ideas. The requirements of GUI programming are complex, to say the least. First of all, there is the issue of layout. How to write a program so that the layout displayed on a computer terminal maintains its visual aesthetic and functionality as the user resizes a GUI to suit his/her particular needs? Then there is the issue of rendering graphics, displaying images, playing video clips and sounds files — all compute-intensive operations. Additionally, a GUI must be programmed in such a way that it remains responsive to user interaction even as it is engaged in compute-intensive operations. Over the years, OO has emerged as the best way to meet these diverse requirements of GUI programming.

With regard to what the various OO toolkits can do for GUI design, it is instructive to ponder the similarities between programming up a functional and aesthetically pleasing GUI, on the one hand, and designing and constructing a beautiful building, on the other. There is no science of GUI design, just as there is no science of architecture. Yet, over the years we have learned that humans have distinct preferences with regard to how a GUI is laid out and how its functionality is engineered, just as we know about our distinct preferences concerning the various dimensions of living spaces and how the spaces are put to use. We could refer to these human preferences as *invariances*.[1]

---

[1] The notion that the author is trying to convey through *invariances* is different from the notion of *patterns* as in [1]. Invariances are meant to refer to human preferences at a more basic level than what is addressed by patterns. The "golden proportion" could be an example of an invariance.

This analogy with architecture is important to us for two reasons: First, the programming tools for GUI must not allow easy violation of the universal human preferences I referred to as invariances, in the same sense that the written and the unwritten rules of architecture do not allow for living spaces that are aesthetically and functionally offensive to humans. As we will see in this chapter, the GUI toolkits of various kinds provide *layout managers* that in some cases come with built-in smarts to keep a spatial layout from looking grotesque as a programmer packs more and more graphical components into a GUI or as a user tries to change the horizontal and the vertical dimensions of a GUI. With regard to the human preferences concerning the responsiveness of a GUI, modern GUI programming languages permit a programmer to deploy separate threads of computation if an interaction between a human and the GUI calls for intensive computing.

The second reason for the importance of the architecture analogy is that just as a study of the history of building construction and design is important to inculcate in a student a sense of what has worked in the past and what serves as a foundation for the future, a study of the history of the GUI toolkits is likely to serve the same purpose. In what follows, therefore, we will start with a brief history of the GUI toolkits. An interesting detail that emerges from this history is the important role that was played by object-orientation in GUI programming even before OO became mainstream.

The section on history will be followed by a presentation of the main features of three high-level toolkits for GUI design: one from Java (AWT/Swing), one from C++ (Qt), and one using simulated object-orientation in C (GNOME/GTK+),[2] the last because GTK+ has emerged as an important GUI toolkit and because it is educational to see the power of simulated object-orientation directly in C.

The reader will not find this chapter exhaustive — since, after all, one could write an entire book on GUI programming in Java alone, or in C++ alone, or in C alone. Our focus will be more on capturing the essential ideas of each toolkit, providing a reader with sufficient information to get started with his or her own efforts at GUI design, leaving the rest to extensive information available on the web and to other excellent books devoted solely to GUI issues. This chapter leaves unaddressed important topics such as the playing of sounds files and video clips.

17.1   A BRIEF HISTORY OF GUI TOOLKITS

It is probably not far from the truth that modern GUI programming for graphical workstations started with X in the mid-eighties. The X window system gave us a network-transparent method of working on remote computers through virtual termi-

---

[2]In the GNOME/GTK+ pairing, GNOME is a desktop environment that is based on the GTK+ GUI toolkit. But since it is convenient to use some of the functions of GNOME for constructing GTK+ based GUIs, we consider them paired in this chapter.

nals on workstations. Using X, the interaction with the remote machine is such that it appears to run locally. The remote machine presents its output in an X window and accepts keystrokes and other user interactions made available through the window. Although X was developed originally for Unix environments, it's now available for practically all the other operating systems.

Although X was without doubt an enormous development in its own right, the support it contains for GUI programming consists essentially of low-level function calls for drawing lines and rectangles, for setting foreground and background colors, and for having events, such as those produced by a mouse, reported back to you. It does not provide facilities for direct creation of what we now take for granted in modern GUI design — buttons, scrollbars, dialog boxes, pop-ups, toolbars, tabbed pages, and so on. The first X-based GUI toolkit that facilitated high-level programming of these graphical components was Motif, which is a combination of both a toolkit and a GUI design specification. Motif makes calls to a lower-level toolkit called Xt (for X toolkit) that sits on top of Xlib, the X library. Xlib is the lowest-level programming API (Application Programming Interface) for working with X. Xt, which was one of the first large software systems to simulate object-orientation directly in C, allows one to create a graphical object, such as a window, but does not require that the window object come with a title bar and have a certain "look-and-feel" to it. The "look-and-feel" specification was supplied by Motif and is now known as the Motif "look-and-feel." The modern Common Desktop Environment (CDE) that ships with most Unix workstations is based on Motif.

While Motif was gaining steam within Unix circles, Win32 API was introduced by Microsoft for PC's. Although the main goal of Win32 API differed from Motif's goal of performing network-transparent computing through virtual terminals on graphics-enabled machines, they both provided the basic programming tools for creating graphical interfaces that users could interact with either by mouse clicking or through keystrokes. But as demands arose for creating more and more sophisticated user interfaces, programmers found it cumbersome to work with Motif and Win32. Programs written using these API's were often error-prone and difficult to debug. Additionally, and perhaps even more importantly, using either Motif or Win32 API's directly meant that a programmer had to spend far too much time on getting the GUI syntax and program-flow to work correctly in relation to the time required for the programming of the core functionality of an application.

Thus there arose a need for even higher-level toolkits that could hide bothersome details concerning layout management, event processing, multithreading, and the like. This need was also fueled by a desire for toolkits that would be portable across diverse platforms. The higher-level toolkits that have come into existence during the last few years include Java-based AWT and Swing, C++-based Qt, C-based GTK+, C++- based wxWindows, also C++-based MFC (Microsoft Foundation Classes), and many others.

While going through the different GUI toolkits in this chapter, the reader should bear in the mind the fact that a high-level toolkit of the kind we present in this chapter often sits on top of a more native GUI toolkit. It can also happen that a high-level toolkit may sit on top of a "tower" of toolkits. The chaining of toolkits in a tower of API's sometimes creates robustness problems caused by the not well-understood and undocumented incompatibilities between the API's. But, more importantly, what visual effects can be achieved with the topmost API become dependent on the capabilities of the API's underneath.

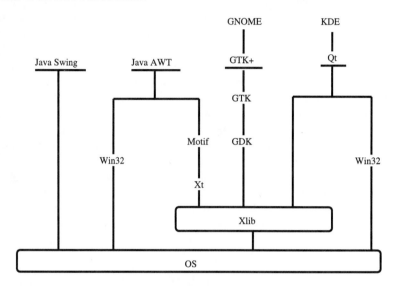

Fig. 17.1

For example, if a high-level API has to call on Motif to process its GUI widget construction code, the final look-and-feel will correspond to Motif. On the other hand, if a high-level API reaches directly into Xlib or directly into the operating system, it could generate its own look-and-feel. Figure 17.1 should give the reader a sense of this aspect of what we will be studying in the rest of the chapter. The high-level GUI toolkits of importance to us that are mentioned in this figure are Swing, AWT, GTK+, and Qt.

Figure 17.1 also includes GNOME and KDE, both desktop environments based on the GUI toolkits listed underneath them. But since, while working with GTK+, it is common to include some of GNOME'S functionality, we will refer to both of them as GNOME/GTK+. A paired up name, AWT/Swing, will also be used for the Swing and AWT toolkits since a modern GUI program in Java will include both Swing and and AWT classes.

Note that Figure 17.1 is only approximately correct, in the sense that it shows only the dominant dependencies. For example, Java Swing, while reaching directly into the operating system for most of its GUI construction, depends on Win32 and Xlib for some of its functionality. However, by contrast, Java AWT gets all its work done through calls to the native GUI API's, which is Motif for Unix-like platforms and

Win32 for Windows platforms. So the look-and-feel generated by Java AWT (if used without Swing) would correspond strictly to Motif on Unix-like workstations and to Win32 on Windows platforms.

As Figure 17.1 shows, the C-based GNOME/GTK+ system sits on top of GDK, which makes calls to Xlib. (Section 17.3 describes what the acronyms GNOME, GTK, GDK, and so on, stand for.) The C++-based Qt system comes in two versions. The version that works for Unix-like platforms makes calls to Xlib and the version that works for Windows platforms makes calls to the Win32 API.

17.2 AWT/SWING COMPONENTS

In Java, the GUI components one places on a screen come from either the packages that begin with the prefix `java.awt` [3] or the packages that begin with the prefix `javax.swing`. The components are designed so as to generate events when subject to human interaction. These events can be captured and processed by objects that implement certain interfaces defined in the `java.awt.event` and the `javax.swing.event` packages.

The more commonly used AWT and Swing types in a Java based GUI program can be broadly divided into the following four categories:

Top-Level Containers: AWT/Swing components that are top-level containers are meant for holding other graphical objects, which can be intermediate-level containers or atomic components. Graphical components including other graphical components within them gives rise to *containment hierarchies*. Every AWT/Swing program must have at least one top-level container and every containment hierarchy in an AWT/Swing program must have a top-level container at its root. Moreover, an atomic GUI component cannot be made visible on a screen unless it is in some containment hierarchy. Examples of the commonly used Swing top-level containers are `JFrame`, `JDialog`, and `JApplet`. All of these are heavyweight[4] containers. The heavyweight Swing containers are extensions of their AWT counterparts, which are all heavyweight. For example,

---

[3]The acronym `AWT` stands for Abstract Window Toolkit.

[4]A component is considered heavyweight if it has associated with it a *peer* class that acts like a wrapper for the corresponding native API component. Many of the AWT components are heavyweight. Let's say the native API is Motif. Then to draw an AWT button, Java will actually invoke a peer class to call on a Motif button. By contrast, lightweight components are *peerless*. Since a lightweight component is drawn without invoking any native GUI API code, it is possible to achieve the same look-and-feel across platforms. Given a choice between a lightweight component from one of the Swing packages and a heavyweight component from an AWT package, you should choose the former since the lightweight components are computationally less demanding. Another reason for preferring a Swing lightweight component over an AWT heavyweight component that does the same thing is that the former gives you *transparent* pixels. Because of transparent pixels, a lightweight component can *appear* to be nonrectangular. On the other hand, a heavyweight component is always rectangular.

the Swing container JFrame is derived from the AWT container Frame. It is possible and common for a program written in Swing to have more than one containment hierarchy. For example, an applet that brings up a dialog will have at least two containment hierarchies, one rooted at JApplet and the other at JDialog.

Intermediate Containers: Intermediate containers are often not directly visible but are nonetheless useful for organizing the visual layout of the graphical objects they hold. Examples: JPanel, JScrollPane, JTabbedPane, and so on. The intermediate container InternalFrame mimics a frame. However, unlike JFrame, which is heavyweight, InternalFrame is lightweight.

Atomic Components: The self-contained graphical components — referred to as the atomic components — are held by top-level and intermediate containers. Examples of these are JButton, JTextField, JScrollBar, and so on. All atomic components in the Swing packages are lightweight.

Miscellaneous Classes: These include classes for managing the layout of the components, for controlling the look and feel, for fetching information from the underlying operating system, and so on. Examples of these are GridLayout, FlowLayout, Toolkit, Graphics, and so on.

Now for a bit of background on AWT and Swing in the evolution of the Java language, first came AWT with Java in 1995. From the standpoint of designing sophisticated GUI and applets, AWT was fairly rudimentary. Under AWT, each Java component created a corresponding component using the native GUI API.[5] This meant that Java could only support those components that existed in all the important platforms of the day. This fact — referred to as the "least common denominator" approach — caused a Java button on a Unix platform to look like a Motif button, and on a Windows platform to look like a Windows button. While early on, this property of Java to create a native look-and-feel was considered to be a positive point, the thinking in the community changed as time went on. Software developers began to see the benefits of a programmable approach to look-and-feel that would allow a GUI to look the same and to work the same across diverse platforms. Enter Swing at this juncture. The Swing packages (which form a large part of the *Java Foundation Classes (JFC)*), besides giving the application developers a programmable look-and-feel, contain many other innovations over AWT, such as the computationally more efficient lightweight components, better debugging support, more efficient event handling, decorative borders, ability to place icons on components, double buffering, and so on.

---

[5] See the footnote discussion earlier in this section about "peered" components.

17.3 Qt WIDGETS

What is referred to as a component in Java AWT/Swing is usually called a *widget* in the C++-based Qt (and also in the C-based GNOME/GTK+ to be discussed in the next section).[6] Qt widgets are objects of type `QObject`. These widgets lend themselves to the same sort of categorization that we showed earlier for AWT/Swing. Examples of top-level widgets would be `QFrame`, `QDialog`, `QFileDialog`, and so on. Intermediate containers, intended mostly for organizing the more atomic widgets, include `QGroupBox`, `QHBox`, `QVBox`, and so on. There are very many atomic widgets; for example, `QButton`, `QStatusBar`, `QLabel` and so on. Example of the utility classes include `QApplication`, `QSocket`, `QLayout`, and so on.

As will be illustrated later with the help of examples, every Qt GUI program must at the very outset create a `QApplication` object whose job is to provide default initializations for the various parameters of an interface and to manage the flow of events between the various widgets as a human interacts with the widgets. The widgets that you actually display are objects of type `QWidget`.

17.4 GNOME/GTK+ WIDGETS

In Chapter 3, we showed that it is possible to simulate object-oriented behavior directly in C, provided one rigidly obeys certain programming and naming conventions (and also provided one is willing to accept the resulting somewhat more tortured programming syntax). The C-based package of software that goes under the name GNOME/GTK+ uses such object orientation for GUI design.

GNOME, which stands for *GNU Object Modeling Environment*, was designed for creating desktop environments. In functionality and in terms of the widgets included, GNOME is an extension of the GTK+ toolkit. The GTK+ toolkit contains two libraries: GTK and GDK. GTK, which stands for the *GIMP[7] Tool Kit*, consists of a large collection of functions and structures for creating different kinds of GUI widgets and for controlling various aspects of the widgets included in a GUI, such as their spatial layout. The GDK library — GDK stands for *GIMP Drawing Kit* — provides numerous drawing functions and facilities for managing colors, fonts, and so on.

The fundamental data types used in GNOME, GTK+, GDK, GIMP, and so on, are defined in the library `glib` of low-level C functions, macros, and structures. The glib library was created as a part of GIMP development for the purpose of standardization

---

[6]We will use the terms 'widget' and 'component' interchangeably from now on in the context of GUI programming.

[7]GIMP stands for the *GNU Image Manipulation Program*. GIMP, available as *open source* software, is to a Unix-like platform what Photoshop is to a Windows-based system.

and portability. For example, an int in C may be represented by 16 bits in some machines and 32 in others. Similarly, a char may be signed in some and unsigned in others. By contrast, glib defines a type called gint for representing integers; a gint is always 32 bits. If your GNOME/GTK+ code needs a shorter integer, you can use gint8 for an 8-bit integer, or a gint16 for a 16-bit integer. Similarly, a gchar will always be signed. If you need an unsigned char, you can use guchar. The glib library also comes with utility functions for memory management, string manipulation, and the formatting of textual output. GNOME/GTK+ programs will, for example, use g_print() instead of printf(), g_malloc() instead of malloc(), and so on.

GtkObject is the root of the GNOME/GTK+ type hierarchy. The GNOME/GTK+ widgets are all in the subtree that hangs from GtkWidget, a direct subtype of GtkObject. While many of these widgets can be displayed, others are intended to serve either as containers for the displayable widgets or just to serve as base types for lending organization to the displayable widgets. A widget type whose instances can be displayed must have associated with it a function that has '_new_' somewhere in the name of the function and this function must return a pointer to the newly constructed instance. If no such function exists for a widget type, it can only be used as a base type to create other subtypes.

The GNOME/GTK+ widget types can be categorized in the same way that was shown earlier for AWT/Swing and for Qt. There are the top-level containers like GtkWindow that get displayed as windows on a terminal; intermediate level containers like GtkTable, GtkHBox, and so on, for creating different kinds of groupings of the more atomic widgets; atomic widgets like GtkButton, GtkEditable, GtkLabel, and so on, that actually get displayed in a window; and utility widgets like GtkLayout, GtkSeparator, and so on.

17.5 MINIMALIST GUI PROGRAMS IN AWT/SWING

Here is a minimalist GUI program in Java's AWT/Swing. All it does is to display a top-level window of a certain size and at a certain location on the terminal screen.

```
//FirstWindow.java

import javax.swing.*;

class FirstWindow {
    public static void main(String[] args)  {
        JFrame f = new JFrame( "FirstWindow" );
        f.setSize( 300, 200 );
        f.setLocation( 200, 300 );
        f.setVisible( true );
    }
}
```

The program shown above will create a window from the top-level container JFrame from the javax.swing package. This window, of width 300 pixels and height 200 pixels, has its upper left-hand corner located at the pixel coordinates (200, 300), with 200 being the x-coordinate (the horizontal coordinate) and 300 the y-coordinate (the vertical coordinate). The origin of the (x,y) coordinate frame is the top left corner of the screen for a top-level window, meaning a window that is not contained in any other container. The coordinate x increases to the right horizontally and the coordinate y increases downwards vertically from the origin.[8] The last statement in the program, the call to setVisible, makes the window appear on the screen.[9] Figure 17.2 shows the window created by the above program.

Fig. 17.2

The program shown above is much too rudimentary — you won't even be able to exit the program when you click on the close button of the displayed window. To exit, you'll have to "kill" the process in which the program is running. Later we will discuss how we can rectify this shortcoming. For now, let's first discuss the composition of top-level windows in Swing.

A top-level container in Swing, such as JFrame, JDialog, JApplet, and so on, consists of a JRootPane lightweight container object that does behind-the-scenes work for the top-level container for managing the layout, the visibility, the look-and-feel, and so on, of the components that go into the top-level container.[10] As shown in Figure 17.3, in general a root pane container consists of a three panes: a layered pane of type JLayeredPane, a content pane, and a glass pane. The root pane can create and manage the other panes. The important point to remember is that a top-level Swing container always has these three panes associated with it: a layered pane, a content pane, and a glass pane.

---

[8]When the method setLocation is invoked on a Component that is inside another Container, the coordinates x and y are with respect to the upper left-hand corner of the enclosing container.

[9]Instead of f.setVisible(true), we could also have invoked f.show(). The two usages do the same thing before a window is "realized," a concept we will discuss in the next chapter. After a window is realized, one should invoke setVisible(true).

[10]The Swing top-level containers like JFrame, JDialog, and JApplet are obtained by extending their AWT counterparts and implementing the RootPaneContainer interface.

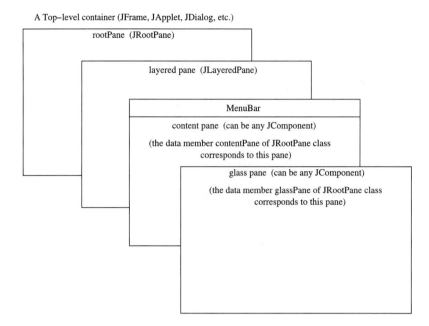

Fig. 17.3

The layered pane and the glass pane can be used to create novel and interesting user-interface effects. For example, the layered pane accepts the notion of "depth." When you add a widget to a layered pane, you can specify a depth value for it. This is done with the help of an integer argument to the method that adds a widget to the pane, the integer argument serving as a depth index. The larger the value of this index, the closer the widget is to the front. Certain values of this index are reserved. For example, the value of -300 for the depth index corresponds to the instance that holds the content pane. The depth index of 0 is also important; if you do not specify a depth index when adding widgets to a layered pane, the depth index of 0 will be used by default. The depth index of 100 is used for floating toolbars and pallets. The depth index associated with a widget in a layered pane can be changed dynamically. So if a widget A was in front of widget B, that fact could be reversed after some specified user interaction.

If you do not want depth effects, you'd use the content pane and its optional menu bar for the widgets you want displayed through the top-level container. A content pane can be any arbitrary `JComponent` object. After constructing a `JComponent` object, you can make it a root pane's content pane by invoking `setContentPane()` on the root pane object. A `JPanel` usually makes a good candidate for constructing one's own content pane. However, a more common approach consists of first bringing up the default content pane associated with the root pane of a top-level container by invoking the `getContentPane()` method and then adding widgets to the returned object by using "add" methods, as in

```
rootPane.getContentPane().add( myWidget );
```

Although the subject of layout managers will be taken up later, we want to mention quickly here that the default layout manager associated with the default content pane is BorderLayout. It is however permissible to customize a content pane — including the default content pane — by changing its layout manager and also by changing its border. In line with the above syntax, the layout manager associated with the default content pane can be changed by

```
rootPane.getContentPane().setLayout( myLayoutManager );
```

The glass pane, which can also be any arbitrary JComponent object, sits on top of all other panes associated with a top-level container. By default, a glass pane is transparent for obvious reasons. A glass pane can be used to trap mouse events sourced by multiple widgets underneath. It can also be used to paint or draw images over multiple widgets underneath without being limited by their boundaries.

We will now show a simple Swing/AWT program that illustrates the content-pane feature of a top-level container. The program below extends our earlier program by adding a button to it. The syntax of how a button is added to the top-level container in line (G) should be clear from our above discussion, as should the statement about setting the layout manager in line (F). With regard to the rest of the program, the reader should at this time gloss over the addWindowListener and the addActionListener statements in lines (A) and (E). Suffice it to say here that the former causes the window to close and the program to quit when you click on the close button of the window, and the latter causes the message "Have a Good Day!" to be printed out on your terminal window when you click on the button.

```
//FirstWindowWithButton.java

import javax.swing.*;
import java.awt.*;                      // for FlowLayout
import java.awt.event.*;               // for ActionListener

class FirstWindowWithButton {
    public static void main(String[] args) {
        JFrame f = new JFrame( "FirstWindowWithButton" );

        f.addWindowListener(new WindowAdapter() {              //(A)
            public void windowClosing(WindowEvent e) {
                System.exit(0);
            }
        });

        JButton b = new JButton("Click Here for a Message");   //(B)
        b.setVerticalTextPosition( AbstractButton.CENTER );    //(C)
        b.setHorizontalTextPosition( AbstractButton.CENTER );  //(D)
```

```
    b.addActionListener( new ActionListener() {              //(E)
        public void actionPerformed( ActionEvent evt ) {
            System.out.println( "Have a Good Day!" );
        }
    });


    f.getContentPane().setLayout( new FlowLayout() );        //(F)
    f.getContentPane().add( b );                             //(G)
    f.setLocation( 100, 50);                                 //(H)
    f.pack();                                                //(I)
    f.setVisible( true );                                    //(J)
    }
}
```

We will also explain later the reason for the use of FlowLayout in line (F) when we explain the difference between different types of layout managers. All we want to say here is that if you use the default layout manager that comes with a content pane — the BorderLayout — the button you create may end up occupying the entire width of the window if you should enlarge the window by dragging one of its corners. Using FlowLayout makes a button look like a button and causes it to be displayed in the top middle of the window.

The reader should note that instead of the setSize invocation in FirstWindow.java, we now invoke pack in line (I) to size the window. The pack method automatically sizes a top-level window so that all its contents are at or above their preferred minimum sizes. In this case, since it contains only a single button, the top-level window will be just large enough to hold the button. For complex top-level windows, we usually get a superior presentation with pack than with setSize since the former lets the layout manager decide how to size the window. The layout managers have built-in smarts to account for platform and other dependencies that affect component size.

Figure 17.4 shows the window created by the above program.

Fig. 17.4

17.6   MINIMALIST GUI PROGRAMS IN QT

Every GUI program in Qt must have the following two features:

- It must consist of exactly one object of type `QApplication`. This object initializes GUI features such as colors, fonts, cursor, and so on. This object is also in charge of all event handling, a topic we will discuss in a later section. The `QApplication` object must be brought into existence before any other graphical object is created.

- Every GUI program in Qt must also specify one "main widget." Usually, the `show()` command will be invoked on this main widget, which would also automatically "show" the child widgets in the containment hierarchy of the main widget. When the main widget is closed, it causes the system to exit the GUI program. If a main widget has not been specified for a GUI program, closing the window on the terminal screen by, say, clicking on the "Close" button of the system-supplied window menu will not terminate the GUI program — it will continue to run in the background.

The following example displays a window whose width is 500 pixels and height 300 pixels and whose upper left-hand corner is located at pixel coordinates (200, 100) with respect to the upper left-hand corner of the terminal screen:

```
//FirstWindow.cc

#include <qapplication.h>
#include <qmainwindow.h>

int main( int argc, char **argv )                          //(A)
{
    QApplication myApp( argc, argv );                      //(B)

    QMainWindow* myWin = new QMainWindow( 0, 0, 0 );       //(C)
    myWin->resize( 500, 300 );                             //(D)
    myWin->move( 200, 100 );                               //(E)

    myApp.setMainWidget(myWin );                           //(F)
    myWin->show();                                         //(G)
    return myApp.exec();                                   //(H)
}
```

First note that `main` is written as if we want to invoke the program with command line arguments for the parameters `argc` and `argv` in line (A). Despite the syntax in line (A), the executable is called without command line arguments. The parameters `argc` and `argv` are provided because the compiler synthesizes arguments for these parameters that are then passed on to the QApplication constructor in line (B) where we create the mandatory QApplication object.

In line (C), we then invoke a constructor for QMainWindow. This creates a top-level window, with a menu bar, some tool bars and a status bar. To understand the arguments of the constructor in line (C), we need to show the prototype of the constructor:

```
QMainWindow::QMainWindow( QWidget* parent = 0,
                          const char* name = 0,
                          WFlags f = WType_TopLevel );
```

The first parameter, parent, is used to establish a parent–child containment hierarchy of widgets for a graphical interface on the basis of what contains what.[11] In our simple example, we can set this to the null pointer, the symbol 0. The second parameter, name, is the nominal name of the QMainWindow object being created; this name can be used as a handle to the object. The last parameter, f, permits special flags to be designated for giving a custom look to the top-level window. For most applications of Qt, this parameter will also be set to 0.

Lines (D) and (E) establish the size and the position of the window on the user's terminal screen. Both are in pixels from the upper left-hand corner of the terminal screen. The first argument is for the horizontal dimension and the second for the vertical. As with Java, the horizontal coordinate increases to the right and the vertical coordinate from top to bottom.

Line (F) declares the QMainWindow object to be the main widget of the program. As was mentioned earlier, *a widget is the main widget if its deletion would cause the application to be terminated.*

To make the window just created visible on a terminal screen, we invoke its show() method in line (G). Finally, main passes the control to the exec() method of the QApplication object in line (H). As we will see later in further detail, invoking exec() causes the control to enter the *event processing loop* for user interaction. In our example, the control will stay in this loop until the displayed window is destroyed.

Assuming the above program was stored in a file called FirstWindow.cc, it can be compiled by the following command line[12]

```
g++ -o FirstWindow FirstWindow.cc -I$QTDIR/include -L$QTDIR/lib -lqt
```

---

[11] In a class hierarchy in an OO program, it is not uncommon to refer to a base class as a parent and a derived class as a child. But that is not what is meant by a parent-child relationship between the widgets of a GUI program. In a GUI program, a widget B is a child of a parent widget A if A is serving as a "container" for B.

[12] This command line invocation may not work if the compiler cannot locate the X11 libraries in your machine. As a case in point, with the Mandrake packaging of Linux, you have to add /usr/X11R6/lib to the file ld.so.conf in the /etc directory and run the ldconfig command before the command-line invocation of the compiler shown here will work. Another option, the only option if you do not have root access, would be to add the path /usr/X11R6/lib to the user-defined environment variable LD_LIBRARY_PATH.

where the environment variable QTDIR points to the directory containing the Qt software.

Figure 17.5 shows the window created by FirstWindow.cc.

Fig. 17.5

As written, the above program does not respond to any interaction with a human. Let's now consider another minimalist Qt program that shows a button in a window and, if you click on the button, actually causes the entire program to quit.

```
//FirstWindowWithButton.cc

#include <qapplication.h>
#include <qmainwindow.h>
#include <qpushbutton.h>
#include <qfont.h>

int main( int argc, char **argv )
{
    QApplication myApp( argc, argv );                        //(A)
    QMainWindow* myWin = new QMainWindow( 0, 0, 0 );         //(B)
    myWin->resize( 500, 300 );                               //(C)
    myWin->move( 200, 100 );                                 //(D)

    QPushButton* quitButton = new QPushButton( "Quit", myWin );   //(E)
    quitButton->resize( 60, 30 );                            //(F)
    quitButton->move( 220, 135 );                            //(G)
    quitButton->setFont( QFont( "Times", 18, QFont::Bold ) );     //(H)

    QObject::connect( quitButton,
                      SIGNAL(clicked()),
                      &myApp,
                      SLOT(quit()) );                        //(I)
    myApp.setMainWidget( myWin );                            //(J)
    myWin->show();                                           //(L)
    return myApp.exec();                                     //(M)
}
```

Lines (A) through (D) are the same as in the previous program. In line (E), we create a pushbutton object and, via the second argument of the QPushButton constructor, we cause the pushbutton object to be a child widget of the parent QMainWindow widget constructed in line (B). The pixel coordinates for sizing and positioning as specified in the lines (F) and (G) are with respect to the upper left-hand corner of the parent widget myWin, whereas those specified for the parent widget in lines (C) and (D) are with respect to the upper left-hand corner of the terminal window.

It is the code in line (I) that tells the program how to respond to a click on the button. As we will explain in greater detail in Section 17.14, this statement connects the *signal* produced by the button when it is clicked with the *slot* quit() of the QApplication object myApp.

Figure 17.6 shows the window created by the above program.

Fig. 17.6

17.7 MINIMALIST PROGRAMS IN GNOME/GTK+

A GUI program in GNOME/GTK+ starts most commonly by invoking the function gnome_init for the initialization of both GNOME and GTK+. As with Qt, the top-level main is written as if we want to use it with command line arguments, that is with the parameters argc and argv as shown in line (A) of the program below. The compiler synthesizes these command line arguments and then passes them on to gnome_init in line (C). Regarding the syntax of the call to gnome_init in line (C), the first argument supplies a symbolic name you'd want GNOME to associate with the graphical application being created, and the second a version number, in the form of a character string. As mentioned already, the last two arguments acquire compiler-synthesized values from the parameters of main.

The initialization step is usually followed by the construction of a top-level window by invoking gnome_app_new().[13] In the following program, the top-level window is

---

[13]This function actually calls gtk_window_new() using GTK_WINDOW_TOPLEVEL as its argument.

constructed in line (D). While the first argument here is the name of the application declared in line (C), the second a text string that will be displayed in the title bar of the top-level window,

```
//FirstWindow.c

#include <gnome.h>

int main( int argc, char* argv[] )                          //(A)
{
    GtkWidget*  topLevelWindow;                              //(B)

    gnome_init( "gnomewin", "1.0", argc, argv );            //(C)
    topLevelWindow = gnome_app_new( "gnomewin",
                                    "Gnome Window" );       //(D)
    gtk_container_set_border_width(
                GTK_CONTAINER( topLevelWindow ), 200 );     //(E)
    gtk_widget_show( topLevelWindow );                      //(F)
    gtk_main();                                             //(G)
    exit( 0 );                                              //(H)
}
```

In line (E), we establish the size of the window by invoking the function `gtk_container_set_border_width()`. Note how the first argument to this function call has a C style cast from `GtkWidget*` to `GTK_CONTAINER`. The function called demands that its first argument be of type `GTK_CONTAINER`. The command in line (F) then displays the top-level window on a terminal.

As we will see later in greater detail, the statement in line (G) is very important to a GNOME/GTK+ program because it is the invocation of `gtk_main()` that starts the event processing loop. Even though for this first GNOME/GTK+ exercise we do not wish to provide for user interaction, we must still include this statement since otherwise the displayed window will get destroyed the moment it is created. Calling `gtk_main()` parks the flow of control in an infinite loop and the window stays visible. The event processing loop can only be terminated by invoking `gtk_main_quit()`. Since we have not included that call in our program, even if we close the displayed window the program will keep on running in the background and you'll have to kill the process to terminate the program.

The compilation of the above program — as of all GNOME/GTK+ programs — is best done with the help of a makefile. The developers of GNOME/GTK+ have provided a utility program called `gnome-config` that can automatically figure out the locations of the libraries needed for compilation and dynamic linking. To illustrate, the command line invocation

```
gnome-config --cflags gnomeui
```

returns the following string for the locations of the 'include' files needed for the compilation of a GNOME program

```
-I/usr/include -DNEED_GNOMESUPPORT_H -I/usr/lib/gnome-libs/include
-I/usr/lib/glib/include -I/usr/X11R6/include
```

Shown below is a makefile that would work for the program FirstWindow.c:

```
#Makefile_GTK_FirstWindow

CC=gcc
LDLIBS='gnome-config --libs gnomeui'
CFLAGS=-Wall -g 'gnome-config --cflags gnomeui'

FirstWindow:  FirstWindow.o Makefile_FirstWindow
        $(CC) $(LDLIBS) FirstWindow.o -o FirstWindow

FirstWindow.o: FirstWindow.c
        $(CC) $(CFLAGS) -c FirstWindow.c

clean:
        rm -f FirstWindow
        rm -f FirstWindow.o
```

---

assuming that you want to use the Gnu C compiler gcc. Figure 17.7 shows the window created by FirstWindow.c.

Fig. 17.7

The above example did not incorporate any human interaction. Paralleling our minimalist examples for Java and Qt, we now present a GNOME/GTK+ program that contains a button which when pushed will terminate the program.

```
//FirstWindowWithButton.c

#include <gnome.h>

gint eventDestroy( GtkWidget* widget,
                        GdkEvent* event,  gpointer data );          //(A)

int main( int argc, char* argv[] )                                 //(B)
{
    GtkWidget*  topLevelWindow;                                     //(C)
    GtkWidget*  myButton;                                           //(D)

    gnome_init( "buttonwin", "1.0", argc, argv );                  //(E)
    topLevelWindow = gnome_app_new(
                        "buttonwin", "My Window" );                //(F)
    gtk_container_set_border_width(
                        GTK_CONTAINER( topLevelWindow ), 100 );    //(G)

    myButton = gtk_button_new_with_label( "Quit" );                //(H)
    gtk_signal_connect( GTK_OBJECT( myButton ),                    //(I)
                        "clicked",
                        GTK_SIGNAL_FUNC( eventDestroy ),
                        NULL );
    gnome_app_set_contents(
                        GNOME_APP( topLevelWindow ), myButton );   //(J)

    gtk_widget_show( topLevelWindow );                             //(K)
    gtk_main();                                                     //(L)
    exit( 0 );                                                      //(M)
}

gint eventDestroy( GtkWidget* widget,
                        GdkEvent* event,  gpointer data ) {         //(N)
    gtk_main_quit();                                               //(O)
    return( 0 );                                                    //(P)
}
```

As in our first GNOME/GTK+ program, we first carry out the initialization in line (E), followed by the construction of a top-level main window in line (F) and then the setting of the size of the top-level window in line (G). In line (H), we construct a button object by invoking its constructor gtk_button_new_with_label and provide the constructor with a label to put on the button.

Line (I) is crucial to how this program will respond to an interaction with the button. This line registers what's known as a *callback function* or just *callback* — in this case this function is eventDestroy() — with the signal "clicked" that is emitted by a button. We will have more to say about signals and callbacks later in Section 17.14. At this point, all we want the reader to do is to look at the definition of the callback function in lines (N) through (P). This function invokes gtk_main_quit(). While the function gtk_main() invoked in line (L) starts the event processing loop, the invocation of gtk_mail_quit() in line (O) terminates it. Termination of the event processing loop causes the control to shift back to line (M), which brings the execution to an end.

To compile this program, you'd again need the makefile that was shown for the program FirstWindow.c after it is changed to reflect the name of the new source file, the executable, and so on. The window created by this program is shown in Figure 17.8.

Fig. 17.8

17.8 LAYOUT MANAGEMENT IN GUI PROGRAMS

One of the first things a GUI designer has to think about is where to place a GUI component in a window with regard to the window frame and with regard to the placement of the other components. This issue is more complex than it seems at first thought.

Let's say we want to place a few buttons in a top-level window. One's first thought would be to place the buttons at certain predesignated locations. But that would seem like a poor GUI design if the choice of the fixed locations for the buttons caused the window to look appalling when it is resized by a user.

Another option, it would seem, would be to place the buttons at locations relative to the dimensions of a window. So if a window was reduced to, say, half its width and half its height, the coordinates of the button locations would be reduced to half their original values. This is certainly better than the first solution, but it still suffers from a shortcoming. As the locations of the buttons change proportionately to the resized dimensions of a window, if the button sizes remain fixed, we could end up with overlapping buttons if the window size became small enough. Resizing of the top-level window with fixed-sized buttons could also lead to a poor-looking window in which the spaces between the buttons would acquire forms not appropriate for displaying the information that needed to be displayed there. On the other hand, if we allow the sizes of the buttons to also change as a window is resized, a button may stop looking like a button.

While there are no perfect solutions to the difficulties listed above, many of the problems can be alleviated by using a layout manager supplied with a GUI toolkit. As an example of the smarts incorporated in modern layout managers, some of them can "float" the components inside a container. By "float" we mean that the layout manager will automatically resize, reposition, or, in some cases, even rearrange the components as a window is resized so that the layout of the components maintains a certain visual form. To illustrate this idea better, one of the layout managers in Java arranges the components symmetrically along a row. But if upon resizing, the width of the window becomes too small to accommodate all the components in that row, the layout manager automatically places one or more components symmetrically in the next row.

Layout managers often accept user-supplied recommendations regarding the default, the minimum, and the maximum sizes to use for the components. This can prevent a graphical application from looking too ghastly if the user chooses an "unnatural" size for the top-level window.

In the subsections that follow, we will present the main classes for layout management in Java-based AWT/Swing, in C++-based Qt, and in C-based GNOME/GTK+. We will illustrate each class with a simple example. But note that more complex layouts can be produced by nesting the layouts. For example, a particular cell in a grid-like positioning of the GUI components could be a holder for a horizontal arrangement of other components, and so on.

17.9 LAYOUT MANAGEMENT IN AWT/SWING

AWT/Swing provides the following layout managers:

```
BorderLayout
FlowLayout
BoxLayout
CardLayout
GridLayout
GridBagLayout
```

Each layout manager embodies a different layout approach that we will illustrate with the help of simple examples below. Before getting into the examples, we want to say here that every container comes with a default layout manager. For example, the content pane, which, as mentioned previously, is the main container used in Swing frames, applets, and dialogs, uses BorderLayout as its default layout manager, the panels use FlowLayout by default, and so on.

It is, of course, possible to position components inside a container without using a layout manager class — by absolute positioning. But then one has to pay the price that the placement of the components could look awkward if the top-level window is resized.

17.9.1 Border Layout

The BorderLayout class recognizes five different areas — north, south, east, west, and center — for placing a component. These areas are designated, naturally, by the integer constants NORTH, SOUTH, EAST, WEST, and CENTER of the BorderLayout class. The following example shows how the space inside a content pane is allocated to these five areas.[14] The program places four JLabel objects in the north, south, east, and west portions of the top-level window and another JLabel object in the center, all with the help of BorderLayout. Each of the first four labels consists of an image icon and a text string. The JLabel object in the center consists of just a text string. The east, west, and center labels have been given borders to separate them visually from the other displayed objects.

```
//BorderLayoutTest.java
//additional files needed: snlowflake.gif, zwthr14.gif,
//thunderstormanim.gif, sunanim.gif

import java.awt.*;            // for Container, BorderLayout
import java.awt.event.*;      // for WindowAdapter
import javax.swing.*;
import javax.swing.border.*;  // Border, BorderFactory

public class BorderLayoutTest {
    public static void main( String[] args ) {
        JFrame f = new JFrame( "BorderLayoutTest" );

        f.addWindowListener(new WindowAdapter() {
            public void windowClosing(WindowEvent e) {
                System.exit(0);
            }
        });
```

---

[14] Since we will not be discussing the JLabel class separately in this chapter, this example will also serve as our introduction to JLabel. A JLabel can be used to show noneditable information in the form of a string and/or an image. In the program shown, please note how a string can be positioned within a JLabel's drawing area. By default, text is centered vertically and positioned to the left side. Also, by default, an image is centered both vertically and horizontally. Note how we get an image in the center and a string below it.

```
Container contentPane = f.getContentPane();

//the following is unnecessary since BorderLayout is default:
// contentPane.setLayout( new BorderLayout() );

//NORTH:
ImageIcon northIcon = new ImageIcon( "image/snowflake.gif" );
JLabel northLabel = new JLabel( "Frigid in the North",
                                northIcon,
                                JLabel.CENTER );
northLabel.setVerticalTextPosition( JLabel.BOTTOM );
northLabel.setHorizontalTextPosition( JLabel.CENTER );
contentPane.add( northLabel , BorderLayout.NORTH );

//SOUTH:
ImageIcon southIcon = new ImageIcon( "image/zwthr14.gif" );
JLabel southLabel = new JLabel( "Balmy in the South",
                                southIcon,
                                JLabel.CENTER );
southLabel.setVerticalTextPosition( JLabel.BOTTOM );
southLabel.setHorizontalTextPosition( JLabel.CENTER );
contentPane.add( southLabel, BorderLayout.SOUTH );

//EAST:
ImageIcon eastIcon =
            new ImageIcon( "image/thunderstormanim.gif" );
JLabel eastLabel = new JLabel( "Stormy In the East",
                               eastIcon,
                               JLabel.CENTER );
eastLabel.setVerticalTextPosition( JLabel.BOTTOM );
eastLabel.setHorizontalTextPosition( JLabel.CENTER );
Border borderEastLabel =
            BorderFactory.createLineBorder( Color.blue );
eastLabel.setBorder( borderEastLabel );
contentPane.add( eastLabel, BorderLayout.EAST );

//WEST:
ImageIcon iconWest = new ImageIcon( "image/sunanim.gif" );
JLabel westLabel = new JLabel( "Sunny in the West",
                               iconWest,
                               JLabel.CENTER );
westLabel.setVerticalTextPosition( JLabel.BOTTOM );
westLabel.setHorizontalTextPosition( JLabel.CENTER );
Border borderWestLabel =
            BorderFactory.createLineBorder( Color.black );
westLabel.setBorder( borderWestLabel );
contentPane.add( westLabel, BorderLayout.WEST );
```

```
        //CENTER:
        JLabel centerLabel =
                new JLabel( "The Weather Compass", JLabel.CENTER );
        Border borderCenterLabel =
                BorderFactory.createLineBorder( Color.red );
        centerLabel.setBorder( borderCenterLabel );
        contentPane.add( centerLabel , BorderLayout.CENTER );

        f.pack();
        f.setLocation( 200, 300 );
        f.setVisible( true );
    }
}
```

The window produced by the above program is shown in Figure 17.9.

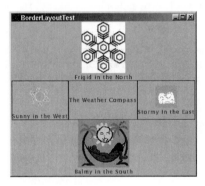

Fig. 17.9

17.9.2 Flow Layout

FlowLayout arranges the components from left to right and from top to bottom, displaying each component at its preferred size. The first component that the manager is given is displayed in the middle of the first row at the top. When it is given a second component, the layout manager arranges for the two components to appear symmetrically with respect to the middle in the top row. When it is given a third component, the manager tries to arrange all three symmetrically in the top row. As more components are added, at some point the manager will run out of room in the top row. Then it starts the same process of arranging the components in the second row, and so on. When a window is resized, the layout manager automatically rearranges the components symmetrically even if that means shifting a component from one row to another.

Shown below is the `FlowLayout` version of the program we showed previously. Now that we do not want to use the default layout manager specified for a content pane, we use the following `set` invocation:

```
Container contentPane = f.getContentPane();
contentPane.setLayout( new FlowLayout() );
```

in lines (A) and (B) of the program. Since the cardinal directions do not carry any meaning for `FlowLayout`, we have also changed the names of the labels and the icons accordingly.

```java
//FlowLayoutTest.java

import java.awt.*;              // for Container, BorderLayout
import java.awt.event.*;       // for WindowAdapter
import javax.swing.*;
import javax.swing.border.*;   // for Border, BorderFactory

public class FlowLayoutTest {
    public static void main( String[] args ) {
        JFrame f = new JFrame( "FlowLayoutTest" );

        f.addWindowListener(new WindowAdapter() {
            public void windowClosing(WindowEvent e) {
                System.exit(0);
            }
        });

        Container contentPane = f.getContentPane();              //(A)
        contentPane.setLayout( new FlowLayout() );               //(B)

        //ITEM 1:
        ImageIcon firstIcon = new ImageIcon( "snowflake.gif" );
        JLabel firstLabel = new JLabel( "Frigid in the North",
                                        firstIcon,
                                        JLabel.CENTER );
        firstLabel.setVerticalTextPosition( JLabel.BOTTOM );
        firstLabel.setHorizontalTextPosition( JLabel.CENTER );
        contentPane.add( firstLabel );

        //ITEM 2:
        ImageIcon secondIcon = new ImageIcon( "zwthr14.gif" );
        JLabel secondLabel = new JLabel( "Balmy in the South",
                                         secondIcon,
                                         JLabel.CENTER );
        secondLabel.setVerticalTextPosition( JLabel.BOTTOM );
        secondLabel.setHorizontalTextPosition( JLabel.CENTER );
```

```
// secondLabel.setPreferredSize(new Dimension(50, 50));   //(C)
contentPane.add( secondLabel );

//ITEM 3:
ImageIcon thirdIcon = new ImageIcon( "thunderstormanim.gif" );
JLabel thirdLabel = new JLabel( "Stormy In the East",
                                thirdIcon,
                                JLabel.CENTER );
thirdLabel.setVerticalTextPosition( JLabel.BOTTOM );
thirdLabel.setHorizontalTextPosition( JLabel.CENTER );
Border borderThirdLabel =
                BorderFactory.createLineBorder( Color.blue );
thirdLabel.setBorder( borderThirdLabel );
contentPane.add( thirdLabel );

//ITEM 4:
ImageIcon fourthIcon = new ImageIcon( "sunanim.gif" );
JLabel fourthLabel = new JLabel( "Sunny in the West",
                                 fourthIcon,
                                 JLabel.CENTER );
fourthLabel.setVerticalTextPosition( JLabel.BOTTOM );
fourthLabel.setHorizontalTextPosition( JLabel.CENTER );
Border borderFourthLabel =
                BorderFactory.createLineBorder( Color.black );
fourthLabel.setBorder( borderFourthLabel );
contentPane.add( fourthLabel );

//ITEM 5:
JLabel fifthLabel =
        new JLabel( "The Weather Compass", JLabel.CENTER );
Border borderFifthLabel =
                BorderFactory.createLineBorder( Color.red );
fifthLabel.setBorder( borderFifthLabel );
contentPane.add( fifthLabel );

f.pack();
f.setLocation( 200, 300 );
f.setVisible( true );
    }
}
```

If you run this program, all five JLabel object may appear in a single row. If you resize the window to make it smaller, one or more of the rightmost entries will "float" down to the second row, while remaining symmetrical with respect to the middle of the window.

A noteworthy aspect of FlowLayout is that it respects any hints you provide for the preferred size of a component (whereas BorderLayout ignores such hints). For example, if in the above program, we uncomment the following statement in line (C):

```
secondLabel.setPreferredSize( new Dimension( 50, 50 ) );
```

then the size used for this component will be 50×50 pixels. This size remains fixed if you enlarge or shrink the top-level window.[15] In general, layout managers can also be provided with recommendations for the minimum and the maximum sizes to use for a component by invoking

```
component.setMinimumSize( size );
component.setMaximumSize( size );
```

While you are free to provide such hints, a layout manager may or may not pay attention to them. For example, only the BoxLayout to be presented next respects the maximum size hint.

The GUI produced by the above program is shown in Figure 17.10.

Fig. 17.10

17.9.3 Box Layout

BoxLayout can create either a horizontal or a vertical arrangement of its components. The horizontal option arranges the components in a left-to-right order and the vertical option in a top-to-bottom order. The BoxLayout class also comes with the means to create empty spaces in a spatial layout to bring about a desired visual effect. There are three types of empty spaces:

1. Rigid area, created by invoking

```
Box.createRigidArea( size )
```

As its name implies, a rigid area gives you a fixed number of pixels as empty space. Say you are using BoxLayout for creating a horizontal arrangement of components and you want a space of 10 pixels between a pair of adjacent components, you can say:

---

[15]For the example shown, what will be displayed with the preferred-size hint is the central 50×50 portion of the component bound to secondLabel, as opposed to a resized version of the original component.

```
container.add( firstComponent );
container.add( Box.createRigidArea( new Dimension( 10, 0 ) ) );
container.add( secondComponent );
```

The same goes for vertical spacing in a vertical arrangement of components. For vertical spacing, the argument supplied to createRigidArea would be like new Dimension(0, 10).

2. Glue, created by invoking either

```
Box.createHorizontalGlue()
```

or

```
Box.createVerticalGlue()
```

Glue gives you expandable empty space. Suppose you want a couple of buttons to show up at the right end of a row that is constrained by the rest of the layout to be longer than what is needed to hold the two buttons. You could do so by

```
rowContainer.add( Box.createHorizontalGlue() );
rowContainer.add( firstButton );
rowContainer.add( secondButton );
```

Without the glue, both buttons would end up at the left end of the row.

3. Invisible component, created by invoking

```
new Box.Filler( minSize, prefSize, maxSize )
```

By incorporating an invisible component with appropriate size hints, you can force the layout manager to create an empty space that varies in size like the glue but that will not violate the min-size and the max-size constraints.

The example below uses BoxLayout to create the GUI whose outline is shown in Figure 17.11. The BoxLayout is used specifically in this example in the intermediate containers named listPanel and buttonPanel, both of type JPanel that are created in lines (E) and (I) of the program below. The container listPanel uses BoxLayout in the vertical mode to arrange a JLabel and a JScrollPane vertically. On the other hand, the container buttonPanel uses BoxLayout in the horizontal mode to arrange the two buttons as shown. The container buttonPanel also uses glue left of the buttons to push the buttons to the right end of the container.

The JScrollPane object, called listScroller in the program, that resides inside the listPanel displays a JList object consisting of the data declared in line (B). A JList allows a user to select one or more items from a list. Since a JList does not support scrolling directly, if scrolling is needed you need to construct a JScrollPane object from a JList, as we have done in line (D), and thus make the JList object the *viewport view* of the JScrollPane object.

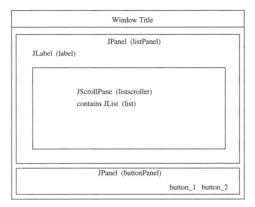

Fig. 17.11

The two JPanel components, listPanel and buttonPanel, are inserted into the top-level window with BorderLayout in lines (H) and (J). Note how the listPanel component includes a a 10-pixel vertical space — in the form of a rigid area — between the JLabel and the JScrollPane in line (F). The component listPanel is also given a 10-pixel empty border all around in line (G).

```
//BoxLayoutTest.java

import java.awt.*;          // for Container, BorderLayout
import java.awt.event.*;    // for WindowAdapter
import javax.swing.*;

public class BoxLayoutTest {
    public static void main( String[] args ) {
        JFrame f = new JFrame( "BoxLayoutTest" );

        f.addWindowListener(new WindowAdapter() {
            public void windowClosing(WindowEvent e) {
                System.exit(0);
            }
        });

        Container contentPane = f.getContentPane();              //(A)

        String[] data = {"sunny", "hot", "stormy", "balmy",      //(B)
                         "cold",  "frigid", "rainy", "windy",
                         "snowy", "blistery", "blizzardy"};

        JList list = new JList( data );                          //(C)
```

```
//this makes list the viewport of listscroller:
JScrollPane listScroller = new JScrollPane( list );        //(D)

listScroller.setPreferredSize( new Dimension( 300, 100 ) );
listScroller.setMinimumSize( new Dimension( 300, 100 ) );
listScroller.setAlignmentX( Component.LEFT_ALIGNMENT );

JPanel listPanel = new JPanel();                           //(E)
listPanel.setLayout(
            new BoxLayout( listPanel, BoxLayout.Y_AXIS ) );
JLabel label = new JLabel( "Select today's weather:" );
listPanel.add( label );
listPanel.add(
        Box.createRigidArea( new Dimension( 0, 10 ) ) );   //(F)
listPanel.add( listScroller );
listPanel.setBorder(
    BorderFactory.createEmptyBorder( 10, 10, 10, 10 ) );   //(G)

contentPane.add( listPanel, BorderLayout.CENTER );         //(H)

JButton cancelButton = new JButton( "Cancel" );
JButton selectButton = new JButton( "Select" );

JPanel buttonPanel = new JPanel();                         //(I)
buttonPanel.setLayout(
        new BoxLayout( buttonPanel, BoxLayout.X_AXIS ) );
buttonPanel.setBorder(
        BorderFactory.createEmptyBorder(0,10,10,10 ) );
buttonPanel.add( Box.createHorizontalGlue() );
buttonPanel.add( cancelButton );
buttonPanel.add(
        Box.createRigidArea( new Dimension( 10, 0 ) ) );
buttonPanel.add( selectButton );

contentPane.add( buttonPanel, BorderLayout.SOUTH );        //(J)

f.pack();
f.setLocation( 200, 300 );
f.setVisible( true );
    }
}
```

The window produced by this program looks like what is shown in Figure 17.12.

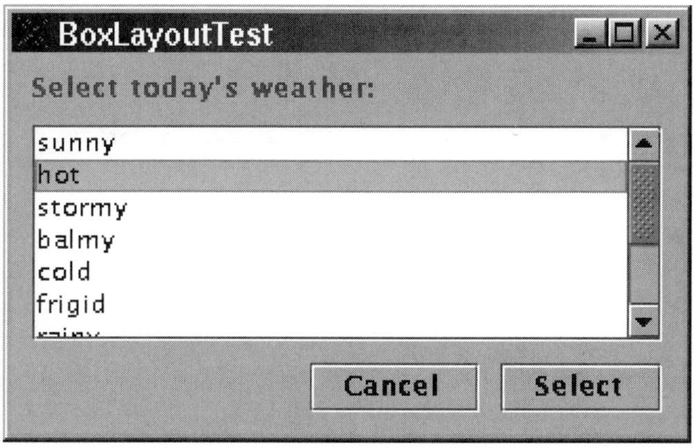

Fig. 17.12

17.9.4 Grid Layout

GridLayout divides the container into a grid of equal-sized cells. Each component is assigned a cell in a left-to-right and top-to-bottom fashion. The components may be enlarged by padding them with empty space so as to fill each cell. For this reason, GridLayout, like BorderLayout, usually ignores any size hints you may provide.

The GridLayout constructor can be invoked either with two arguments or with four arguments:

```
public GridLayout( int rows, int columns )
```

and

```
public GridLayout( int rows,
                   int columns,
                   int horizontalGap,
                   int verticalGap )
```

In both these constructor calls, either the rows or the columns arguments must be nonzero. A zero value for rows means that any number of rows is allowed in the grid. Similarly, when columns is set to zero, any number of columns is permissible. Ordinarily, the adjacent cells abut each other. However, nonzero values given to the arguments horizontalGap and/or verticalGap create that much space in pixels between the cells.

It is educational to compare the GUI constructed by the following program with that for FlowLayoutTest.java. The reader will notice that while FlowLayout produces unequal sized components, the GridLayout makes them all equal-sized. This is especially evident for the components with borders.

```java
//GridLayoutTest.java

import java.awt.*;            // for Container, BorderLayout
import java.awt.event.*;      // for WindowAdapter
import javax.swing.*;
import javax.swing.border.*;  // for Border, BorderFactory

public class GridLayoutTest {
    public static void main( String[] args ) {
        JFrame f = new JFrame( "GridLayoutTest" );
        f.addWindowListener(new WindowAdapter() {
            public void windowClosing(WindowEvent e) {
                System.exit(0);
            }
        });
        Container contentPane = f.getContentPane();
        contentPane.setLayout( new GridLayout( 0, 2 ) );

        //ITEM 1:
        ImageIcon firstIcon = new ImageIcon( "snowflake.gif" );
        JLabel firstLabel = new JLabel( "Frigid in the North",
                                        firstIcon,
                                        JLabel.CENTER );
        firstLabel.setVerticalTextPosition( JLabel.BOTTOM );
        firstLabel.setHorizontalTextPosition( JLabel.CENTER );
        contentPane.add( firstLabel );

        //ITEM 2:
        ImageIcon secondIcon = new ImageIcon( "zwthr14.gif" );
        JLabel secondLabel = new JLabel( "Balmy in the South",
                                         secondIcon,
                                         JLabel.CENTER );
        secondLabel.setVerticalTextPosition( JLabel.BOTTOM );
        secondLabel.setHorizontalTextPosition( JLabel.CENTER );
        contentPane.add( secondLabel );

        //ITEM 3:
        ImageIcon thirdIcon = new ImageIcon( "thunderstormanim.gif" );
        JLabel thirdLabel = new JLabel( "Stormy In the East",
                                        thirdIcon,
                                        JLabel.CENTER );
        thirdLabel.setVerticalTextPosition( JLabel.BOTTOM );
        thirdLabel.setHorizontalTextPosition( JLabel.CENTER );
        Border borderThirdLabel =
                    BorderFactory.createLineBorder( Color.blue );
        thirdLabel.setBorder( borderThirdLabel );
        contentPane.add( thirdLabel );
```

```
    //ITEM 4:
    ImageIcon fourthIcon = new ImageIcon( "sunanim.gif" );
    JLabel fourthLabel = new JLabel( "Sunny in the West",
                                     fourthIcon,
                                     JLabel.CENTER );
    fourthLabel.setVerticalTextPosition( JLabel.BOTTOM );
    fourthLabel.setHorizontalTextPosition( JLabel.CENTER );
    Border borderFourthLabel =
            BorderFactory.createLineBorder( Color.black );
    fourthLabel.setBorder( borderFourthLabel );
    contentPane.add( fourthLabel );

    //ITEM 5:
    JLabel fifthLabel =
        new JLabel( "The Weather Compass", JLabel.CENTER );
    Border borderFifthLabel =
                BorderFactory.createLineBorder( Color.red );
    fifthLabel.setBorder( borderFifthLabel );
    contentPane.add( fifthLabel );

    f.pack();
    f.setLocation( 200, 300 );
    f.setVisible( true );
    }
}
```

Figure 17.13 shows the layout produced by the above program.

17.9.5 Card Layout

CardLayout is useful for displaying multiple components in the same space. Each component can be thought of as residing on a separate card, as if in a deck of cards. The user gets to see only one card at a time. Therefore, a GUI that uses CardLayout generally includes a selection mechanism for choosing the card for display.[16]

The following program places the four weather JLabel objects you have seen before on four different cards of a CardLayout. The program provides a JComboBox to enable a user to select the card to see.[17] The JComboBox object, created in line (A),

---

[16]The functionality that we get from CardLayout can sometimes be achieved more easily by using a tabbed pane as provided by the class JTabbedPane.

[17]When space is limited, a JComboBox is a convenient way to give the user a one-of-many selection mechanism. When the user clicks on the component, a drop-down menu of items is made visible. The user can select the item desired by clicking on it. By default, a JComboBox is uneditable. But if made editable, a textfield is also displayed to give the user the option of entering his/her own choice, besides the choices

Fig. 17.13

is provided with an empty border 20 pixels wide in line (C) and encased in a JPanel in line (D) to create a pleasing visual effect.

The syntax of and the need for addItemListener in line (B) will become clear from our discussion on event processing in Section 17.13. Suffice it to say here that when the user clicks on one of the JComboBox items, this statement enables automatic invocation of the itemStateChanged method in line (F), which causes the selected card to be displayed.

While the part of the program where we create the different cards and add them to the cards panel is self-explanatory, note how we force the cards panel to be of size 200 × 200 pixels in the override definition for the getPreferredSize method in line (E).

```
//CardLayoutTest.java

import java.awt.*;            // for Container, BorderLayout
import java.awt.event.*;      // for WindowAdapter
import javax.swing.*;
import javax.swing.border.*;  // for Border, BorderFactory

public class CardLayoutTest extends JFrame implements ItemListener {
    JPanel cards;
```

made available through the drop-down menu. When space is not an issue, other mechanisms that can be used for one-of-many selection include JList and JRadioButton.

```
final static String[] comboBoxItems
            = {"frigid","balmy","stormy","sunny" };

public CardLayoutTest() {
    Container contentPane = getContentPane();

    JPanel comboPanel = new JPanel();
    JComboBox c = new JComboBox( comboBoxItems );          //(A)
    c.setEditable( false );
    c.addItemListener( this );                             //(B)
    c.setBorder(
        BorderFactory.createEmptyBorder( 20, 20, 20, 20 ) ); //(C)
    comboPanel.add( c );                                   //(D)

    contentPane.add( comboPanel, BorderLayout.NORTH );

    cards = new JPanel() {
            public Dimension getPreferredSize() {          //(E)
                Dimension size = super.getPreferredSize();
                size.width = 200;
                size.height = 200;
                return size;
            }
    };

    cards.setLayout( new CardLayout() );

    //Card 1:
    ImageIcon firstIcon = new ImageIcon( "snowflake.gif" );
    JLabel firstLabel = new JLabel( "Frigid in the North",
                                    firstIcon,
                                    JLabel.CENTER );
    firstLabel.setVerticalTextPosition( JLabel.BOTTOM );
    firstLabel.setHorizontalTextPosition( JLabel.CENTER );
    firstLabel.setBorder(
            BorderFactory.createLineBorder( Color.blue ) );
    cards.add( firstLabel, "frigid" );

    //Card 2:
    ImageIcon secondIcon = new ImageIcon( "zwthr14.gif" );
    JLabel secondLabel = new JLabel( "Balmy in the South",
                                     secondIcon,
                                     JLabel.CENTER );
    secondLabel.setVerticalTextPosition( JLabel.BOTTOM );
    secondLabel.setHorizontalTextPosition( JLabel.CENTER );
    secondLabel.setBorder(
            BorderFactory.createLineBorder( Color.green ) );
    cards.add( secondLabel, "balmy" );
```

```
    //Card 3:
    ImageIcon thirdIcon = new ImageIcon( "thunderstormanim.gif" );
    JLabel thirdLabel = new JLabel( "Stormy In the East",
                                    thirdIcon,
                                    JLabel.CENTER );
    thirdLabel.setVerticalTextPosition( JLabel.BOTTOM );
    thirdLabel.setHorizontalTextPosition( JLabel.CENTER );
    thirdLabel.setBorder(
                  BorderFactory.createLineBorder( Color.red ) );
    cards.add( thirdLabel, "stormy" );

    //Card 4:
    ImageIcon fourthIcon = new ImageIcon( "sunanim.gif" );
    JLabel fourthLabel = new JLabel( "Sunny in the West",
                                    fourthIcon,
                                    JLabel.CENTER );
    fourthLabel.setVerticalTextPosition( JLabel.BOTTOM );
    fourthLabel.setHorizontalTextPosition( JLabel.CENTER );
    fourthLabel.setBorder(
                  BorderFactory.createLineBorder( Color.white ) );
    cards.add( fourthLabel, "sunny" );

    contentPane.add( cards, BorderLayout.CENTER );

    addWindowListener(new WindowAdapter() {
        public void windowClosing(WindowEvent e) {
            System.exit(0);
        }
    });
}

public void itemStateChanged( ItemEvent evt ) {                  //(F)
    CardLayout cl = (CardLayout) ( cards.getLayout() );
    cl.show( cards, (String) evt.getItem() );
}

public static void main( String[] args ) {
    CardLayoutTest window = new CardLayoutTest();
    window.setTitle( "CardLayoutTest" );
    window.setLocation( 200, 300 );
    window.pack();
    window.setVisible( true );
}
}
```

Figure 17.14 illustrates the layout produced by the above program.

Fig. 17.14

17.9.6 Grid-Bag Layout

GridBagLayout is the most versatile of the layout managers that come with the Java platform. Like GridLayout, it divides the display area into an array of cells. But, it accomplishes much more than what GridLayout can do. GridBagLayout gives you the following in a row-column presentation of components:

- The display area assigned to a component can span multiple rows, multiple columns, or multiple rows and multiple columns simultaneously.

- Each row can be of a different height, and each column of a different width.

- As a window is resized, the resizing behavior of the display area allocated to each component in relation to that of the display areas assigned to the other components can be tuned on an individual basis.

- Within the display area allocated to each component, how the component expands or shrinks as a window is resized can again be controlled on an individual basis. While the previous property was about the resizing behavior of the display area allocated to a component, we are now talking about the resizing behavior of the component itself within its allocated display area.

All of this is done with the help of the GridBagConstraints class whose various data members provide control over the various aspects of the display. One first creates an instance of GridBagConstraints, sets its data members to desired values, and then informs the GridBagLayout manager which component is to be impacted by those constraints. Before we illustrate this process with an example, here is a list of the data members of GridBagConstraints that can be set to provide control over a display:

gridx, gridy These decide which cell in the array a component goes into. You can think of them as the row and column "coordinates" of the top-left corner of the display area assigned to a component. For example, if you wanted the display area assigned to a component to occupy the leftmost cell in the topmost row, you'd set both gridx and gridy to 0. For the next component on the right, gridx would be 1 and gridy would still be 0, and so on.

gridwidth, gridheight These control the number of cells the display area assigned to a component can occupy in width and in height. The default value for each is 1, as you'd expect. Note that the constraints specified by these two variables do not work for the topmost row and for the leftmost column. This is for the simple reason that the column decomposition of a row is not defined until the objects are placed in the first row. Similarly, the row decomposition of a column is not defined until the objects are placed in the left column. After the first row and the first column are fully occupied, the layout manager can make sense of an interior cell occupying a certain number of columns in width and a certain number of rows in height.

weightx, weighty These control the resizing behavior of the display area assigned to a component as the top-level window is resized manually.[18] If you wanted all the components to resize proportionately as the top-level window is resized, you'd set both weightx and weighty equal to 1 at the beginning of constraint specifications, as we do in the example below. However, you can selectively specify a different resizing behavior of the display area for each component by varying the values of these two constraints. The values can be between 0 and 1 and the default is 0, which means that the display area will not expand as the top-level window is made larger; the extra space simply appears as empty space around the component.

fill This controls the resizing behavior of a component within its allocated display area when the top-level window is resized. The four possible values for this variable are NONE, which is the default, HORIZONTAL, VERTICAL, and BOTH. When the value is set to HORIZONTAL, a component expands or shrinks as necessary to horizontally fill the display area assigned to the component. If you want to confine the filling behavior to the vertical direction, you'd use VERTICAL. But if you wanted the fill to take place in both dimensions (which is

---

[18]Note that whereas fill controls the resizing behavior of a component within its own display area as the display area expands or shrinks, weightx and weighty control how the display area assigned to a component expands or shrinks when the top-level window is resized.

probably what you would want to see happen in most cases), you'd use BOTH. With the default filling behavior provided by NONE, the component would stay at its preferred size even when its allocated display area expands as the window is made larger.

ipadx, ipady Through these variables, you can make columns of unequal width and rows of unequal height. These, referred to as the padding variables, have a default value of 0. When ipadx is nonzero, the width of that component will be at least its minimum width plus 2*ipadx, since the padding is applied symmetrically at both ends. Similarly for ipady in the vertical direction.

insets This specifies the extent of the empty space between the boundary of the component and the edges of its display area. The default is 0.

anchor If a component is smaller than its allocated display area, this controls where in the display area the component will be placed. The default value is CENTER. Other possible values are NORTH, NORTHEAST, EAST, SOUTHEAST, SOUTH, SOUTHWEST, WEST, and NORTHWEST.

We will now show how GridBagConstraints is actually used in a program. First, we create an instance of the layout manager and an instance of GridBagConstraints, as illustrated by

```
Container contentPane = frame.getContentPane();
GridBagLayout gridbag = new GridBagLayout();
contentPane.setLayout( gridbag );
GridBagConstraints constraints = new GridBagConstraints();
```

Now suppose you wanted all your components to fill out their assigned display areas and you also wanted the display areas to expand and shrink proportionately as the top-level window is resized, you could say at the very outset (before getting into the details of constraint specification at the level of individual components):

```
constraints.fill = GridBagConstraints.BOTH;
constraints.weightx = 1.0;
constraints.weighty = 1.0;
```

Now let's say you'd like to add a wider-than-usual JButton at the top-left corner of the display. You would say

```
JButton button = new JButton( "Button 1" );
constraints.gridx = 0;
constraints.gridy = 0;
constraints.ipadx = 100;
gridbag.setConstraints( button, constraints );
contentPane.add( button );
```

After using the GridBagConstraints object for one component, you have the option of using the same constraint object for the next component or creating a new constraint object. If you use the same constraint object, you have to remember to reset the values of those constraints that were set previously. The example below uses the following code for the next component in the same row:

```
button = new JButton( "Button 2" );
constraints.gridx = 1;
constraints.gridy = 0;
constraints.ipadx = 0;
gridbag.setConstraints( button, constraints );
contentPane.add( button );
```

Since, in relation to the previous button, we want this button to appear at its regular width, we reset ipadx to 0. This process can be continued as we do in the example shown below that creates three rows of buttons. There are three buttons in the first row, two in the second, and one in the last. Of the three buttons in the first row, the leftmost button is wider than the other two, which causes the first column to be wider than the other two columns. By setting ipady, all the buttons in the second row appear taller than the buttons in the other rows.

```
//GridBagLayoutTest.java

import java.awt.*;           // for Container, BorderLayout
import java.awt.event.*;     // for WindowAdapter
import javax.swing.*;

public class GridBagLayoutTest {
    public static void main( String[] args ) {

        JButton button;

        JFrame f = new JFrame( "GridBagLayoutTest" );
        f.addWindowListener(new WindowAdapter() {
            public void windowClosing(WindowEvent e) {
                System.exit(0);
            }
        });

        Container contentPane = f.getContentPane();
        GridBagLayout gridbag = new GridBagLayout();
        contentPane.setLayout( gridbag );
        GridBagConstraints cons = new GridBagConstraints();
        cons.fill = GridBagConstraints.BOTH;
        cons.weightx = 1.0;
        cons.weighty = 1.0;

        // ROW 1:
        button = new JButton( "Button 1" );
```

```
        cons.gridx = 0;
        cons.gridy = 0;
        cons.ipadx = 100;
        gridbag.setConstraints( button, cons );
        contentPane.add( button );

        button = new JButton( "Button 2" );
        cons.gridx = 1;
        cons.gridy = 0;
        cons.ipadx = 0;
        gridbag.setConstraints( button, cons );
        contentPane.add( button );

        button = new JButton( "Button 3" );
        cons.gridx = 2;
        cons.gridy = 0;
        gridbag.setConstraints( button, cons );
        contentPane.add( button );

        // ROW 2:
        button = new JButton( "Button 4" );
        cons.gridwidth = 2;
        cons.gridx = 0;
        cons.gridy = 1;
        cons.ipady = 50;
        gridbag.setConstraints( button, cons );
        contentPane.add( button );

        button = new JButton( "Button 5" );
        cons.gridwidth = 1;
        cons.gridx = 2;
        cons.gridy = 1;
        gridbag.setConstraints( button, cons );
        contentPane.add( button );

        // ROW 3:
        button = new JButton( "Button 6" );
        cons.gridwidth = 3;
        cons.gridx = 0;
        cons.gridy = 2;
        cons.ipady = 0;
        gridbag.setConstraints( button, cons );
        contentPane.add( button );

        f.pack();
        f.setLocation( 200, 300 );
        f.setVisible( true );
    }
}
```

Figure 17.15 shows the layout produced by the above program.

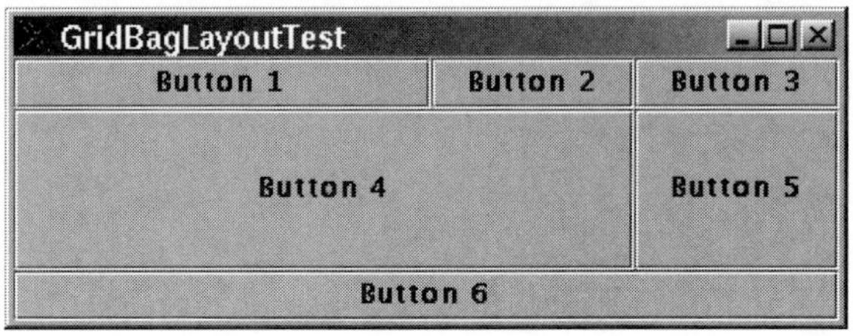

Fig. 17.15

As was mentioned earlier, one also has the option of not using a layout manager at all and instead using specific designated positions for the components. Since some components come with default layout managers, in order to not use a layout manager, you must first "de-select" the default layout manager by invoking setLayout(null). The absolute position and size of a component can then be specified by the invocation of setBounds(int x, int y, int size_x, int size_y) where x and y are the absolute coordinates of the new component and size_x and size_y its size. Yet another option is to custom design your own layout manager by implementing the LayoutManager interface.

17.10   LAYOUT MANAGEMENT IN QT

The C++-based Qt toolkit provides the following classes to serve as layout managers:

```
QHBox
QHBoxLayout
QVBox
QVBoxLayout
QGrid
QGridLayout
QLayout
```

Of these, QHBox, QVBox, and QGrid insert *automatically* a new widget[19] into the next available cell in the layout. The other four give the programmer greater control over where a given widget will be in the overall layout controlled by the manager.

---

[19]Recall that the terms "widget" and "component" are used interchangeably in this chapter. What a component is to AWT/Swing, a widget is to Qt and to GNOME/GTK+.

17.10.1 Box Layout

If we wish for all the child widgets to be arranged horizontally, regardless of how the window is resized, we use either the QHBox or the QHBoxLayout classes. The following example illustrates the notion of automatic layout with QHBox. The child widgets in lines (C), (D), and (E) as they are created get automatically inserted into a horizontal arrangement without the invocation of any sort of an "add" function:

```
//QHBoxTest.cc
#include <qpushbutton.h>
#include <qhbox.h>
#include <qapplication.h>

class MyHBox : public QHBox {
public:
    MyHBox();
};

MyHBox::MyHBox() {
    setSpacing( 5 );                                         //(A)
    setMargin( 10 );                                         //(B)

    new QPushButton( "button1", this );                      //(C)
    new QPushButton( "button2", this );                      //(D)
    new QPushButton( "button3", this );                      //(E)
}

int main( int argc, char* argv[] )
{
    QApplication a( argc, argv );

    MyHBox* hb = new MyHBox();
    hb->show();
    a.setMainWidget( hb );

    return a.exec();
}
```

No matter how many widgets we create in the constructor MyHBox::MyHBox(), they will all be arranged horizontally and will appear in the order in which they are created. The spacing between adjoining widgets in the horizontal arrangement is controlled by invoking setSpacing with its argument set to the desired spacing in pixels, as we do in line (A). If you'd like blank space to show around the horizontal arrangement, that can be done by invoking setMargin in the manner shown in line (B). Using the g++ compiler, this program can be compiled by the command line

```
g++ -o QHBoxTest QHBoxTest.cc -I$QTDIR/include -L$QTDIR/lib -lqt
```

The output of the program is shown in Figure 17.16.

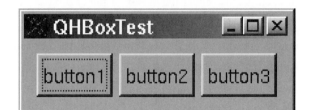

Fig. 17.16

If you wish to exercise greater control over the placement of a widget as it is created for a horizontal arrangement of widgets, you'd use QHBoxLayout. The following example from Dalheimer [14] accomplishes exactly the same as the previous example, but with the QHBoxLayout layout manager:

```
//QHBoxLayoutTest.cc

#include <qdialog.h>
#include <qpushbutton.h>
#include <qlayout.h>
#include <qapplication.h>

class MyDialog : public QDialog {
public:
    MyDialog();
};

MyDialog::MyDialog() {
    QPushButton* b1 = new QPushButton( "button1", this );        //(A)
    b1->setMinimumSize( b1->sizeHint() );                        //(B)
    QPushButton* b2 = new QPushButton( "button2", this );
    b2->setMinimumSize( b2->sizeHint() );
    QPushButton* b3 = new QPushButton( "button3", this );
    b3->setMinimumSize( b3->sizeHint() );

    QHBoxLayout* layout = new QHBoxLayout( this );
    layout->addWidget( b1 );                                     //(C)
    layout->addWidget( b2 );
    layout->addWidget( b3 );
    layout->activate();                                          //(D)
}
```

```
int main( int argc, char* argv[] )
{
    QApplication a( argc, argv );

    MyDialog* dlg = new MyDialog();
    dlg->show();
    a.setMainWidget( dlg );

    return a.exec();
}
```

Note that for each button created inside the `MyDialog` constructor, as in line (A), we declare its parent widget via the second argument to the button constructor and we add it to the layout by invoking the `addWidget` function, as in line (C). The buttons will appear in a horizontal arrangement in the order in which they are added to the layout. By supplying additional arguments to the `addWidget` function, one can specify *stretch* and *alignment* for each child widget. The prototype of the `addWidget` function is

```
void QBoxLayout::addWidget( QWidget* widget,
                            int stretch = 0,
                            int alignment = 0 );
```

The value assigned to `stretch` dictates how much a child widget will grow or shrink in relation to the other child widgets as the parent window is resized. And the value assigned to `alignment` dictates how much a child widget will stay centered in the portion of the space allocated to it as the parent window is resized. The actual values assigned to `stretch` and `alignment` are not important; what's important is how these values compare against the values assigned to the same variables for the other child widgets.

The above example also illustrates how we can establish a minimum size for a child widget. The minimum size for button b1 is set in line (B) to the value returned by `sizeHint`. Presumably, this is the size at which the displayed child widget will look the best. If we also wanted to tell the layout manager what maximum size to use for the widget, we would invoke `setMaximumSize`. Layout management in the above program is activated by invoking `activate` in the manner shown in line (D).

The program shown above can be compiled with the following command line:

```
g++ -o QHBoxLayoutTest QHBoxLayoutTest.cc                   \
             -I$QTDIR/include -L$QTDIR/lib -lqt
```

The GUI produced by this program looks like what's shown in Figure 17.17.

Fig. 17.17

Our discussion above applies identically to QVBox and QVBoxLayout, except that these two classes produce vertical arrangements of their child widgets, as opposed to horizontal arrangements.

17.10.2 Grid Layout

Our next example illustrates the use of QGrid for placing the child widgets in a row–column arrangement. The int argument to a QGrid constructor, as in line (A) below, specifies how many columns to use. The number of rows is arbitrary. A new row of widgets is added if warranted by the addition of a new widget. The example below shows the buttons arranged in two columns. There are three rows, but the last row contains only one button since the program creates only five child widgets.

```
//QGridTest.cc

#include <qpushbutton.h>
#include <qgrid.h>
#include <qapplication.h>

class MyGrid : public QGrid {
public:
    MyGrid( int );
};

MyGrid::MyGrid( int cols ) :  QGrid( cols ) {
    setSpacing( 5 );
    setMargin( 10 );

    new QPushButton( "button1", this );
    new QPushButton( "button2", this );
    new QPushButton( "button3", this );
    new QPushButton( "button4", this );
    new QPushButton( "button5", this );
}
```

```
int main( int argc, char* argv[] )
{
    QApplication a( argc, argv );

    MyGrid* mg = new MyGrid( 2 );                              //(A)
    mg->show();
    a.setMainWidget( mg );

    return a.exec();
}
```

This program produces the output shown in Figure 17.18.

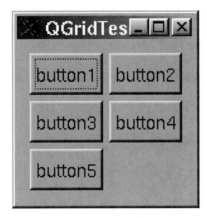

Fig. 17.18

With QGridLayout, we can specify both the number of rows and the number of columns for a table-like display of widgets. In the following program, the invocation

```
QGridLayout* layout = new QGridLayout( this, 2, 3 );
```

in line (A) creates a grid of cells consisting of 2 rows and 3 columns. Other versions of this constructor allow for the specification of spacing to be used between the cells of the grid. When spacing is not specified, the default is for a QGridLayout to inherit the parent's spacing.

The cells in a layout produced by QGridLayout use matrix indexing. The index of the top left cell is (0,0), of the next cell in the top row (0,1), and so on. The row and column indices are used by the addWidget function, as in the invocation

```
layout->addWidget( b3, 0, 2 );
```

in line (B), which says to insert the widget b3 in the first row of cells in the third column. Widgets in a grid layout are also allowed to occupy multiple cells by the invocation of `addMultiCellWidget`.

```
//QGridLayoutTest.cc

#include <qdialog.h>
#include <qpushbutton.h>
#include <qlayout.h>
#include <qapplication.h>

class MyDialog : public QDialog {
public:
    MyDialog();
};

MyDialog::MyDialog() {
    QPushButton* b1 = new QPushButton( "button1", this );
    b1->setMinimumSize( b1->sizeHint() );
    QPushButton* b2 = new QPushButton( "button2", this );
    b2->setMinimumSize( b2->sizeHint() );
    QPushButton* b3 = new QPushButton( "button3", this );
    b3->setMinimumSize( b3->sizeHint() );
    QPushButton* b4 = new QPushButton( "button4", this );
    b4->setMinimumSize( b4->sizeHint() );

    QGridLayout* layout = new QGridLayout( this, 2, 3 );        //(A)
    layout->addWidget( b1, 0, 0 );                             //(B)
    layout->addWidget( b2, 0, 1 );
    layout->addWidget( b3, 0, 2 );
    layout->addWidget( b4, 1, 1 );
    layout->activate();
}


int main( int argc, char* argv[] )
{
    QApplication a( argc, argv );

    MyDialog* dlg = new MyDialog();
    dlg->show();
    a.setMainWidget( dlg );

    return a.exec();
}
```

The output of the program is shown in Figure 17.19.

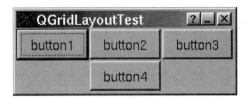

Fig. 17.19

For specialized effects, it is also possible to create your own layout manager by extending the class QLayout.

Finally, when you create your widget class, you'd also need to specify its layout properties. In most cases, this requires providing implementations for sizeHint(), minimumSizeHint(), and sizePolicy() methods.

17.11 LAYOUT MANAGEMENT IN GNOME/GTK+

GNOME/GTK+ uses the following layout managers for controlling the layout:

```
GtkHbox
GtkVBox
GtkTable
```

GtkHBox and GtkVBox work much the same way as QHBox and QVBox layout managers in Qt. And GtkTable is similar to QGridLayout of Qt.

17.11.1 Box Layout

A GtkHBox arranges all of its children in a single row, and all the children are allocated the same height. The following program illustrates this by packing buttons into a GtkHBox. As shown in line (A) of the program, the layout manager is constructed by a call to gtk_hbox_new whose prototype is

```
GtkWidget* gtk_hbox_new( gboolean homogeneous, gint spacing )
```

The second parameter is the number of pixels of empty space around each child widget. If the first parameter, homogeneous, is set to TRUE, each child widget will occupy an equal amount of space horizontally. This means that the amount of horizontal space alloted to a button with a short label will the same as to a button with a long label. The size of each child widget in its allocated space in the layout and how that size changes as the top-level window is resized is specified at the time a component is inserted into the layout, as shown by line (B) of the program. The prototype of the function gtk_box_pack_start() invoked in line (B) is

```
void gtk_box_pack_start( GtkBox* box,
                         GtkWidget* child,
                         gboolean expand,
                         gboolean fill,
                         guint padding );
```

For the case of arranging buttons in the following program, if the expand parameter is set to TRUE, a button would be made just large enough to fit the label for the button (the label length has to exceed a threshold for this to be true). If the fill parameter is set to TRUE, the button will occupy as much space as possible (taking into account the value assigned to padding) within the horizontal space alloted to the button.

```
//GHBoxTest.c

#include <gnome.h>

gint eventDestroy( GtkWidget* widget, GdkEvent* event, gpointer data );

int main( int argc, char* argv[] )
{
    GtkWidget* window;
    GtkWidget* hbox;
    GtkWidget* button;

    gnome_init( "HorizBoxTest", "1.0", argc, argv );

    window = gtk_window_new( GTK_WINDOW_TOPLEVEL );

    gtk_signal_connect( GTK_OBJECT( window ),
                        "destroy",
                        GTK_SIGNAL_FUNC( eventDestroy ),
                        NULL );

    gtk_container_set_border_width( GTK_CONTAINER( window ), 25 );

    hbox = gtk_hbox_new( TRUE, 10 );                             //(A)

    button = gtk_button_new_with_label( "Hi" );
    gtk_box_pack_start( GTK_BOX(hbox), button, FALSE, TRUE, 0 );  //(B)

    button = gtk_button_new_with_label( "Hello" );
    gtk_box_pack_start( GTK_BOX( hbox ), button, TRUE, FALSE, 0 );

    button = gtk_button_new_with_label( "Hi There" );
```

```
    gtk_box_pack_start( GTK_BOX( hbox ), button, FALSE, FALSE, 0 );

    button = gtk_button_new_with_label( "Hello There" );
    gtk_box_pack_start( GTK_BOX( hbox ), button, TRUE, TRUE, 0 );

    gtk_container_add( GTK_CONTAINER( window ), hbox );

    gtk_widget_show_all( window );
    gtk_main();
    exit( 0 );
}

gint eventDestroy( GtkWidget* widget, GdkEvent* event, gpointer data ){
    gtk_main_quit();
    return 0;
}
```

The _start in the function name gtk_box_pack_start means that the child widgets
will be inserted left to right in a horizontal layout. For inserting the child widgets
right to left, one can use the function gtk_box_pack_end. The window created by
the above program is shown in Figure 17.20.

Fig. 17.20

The discussion above applies equally to GtkVBox, except that now the child widgets will be arranged vertically. This layout manager is constructed with a call to
gtk_vbox_new whose prototype is similar to that shown earlier for gtk_hbox_new.

17.11.2 Table Layout

Our next example shows how the GtkTable layout manager can be used for creating
a grid-like arrangement of child widgets. The layout manager itself is constructed
with a call whose prototype is

```
    GtkWidget* gtk_table_new( guint rows,
                              guint columns,
                              gboolean homogeneous );
```

where the parameters rows and columns have obvious meanings. The meaning of homogeneous is the same as before; that is, the cell sizes will all be the equal regardless of the actual sizes of the child widgets if this parameter is set to TRUE.

As the following program shows in line (A), an easy way to enter a child widget into a cell is by invoking gtk_table_attach_defaults; this function is of prototype

```
void gtk_table_attach_defaults( GtkTable* table,
                                GtkWidget* widget,
                                guint left_attach,
                                guint right_attach,
                                guint top_attach,
                                guint bottom_attach );
```

where left_attach, right_attach, top_attach, and bottom_attach refer to the grid lines partitioning the table into cells. The leftmost edge of the table corresponds to the vertical grid line 0, the edge between the first column and the second column to the vertical grid line 1, and so on. So for the top left cell, the value of left_attach will always be 0 and that of right_attach 1. For the next cell in the top row, the left_attach will be 1 and the right-attach will be 2, and so on. Similarly for the values of top_attach and bottom_attach.

It is important to realize that a single widget can cover multiple cells in the table. In the program below, we show at (B) that the last button is constructed with the calls

```
button = gtk_button_new_with_label( "Hello There" );
gtk_table_attach_defaults( GTK_TABLE( table ), button, 0, 3, 1, 2 );
```

which by giving a value of 0 to left_attach and 3 to right_attach would cause this button to occupy three cells horizontally in the second row of the table.

The reason for "defaults" in the function name gtk_table_attach_defaults shown above is that it is a defaults-assuming abbreviated version of a function whose prototype is

```
void gtk_table_attach( GtkTable* table,
                       GtkWidget* widget,
                       guint left_attach,
                       guint right_attach,
                       guint top_attach,
                       guint bottom_attach,
                       GtkAttachOptions xoptions,
                       GtkAttachOptions yoptions,
                       guint xpadding,
                       guint ypadding );
```

where the parameters xoptions and yoptions are used to specify the expansion properties of the child widget when the table is resized horizontally or vertically. GtkAttachOptions is an enum defined by

```
typedef enum {
    GTK_EXPAND = 1 << 0,
    GTK_SHRINK = 1 << 1,
    GTK_FILL   = 1 << 2,
} GtkAttachOptions;
```

When xoptions is set to 0, the child widget will not be resized horizontally as the size of the table is changed; the child widget will appear at its minimum horizontal size. Additionally, if the size of the cell (or cells for multicell widgets) is larger than the minimum horizontal size of the widget, the widget will be centered. The same for yoptions set to 0 for vertical adjustments. When xoptions and/or yoptions is set to GTK_FILL, the child widget will expand, horizontally and/or vertically, to fill the available space. When set to GTK_SHRINK, the child widget will shrink to fit inside the cell (or cells) if the cell is smaller than the minimum size of the widget. And when set to GTK_EXPAND, the child widget will expand proportionately to the change in the size of the table. The parameters xpadding and ypadding stand for the margins to be used around the child widgets. The default for both xoptions and yoptions is GTK_EXPAND | GTK_FILL, and the default for both xpadding and ypadding is 0.

```
//TableLayoutTest.c

#include <gnome.h>

gint eventDestroy( GtkWidget* widget, GdkEvent* event, gpointer data );

int main( int argc, char* argv[] )
{
    GtkWidget* window;
    GtkWidget* table;
    GtkWidget* button;

    gnome_init( "TableLayoutTest", "1.0", argc, argv );

    window = gtk_window_new( GTK_WINDOW_TOPLEVEL );
    gtk_signal_connect( GTK_OBJECT( window ),
                        "destroy",
                        GTK_SIGNAL_FUNC( eventDestroy ),
                        NULL );
    gtk_container_set_border_width( GTK_CONTAINER( window ), 25 );

    table = gtk_table_new( 2, 3, TRUE );  //rows, cols, homogeneous

    button = gtk_button_new_with_label( "Hi" );
    gtk_table_attach_defaults( GTK_TABLE(table), button, 0, 1, 0, 1 );
                                                                    //(A)
    button = gtk_button_new_with_label( "Hello" );
    gtk_table_attach_defaults( GTK_TABLE(table), button, 1, 2, 0, 1 );
```

```
    button = gtk_button_new_with_label( "Hi There" );
    gtk_table_attach_defaults( GTK_TABLE(table), button, 2, 3, 0, 1 );

    button = gtk_button_new_with_label( "Hello There" );          //(B)
    gtk_table_attach_defaults( GTK_TABLE(table), button, 0, 3, 1, 2 );

    gtk_container_add( GTK_CONTAINER( window ), table );

    gtk_widget_show_all( window );
    gtk_main();
    exit( 0 );
}

gint eventDestroy( GtkWidget* widget, GdkEvent* event, gpointer data ){
    gtk_main_quit();
    return 0;
}
```

The window produced by the above program is shown in Figure 17.21.

Fig. 17.21

17.12 EVENT PROCESSING IN GUI PROGRAMS

When you run a GUI program, at its most basic level the interaction between a human user and the computer consists of *events*. To get a good sense what an event is, let's examine closely through Figure 17.22 as to what happens when you press a mouse button to interact with a GUI. An event is the information packet that is placed by the window manager in the event queue of the window in which the event was generated. This information packet contains the values for the x and the y coordinates of the mouse pointer when the mouse button was pressed and the identity of the button. The window manager's job is to keep track of the stacking order of the windows on a terminal screen and to ascertain from the coordinates of the mouse pointer as to which window generated the event. The window manager then simply places the event in the event queue of that window.

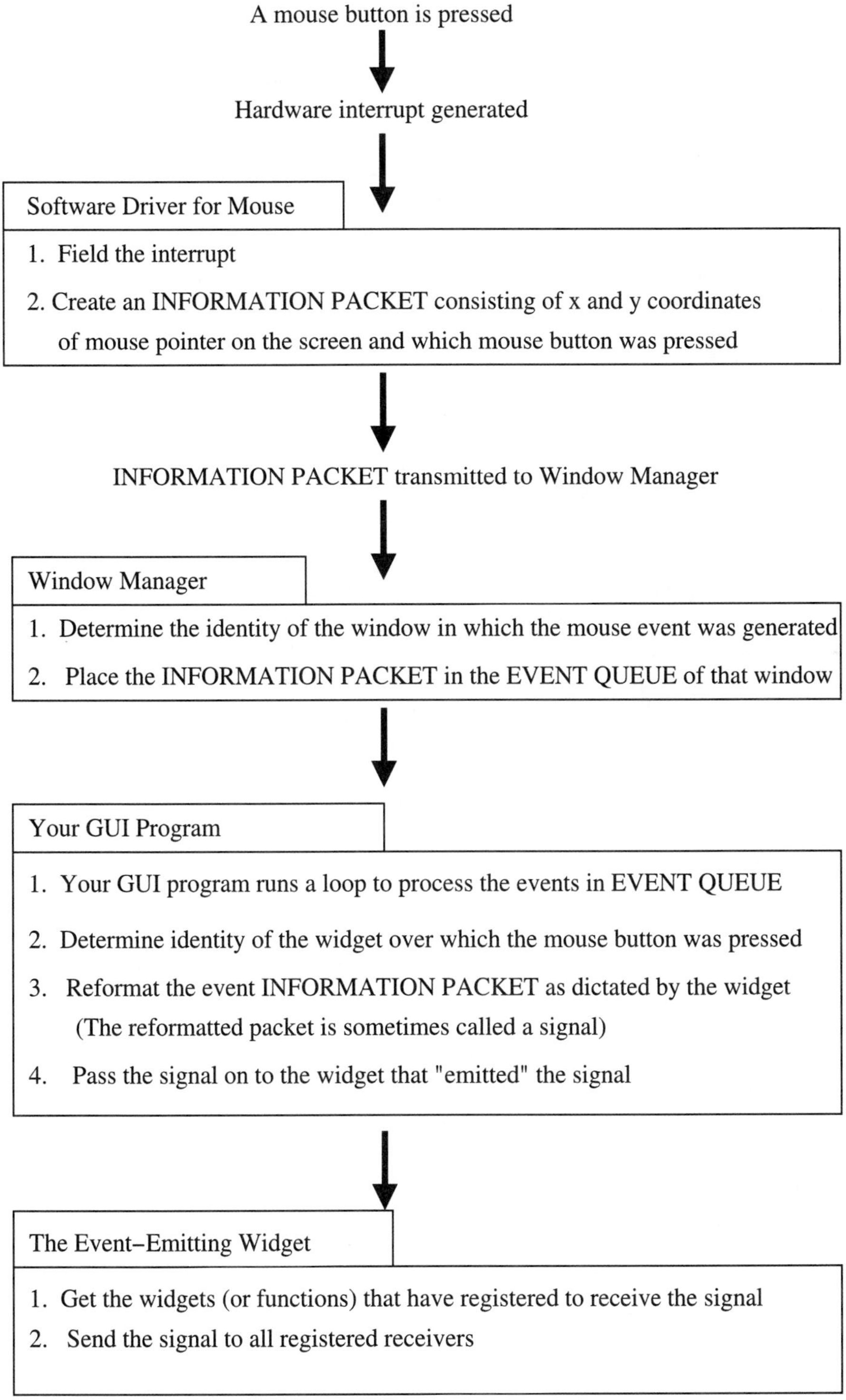

A mouse button is pressed

Hardware interrupt generated

Software Driver for Mouse

1. Field the interrupt

2. Create an INFORMATION PACKET consisting of x and y coordinates
   of mouse pointer on the screen and which mouse button was pressed

INFORMATION PACKET transmitted to Window Manager

Window Manager

1. Determine the identity of the window in which the mouse event was generated
2. Place the INFORMATION PACKET in the EVENT QUEUE of that window

Your GUI Program

1. Your GUI program runs a loop to process the events in EVENT QUEUE

2. Determine identity of the widget over which the mouse button was pressed

3. Reformat the event INFORMATION PACKET as dictated by the widget
   (The reformatted packet is sometimes called a signal)

4. Pass the signal on to the widget that "emitted" the signal

The Event–Emitting Widget

1. Get the widgets (or functions) that have registered to receive the signal
2. Send the signal to all registered receivers

Fig. 17.22

One of the main jobs of a GUI program is to run an *event processing loop* for a window for reacting to the events placed in the event queue of that window by the window manager. The very first step in event processing consists of determining the identity of the widget that is responsible for the event. If the event was caused by a user pressing a mouse button when the mouse pointer was on top of a GUI button, the GUI program would need to associate the event with that specific GUI button. Once this association is established, we could say loosely that the widget — the specific GUI button in this case — "emitted" the event or the signal.

After the source of an event is identified, one or more appropriate functions must be invoked in response to that event. Most modern GUI systems require a programmer to specify these functions explicitly in a program. These functions, called *callbacks* or *callback functions*, must somehow be "registered" with the widget that emitted the event. They are called callback functions because the GUI program does not invoke them explicitly. All a GUI program does is to set up an association between the event types that can be emitted by a widget and the callbacks that are to be executed in response to those event types. It is the underlying operating system that hands the flow of execution to a callback function when an event specific to a widget has been emitted.

How a callback function is registered with the source of an event varies considerably from system to system. In AWT/Swing, the callback functions are a programmer's implementations of functions in certain "listener" interfaces. An object must implement such an interface if it wishes to be notified of the occurrence of an event. Such an object must then be registered with the event-emitting widget with an "add" function. Qt, on the other hand, has a system of signals and slots for processing "high-level" events. Any object that wishes to be notified of a signal emitted by a widget must provide a slot for that signal. A slot is merely a function that can be made to respond to a particular signal by including both in a "connect" declaration. The signal from the emitting widget goes directly to the slot designated in the "connect" invocation. GNOME/GTK+ also uses a connect declaration for associating a signal with a callback.

An alternative to explicit registration of a callback with a signal is the use of polymorphic functions associated with signal-emitting widgets. So when a widget emits a signal, certain such functions are automatically invoked by the operating system. But being polymorphic, it is the override definitions that you provide in your code that actually get executed. This approach is used for the processing of "low-level" events in Qt. This approach is also used in wxWindows, a C++-based GUI toolkit for Unix and Windows, where virtual functions are invoked for processing the events generated by widgets. If an object needs to be informed of an event emitted by a widget, the object must be constructed from a class that extends the widget class and the class derivation must override certain virtual functions of the original widget class.

Yet other systems, Microsoft Foundation Classes (MFC) being a case in point, use macros and messages for event processing. Macros are used to link designated C++

methods to the various kinds of events that can be generated by the window system. The macros translate the events into "messages." Microsoft provides a graphical tool called IDE (for Interactive Design Environment) to help create the macros and messages.

17.13   EVENT PROCESSING IN AWT/SWING

As was mentioned earlier, the interaction of a user with a GUI program takes the form of events. Every event has a source, which is the component that produced it. Only certain kinds of objects can trap events — objects that have implemented certain designated *listener* interfaces. For example, when a user clicks the mouse on a GUI button, the resulting event produced by the button can be trapped by any object whose class has implemented the `ActionListener` interface. Objects that are able to trap an event have to be registered with the source of that event.

Table 17.1 lists some typical user actions that result in events, the event type generated, and the type of listener needed for trapping the event. The last column shows whether or not there exists an *adapter* class for a given *listener* class. Every listener interface with more than one method declared for it has a corresponding adapter class purely for convenience. The adapter class for a listener interface provides *do-nothing* implementations for all of the methods of the interface. Ordinarily, if you wanted to implement a listener interface but were interested in only one of the methods declared in the interface, you'd have to provide *do-nothing* implementations for all other methods of the interface. An adapter class saves you from having to do all that extra typing.[20]

Of the different types of events listed in Table 17.1, `KeyEvent` and `MouseEvent`, both derived from `InputEvent`, are low-level, while the rest are high-level. When you click a mouse anywhere on a terminal screen, if you only wanted to gain access to the coordinates of the mouse pointer and the identity of the mouse button that was clicked, you'd need to think of the event as a low-level event and trap it as a `MouseEvent`. On the other hand, if you clicked the mouse over a GUI button, now it is possible to think of the same user action as a high-level event, of type `ActionEvent`, as having been emitted by the GUI button itself. Obviously, if a user action can be interpreted at both a low level and a high level, consuming the event at a low level event would make it unavailable for high-level interpretation.

About the `FocusEvent` listed in Table 17.1, a component gains the keyboard focus if it can receive and process keypresses. A user can give focus to a component by a

---

[20]Obviously, when you use an adapter class, your listener class must extend the adapter class. But if the listener class is already extending some other class, the listener class will not be able to extend the adapter class also because of Java's only-one-superclass rule. In such cases, you have no choice but to have your listener class implement the original listener interface.

Nature of user interaction	Type of event generated	Listener type needed for trapping the event	Adapter class, if available
User clicks a button.	ActionEvent	ActionListener	
User chooses a menu item.	ActionEvent	ActionListener	
User presses RETURN while typing in a text field.	ActionEvent	ActionListener	
User drags the slider of a scrollbar or clicks one of the arrows at the two ends of a scrollbar or clicks in the gutter on either side of the slider.	AdjustmentEvent	AdjustmentListener	
Component becomes visible or loses visibility.	ComponentEVent	ComponentListener	ComponentAdapter
User changes the size or location of a component.	ComponentEVent	ComponentListener	ComponentAdapter
User enters a character in a text component.	DocumentEvent	DocumentListener	
Component gets or loses the keyboard focus.	FocusEvent	FocusListener	FocusAdapter
User selects an item by clicking on a checkbox, or a checkbox menu item, or a combo box.	ItemEvent	ItemListener	
A component has keyboard focus and the user types on the keyboard.	KeyEvent	KeyListener	KeyAdapter
User presses a mouse button while the cursor is over a component such as a canvas.	MouseEvent	MouseListener	MouseAdapter
The mouse pointer enters or exits a component.	MouseEvent	MouseListener	MouseAdapter
User moves or drags the mouse over a component such as a canvas for the of painting.	MouseEvent	MouseMotionListener	MouseMotionAdapter
User closes a window such as a frame or a dialog.	WindowEvent	WindowListener	WindowAdapter

Table 17.1

variety of means, including clicking in a window, by tabbing between components, and so on.

In accordance with what was stated previously, Table 17.1 does not list all possible interactions between a user and a Java GUI. In particular, we have not listed, except for the row with the entries DocumentEvent and DocumentListener, the various types of interactions available through the javax.swing.event package.[21]

To illustrate how one creates listener objects, let's write a program that uses three GUI buttons to do the following:[22]

1. The GUI program should contain a "Start" button that when clicked activates the other two buttons.

2. The second button, when clicked, should result in the printing of the message "Good Morning to you!" in the terminal window.

3. Clicking on the third button should result in the printing out of the message "Good Bye!" and should cause the program to terminate.

4. It should also be possible to terminate the program when the user tries to close the window by selecting the "Close" item in the system-supplied window menu.

From Table 17.1, our GUI program will have to provide two listener objects, one for trapping button events and the other for trapping the window closing event. The first must implement the ActionListener interface, and the second must implement the WindowListener interface. As the reader will recall from Chapter 15, implementing an interface basically means providing implementation code for all the methods declared in that interface.

The program below first declares the three buttons in lines (A), (B), and (C) and then goes on to define two *static nested classes* MyActionListener and MyWindowListener in lines (D) and (E). As mentioned in Chapter 3, a static nested class acts just like any top-level class except that its accessibility can be controlled by using an access control modifier. Since we do not foresee that access to the two nested classes would be needed outside the class WindowWithButtons or in any extensions of this class, we have declared the nested classes private. The program creates listener objects and registers them with the sources of events in lines (I), (J), (K), and (L). This is accomplished by statements like

```
startButton.addActionListener( new MyActionListener() );
```
and
```
JFrame jf = new JFrame();
jf.addWindowListener( new MyWindowListener() );
```

---

[21]A complete listing of all the event types and their corresponding listener interfaces is available at the java.sun.com site.

[22]We will also use this example to illustrate the various features of the Swing JButton class.

Notice the two *add* functions: addWindowListener for *registering* the window listener object MyWindowListener with the source of window events, and addActionListener for registering the action listener object MyActionListener with the source of button events.

```java
//WindowWithButtons.java

import javax.swing.*;
import java.awt.*;
import java.awt.event.*;

class WindowWithButtons {
    static JButton startButton;                                    //(A)
    static JButton greetingButton;                                 //(B)
    static JButton closeButton;                                    //(C)

    private static class MyActionListener
                    implements ActionListener {                    //(D)
        public void actionPerformed( ActionEvent e )  {
            if ( e.getActionCommand().equals( "start" ) ) {
                greetingButton.setEnabled( true );
                closeButton.setEnabled( true );
            }
            else if ( e.getActionCommand().equals("print greeting") ) {
                startButton.setEnabled( false );
                System.out.println( "Good Morning to you!" );
            }
            else if ( e.getActionCommand().equals( "close window" ) ) {
                System.out.println( "Good Bye!" );
                System.exit( 0 );
            }
        }
    }

    private static class MyWindowListener extends WindowAdapter { //(E)
        public void windowClosing( WindowEvent e ) {
            System.exit( 0 );
        }
    }

    public static void main(String[] args)
    {
        JPanel buttonPanel = new JPanel();
        buttonPanel.setLayout( new GridLayout( 1, 3, 10, 0 ) );   //(F)
        ImageIcon icon1 = new ImageIcon( "images/smiley.gif" );
        ImageIcon icon2 = new ImageIcon( "images/happyface.gif" );
```

```
            startButton = new JButton("Start here" );
            startButton.setActionCommand( "start" );
            startButton.setToolTipText(
                    "Click to enable the other buttons." );        //(G)
            startButton.setMnemonic( KeyEvent.VK_S );              //(H)
            startButton.addActionListener( new MyActionListener() );  //(I)
            buttonPanel.add( startButton );

            greetingButton = new JButton( "Click for Greeting", icon1 );
            greetingButton.setVerticalTextPosition(AbstractButton.BOTTOM);
            greetingButton.setHorizontalTextPosition(
                                        AbstractButton.CENTER );
            greetingButton.setToolTipText( "First \"Start\","
                        + " then click this to see greetings." );
            greetingButton.setMnemonic( KeyEvent.VK_C );
            greetingButton.setActionCommand( "print greeting" );
            greetingButton.addActionListener(new MyActionListener()); //(J)
            buttonPanel.add( greetingButton );

            closeButton = new JButton( "Time to quit", icon2 );
            closeButton.setToolTipText( "First \"Start\","
                            + " then click here to close window." );
            closeButton.setActionCommand( "close window" );
            closeButton.setMnemonic(KeyEvent.VK_T);
            closeButton.addActionListener( new MyActionListener() );  //(K)
            buttonPanel.add( closeButton );

            greetingButton.setEnabled( false );
            closeButton.setEnabled( false );

            buttonPanel.setBorder(
                    BorderFactory.createEmptyBorder( 20, 20, 20, 20 ) );

            JFrame f = new JFrame();
            f.addWindowListener( new MyWindowListener() );           //(L)
            f.getContentPane().add( buttonPanel );
            f.setLocation( 100, 50);
            f.pack();
            f.setVisible( true );
    }
}
```

The program used a 4-argument constructor for GridLayout in line (F); the third and the fourth arguments are for specifying the horizontal and the vertical gaps, respectively, between the components. The horizontal gaps are also placed at the beginning and the end of each row; and the vertical gaps are placed at the top and the bottom of each column. The program also showed how setToolTipText and setMnemonic are invoked for a button in statements like those shown in lines (G) and (H). The setToolTipText method, inherited by JButton from JComponent, specifies the tooltip text, meaning the text that will be displayed when the mouse pointer lingers over a button. The setMnemonic specifies a keyboard shortcut — also referred to as a "hot key" — for a button. For example, pressing the "Alt" and the "s" keys simultaneously will elicit the same behavior from the GUI as clicking on the "Start" button. The GUI for this program is shown in Figure 17.23.

Fig. 17.23

By using the notion of an *anonymous class*, we will now show how one can do away with the need for defining separate listener classes like the MyActionListener class in line (D) and the MyWindowListener class in line (E) of the above program. In the following version of the previous program, we have brought the definitions of the listener classes to where they are needed — inside the *add* functions for registering the listener objects with the sources of events. This we do in lines (M), (N), (O), and (P) of the next program. The argument supplied to the method addWindowListener in line (P) now consists of an object made from a nameless class that extends the WindowAdapter class and that overrides its windowClosing method. Similarly, the argument supplied to the addActionListener method in lines (M), (N), and (O) now consists of a nameless class that implements the ActionListener interface by providing an implementation of its only method, actionPerformed.

```
//WindowWithButtons2.java

import javax.swing.*;
import java.awt.*;
import java.awt.event.*;

class WindowWithButtons {
    static JButton startButton;
    static JButton greetingButton;
    static JButton closeButton;

    public static void main(String[] args)
    {
        JPanel buttonPanel = new JPanel();
        buttonPanel.setLayout( new GridLayout( 1, 3, 10, 0 ) );
        ImageIcon icon1 = new ImageIcon( "images/smiley.gif" );
        ImageIcon icon2 = new ImageIcon( "images/happyface.gif" );

        startButton = new JButton("Start here" );
        startButton.setToolTipText(
```

```java
                          "Click to enable the other buttons." );
startButton.setMnemonic( KeyEvent.VK_S );
startButton.addActionListener( new ActionListener() {      //(M)
    public void actionPerformed( ActionEvent e ) {
            greetingButton.setEnabled( true );
            closeButton.setEnabled( true );
    }
} );
buttonPanel.add( startButton );

greetingButton = new JButton( "Click for Greeting", icon1 );
greetingButton.setVerticalTextPosition(AbstractButton.BOTTOM );
greetingButton.setHorizontalTextPosition(
                                    AbstractButton.CENTER);
greetingButton.setToolTipText( "First \"Start\","
                + " then click this to see greetings." );
greetingButton.setMnemonic( KeyEvent.VK_C );
greetingButton.addActionListener( new ActionListener() {  //(N)
    public void actionPerformed( ActionEvent e ) {
            startButton.setEnabled( false );
            System.out.println( "Good Morning to you!" );
    }
} );
buttonPanel.add( greetingButton );

closeButton = new JButton( "Time to quit", icon2 );
closeButton.setToolTipText( "First \"Start\","
                + " then click here to close window." );
closeButton.setMnemonic(KeyEvent.VK_T);
closeButton.addActionListener( new ActionListener() {      //(O)
    public void actionPerformed( ActionEvent e ) {
            System.out.println( "Good Bye!" );
            System.exit( 0 );
    }
} );
buttonPanel.add( closeButton );

greetingButton.setEnabled( false );
closeButton.setEnabled( false );

buttonPanel.setBorder(
        BorderFactory.createEmptyBorder( 20, 20, 20, 20 ) );

JFrame f = new JFrame();
f.addWindowListener( new WindowAdapter() {                 //(P)
        public void windowClosing( WindowEvent e ) {       //(Q)
            System.exit( 0 );
        }
} );
```

```
        f.getContentPane().add( buttonPanel );
        f.setLocation( 100, 50);
        f.pack();
        f.setVisible( true );
    }
}
```

Different modes of interaction with a component may generate the same type of an event, but associated with an event will be an attribute specific to each different interaction. For example, the acts of opening a window, iconifying or deiconifying a window, closing a window, and so on, all generate events of type WindowEvent, but associated with each event object will be a symbolic constant specific to the interaction. A WindowEvent has the following symbolic constants defined for it: WINDOW_OPENED, WINDOW_CLOSING, WINDOW_CLOSED, WINDOW_ACTIVATED, WINDOW_DEACTIVATED, WINDOW_ICONIFIED and WINDOW_DEICONIFIED. The symbolic constant associated with a WindowEvent can be retrieved by invoking the getID() method on the event. To illustrate, we could have written the definition of the windowClosing method in the above program in line (Q) as

```
    public void windowClosing( WindowEvent e ) {
        if ( e.getID() == WindowEvent.WINDOW_CLOSING )
            System.out.println("Request received for closing window");
        System.exit( 0 );
    }
```

In this implementation, we are using the getID() method to determine which event specifically was generated by our Window object. Now the message "Request received for closing window" will be printed out on the terminal any time you close the window. The reason our implementation of windowClosing works without explicitly invoking getID() is that this method is invoked only if the "signal" put out by the window event is the symbolic constant WINDOW_CLOSING.

Now that the reader understands how an event is trapped by a listener object and how a listener object must be registered with the source of the event, we will address the question, What are all the different event types that a given component can emit? This question is answered by looking at all the different kinds of listeners that can be registered with the component. For example, the following listener registration methods are defined for the Component class:

```
    addComponentListener
    addFocusListener
    addKeyListener
    addMouseListener
    addMouseMotionListener
```

This means that every Component object — all Swing widgets are Component objects — is *capable of* producing events of types ComponentEvent, FocusEvent, KeyEvent, and MouseEvent. While a component is capable of emitting all these different kinds of events, it does not mean that it will necessarily emit those events in response to user interactions. A component *will* only emit those events for which the appropriate listeners are registered with the component. So only if either a MouseListener or a MouseMotionListener is registered with a component, will the component emit events of type MouseEvent.

17.13.1 An Example in Inter-Component Communication in AWT/Swing

Our next example shows how to set up a communication link between two components so that events in one component can cause things to happen in another component. In this specific example, our two components will be two JPanel objects. We will associate a set of keywords — names of colors — with the left panel. As a user types in some sort of a story in the left panel, an occurrence of any of the keywords would cause a square of that color to pop up at some random place in the second panel.

The panel on the left will be of type MyTextPanel and the one on the right where the colored squares will pop up of type MyDrawPanel, as depicted in Figure 17.24.

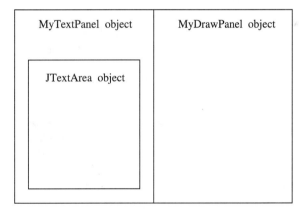

Fig. 17.24

The panels MyTextPanel and MyDrawPanel are declared in lines (A) and (B) and are created in lines (C) and (D) of the program below. If a user enters something like the following text in MyTextPanel:

```
The red herring became green with envy when it saw the
orange fox jump over a blue fish ......
```

then this would cause red, green, orange, and blue squares to pop up automatically at random locations in the right panel as the names of the colors are entered in the left panel.

In the program we show below, this communication link between the two panels is the work of the class `MyDocumentListener`, defined in line (E), that traps the text change events in the `JTextArea` object on the left. `MyDocumentListener` implements the interface `DocumentListener` and provides implementations in lines (G), (K), and (N) for the following methods declared in the interface:[23]

```
public void insertUpdate( DocumentEvent e )
public void removeUpdate( DocumentEvent e )
public void changeUpdate( DocumentEvent e )
```

A `DocumentEvent` is generated any time there is a change in the text content of a `JTextArea` object. If this event is caused by a new insertion into the document, the event will be sent for processing to the `insertUpdate` method. If the event is caused by the removal of previously inserted text, it will be sent for processing to the `removeUpdate` method. Since the method `changeUpdate` is triggered only by style changes in a text component that supports a *StyledDocument* model and since the default of the *PlainDocument* model will suffice for our example here, we can give this method a do-nothing implementation.[24]

The main job assigned to `MyDocumentListener` is carried out in the `insertUpdate` method in line (G) with the help of the data member `word` that is declared and initialized in line (F). As a user enters characters in the text component, these are joined together in `word` in line (J) until the user enters a space or a newline character. When that happens, we compare `word` with certain designated color names through statements like the one shown in line (H). If `word` points to the name of a color, we call on the `drawColoredSquare` method of the `MyDrawPanel` class to draw a square of that color in the panel on the right and reinitialize `word` for the next series of characters to be entered by the user.

The reader should also examine the implementation of the `removeUpdate` method of the `DocumentListener` interface in line (K). If the user hits the backspace key, this method deletes in line (M) the last character appended to `word`. If, as a result, the last character of what is left in the text component is a blank space or a newline character, we reinitialize `word` in line (L).

In the panel on the right where the colored squares pop up, the actual drawing of the squares is accomplished with the help of a `Graphics` object whose various values are set in the `drawColoredSquare` method of the `MyDrawPanel` class. This `Graphics` object is supplied as an argument to the `paintComponent` method in line (P). Invocation of `paintComponent` in line (P) causes the `MyDrawPanel` to be

---

[23]The text that you enter into a Swing text component such as `JTextArea` is actually held in an object of type Document. An event of type `DocumentEvent` occurs when the text held by a Document changes in any way. You can trap these events by a `DocumentListener` object, which must be registered with the Document object directly.

[24]For document models of Swing, see the interfaces Document and StyledDocument and the class PlainDocument in the `java.swing.text` package.

repainted. We will have more to say about the `Graphics` class and how shapes can be drawn in AWT/Swing in Section 17.19.

```java
//CrazyWindow.java

import javax.swing.*;              // for JTextArea, JPanel, etc.
import javax.swing.event.*;        // for DocumentListener
import javax.swing.text.*;         // for Document interface
import java.awt.*;                 // for Graphics, GridLayout, etc.
import java.awt.event.*;           // for WindowAdapter

class CrazyWindow extends JFrame {
    MyTextPanel panel1;                                             //(A)
    MyDrawPanel panel2;                                            //(B)

    public CrazyWindow() {
        super( "Crazy Window" );
        addWindowListener( new WindowAdapter() {
                public void windowClosing( WindowEvent e ) {
                    System.exit( 0 ) ;
                }
        });
        JPanel contentPane = new JPanel();
        contentPane.setLayout(new GridLayout(1, 2));
        panel1 = new MyTextPanel();                                 //(C)
        panel2 = new MyDrawPanel();                                 //(D)
        contentPane.add( panel1 );
        contentPane.add( panel2 );
        setContentPane( contentPane );
    }

    class MyTextPanel extends JPanel  {
        class MyDocumentListener implements DocumentListener {      //(E)
            int lengthText;
            StringBuffer word = new StringBuffer("");               //(F)
            public void insertUpdate( DocumentEvent e ) {           //(G)
                Document doc = (Document) e.getDocument();
                try {
                    lengthText = doc.getLength();
                    String currentChar =
                            doc.getText( lengthText - 1, 1 );
                    char ch =
                        currentChar.charAt( currentChar.length() - 1 );
                    if ( currentChar.equals( " " ) || ch == '\n' ) {
                        if ( word.toString().equals( "red" ) ) { //(H)
                            panel2.drawColoredSquare( "red" );   //(I)
                        }
```

```
                    if ( word.toString().equals( "green" ) ) {
                        panel2.drawColoredSquare( "green" );
                    }
                    if ( word.toString().equals( "blue" ) ) {
                        panel2.drawColoredSquare( "blue" );
                    }
                    if ( word.toString().equals( "magenta" ) ) {
                        panel2.drawColoredSquare( "magenta" );
                    }
                    if ( word.toString().equals( "orange" ) ) {
                        panel2.drawColoredSquare( "orange" );
                    }
                    word = new StringBuffer();
                }
                else                                        //(J)
                    word = word.append( currentChar );
            } catch( BadLocationException bad ) {
                bad.printStackTrace();
            }
        }
        public void removeUpdate( DocumentEvent e )  {      //(K)
            try {
                Document doc = (Document) e.getDocument();
                lengthText = doc.getLength();

                String currentChar =
                            doc.getText( lengthText - 1, 1 );
                char ch =
                  currentChar.charAt( currentChar.length() - 1 );
                if ( currentChar.equals( " " ) || ch == '\n'  ) {
                    word = new StringBuffer();              //(L)
                }
                else if ( word.length() >= 1 )
                    word =
                        word.deleteCharAt( word.length() - 1 );   //(M)
            } catch( BadLocationException bad ) {
                bad.printStackTrace();
            }
        }
        public void changedUpdate( DocumentEvent e ) {}     //(N)
    }

    public MyTextPanel() {
        JTextArea ta = new JTextArea( 100, 60);
        ta.getDocument().addDocumentListener(
                        new MyDocumentListener() );
        ta.setEditable(true);
        JScrollPane jsp = new JScrollPane( ta );
        jsp.setPreferredSize(new Dimension( 150, 150));
```

```
            add(jsp, "Center");
            setBorder( BorderFactory.createCompoundBorder(
                BorderFactory.createTitledBorder("My Text Window"),
                BorderFactory.createEmptyBorder( 5, 5, 5, 5 ) ) );
        }
    }

    // panel2
    class MyDrawPanel extends JPanel {
        protected void paintComponent( Graphics g ) { }
        public void drawColoredSquare( String color ) {              //(O)
            Graphics g = getGraphics();
            g.translate( getInsets().left, getInsets().top );
            int width = getBounds().width;
            int height = getBounds().height;
            if ( color.equals( "red" ) ) g.setColor( Color.red );
            if ( color.equals( "green" ) ) g.setColor( Color.green );
            if ( color.equals( "blue" ) ) g.setColor( Color.blue );
            if ( color.equals( "orange" ) ) g.setColor( Color.orange );
            if ( color.equals("magenta") ) g.setColor( Color.magenta );
            int x = (int) ( Math.random() * width );
            int y = (int) ( Math.random() * height );
            if ( x > width - 30 ) x = x - 30;
            if ( y > height - 30 ) y = y - 30;
            g.fillRect( x, y, 30, 30 );
            paintComponent( g );                                     //(P)
        }
    }

    public static void main(String[] args)
    {
        JFrame wg = new CrazyWindow();
        wg.setSize( 500, 400 );
        wg.show();
    }
}
```

The GUI created by this program is shown in Figure 17.25.

This concludes this chapter's discussion on how events are processed in the AWT/Swing framework. We will take up this subject again in the next chapter when we address the very important topic of **Event Dispatch Thread** in which the event processing loop of AWT/Swing programs is executed.

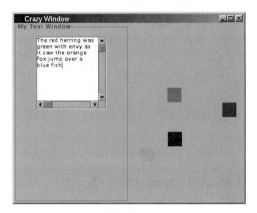

Fig. 17.25

17.14   EVENT PROCESSING IN Qt

Event processing in C++-based Qt is carried out in two different ways, depending on whether an event is high-level or low-level. The distinction between the two is the same here as it was for Java. But since Qt uses two different modes of processing for these two different types of events, we will revisit this distinction.

When a user clicks the mouse on a GUI button, we have a high-level event, in the sense that the GUI button stands for some action that is supposed to be initiated by the mouse click. Similarly, selecting a menu item gives rise to a high-level event. Entering text in a text window would also constitute a high-level event. In fact, as was the case with Java, most widgets in Qt when subject to human interaction produce high-level events in the form of signals. *High-level events are handled by the signal-slot mechanism of Qt.*

On the other hand, clicking a mouse or dragging a mouse inside a widget for the purpose of, say, free-form drawing gives rise to a low-level event; low-level in the sense that all we want to know is the position of the mouse pointer on the screen and, in some cases, the identity of the mouse button pressed. *Low-level events in Qt are handled through the mechanism of virtual functions.* Certain virtual functions defined for a widget are automatically invoked upon the occurrence of low-level events. Since the functions are virtual, it's the user-defined override definitions for the functions that would actually be invoked. In this manner, a given application can exhibit a desired behavior in response to low-level events.

This section will only deal with the signal-slot mechanism for the handling of high-level events, since that is the dominant mode for dealing with events in Qt. The virtual function mechanism for handling low-level events will be presented in Section 17.20.

Section 17.6 showed a Qt program in which the signal emitted by a GUI button was used to terminate the event processing loop and the program. To further illustrate high-level event processing in Qt, in this section we will discuss two programs. In the first, we will illustrate how a signal emitted by one widget can be used to affect the behavior of another widget. Next, in a more elaborate program, we will show how the user can create his/her own widget class with its own signals and slots. That example will also take us to the topic of *meta object compilation* in Qt. However, before getting into these two examples, we will explain in greater detail the signal-slot mechanism of Qt.

As explained in the previous two sections, every widget available for human inter-action emits a signal in response to that interaction. In Qt, if an object wishes to be notified of a signal emitted by a widget, the class corresponding to the object must provide a slot for the signal and you must explicitly connect the signal with the slot. The minimal syntax for connecting a signal with a slot is

```
QObject::connect( pointerToWidgetEmittingSignal,
                  SIGNAL( signalName( paramTypeOnly ) ),
                  pointerToObjectReceivingSignal,
                  SLOT(  slotName( paramTypeOnly ) ) );
```

where the first argument is a pointer to the object emitting the signal; the second, enveloped by the keyword SIGNAL, is the name of the signal together with its parameter type(s); the third is a pointer to the object that wants to be notified of the signal; and the fourth, enveloped by the keyword SLOT, is the name of the slot function in the destination object. So, as we did in the example in Section 17.6, if we want our top-level QApplication object to include a pushbutton for closing the top-level application, we'd need to connect the clicked() signal of the pushbutton with the quit() slot of the QApplication object:

```
QApplication myapp( argc, argv );      //argc, argv from main header
QPushButton* myButton = new QPushButton( "Quit");
QObject::connect( myButton,
                  SIGNAL( clicked() ),
                  &myapp,
                  SLOT( quit() ) );
```

For another example,

```
QObject::connect( myMenu,
                  SIGNAL( activated( int ) ),
                  pointerToObjectReceivingSignal,
                  SLOT( slotDoMenuFunction( int ) ) );
```

In the example that follows, we use predefined classes with signals and slots and therefore we do not need to invoke the meta object compiler. This example, which is only a slight variation of an example provided by Dalheimer [14], consists of connecting a signal from the QSlider widget with a slot of the QLCDNumber widget. The program constructs a QSlider object in line (A) and a QLCDNumber object in line (B). The statement in line (D) connects the valueChanged(int) signal of the QSlider object with the slot display(int) of the QLCDNumber object. Note how, in line (C), the number displayed initially by the QLCDNumber object is set by a direct invocation of the slot function display(int).

```cpp
//SignalSlotLCD.cc
//Based on a program by Dalheimer with
//inconsequential made by the author

#include <qapplication.h>
#include <qslider.h>
#include <qlcdnumber.h>

int main( int argc, char **argv )
{
    QApplication myApp( argc, argv );
    QWidget* myWidget= new QWidget();
    myWidget->setGeometry( 400, 300, 170, 110 );

    QSlider* myslider =
                new QSlider( 0,          // minimum value            //(A)
                9,                       // maximum value
                1,                       // step
                1,                       // initial value
                QSlider::Horizontal,     // orient.
                myWidget );              // parent

    myslider->setGeometry( 10, 10, 150, 30 );

    //first arg below is the number of digits to display:
    QLCDNumber* mylcdnum = new QLCDNumber( 1, myWidget );           //(B)
    mylcdnum->setGeometry( 60, 50, 50, 50 );
    //manual invocation of slot:
    mylcdnum->display( 1 );                                         //(C)

    // connect slider and number display
    QObject::connect( myslider,                                     //(D)
                      SIGNAL( valueChanged( int ) ),
                      mylcdnum,
                      SLOT( display( int ) ) );

    myApp.setMainWidget( myWidget );
    myWidget->show();

    // starts event loop
    return myApp.exec();
}
```

This program can be compiled with a simple command line call to the compiler, as in

```
g++ -o SignalSlotLCD SignalSlotLCD.cc                    \
                 -I$QTDIR/include -L$QTDIR/lib -lqt
```

The program produces a GUI that looks like what is shown in Figure 17.26.

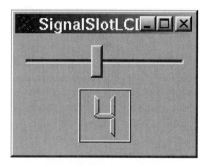

Fig. 17.26

17.14.1   A Qt Example that requires Meta Object Compilation

In this subsection we will consider a more elaborate example consisting of a class for which we define our own signals and slots. The syntax of a class for which you want to define your own signals or slots looks like

```
class MyClass : public QObject {

    Q_OBJECT
    // ..

    signals:
        void userDidSomething();
        // other signals ..

    public slots:
        void doSomethingReactToSignal();
        // other public slots ..

    private slots:
        void doSomethingInternally();
        // other private slots

    // rest of code

};
```

where Q_OBJECT is a macro that must be declared inside the private section of the class. Qt has a special procedure for compiling such classes. Before regular compilation, such classes must first be run through a *meta object compiler*. The meta object compiler, moc, generates *meta object code*, also referred to as "glue code," that is needed for the signal/slot mechanism to work. This meta object code is in the form of another source file that is subsequently subject to regular compilation, as explained further in the following list of compilation steps for a Qt class with signals and/or slots:

1. Separate the class declaration from its implementation. So if MyWidget has signals and/or slots, create the following three files:

   ```
   MyWidget.h
   MyWidget.cc
   main.cc
   ```

2. Run the declaration file, MyWidget.h, through the meta object compiler, moc. The moc compiler will output a source file containing meta object code. The name of the output file will be moc_MyWidget.cc.

3. Now compile the meta object file moc_MyWidget.cc to create the binary file moc_MyWidget.o.

4. Compile the implementation source file MyWidget.cc to create the binary file MyWidget.o.

5. Compile the source file main.cc to create a binary file main.o.

6. Link the binary files moc_MyWidget.o, MyWidget.o and main.o to create the executable.

In the example that follows, we will now present a Qt version of the Java Crazy-Window program of Section 17.13.1. As with the Java program, the Qt program creates two side-by-side panels, one for a user to enter text in and the other for drawing shapes. As the reader will recall from our Java discussion, the idea behind the example is that the user enters some sort of a story in the left panel — let's say a story involving the names of various colors. Each time the user mentions the name of a color, a square block of that color pops up at a random location in the right panel.

The top-level header file is CrazyWindow.h and its implementation CrazyWindow.cc. Following the declaration in line (A) of the header file, the implementation in CrazyWindow.cc first declares a layout manager for the top-level window in line (C) and then creates an instance of MyTextPanel for the left panel and an instance of MyDrawPanel for the right panel in lines (D) and (E), respectively.

As shown in line (F), another important task of the top-level CrazyWindow class is to establish a connection between the signal userTypedKeyword(char*) of the MyTextPanel object and the slot function drawColoredSquare(char*) of the MyDrawPanel object. The overall "flow" of signals in the program is as shown in Figure 17.27.

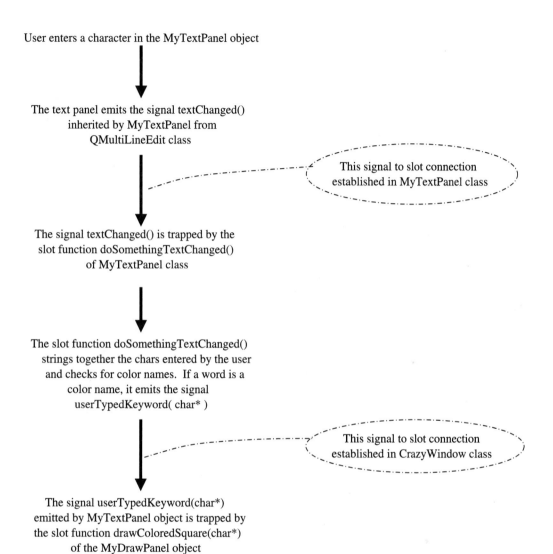

User enters a character in the MyTextPanel object

The text panel emits the signal textChanged()
inherited by MyTextPanel from
QMultiLineEdit class

This signal to slot connection
established in MyTextPanel class

The signal textChanged() is trapped by the
slot function doSomethingTextChanged()
of MyTextPanel class

The slot function doSomethingTextChanged()
strings together the chars entered by the user
and checks for color names. If a word is a
color name, it emits the signal
userTypedKeyword(char*)

This signal to slot connection
established in CrazyWindow class

The signal userTypedKeyword(char*)
emitted by MyTextPanel object is trapped by
the slot function drawColoredSquare(char*)
of the MyDrawPanel object

Fig. 17.27

```
///////////////////////  file:  CrazyWindow.h  ///////////////////////
#ifndef CRAZYWINDOW_H
#define CRAZYWINDOW_H

#include <qwidget.h>

class CrazyWindow: public QWidget {                               //(A)
public:
    CrazyWindow( QWidget *parent=0, const char* name= 0 );
};
#endif

///////////////////////  file:  CrazyWindow.cc  ///////////////////////
#include "CrazyWindow.h"
#include <qpainter.h>
#include <qlayout.h>
#include "MyTextPanel.h"
#include "MyDrawPanel.h"

CrazyWindow::CrazyWindow( QWidget* parent, const char* name )     //(B)
    : QWidget( parent, name )
{
    QGridLayout* grid = new QGridLayout( this, 0, 1 );            //(C)
    MyTextPanel* textPanel =
            new MyTextPanel( this, "for text only" );             //(D)
    MyDrawPanel* drawPanel =
            new MyDrawPanel( this, "for graphics only" );         //(E)

    grid->addWidget( textPanel, 0, 0 );
    grid->addWidget( drawPanel, 0, 1 );

    QObject::connect( textPanel,                                  //(F)
                    SIGNAL( userTypedKeyword( char* ) ),
                    drawPanel,
                    SLOT( drawColoredSquare( char* ) ) );
}
```

It is the job of the MyTextPanel object to receive the keystrokes from the user, to trap the signal textChanged() via the slot function textChangedDoSomething(), test the words entered by the user for the color names, and to emit the signal userTypedKeyword(char*) when the user has entered a color name. The class must therefore define its own signal userTypedKeyword(char*), as done in line (G) below, and its own slot function textChangedDoSomething(), as declared in

line (H) and implemented in line (J). The logic in textChangedDoSomething is the
same as for insertUpdate for the Java example.

```
/////////////////////// file: MyTextPanel.h ///////////////////////
#ifndef MYTEXTPANEL_H
#define MYTEXTPANEL_H

#include <qmultilineedit.h>

class MyTextPanel: public QMultiLineEdit {
    Q_OBJECT
public:
    MyTextPanel( QWidget *parent=0, const char* name= 0 );
signals:
    //This signal is connected in class CrazyWindow
    //with slot function drawColoredSquare of class
    //MyDrawPanel in line (F)
    void userTypedKeyword( char* );                           //(G)
public slots:
    //The signal textChanged() emitted by an object
    //of type "this" is connected to this slot function
    //in this class in line (I)
    void doSomethingTextChanged();
private:
    QString word;
};
#endif

/////////////////////// file: MyTextPanel.cc ///////////////////////
#include "MyTextPanel.h"
#include <qtextstream.h>
#include <stdlib.h>                    // for malloc()

MyTextPanel::MyTextPanel( QWidget* parent, const char* name )
    : QMultiLineEdit( parent, name )
{
    word = QString( "" );
    setPalette( QPalette( QColor( 250, 250, 200 ) ) );

    //MyTextPanel inherits the signal textChanged()
    //from its superclass QMultiLineEdit
    QObject::connect( this,                                    //(I)
                      SIGNAL( textChanged() ),
                      this,
                      SLOT( doSomethingTextChanged( ) ) );
}
```

```
void MyTextPanel::doSomethingTextChanged() {                              //(J)
    QString qstr = text();
    QChar c = qstr[ (int) qstr.length() - 1 ];
    if ( c == ' ' || c == '\n' ) {
        if ( word == "red"    ||
             word == "blue"   ||
             word == "orange"||
             word == "green"  ) {
            char* keyword = (char*) malloc( word.length() + 1 );
            strcpy( keyword, word );
            emit( userTypedKeyword( keyword ) );
        }
        word = QString( "" );
    }
    else
        word += c ;
}
```

Finally, we will present the MyDrawPanel class which corresponds to the right panel in the top-level display. The class has defined for it one slot function, drawColoredSquare(char*), whose job is to trap the signal userTypedKeyword(char*) emitted by a MyTextPanel object. The rest of the class is self-explanatory, save for the function sizePolicy(). The implementation code provided in MyDrawPanel.cc includes invocation of the following QSizePolicy constructor in line (K) in the code for sizePolicy():

```
QSizePolicy MyDrawPanel::sizePolicy() const {
    return QSizePolicy(QSizePolicy::Expanding, QSizePolicy::Expanding);
}
```

The QSizePolicy object returned by sizePolicy() function says that the MyDrawPanel object is to occupy as much space as possible both horizontally and vertically. The prototype of the constructor is

```
QSizePolicy( SizeType hor, SizeType ver, bool hvw = FALSE )
```

where SizeType is the following enum

```
enum SizeType {
    Fixed = 0,
    Minimum = MayGrow,
    Maximum = MayShrink,
    Preferred = MayGrow|MayShrink,
    MinimumExpanding = Minimum|ExpMask,
    Expanding = MinimumExpanding | MayShrink
};
```

where the identifiers used on the right of the assignment operators are defined by the following enum:

```
enum { HSize   = 6.
    HMask = 0x3f,
    VMask = HMask << HSize,
    MayGrow = 1,
    ExpMask = 2,
    MayShrink = 4
};
```

Both these enumerations are defined in the header file qsizepolicy.h. Assigning Expanding to the first two arguments in the QSizePolicy constructor causes the MyDrawWindow to occupy all the space that can be assigned by the layout manager. Without setting the sizing policy in the manner shown, it would be possible for the first widget, a MyTextPanel object, to occupy all the visible space in the top-level object.

```
/////////////////////// file: MyDrawPanel.h ///////////////////////
#ifndef MYDRAWPANEL_H
#define MYDRAWPANEL_H

#include <qwidget.h>

class MyDrawPanel: public QWidget {
    Q_OBJECT
public:
    MyDrawPanel( QWidget *parent=0, const char* name= 0 );
    QSizePolicy sizePolicy() const;
    void paintEvent( QPaintEvent* );
public slots:
    void drawColoredSquare( char* );
};
#endif

/////////////////////// file: MyDrawPanel.cc ///////////////////////
#include "MyDrawPanel.h"
#include <string.h>
#include <qpainter.h>
#include <qwidget.h>
#include <stdlib.h>        // for rand()
#include <time.h>          // for time(NULL) to seed rand()

MyDrawPanel::MyDrawPanel( QWidget* parent, const char* name )
    : QWidget( parent, name )
{
    setPalette( QPalette( QColor( 250, 250, 200 ) ) );
```

```
    srand( (unsigned) time(NULL) );
}

void MyDrawPanel::paintEvent( QPaintEvent* ) {
    QPainter p( this );
}

void MyDrawPanel::drawColoredSquare( char* key ) {
    QPainter p( this );
    p.setBrush( QString( key ) );
    p.setPen( NoPen );
    int x = rand() % 250 + 1;
    int y = rand() % 300 + 1;
    p.drawRect( QRect( x, y, 30, 30 ) );
}

QSizePolicy MyDrawPanel::sizePolicy() const {                    //(K)
    return QSizePolicy( QSizePolicy::Expanding,
                                QSizePolicy::Expanding );
}
```

We also need a main for the entire program to work:

```
///////////////////// file: main_CrazyWindow.cc //////////////////////
#include <qapplication.h>
#include "CrazyWindow.h"

int main( int argc, char ** argv ) {
    QApplication::setColorSpec( QApplication::CustomColor );
    QApplication a( argc, argv );

    CrazyWindow w;
    w.setGeometry( 0, 0, 700, 500 );
    a.setMainWidget( &w );
    w.show();
    a.connect( &a, SIGNAL(lastWindowClosed()), &a, SLOT(quit()) );
    return a.exec();
}
```

We will now show the makefile that can be used with this program. If you name the makefile Makefile_Qt_CrazyWindow, you can build the executable by

```
    make -f Makefile_Qt_CrazyWindow
```

```
#Makefile_Qt_CrazyWindow

CC=g++
LDLIBS=-L$(QTDIR)/lib -lqt
CFLAGS=-g -I$(QTDIR)/include

CrazyWindow: moc_CrazyWindow.o moc_MyDrawPanel.o moc_MyTextPanel.o    \
             CrazyWindow.o MyDrawPanel.o MyTextPanel.o                \
             main_CrazyWindow.o Makefile_Qt_CrazyWindow
        $(CC) $(LDLIBS)  -o CrazyWindow moc_CrazyWindow.o            \
             moc_MyDrawPanel.o moc_MyTextPanel.o CrazyWindow.o       \
             MyDrawPanel.o MyTextPanel.o main_CrazyWindow.o

moc_CrazyWindow.cc: CrazyWindow.h
        moc -o moc_CrazyWindow.cc CrazyWindow.h
moc_MyDrawPanel.cc: MyDrawPanel.h
        moc -o moc_MyDrawPanel.cc MyDrawPanel.h
moc_MyTextPanel.cc: MyTextPanel.h
        moc -o moc_MyTextPanel.cc MyTextPanel.h

moc_CrazyWindow.o: moc_CrazyWindow.cc
        $(CC) -c $(CFLAGS) -O2 moc_CrazyWindow.cc
moc_MyDrawPanel.o: moc_MyDrawPanel.cc
        $(CC) -c $(CFLAGS) -O2 moc_MyDrawPanel.cc
moc_MyTextPanel.o: moc_MyTextPanel.cc
        $(CC) -c $(CFLAGS) -O2 moc_MyTextPanel.cc

CrazyWindow.o: CrazyWindow.cc
        $(CC) -c $(CFLAGS) -O2 CrazyWindow.cc
MyDrawPanel.o: MyDrawPanel.cc
        $(CC) -c $(CFLAGS) -O2 MyDrawPanel.cc
MyTextPanel.o: MyTextPanel.cc
        $(CC) -c $(CFLAGS) -O2 MyTextPanel.cc

main_CrazyWindow.o: main_CrazyWindow.cc
        $(CC) -c $(CFLAGS) -O2 main_CrazyWindow.cc

clean:
        rm -f CrazyWindow
        rm -f *.o
        rm -f moc*.*
```

The GUI produced by this program is shown in Figure 17.28.

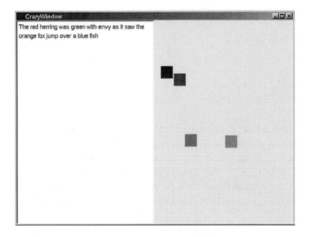

Fig. 17.28

17.14.2 Summary of Facts about Signals and Slots

Here is a list of important facts about Qt's signals and slots. This list is reproduced from [14]:

- You never have to implement signals directly. You just declare them. In other words, there is no implementation code associated with the signals.
- Slots are declared and implemented just like any other C++ member function. They can also be called and used like any other member function.
- A slot will generally be public, but you can make it protected. It does not make much sense for a slot to be private.
- A slot function can be virtual.
- A slot function cannot be static.
- You can connect any number of slots to a signal, and you can connect any number of signals to a slot.
- If more than one slot is connected to a signal, the order in which the slots are called is not guaranteed.
- In order to be connected to a signal, a slot must have the same parameter types as the signal.
- Signals and slots are only available within a C++ class; you cannot make a stand-alone function a slot.
- Every class that wants to define its own signals or slots must be derived, directly or indirectly, from QObject.
- Every class that wants to define its own signals or slots must contain the macro Q_OBJECT somewhere.
- Do not put a semicolon after the Q_OBJECT macro.

17.15   EVENT PROCESSING IN GNOME/GTK+

An event processing loop in a GNOME/GTK+ program is started by invoking gtk_main() and terminated by invoking gtk_main_quit(). Invocation of gtk_main() basically wrests the control away from the GUI program and gives it to the GNOME/GTK+ system. The system waits for the events to appear in the event queue, where they are placed by the window manager (see Section 17.12). When an event is retrieved from the event queue, the GNOME/GTK+ system first determines the identity of the generating widget. After ascertaining the identity of the widget, GTK+ passes the event information packet to a function such as

```
gtk_signal_emit()
```

where the information packet is reformatted into a signal and then passed onto the widget that generated it.[25] The widget looks at the list of all the callback functions that have been connected to this signal and invokes them all.

In the example that follows, we have a single button, created in line (B), in the middle of a top-level window. When the mouse is clicked on the button, we want the following message to be displayed on the terminal screen: "Hello from GNOME/GTK+." So we need a callback function that would respond to a button click and print out the message. In the following program, the callback function, sayHello(), is defined in line (D). This callback is connected in line (C) to the clicked signal of the button by

```
gtk_signal_connect( GTK_OBJECT( myButton ),
                    "clicked",
                    GTK_SIGNAL_FUNC( sayHello ),
                    NULL );
```

where the first argument points to the source of the signal, the second is the name of the signal, the third is a pointer to the callback function, and the last, when non-null, is a pointer to an object for providing the callback with arguments. The "connect" function expects the first argument to be of type GTK_OBJECT and the third of type GTK_SIGNAL_FUNC, hence the casts shown.

```
//WindowWithHelloButton.c


#include <gnome.h>
```

---

[25]This function can also be used to simulate a signal corresponding to an event by supplying it with a signal ID number. An alternative to using a signal ID number in simulations is to invoke the following version of the function:

```
gtk_signal_emit_by_name()
```

Both these functions need a pointer to the widget that is to receive the signal.

```
gint eventDestroy( GtkWidget* widget, GdkEvent* event, gpointer data );
void sayHello( GtkWidget* widget, GdkEvent* event, gpointer data );

int main( int argc, char* argv[] )
{
    GtkWidget* window;
    GtkWidget* myButton;

    gnome_init( "hellobutton", "1.0", argc, argv );
    window = gnome_app_new(
                     "hellobutton", "Window with Hello Button" );
    gtk_container_set_border_width(
                     GTK_CONTAINER( window ), 100 );             //(A)
    gtk_signal_connect( GTK_OBJECT( window ),
                     "destroy",
                     GTK_SIGNAL_FUNC( eventDestroy ),
                     NULL );
    myButton = gtk_button_new_with_label( "Say Hello" );         //(B)
    gtk_signal_connect( GTK_OBJECT( myButton ),                  //(C)
                     "clicked",
                     GTK_SIGNAL_FUNC( sayHello ),
                     NULL );
    gnome_app_set_contents( GNOME_APP( window ), myButton );
    gtk_widget_show_all( window );
    gtk_main();
    exit( 0 );
}

void sayHello(GtkWidget* widget, GdkEvent* event, gpointer data){ //(D)
    g_print( "Hello from GNOME/GTK+\n" );
}

gint eventDestroy(GtkWidget* widget, GdkEvent* event, gpointer data) {
    gtk_main_quit();
    return 0;
}
```

The window produced by this program is shown in Figure 17.29.

17.15.1 Communicating Events to Other Widgets in GNOME/GTK+

We will now present a more elaborate example of event processing in GNOME/GTK+.
The example presented here, CrazyWindow, parallels the examples presented earlier
in Section 17.13.1 for AWT/Swing and in Section 17.14.1 for Qt.

Fig. 17.29

In the AWT/Swing and Qt implementations of CrazyWindow, we used the grid layout for the two panels. What a grid layout does in AWT/Swing and Qt, a table layout does in GNOME/GTK+. In main below, in line (A) we call on the makeTable() function to create a two-paneled widget, the left side of which will accept text from a user and the right side of which will then display colored squares at random positions, the color of each block corresponding to the color name entered by the user in the left panel. Before invoking makeTable(), main carries out the usual top-level initializations, constructs a top-level window by invoking gtk_window_new(GTK_WINDOW_TOPLEVEL), sets a default size for the window, and connects the "destroy" signal of the top-level window with the eventDestroy() callback function.

In the makeTable() function, we first declare the two panels, textPanel and drawPanel in lines (C) and (D). For textPanel, we invoke in line (E) the constructor gtk_scrolled_window_new(NULL,NULL), where the two NULL arguments are for the adjustments for the horizontal and the vertical scrollbars. By setting these to NULL, we let the panel create its own scrollbars but only if needed. To allow for automatic creation of the scrollbars should the user enter text whose width exceeds that of the viewable area, we also invoke in line (H) the function gtk_scrolled_window_set_policy() with the automatic option for its second and the third arguments.

For the left panel, we create in line (F) a text area by invoking gtk_text_new(NULL,NULL) where, as for textPanel, the two arguments are supposed to be pointers to adjustment objects for the scrollbars; we set these to NULL to elicit the default behavior. To take advantage of the scrolling for the enclosing widget, we turn off the automatic line wrapping option in the text area by invoking gtk_text_set_line_wrap((GtkText*) textarea, FALSE) in line (G). In line (I), the text area is made a child of textPanel by the invocation of gtk_scrolled_window_add_with_viewport().

The rest of the code for the left panel consists of setting the text area to be editable in line (J) so that the user can enter/modify text in it and, in line (K), inserting the scrollable container containing the text area in the left cell of the table.

The last thing we do for the text panel is to connect in line (L) the `insert-text` signal of the text widget with the callback `textEnteredDoSomething()` defined in the code at line (S).

For the draw panel, we create in line (M) a window as before, but make it nonscrollable by invoking in line (N) the option `GTK_POLICY_NEVER` for the last two arguments of the function `gtk_scrolled_window_set_policy()`. In line (R), we then make a child of this window a canvas for drawing colored squares. The canvas is created in line (O). A canvas has associated with it an object of type GnomeCanvasGroup, in our example called `rootGroup` in line (Q), into which you add widgets of type GnomeCanvasItem if you'd like to see them drawn on the canvas. In line (R), we instantiate `rootGroup` by the call

```
rootGroup = gnome_canvas_root( GNOME_CANVAS( canvas ) );
```

This brings us to the callback `textChangedDoSomething` which is fired each time the user enters a new character into the text area of the left panel. This function retrieves the latest character entered by the user by invoking the following two function calls in lines (T) and (U):

```
gint end_pos = gtk_editable_get_position((GtkEditable*) widget );
gchar* str = gtk_editable_get_chars( (GtkEditable*) widget,
                                     end_pos - 1,
                                     end_pos );
```

where the first call retrieves the current cursor position and the second call retrieves the last character by virtue of how the second and the third arguments are set.

The logic in the callback `textChangedDoSomething()` is based on joining together the characters entered by the user, looking for word breaks, and comparing the words with the names of the colors. When the word retrieved is, say, "red", we invoke the following function in line (V):

```
item = gnome_canvas_item_new( rootGroup,
                gnome_canvas_rect_get_type(),
                "x1", xpos,
                "y1", ypos,
                "x2", xpos + 20.0 ,
                "y2", ypos + 20.0 ,
                "fill_color", "red",
                "outline_color", "white",
                NULL );
```

to actually draw a red colored square of size 20×20 pixels on the canvas. This function returns an object of type GnomeCanvasItem, which is then added to the `rootGroup` object associated with the canvas.

```
//CrazyWindow.c

#include <gnome.h>
#include <stdio.h>
#include <stdlib.h>        // for rand()
#include <time.h>          // for seed for rand()

GtkWidget* makeTable();

gint eventDestroy( GtkWidget* widget, GdkEvent* event, gpointer data );
void textEnteredDoSomething( GtkWidget* widget,
                             GdkEvent* event, gpointer data );
char* word = NULL;              // for the keyword
GtkWidget* textarea;            // for incorporation in textPanel
GtkWidget* canvas;              // for incorporation in drawPanel
GnomeCanvasGroup* rootGroup;    // for canvas
GnomeCanvasItem* item;          // for canvas

int main( int argc, char* argv[] )
{
    GtkWidget* window;
    GtkWidget* table;
    gnome_init( "aspect", "1.0", argc, argv );
    srand( (unsigned) time( NULL ) );
    window = gtk_window_new( GTK_WINDOW_TOPLEVEL );
    gtk_window_set_default_size( GTK_WINDOW( window ), 300, 200 );
    gtk_signal_connect( GTK_OBJECT( window ),
                        "destroy",
                        GTK_SIGNAL_FUNC( eventDestroy ),
                        NULL );
    table = makeTable();                                    //(A)
    gtk_container_add( GTK_CONTAINER( window ), table );
    gtk_widget_show_all( window );
    gtk_main();
    exit( 0 );
}

GtkWidget* makeTable() {
    GtkWidget* table = gtk_table_new( 1, 2, TRUE );         //(B)
    GtkWidget* textPanel;                                   //(C)
    GtkWidget* drawPanel;                                   //(D)


    // textPanel:
    textPanel = gtk_scrolled_window_new( NULL, NULL );      //(E)
    textarea = gtk_text_new( NULL, NULL );                  //(F)
    gtk_text_set_line_wrap( (GtkText*) textarea, FALSE );   //(G)
```

```
    gtk_scrolled_window_set_policy(GTK_SCROLLED_WINDOW(textPanel),//(H)
                            GTK_POLICY_AUTOMATIC,
                            GTK_POLICY_AUTOMATIC);
    gtk_scrolled_window_add_with_viewport(                    //(I)
            GTK_SCROLLED_WINDOW( textPanel ), textarea );
    gtk_text_set_editable( (GtkText*) textarea, TRUE );       //(J)
    gtk_table_attach_defaults(                                //(K)
                GTK_TABLE( table ), textPanel, 0, 1, 0, 1 );
    gtk_widget_show( textPanel );
    gtk_signal_connect( GTK_OBJECT( textarea ),               //(L)
                    "changed",
                    GTK_SIGNAL_FUNC( textEnteredDoSomething ),
                    NULL );

    // drawPanel:
    drawPanel = gtk_scrolled_window_new( NULL, NULL );        //(M)
    gtk_scrolled_window_set_policy(GTK_SCROLLED_WINDOW(drawPanel),//(N)
                            GTK_POLICY_NEVER,
                            GTK_POLICY_NEVER);
    canvas = gnome_canvas_new();                              //(O)
    gtk_widget_set_usize( canvas, 100, 100 );                 //(P)
    rootGroup = gnome_canvas_root( GNOME_CANVAS( canvas ) );  //(Q)
    gtk_container_add( GTK_CONTAINER( drawPanel ), canvas );  //(R)
    gtk_table_attach_defaults( GTK_TABLE( table ),
                            drawPanel, 1, 2, 0, 1 );
    return table;
}


gint eventDestroy( GtkWidget* widget,
                GdkEvent* event, gpointer data ) {
    gtk_main_quit();
    return 0;
}



void textEnteredDoSomething( GtkWidget* widget,              //(S)
                        GdkEvent* event,
                        gpointer data ) {
    double xpos;
    double ypos;
    gint end_pos = gtk_editable_get_position(
                            (GtkEditable*) widget );          //(T)
    gchar* str = gtk_editable_get_chars( (GtkEditable*) widget,  //(U)
                                    end_pos - 1,
                                    end_pos );
    if ( word == NULL) {
        word = malloc( 50 );
        *word = '\0';
    }
```

```
if (strlen (word) >= 50) { //guard against buffer breaking 50 chars
    free (word);
    word = malloc ( 50 );
    *word = '\0';
}
if ( str != NULL ) {
    if ( *str == ' ' || *str == '\n') {
        if ( strcmp( word, "red" ) == 0 ) {
            xpos = rand() %75;
            ypos = rand() %75;
            item = gnome_canvas_item_new( rootGroup,          //(V)
                            gnome_canvas_rect_get_type(),
                            "x1", xpos,
                            "y1", ypos,
                            "x2", xpos + 20.0 ,
                            "y2", ypos + 20.0 ,
                            "fill_color", "red",
                            "outline_color", "white",
                            NULL );
            gnome_canvas_item_show( item );
        }
        if ( strcmp( word, "green" ) == 0 ) {
            xpos = rand() %75;
            ypos = rand() %75;
            item = gnome_canvas_item_new( rootGroup,
                            gnome_canvas_rect_get_type(),
                            "x1", xpos,
                            "y1", ypos,
                            "x2", xpos + 20.0 ,
                            "y2", ypos + 20.0 ,
                            "fill_color", "green",
                            "outline_color", "white",
                            NULL );
            gnome_canvas_item_show( item );
        }
        if ( strcmp( word, "blue" ) == 0 ) {
            xpos = rand() %75;
            ypos = rand() %75;
            item = gnome_canvas_item_new( rootGroup,
                            gnome_canvas_rect_get_type(),
                            "x1", xpos,
                            "y1", ypos,
                            "x2", xpos + 20.0 ,
                            "y2", ypos + 20.0 ,
                            "fill_color", "blue",
                            "outline_color", "white",
                            NULL );
            gnome_canvas_item_show( item );
        }
```

```
            if ( strcmp( word, "magenta" ) == 0 ) {
                xpos = rand() %75;
                ypos = rand() %75;
                item = gnome_canvas_item_new( rootGroup,
                                    gnome_canvas_rect_get_type(),
                                    "x1", xpos,
                                    "y1", ypos,
                                    "x2", xpos + 20.0 ,
                                    "y2", ypos + 20.0 ,
                                    "fill_color", "magenta",
                                    "outline_color", "white",
                                    NULL );
                gnome_canvas_item_show( item );
            }
            free (word);
            word = NULL;
            gnome_canvas_update_now( (GnomeCanvas*) canvas );
        }
        else strcat( word, str );
    }
    g_free( str );
}
```

Here is a makefile that produces the executable for this program:

```
#Makefile_GTK_CrazyWindow

CC=gcc
LDLIBS=`gnome-config --libs gnomeui`
CFLAGS=-Wall -g `gnome-config --cflags gnomeui`

CrazyWindow:  CrazyWindow.o Makefile_GTK_CrazyWindow
        $(CC) $(LDLIBS) CrazyWindow.o -o CrazyWindow

CrazyWindow.o: CrazyWindow.c
        $(CC) $(CFLAGS) -c CrazyWindow.c

clean:
        rm -f CrazyWindow
        rm -f CrazyWindow.o
```

The GUI for this program is shown in Figure 17.30.

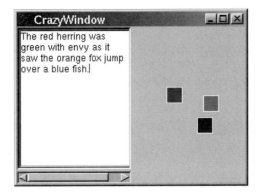

Fig. 17.30

17.15.2   Summary of Facts about Callbacks in GNOME/Gtk+

The following list, from Griffith [25], summarizes the important facts about the callbacks in GNOME/GTK+:

1. The callback function you write for a given signal must have its return type, the argument types, and the number of arguments exactly the same as are specified for the signal.

2. The header format of a callback function is not standardized.

3. Since the call to a callback function is generated at run time, there is no way for a compiler to make sure that your callback function has the correct return type and the number of arguments. All that the compiler can do is to make sure that the header of your callback function matches the prototype. In fact, at compile time, the system does not really know that what you have written as a callback function is really a callback function. To the compiler, it is like any other function. However, at run time, when the function gtk_signal_connect() is invoked and the name of the callback function is encountered as one of the arguments, the system knows that it is dealing with a callback function. It is at that time that the system first checks that your callback function meets the specifications for the signal in question.

4. Each widget class defines its own set of signals. For example, the class GtkButton has defined for it directly the following five signals:

        clicked
        pressed
        released
        enter
        leave

5. A widget class also inherits all the signals from all its parent classes. `GtkButton` inherits from `GtkBin`, `GtkContainer`, `GtkWidget`, and `GtkObject`. `GtkBin` has no signals defined for it directly, `GtkContainer` has 5, `GtkWidget` 54, and `GtkObject` 1. So `GtkButton` inherits 60 signals from its parents. Together with its own 5, `GtkButton` has 65 signals.

6. Every callback function has at least the two parameters, but many have many more. The prototype of the simplest callback function looks like

   ```
   void callBack( GtkWidget*, gpointer );
   ```

7. If a callback function has additional parameters, they are always between the two standard ones shown above. For example, a callback function that includes a GdkEvent* in its parameter list is

   ```
   void callBack( GtkWidget*, GdkEvent*, gpointer );
   ```

8. A callback function will have one of the following return types:

   ```
   void
   gint
   gboolean
   ```

9. When a new widget is constructed at run time, the signals for that widget are automatically registered by entering them into an internal table. Each signal is assigned an ID number in this table. The entries in this table can be queried by invoking

   ```
   gtk_signal_query( i )
   ```

   This will return the information on the signal which was assigned the ID number i. The returned information is a pointer to a struct of type `GtkSignalQuery`. This struct contains the the following fields

   ```
   object_type
   return_val
   signal_name
   nparams
   params[j]
   ```

   The following invocations on these fields return the information shown below:

   ```
   GtkSignalQuery* q = gtk_signal_query( i );
   gtk_type_name( q->object_type );
                       //returns the name of the object for
                       //which the signal is directly defined
   gtk_type_name( q->return_val );
                       //returns the type of the value
                       //returned by the callback function
   ```

   The value stored in field `nparams` is the number of parameters in the callback for the signal whose names is stored in `signal_name`. This number is in addition to the two default parameters that every callback must have. The names of these additional parameters are stored in the array `params[]`.

As was mentioned before, once you invoke `gtk_main()` in your program, you are handing over the control to the GNOME/GTK+ system for the event processing loop. The system will wait (unless terminated by the invocation of `gtk_main_quit()`) for the next event to show up in the event queue for the window. Ordinarily, while waiting for the next event, the system will simply block, meaning it will sit idle. That can result in a waste of computing resources on modern fast machines. To get around this problem, GTK makes available a special facility for invoking background processing of whatever you'd want the computer to do in the background should the event queue become and remain empty. This background activity can be invoked by calling

```
gtk_idle_add( functionName, pointerToData )
```

where `functionName` is a pointer to the function you'd want to invoke in the background. If the function needs some input data for processing, that can be sent to it via the parameter `pointerToData`.

A function that is executed in the background in this manner is called an *idle function*, not because the function is idling — it could actually be engaged in some very important task such as accessing and retrieving information from a database — but because the function is invoked while the event queue is idle. However, this solves only half of the problem. The other half of the problem is reacquiring the control of the CPU when the window manager deposits something in the event queue while the idle function is being executed. This problem can be solved by having the idle function relinquish control back to `gtk_main()` periodically. The reader is referred to Griffith [25] for further details regarding the implementation of idle functions.

17.16 WINDOWS WITH MENUS IN AWT/SWING

User interfaces frequently require pull-down menus. To explain how these can be programmed, let's try to construct a window that can be used for editing a small text file. To keep this interface simple, we will provide this window with a bare minimum functionality. Basically, we want a menu bar at the top of the window. The menu bar should contain one menu object labeled "File" and this object should consist of the following menu items:

```
File:
        New
        Open
        Save
```

Clicking on "New" should result in our being able to enter text into the window, clicking on "Open" should enable us to download a designated file into the window, and clicking on "Save" should enable us to write the contents of the window into a designated file.

In order for the menu items to possess the functionality stated above, we'd need to associate an `ActionListener` object with each menu item; this object will trap the mouse clicks on that item and take appropriate action. As was the case with `JButton` objects, when a menu item is clicked on, it delivers an `ActionEvent` object.

The editing of text in the window can be done with the help of a `TextArea` object. For example, we can create a new `TextArea` object by

```
TextArea ta = new TextArea( 45, 40 );                        //(A)
```

which will create an editable subwindow, 45 lines high and 40 columns wide, inside our window. The `TextArea` constructed with this constructor call comes with both horizontal and vertical scroll bars.[26] Simple editing in this area can be done by moving the cursor to the desired location by using the cursor control keys of the keyboard and then by adding or deleting characters as needed.

With the overview of what needs to be done as presented above, let's see how one would write up the code. The menu bar itself can be created by the invocation

```
MenuBar menuBar = new MenuBar();
```

and added to the window by

```
setMenuBar( menuBar );
```

But before we can invoke the `setMenuBar()` function to set the menu bar in place at the top of the window, we must insert menu objects into the menu bar. The following steps have to be gone through in order to add a menu object to the menu bar:

1. Construct an object of type `Menu`. Supply the name of the menu object as an argument to the constructor. In our case, that would be

   ```
   Menu menuObject = new Menu( "File" );
   ```

2. Create menu items for the menu object. For our example, for the first menu item "New," we would say

   ```
   MenuItem menuItem = new MenuItem( "New" );
   ```

   Associate an `ActionListener` object with each menu item. This could be done in the same manner as for button objects in our earlier programs. For example, for the `menuItem` we just created, we could associate an `ActionListener` object with it via an anonymous class that provides an implementation for the `actionPerformed` method:

   ```
   menuItem.addActionListener( new ActionListener() {
           public void actionPerformed( ActionEvent evt ) {
               String arg = evt.getActionCommand();
               if ( arg.equals( "New" ) ) ta.setEditable( true );
           }
   });
   ```

---

[26]Scrolling is handled internally by a `TextArea` object. No scroll events are generated.

The action performed here is that we want the `TextArea` window to become editable. This we accomplished by

```
ta.setEditable( true );
```

Recall from line (A) above, `ta` is the `TextArea` object in our example. But this is not the approach we will use in the program that is shown below. Instead, we will have the class `WindowWithMenu` implement the `ActionListener` interface and then we will write a single `actionPerformed` method for all three menu items (see line (G) of the program). Now a menu item's `ActionListener` object can be declared by

```
menuItem.addActionListener( this );
```

which says that the `WindowWithMenu` object itself will be the menu item's `ActionListener`. These "add" statements are in lines (D), (E), and (F) of the program.

3. Now all that remains to be done is to add the menu item to the menu object by

```
menuObject.add( menuItem );
```

Of the three menu items, "New" is simplest to deal with. For the other two menu items, "Open" and "Save," we need to be able specify the files that for the former case would be loaded into the `TextArea` object and in the latter case would be used for storing the text in the `TextArea` object. This is best done by using a `FileDialog` object. For example, for designating a file for loading into the `TextArea`, we could say

```
FileDialog loadDialog = new FileDialog( this,
                             "Load File Dialog:",
                             FileDialog.LOAD );
```

as we do in line (B) of the program. Interaction with this `FileDialog` object is initiated with the following statement in line (H) of the program:

```
String filename = loadDialog.getFile();
```

This statement causes a file dialog to pop up on the terminal screen. The user can either click on one of the files in the list shown or enter the name of the file in the space provided. In the `FileDialog` constructor call, the first argument is the parent `Frame` object through which the `FileDialog` object will be constructed. The second argument, the string "Load File Dialog:," is used as a title for the file dialog window. The third argument is the constant `LOAD` from for the `FileDialog` class. This argument becomes `SAVE` for a file dialog window in which we wish to name a file for writing into. See line (C) of the program.

In the program shown below, the part of the implementation of `actionPerformed` which deals with the menu item "Open" includes the code needed for setting up an input stream and for reading the characters from this stream. In line (I), we use `read` to read one character at a time. The entire content of the file is used to construct a single large string, called superString. This string object is then inserted into the TextArea sub-window by

```
String superString;
...
superString += (char) ch;
ta.append( superString )
```

where ch is the character returned by the read function and where, as the reader will recall, ta is the TextArea subwindow in our example. See lines (I) through (K).

For the "Save" menu item, the actionPerformed() method needs to write the contents of the TextArea subwindow into the designated file. As shown in line (L), the entire content of the subwindow can be extracted as a single String object by

```
String str = ta.getText();
```

and, as we have done in line (M), this object can then be deposited into the designated file by

```
FileOutputStream fout = new FileOutputStream( filename );
for (int i=0; i<superString.length(); i++)
    fout.write( superString.charAt(i) );
```

The source code follows:

```
//WindowWithMenu.java

import javax.swing.*;
import java.awt.*;
import java.awt.event.*;
import java.io.*;

class WindowWithMenu extends JFrame implements ActionListener {
    TextArea ta = new TextArea( 45, 40 );                       //(A)
    String filename;
    FileDialog loadDialog = new FileDialog( this,               //(B)
                                  "Load File Dialog:",
                                  FileDialog.LOAD );
    FileDialog saveDialog = new FileDialog( this,               //(C)
                                  "Save File Dialog:",
                                  FileDialog.SAVE );
    public WindowWithMenu() {
        super( "Window with Menu" );
        addWindowListener( new WindowAdapter() {
            public void windowClosing( WindowEvent e ){
                System.exit( 0 ) ;
            }
        });
```

```
    MenuBar menuBar = new MenuBar();

    ta.setEditable( false );
    getContentPane().add( ta, "North" );

    Menu menu = new Menu( "File" );

    MenuItem menuItem = new MenuItem( "New" );
    menuItem.addActionListener( this );                      //(D)
    menu.add( menuItem );

    menuItem = new MenuItem( "Open" );
    menuItem.addActionListener( this );                      //(E)
    menu.add( menuItem );

    menuItem = new MenuItem( "Save" );
    menuItem.addActionListener( this );                      //(F)
    menu.add( menuItem );

    menuBar.add (menu );
    setMenuBar( menuBar );
}

public void actionPerformed( ActionEvent evt ) {            //(G)
    String arg = evt.getActionCommand();
    if ( arg.equals( "New" ) ) ta.setEditable( true );
    if ( arg.equals( "Open" ) ) {
        loadDialog.setDirectory(".");
        loadDialog.show();
        filename = loadDialog.getFile();                     //(H)
        String superString = "";
        if (filename != null) {
            try {
                FileInputStream fin =
                        new FileInputStream( filename );
                while (true) {
                    int ch = fin.read();                     //(I)
                    if ( ch == -1 ) break;
                    superString += (char) ch;                //(J)
                }
                fin.close();
            } catch( IOException e ) {
                System.out.println( "IO error" );
            }
        }
        ta.append( superString );                            //(K)
        ta.setEditable( true );
    }
```

```
       if ( arg.equals( "Save" ) ) {
           saveDialog.setDirectory(".");
           saveDialog.show();
           filename = saveDialog.getFile();
           String superString = ta.getText();                    //(L)
           if (filename != null) {
               try {
                   FileOutputStream fout =
                           new FileOutputStream( filename );
                   for (int i=0; i<superString.length(); i++)
                       fout.write( superString.charAt(i) );       //(M)
                   fout.close();
               } catch( IOException e ) {
                   System.out.println( "IO error" );
               }
           }
       }
   }

   public static void main(String[] args){
       Toolkit tk = Toolkit.getDefaultToolkit();
       Dimension d = tk.getScreenSize();
       int screenHeight = d.height;
       int screenWidth = d.width;
       Frame wb = new WindowWithMenu();
       wb.setSize( 2*screenWidth/3, 3*screenHeight/4 );
       wb.setLocation(screenWidth / 5, screenHeight / 5);
       wb.show();
   }
}
```

Figure 17.31 shows the GUI produced by this program. The screen shot for the figure was taken with the "File" pull-down menu visible.

17.17 WINDOWS WITH MENUS IN Qt

To convey the basics of how menus and menu items are specified in Qt, we will now show a Qt implementation of the example of the previous section. Our top-level window, an object of type WindowWithMenu, will be equipped with a menu bar and will contain a text area of type QMultiLineEdit for entering and editing text as in the previous example. Since there are two very different ways of specifying an action for a menu item in Qt, this time we will incorporate two separate menus in the menu bar to illustrate the two different ways. Now the menu bar will include, as before, a File menu consisting of the usual items — New, Open, Save — and a Color menu,

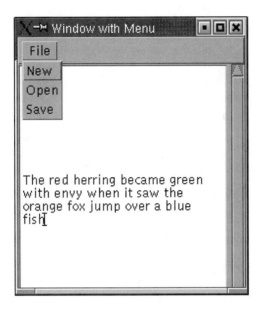

Fig. 17.31

consisting of four different colors. When a user selects an item from the Color menu, the border of the text area would change to that color.

In the program below, the header file for the WindowWithMenu class declares two functions, load() and save(), in lines (B) and (C). These are, respectively, for loading into the text area the contents of a disk file and saving the contents of the text area into a disk file. The slots defined in lines (D) through (G) are:

```
void allowTextEntry();
void getTextFromFile();
void saveTextToFile();

void selectColor( int );
```

The first three of the slot functions are for the three items of the File menu. And the last for the four color items of the Color menu. Note that whereas we provide a separate slot function for each item of the File menu, we provide only one slot function for all the four items of the Color menu. Actually, as we will show in greater detail later, we get multiple uses from the single slot function for the Color menu by virtue of providing it with an int parameter. Selecting each item from the Color menu will invoke selectColor(int) with a different argument.

Looking at the data members of the WindowWithMenu class

```
QMultiLineEdit* textarea;
QMenuBar* menubar;
```

```
QPopupMenu* filemenu;
QPopupMenu* colormenu;
const QColor* borderColor;
```

the first two are the two different components of the top-level window, the menubar at the top of the window and the text area. Then come the two menus. Finally, we have a variable for the color of the border of the text area.

We are now ready to show how menus are created in Qt. We have basically two choices, the first exemplified by how we create filemenu, and the second by how we create colormenu. In either case, we start out by creating a QPopupMenu object:

```
filemenu =   new QPopupMenu( this );
   . . .
   . . .
colormenu =  new QPopupMenu( this );
```

where the argument, this, establishes the parent–child relationship of the menu item (so that when the parent is destroyed, the child will be also). The program creates these two objects in lines (H) and (J).

For the filemenu case, we insert items into the menu by statements of the kind

```
filemenu->insertItem( "New", this, SLOT( allowTextEntry() ) );
```

as shown in line (I). In the statement in line (I), the first argument, "New", is the character string that will be displayed for the menu item, and the second argument declares the object that will supply the slot function for handling the signal emitted by selecting this menu item. Finally, the last argument is for naming the slot function.

The second approach to specifying a menu item is exemplified by the following group of statements for the Color menu in lines (K) through (L) of the program:

```
colormenu->insertItem( "blue", BLUE );
colormenu->insertItem( "yellow", YELLOW );
colormenu->insertItem( "magenta", MAGENTA );

QObject::connect( colormenu,
                  SIGNAL( activated( int ) ),
                  this,
                  SLOT( selectColor( int ) ) );
```

where the symbolic constants BLUE, YELLOW, and MAGENTA are defined in the enumeration in line (A) of the header file WindowWithMenu.h. In this manner, we are associating with each menu item an integer that in the example here is supplied by the enumeration definition. When a user clicks on one of these menu items, the signal activated(int) will be issued, with the parameter set to the integer value associated with the menu item. As to which function gets to trap this signal, that is supplied by the connect invocation above. So if the user clicks on the item "blue", the signal activated(0) will be invoked, causing the invocation of selectColor(0).

In lines (M) through (O), we insert the menus thus constructed into the menu bar, and at the same time give names to the menus, by the following statements:

```
menubar = new QMenuBar( this );
menubar->insertItem( "&File", filemenu );
menubar->insertItem( "Color", colormenu );
```

Attaching an & to the name of the menu, as we have done for the menu "File," means that we can associate a keyboard accelerator with this menu.

The rest of the program is self-explanatory. The executable can be built by

```
make -f Makefile_Qt_WindowWithMenu
```

and, if needed, the binaries can be cleaned up by

```
make -f Makefile_Qt_WindowWithMenu clean
```

```
/////////////////////// file: WindowWithMenu.h ///////////////////////
#ifndef WINDOWWITHMENU_H
#define WINDOWWITHMENU_H

#include <qmultilineedit.h>
#include <qmenubar.h>
#include <qpopupmenu.h>
#include <qcolor.h>
#include <qtextstream.h>
#include <qstatusbar.h>

enum BackgroundColor {                                         //(A)
    BLUE,
    YELLOW,
    MAGENTA
};

class WindowWithMenu: public QWidget {
    Q_OBJECT
public:
    WindowWithMenu( QWidget *parent=0, const char* name= 0 );
    ~WindowWithMenu();
    void load( const char *fileName );                        //(B)
    void save( const char *fileName );                        //(C)

public slots:
    void allowTextEntry();                                    //(D)
    void getTextFromFile();                                   //(E)
    void saveTextToFile();                                    //(F)
    void selectColor( int );                                  //(G)
```

```
private:
    QMultiLineEdit* textarea;
    QMenuBar* menubar;
    QPopupMenu* filemenu;
    QPopupMenu* colormenu;
    const QColor* borderColor;
};
#endif

//////////////////////// file: WindowWithMenu.cc ////////////////////////
#include "WindowWithMenu.h"
#include <qfiledialog.h>
#include <iostream>

WindowWithMenu::WindowWithMenu( QWidget* parent, const char* name )
    : QWidget( parent, name )
{
    setPalette( QPalette( QColor( 250, 250, 200 ) ) );

    filemenu = new QPopupMenu( this );                              //(H)
    filemenu->insertItem( "New", this, SLOT(allowTextEntry()) );   //(I)
    filemenu->insertItem( "Open", this, SLOT( getTextFromFile() ) );
    filemenu->insertItem( "Save", this, SLOT( saveTextToFile() ) );

    colormenu = new QPopupMenu( this );                            //(J)
    colormenu->insertItem( "blue", BLUE );                         //(K)
    colormenu->insertItem( "yellow", YELLOW );
    colormenu->insertItem( "magenta", MAGENTA );

    QObject::connect( colormenu,                                   //(L)
                      SIGNAL( activated( int ) ),
                      this,
                      SLOT( selectColor( int ) ) );

    menubar = new QMenuBar( this );                                //(M)
    menubar->insertItem( "&File", filemenu );                      //(N)
    menubar->insertItem( "Color", colormenu );                     //(O)

    QRect rect = menubar->frameGeometry();
    int h = rect.height();

    textarea = new QMultiLineEdit( this );
    textarea->setGeometry( 0, h, 300, 350 );
    textarea->setReadOnly( TRUE );
}

WindowWithMenu::~WindowWithMenu() {}
```

```
void WindowWithMenu::allowTextEntry() {
    cout << "New selected" << endl;
    textarea->setReadOnly( FALSE );
}

void WindowWithMenu::getTextFromFile() {
    QFileDialog* fd = new QFileDialog();
    QString fileName =
        fd->getOpenFileName( QString::null, QString::null, this );
    cout << "file selected: " + fileName << endl;
    if ( !fileName.isEmpty() && !fileName.isNull() )
        load( fileName );
    else
        cout << "File is either empty or does not exist" << endl;
}

void WindowWithMenu::saveTextToFile() {
    QString fileName =
      QFileDialog::getSaveFileName(QString::null, QString::null, this);
    save( fileName );
}

void WindowWithMenu::selectColor( int item ) {
    switch( item ) {
        case BLUE:
            borderColor = &blue;  // predefined QColor object
            textarea->setPalette( QPalette( *borderColor ) );
            textarea->repaint();
            break;
        case YELLOW:
            borderColor = &yellow;
            textarea->setPalette( QPalette( *borderColor ) );
            textarea->repaint();
            break;
        case MAGENTA:
            borderColor = &magenta;
            textarea->setPalette( QPalette( *borderColor ) );
            textarea->repaint();
            break;
        default:
            borderColor = &white;
            textarea->setPalette( QPalette( *borderColor ) );
            textarea->repaint();
    }
}

void WindowWithMenu::load( const char* fileName ) {
    QFile f( fileName );
    if ( !f.open( IO_ReadOnly ) ) return;
```

```
    textarea->setAutoUpdate( FALSE );

    QTextStream t(&f);
    while ( !t.eof() ) {
        QString s = t.readLine();
        textarea->append( s );
    }
    f.close();

    textarea->setAutoUpdate( TRUE );
    textarea->repaint();
    textarea->setEdited( FALSE );
    textarea->setReadOnly( FALSE );
}

void WindowWithMenu::save( const char* filename ) {
    QString text = textarea->text();
    QFile f( filename );
    if ( !f.open( IO_WriteOnly ) ) {
        cout << "Could not write to the file" << endl;
        return;
    }
    QTextStream t( &f );
    t << text;
    f.close();
    textarea->setEdited( FALSE );
}


/////////////////// file: main_WindowWithMenu.cc ///////////////////
#include <qapplication.h>
#include "WindowWithMenu.h"

int main( int argc, char ** argv ) {
    QApplication a( argc, argv );
    WindowWithMenu* m = new WindowWithMenu();
    m->setGeometry( 100, 200, 400, 400 );
    m->setCaption( "Window with Menu" );
    a.setMainWidget( m );
    m->show();
    a.connect( &a, SIGNAL(lastWindowClosed()), &a, SLOT(quit()) );
    return a.exec();
}


/////////////////// file: Makefile_Qt_WindowWithMenu ///////////////////
CC=g++

LDLIBS=-L$(QTDIR)/lib -lqt
```

```
CFLAGS=-g -I$(QTDIR)/include

WindowWithMenu: moc_WindowWithMenu.o WindowWithMenu.o \
                main_WindowWithMenu.o Makefile_Qt_WindowWithMenu
        $(CC) $(LDLIBS)  -o WindowWithMenu moc_WindowWithMenu.o \
                WindowWithMenu.o main_WindowWithMenu.o

moc_WindowWithMenu.cc: WindowWithMenu.h
        moc -o moc_WindowWithMenu.cc WindowWithMenu.h

moc_WindowWithMenu.o: moc_WindowWithMenu.cc
        $(CC) -c $(CFLAGS) -O2 moc_WindowWithMenu.cc

WindowWithMenu.o: WindowWithMenu.cc
        $(CC) -c $(CFLAGS) -O2 WindowWithMenu.cc

main_WindowWithMenu.o: main_WindowWithMenu.cc
        $(CC) -c $(CFLAGS) -O2 main_WindowWithMenu.cc

clean:
        rm -f WindowWithMenu
        rm -f moc*.*
        rm -f *.o
```

The GUI for this program looks like what is shown in Figure 17.32. The screen shot for the figure was taken with the pull-down "File" menu visible.

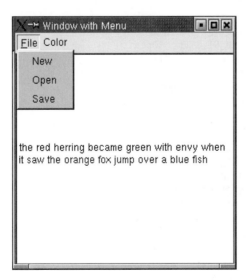

Fig. 17.32

17.18 WINDOWS WITH MENUS IN GNOME/GTK+

We will use the same example as in Section 17.16 for Java to illustrate how menus and menu items are specified in GNOME/GTK+. Basically, we want a rudimentary GUI that would help us edit a small text file. So we want a GNOME/GTK+ program that will create a window with a menu bar at the top containing one menu item named "File". As for the case of Java, we want to associate with "File" a pull-down menu consisting of the following items:

```
New
Open
Save
Exit
```

In GNOME, a menu is simply an array of GnomeUIInfo objects, one for each menu item. For example, the pull-down menu associated with "File" consists of the following array of GnomeUIInfo objects. As the reader can tell, the first element of this array is the GnomeUIInfo object for the menu item "New," the second for the menu item "Open," and so on.

```
GnomeUIInfo fileMenu[] = {                              //(A)
    { GNOME_APP_UI_ITEM,                                //(A1)
      "New",                                            //(A2)
      "Allow text entry into window",                   //(A3)
      allowTextEntry,                                   //(A4)
      NULL,                                             //(A5)
      NULL,                                             //(A6)
      GNOME_APP_PIXMAP_NONE,                            //(A7)
      NULL,                                             //(A8)
      0,                                                //(A9)
      0,                                                //(A10)
      NULL },                                           //(A11)
    { GNOME_APP_UI_ITEM, "Open",
      "Open an existing file",
      selectFileForLoad, NULL, NULL,
      GNOME_APP_PIXMAP_NONE,
      NULL, 0, 0, NULL },
    { GNOME_APP_UI_ITEM, "Save",
      "save contents to the current file",
      selectFileForSave, NULL, NULL,
      GNOME_APP_PIXMAP_NONE,
      NULL, 0, 0, NULL },
    GNOMEUIINFO_SEPARATOR,                              //(B)
    { GNOME_APP_UI_ITEM, "Exit",
      "Close the window and cease",
      eventDestroy, NULL, NULL,
      GNOME_APP_PIXMAP_NONE,
      NULL, 0, 0, NULL },
    GNOMEUIINFO_END
};
```

In the above declaration, we have written the first `GnomeUIInfo` object with one field value per line, and the rest more compactly.[27] As should be evident from the `GnomeUIInfo` object created for the menu item "New", the `GnomeUIInfo` struct has 11 fields:

1. Th first field requires a type label for the menu item. The different possible type labels are

   ```
   GNOME_APP_UI_ITEM                                          //(C)
   GNOME_APP_UI_SEPARATOR                                     //(D)
   GNOME_APP_UI_SUBTREE                                       //(E)
   GNOME_APP_UI_ENDOFINFO                                     //(F)
   GNOME_APP_UI_HELP                                          //(G)
   GNOME_APP_UI_RADIOITEMS
   GNOME_APP_UI_TOGGLEITEM
   etc.
   ```

   For the `GnomeUIInfo` object corresponding to "New," line (A1) declares the menu item to be of type `GNOME_APP_UI_ITEM`. This is also the case for the `GnomeUIInfo` objects for the menu items "Open", "Save" and "Exit".

2. The second field requires a character string, of type `gchar*`,[28] that is actually displayed in the menu for the menu item. Line (A2) shows this character string for the "New" menu item. When this string is preceded by an underscore, the menu item has an accelerator key associated with it. For illustration, if for the first menu item shown above we changed the second field from `New` to `_New` in line (A2), we'd be able to select this menu item by pressing on the keyboard either `Alt-N` or `Meta-N`, depending on the operating system.

3. A character string, of type `gchar*`, that appears in the status bar of a window, if one is provided, when the mouse pointer is on the menu item. This string, shown in line (A3) for the "New" menu item, serves as an elaboration of the label that actually appears in the menu.

4. This is a pointer whose meaning is predicated on the type label used for the first field. When the type label in the first field is `GNOME_APP_UI_ITEM`, this field is a pointer to the callback function to invoke when the menu item in question is selected. When the type label in the first field is `GNOME_APP_UI_SUBTREE`, this field points to another array of `GnomeUIInfo` objects. (In this manner, one can create hierarchical menus.) When the type label in the first field points to `GNOME_APP_UI_HELP`, this field specifies the name of the help node to be

---

[27]In the array of five `GnomeUIInfo` objects shown above starting at line (A), there is an odd-looking object in line (B) — odd since it does not correspond to the structure of the `GnomeUIInfo` struct. The object `GNOMEUIINFO_SEPARATOR` is actually a macro that we will talk about later.

[28]Section 17.4 briefly mentions the different data types of GNOME/GTK+.

loaded, and so on. In our example above, this entry in line (A4) is a pointer to a callback function.

5. If the previous field specifies a callback function and the function expects arguments, this field can be used to specify a pointer to the arguments. As line (A5) shows, this value is NULL for the "New" menu item since the callback does not expect any arguments.

6. Reserved for future use.

7. The type of pixmap to be used for the menu button. A pixmap for a menu button may be incorporated directly within the program as data, or supplied through a separate file, or retrieved from an icon source, and so on. This field tells the program which of these is true. The type can be one of

```
GNOME_APP_PIXMAP_DATA
GNOME_APP_PIXMAP_FILENAME
GNOME_APP_PIXMAP_STOCK
GNOME_APP_PIXMAP_NONE
```

In our menu example, line (A7) declares this field to be GNOME_APP_PIX-MAP_NONE to signify that the menu button for "New" will not display a pixmap icon.

8. If the previous field causes a program to expect a pixmap for a menu button, this field supplies a pointer to the pixmap. If the previous field mentions GNOME_APP_PIXMAP_FILENAME, this field is a pointer to the character string that is the name of the file containing the XPM data.

9. This field specifies the accelerator key, which must be of type gint. The symbol 0 means no accelerator key for the menu item. Line (A9) in our example declares 0 for this field.

10. This is a mask of the modifier keys for the accelerator. Must be of type GtkModifierType.

11. If access to the widget corresponding to the menu button is desired, this field can serve as a pointer to the widget.

Once an array of GnomeUIInfo objects is declared, as we did for fileMenu above in line (A), it can be directly incorporated into a top level window by

```
gnome_app_create_menus( GNOME_APP( app ), fileMenu );
```

where app is a pointer to the GNOME application window, which must be of type GNOME_APP. The above invocation will display all the menu buttons horizontally at the top of the application window. If the menu created through the array fileMenu in line (A) is to be a pop-down menu, you'd need to incorporate it within a "higher level" menu which could be a menu bar consisting of buttons corresponding to the names of the individual menus. For the simple case here, the menu corresponding to the menu bar can be declared by

```
GnomeUIInfo mainMenu[] = {
    GNOMEUIINFO_SUBTREE( "File", fileMenu ),                    //(H)
    GNOMEUIINFO_END                                            //(I)
};
```

where the second argument, `fileMenu`, to the macro `GNOMEUIINFO_SUBTREE` in line (H) is as defined in line (A) previously. This would cause a button labeled "File" to show up in the menubar at the top of the window. Clicking on this button would then reveal the menu declared through the array `fileMenu` in line (A). To include another menu in the menubar, say a menu declared through a `GnomeUIInfo` array named `helpMenu`, we could do that by expanding the above declaration as

```
GnomeUIInfo mainMenu[] = {
    GNOMEUIINFO_SUBTREE( "File", fileMenu ),
    GNOMEUIINFO_SUBTREE( "Help", helpMenu ),
    GNOMEUIINFO_END                                            //(J)
};
```

The important thing to note here is that all menus are arrays of `GnomeUIInfo` objects. This applies as much to the menu consisting of the buttons that are usually displayed horizontally in a menubar as it does to a pop-down menu that becomes visible when you select a menu item from a "higher level" menu.

Note that the invocation `GNOMEUIINFO_SUBTREE` in line (H) above is a macro that creates a `GnomeUIInfo` object of type `GNOME_APP_UI_SUBTREE`, a menu item type listed in line (E). There are many other macros available that mitigate the task of having to specify values for all eleven fields of a `GnomeUIInfo` object. For another illustration, the macro `GNOMEUIINFO_HELP( app_name )` directly constructs a `GnomeUIInfo` object of type `GNOME_APP_UI_HELP` of line (G) without having to specify the other 10 fields. The identifiers `GNOMEUIINFO_END` in lines (I) and (J) and `GNOMEUIINFO_SEPERATOR` used in line (B) are also macros. These macros can also be used for constructing toolbars; a toolbar is the same as a menu except that it uses graphics for buttons instead of labels.

To provide an explanation of the program shown below, the initial part of the code in `main` is similar to what we have shown before for other GNOME/GTK+ programs. Lines (N1) through (N3) of `main` first construct a text area (using a call that was explained earlier in the `CrazyWindow.c` program of Section 17.15.1), set the text area to be uneditable to begin with, and insert the text area into the top-level window. Line (N4) endows the top-level window with the menu defined previously in global scope in line (M). Apart from `main`, the program shown below consists of the following callback functions:

`allowTextEntry,` declared in line (K2) and defined in line (O). This callback is
   associated with the menu button "New" of the "File" menu by virtue of its ap-

pearing in line (L1) at the position shown. The definition of this callback makes the text area editable and thus allows a user to enter text from the keyboard.

selectFileForLoad, declared in line (K3) and defined in line (P). This callback is associated with the menu button "Open" of the "File" menu by virtue of its appearing in line (L2) at the position shown. The definition of this callback first brings up a file dialog window through the invocation of the function gtk_file_selection_new in line (P1). The rest of the code for selectFileForLoad is for managing the interaction of the user with the file dialog window. As implied by the "connect" statement that begins in line (P1), if the user clicks on the "OK" button of the file dialog window, the signal produced invokes getTextFromFile, a callback declared in line (K5) and defined in line (Q). The other two "connect" statements, in lines (P2) and (P3), are for the responses needed from the file dialog window if the user either hits the "Cancel" button or simply closes the window.

selectFileForSave, declared in line (K4) and defined in line (R). This callback is associated with the menu button "Save" of the "File" menu by virtue of its appearance in line (L3) at the position shown. The invocation of gtk_file_selection_new in line (R1) again brings up a file dialog window to make it convenient for the user to choose or name a file in which to save the content of the text area. As the statement that begins in line (R2) shows, if the user clicks on the "OK" button of the file dialog window, the callback saveTextToFile, declared in line (K6) and defined in line (S), is invoked.

getTextFromFile is declared in line (K5) and defined in line (Q). As mentioned previously, this callback is invoked when the user clicks on the "OK" button in a file dialog window that pops up as a result of the user clicking on the "Open" menu button. Regarding its implementation, the statement in line (Q1) first retrieves the file name from the file dialog window. This file is opened in read mode in line (Q2). The function reads the file one character at a time and inserts it in the text area of the GUI in the loop in line (Q3).

saveTextToFile is declared in line (K6) and defined in line (S). Its implementation is straightforward, being similar to that of getTextFromFile, except for the fact it writes out the content of the text area into a file chosen through the file dialog window.

eventDestroy The reader has already seen this callback in all the GNOME/GTK+ programs shown so far. This function is declared in line (K1) and defined at the end of the program. This callback is associated with the menu button "Exit" because it appears in line (L4) as shown.

The source code follows:

```
//WindowWithMenu.c

#include <gnome.h>

GtkWidget* textarea;
gchar* selected_filename;
GtkWidget* file_selector;

gint eventDestroy( GtkWidget* widget, GdkEvent* event,
                                      gpointer data );    //(K1)
void allowTextEntry( GtkObject* object, gpointer data );  //(K2)
void selectFileForLoad( GtkObject* object, gpointer data );  //(K3)
void selectFileForSave( GtkObject* object, gpointer data );  //(K4)

int getTextFromFile( GtkFileSelection* selector, gpointer data );//(K5)
int saveTextToFile( GtkFileSelection* selector, gpointer data ); //(K6)

GnomeUIInfo fileMenu[] = {                                //(L)
    { GNOME_APP_UI_ITEM, "New",
      "Allow text entry into window",
      allowTextEntry, NULL, NULL,                         //(L1)
      GNOME_APP_PIXMAP_NONE,
      NULL, 0, 0, NULL },
    { GNOME_APP_UI_ITEM, "Open",
      "Open an existing file",
      selectFileForLoad, NULL, NULL,                      //(L2)
      GNOME_APP_PIXMAP_NONE,
      NULL, 0, 0, NULL },
    { GNOME_APP_UI_ITEM, "save",
      "save contents to the current file",
      selectFileForSave, NULL, NULL,                      //(L3)
      GNOME_APP_PIXMAP_NONE,
      NULL, 0, 0, NULL },
    GNOMEUIINFO_SEPARATOR,
    { GNOME_APP_UI_ITEM, "Exit",
      "Close the window and cease",
      eventDestroy, NULL, NULL,                           //(L4)
      GNOME_APP_PIXMAP_NONE,
      NULL, 0, 0, NULL },
    GNOMEUIINFO_END
};

GnomeUIInfo mainMenu[] = {                                //(M)
    GNOMEUIINFO_SUBTREE( "File", fileMenu ),
    GNOMEUIINFO_END
};
```

```
int main( int argc, char* argv[] )
{
    GtkWidget* app;
    gnome_init( "aspect", "1.0", argc, argv );
    app = gnome_app_new( "menudemo", "Menu Demo Window" );
    gtk_window_set_default_size( GTK_WINDOW( app ), 300, 200 );
    gtk_signal_connect( GTK_OBJECT( app ),
                        "destroy",
                        GTK_SIGNAL_FUNC( eventDestroy ),
                        NULL );
    textarea = gtk_text_new( NULL, NULL );                     //(N1)
    gtk_text_set_editable( (GtkText*) textarea, FALSE );       //(N2)
    gnome_app_set_contents( GNOME_APP( app ), textarea );      //(N3)
    gnome_app_create_menus( GNOME_APP( app ), mainMenu );      //(N4)
    gtk_widget_show_all( app );
    gtk_main();
    exit( 0 );
}

void allowTextEntry( GtkObject* object, gpointer data ) {       //(O)
    gtk_text_set_editable( (GtkText*) textarea, TRUE );
}

void selectFileForLoad( GtkObject* object, gpointer data ) {     //(P)
    file_selector = gtk_file_selection_new( "Load Dialog" );
    gtk_signal_connect(                                         //(P1)
        GTK_OBJECT( GTK_FILE_SELECTION( file_selector )->ok_button ),
        "clicked",
        GTK_SIGNAL_FUNC( getTextFromFile ), NULL );
    gtk_signal_connect_object(                                  //(P2)
        GTK_OBJECT( GTK_FILE_SELECTION( file_selector )->ok_button ),
        "clicked",
        GTK_SIGNAL_FUNC( gtk_widget_destroy ),
        (gpointer) file_selector );
    gtk_signal_connect_object(                                  //(P3)
        GTK_OBJECT(GTK_FILE_SELECTION( file_selector )->cancel_button),
        "clicked",
        GTK_SIGNAL_FUNC( gtk_widget_destroy ),
        (gpointer) file_selector );
    gtk_widget_show( file_selector );
}

int getTextFromFile( GtkFileSelection* selector, gpointer data ){ //(Q)
    FILE* fp;
    gint ch;
    gchar* str = g_malloc( 1 + 1 );
    selected_filename = gtk_file_selection_get_filename(        //(Q1)
        GTK_FILE_SELECTION( file_selector ) );
    g_print( "Filename retrieved: %s\n", selected_filename );
```

```
    if ( ( fp = fopen( selected_filename, "r" ) ) == NULL ) {     //(Q2)
        g_print( "Unable to open the file" );
        return 1;
    }
    str[ 1 ] = '\0';
    while ( ( ch = getc( fp ) ) != EOF ) {                        //(Q3)
        str[ 0 ] = (gchar) ch;
        gtk_text_insert( GTK_TEXT( textarea ),
                                NULL, NULL, NULL, str, -1 );
    }
    gtk_text_set_editable( (GtkText*) textarea, TRUE );
    fclose( fp );
    g_free( str );
    return 0;
}


void selectFileForSave( GtkObject* object, gpointer data ) {      //(R)
    file_selector = gtk_file_selection_new( "Save Dialog" );     //(R1)
    gtk_signal_connect(                                          //(R2)
        GTK_OBJECT( GTK_FILE_SELECTION( file_selector )->ok_button ),
        "clicked",
        GTK_SIGNAL_FUNC( saveTextToFile ), NULL );
    gtk_signal_connect_object(
        GTK_OBJECT( GTK_FILE_SELECTION( file_selector )->ok_button ),
        "clicked",
        GTK_SIGNAL_FUNC( gtk_widget_destroy ),
        (gpointer) file_selector );
    gtk_signal_connect_object(
        GTK_OBJECT( GTK_FILE_SELECTION(file_selector)->cancel_button ),
        "clicked",
        GTK_SIGNAL_FUNC( gtk_widget_destroy ),
        (gpointer) file_selector );
    gtk_widget_show( file_selector );
}


int saveTextToFile( GtkFileSelection* selector, gpointer data ) { //(S)
    FILE* fp;
    int len;
    int i = 0;
    gchar* str = gtk_editable_get_chars((GtkEditable*) textarea,0, -1);
    len = strlen( str );
    selected_filename = gtk_file_selection_get_filename(
        GTK_FILE_SELECTION( file_selector ) );
    if ( ( fp = fopen( selected_filename, "w" ) ) == NULL ) {
        g_print( "Unable to open the file for save" );
        return 1;
    }
    while ( i < len ) fputc( str[ i++ ], fp );
    fclose( fp );
```

```
    g_free( str );
    return 0;
}

gint eventDestroy( GtkWidget* widget, GdkEvent* event, gpointer data ) {
    gtk_main_quit();
    return 0;
}
```

This program can be compiled using the following makefile that is named Makefile_GTK_WindowWithMenu. The makefile is invoked by

```
    make -f Makefile_gtk_WindowWithMenu
```

```
CC=gcc
LDLIBS='gnome-config --libs gnomeui'
CFLAGS=-Wall -g 'gnome-config --cflags gnomeui'

WindowWithMenu:  WindowWithMenu.o Makefile_gtk_WindowWithMenu
        $(CC) $(LDLIBS) WindowWithMenu.o -o WindowWithMenu

WindowWithMenu.o: WindowWithMenu.c
        $(CC) $(CFLAGS) -c WindowWithMenu.c

clean:
        rm -f WindowWithMenu
        rm -f WindowWithMenu.o
```

The window produced by this program is shown in Figure 17.33. The screen shot was taken with the "File" pull-down menu visible.

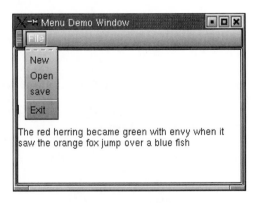

Fig. 17.33

17.19 DRAWING SHAPES, TEXT, AND IMAGES IN AWT/SWING

An understanding of the abstract class Graphics and its subclass Graphics2D is central to the programming required for drawing shapes, strings, and images in Java. An object of type Graphics is like a drawing instrument that knows what sized pen to use for the draw operation desired; what colors to use; how to draw a string and what font to use for that purpose; what origin and axes to use for the coordinates needed for all sorts of drawing; how to transform the coordinates if it is desired to draw transformed versions of the shapes, strings, and images; and so on. The process of drawing is usually referred to as *rendering*, and all of the information that is needed before a graphics object can be rendered is referred to as the *graphics context*.

To explain how an object of type Graphics is used in a program, it is best to start with a discussion of the paint method that is defined as a do-nothing method for the java.awt.Component class, which, besides being the ancestor class of all AWT components, is also the ancestor of the JComponent class from which the Swing components are derived. The header of this method is

```
public void paint( Graphics g )
```

The paint method must be overridden by the programmer for the rendering of graphical objects inside AWT components. It is in the override definition of paint that we tell the system what shapes, strings, or images we wish to see drawn inside an AWT component. What is particularly interesting is that even when we provide an override definition for paint, this function is almost never called directly in a program. The override definition will be invoked by the system automatically when it needs to render the component, which could happen when the system is trying to display the component for the first time, or if the system is trying to redraw the component because the user has resized the top-level window, and so on.[29] For each such event-driven invocation of paint, the system first automatically constructs a Graphics object needed for the argument of paint. Note that since Graphics is an abstract class, objects of this class cannot be created directly.

Whereas we provide an override definition for paint for drawing graphical objects inside an AWT component, for doing the same inside a Swing component we provide override definition for paintComponent. While it is true that the system automatically invokes paint(Graphics g) for rendering both AWT and Swing components, for the latter case the invocation of paint(Graphics g) is further decomposed into the following three invocations:

```
protected void paintComponent( Graphics g )
protected void paintBorder( Graphics g )
protected void paintChildren( Graphics g )
```

---

[29]If you provide an override definition for paint for an applet, it will automatically be called after the init and start methods. Java applets are discussed in Section 17.22.

This means that if we wish to include the drawing of a shape, a string, or an image in the rendering of a Swing component, we must provide code to that effect in the override definition of paintComponent.

Since paint is almost never directly invoked by a programmer, then how is one to force re-rendering of a component. Let's say that we want a certain shape to appear inside a component *after* the user has clicked on some button. This would call for a re-rendering of the component. If we want a component to be re-rendered during user interaction, we must call repaint. The method repaint automatically calls the method update of the Component class, which in turn calls our override definition of paint. One never provides an override definition for repaint since it has to perform certain system-dependent tasks. However, in some cases involving animation, it may be necessary to provide an override definition for update. The headers for repaint and update are

```
public void repaint()
public void update( Graphics g )
```

While a Graphics object renders shapes, strings, and images by coloring the pixels made available by the underlying output device, deciding which specific pixels to use is not always as straightforward as it seems. Suppose we want a straight line to be drawn between two points whose locations are specified using high-precision floating-point numbers. The straight line joining the two end points would in most cases pass between the pixels for the most part. The question then becomes as to which pixels should be colored by the Graphics object in order to display the line. One could, for example, color all pixels that are within a half-pixel distance of the analog line. The problem with this strategy is that we could end up with a two-pixel wide line if the analog line is exactly between two rows of pixels. Java uses the policy that the Graphics object will render such a straight line by a pixel-sized pen that colors the nearest pixel on the right side of the line. The same policy is applied to the rendering of outlines of all shapes. Filled shapes are created by filling the interiors of the analog (infinitely thin) closed curves.

Coloring pixels for drawing requires that the locations of those pixels be specified with respect to some coordinate system. Java uses (x, y) coordinates for this purpose, with the default location of the origin situated at the upper left *outside* corner of the component, and with x measured horizontally in pixels to the right and y measured vertically in pixels towards the bottom of the component. Let's say we want an ellipse to be drawn inside a component. The coordinates of the center of the ellipse will by default be set with respect to the outer upper left corner of the component for which we provide an override definition for either paint or paintComponent. This default location of the origin can sometimes be inconvenient if we are drawing inside a top-level window with a title bar. Say we want to place an ellipse in the center of the inside borders of the window, it would be difficult to do so with respect to the outside upper-left corner of the top-level window. To get around this difficulty, we would want to shift the origin to the upper left corner of the *inside* of the component. The getInsets() method, inherited from the Container class, returns an Insets object whose top, left, bottom, and right data members hold four values corresponding to the respective margins of the Container object. The margin at the top includes the title bar, the other margins being the border that surrounds the window. Therefore, the pixel coordinates given by the pair getInsets().left, getInsets().top corresponds to the top left corner of the drawable area of a window. To illustrate how getInsets is used to translate the origin, here is an override definition for paint that seeks to draw a rectangular shape at the pixel coordinates (180, 80) with respect to the upper left corner of the drawable part of an AWT component. The rectangle will be of width 60 pixels and height 40 pixels.

```
public void paint( Graphics g ) {
    g.translate( getInsets().left, getInsets().top );        //(A)
    g.setColor( Color.red );                                 //(B)
    g.drawRect( 180, 80, 60, 40 );                           //(C)
}
```

The translate method of the Graphics object is used in line (A) to shift the default location of the origin to the upper left of the drawable area of the component. The method drawRect defined for the Graphics class does the actual drawing of the rectangular shape.

The statement in line (B) above changes the *current* color. Unless otherwise changed, all future graphics will be drawn using the color set by the setColor() method defined for the Graphics class. The argument to this is an object of type Color. A color can be specified by choosing one of the thirteen colors that are defined as constant members of the Color class, these being black, blue, cyan, darkGray, gray, green, lightGray, magenta, orange, pink, red, white, and yellow. A more general way to specify color is by its red, green, and blue constituents. For example, if we so wished, we could replace the statement in line (B) above by

```
g.setColor( new Color( 128, 0, 128 ) );
```

which by assigning a value of 128 to *red*, 0 to *green*, and 128 to *blue* results in a purplish-red sort of a color. Each color constituent takes a value between 0 and 255. If a particular color needs to be made brighter or darker, one can do so by using the brighter and darker methods of the Color class. For example, the above call to the setColor method could be replaced by

```
Color c = new Color( 128, 0, 128 );
g.setColor( c.brighter().brighter().brighter() );
```

Shown below is a program that draws a sampling of shapes on a screen. Each shape has been drawn inside its own anonymous JPanel object. The syntax used for the drawing of the various shapes is further explained after the program.

```java
//RenderGraphics.java

import java.awt.*;            // for Color, GridLayout, Graphics, etc.
import java.awt.event.*;      // for WindowAdapter
import javax.swing.*;

public class RenderGraphics {
    static final int maxCharHeight = 15;
    static final Color bg = Color.lightGray;
    static final Color fg = Color.black;
    static int width;          // for width of a shape panel
    static int height;         // for height of a shape panel
    static int rectWidth;      // width of shape's bounding rect
    static int rectHeight;     // height of shape's bounding rect

    public static void main( String[] args ) {
        JFrame f = new JFrame( "Draw Shape Samples" );
        f.addWindowListener(new WindowAdapter() {
            public void windowClosing(WindowEvent e) {
                System.exit(0);
            }
        });

        f.setBackground(bg);                                    //(D)
        f.setForeground(fg);                                    //(E)

        Container contentPane = f.getContentPane();
        contentPane.setLayout( new GridLayout( 0, 3 ) );

        //polyline:
        contentPane.add( new JPanel() {
            public void paintComponent(Graphics g) {
                super.paintComponent(g);      //clears the background
                width = getWidth();
                height = getHeight();
                int stringY = height - 10;
                rectWidth = width - 20;
                rectHeight = stringY - maxCharHeight - 10;
                int x2Points[] =
                    {10, 10+rectWidth, 10, 10+rectWidth};
                int y2Points[] =
                    {10, 10+rectHeight, 10+rectHeight, 10};
                g.drawPolyline(x2Points,
                    y2Points, x2Points.length);                 //(F)
                g.drawString("drawPolyline", 10, stringY);      //(G)
            }
        });
```

```
        //rounded rectangle:
        contentPane.add( new JPanel() {
            public void paintComponent(Graphics g) {
                super.paintComponent(g);
                width = getWidth();
                height = getHeight();
                int stringY = height - 10;
                rectWidth = width - 20;
                rectHeight = stringY - maxCharHeight - 10;
                g.drawRoundRect(10,
                        10, rectWidth, rectHeight, 10, 10);      //(H)
                g.drawString("drawRect", 10, stringY);
            }
        });

        //filled oval:
        contentPane.add( new JPanel() {
            public void paintComponent(Graphics g) {
                super.paintComponent(g);
                width = getWidth();
                height = getHeight();
                int stringY = height - 10;
                rectWidth = width - 80;
                rectHeight = stringY - maxCharHeight - 10;
                g.fillOval(40, 10, rectWidth, rectHeight);       //(I)
                g.drawString("drawOval", 10, stringY);
            }
        });

        f.setSize(new Dimension(550, 200));
        f.setVisible(true);
    }
}
```

The output of the program is shown in Figure 17.34.

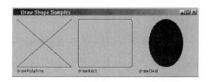

Fig. 17.34

Note that for each "draw" method that draws a closed shape, there is a "fill" method in the Graphics class that draws a filled shape. The method calls are similar for the two cases. In addition to taking note of the syntax of the "draw" and "fill" calls, as in lines (H) and (I) above, the reader should also note how the pen color for the draw operation is set in line (E).

After paintComponent is invoked, the pen color can be changed as desired by invoking setColor on the graphics context, as shown previously in line (B).

Note that in the "fill" call for drawing the oval shape in line (I), the first argument to fillOval is the *x*-coordinate of the top left corner of the bounding rectangle of the oval, the second argument the *y*-coordinate of the same point, and the third and the fourth arguments are the width and the height of the bounding rectangle.

The reader should also take note of the call to drawString for drawing a string under each shape, as in line (G). The first argument to drawString is the string that needs to be drawn, and the second and the third arguments are the horizontal and the vertical coordinates in pixels for the leftmost point for the imaginary *baseline* under the drawn string. The method drawString uses the system-supplied default font for drawing the string. However, one can choose from a number of fonts that Java makes available through the Font class. For example, if we wished for a string to be drawn using the SansSerif font in italics with size 14, before invoking the drawString method, we'd first set the font by

```
Font f = new Font( "SansSerif", Font.ITALIC, 14 );
g.setFont( f );
```

where, as before, g is the Graphics object in the argument to the paint method.

A list of all font families available to Java can be retrieved by invoking one of the following methods

```
Font[]   getAllFonts()
String[] getAvailableFontFamilyNames()
String[] getAvailableFontFamilyNames(Locale l)
```

on a GraphicsEnvironment object. The first call, getAllFonts, returns an array of one-point sized instances of all the available fonts. The second call above returns the names of all the font families. And the last call returns an array of the localized names of the available font families. The GraphicsEnvironment class is abstract. The GraphicsEnvironment object for your current environment can only be constructed by invoking the getLocalGraphicsEnvironment method as shown below:

```
GraphicsEnvironment ge =
    GraphicsEnvironment.getLocalGraphicsEnvironment();
```

The names of all the available fonts may now be retrieved by

```
String[] fontList = ge.getAvailableFontFamilyNames();
```

The following program will display all the fonts available to Java on a given platform:

```
//FontFamilies.java

import javax.swing.*;
import java.awt.*;
import java.awt.event.*;

class FontFamilies extends JPanel {

    public void paintComponent( Graphics g ) {
        super.paintComponent( g );
        g.translate( getInsets().left, getInsets().top );
        GraphicsEnvironment ge =
            GraphicsEnvironment.getLocalGraphicsEnvironment();
        String[] fontList = ge.getAvailableFontFamilyNames();
        Font defaultFont = g.getFont();
        for (int i = 0; i < fontList.length; i++ ) {
            g.setFont( defaultFont );
            g.drawString( fontList[ i ], 10, i * 14 );
            Font f = new Font( fontList[ i ], Font.PLAIN, 12 );
            g.setFont( f );
            g.drawString( "Purdue", 200 , i * 14 );
        }
    }

    public static void main( String[] args ) {
        JFrame f = new JFrame();
        f.addWindowListener(new WindowAdapter() {
            public void windowClosing(WindowEvent e) {
                System.exit(0);
            }
        });
        FontFamilies fd = new FontFamilies();
        f.getContentPane().add( fd, BorderLayout.CENTER );
        f.setSize( 300, 300 );
        f.setLocation( 200, 300 );
        f.setVisible( true );
    }
}
```

The output of this program on the author's Linux machine is shown in Figure 17.35.

In addition to maintaining a list of all the available fonts, a GraphicsEnvironment object also maintains a list of GraphicsDevice objects available. Graphics-Device objects can be screens, printers, or image buffers and are the destinations of the Graphics2D drawing methods.

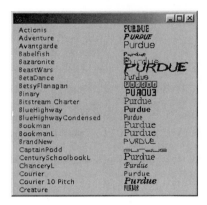

Fig. 17.35

We will now discuss graphics rendering when a user's interaction alters the state of the GUI in such a way that it would need to be re-rendered by a call to `repaint`. The following program displays a yellow square in the middle of a top-level window. A corner of the square always stays pointed towards where the user clicks in the window. So as the user clicks at different points in the window, the yellow square rotates through an angle that keeps one of its corners pointed toward the point clicked on.

This program uses a `Graphics2D` object to rotate the square to its new position as the user clicks anywhere in the window. As mentioned earlier, `Graphics2D` extends `Graphics` to allow for coordinate transformations prior to and during the rendering process, and to give more sophisticated control over colors and fonts.

In our program, after the user has clicked somewhere inside the window, the new orientation of the yellow square is calculated from the *x* and the *y* coordinates of the point clicked on. This orientation is designated by the variable `theta` in the program. The variable name `thetaPrevious` denotes the orientation of the square prior to the user click. Therefore, after the user has clicked, the square needs to be rotated through an angle `theta−thetaPrevious`. The following statements extracted from the program show how a `Graphics2D` object is used to bring about this rotation of the square:

```
Graphics g;
....
....
Graphics2D g2d = (Graphics2D) g;
....
....

//previous orientation of square:
double thetaPrevious = ...                              //(J)
```

```
        //next orientation of square:
        double theta = ...                                     //(K)
        ....
        ....
        g2d.translate( halfWindowWidth, halfWindowHeight );    //(P)
        g2d.rotate( theta - thetaPrevious );                   //(Q)
        g2d.translate( - halfWindowWidth, - halfWindowHeight ); //(R)
        ....
        ....
        g2d.setColor(Color.yellow);
        g2d.fillRect(rectOriginX, rectOriginY, rectWidth, rectHeight);
        thetaPrevious = theta;
```

In order to bring about an *in-place* rotation of the yellow square, we first translate
the origin to the center of the square in line (P); we then rotate the square in line
(Q) about the new origin; and then move the origin back to where it was originally
in line (R). All of these transformation steps are stored away in the Graphics2D
object g2d. Subsequently, when a "draw" or a "fill" function is invoked, the actual
drawing will incorporate those transformations. The rest of the program shown below
is self-explanatory.

```
//RotatingRect.java

import javax.swing.*;
import java.awt.*;
import java.awt.event.*;

public class RotatingRect {
    public static void main(String[] args) {
        JFrame f = new JFrame("Rotating Rectangle");
        f.addWindowListener(new WindowAdapter() {
            public void windowClosing(WindowEvent e) {
                System.exit(0);
            }
        });
        Container container = f.getContentPane();
        container.add( new RotatingRectPanel() );
        f.setLocation( 300, 300 );
        f.pack();
        f.setVisible(true);
    }
}

class RotatingRectPanel extends JPanel {
    Graphics2D g2d;
    Point point = null;          // point in window clicked on
    Dimension preferredSize = new Dimension(300, 300);
```

```
//width and height of the rotating yellow square:
int rectWidth = 60;
int rectHeight = 60;

//the following two data members needed for computing
//rotation angles around the center of the square:
int halfWindowWidth = preferredSize.width / 2;
int halfWindowHeight = preferredSize.height / 2;

//theta is desired orientation of the square
//thetaPrevious is current orientation of the square
double theta  = 0.0;                                         //(J)
double thetaPrevious = 0.0;                                  //(K)

//constructor:
public RotatingRectPanel( ) {
    addMouseListener(new MouseAdapter() {                   //(L)
        public void mousePressed(MouseEvent e) {            //(M)
            //coordinates of the pointed clicked on:
            int x = e.getX();                               //(N)
            int y = e.getY();                               //(O)
            if (point == null) {
                point = new Point(x, y);
            } else {
                point.x = x;
                point.y = y;
            }
            repaint();
        }
    });
}

//important for panel sizing:
public Dimension getPreferredSize() {
    return preferredSize;
}

public void paintComponent(Graphics g) {
    super.paintComponent(g);                    //paint background
    int xFromCenter = 0;
    int yFromCenter = 0;
    int rectOriginX = halfWindowWidth - rectWidth / 2;
    int rectOriginY = halfWindowHeight - rectHeight / 2;

    if ( g2d == null ) g2d = (Graphics2D) g;
    if ( point != null ) {
        xFromCenter = point.x - halfWindowWidth;
        yFromCenter = point.y - halfWindowHeight;
```

```
        theta = Math.atan2( (double) yFromCenter,
                            (double) xFromCenter ) + Math.PI/4.0;
    }

    g2d.translate( halfWindowWidth, halfWindowHeight );        //(P)
    g2d.rotate( theta - thetaPrevious );                       //(Q)
    g2d.translate( - halfWindowWidth, - halfWindowHeight );    //(R)
    g2d.setColor(Color.yellow);
    g2d.fillRect(rectOriginX, rectOriginY, rectWidth, rectHeight);

    thetaPrevious = theta;
  }
}
```

The GUI for the above program looks as shown in Figure 17.36. As mentioned before, the user can click anywhere in the window and the rectangle will automatically rotate so that one of its corners points towards the direction of the mouse click.

Fig. 17.36

The above program provided an implementation for the `mousePressed` method of the `MouseListener` interface in line (M). This method is used to trap the `MOUSE_PRESSED` event. The `MouseListener` interface declares other methods for trapping other types of mouse events, such as mouse move, click, and drag, the last corresponding to the situation when you move a mouse with one of the mouse buttons pressed. The mouse events are delivered to an object of a class that implements either the `MouseListener` interface or the `MouseMotionListener` interface from the `java.awt.event` package. It is instructive to look at the definitions of these two interfaces to get a good sense of which interface to use for what application:

```
public abstract interface MouseListener extends EventListener {
  public abstract void mouseClicked( MouseEvent e );
  public abstract void mouseEntered( MouseEvent e );
  public abstract void mouseExited( MouseEvent e );
  public abstract void mousePressed( MouseEvent e );
  public abstract void mouseReleased( MouseEvent e );
}

public abstract interface MouseMotionListener extends EventListener {
  public abstract void mouseDragged( MouseEvent e );
  public abstract void mouseMoved( MouseEvent e );
}
```

As to what specific type of a mouse event has taken place can be ascertained by invoking the getID() method on the MouseEvent object. Depend on the nature of the mouse event, the getID() method will return one of the following seven symbolic constants:

```
                             _
  MOUSE_CLICKED            |
  MOUSE_PRESSED            |
  MOUSE_RELEASED          |   trapped by a MouseListener object
  MOUSE_ENTERED           |
  MOUSE_EXITED            |
                             _

                             _
  MOUSE_MOVED             |   trapped by a MouseMotionListener object
  MOUSE_DRAGGED           |
                             _
```

A MouseEvent object corresponding to the first five events listed above can be trapped by a GUI component that implements the MouseListener interface. There corresponds a MouseListener method for each of these five mouse events. The method mouseClicked traps the MOUSE_CLICKED mouse event that is delivered when a button is pressed and released without intervening mouse drag. The method mousePressed traps the mouse event MOUSE_PRESSED that is generated when the user presses a mouse button. The method mouseReleased traps the event MOUSE_RELEASED that is generated when the user releases a mouse button. The method mouseEntered traps the mouse event MOUSE_ENTERED that is delivered when the mouse pointer has entered the GUI component on which is invoked an "add" method for a MouseListener object. The method mouseExited traps the mouse event MOUSE_EXITED that is generated when the mouse pointer exits the component.

The other two types of mouse events listed above, MOUSE_MOVED and MOUSE_DRAGGED, can be trapped by a GUI component if it implements the MouseMotionListener interface. The method mouseMoved of this interface traps the former and the method mouseDragged traps the latter.

When a `MouseEvent` is trapped by any of the methods, the coordinates of the mouse pointer on the screen at that moment can be determined, as we do in lines (N) and (O) of the previous program, by invoking the methods `getX` and `getY` defined for the `MouseEvent` class of the `java.awt.event` package. One can also use the method `getPoint` defined for the same class and retrieve the pixel coordinates from the `Point` object returned.

Of course, as with other event listener interfaces, if an interface has more than one method, it is easier to use the corresponding adapter class in which the methods have been given the trivial do-nothing implementations, as we have done in line (L) of `RotatingRect.java`.

We will now discuss the "drawing" of gray-scale or color images in a window. Java accepts both of the commonly used image file formats, JPEG and GIF, for this purpose. An image file is read into a Java program by creating an object of type `Image` with the help of the `getImage` method of the `Toolkit` class in the following manner

```
Image image = Toolkit.getDefaultToolkit().getImage("filename.jpg");
```

Of course, as the reader would expect, for GIF files, the suffix for the file name must be ".gif".

Images are loaded into Java "asynchronously," a concept that will become clearer when we delve into multithreaded computing in Chapter 18. But basically what that means is that `getImage` returns immediately because the image is loaded in a separate thread of computation. So if you don't wait for this separate thread to complete its job, you could end up processing only a part of the image. This potential source of difficulty is gotten around by tracking the progress of image loading with the help of a `MediaTracker` object. This is done by first creating a `MediaTracker` object by

```
MediaTracker tracker = new MediaTracker( this );
```

and then registering with the `tracker` the image whose loading we want to monitor. This is done by

```
tracker.addImage( image, 0 );
try {
    tracker.waitForID( 0 );
} catch( InterruptedException e ) {}
```

The method `addImage` assigns an ID, in this case 0, to the image. Subsequently, we can invoke the method `waitForID(0)` to make sure that the image is completely loaded in. One can add any number of images to a `MediaTracker` object, by simply assigning a different identification number to each image with the `addImage` method. When multiple images need to be kept track of, inside the `try` block one can also invoke the `waitForAll` method for all the images together, instead of `waitForID` for each image separately.

After an image is fully loaded in, its various attributes, such as its width and height, can be retrieved through calls like

```
int width = image.getWidth( this );                        //(S)
int height = image.getHeight( this );                      //(T)
```

To understand the argument this in the calls to getWidth and getHeight, you have to examine the prototypes of these two methods as defined for the abstract class Image in the java.awt package:

```
public abstract int getWidth( ImageObserver observer )     //(U)
public abstract int getHeight( ImageObserver observer )    //(V)
```

where ImageObserver, an interface defined in the java.awt.image package, has been implemented by java.awt.Component. An object of type ImageObserver can keep track of asynchronous loading of an image and inform the rest of the GUI program about the availability of the various attributes of the image as its loading proceeds and as the attribute values become available. Since all AWT components descend from java.awt.Component, therefore all such components are ImageObserver objects. So by supplying this as an argument to the method calls in lines (S) and (T), we conform to the prototypes in lines (U) and (V). If the image has not yet been fully loaded and the method getWidth as in line (S) above is invoked, the method will return -1. The same applies to the method getHeight in line (T).

Now we are ready to actually draw an image in a window. Let's assume that we wish for the top left corner of the image to coincide with the origin of the drawable area. We will assume that the Graphics object associated with the window is g. Then the following invocation will do the job:

```
g.drawImage( image, 0, 0, this );
```

where the first argument, image, is the Image object corresponding to the image file read into Java, and the next two arguments the coordinates of the point corresponding to the top left corner of the displayed image. The last argument, this, is, as before, the component in its capacity as an ImageObserver object.

Sometimes we want a displayed image to expand or shrink as the user changes the window size. This can be accomplished by incorporating the following version of drawImage in the paint method:[30]

---

[30]This can also be accomplished by invoking the following method

```
public Image getScaledInstance(int width, int height, int hints)
```

defined for the Image class in java.awt package. When invoked on an Image object that was previously loaded in, this method returns a scaled version of the image whose new width and new height are the parameters of this method. If a negative value is given to either of the width and height parameters, then a value will be substituted for that parameter so as to maintain the aspect ratio of the image. The last parameter is a flag that controls the choice of algorithm to use for interpolation. This parameter can be set to one of the following symbolic constants: SCALE_DEFAULT, SCALE_FAST, SCALE_SMOOTH, SCALE_REPLICATE.

```
        g.drawImage( image, 0, 0, clientWidth, clientHeight, this );
```

The difference between this call to drawImage and the call shown earlier is that we now have two additional arguments in the fourth and the fifth positions. Both of these are of type int and represent the scaled width and height to which we want the image to be drawn. Obviously, one could use a fixed relationship between the two so that the image does not get distorted as it is drawn to different scales. The following paint method uses this version of drawImage:

```
//ImageLoadAndDisplay.java

import javax.swing.*;
import java.awt.*;
import java.awt.event.*;

class ImageLoadAndDisplay extends JPanel {

    public void paintComponent( Graphics g ) {
        super.paintComponent( g );
        g.translate( getInsets().left, getInsets().top );
        Dimension d = getSize();
        Insets in = getInsets();
        Image image = Toolkit.getDefaultToolkit().getImage(
                            "images/slideshow/flower16.jpg");
        MediaTracker tracker = new MediaTracker( this );
        tracker.addImage( image, 0 );
        try {
            tracker.waitForID( 0 );
        } catch( InterruptedException e ) {}

        int imageWidth = image.getWidth( this );
        int imageHeight = image.getHeight( this );
        int clientWidth = d.width - in.right - in.left;
        int clientHeight = d.height - in.bottom - in.top;
        g.drawImage( image,
                     in.left, in.top,
                     clientWidth, clientHeight,
                     this );
    }


    public static void main( String[] args ) {
        JFrame f = new JFrame( "ImageLoadAndDisplay" );
        f.addWindowListener(new WindowAdapter() {
            public void windowClosing(WindowEvent e) {
                System.exit(0);
            }
        });
```

```
        ImageLoadAndDisplay im = new ImageLoadAndDisplay();
        f.getContentPane().add( im, BorderLayout.CENTER );
        f.setSize( 1000, 600 );
        f.setLocation( 200, 300 );
        f.setVisible( true );
    }
}
```

The output of this program is shown in Figure 17.37 for an example image file.

Fig. 17.37

17.20   DRAWING SHAPES, TEXT, AND IMAGES IN Qt

As mentioned previously, graphics programming deals with rendering geometric shapes, displaying images, playing animation, sketching free-form figures with a mouse pointer, and so on. Central to graphics programming in Qt is the polymorphic behavior of those virtual functions that are automatically invoked in response to certain low-level events. For example, when a QWidget object needs to be drawn on a computer screen, the low-level event QPaintEvent is sent to the widget, where its receipt causes automatic invocation of the paintEvent method. So, as with the paint method for AWT components and the paintComponent method for Swing components, if a programmer extends the QWidget class and supplies an override definition for paintEvent, it's the programmer's definition of paintEvent that will be invoked any time the new widget needs to be drawn. Thus, by incorporating calls to the rendering routines in the override definition of paintEvent, one can display shapes, images, text, and so on, in the new widget.

A typical override definition for paintEvent consists of first constructing a QPainter object and then invoking one of the many methods defined for this class for graphical programming. The QPainter class plays an important role in practically all graphical programming in Qt as it has been provided with a large number of methods whose functionality runs the gamut from rendering geometrical shapes, to displaying images, to drawing text strings, to affecting coordinate transformations, and so on.

Other graphical applications, such as those involving free-form sketching in a QWidget object, depend on the programmer supplying override definitions for virtual event handlers such as mousePressEvent, mouseMoveEvent, and so on, that are automatically invoked upon receipt of low-level mouse events of the type QMouseEvent.

In the rest of this section, we will first show code that renders shapes, images, text, and so on, in a widget via the override definition for the paintEvent method. Next we will show how low-level mouse events can be handled for sketching, and so on.

In the following example, all of the graphics code for the class RenderGraphics-Widget is invoked through the override definition for the paintEvent method in line (M). This method is invoked whenever a RenderGraphicsWidget object is displayed for the first time, or whenever it is resized, or when it is exposed because an overlying widget was moved away. Also, the methods update and repaint defined for the QWidget class can be used to force a paint event and to thus cause paintEvent to be invoked.

Basic to shape rendering in Qt is the specification of the following three items;

1. **Coordinate Transformation:** A coordinate transformation specifies the location of the origin and the directions of the x and y axes for the purpose of drawing a shape. Ordinarily, if no coordinate transformation is specified, the origin is taken to be the upper left corner of the widget (excluding the space occupied by the title bar and the borders); the x direction is taken to increase to the right; and the y direction is taken to increase downwards.

   The default location of the origin and the default directions of the axes can be changed by specifying a 3×3 affine matrix:

   ```
   m11   m12   0

   m21   m22   0

   dx    dy    1
   ```

   In Qt, this matrix defines an object of type QWMatrix. The elements dx and dy control the translation of the origin; the elements m11 and m22 specify the horizontal and the vertical scaling; the elements m12 and m21 specify horizontal and vertical shear; and, provided certain mathematical conditions are satisfied, the elements m11, m12, m21, m22 together control the rotation.

   A QMatrix object may be constructed by directly specifying all the elements, as in

   ```
   QWmatrix matrix;                                    //(A)
   matrix.setMatrix( 1.0, 0.0, 0.0, 1.0, 0.0, 0.0 );   //(B)
   ```

for specifying what's knows as the *identity transformation*, which leaves the coordinate frame unchanged. The order of appearance of the arguments in the call to setMatrix is m11, m12, m21, m22, dx, and dy. However, in most situations, it is more convenient to set the coordinate transformation by invoking translate, rotate, scale, and so on, on a QWMatrix object:

```
QWMatrix matrix;
matrix.translate( 150, 0 );                        //(C)
matrix.rotate( (float)3*10 );                      //(D)
painter.setWorldMatrix( matrix );                  //(E)
```

As one would expect, translate shifts the origin along the *x* and the *y* directions by the number of pixels that are supplied to it as arguments. In the code snippet shown, the origin will be shifted by 150 pixels along *x* and none along *y*. Similarly, rotate rotates the coordinate frame in a clockwise direction by the number of degrees supplied to it as argument. After a QWMatrix object is given values either directly by invoking setMatrix, or indirectly by the invocations of translate, rotate, and scale as shown, the QPainter object in charge of rendering in the window must be informed of the new coordinate transformation by calling setWorldMatrix, as we do in line (E) above.

After the coordinate frame used by the QPainter object is transformed, any invocations of a "draw" function would be in the new coordinate frame. For example, if we invoke

```
painter.drawRect( 10, 10, 100, 50 );               //(F)
```

the first two arguments to drawRect, which stand for the pixel coordinates of the upper left corner of the rectangle, will be interpreted with respect to the new coordinate frame. The next two arguments, for the width and the height of the rectangle, will now be the width along the new *x* axis and the height along the new *y* axis.

After one or more transformations, it sometimes becomes necessary to reset the coordinate frame to its default. As we show in line (T) in the example code below, this can be achieved by invoking reset on the QWMatrix object. This can also be achieved by invoking setMatrix with values corresponding to the identity matrix. This latter approach is shown commented out after the line labeled (T).

2. **The Fill Pattern:** The fill pattern refers to how to display the interior of a shape. The interior of a shape could be rendered with a solid color, or with some sort of shading or hatching, or it could be left blank to show the background pixels. A fill pattern is specified by constructing a QBrush object and then informing the painter of that fact, as in

```
QBrush b3( Qt::red, Qt::Dense2Pattern );           //(G)
painter.setBrush( b3 );                            //(H)
```

This tells the `QPainter` object, `painter`, that the brush to use for the interior of a shape is the b3 object. That would cause the interior to be dotted red, the dot density being 20%.[31] Lines (P1) through (P5) of the program below show five different fill pattern specifications.

3. The Border: The border of a shape can be drawn in different styles by invoking setPen on the painter object, as in line (Q) of the program. Ordinarily, a one-pixel thick border consisting of a solid line is drawn, but that can be changed by giving appropriate arguments to `setPen`.

Shown below is a Qt example that renders a sampling of shapes and an image:

```
//RenderGraphics.cc

#include <qwidget.h>
#include <qpainter.h>
#include <qapplication.h>
#include <qpixmap.h>

class RenderGraphicsWidget : public QWidget {              //(I)
public:
    RenderGraphicsWidget();                                //(J)
protected:
    void   paintEvent( QPaintEvent * );                    //(K)
};

RenderGraphicsWidget::RenderGraphicsWidget() {             //(L)
    setCaption( "Render Graphics with Qt" );
    setBackgroundColor( white );
}

void RenderGraphicsWidget::paintEvent( QPaintEvent* ) {    //(M)
    QWMatrix matrix;                                       //(N)
    QPainter painter( this );                              //(O)

    QBrush b1( Qt::NoBrush );                              //(P1)
    QBrush b2( Qt::magenta );                              //(P2)
```

---

[31]The class Qt serves as a repository of identifiers that are needed on a global basis by the Qt toolkit. For example, via the header file `namespace.h`, the class Qt makes available the identifiers `black`, `white`, `darkGray`, `gray`, `lightGray`, `red`, `green`, `blue`, `cyan`, `magenta`, `yellow`, `darkRed`, `darkGreen`, `darkBlue`, `darkCyan`, `darkMagenta`, `darkYellow`, and so on, for convenient-to-use color names. Of course, one can also specify an arbitrary color by constructing a `QColor` object. The identifiers made available in a similar manner for brush styles include `NoBrush`, `Dense1Pattern`, `Dense2Pattern`, ..., `Dense7Pattern`, `Crosspattern`, and so on, where the middle numeral in the dense pattern name refers to the fill density of the dots. For specifying the border of a shape, the class Qt makes available the identifiers `NoPen`, `SolidLine`, `DashLine`, `DotLine`, `DashDotLine`, and so on.

```
    QBrush b3( Qt::red, Qt::Dense2Pattern );                    //(P3)
    QBrush b4( Qt::blue, Qt::Dense7Pattern );                   //(P4)
    QBrush b5( Qt::CrossPattern );                              //(P5)

    painter.setPen( Qt::red );                                  //(Q)
    painter.setBrush( b1 );                                     //(R)
    painter.drawRect( 10, 10, 100, 50 );                        //(S)

    matrix.translate( 150, 0 );
    matrix.rotate( (float)3*10 );
    painter.setWorldMatrix( matrix );
    painter.setBrush( b2 );
    painter.drawRoundRect( 10, 10, 100, 50, 30, 30 );

    matrix.rotate( - (float)3*10 );
    matrix.translate( - 150, -30 );
    matrix.shear( 0.8, 0.2 );
    painter.setWorldMatrix( matrix );
    painter.setBrush( b3 );
    painter.drawRect( 250, 0, 100, 50 );

    matrix.reset();                                             //(T)
    //  matrix.setMatrix( 1.0, 0.0, 0.0, 1.0, 0.0, 0.0 );
    painter.setWorldMatrix( matrix );
    painter.setBrush( b4 );
    painter.drawRect( 10, 200, 100, 50 );

    painter.setBrush( b5 );
    painter.drawEllipse( 130, 200, 100, 50 );

    painter.setPen( Qt::NoPen );
    QPixmap pix( "allthatjazz.xpm" );
    pix.resize( 100, 50 );
    painter.drawPixmap( 260, 200, pix );

    int y = 300;
    painter.setWorldMatrix( matrix );
    QFont font( "Times", 18 );
    painter.setFont( font );
    QFontMetrics fm = painter.fontMetrics();
    y += fm.ascent();
    painter.drawText( 70, y,
                    "Graphics rendered using QPainter methods" );
}

int main( int argc, char **argv )
{
    QApplication app( argc, argv );
    RenderGraphicsWidget drawdemo;
```

```
      drawdemo.setGeometry( 200, 200, 450, 400 );
      app.setMainWidget( &drawdemo );
      drawdemo.show();
      return app.exec();
}
```

This program can be compiled with the following command line

```
    g++ -o RenderGraphics RenderGraphics.cc -I$QTDIR/include      \
                          -L$QTDIR/lib -lqt
```

The window produced by this program is shown in Figure 17.38.

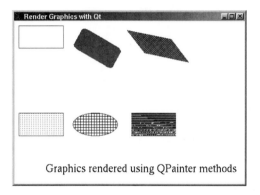

Fig. 17.38

Our next example shows how low-level mouse events can be put to use for free-form sketching. An event of type MouseEvent occurs when a button is pressed or released inside a widget or when the mouse cursor is moved. When such an event occurs, the following virtual and protected functions of the QWidget class are automatically invoked:

```
    mousePressEvent( MouseEvent* )

    mouseReleaseEvent( MouseEvent* )

    mouseDoubleClickEvent( MouseEvent* )

    mouseMoveEvent( MouseEvent* )
```

By providing override definitions for one or more of these functions in your own extension of the QWidget class you can put the mouse to use for various graphics-related activities — sketching, for example.

In the following program, the user clicks the mouse at different points in a window and, when the user double clicks, the points are joined together by straight lines in the order in which they were clicked, forming a polyline. As the user clicks away, the coordinates of the mouse cursor are retrieved in the `mousePressEvent` function in line (V) by invoking pos on the `MouseEvent` object that is the argument of the function. The pos function returns an object of type `QPoint`, which is basically a pairing of the *x* and the *y* coordinates of a point, the coordinates being measured relative to the upper left corner of the widget that receives the mouse event.

When the user double-clicks the mouse, note how we force a paint event by invoking repaint in line (W). The occurrence of this event triggers the automatic invocation of the event handler `paintEvent` of line (U), which causes the sketch to be displayed.

```
//Sketch.cc

#include <qapplication.h>
#include <qpainter.h>
#include <qwidget.h>

const int MAXPOINTS = 200;

class SketchWidget : public QWidget {
public:
    SketchWidget( QWidget *parent=0, const char *name=0 );
    ~SketchWidget();
protected:
    void        paintEvent( QPaintEvent * );
    void        mousePressEvent( QMouseEvent *);
    void        mouseDoubleClickEvent( QMouseEvent* );
private:
    QPoint      *points;
    int         count;
};

SketchWidget::SketchWidget( QWidget *parent, const char *name )
    : QWidget( parent, name ) {
    setBackgroundColor( white );
    count = 0;
    points = new QPoint[MAXPOINTS];
}

SketchWidget::~SketchWidget() {
    delete[] points;
}
```

```
void SketchWidget::paintEvent( QPaintEvent* ) {                    //(U)
    QPainter paint( this );
    for ( int i=0; i<count - 2; i++ ) {
        paint.drawLine( points[i], points[ i + 1 ] );
    }
}

void SketchWidget::mousePressEvent( QMouseEvent* mouse ) {         //(V)
    points[count++] = mouse->pos();
}

void SketchWidget::mouseDoubleClickEvent( QMouseEvent* mouse ) {
    points[count++] = mouse->pos();
    repaint();                                                     //(W)
}

int main( int argc, char* argv[] )
{
    QApplication app( argc, argv );

    SketchWidget* sketchWidget = new SketchWidget();
    sketchWidget->setGeometry( 200, 200, 200, 200 );
    sketchWidget->show();
    app.setMainWidget( sketchWidget );
    return app.exec();
}
```

This program can be compiled with the following command line

```
g++ -o Sketch Sketch.cc -I$QTDIR/include -L$QTDIR/lib -lqt
```

Figure 17.39 shows a sample sketch in a window created by this program.

Fig. 17.39

17.21 DRAWING SHAPES, TEXT, AND IMAGES IN GNOME/GTK+

Graphics programming in GNOME/GTK+ is done with the help of the GnomeCanvas widget. This widget knows how to display the items that are supplied to its container widget, which is an object of type GnomeCanvasGroup. One first constructs a canvas object and then retrieves its container widget by

```
GtkWidget* canvas;                                        //(A)
GnomeCanvasGroup* rootGroup;                              //(B)
...
...
canvas = gnome_canvas_new();                             //(C)
rootGroup = gnome_canvas_root( GNOME_CANVAS( canvas ) ); //(D)
```

where rootGroup is the container widget for the canvas object constructed in line (C). A graphics object, such as a shape, can then be added to the container widget by

```
item = gnome_canvas_item_new( rootGroup,                  //(E1)
                        gnome_canvas_rect_get_type(),      //(E2)
                        // now specify values for the
                        // attributes of a rectangular
                        // shape
        );
```

where the invocation gnome_canvas_item_new in line (E1) causes a graphics item to be added to the rootGroup, the type of the item determined by the second argument (in line (E2)), and its various properties — such as the location, the fill pattern, the type of border — by the rest of the arguments.[32]

Typically, after creating a GnomeCanvas object, you would set its width and height and declare the location of the origin and the size of the viewable area through invocations such as

```
...
canvas = gnome_canvas_new();
gtk_widget_set_usize( canvas, WIDTH, HEIGHT );            //(F)
gnome_canvas_set_scroll_region( GNOME_CANVAS( canvas ),   //(G1)
                        0.0,                               //(G2)
                        0.0,                               //(G3)
                        WIDTH,                             //(G4)
                        HEIGHT );                          //(G5)
...
```

---

[32]An item in a grouping, such as the rootGroup above, can be another group. In this fashion, one can create of a hierarchical arrangement of groups of graphics objects. Each group in such a hierarchy can be manipulated as a unit.

In this case, the viewable area, as set by `gnome_canvas_set_scroll_region`, in line (G1) fills the entire canvas. However, in general, by making the viewable area smaller than the canvas, one can create and manipulate a large graphics object even though only a portion of the object can be seen at a time. Through the arguments in lines (G2) through (G5), the above declaration also sets the origin at the upper left corner of the viewable area; the location coordinates specified for the graphics items are with respect to this origin. Sometimes it is more convenient to place the origin at the center of the viewable area, which can be done by the following statements:

```
...
canvas = gnome_canvas_new();
gtk_widget_set_usize( canvas, WIDTH, HEIGHT );
gnome_canvas_set_scroll_region( GNOME_CANVAS( canvas ),
                                -WIDTH/2,
                                -HEIGHT/2,
                                WIDTH/2,
                                HEIGHT/2 );
...
```

The following example places on a canvas a filled rectangle in line (H1), an ellipse in line (I1), a hollow rectangle in line (J), a text string in line (K1), an image in line (L), and a rotated polygon in line (N1). The statements that create each of these items are mostly self-explaining. The four coordinate values supplied to the rectangle item in lines (H2) through (H6) specify the coordinates of the top left corner and the bottom right corner. The four coordinates values supplied to the ellipse item in lines (I2) through (I6) do the same for the minimum bounding rectangle of the ellipse. An unfilled shape can be obtained by leaving out the specification of the `fill_color` field, as we do for the rectangle in line (J).

For the text string item in line (K1), the exact positioning of the string in relation to the coordinates specified by the ''x'' and the ''y'' fields in lines (K6) and (K7) is controlled by the symbolic constant value of the ''anchor'' field in line (K9). For the value shown, `GTK_ANCHOR_W`, the west end (meaning, the left end) of the string will coincide with the pixel coordinates (20, 100).[33]

An image is displayed in a canvas by first creating a `GdkImlibImage` object from the pixel data file. In line (L) of the program, we refer to an XPM image[34] which consists of a string array named `allthatjazz`. This array is supplied by the file

---

[33] Other possible values for the ''anchor'' field are `GTK_ANCHOR_E`, `GTK_ANCHOR_CENTER`, `GTK_ANCHOR_N`, `GTK_ANCHOR_S`, `GTK_ANCHOR_NE`, `GTK_ANCHOR_NW`, `GTK_ANCHOR_SE`, and `GTK_ANCHOR_SW` with obvious meanings.

[34] XPM stands for X PixMap. An XPM stores a color image using an ASCII character based format — very much like what XBM does for black-and-white images. XPM allows you to define symbolic names for the colors needed in an image. More precisely, an XPM file is an array of strings. The name of this array is the argument to the `gdk_imlib_create_image_from_xpm_data` function. Since all the information in an XPM file is contained in a C-legal data structure — an array — an XPM file can be #included in a C program, as we have done in the example here.

allthatjazz.xpm that is pulled into the program through an include declaration at the beginning. The image object thus created can then be rendered by a call shown in lines (M1) through (M9).

As was the case with the text item, the exact positioning of a rendered image in relation to the coordinates supplied to the fields ''x'' and ''y'' is controlled by the value of the field ''anchor''. With the value GTK_ANCHOR_W, the left edge of the image will have its middle pixel at the coordinates (200, 200).

The last item placed on the canvas consists of a polygon item created in line (N1). A general polygon is supplied as an array of GnomeCanvasPoints to the ''points'' field. As shown in line (N3), this array is constructed by a call to the function makePolygon that is defined in line (S).

We have used the polygon item to also illustrate how affine transformations can be specified in GNOME/GTK+. As was the case with Qt, a 3×3 affine transformation matrix is specified by constructing an array of its six elements m11, m12, m21, m22, dx, and dy, where m11 and m22 control scale; m11, m12, m21 and m22 together control rotation provided certain constraints are satisfied by the four numbers; and where dx and dy control the translation of the origin. The easiest way to specify an affine transform in GNOME/GTK+ is to first declare an array of six doubles and to then specify the rotations, translations, or scale, as needed:

```
double affine[6];
...
item = ....;
art_affine_rotate( affine, 45.0 );
gnome_canvas_item_affine_relative( item, affine );
art_affine_translate( affine, 400, 250 );
gnome_canvas_item_affine_relative( item, affine );
```

These statements would cause the graphical item item to rotate by 45 degrees clockwise around the origin of the viewable area and to then get translated by 400 pixels horizontally and 250 pixels vertically. The statements in lines (O) through (R) of the program create this rotation and translation for the polygon item of line (N1).

```
//RenderGraphics.c

#include <gnome.h>
#include "allthatjazz.xpm"

gint eventDestroy( GtkWidget* widget, GdkEvent* event, gpointer data );
GnomeCanvasPoints* makePolygon( gint h, gint v );

#define HORIZ 100
#define VERT 50
#define WIDTH 550
#define HEIGHT 400
```

```
double affine[6];

int main( int argc, char* argv[] )
{
    GtkWidget* app;
    GtkWidget* canvas;
    GnomeCanvasGroup* rootGroup;
    GnomeCanvasItem* item;
    GdkImlibImage* image;

    gnome_init( "Graphics Demo", "1.0", argc, argv );
    app = gnome_app_new( "canvasorder", "Gnome Canvas Order" );
    gtk_signal_connect( GTK_OBJECT( app ),
                        "destroy",
                        GTK_SIGNAL_FUNC( eventDestroy ),
                        NULL );

    canvas = gnome_canvas_new();
    gtk_widget_set_usize( canvas, WIDTH, HEIGHT );
    gnome_canvas_set_scroll_region( GNOME_CANVAS( canvas ),
                                    0.0,
                                    0.0,
                                    WIDTH,
                                    HEIGHT );
    rootGroup = gnome_canvas_root( GNOME_CANVAS( canvas ) );
    gnome_app_set_contents( GNOME_APP( app ), canvas );

    item = gnome_canvas_item_new( rootGroup,                     //(H1)
                                  gnome_canvas_rect_get_type(),  //(H2)
                                  "x1", (double) ( 20 ),         //(H3)
                                  "y1", (double) ( 20 ),         //(H4)
                                  "x2", (double) ( 20 + HORIZ ), //(H5)
                                  "y2", (double) ( 20 + VERT ),  //(H6)
                                  "fill_color", "red",           //(H7)
                                  "outline_color", "black",      //(H8)
                                  NULL );                        //(H9)
    item = gnome_canvas_item_new( rootGroup,                     //(I1)
                                  gnome_canvas_ellipse_get_type(),//(I2)
                                  "x1", (double) ( 220 ),        //(I3)
                                  "y1", (double) ( 20 ),         //(I4)
                                  "x2", (double) ( 220 + HORIZ ),//(I5)
                                  "y2", (double) ( 20 + VERT ),  //(I6)
                                  "fill_color", "blue",          //(I7)
                                  "outline_color", "black",      //(I8)
                                  NULL );                        //(I9)
    item = gnome_canvas_item_new( rootGroup,                     //(J)
                                  gnome_canvas_rect_get_type(),
                                  "x1", (double) 400,
                                  "y1", (double) 20,
```

```
                                    "x2", (double) 400 + HORIZ,
                                    "y2", (double) 20 + VERT,
                                    "outline_color", "white",
                                    NULL );
        item = gnome_canvas_item_new( rootGroup,                      //(K1)
                                    gnome_canvas_text_get_type(),   //(K2)
                                    "text", "The hungry brown fox"  //(K3)
                                    " jumped over a lazy dog.",      //(K4)
                                    "font", "12x24",                 //(K5)
                                    "x", (double) 20,                //(K6)
                                    "y", (double) 100,               //(K7)
                                    "fill_color", "magenta",         //(K8)
                                    "anchor", GTK_ANCHOR_W,          //(K9)
                                    NULL );                          //(K10)
        image = gdk_imlib_create_image_from_xpm_data( allthatjazz );  //(L)
        item = gnome_canvas_item_new( rootGroup,                      //(M1)
                                    gnome_canvas_image_get_type(),  //(M2)
                                    "image", image,                  //(M3)
                                    "x", (double) 20,                //(M4)
                                    "y", (double) 250,               //(M5)
                                    "width", (double) 200,           //(M6)
                                    "height", (double) 200,          //(M7)
                                    "anchor", GTK_ANCHOR_W,          //(M8)
                                    NULL );                          //(M9)
        item = gnome_canvas_item_new( rootGroup,                      //(N1)
                                    gnome_canvas_polygon_get_type(),//(N2)
                                    "points", makePolygon( 50, 50 ),//(N3)
                                    "fill_color", "red",             //(N4)
                                    "outline_color", "black",        //(N5)
                                    NULL );                          //(N6)
        art_affine_rotate( affine, 45.0 );                           //(O)
        gnome_canvas_item_affine_relative( item, affine );           //(P)
        art_affine_translate( affine, 400, 250 );                    //(Q)
        gnome_canvas_item_affine_relative( item, affine );           //(R)

        gtk_widget_show_all( app );
        gtk_main();
        gdk_imlib_destroy_image( image );
        exit( 0 );
}

gint eventDestroy(GtkWidget* widget, GdkEvent* event, gpointer data) {
        gtk_main_quit();
        return 0;
}

GnomeCanvasPoints* makePolygon( gint h, gint v ) {                    //(S)
        int i;
        GnomeCanvasPoints* points;
```

```
        static const gint xy[ 10 ] = {-1,-1, 1,-1,1,1,-1,1,-1,-1};
        points = gnome_canvas_points_new( 5 );
        for ( i=0; i < 10; i += 2 ) {
            points->coords[i] = ( xy[i] * h );
            points->coords[i + 1] = ( xy[i + 1] * v );
        }
        return points;
}
```

The executable for this code can be generated by the following makefile

```
#Makefile_GTK_RenderGraphics

CC=gcc
LDLIBS='gnome-config --libs gnomeui'
CFLAGS=-Wall -g 'gnome-config --cflags gnomeui'

RenderGraphics:  RenderGraphics.o Makefile_gtk_RenderGraphics
        $(CC) RenderGraphics.o $(LDLIBS) -o RenderGraphics

RenderGraphics.o: RenderGraphics.c
        $(CC) $(CFLAGS) -c RenderGraphics.c

clean:
        rm -f RenderGraphics
        rm -f RenderGraphics.o
```

The program produces the output shown in Figure 17.40.

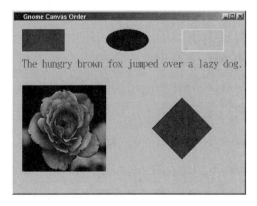

Fig. 17.40

Our next program will show how to trap the mouse events for a rudimentary free-form sketching program in GNOME/GTK+. The mouse events are of the following types in GNOME/GTK+:

```
GDK_BUTTON_PRESS          Mouse button pressed
GDK_2BUTTON_PRESS         Double-click any mouse button
GDK_3BUTTON_PRESS         Triple-click any mouse button
GDK_BUTTON_RELEASE        Mouse button released
GDK_DRAG_ENTER            A dragging mouse entered window
GDK_DRAG_LEAVE            A dragging mouse left the window
GDK_DRAG_MOTION           A dragging mouse moved within window
GDK_MOTION_NOTIFY         Mouse moved
```

Of these, our program would need to capture and process only the events GDK_BUTTON_PRESS and GTK_2BUTTON_PRESS since, like in the earlier Qt program, we wish to use one click to record the location of the mouse cursor in the window and a double-click to show a polyline connecting all the points recorded so far.[35] The occurrence of any mouse event generates the signal event. So, in line (T) of the program below, we connect this signal with our event processing function canvasEvent as shown here:

```
gtk_signal_connect( GTK_OBJECT(canvas), "event",
                    GTK_SIGNAL_FUNC( canvasEvent ), NULL );
```

As for the event processing function itself, its header looks like

```
gboolean canvasEvent(GtkWidget* widget, GdkEventButton* eventButton);
```

If we had wanted to capture other mouse events, such as those related to the motion and the dragging of the mouse, to whether or not the mouse cursor was inside the window, and so on, the parameter would be of type GdkEvent*. But since we are only interested in mouse button action here, making it of type GdkEventButton* is sufficient.

The switch block inside the callback function in line (U) checks the type of the GdkEventButton object received by the function for the following types: GDK_BUTTON_PRESS, GDK_2BUTTON_PRESS, and GDK_3BUTTON_PRESS. For each of these cases, the callback function tries to determine the identity of the button pressed by testing the value of the button field, as in

```
GdkEventButton* eventButton;
...
if ( eventButton->button == 1 )
    ...
```

---

[35]We should mention that a GnomeCanvas widget has the ability to pass those mouse events to the graphics items it contains that have the *x* and the *y* coordinate information associated with them. This makes it possible to write callback functions for the graphical items displayed in a window. Such functions can be used, for example, to drag a graphics item in the window.

The button equals 1 for the left button, 2 for the middle button, and 3 for the right button.

In lines (V2) and (V3), the x and the y fields of a button action event return the two coordinates of the mouse cursor at the moment the event was generated. The program below stores away these coordinates in the array points, which is of type GnomeCanvasPoints*. When the user double-clicks the left button, this array is copied over into another array of the same type, but whose size equals the number of points entered by the user. This copying over is done by the function makePolyline in line (X). Double-clicking also causes the points to be joined by a segmented straight line by the invocation of gnome_canvas_line_get_type in line (W).

```
//Sketch.c

#include <gnome.h>

#define WIDTH 400
#define HEIGHT 300

int pointIndex = 0;
GnomeCanvasPoints* points;
GtkWidget *canvas;
GnomeCanvasGroup* rootGroup;
GnomeCanvasItem* item;

gint eventDestroy(GtkWidget *widget, GdkEvent *event,gpointer data);
gboolean canvasEvent(GtkWidget *widget, GdkEventButton* event );
GnomeCanvasPoints* makePolyline();

int main(int argc,char *argv[])
{
    GtkWidget *app;
    gnome_init("Sketch","1.0",argc,argv);
    app = gnome_app_new("sketch", "Make a free-form sketch");

    gtk_signal_connect(GTK_OBJECT(app),"destroy",
                            GTK_SIGNAL_FUNC(eventDestroy),NULL);
    points = gnome_canvas_points_new( 1000 );
    canvas = gnome_canvas_new();
    gtk_widget_set_usize(canvas,WIDTH,HEIGHT);
    gnome_canvas_set_scroll_region( GNOME_CANVAS( canvas ),
                                    0.0,
                                    0.0,
                                    WIDTH,
                                    HEIGHT );
    rootGroup = gnome_canvas_root( GNOME_CANVAS( canvas ) );
    gnome_app_set_contents( GNOME_APP(app), canvas );
```

```
        gtk_signal_connect( GTK_OBJECT(canvas), "event",              //(T)
                            GTK_SIGNAL_FUNC( canvasEvent ), NULL );
        gtk_widget_show_all(app);
        gtk_main();
        exit(0);
}

gboolean canvasEvent(GtkWidget* widget, GdkEventButton* eventButton) {
        gint xpoint;
        gint ypoint;

        switch( eventButton->type ) {                                 //(U)
            case GDK_BUTTON_PRESS:
                if ( eventButton->button == 1 ) {                     //(V1)
                    xpoint = eventButton->x;                          //(V2)
                    ypoint = eventButton->y;                          //(V3)
                    points->coords[ pointIndex ] = xpoint;           //(V4)
                    points->coords[ pointIndex + 1] = ypoint;        //(V5)
                    pointIndex += 2;
                }
                break;
            case GDK_2BUTTON_PRESS:
                if ( eventButton->button == 1 ) {
                    item = gnome_canvas_item_new( rootGroup,
                                    gnome_canvas_line_get_type(),    //(W)
                                    "points", makePolyline(),
                                    "fill_color", "red",
                                    "width_pixels", 4,
                                    NULL );
                }
                break;
            case GDK_3BUTTON_PRESS:
                if ( eventButton->button == 2 ) {
                    gnome_canvas_points_free( points );
                    exit(0);
                }
                break;
            default:
                break;
        }
        return(TRUE);
}

gint eventDestroy( GtkWidget* widget, GdkEvent* event, gpointer data){
        gtk_main_quit();
        gnome_canvas_points_free( points );
        return(0);
}
```

```
GnomeCanvasPoints* makePolyline() {                                //(X)
    int i;
    int N = pointIndex/2 - 1;
    GnomeCanvasPoints* newPoints = gnome_canvas_points_new( N );
    for ( i = 0; i < pointIndex - 2; i++ )
        newPoints->coords[ i ] = points->coords[ i ];
    return newPoints;
}
```

The following make file can be used to create an executable for this program:

```
CC=gcc
LDLIBS=`gnome-config --libs gnomeui`
CFLAGS=-Wall -g `gnome-config --cflags gnomeui`

Sketch:   Sketch.o Makefile_Sketch
          $(CC) Sketch.o $(LDLIBS) -o Sketch

Sketch.o: Sketch.c
          $(CC) $(CFLAGS) -c Sketch.c

clean:
          rm -f Sketch
          rm -f Sketch.o
```

Figure 17.41 shows the GUI for this program and a partial sketch made on it.

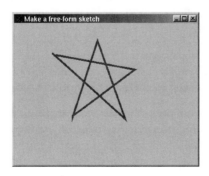

Fig. 17.41

17.22   JAVA APPLETS

A JApplet in Swing and an Applet in AWT are graphical objects that can be embedded in a web page and viewed at a remote site when a web browser points to the web page. Practically any graphical application in Java can be converted into an applet. While a generic web page shows mostly textual information and images, you can use applets to show animated clips, play sound files, and so on, and, to elicit information from the viewer of a web page. When an applet is used for displaying animated clips or playing sound files, the computing that is required for doing so is carried out on the local machine where the web page is viewed. Since such computing may require access to other Java classes (for example, the math classes that are often needed for graphical rendering and animation of 3D scenes) and system resources on the local machine, an important issue concerning applets is security regarding the level of access available to an applet.

That a graphical application in Java, written for command line execution, can be converted very simply into an applet is a consequence of the fact that Applet is a subclass of the AWT class Panel and the Swing class JApplet is a subclass of Applet. That makes an applet an AWT/Swing component, just like a button, a text area, and so on, with the difference that an applet is meant to be executed by a special version of the Java Virtual Machine that is embedded in a Java-enabled web browser. The reason that a special version of JVM is needed for executing applets is because, unlike regular AWT/Swing classes, an applet should be executable without the function main and because of the security issues that surround the invocation of applets.

There are basically four steps to go through to convert a graphical application that is invoked from a command line into an applet that is invoked automatically by a web browser at a remote workstation:

1. Change the header of the class so that the class now extends JApplet or Applet as opposed to, say, JFrame or Frame. If you plan to use Swing components in your applet, you must extend JApplet.

2. The code that was in the constructor is now placed in init. What a constructor does for a regular Java graphical program, init does for an applet — it carries out the initializations needed when the applet is first loaded in.

3. Eliminate the function main.[36] The work that was done by main now gets distributed. The job of creating a frame object in main is now carried out implicitly by the web browser. The sizing as established by the invocation

---

[36]Actually, it is not even necessary to eliminate main, but in general it would need to be modified. Later we will see how by embedding a suitable main inside an applet, we can use the same program as a graphical application that can be invoked from a command line and as an applet that would be viewable from a remote workstation through a web browser.

of setSize is now taken care of by assigning values to the WIDTH and the HEIGHT fields of the APPLET tag in an associated HTML file that we will discuss shortly. The location of the display on the screen, as established by the invocation of setLocation, is now left to the discretion of the web browser, determined mostly by the value of the ALIGN field of the APPLET tag in the HTML file.

4. Declare the applet class public so that the program that runs the applet, which will either be a browser JVM or the appletviewer tool, can access it.

17.22.1   Life Cycle of an Applet

The Applet class provides the following methods that can be used to control the different phases of an applet:

```
init()
start()
stop()
destroy()
```

As mentioned before, the init method is used to carry out the sort of initializations for an applet that a constructor carries out for an AWT/Swing application. The other three methods become important when an applet is used for displaying animation or for playing a sound file, activities that require continuous computations.

The start method is called automatically after the init method. It is also called automatically whenever a user revisits the page containing the applet. The start method is therefore useful for starting, for example, animation threads after they have been initialized by the init method.[37]

If an applet needs a start method, in most situations it would also need a stop method. The stop is invoked automatically if the applet becomes invisible for some reason, such as when it is iconified or when the user goes off to another web page. The stop methods can therefore be used for suspending the threads of computations needed for animation, sounds, and so on. When the applet is made visible again, the start method will again be automatically invoked to restart the suspended threads. There is almost never a reason to invoke the stop method directly. That is, its invocation is at the discretion of the browser.

The destroy method is invoked automatically when the browser gets ready to shut down normally. For most applets you would not need to override the destroy method since the stop method that will always be invoked prior to the destroy method would have stopped the execution of the applet anyway. This method has been provided in case an applet needs to free up other system resources.

---

[37]In the next chapter we will discuss how to write applets for displaying animation.

17.22.2 The Applet Tag

To embed an applet in a web page, you need to invoke the applet class within the
<APPLET> and </APPLET> HTML tags. As shown below, the <APPLET> tag comes
with a number of attributes, some of which are mandatory and other optional, the
latter kind are shown bracketed:

```
< APPLET
    [CODEBASE = codebaseURL]
    CODE = appletFile
    [ALT = alternateText]
    [NAME = appletInstanceName]
    WIDTH = pixels
    HEIGHT = pixels
    [ALIGN = alignment]
    [VSPACE = pixels]
    [HSPACE = pixels]
>
[< PARAM NAME = appletParameter1 VALUE = value >]
[< PARAM NAME = appletParameter2 VALUE = value >]
. . .
[alternateHTML]
</APPLET>
```

The CODE, WIDTH, and HEIGHT attributes of the <APPLET> tag are mandatory, in the
sense that they must be specified in an HTML file.

Although we have shown all the attributes, such as CODEBASE, CODE, and so on, in
uppercase, they can be in any mixture of uppercase and lowercase. The CODEBASE
attribute can be used to specify the base URL of the applet. By default, the browser
that displays the applet looks for the applet code in the same directory (of the remote
host) that contains the HTML file containing the applet tag. But sometimes it is more
convenient for the applet code to be stored elsewhere. By giving a value to CODEBASE,
you can tell the browser where to find the code for the applet. The value given to
CODEBASE can be either relative or absolute. A relative value is a pathname with
respect to the location of the folder that contains the HTML file. When the value of
CODEBASE is a full http address, it is called absolute. With an absolute value, you
could use an applet situated anywhere on the web in your HTML file.

When the applet code is in the same directory as the HTML file that invokes it,
the value of the required attribute CODE is just the name of the applet class. However,
if the applet code is in some other directory, the value of the CODE attribute must be
the full pathname to the file containing the applet code. So if your applet class file
is in a subdirectory of the directory containing the HTML file, that fact can be made
known to the browser either via the CODEBASE attribute or via the CODE attribute.
But note that while CODEBASE is allowed to be absolute, making possible retrieval of
applets from virtually anywhere on the web, CODE can only be relative with respect

to the base URL of the applet, meaning the http address of the HTML file invoking the applet.

The optional attribute ALT specifies text that will be displayed if the browser understands the <APPLET> tag but is not equipped to run the Java applet.

The optional attribute NAME can be used to associate a handle with the applet. Such handles permit inter-applet communication between applets running in the same web page.

The required attributes WIDTH and HEIGHT are used to specify in pixels the width and the height of the applet.

The optional attributes ALIGN, VSPACE, and HSPACE work the same way as they do for the <IMG> HTML tag. ALIGN can be used to help the browser decide where to place the applet in relation to the rest of the material on the web page. The various possible values for the ALIGN attribute are: left, right, top, texttop, middle, absmiddle, baseline, bottom, absbottom. The attributes VSPACE and HSPACE control the amount space in pixels to be left above, below, and to the sides of an applet.

The <PARAM> tag can be used to put the same applet program to multiple uses, each with a different set of parameters that characterize different aspects of the information displayed in the applet. For example, the parameters may specify image locations and their sizes, locations and sizes of graphical objects displayed in the applet, URL's of web resources to be downloaded and displayed, and so on. The PARAM tag if used must appear immediately after the APPLET tag. The parameter values are always strings even if they are not specified as strings in the HTML file. The following usage shows how the parameters are interpreted in the applet code:

```
String boxWidthString = getParameter( "BOX_WIDTH" );        //(A)
if ( boxWidthString != null )                               //(B)
    boxWidth = Integer.parseInt( boxWidthString );          //(C)
else boxWidth = 200;                                        //(D)
```

In line (A), the method getParameter gets from the HTML file the value of the parameter BOX_WIDTH. Since the returned value is always a string, it is used to instantiate a String variable boxWidthString. To make sure that a value for this parameter was indeed specified in the HTML file, we compare the value of boxWidthString against null in line (B). If non-null, we convert it into an integer in line (C), which then becomes the value of the variable boxWidth in the applet program. We also provide a default value in line (D) just in case a value for the parameter BOX_WIDTH was not specified in the HTML file.

For browsers that do not understand the <APPLET> tag, it is useful to include some HTML code, referred to by alternateHTML in the syntax specification shown above, to inform the viewer as to the nature of the applet that the browser is not able to display. Java enabled browsers will ignore this additional HTML.

17.22.3   An Applet Example

We will now design an applet that does the following:

1. The applet should display a sequence of images to a user whose browser has invoked the applet at a remote site. The nature of the display should be as if the user was watching a slide show presentation on his/her browser. For that reason, the applet will be called `SlideShowApplet`.

2. Since it can take a while to load all the images into the browser Java Virtual Machine, the applet should display status messages like *"Loading image i"* for different value of i as the ith image is loaded in.

3. The images should be displayed a fixed time interval apart. The time interval between successive images should be a parameter value supplied by the HTML code associated with the applet.

4. If an image is larger than the size of the applet window as specified in the HTML file, then the image should appear with scrollbars so that all parts of the image can be examined.

The program below shows an applet that meets the above specifications. The special features of the program are as follows:

- Use of the `Timer` class to display the images at fixed intervals.

- The loading of images into the program in a separate thread of computation. (What's meant by a separate thread of computation will be made clear in the next chapter.)

- Use of the `ImageIcon` class (as opposed to the `Image` class) for representing the images.

- The use of a `JLabel` as a `Scrollable` object for displaying scrollable images when the image size is larger than the size of the applet window.

In what follows, each of these features will be discussed separately.

In order to show the images at fixed time intervals, the program uses the `Timer` class, the first argument to whose constructor is the time interval between the successive images:

```
Timer timer;                                               //(A1)
....
timer = new Timer( pause, new ActionListener() {           //(A2)
        public void actionPerformed( ActionEvent evt ) {   //(A3)
            ....
            contentPane.repaint();                         //(A4)
        }
    });
timer.setInitialDelay( 0 );                                //(A5)
```

```
timer.setCoalesce(false);                                      //(A6)
....
timer.start();                                                 //(A7)
....
timer.stop();                                                  //(A8)
....
timer.restart();                                               //(A9)
```

The second argument to the `Timer` constructor in line (A2) is an `ActionListener` object whose `actionPerformed` method traps the timing signals issued after every interval equal to the value of pause in milliseconds. Note that pause is the first argument to the constructor invocation in line (A2).

If `contentPane` is the content pane of the applet, then the invocation of `contentPane.repaint` can be used to paint a new image in the applet window at the receipt of a timing signal, as we do in line (A4). The invocations `setInitialDelay` in line (A5) and `setCoalesce` in line (A6) are further initializations of the timer before the timing action is actually started by calling `start`. By default, a timer issues its first timing signal after a delay equal to the value of pause; but the exact moment of this first signal can be controlled by invoking `setInitialDelay`. The invocation `setCoalesce` deals with the situation of multiple pending invocations of `actionPerformed`, corresponding to consecutive timing signals, getting bunched up because the system was too busy to trap each timing signal separately. When the argument to `setCoalesce` is true, all the pending invocations of `actionPerformed` are coalesced into a single call. This is the default behavior. However, when the argument is false, any pending invocations of `actionPerformed` will be processed separately no matter what.

About the other calls shown above, we have already mentioned that the timer is started by invoking `start`, as in line (A7). It is stopped by invoking `stop`, as in line (A8). After stopping, the timer can be restarted by invoking `restart`, as in line (A9). A restart cancels any timing signals between the moment the timer was stopped and the moment it is restarted. After a restart, the first timing signal is issued after the delay specified by `setInitialDelay`.

That brings us to the subject of image loading, which in the program shown below is carried out by the `loadImages` method, defined in the program at line (O). Note how this method is run in a separate thread in `init` in line (M):

```
new Thread() {
    public void run() {
        loadImages();
    }
}.start();
```

The syntax used for creating a new thread of computation will become clear in the next chapter. Suffice it to say here that without running the loading of images in a separate thread, the viewer of the applet may not be able to see the load status messages in the applet window.[38]

The applet program shown below uses the `ImageIcon` class for representing images, as opposed to the `Image` class. As was mentioned earlier in Section 17.9, the advantage of the former is that it automatically uses a `MediaTracker` for image loading. So, unless there is a need to keep track of the progress of loading for each image, it is more efficient to use `ImageIcon` for image representation.

To deal with the requirement that images larger than the applet window show up with scrollbars, the program `SlideShowApplet.java` "paints" each image inside a `JLabel` object. A `JLabel` is a `Scrollable` object, and can therefore be displayed in a `JScrollPane`. Shown below is the part of the applet program that first loads an image into a `JLabel` object and then places the `JLabel` object inside a `JScrollPane` (see line (E)). The images are stored in an `ImageIcon` array called `images` (see program line (I)).

```
ImageIcon[] images[ numImages ];
....
JScrollPane scrollableImage;
....
scrollableImage =
    new JScrollPane( new JLabel( images[ frameIndex - 1 ],
                    JLabel.CENTER ) );
scrollableImage.setPreferredSize( new Dimension( displayWidth,
                                displayHeight - 8 ) );
```

Each scrollable image formed in this manner is painted in the content pane of the applet by the following override definition of the `paintComponent` method (see line (D)):

```
public void paintComponent( Graphics g ) {
    super.paintComponent( g );
    ....
    ....
    if ( scrollableImage != null ) {
        contentPane.removeAll();
        contentPane.add( scrollableImage );
    }
    contentPane.revalidate();
    contentPane.setVisible( true );
    ....
}
```

---

[38]The reason has to do with the priorities accorded to the different threads by a browser JVM. If the applet has to load images in the main thread, then it is a matter of the priority of the main thread vis-à-vis the priority of what's known as the Event Dispatch Thread that we will discuss in detail in the next chapter. The Event Dispatch Thread handles tasks related to the display of information in the applet window and the user interaction with the display.

As you'd expect, the call to removeAll removes the previous image from the content pane of the applet and the call to add inserts the next image. The invocation of revalidate is a request to the layout manager to do its job again with regard to the newly inserted or modified component.

Recall that the paintComponent method will be invoked by the Timer object at the issuance of each timing signal. So all we have to do is to increment image index variable frameIndex to load a fresh image into the content pane. This is done in line (H) of the program.

Finally, the reader should note in the loadImages method in line (L) the syntax of the command used for loading the images from the web site where the applet is posted. The code for this method is reproduced here:

```
public void loadImages() {
    String prefix = dir + "/flower";
    for ( int i = 0; i < numImages; i++ ) {
        ....
        ....
        try {
          images[i] = new ImageIcon( new URL( getCodeBase() +
                                    prefix + (i+1) + ".jpg" ) );
        } catch( MalformedURLException m ) {
            System.out.println(
                "Couldn't create image: badly formed URL" );
        }
    }
    ....
    ....
}
```

Note in particular the invocation:

```
images[i] = new ImageIcon(
            new URL( getCodeBase() + prefix + (i+1) + ".jpg" ) );
```

For command line applications, it is possible to construct an ImageIcon object simply by

```
String imageFileName;
ImageIcon image = new ImageIcon( imageFileName );
```

but an applet needs the more elaborate invocation because the image loader in the web browser JVM must establish a communication link with the site hosting the applet and the associated images. This requires that the ImageIcon constructor be supplied with a URL object containing the network address of the site hosting the applet. The method getCodeBase plays a critical role in this, as it is this method that supplies the base URL to the directory containing the applet web page.

Shown below is the program for the applet:

```java
//SlideShowApplet.java

import javax.swing.*;
import java.awt.*;                  //for Graphics, Color, Dimension, etc.
import java.awt.event.*;
import java.net.*;                  //for URL needed for image loading

public class SlideShowApplet extends JApplet {                      //(B)
    int frameIndex = 0;            //current frame number
    String dir;                    //directory relative to the codebase
    Timer timer;                   //timer for sequencing through images
    int pause;                     //time interval between images
    int numImages;                 //number of images to display
    int width;                     //width of the applet
    int height;                    //height of the applet
    int displayWidth;
    int displayHeight;
    JComponent contentPane;        //the applet's content pane
    ImageIcon images[];            //the images
    boolean finishedLoading = false;
    JLabel statusLabel;
    JScrollPane scrollableImage;
    boolean newFrameAvailable = false;

    public void init() {                                            //(C)
        //Get the applet parameters.
        String at = getParameter("dir");
        dir = (at != null) ? at : "images/slideshow";
        at = getParameter("pause");
        pause = (at != null) ? Integer.valueOf(at).intValue() : 2000;
        at = getParameter("numImages");
        numImages = (at != null) ? Integer.valueOf(at).intValue() : 10;

        width = getWidth();
        height = getHeight();
        displayWidth = width - getInsets().left - getInsets().right;
        displayHeight = height - getInsets().top - getInsets().bottom;

        contentPane = new JPanel() {
            public void paintComponent( Graphics g ) {              //(D)
                super.paintComponent( g );
                if ( finishedLoading && newFrameAvailable ) {
                    scrollableImage =
                        new JScrollPane(
                            new JLabel(
                                images[ frameIndex - 1 ],           //(E)
                                    JLabel.CENTER ) );
```

```
                    scrollableImage.setPreferredSize(
                      new Dimension(
                            displayWidth, displayHeight - 8 ) );
                }
                if ( scrollableImage != null ) {
                    contentPane.removeAll();
                    contentPane.add( scrollableImage );
                }
                contentPane.revalidate();
                contentPane.setVisible( true );
                newFrameAvailable = false;
            }
        };
        contentPane.setBackground(Color.white);              //(F)
        setContentPane(contentPane);

        statusLabel = new JLabel("Loading Images...", JLabel.CENTER);
        statusLabel.setForeground( Color.red );
        contentPane.add(statusLabel);

        timer = new Timer( pause, new ActionListener() {      //(G)
                public void actionPerformed( ActionEvent evt ) {
                    frameIndex++;                             //(H)
                    if ( frameIndex == numImages )
                        frameIndex = 1;
                    newFrameAvailable = true;
                    contentPane.repaint();
                }
        });
        timer.setInitialDelay( 0 );
        timer.setCoalesce(false);

        images = new ImageIcon[numImages];                    //(I)
        new Thread() {                                        //(J)
                public void run() {
                    loadImages();
                }
        }.start();
}

public void start() {                                        //(K)
    if ( finishedLoading )
        timer.restart();
}

public void loadImages() {                                    //(L)
    String prefix = dir + "/flower";
    for ( int i = 0; i < numImages; i++ ) {
        statusLabel.setText( "loading image " + ( i + 1 ) );
```

```
            try {
                images[i] =                                     //(M)
                    new ImageIcon( new URL( getCodeBase() +
                                       prefix + (i+1) + ".jpg" ) );
            } catch( MalformedURLException m ) {
                System.out.println(
                        "Couldn't create image: badly formed URL" );
            }
        }
        finishedLoading = true;
        statusLabel.setText( null );
        timer.start();
    }

    public void stop() {                                        //(N)
        timer.stop();
    }

    public String getAppletInfo() {                             //(O)
        return "Title: A SlideShow Applet\n";
    }

    public String[][] getParameterInfo() {                      //(P)
        String[][] info = {
            {"dir",
             "String",
             "the directory containing the images to loop"},
            {"pause",
             "int",
             "the time interval between successive frames"},
            {"numImages",
             "int",
             "the number of images to display; default is 10 " },
        };
        return info;
    }
}
```

The applet shown above also includes code for the methods getAppletInfo in line (O) and getParameterInfo in line (P). Presumably, browsers of the future will use the former for giving the viewer a brief description of what the applet does and the latter for helping the viewer set interactively the values of the various applet parameters.

To embed this applet in a web page, we need to invoke the SlideShowApplet class within the <APPLET> and /APPLET> HTML tags as shown by the HTML code below. This code is placed in file that is conveniently named SlideShowApplet.html:

```
<!DOCTYPE HTML PUBLIC "-//W3C//DTD HTML 3.2//EN">
<html>
<head>
<title>Run Slide Show</title>

<body>
<APPLET  CODE = "SlideShowApplet.class"  WIDTH = "600" HEIGHT = "500" >
<PARAM NAME = "numImages" VALUE ="21">
<PARAM NAME = "pause" VALUE ="8000">
<PARAM NAME = "dir" VALUE ="images/slideshow">
Your browser is completely ignoring the &lt;APPLET&gt; tag!
</APPLET>

</body>
</html>
```

If you move the code compiled from the `SlideShowApplet.java` file and the `SlideShowApplet.html` file into a directory available for HTTP access, a remote user downloading the `SlideShowApplet.html` page would be able to watch the slide show.[39] However, for code development, it is more convenient to use the *appletviewer* tool for testing applets on your local machine without having to invoke them through a web browser. To use the appletviewer for the above example, we'd say

```
appletviewer SlideShowApplet.html
```

The window created by the applet with one of the images displayed therein is shown in Figure 17.42.

---

[39]The reader should note that many browsers were not Swing-enabled as of the middle of 2002. For obvious reasons, downloading and executing a `JApplet` can be a problem for users of such browsers. There are two options to deal with this situation: Either you must create purely AWT-based applets or, for a solution that would work for a vast majority of Netscape Navigator and Microsoft Internet Explorer users, you can get the users to deploy automatically a Java Plug-in to run Swing applets. A Java Plug-in enables a browser to use the Sun's Java 2 JRE (Java Runtime Environment) when encountering an applet, rather than the default JRE that comes with the browser. However, the JRE supplied by a Java Plug-in will only be invoked if the applet is included in an HTML page with the `<OBJECT>` tag for the Internet Explorer browsers and with the `<EMBED>` tag for the Netscape Navigator browsers. Sun provides an HTML converter tool, called HTMLConverter, that automatically converts a regular HTML file with `<APPLET>` tags into a file with both `<OBJECT>` and `<EMBED>` tags so that with the converted HTML file an applet would run on both Netscape Navigator and Internet Explorer browsers.

Fig. 17.42

17.22.4 Dual-Purpose Programming for Applets

It is interesting and useful to note that it is possible to write an applet program in such a way that the same program can be used as an application, executable with the command-line application launcher *java*, and as an applet that would be viewable at a remote workstation through a web browser (or locally with the *appletviewer* tool). Evidently, for command-line invocation, a class must have main since that's the function which is invoked when you execute a class. But one has to be careful when one writes main for a Java program that must serve both as an applet and as a command-line executable graphical application.

In this subsection, we will use the SlideShowApplet.java program of the previous subsection as an example and show how such a program must be modified if it is to run both as an applet and as a standalone command-line executable graphical application.

As we mentioned already, one has to exercise care in writing a main that could be embedded in an applet program so that it can be executed with the *java* tool. For example, it would not work if we added the following main to the code for SlideShowApplet.java:

```
public static void main( String[] args )    // WRONG
{
    SlideShowApplet s = new SlideShowApplet();
    s.setSize( 600, 500 );
    s.setVisible( true );
}
```

That's because a JApplet is merely a Panel and a Panel object cannot be displayed on a terminal unless it is embedded in a JFrame. To get around this difficulty, we must create a JFrame in main, as we do in line (A) below, and then embed the applet panel in the frame, as in line (D):

```
//needed for running SlideShowApplet as a
//stand-alone application
public static void main( String[] args ) {
    JFrame f = new JFrame( "slide show" );                  //(A)
    f.addWindowListener(new WindowAdapter() {
        public void windowClosing(WindowEvent e) {
            System.exit(0);
        }
    });
    Container cPane = f.getContentPane();                   //(B)
    SlideShowApplet slideshow = new SlideShowApplet();     //(C)
    cPane.add( slideshow, BorderLayout.CENTER );           //(D)
    f.pack();
    f.setSize( 600, 500 );
    f.setVisible( true );
}
```

There is also the issue of the constructor: While a graphical application needs a constructor, the work of the constructor will most likely be done by init for an applet. To get around this problem, we can include the following constructor in the code shown for SlideShowApplet.java. Note that the constructor in line (E) calls the init method in line (G). In this manner, the browser JVM can use the code in the init method directly for constructing the applet and the regular JVM will use the constructor.

```
//constructor needed to run SlideShowApplet.java
//as a stand-alone application
public SlideShowApplet() {                                 //(E)
    inApplet = false;                                      //(F)
    init();                                                //(G)
}
```

The boolean variable inApplet that makes its appearance in line (F) is to control the behavior of init in the two separate modes in which it will be invoked — directly by the browser JVM and indirectly by the above constructor in line (G). For the goals of this subsection, the class SlideShowApplet would be defined with this boolean variable default-initialized to true as follows:

```
public class SlideShowApplet extends JApplet {
    boolean inApplet = true;    //needed to switch between
                                //execution as an applet and
                                //as a stand-alone application
    // the rest of the data
    // members the same as
    // before
        .....
```

The following implementation for the new dual-use `init` method should now make sense:

```
public void init() {
    //check if running as an applet
    //or as a stand-alone application
    if ( inApplet ) {                                                   //(H)
        String at = getParameter("dir");
        dir = (at != null) ? at : "images/slideshow";
        at = getParameter("pause");
        pause =
            (at != null) ? Integer.valueOf(at).intValue() : 15000;
        at = getParameter("numImages");
        numImages =
            (at != null) ? Integer.valueOf(at).intValue() : 21;
        width = getWidth();
        height = getHeight();
    }
    else {                                                              //(I)
        dir = "images/slideshow";
        pause = 15000;
        numImages = 21;
        width = 600;
        height = 500;
    }

    // the rest of the code for init() remains the same as before
    ....
    ....
```

So when `init` is called directly by a browser JVM, the `if` block starting in line (H) will be executed. This is the same code that you saw in the beginning section of `init` in `SlideShowApplet.java`. On the other hand, if `init` is called indirectly by the constructor of line (E) above when the class `SlideShowApplet` is executed as a command-line application, it is the `else` block starting in line (I) that will be executed.

The last change we need to make is to the `loadImages` method of `SlideShowApplet.java`. Recall that this method loaded each image into an `ImageIcon` object and that the `ImageIcon` constructor was supplied with the network address of the site hosting the images for the applet. That is obviously unnecessary when the same program is run as a standalone application. Shown below is modified implementation for `loadImages` whose behavior is again controlled by the boolean flag `inApplet`. When the modified `SlideShowApplet.java` is run as an applet, the code in the `if` block starting in line (J) will be executed. And when run as a standalone application, the simpler invocation of the `ImageIcon` constructor in the `else` block in line (K) will be used.

```
public void loadImages() {
    String prefix = dir + "/flower";
    for ( int i = 0; i < numImages; i++ ) {
        statusLabel.setText( "loading image " + ( i + 1 ) );
        //check if running as an applet or
        //as a standalong application:
        if ( inApplet ) {                                    //(J)
            try {
                images[i] = new ImageIcon( new URL( getCodeBase() +
                                         prefix + (i+1) + ".jpg" ) );
            } catch( MalformedURLException m ) {
                System.out.println("badly formed URL" );
            }
        }
        else {                                               //(K)
            images[i] = new ImageIcon( prefix + (i+1) + ".jpg" );
        }
    }
    finishedLoading = true;
    statusLabel.setText( null );
    timer.start();
}
```

With all these changes, the code of SlideShowAppliet.java can be made to run both as an applet and as a standalone command-line graphical application.

17.22.5 The AppletContext Interface

There is an *applet context* of type AppletContext associated with a Java applet. AppletContext is defined as an interface in the java.applet package. The context refers to the document containing the applet. An object of type AppletContext is constructed by invoking the following method that is defined for the class Applet:

```
getAppletContext()
```

The interface AppletContext declares many useful methods that an applet can call to get a list of all the applets referred to in the same web page, to get by name a specific applet in the same web page, to fetch other documents and multi-media information available on the web, and so on.

This subsection shows how an applet can use the AppletContext object to pull in other web pages available on the web. This we will do by designing a frame-based web page that pulls in some of the on-line GUI tutorials. The format of the page will be as shown in Figure 17.43. Each of the three frames of the browser window has a name, shown double-quoted in the figure. In the frame named "top" will go the title of the web page. The frame named "left" will show a list of items, each associated with a URL. The display in the "left" frame will be created by an applet. The applet will respond to double clicks on the items of the list by displaying in the "right" frame the document corresponding to that item.

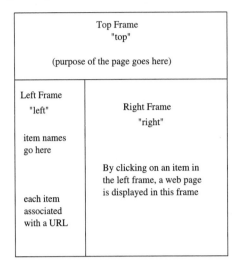

Fig. 17.43

We will first show the HTML code needed to split the web browser window into three frames. We will place this code in a file called GUITutorials.html in an HTTP accessible directory.

```
<!doctype html public "html2.0">
<html>
<head>
<title>Experimental HomePage</title>
<meta name="Author" content="Ehtee Emel">
<meta name="security" content="public">
</head>
<FRAMESET ROWS="90,*">
<FRAME NAME="top" SRC="top.html" MARGINHEIGHT=2
               MARGINWIDTH=2 SCROLLING="no" NORESIZE>
<FRAMESET COLS="180,*">
<FRAME NAME="left" SRC="Left.html" MARGINHEIGHT=2
               MARGINWIDTH=2 SCROLLING="yes" NORESIZE>
<FRAME NAME="right" SRC="Right.html" MARGINHEIGHT=2
               MARGINWIDTH=2 SCROLLING="yes" NORESIZE>
</FRAMESET>
</FRAMESET>
</HTML>
```

Each statement that begins with the tag FRAMESET sets up a division of the web page at that point. For example, the first such statement

```
<FRAMESET ROWS="90,*">
```

says that the rest of the window is to be divided horizontally, with the top portion of height 90 pixels and the bottom portion of height that can be arbitrary. Next, we must declare a name and an HTML file associated with each of these divisions. The statement

```
<FRAME NAME="top" SRC="top.html" MARGINHEIGHT=2
          MARGINWIDTH=2 SCROLLING="no" NORESIZE>
```

says that the top frame of the horizontally divided window will be called "top" and that its contents will be controlled by the file "top.html". What follows are the values for the various parameters of this frame. We can choose whether or not to make this frame scrollable and whether or not to make it resizable.

If all we wanted to do was to divide the browser window into two frames horizontally, the next statement in GUITutorials.html would be similar to the one we just showed, except that it would refer to the bottom portion of the horizontally divided window. But we now want to create a vertical division. This we do with another FRAMESET statement:

```
<FRAMESET COLS="180,*">
```

This statement says that the rest of the window is to be divided vertically into two frames. The left frame will be 180 pixels wide, and the width of the right frame is arbitrary. The next two statements in the GUITutorials.html file do for each of the partitions created by the vertical division what we showed previously for the "top" frame.

As was mentioned before, the purpose of the "top" frame is to show the purpose of the page. So the contents of the file top.html could be something like this:

```
<HTML>
<!--- <body bgcolor="#ffffdd">  ----->
<BODY BGCOLOR="#aadddd">
<font size=4>
<B>Online GUI Tutorials</B>
</font>
<pre>

</pre>
</BODY>
</HTML>
```

By comparison, the file left.html for the "left" frame is a bit more complicated because it must invoke the applet Left.java. The way this HTML file is set up, the GUI tutorial names and their associated URL's are all contained in this file in the form of parameters declared by PARAM tags. For example, the first item we'd like to show in the left frame is "Swing Tutorial". This is our "item_1". Following the declaration of this item, we have another parameter, "url_1", whose value is a web address of where the Swing tutorial is located. We repeat this paired declarations for two more items — for "Qt Tutorial" and for "GTK+ Tutorial." In this manner, all of the items that need to be displayed in the left frame and their associated URL's stay in the HTML file itself.

```
<HTML>
<TITLE>A Trial Applet</TITLE>
<BODY BGCOLOR="#ffffff">
<pre>

</pre>
<font size=2>
<P>
<APPLET CODE="Left.class" WIDTH=180 HEIGHT=480>
<PARAM NAME=item_1 VALUE="Swing Tutorial">
<PARAM NAME=url_1 VALUE=
      "http://java.sun.com/docs/books/tutorial/uiswing/index.html">
<PARAM NAME=item_2 VALUE="Qt Tutorial">
<PARAM NAME=url_2 VALUE=
   "http://doc.trolltech.com/2.3/tutorial.html">
<PARAM NAME=item_3 VALUE="GTK+ Tutorial">
<PARAM NAME=url_3 VALUE="http://www.gtk.org/tutorial/">
</APPLET>
</BODY>
</HTML>
```

The purpose of the applet Left.java invoked in the above HTML file is to actually show a list of the names of the tutorials in the left frame and then to be responsive to mouse clicks on the names for displaying the corresponding web pages in the right frame. We will show the tutorial names in the form of a list by using the AWT component List that will be constructed by the invocation:

```
private List links = new List( 3, false );
```

for the three tutorials whose names we want displayed. (If a List component contains more items than the integer that is the first argument in the constructor, the displayed list is made scrollable.) The second argument, a boolean, specifies whether the user is allowed to select more than one item at a time from the list. By making it false, the user will be able to select only one item at a time. Every time the user selects an item, by double-clicking on it, Java generates an ActionEvent that when trapped can be used to determine the identity of the item clicked on. In the following code, the applet itself is a listener for ActionEvents because it implements the ActionListener interface.

```java
//Left.java

import java.awt.*;
import java.awt.event.*;
import java.applet.*;
import java.net.*;
import java.io.*;

public class Left extends Applet implements ActionListener {
    private List links = new List( 3, false );

    public void init() {
        setLayout( new BorderLayout() );
        setBackground( Color.red );
        Font f = new Font( "SansSerif", Font.BOLD, 14 );
        setFont( f );

        Panel p = new Panel();
        p.setLayout( new BorderLayout() );
        p.add( links, "Center" );
        links.addActionListener( this );
        int i = 1;
        String s;
        while ( ( s = getParameter( "item_" + i ) ) != null ) {
            links.add( s );
            i++;
        }
        add( p, "Center" );

    }

    public void actionPerformed( ActionEvent evt ) {
        try {
            String str = evt.getActionCommand();
            AppletContext context = getAppletContext();
            int i = 1;
            String s;
            while ( ( s = getParameter( "item_" + i ) ) != null ) {
                if ( str.equals( s ) ) {
                    URL u = new URL( getParameter( "url_" + i ) );
                    context.showDocument( u, "right" );
                }
                i++;
            }
        } catch( Exception e ) { showStatus( "Error " + e ); }
    }
}
```

In order to download a web document, the above applet first constructs an object of Java class URL by

```
URL u = new URL( getParameter( "url_" + i ) );
```

where the argument to the URL constructor is the actual web address that is returned by the getParameter method. The web document is then downloaded into the right frame by

```
AppletContext context = getAppletContext();
context.showDocument( u, "right" );
```

It is through the AppletContext object context that the showDocument method becomes aware of the fact that "right" is the name of the right frame. The method then proceeds to show the web document in that frame.

That leaves only the file Right.html yet to be described. Since the right frame's sole function is to display the web documents when a user clicks on the items in the left frame, the contents of this file can be as simple as

```
<HTML>
<TITLE>
Web pages will be displayed here
</TITLE>
<BODY BGCOLOR="#dddddd">
double click on any of the items on the left
</BODY>
</HTML>
```

17.22.6 Security Issues Related to Applets

As was mentioned earlier, security is an important issue related to applets since they are downloaded from remote hosts and require local computing resources. So it becomes an important issue as to what local resources an applet can gain access to. The security considerations are different depending on whether an applet is viewed through a web browser or by using the appletviewer tool. For obvious reasons, the security restrictions are more stringent when an applet is viewed through a browser.

In general, an applet loaded into a browser cannot read a local file or write into a local file, nor can it execute a local executable file. An applet is not allowed to even check for the existence of a local file, or rename a local file, or check a file's size, or create a directory on the local disk, and so on. However, when an applet is viewed with appletviewer, the applet can be allowed to read files and directories, provided that those files and directories are named in the acl.read property in the `~/.hotjava/properties` file. An applet viewed with appletviewer is also allowed to write into files provided such files are named in `acl.write` property in the `~/.hotjava/properties` file.

An applet, when viewed either through a browser or with appletviewer, can read the following system properties by invoking `System.getProperty(String key)` or `System.getProperty(String key, String default)` where the string key stands for one of the following arguments on the left:[40]

```
key                     meaning
-----------             -----------------------------
java.version            Java version number
java.vendor             Java vendor-specific string
java.vendor.url         Java vendor URL
java.class.version      Java class version number
os.name                 Operating system name
os.arch                 Operating system architecture
os.version              Operating system version
file.separator          File separator (eg, "/")
path.separator          Path separator (eg, ":")
line.separator          Line separator
```

Applets, when viewed either through a web browser or with appletviewer, are prevented by default from reading these system properties:

```
key                     meaning
-----------             -----------------------------
java.home               Java installation directory
java.class.path         Java classpath
user.name               User account name
user.home               User home directory
user.dir                User's current working directory
```

However, this default behavior, with regard to both the access and the denial of access to the various system properties, can be gotten around for the case when an applet is loaded into an `appletviewer` by suitable changes to the `~/.hotjava/properties` file.

Applets, regardless of whether they are loaded into a browser or an `appletviewer`, are not allowed to open network connections to any computer except for the host that supplied the class file for the applet.

---

[40]Both of the tables shown are reproduced here from `www.java.sun.com`.

17.23   CREDITS AND SUGGESTIONS FOR FURTHER READING

The historical remarks in Section 17.1 are based partly on Dalheimer's [14] introduction to GUI toolkits. The API layering figure in the same section incorporates corrections received by the author from Dalheimer via personal communication. The introductory material on event processing in Section 17.12 is derived partly from Dalheimer [14], partly from Griffith [25].

Some of the more basic GUI examples shown for Java and Qt in this chapter are patterned after the examples in the on-line tutorials provided by the developers of the toolkits. To put this chapter's code examples in perspective, they should serve as good introductions to the more extensive examples posted on-line by toolkit developers. A reader who wishes to develop advanced proficiency in any of the toolkits discussed here is encouraged to visit and learn from the on-line material. For AWT/Swing, there is the Swing tutorial at [32]. The on-line tutorial for Qt is available at [30]. For hard-copy sources of more advanced help with AWT and Swing, the reader is referred to [26, 27, 18, 55, 17]. For a hard-copy source of more advanced help with Qt, Dalheimer's book [14] is a recommended must-read.

Our presentation of the GNOME/GTK+ material is essentially a paraphrase of the first half of the extensive book on the subject by Griffith [25]. Many of the GNOME/GTK+ examples shown, especially those dealing with layout, are derived directly from Griffith's examples. For an on-line tutorial on GTK+, the reader is referred to [34].

Our discussion of Java applets assumed that the reader is already familiar with the Hypertext Markup Language (HTML) used for creating web pages. If that's not the case, a recommended reading on the subject is the book by Castro [12].

17.24   HOMEWORK

1. As an exercise in using a panel to organize components in a window, write a Java program that allows you to enter text in a JTextArea component and then to fetch the text thus entered so that it can be displayed in a terminal window. Your top-level frame should consist of two JPanel objects arranged vertically. The top JPanel object should contain a label at the very top announcing the purpose of the window, and a text-entry area below that. The text-entry area can be an object of type JTextArea. The bottom panel should consist of three buttons as follows:

   (a) A button, with label "Start," that allows text to be entered in the text-area part of the window.

   (b) A button, labeled "Stop," that when pressed disallows any further keyboard entry of text.

(c) A button, labeled "Get Text," that extracts the entire text entered by the user in the text window and then displays the text in the user's terminal.

2. Design a `ColorMixer` applet for your web page. As depicted in Figure 17.44, the upper half of the applet should consist of a `Canvas` object that shows the result of mixing R, G, and B color components. The lower half of the applet should be a panel consisting of three subpanels, as depicted in greater detail in Figure 17.45. Each of these three subpanels should look like what is shown in Figure 17.46 — that is, each subpanel should consist of a `Canvas` object at the top and a `Scrollbar` and a `TextField` objects at the bottom. The scrollbar is for altering the color value of a color component. The text field is for displaying a numerical readout of the current value of that component.

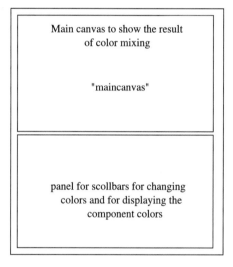

Fig. 17.44

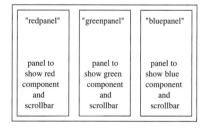

Fig. 17.45

Fig. 17.46

3. Create a simple two function (add/subtract) calculator using Qt. It should also include an all-clear (AC) button. Use QGridLayout to manage the positioning of the buttons and the display. A QLineEdit object can be used for the display, and QPushButton objects for the buttons.

4. Design a countdown timer using Qt. A slider should control the length of time the timer is set for, an LCD display to show how much time is left, and buttons to start, stop, and reset the timer. When the timer is started, the start and reset buttons should be disabled and the stop button enabled. When the timer expires or is stopped, the stop button should be disabled and the start and reset buttons should be enabled.

5. Write a program using GNOME/GTK+ that creates a window divided into two main parts. The top part should be an empty area where the user can click the mouse. The bottom part should be a label where the coordinates of the mouse click in the upper area are displayed. The displayed coordinates should be relative to the top left corner of the window.

6. Write a program using GNOME/GTK+ that can display images. The program should include a menu with "Open" (open a picture), "Close" (close a picture), "Exit" (exit the program), and "About" (a short message about the author) items. The image should be displayed inside a scrolled window.

7. Write a Java applet that allows the viewer at a client machine to see a "picture postcard" that consists of an image and a brief greetings, both as specified in the HTML file. More specifically, the applet should do the following:

    (a) Display an image retrieved from a URL that is specified in the HTML file.

    (b) Draw a rectangular box whose width, height, and location are specified by appropriate parameters in the HTML file.

    (c) Display the greetings inside the box. The message is supplied as a string in the HTML file.

    Your applet should work with an HTML file similar to the following:

```
<HTML>
<TITLE>
A Flexible Applet
</TITLE>
<BODY BGCOLOR="#000000">
<APPLET CODE="FlexiApplet.class"  WIDTH=650 HEIGHT=400>
<PARAM NAME=BOX_WIDTH VALUE="170">
<PARAM NAME=BOX_HEIGHT VALUE=50>
<PARAM NAME=BOX_X VALUE=80>
<PARAM NAME=BOX_Y VALUE=220>
<PARAM NAME=MESSAGE VALUE="Greetings from the Land of Objects ">
<PARAM NAME=IMAGE_URL VALUE="http://machine-name/Portrait.jpg">
</APPLET>
</BODY>
</HTML>
```

8. Write a Java applet that allows a remote user to draw a free-form sketch by clicking the mouse at different points in the applet window. It should also be possible to run the program as a graphical application for command-line invocation.

18

Multithreaded Object-Oriented Programming

Unlike C++, Java has support for multithreading built right into the language. However, even with C++, it is possible to write multithreaded programs by using external thread classes, as we will show in this chapter.

Multithreading facilitates the design of more responsive graphical interfaces, especially when they are intended for multimedia applications. Imagine you are downloading a long video or audio clip over the internet. If the download could be implemented in a separate thread, you would be able to start viewing the clip soon after downloading starts, as opposed to having to wait until the end. For another example, multiple threads of execution could allow many users to simultaneously access a common database, something that could be very useful for applications such as inventory management and airline reservation systems. To prevent corruption of data when multiple users are authorized to read and write into a common database, multithreading would need to allow for locks to be placed on objects so that only one thread modifies the state of an object at a time.

To the reasons we have listed above for multithreading, a reader might say how about using multiple processes for achieving similar results. The distinction between multiple processes running concurrently and multiple threads running concurrently is crucial. A thread of execution takes place within a process. While a process typically requires its own address space, multiple threads of execution share the same address space, which is the address space of the process in which they reside. This permits multiple threads to more easily access the same data in the memory. Also, the time it takes to switch between threads is shorter than the time it takes to switch between processes. Additionally, interthread communication is faster than interprocess communication.[1]

In a multithreaded program, different priority levels can be attached to different threads. But how these priority levels are actually taken into account varies considerably from system to system. Ordinarily, the highest priority thread is selected for execution. Such a thread continues running until a thread of higher priority seeks attention. However, in systems that use *preemptive scheduling*, the threads are timesliced so that every thread gets a chance at the processor. When timesliced, equal-priority threads get scheduled for execution in a round-robin fashion. An alternative way of dealing with threads of equal priority consists of letting a thread run to completion, unless the execution is preempted by a higher priority thread seeking time on the processor (in what may be referred to as *priority-preemptive* scheduling) or by a `sleep` or a `wait` command.

The performance of a multithreadable programming language depends ultimately on how the threads are mapped to the native threads of the underlying operating system. This mapping, kept mostly hidden from the application programmer, can vary from one implementation to another of a programming language. For example, for the case of Java, some implementations of the Java Virtual Machine use what are known as *green threads*,[2] which are all executed in a single native thread of the operating system. Other implementations of JVM may use directly the native threads, which allows Java threads to execute in parallel on multiprocessor machines. Yet other implementations may map n Java threads to m native threads dynamically at the discretion of the scheduler. In Linux, each Java thread may be mapped to a separate process of the operating system.

This chapter first uses Java to introduce the vocabulary of multithreading. This is followed by an introduction to POSIX threads. It is necessary to understand POSIX threads because they can be used directly in C++ programs and because they are important for gaining a full understanding of the C++-based thread classes. The Java part of this chapter also discusses the Event Dispatch Thread in Swing and how multithreading can be used to design animated applets.

18.1 CREATING AND EXECUTING SIMPLE THREADS IN JAVA

Before showing how one can write a multithreadable program in Java, we wish to point out that even the simplest Java programs execute in a multithreaded mode without any conscious effort by the programmer. That's because the garbage collection for reclaiming the dynamically allocated memory occupied by unreferenced objects takes

---

[1] According to Stevens [53], thread creation can be 10 to 100 times faster than process creation.

[2] Apparently, green in green threads dates back to the Sun's Green Project, whose goal was to implement Java in a hand-held computer based on the Sparc chip (source: John Brewer at jGuru.com).

place in a separate low-priority thread running in the background.[3] To see all of the threads running as you execute any Java class, you could embed the following two statements in the `main` of your program:

```
ThreadGroup topGroup =
    Thread.currentThread().getThreadGroup().getParent();
topGroup.list();
```

where, as the method names imply, we first get the thread group of which the thread executing the `main` is a member, then we get its parent thread group, and, finally, in the second statement we ask the system to display the thread group tree. The reason for why we need to get hold of the `ThreadGroup` object is that the threads are organized in the form of a tree of thread groups. (Of course, it is possible for a thread group to consist of a single thread.) To actually see an example of this thread-group tree, you can run the following program which does nothing but display the currently running threads in the Java Virtual Machine:

```
class DisplayThreads {
    public static void main( String[] args )
    {
        ThreadGroup topGroup =
                Thread.currentThread().getThreadGroup().getParent();
        topGroup.list();
    }
}
```

Compiling and running this program on a Linux machine yields the following output:

```
java.lang.ThreadGroup[name=system,maxpri=10]
    Thread[Reference Handler,10,system]
    Thread[Finalizer,8,system]
    Thread[Signal Dispatcher,10,system]
    Thread[CompileThread0,10,system]
    java.lang.ThreadGroup[name=main,maxpri=10]
        Thread[main,5,main]
```

As shown by the names of the threads inside the square brackets, at the top we have a system thread group. This thread group consists of a "Reference Handler" thread for keeping track of object reference counts, a "Finalizer" thread for automatic garbage collection, a "Signal Dispatcher" thread in which the Event Dispatch Thread (see Section 18.11) is run, a "CompileThread0" for JIT compilation we talked about in Chapter 2, and, finally, another thread group called "main." The thread group "main" has a single thread running in it, also called "main."

---

[3]Compare this with C++, where a programmer must explicitly invoke the destructor of an object to free up the dynamically allocated memory. Should a programmer forget to do so, a program could potentially suffer from memory leaks. Java's automatic garbage collection mechanism running in a separate thread, although not as efficient as the deliberate and immediate freeing up of memory in C++, results nonetheless in simplification of the programming effort.

That brings us to the main goal of this section, which is to show how to create and execute a simple multithreadable program in Java. To be multithreadable, a class must extend the class `Thread` of the `java.lang` package and override its `run` method. The code that needs to be run in the form of separate threads is placed in the `run` method. This code is invoked for execution by calling the `start` method.

To illustrate Java multithreading in its most rudimentary form, the following example shows a multithreadable class `HelloThread`.[4] All that the `run` method of this class does is to print out a message that is supplied as an argument to the class constructor. In the `main` of this class, we create three threads, and start the execution of each thread by invoking `start` on each. The overall goal of the program is to print out the following string on the terminal:

```
Good morning to you!
```

The first three words of this string will be printed out by the three child threads created in `main` and the last, *you!* by the parent thread (or the process) in which `main` is being executed.

```
//ThreadsBasic.java

class HelloThread extends Thread {
    String message;

    HelloThread( String message ) { this.message = message; }

    public void run() {
        //int sleeptime = (int) ( Math.random() * 3000 );        //(A)
        //try {                                                  //(B)
        //    sleep( sleeptime );                                //(C)
        //} catch( InterruptedException e ){}                    //(D)
        System.out.print( message );
    }

    public static void main( String[] args )
    {
        HelloThread ht1 = new HelloThread( "Good" );
        HelloThread ht2 = new HelloThread( " morning" );
        HelloThread ht3 = new HelloThread( " to" );
        ht1.start();
        ht2.start();
        ht3.start();
```

---

[4]Strictly speaking, this is an inappropriate example for multithreading since the words of the message must be printed out in a specific order. Nonetheless, this class will help us convey in a compact fashion some of the more basic aspects of multithreading.

```
    try {                                          //(E)
        sleep( 1000 );                             //(F)
    } catch( InterruptedException e ){}            //(G)

    System.out.println( " you!" );
  }
}
```

If you compile and run this program, it will in most cases print out the *Good morning to you!* string. But, at least theoretically, there would be no guarantee that the words would be printed out in the correct order. Since the three threads and the process in which they reside will be executed concurrently, the words *could* be printed out in a jumbled order. To underscore this point, suppose we comment out the try–catch block in lines (E) through (G), in most cases the word you! would be printed out before one or more of the three other words. Also, if you uncomment the commented out block in lines (A) through (D) to introduce random sleep times in each of the threads, the words would definitely be printed out in a jumbled order. The sleep times introduced in each thread could correspond to some background activity that a thread might engage in before executing output producing code.

As soon as a thread is created by invoking the constructor of the HelloThread class, the thread is considered to be in the *born* state. And then when the method start is invoked on the thread, it is in the *runnable* state and waiting for the scheduler to assign it a processor. Taking thread priorities into account, which can be set by invoking setPriority on a thread, the scheduler assigns the processor to each thread for a fixed interval of time, called a *quantum*. Assigning quanta of time to the different threads is referred to as *timeslicing*.

As mentioned previously, a serious problem with the HelloThread class is that the three threads and the parent thread are all competing with one-another for time on the processor and there is no guarantee which will finish first. One simple way to regulate this race condition is to invoke join on another thread, as we do in lines (H) through (J) in the following version of the program. The thread that invokes join on another thread has its own execution halted until the thread on which join was invoked has finished its execution. In the code presented below, main is invoking join on the threads ht1, ht2, and ht3. This implies that the execution of main will come to a halt until the threads ht1, ht2, and ht3 are done.

Using join in this manner will at least guarantee that the word *you!* will be printed out *after* the other three words of the message. But we still have no guarantee that the first three words will be printed out in the correct order. But, from the standpoint of general multithreaded programming, we would not want that sort of a guarantee anyway because concurrency through multithreading is not intended for the sort of serial control you need to get the words to print out in the correct order. It is for this reason we said at the very beginning of this section that HelloThread was an inappropriate example for multithreading even though it gave us a compact example for illustrating the more basic notions of multithreading in Java.

```java
//ThreadsBasicWithJoin.java

class HelloThread extends Thread {
    String message;

    HelloThread( String message ) { this.message = message; }

    public void run() {
        //int sleeptime = (int) ( Math.random() * 3000 );
        //try {
        //     sleep( sleeptime );
        //   } catch( InterruptedException e ){}
        System.out.print( message );
    }

    public static void main(String[] args) throws InterruptedException
    {
        HelloThread ht1 = new HelloThread( "Good" );
        HelloThread ht2 = new HelloThread( " morning" );
        HelloThread ht3 = new HelloThread( " to" );

        ht1.start();
        ht2.start();
        ht3.start();

        ht1.join();                                                    //(H)
        ht2.join();                                                    //(I)
        ht3.join();                                                    //(J)

        System.out.println( " you!" );
    }
}
```

18.2 THE RUNNABLE INTERFACE IN JAVA

It is not always possible to extend Thread to create a user-defined multithreadable class. What if your user-defined class already extends some other class? To get around this difficulty, Java also allows us to create a multithreadable class by directly implementing the Runnable interface, as we show in this section.[5]

The following version of the HelloThread class implements the Runnable interface by providing an implementation for run, the only method that is declared in the interface. In main, Runnable objects of type HelloThread are then passed to the Thread constructor for the creation of threads:

```
//ThreadBasicWithRunnable.java

class HelloThread implements Runnable {
    String message;
    HelloThread( String message ) { this.message = message; }

    public void run() {                                          //(A)
        //int sleeptime = (int) ( Math.random() * 3000 );        //(B)
        //try {                                                  //(C)
        //    Thread.sleep( sleeptime );                         //(D)
        //} catch( InterruptedException e ){}                    //(E)
        System.out.print( message );
    }

    public static void main( String[] args )
    {
        HelloThread ht1 = new HelloThread( "Good" );             //(F)
        Thread t1 = new Thread( ht1 );                           //(G)

        HelloThread ht2 = new HelloThread( " morning" );
        Thread t2 = new Thread( ht2 );

        HelloThread ht3 = new HelloThread( " to" );
        Thread t3 = new Thread( ht3 );

        t1.start();                                              //(H)
        t2.start();
        t3.start();

        try {
            Thread.sleep( 1000 );                                //(I)
        } catch( InterruptedException e ){}

        System.out.println( " you!" );
    }
}
```

---

[5]In fact, Thread also implements the Runnable interface. So every Thread is an object of type Runnable.

The implementation of the run method in line (A) is the same as before, except that (if you uncomment the commented out part) you must now invoke Thread.sleep in line (D), as opposed to just sleep, since HelloThread does not inherit from Thread any longer.

One of the main differences between the code of the previous section and the code shown here is in how main is set up. For our first thread, we construct in line (F) a HelloThread object ht1. We then pass ht1 as an argument to the Thread constructor in line (G). This allows us to invoke the Thread method start in line (H) to make the thread runnable. This is repeated in the rest of main for the other two threads.

18.3 THREAD STATES

Although some of the thread states have already been mentioned in our description of the program ThreadsBasic.java, here is a more complete list:

- born
- runnable
- running
- waiting
- sleeping
- blocked
- dead

When the constructor of a Runnable type is first invoked,[6] a new thread is born. Unless the method start is inside the constructor, the new thread just stays in the memory as a new object, basically doing nothing. When start is invoked on the thread either inside a constructor or in main, or at any other place in a program, the status of the thread changes from *born* to *runnable*, meaning that the thread can now be assigned a processor by the scheduler.

Assignment of a processor to a thread in a *runnable* state changes the state to *running*.[7] If a running thread is able to run to completion, its state changes to *dead*. Otherwise, the fate of the thread depends on whether there are other threads waiting for their turn at the processor. If the thread has the highest priority of all the currently *runnable* threads, it continues to be executed, unless the threads are timesliced by the

---

[6]As mentioned earlier in this chapter, an object of type Thread is also an object of type Runnable since the class Thread implements the Runnable interface.

[7]In the official Java documentation, both the *runnable* and the *running* states are referred to as *runnable*. But it makes practical sense to make a distinction between the two.

platform. When threads are timesliced, as previously mentioned, a running thread is allocated a fixed time interval on the processor — a quantum. Timeslicing of equal-priority threads results in the processor being assigned to them in a round-robin fashion. If the code that a thread is executing contains `yield`, that would also cause a running thread to stop executing and yield the processor to another thread.

A running thread can be put to sleep by the `sleep` method. If threads contain long loops, putting threads to sleep in each iteration is a good strategy to ensure that no threads will have to wait unduly long to get their turn at the processor. When a running thread goes to sleep, one of the waiting threads gets a turn at the processor. An alternative to using `sleep` in long loops is to use `yield`.

The processor cannot be wrested away from a thread during an I/O operation in the `run` method, that being the case even for timesliced system. So we say that a thread blocks on I/O.

18.4 THREAD INTERFERENCE IN JAVA

Multithreaded programming is simplest to implement when the various threads can operate independently, meaning when they share no data objects during their execution. That has been the case with all the programs we have shown so far. When the threads are given the ability to access and modify the same data, there is always a potential for a program to exhibit incorrect behavior.

In this section, we will present two examples of thread interference. The first example shows a subtle and insidious form of thread interference, caused by the threads interfering at the level of low-level instructions that the high-level Java statements get decomposed into. The second example will show thread interference for the special case of I/O.

Example 1:

In this example, all the threads will share the same data object of the following type:

```
class DataObject {
  int dataItem1;
  int dataItem2;
  // ....
}
```

Both the data members of the class, `dataItem1` and `dataItem2`, will be set to 50 initially. When a thread is executed, its job will be to make equal and opposite modifications to the two data members so that their sum will always be equal to 100. So, as shown in lines (A2) and (A3) of the program below, we supply the class DataObject with a constructor where we initialize the two data members. We also supply the class with a method itemSwap in line (B1) for making equal and opposite modifications to the two data members in lines (B3) and (B5). Additional method for DataObject is the method test in line (C1) to test the sum of the values of dataItem1 and dataItem2 after the method itemSwap is invoked. You would expect test to always print out 100 on the console.

Note the invocation of keepBusy(10) inside itemSwap in line (B4). The keepBusy function tries to merely keep the processor busy for the designated number of milliseconds. The purpose of this function is to increase the length of the time the processor would need for completing itemSwap so as to increase the probability that there would be a timeslicing event at some point during the execution of itemSwap. As we will see later, it is this timeslicing action that is responsible for the thread interference we will show for this example.

For the purpose of invoking the method itemSwap repeatedly on an instance of type DataObject and to be able to do so in separate threads, we will define a class RepeatedSwaps in line (E) by subclassing from Thread. The run method of this multithreadable class, in line (G1), goes through 20,000 iterations and, via the statement in line (G4), we print out the sum of the two data members of the data object every 4000 iterations.

Finally, we define a class, UnsynchedSwaps in line (H) for creating different threads of type RepeatedSwaps, as shown in lines (J1) through (J5). Note that all the threads are supplied with the same data object, created in line (I). The source code follows:

```java
//UnsynchedSwaps.java

/////////////////////////  class DataObject  /////////////////////////////
class DataObject {
    int dataItem1;
    int dataItem2;

    DataObject() {                                                  //(A1)
        dataItem1 = 50;                                             //(A2)
        dataItem2 = 50;                                             //(A3)
    }
    void itemSwap() {                                               //(B1)
        int x = (int) ( -4.999999 + Math.random() * 10 );          //(B2)
        dataItem1 -= x;                                             //(B3)
        keepBusy(10);                                              //(B4)
        dataItem2 += x;                                            //(B5)
    }
    void test() {                                                  //(C1)
        int sum = dataItem1 + dataItem2;                           //(C2)
        System.out.println( sum );                                //(C3)
    }
```

```
    public void keepBusy( int howLong ) {                        //(D)
        long curr = System.currentTimeMillis();
        while ( System.currentTimeMillis() < curr + howLong )
            ;
    }
}


/////////////////////// class RepeatedSwaps ///////////////////////
class RepeatedSwaps extends Thread  {                            //(E)
    DataObject dobj;

    RepeatedSwaps( DataObject d ) {                             //(F)
        dobj = d;
        start();
    }
    public void run( ) {                                        //(G1)
        int i = 0;
        while ( i < 20000 ) {                                   //(G2)
            dobj.itemSwap();                                    //(G3)
            if ( i % 4000 == 0 ) dobj.test();                   //(G4)
            try { sleep( (int) (Math.random() * 2 ) ); }        //(G5)
            catch( InterruptedException e ) {}
            i++;
        }
    }
    public void keepBusy() {
        long curr = System.currentTimeMillis();
        while ( System.currentTimeMillis() <
                    curr + (int) (Math.random()*10) )
            ;
    }
}


/////////////////////// class UnsynchedSwaps ///////////////////////
public class UnsynchedSwaps {                                   //(H)
    public static void main( String[] args ) {
        DataObject d = new DataObject();                        //(I)
        new RepeatedSwaps( d );                                 //(J1)
        new RepeatedSwaps( d );                                 //(J2)
        new RepeatedSwaps( d );                                 //(J3)
        new RepeatedSwaps( d );                                 //(J4)
    }
}
```

This program produces the following output:[8]

```
100
98
100
100
105
98
100
99
103
94
98
91
100
97
98
96
100
104
98
105
```

Evidently, something is wrong. Given that the method itemSwap() makes equal and opposite changes to the two data members, dataItem1 and dataItem2, the sum of the two should always add up to 100. So, obviously, it must the case that the threads are interfering with one another.

If you examine the Java code in the above program, it would seem that even if the threads interfered with one another, the sum of the values in dataItem1 and dataItem2 should always add up to 100. One would think that even if a thread, say thread1, was interrupted (on account of timeslicing) after executing the first data-modifying instruction of itemSwap:

```
dataItem1 -= x;
```

and some other thread, say thread2, went ahead executed both of the following instructions

```
dataItem1 -= x;
dataItem2 += x;
```

with possibly a different value of x, after thread1 woke up to execute its own

```
dataItem2 += x;
```

---

[8]This output was produced on a modern multiprocessor machine running the Solaris operating system. The output of this program will vary from platform to platform and from one run to another.

the overall result would still be the same, meaning the sum of the two data members dataItem1 and dataItem2 would still add up to 100.

But, unfortunately, it is not as simple as that, primarily because a single high-level instruction like

```
dataItem2 += x;
```

is decomposed in the Java byte code into more *atomic* operations of the form[9]

1. Load dataItem2 into a register
2. Add x
3. Move the result back to dataItem2

Let's say thread1 is interrupted after it completes the first two steps. After thread1 is interrupted, let's say thread2 is able to complete all three steps. If thread1 wakes up soon after thread2 is done with step 3 and executes its own step 3, the result moved back to dataItem1 will not correspond to thread1 but to thread2.

So, basically, threads can corrupt the shared data any time they get interrupted in the middle of executing high-level source code instructions that access and modify the data.

---

[9]To see this decomposition of high-level Java statements into the low-level instructions of the sort that would be susceptible to thread interference, you can "decompile" a previously compiled class by using the javap tool, as in

```
javap -c -v DataObject
```

This will show the bytecode in human readable form that the source code from the DataObject class got compiled into. The following segment of this bytecode is for the itemSwap method:

```
Method void itemSwap()
   0 ldc2_w #4 <Double -4.999999>
   3 invokestatic #6 <Method double random()>
   6 ldc2_w #7 <Double 10.0>
   9 dmul
  10 dadd
  11 d2i
  12 istore_1
  13 aload_0
  14 dup
  15 getfield #2 <Field int dataItem1>
  18 iload_1
  19 isub
  20 putfield #2 <Field int dataItem1>
  23 aload_0
  24 bipush 10
  26 invokevirtual #9 <Method void keepBusy(int)>
  29 aload_0
  30 dup
  31 getfield #3 <Field int dataItem2>
  34 iload_1
  35 iadd
  36 putfield #3 <Field int dataItem2>
  39 return
```

Example 2:

We will now show an example of thread interference for the case that involves file I/O. In the following program, the class `DataFile` is responsible for two things: (1) Its constructor creates a file named "hello.dat" and then deposits the string "Hello" in the file, as shown in line (B2). And (2) its method `fileIO` first *tries* to read the string that is in the file "hello.dat" and writes *whatever was thus read* back into the file; see lines (C2) and (C3). The class `FileIO` is the same as described in one of the homework problems in Chapter 10.

We next define in line (D) a multithreadable class `ThreadedFileIO` whose sole data member, defined in line (E), is an object of type `DataFile`. By invoking the `fileIO` method on this data member, we can do file I/O in each thread separately, but all the threads will of course be accessing the same file. The `run` method of this class in line (G) calls for four invocations of `fileIO` in each thread. After each invocation of `fileIO`, we print out the name of the thread and the string contained in the file.

Finally, we have in line (H) the class `UnsynchedFileIO` for constructing and launching five `ThreadedFileIO` threads in lines (J1) through (J5), all opening and closing the same file, "hello.dat". Note that each invocation, such as `ThreadedFileIO("t0", dd)` in line (J1), creates a new thread and makes it runnable automatically because the method `start` is embedded in the constructor of `ThreadedFileIO`. If we had not included this method there, our invocations would have to be of the form `ThreadedFileIO("t0", dd).start()`.

Here is the source code for this example:

```
//UnsynchedFileIO.java

/////////////////////////// class DataFile ///////////////////////////
class DataFile {                                           //(A)

    public DataFile() {                                    //(B1)
        try {
            FileIO.writeOneString( "Hello", "hello.dat" );  //(B2)
        } catch( FileIOException e ) {}
    }

    void fileIO() {                                        //(C1)
        try {
            String str = FileIO.readOneString( "hello.dat" );  //(C2)
            FileIO.writeOneString( str  , "hello.dat" );   //(C3)
        } catch( FileIOException e ) {}
    }
}
```

```
///////////////////// class ThreadedFileIO  //////////////////////////
class ThreadedFileIO extends Thread  {                          //(D)
    DataFile df;                                                //(E)

    ThreadedFileIO( String threadName, DataFile d ) {           //(F)
        df = d;
        setName( threadName );
        start();
    }
    public void run( ) {                                        //(G)
        int i = 0;
        while ( i++ < 4 ) {
            try {
                df.fileIO();
                String str = FileIO.readOneString( "hello.dat" );
                System.out.println( getName() + ":      "
                        + "hello.dat contains: " + str );
                sleep( 5 );
            } catch( InterruptedException e ) {}
              catch( FileIOException e ) {}
        }
    }
}


///////////////////// class UnsynchedFileIO  //////////////////////////
public class UnsynchedFileIO {                                  //(H)
    public static void main( String[] args ) {
        DataFile dd = new DataFile();                           //(I)
        new ThreadedFileIO( "t0", dd );                         //(J1)
        new ThreadedFileIO( "t1", dd );                         //(J2)
        new ThreadedFileIO( "t2", dd );                         //(J3)
        new ThreadedFileIO( "t3", dd );                         //(J4)
        new ThreadedFileIO( "t4", dd );                         //(J5)
    }
}
```

As with the previous example, the output of this program depends on which platform you run it on. The following output was produced by a state-of-the-art multiprocessor machine running Solaris:

```
    t1:     hello.dat contains:
    t2:     hello.dat contains:
    t0:     hello.dat contains: Hello
    t4:     hello.dat contains: Hello
    t3:     hello.dat contains: Hello
    t1:     hello.dat contains: Hello
    t2:     hello.dat contains: Hello
```

```
t0:     hello.dat contains: Hello
t3:     hello.dat contains: Hello
t1:     hello.dat contains: Hello
t0:     hello.dat contains:
t2:     hello.dat contains:
t4:     hello.dat contains:
t3:     hello.dat contains: Hello
t0:     hello.dat contains: Hello
t1:     hello.dat contains: Hello
t4:     hello.dat contains:
t2:     hello.dat contains: Hello
t3:     hello.dat contains: Hello
t4:     hello.dat contains: Hello
```

Remember, each thread should make four appearances in the output. And for each thread the content of the file should ideally say "Hello." As is clear from the output, for some of the threads some of the time, the file appears to contain nothing. Evidently, the threads are getting in each other's way once again. The code of the method `fileIO()` of line (C1) where the threads can step on each other's toes consists of the following two statements in lines (C2) and (C3):

```
String str = FileIO.readOneString( "hello.dat" );
FileIO.writeOneString( str  , "hello.dat" );
```

The first statement reads the string that is contained in the file "hello.dat," and the second statement writes the same string back into the same file. But, as in the previous example, each of these high-level statements gets decomposed by the compiler into a number of low-level instructions. One of these low-level instructions for the write statement above erases the previous contents of the file before the file is written into.[10] Suppose one of the threads, call it `t1`, was interrupted immediately after "zeroing out" the file and suppose another thread, call it `t2`, was allowed to read this file next. The read method in `t2` thread would return an empty string. Let's say that `t2` is taken off the processor after this read step. Next, suppose the processor is assigned to `t1` and it writes out the string "Hello" into the file. If `t2` is given the processor soon thereafter, it could overwrite an empty string into the file. The behavior of the other threads subsequently would depend on whether they saw an empty file or the string "Hello" in the file. Also, after all the threads have run to completion, the file "hello.dat" may either contain the string "Hello" or it could be empty.

---

[10]Earlier we said that threads block on I/O operations — that is, the processor cannot be wrested away from a thread until the thread has completed the I/O operation it is engaged in. The reader might now ask, How come the threads do not block on the I/O implied by `readOneString` and `writeOneString`? The answer is that a thread blocks during just the *atomic* I/O steps. A method such as `writeOneString` does many things besides data transfer: It has to either create a new file or open an existing file. In the latter case, it must also erase the contents of the file. Only then can the data be transfered to the file. A thread will block only during the data transfer phase.

18.5 THREAD SYNCHRONIZATION IN JAVA

Java provides a simple-to-use mechanism to prevent thread interference. Methods that require access to shared data are declared `synchronized`. Only one thread at a time is allowed to execute the code in a synchronized method, all other threads must wait. A thread that is executing a synchronized instance method *acquires a lock* on the object on which the method is invoked. When the synchronized method finishes executing, the thread relinquishes its lock on the object. Only one thread may have a lock on an object at any time. Therefore, during the time a thread has a lock on an object, that object is not accessible to any other threads — even via the other methods that might be defined for that object. In other words, if an object possesses several synchronized methods, only one of them will be active at any given time. A thread that is executing a synchronized static method of a class obtains a lock on the class object.

Locking is achieved with the help of *monitors*. Every object with a synchronized instance method has associated with it a *monitor*. By the same token, every class with a static method also has a monitor. A thread becomes the owner of an object's monitor by executing one of its synchronized methods.[11] When a thread is done executing the synchronized method, it relinquishes its ownership of the monitor, which then becomes free to be owned by some other thread. Thread synchronization is achieved with the help of a monitor object maintaining a list of all threads waiting to execute any of its synchronized methods. The monitor then gives access to the waiting threads one at a time.

So to fix the thread interference problem in the `UnsynchedSwap` class of the previous section, all we have to do is to declare the `itemSwap` and the `test` methods synchronized, as we show below in the following thread-safe implementation of the earlier program:

```
//SynchedSwaps.java

/////////////////////////  class DataObject  /////////////////////////
class DataObject {
    int dataItem1;
    int dataItem2;

    DataObject() {
        dataItem1 = 50;
        dataItem2 = 50;
    }
```

---

[11]A thread can also become the owner of an object's monitor by executing the body of a *synchronized block of code* that synchronizes on the object. The end of this section explains what is meant by a synchronized block of code in a method.

```
    synchronized void itemSwap() {
        int x = (int) ( -4.999999 + Math.random() * 10 );
        dataItem1 -= x;
        keepBusy(10);
        dataItem2 += x;
    }
    synchronized void test() {
        int sum = dataItem1 + dataItem2;
        System.out.println( sum );
    }
    public void keepBusy( int howLong ) {
        long curr = System.currentTimeMillis();
        while ( System.currentTimeMillis() < curr + howLong )
            ;
    }
}


//////////////////////// class RepeatedSwaps ////////////////////////
class RepeatedSwaps extends Thread  {
    DataObject dobj;

    RepeatedSwaps( DataObject d ) {
        dobj = d;
        start();
    }
    public void run( ) {
        int i = 0;
        while ( i++ < 20000 ) {
            dobj.itemSwap();
            if ( i % 4000 == 0 ) dobj.test();
            try { sleep( 1 ); } catch( InterruptedException e ) {}
        }
    }
}


//////////////////////// class SynchedSwaps ////////////////////////
public class SynchedSwaps {
    public static void main( String[] args ) {
        DataObject d = new DataObject();
        new RepeatedSwaps(  d );
        new RepeatedSwaps(  d );
        new RepeatedSwaps(  d );
        new RepeatedSwaps(  d );
    }
}
```

The output of this program is free of errors:

```
100
100
100
100
100
100
100
100
100
100
100
100
100
100
100
100
100
100
100
100
```

The interference problem with the UnsynchedFileIO class of the previous section can be fixed in a similar manner — by making the method fileIO() synchronized. We have shown below the source code for a class SynchedFileIO. This code is the same as for UnsynchedFileIO except that the method fileIO() is now synchronized:

```java
//SynchedFileIO.java

//////////////////////////// class DataFile ////////////////////////////
class DataFile {
    public DataFile() {
        try {
            FileIO.writeOneString( "Hello", "hello.dat" );
        } catch( FileIOException e ) {}
    }
    synchronized void fileIO() {
        try {
            String str = FileIO.readOneString( "hello.dat" );
            FileIO.writeOneString( str  , "hello.dat" );
        } catch( FileIOException e ) {}
    }
}
```

```
///////////////////////// class ThreadedFileIO /////////////////////////
class ThreadedFileIO extends Thread  {
    DataFile df;

    ThreadedFileIO( String threadName, DataFile d ) {
        df = d;
        setName( threadName );
        start();
    }
    public void run( ) {
        int i = 0;
        while ( i++ < 4 ) {
            try {
                df.fileIO();
                String str = FileIO.readOneString( "hello.dat" );
                System.out.println( getName() + ":      "
                            + "hello.dat contains: " + str );
                sleep( 5 );
            } catch( InterruptedException e ) {}
              catch( FileIOException e ) {}
        }
    }
}


///////////////////////// class SynchedFileIO /////////////////////////
public class SynchedFileIO {
    public static void main( String[] args ) {
        DataFile dd = new DataFile();
        new ThreadedFileIO( "t0", dd );
        new ThreadedFileIO( "t1", dd );
        new ThreadedFileIO( "t2", dd );
        new ThreadedFileIO( "t3", dd );
        new ThreadedFileIO( "t4", dd );
    }
}
```

The output produced by this program is also free of errors:

```
t0:     hello.dat contains: Hello
t1:     hello.dat contains: Hello
t2:     hello.dat contains: Hello
t3:     hello.dat contains: Hello
t4:     hello.dat contains: Hello
t0:     hello.dat contains: Hello
t1:     hello.dat contains: Hello
t2:     hello.dat contains: Hello
t3:     hello.dat contains: Hello
```

```
t4:     hello.dat contains: Hello
t0:     hello.dat contains: Hello
t1:     hello.dat contains: Hello
t2:     hello.dat contains: Hello
t3:     hello.dat contains: Hello
t4:     hello.dat contains: Hello
t1:     hello.dat contains: Hello
t0:     hello.dat contains: Hello
t2:     hello.dat contains: Hello
t3:     hello.dat contains: Hello
t4:     hello.dat contains: Hello
```

Before ending this section, we must mention that it is also possible to synchronize just blocks of code using the following syntax:

```
synchronized( obj ) {
  // code
}
```

where `obj` is the object to be locked. When synchonization protection is desired vis-à-vis the static members of a class, you'd need to supply the class itself as an argument to `synchronized`.

18.6 JAVA'S `wait–notify` MECHANISM FOR DEALING WITH DEADLOCK

Let's consider again the situation of different threads modifying a common data object. But now let's assume that the different threads produce different types of modifications that could potentially cause the threads to deadlock.

Consider, for example, the case of a bank account that is shared by multiple customers. Some customers may deposit money into the account while others may withdraw money from the account. If a customer finds that the balance in the account is less than the amount he/she wanted to withdraw, the customer would wait until one or more depositors added to the account. If we represent each customer by a thread, then a thread wanting to withdraw money should wait until the threads depositing funds into the account had produced a sufficient balance. In multithreaded programming with Java, this effect can be achieved by using the `wait–notify` mechanism. When a thread wishing to make a certain modification to a data object finds out that the state of the data object does not meet a condition that must be satisfied before the modification can be carried out, the thread executes the `wait` method. And when threads capable of establishing that condition do their job, they execute the `notifiyAll` method, which enables the waiting thread to try to seek a lock on the object again so that it can proceed with data modification.[12]

The reader will recall that every object with at least one synchronized method has a monitor that maintains a list of all the threads wanting to execute any of the synchronized methods in that object. The threads are let into the object one at a time and the thread currently executing a synchronized method becomes the owner of the monitor for the object. When a thread sees `wait` while it is executing a synchronized method, the thread releases its ownership of the monitor and gets placed in the wait list for the object. On the other hand, when a thread executes `notifyAll`, that notification is sent to all the threads in the wait list that were sent there by the `wait` method. The important thing to remember is that if a thread landed in a wait list because it executed `wait`, the only way it can come off the list is if it receives a notification sent by `notifyAll` in some other thread. Instead of `notifyAll`, it is also possible to use `notify`, which sends the notification to a randomly selected thread in the wait list.

The following example illustrates the use of the `wait`–`notify` mechanism. We have a bank account shared by 10 customers, five of whom only deposit money into the account while the other five only like to withdraw money from the account. The shared account is an instance of the class `Account` defined in line (A) with two synchronized methods, `deposit` and `withdraw` in lines (D) and (G), respectively.

Notice how in line (H) the `withdraw` method first makes sure that the amount to be withdrawn is not larger than the current balance in the account. If this condition is not satisfied, the `wait` method is invoked in line (I). The method `wait` throws `InterruptedException`, which must be caught. Execution of this method causes the thread to release its lock on the `Account` object and to be put back in the list of waiting threads maintained by the monitor for the `Account` object. We used the no-arg version of `wait` in line (I). This is one of the following three possible ways to invoke `wait`:

```
void wait() throws InterruptedException;
void wait( long milliseconds ) throws InterruptedException;
void wait( long milliseconds, int nanoseconds )
                        throws InterruptedException;
```

While the first version causes the thread executing the `wait` method to wait indefinitely, the other two versions make for a time-bounded wait in terms of the specified number of milliseconds and nanoseconds.

The only `notifyAll` call in our example that will cause a waiting thread to come off the monitor's list is in line (F) of the `deposit` method of line (D). So each time a deposit is made by any of the threads capable of doing so, a notification is broadcast to all the threads in the monitor list that got put there by the `wait` command.

---

[12]The methods `wait`, `notify`, and `notifyAll` are defined for the class `Object`.

If a thread is again given a lock on the object upon receiving a notification from notifyAll, the flow of control in the thread moves to just beyond the wait statement whose execution put the thread in the wait state in the first place. If the wait statement is placed inside a while loop, as we do in line (H), this will automatically cause the condition of the loop to be tested again. If this condition is not satisfied again, the thread loses once again its lock on the object and gets put back in the monitor's wait list. It is for this reason that the while loop in line (H) cannot be replaced by a statement such as

```
if ( balance < draw ) {                        // WRONG
    try {
    wait();
    } catch( InterruptedException e ) {}
```

Getting back to our example, money will be deposited in the common account by customers of type Depositor as defined in line (K). Note that each deposit, whose amount is generated by the Java random number generator in line (P), consists of a number between 0 and 10. Also, each depositor keeps on adding to the amount indefinitely. As dictated by line (Q), each depositor thread will print out the account balance once every 1000 deposits.

Monies are withdrawn by customers of type Withdrawer defined in line (T). As with the depositors, each thread of type Withdrawer will withdraw monies from the common account indefinitely and will print out the account balance after very 1000 withdrawals. The source code for this example follows:

```
//MultiCustomerAccount.java

///////////////////////// class Account /////////////////////////
class Account {                                            //(A)
    int balance;                                           //(B)

    Account() { balance = 0; }                             //(C)

    synchronized void deposit( int dep ){                  //(D)
        balance += dep;                                    //(E)
        notifyAll();                                       //(F)
    }
    synchronized void withdraw( int draw ) {               //(G)
        while ( balance < draw ) {                         //(H)
            try {
                wait();                                    //(I)
            } catch( InterruptedException e ) {}
        }
        balance -= draw;                                   //(J)
    }
}
```

```
//////////////////////// class Depositor  ////////////////////////
class Depositor extends Thread {                                    //(K)
    private Account acct;                                           //(L)

    Depositor( Account act ){ acct = act; }                         //(M)

    public void run() {                                             //(N)
        int i = 0;
        while ( true ) {                                            //(O)
            int x = (int) ( 10 * Math.random() );                   //(P)
            acct.deposit( x );                                      //(Q)
            if ( i++ % 1000 == 0 )                                  //(R)
                System.out.println(
                    "balance after deposits:  "
                    + acct.balance );                               //(S)
            try { sleep( 5 ); } catch( InterruptedException e ) {}
        }
    }
}

//////////////////////// class Withdrawer  ////////////////////////
class Withdrawer extends Thread {                                   //(T)
    private Account acct;

    Withdrawer( Account act ) { acct = act; }

    public void run() {
        int i = 0;
        while ( true ) {
            int x = (int) ( 10 * Math.random() );
            acct.withdraw( x );
            if ( i++ % 1000 == 0 )
                System.out.println( "balance after withdrawals:  "
                                    + acct.balance );
            try { sleep( 5 ); } catch( InterruptedException e ) {}
        }
    }
}

/////////////////// class MultiCustomerAccount ////////////////////
class MultiCustomerAccount {                                        //(U)
    public static void main( String[] args ) {
        Account account = new Account();
        Depositor[] depositors = new Depositor[ 5 ];
        Withdrawer[] withdrawers = new Withdrawer[ 5 ];
        for ( int i=0; i < 5; i++ ) {
            depositors[ i ] = new Depositor( account );
            withdrawers[ i ] = new Withdrawer( account );
```

```
                depositors[ i ].start();
                withdrawers[ i ].start();
        }
    }
}
```

A typical output of this program is

```
balance after deposits:  5
balance after withdrawals:  4
balance after deposits:  10
balance after withdrawals:  14
balance after deposits:  14
balance after withdrawals:  28
balance after deposits:  31
balance after withdrawals:  10
balance after deposits:  20
balance after withdrawals:  29
balance after deposits:  205
balance after deposits:  214
balance after deposits:  234
  . . . . .
  . . . . .
  . . . . .
```

Since the threads run indefinitely, the program can only be terminated by killing the process.

The wait-notify mechanism is an important tool to resolving potential deadlock between threads. However, just because a program uses this mechanism does not mean that deadlock will not occur — one still has to design with care the logic of a program so that irresolvable deadlock situations do not occur. An irresolvable deadlock occurs when each one of the waiting threads waits indefinitely for the others to proceed.

Evidently, the threads in our MultiCustomerAccount will not deadlock because no conditions need be satisfied for making deposits. So the Depositor threads will continue to make deposits no matter what. Therefore, if a Withdrawer thread blocks for lack of sufficient funds, it will eventually be able to get back into the running.

But now consider the following variation on the MultiCustomerAccount class. Instead of having a single account that could be accessed by multiple customers, let's now consider a single customer with access to multiple accounts. Let's also assume that all that the customer is allowed to do is to shift monies between the accounts. So if the customer is depositing funds in some account, it is because the customer has withdrawn these funds from some other account. If we associate a separate thread with each account, the run method of the thread could then transfer money from its account to one of the other randomly selected accounts. Suppose we have only two accounts A and B. If account A, with a balance of $1000, wants to transfer $2000 to account B, and account B, with a balance of $2000, wants to transfer $3000 to account A, the threads will deadlock. This can also happen with more than two accounts. Say, account A with a balance of $1000 wants to transfer $2000 to account B, account B with a balance of $2000 wants to transfer $3000 to account C, and account C with a balance of $500 wants to transfer $1000 to account A. The three threads corresponding to the three accounts would evidently deadlock.

18.7   DATA I/O BETWEEN THREADS IN JAVA

Java provides special input and output streams for setting up data transfer links between threads. Streams of bytes can be output by a thread through an object of type `PipedOutputStream` and input into a thread through an object of type `PipedInputStream`.

Let's say we have two software modules that we wish to run concurrently in two separate threads. Module 1 generates data that we want Module 2 to read asynchronously. So basically we want Module 1 to output its data when it can and then forget about it. And we want Module 2 to read in this data whenever it can. If, for the sake of discussion, we assume that the type of data is `double`, we could implement this inter-thread data transfer in the following manner:

```
//InterThreadIO.java

import java.io.*;

///////////////////////////// top level /////////////////////////////
class InterThreadIO {
    public static void main( String[] args ) {
        try {
            PipedOutputStream pout = new PipedOutputStream();      //(A)
            PipedInputStream pin = new PipedInputStream( pout );   //(B)

            Module_1 mod1 = new Module_1( pout );                  //(C)
            Module_2 mod2 = new Module_2( pin );                   //(D)

            mod1.start();
            mod2.start();
        } catch( IOException e ){}
    }
}
```

```
///////////////////////// class Module_1 /////////////////////////
class Module_1 extends Thread {
    private DataOutputStream out;

    public Module_1( OutputStream outsm ) {
        out = new DataOutputStream( outsm );                    //(E)
    }
    public void run() {
        for (;;) {
            try {
                double num = Math.random();
                out.writeDouble( num );
                System.out.println(
                    "Number written into the pipe: " + num );
                out.flush();
                sleep( 500 );
            } catch( Exception e ) {
                System.out.println( "Error: " + e );
            }
        }
    }
}

///////////////////////// class Module_2 /////////////////////////
class Module_2 extends Thread {
    private DataInputStream in;

    public Module_2( InputStream istr ) {
        in = new DataInputStream( istr );                      //(F)
    }
    public void run() {
        for (;;) {
            try {
                double x = in.readDouble();
                System.out.println(
                    "  Number received from the pipe: " + x );
            } catch( IOException e ) {
            System.out.println( "Error: " + e );
            }
        }
    }
}
```

Note how the `main` of `InterThreadIO` orchestrates the setting up of the two modules in lines (C) and (D), supplying their constructors with the stream objects they need for data transfer. The constructor for the producer module, `Module_1`, takes an object of type `OutputStream`. Since `OutputStream` is at the root of the output stream hierarchy, every output stream is of type `OutputStream`, and, therefore, an object of type `PipedOutputStream` that is supplied by the call to the `Module_1` constructor in line (C) is also of type `OutputStream`. Similar arguments apply to the constructor invocation for `Module_2` in line (D) since `InputStream` is at the root of the input stream hierarchy.

Also note that locally within the two modules the stream objects are of type `DataOutputStream` and `DataInputStream`, meaning that locally within `Module_1` data is output via a stream object of type `DataOutputStream`, and within `Module_2` the data is read via `DataInputStream`. However, these stream objects can be constructed by supplying the `PipedOutputStream` and `PipedInputStream` objects as arguments to the appropriate stream constructors within the `Module_1` and `Module_2` constructors, as the program does in lines (E) and (F).

18.8 JAVA THREADS FOR APPLETS

We will illustrate how a thread can be used for animating a Java web page. The idea is to construct an applet that loads in a sequence of images sufficiently rapidly so that an illusion of continuous motion is created.

The following example assumes that we have available to us four GIF images `bird0.gif`, `bird1.gif`, `bird2.gif`, and `bird3.gif`, corresponding to four consecutive shots of a bird in flight. We wish to create a thread that would load and display these images consecutively by cycling through them. The thread would be launched by an applet that is called by the following HTML code that resides in a file named `Animator.html`:

```
<HTML>
<TITLE>
Animation Applet
</TITLE>
<BODY BGCOLOR="#000000">
<APPLET CODE="Animator.class"  WIDTH=480 HEIGHT=590>
<PARAM name=imagename value="bird">
<PARAM name=imagecount value="4">
</APPLET>
</BODY>
</HTML>
```

Note the two parameters we pass to the applet: `imagename` and `imagecount`. The former is the base name of our "bird" images, and the latter tells the applet how many images it will need to load for animation.

Regarding the code for the applet itself, we will use the data members shown in lines (A) through (E). The data member `imageNameBase` of line (A) will store the base name of all the image files to be used for animation, and the data member `imageCount` of line (B) the number of images to be displayed in each cycle of animation. The images will be loaded into the `Image[]` array `imageArr` of line (E) whose size will be set to the value of the variable `imageCount`. The image currently being displayed in the animation sequence will be value of the data member `image` of type `Image` in line (D). So, basically, the value of `image` will sequence through the values in the array `imageArr` as each image is displayed in the applet. Finally, the variable `runner` of line (C) will hold a reference to the animation thread.

As was mentioned in Chapter 17, when a web browser launches a new applet for the first time, the initialization code in the `init` method is automatically executed. Our `init` method in line (F) first gets the applet parameters in lines (G) and (H), and then it loads in the images as `Image` objects in line (I). The images are loaded by invoking the `getImage` method of the `Applet` class. As described in the previous chapter, the `MediaTracker` object keeps track of the loading process.

After the `init` method, Java automatically calls the `start` method. This method, defined in line (J), is also called whenever a user returns to the page containing this applet. The animation thread is started afresh each time `start` is invoked, as should be clear from the syntax in lines (K) and (L). When the user goes off the page in which the applet sits, Java automatically calls the `stop` method defined in line (M). By nulling the object reference held by the variable `runner`, as we do in line (N), the execution of the thread is stopped.

The animation itself is carried out by calling the `paint` method defined in line (O). This method is invoked by the call to `repaint` in line (Q) of the `run` method defined in line (P). The source code for this example is shown below:

```
//Animator.java

import java.applet.*;
import java.awt.*;

public class Animator extends Applet implements Runnable {
    private String imageNameBase;                            //(A)
    private int imageCount;                                  //(B)
    private Thread runner;                                   //(C)
    private Image image = null;                              //(D)
    private Image[] imageArr;                                //(E)

    public void init() {                                     //(F)
        imageNameBase = getParameter( "imagename" );         //(G)
        imageCount = Integer.parseInt(
                    getParameter( "imagecount" ) );          //(H)
```

```
        imageArr = new Image[ imageCount ];
        int i = 0;
        while ( i < imageCount  ) {
            String imageName = imageNameBase + i + ".gif";
            imageArr[i] =
                getImage( getDocumentBase(), imageName );        //(I)
            MediaTracker tracker = new MediaTracker( this );
            tracker.addImage( imageArr[i], 0 );
            try {
                tracker.waitForID( 0 );
            } catch( InterruptedException e ) {}
            i++;
        }
    }

    public void start() {                                        //(J)
        runner = new Thread( this );                             //(K)
        runner.start();                                          //(L)
    }

    public void stop() {                                         //(M)
        runner = null;                                           //(N)
    }

    public void paint( Graphics g ) {                            //(O)
        if ( image == null ) return;
        g.drawImage( image, 100, 100, this );
    }

    public void run() {                                          //(P)
        int i = 0;
        while ( true ) {
            image = imageArr[i];
            i = ++i % imageCount;
            try {
                Thread.sleep( 200 );
            } catch( InterruptedException e ){}
            repaint();                                           //(Q)
        }
    }
}
```

18.9 THE EVENT DISPATCH THREAD IN AWT/SWING

We referred to the event processing loop in Chapter 17. This loop, executed in a separate thread in AWT/Swing, is called the *Event Dispatch Thread*.[13] Ideally, all of the interactions of a user with a GUI, such as when the user clicks on a button, or when the user chooses a menu item, and so on, should be handled by this thread.

The following program is a simple demonstration of the fact that ordinarily the event listener code is processed in the Event Dispatch Thread, whereas the code in main is executed in a separate thread. The program creates a window with a text area inside it. The user is allowed to enter text in the text area. (Since the GUI is so simple, a picture of the GUI is not shown.) To demonstrate which thread is handling what part of the code, we have essentially a do-nothing function keepBusy that is invoked both inside main in line (A) and inside the insertUpdate method of the MyDocumentListener class in line (B). The main purpose of keepBusy is to tell us which thread is executing what part of the program. This is accomplished with the help of the if block in line (C) where we test the boolean value of the predicate SwingUtilities.isEventDispatchThread().

```
//EventThreadDemo.java

import java.awt.*;
import java.awt.event.*;
import javax.swing.*;
import javax.swing.text.*;
import javax.swing.event.*;

class EventThreadDemo {

    public static void main( String[] args ) {

        JFrame frame = new JFrame( "Event Thread Demo" );

        frame.addWindowListener( new WindowAdapter() {
                public void windowClosing( WindowEvent e ) {
                    System.exit( 0 );
                }
        });

        JTextArea textArea = new JTextArea();
        textArea.setLineWrap(true);
        textArea.setWrapStyleWord(true);
        textArea.getDocument().addDocumentListener(
                            new MyDocumentListener());
```

---

[13]Sometimes it is also referred to as the AWT thread.

```
        JScrollPane areaScrollPane = new JScrollPane(textArea);
        areaScrollPane.setVerticalScrollBarPolicy(
                    JScrollPane.VERTICAL_SCROLLBAR_ALWAYS);
        areaScrollPane.setPreferredSize(new Dimension(250, 250));
        areaScrollPane.setBorder(
            BorderFactory.createCompoundBorder(
                BorderFactory.createCompoundBorder(
                    BorderFactory.createTitledBorder("Plain Text"),
                    BorderFactory.createEmptyBorder(5,5,5,5)),
                areaScrollPane.getBorder()));

        frame.getContentPane().add(
                    areaScrollPane, BorderLayout.CENTER );
        frame.pack();
        frame.setVisible( true );
        keepBusy( 500, "main" );                                //(A)
    }

    static class MyDocumentListener implements DocumentListener {
        public void insertUpdate( final DocumentEvent e ) {
            String str = null;
            Document doc = e.getDocument();
            int lengthText = doc.getLength();
            try {
                str = doc.getText( lengthText - 1, 1 );
            } catch( BadLocationException badloc ) {
                    badloc.printStackTrace();
            }
            keepBusy( 500, "MyDocumentListener" );              //(B)
            System.out.print( str );
        }
        public void removeUpdate(DocumentEvent e) { }
        public void changedUpdate(DocumentEvent e) { }
    }

    public static void keepBusy( int howLong, String source  ) {
        if (SwingUtilities.isEventDispatchThread() == true )    //(C)
            System.out.println(                                 //(D)
              " using Event Dispatch Thread for keepBusy in " + source);
        else
            System.out.println(                                 //(E)
              "   using the main thread for keepBusy in " + source );
        long curr = System.currentTimeMillis();
        while ( System.currentTimeMillis() < curr + howLong )
            ;
    }
}
```

If you execute the class and enter the string "hello" in the text area of the GUI, lines (D) and (E) of the program will print out the following messages in the terminal:

```
        using the main thread for keepBusy in main

h       using Event Dispatch Thread for keepBusy in MyDocumentListener

e       using Event Dispatch Thread for keepBusy in MyDocumentListener

l       using Event Dispatch Thread for keepBusy in MyDocumentListener

l       using Event Dispatch Thread for keepBusy in MyDocumentListener

o       using Event Dispatch Thread for keepBusy in MyDocumentListener
```

Obviously, the code shown in the `insertUpdate` method of the `MyDocumentListener` class is being executed in the Event Dispatch Thread, while the code in `main()` itself is being executed in a separate thread.

Ordinarily, this would also be the case if we constructed a more complex GUI with multiple top-level components and multiple listeners. All of the code in all the listener methods would get executed in a single thread, the Event Dispatch Thread. The advantages of this are obvious — you do not run into synchronization issues, in the sense that you do not have to worry that the displayed text in a text area may appear as partially old and partially new.

One is naturally curious about the following situation: Suppose we launch multiple GUI windows at the top level, *each in a separate thread of computation,* would *all* of the event processing for *all* of the GUI's be carried in one and the same Event Dispatch Thread? The answer, as demonstrated by the following program, is yes — at least ordinarily.

The following program launches separate GUI's, each in its own thread of computation, in lines (A) and (B) of the program. Each GUI looks the same as in the previous program — it is a window with a text area for the user to enter characters into. The program has also been provided with a utility class `MyTools` in line (L). Its method `printThreadInfo` in line (M) prints out the name of the thread in which the method is invoked. This method is invoked at various places in the program, such as in lines (G), (I), (J), and so on, to determine the identity of the thread executing the code at that point and also in line (O) of the `MyDocumentListener` class.

```
//EventThreadDemo2.java

import java.awt.*;
import java.awt.event.*;
import javax.swing.*;
import javax.swing.text.*;
import javax.swing.event.*;
```

```
///////////////////// class EventThreadDemo ////////////////////////
class EventThreadDemo {
    public static void main( String[] args ) {
        LaunchAFrame laf1 = new LaunchAFrame();                    //(A)
        LaunchAFrame laf2 = new LaunchAFrame();                    //(B)
        laf1.start();                                             //(C)
        laf2.start();                                             //(D)
    }
}

//////////////////////// class LaunchFrame ///////////////////////////
class LaunchAFrame extends Thread {                               //(E)
    public LaunchAFrame() {}

    public void run() {                                           //(F)
        MyTools.printThreadInfo(                                  //(G)
                "Just before creating Frame object:" );
        JFrame frame = new JFrame( "EventThreadsDemo 2" );       //(H)
        MyTools.printThreadInfo(
                "Just after creating Frame object:" );
        frame.addWindowListener( new WindowAdapter() {
                public void windowClosing( WindowEvent e ) {
                    System.exit( 0 );
                }
        });
        JTextArea textArea = new JTextArea();
        textArea.setLineWrap(true);
        textArea.setWrapStyleWord(true);
        textArea.getDocument().addDocumentListener(
                            new MyDocumentListener());
        MyTools.printThreadInfo(                                  //(I)
                "Just after registering document listener:" );
        JScrollPane areaScrollPane = new JScrollPane(textArea);

        MyTools.printThreadInfo(                                  //(J)
                "Just after creating the scroll pane:" );

        areaScrollPane.setVerticalScrollBarPolicy(
                    JScrollPane.VERTICAL_SCROLLBAR_ALWAYS);
        areaScrollPane.setPreferredSize(new Dimension(250, 250));
        areaScrollPane.setBorder(
            BorderFactory.createCompoundBorder(
                BorderFactory.createCompoundBorder(
                    BorderFactory.createTitledBorder("Plain Text"),
                    BorderFactory.createEmptyBorder(5,5,5,5)),
                areaScrollPane.getBorder()));
        frame.getContentPane().add(
                    areaScrollPane, BorderLayout.CENTER );
```

```
            MyTools.printThreadInfo( "Just before calling pack:" );
            frame.pack();
            frame.setLocation( 300, 300 );
            frame.setVisible( true );
            MyTools.printThreadInfo("Just after calling setVisible:");//(K)
        }
    }


/////////////////////////// class MyTools ///////////////////////////
class MyTools {                                              //(L)
    public static void printThreadInfo( String s ) {        //(M)
        System.out.println( s );
//          Thread.currentThread().getThreadGroup().list();
//          System.out.println(
//            "Number of threads in the current thread group: "
//            + Thread.currentThread().getThreadGroup().activeCount() );
        System.out.println( "The current thread is: "
                        + Thread.currentThread() );
    }

    public static void keepBusy( int howLong ) {            //(N)
        long curr = System.currentTimeMillis();
        while ( System.currentTimeMillis() < curr + howLong )
            ;
    }
}


/////////////////////// class MyDocumentListener ///////////////////////
class MyDocumentListener implements DocumentListener {
        public void insertUpdate( final DocumentEvent e ) {
            String str = null;
            Document doc = e.getDocument();
            int lengthText = doc.getLength();
            try {
                str = doc.getText( lengthText - 1, 1 );
            } catch( BadLocationException badloc ) {
                    badloc.printStackTrace();
            }
            MyTools.printThreadInfo("From iniside the listener:");//(O)
            MyTools.keepBusy( 500 );
            System.out.print( str );
        }
        public void removeUpdate(DocumentEvent e) { }
        public void changedUpdate(DocumentEvent e) { }
}
```

As mentioned already, this program creates two separate top-level windows in two separate threads. By executing the class and examining the information printed out in the terminal window, it is easy to see that the event processing for both the top-level windows is carried out in the same Event Dispatch Thread. The program produces the following output before a user starts interacting with either of the top-level windows by entering text into them. The output corresponds to the two threads launched by main, Thread-0 and Thread-1. Each thread executes concurrently its own version of the code in the run method of the LauchAFrame class. Note the timeslicing in action by seeing how the output switches between the two threads as the two top-level GUI's are being constructed:

```
Just before creating Frame object:
    The current thread is: Thread[Thread-0,5,main]

Just before creating Frame object:
    The current thread is: Thread[Thread-1,5,main]

Just after creating Frame object:
    The current thread is: Thread[Thread-1,5,main]

Just after creating Frame object:
    The current thread is: Thread[Thread-0,5,main]

Just after registering document listener:
    The current thread is: Thread[Thread-0,5,main]
....
....
```

But after you start entering text in the text areas of the two top-level GUI windows, you'll see the same Event Dispatch thread executing the two instances of the MyDocumentListener class. Suppose you enter "hello" in one window and "jello" in the other, you'll see the following output

```
From iniside the listener:
    The current thread is: Thread[AWT-EventQueue-0,6,main]
h

From iniside the listener:
    The current thread is: Thread[AWT-EventQueue-0,6,main]
e
....

From iniside the listener:
    The current thread is: Thread[AWT-EventQueue-0,6,main]
j

From iniside the listener:
    The current thread is: Thread[AWT-EventQueue-0,6,main]
e
....
```

Notice that both instances of `MyDocumentListener`, one for each of the top-level GUI windows, are running in the same thread, the thread named `AWT-EventQueue-0`. (The commented out lines in the program will print out additional useful information about the running threads.)

All of the code we have shown so far for `MyDocumentListener` will get executed in the Event Dispatch Thread. We now wish to point out that nothing prevents a programmer from executing any of this code in some other thread, as illustrated by the following version of `MyDocumentListener` in which all of the event handling code is processed by a new thread each time the function `insertUpdate` is invoked because the user typed a new character in the text area. New threads are constructed in line (A) and launched in line (B) of the implementation shown below.

```
class MyDocumentListener implements DocumentListener {

    public void insertUpdate( final DocumentEvent e ) {
        new Thread() {                                          //(A)
            public void run() {
                String str = null;
                Document doc = e.getDocument();
                int lengthText = doc.getLength();
                try {
                    str = doc.getText( lengthText - 1, 1 );
                } catch( BadLocationException badloc ) {
                        badloc.printStackTrace();
                }
                MyTools.printThreadInfo(
                        "From iniside the listener: " );
                MyTools.keepBusy( 500 );
                System.out.print( str );
            }
        }.start();                                             //(B)
    }

    public void removeUpdate(DocumentEvent e) { }

    public void changedUpdate(DocumentEvent e) { }
}
```

Since it is possible to run event handling code in different threads, as the above example illustrates, that raises a very important question: *What if this code needs to change the state of some component of the GUI? Which thread should be responsible for that?* The problem is that if we allow an arbitrary thread to change the state of the GUI, we could produce situations where a component, such as a `JTextArea`, shows information that is partially old and partially new.

To prevent such synchronization problems, it is recommended by the developers of Java that all methods that have the potential of altering the state of the GUI be placed in the Event Dispatch Thread. A GUI state altering method that is automatically placed in the Event Dispatch Thread is called *thread safe*. Most Swing methods are not thread safe. In fact, as of now, there are only two methods that are thread safe — repaint and revalidate — as these are automatically inserted into the Event Dispatch Thread no matter from what thread they are invoked. So, naturally, with the rest of the Swing methods you have to be careful as to how you invoke them.

To make the above recommendation more specific: *"Once a Swing component is realized, all code that might affect or depend on the state of that component should be executed in the Event Dispatch Thread."* A component is considered *realized* when it is either ready to be painted on the screen or has already been painted. A top-level container, such as a JFrame, JDialog, or a JApplet, is realized when any of the following methods is invoked on it: setVisible(true), show() or pack(). When a top-level container becomes realized, all the components it contains also become realized at the same time. A component also becomes automatically realized if it is added to a container that is already realized.

While the upside of all the event handling code being invoked through the Event Dispatch Thread is that one event handler will finish executing before the next one is taken up, the downside is that the code in each event handler must execute quickly so as not to degrade the GUI's overall response to user interaction. Basically, the GUI remains frozen to user interaction during the execution of event handler code. This makes it necessary for the code in an event handler to execute very quickly and that if more extensive processing (of, say, the information elicited from the user) is required, a separate thread be spawned.

Let's say we have spawned a separate thread for some heavy-duty computing needed inside a listener object. What if the result of this computing calls for changing the state of some GUI component?[14] Obviously, threads other than the Event Dispatch Thread would need to be able to place items in the event queue for altering the state of the GUI. The SwingUtilities class of the javax.swing package provides two static methods for this purpose:

```
public static void invokeLater( java.lang.Runnable runnable )

public static void invokeAndWait( java.lang.Runnable runnable )
        throws InterruptedException, InvocationTargetException
```

---

[14]The following scenario should drive home this point more forcefully: The user enters some information in a text component. This information is retrieved in a listener method. But now this information must be used to fetch some other information from a remote site — a process that could take an indeterminate length of time. So you launch a separate thread for the fetching operation so as not to slow down the response of the Event Dispatch Thread to interactions by the user with the other components of the interface. After the other thread has fetched the needed information, you need to update the interface by altering the state of some GUI component. Since the other thread is not the Event Dispatch Thread, how does one do that?

The difference between the two is that while `invokeLater` executes asynchronously, `invokeAndWait` executes synchronously. That means that `invokeLater` will return immediately after it has placed its argument object in the event queue. On the other hand, `invokeAndWait` returns only after the argument object has been processed by the Event Dispatch Thread. In both cases, the Event Dispatch Thread will get to the new object placed in the event queue only after all the pending AWT/Swing events have been processed.

In the following example, the `invokeLater` call queues the `Runnable` object `doHelloWorld` in the Event Dispatch Thread in line (B). Subsequently, we want the message in line (C) to be printed out. The Event Dispatch Thread will first dispose of all the pending items in the event queue before executing the new item. So it is not unlikely that the print statement in line (C) will be executed *before* the print statement in line (A).

```
Runnable doHelloWorld = new Runnable() {
    public void run() {
        System.out.println("Hello World from " +
                Thread.currentThread());                //(A)
    }
};
SwingUtilities.invokeLater(doHelloWorld);               //(B)
System.out.println("This might well be displayed "
            + "before the other message.");             //(C)
```

To compare with the behavior of `invokeAndWait`, in the example code shown below that uses `invokeAndWait` we have a guarantee that the application thread `appThread` will print out the message in line (D) *before* the message in line (E).

```
final Runnable doHelloWorld = new Runnable() {
    public void run() {
        System.out.println("Hello World on " +
                        Thread.currentThread());         //(D)
    }
};
Thread appThread = new Thread() {
    public void run() {
        try {
            SwingUtilities.invokeAndWait(doHelloWorld);
        }
        catch (Exception e) {
            e.printStackTrace();
        }
        System.out.println("Finished on "
                    + Thread.currentThread());            //(E)
    }
};
appThread.start();
```

Both program fragments shown above are from the "Threads and Swing" section of [32].

For complex situations, when a separate thread launched in the event handler is suppose to alter the state of the GUI after finishing some time-consuming operation, it is best to use the SwingWorker class available from the java.sun.com site. This class optionally executes additional code in the Event Dispatch Thread for altering the state of the GUI at the conclusion of the time-consuming operation.

18.10 MULTITHREADED PROGRAMMING IN C/C++

As was mentioned in the introduction to this chapter, one has to use an external thread package to do multithreaded programming in C++ since support for multithreading is not an integral part of the language. This is also true of C — that the language standard itself does not provide for multithreading. Over the years, various thread packages have been proposed for multithreading in C and, through C, for C++. Of these, the POSIX threads have emerged as the *de facto* standard.[15] Since C++ thread packages are generally built on top of C thread packages, it is a good idea to first grasp the POSIX threads in C. That is what we will do in this section.

The main library for POSIX threads in C is pthreads.h. It defines a data type called pthread_t for threads. A new thread is created by a call to pthread_create, a function of four parameters. Its various arguments are set in the following manner:

1. The first argument is a pointer to an object of type pthread_t.

2. The second argument, of type pthread_attr_t, can be used to specify thread attributes, such as the stack size to use, scheduling priority, and so on. If set to NULL, the default values are used for all the thread attributes.

3. The third argument is a pointer to a function that is to be executed by the thread. This function must be of type (void* (*)(void*)) or of a type that can be cast to the specified type.

4. The final argument is a pointer to a data block that can be passed to the function specified in the third argument.

To illustrate:

---

[15]POSIX, which stands for *Portable Operating System Interface*, can be thought of as a portable subset of Unix-like operating systems. It is an IEEE standard that was designed to facilitate the writing of programs that would run on the operating systems from different vendors. The specific standard that deals with thread management is POSIX.4.

```
pthread_t thread1;                                    //(A)
char* message1 = "hello ";                            //(B)
pthread_create( &thread1,                             //(C)
                NULL,
                ( void* (*)(void*) ) &print_message_function,
                (void*) message1);
```

Line (A) declares the identifier `thread1` to be of type `pthread_t` — `thread1` can serve as a convenient name for the thread. Line (B) declares a message that we would want the thread to print out. Line (C) then creates the thread. We assume that the function to be executed by the thread is named `print_message_function`.[16]

In the above example, we used NULL for the second argument in the call to `pthread_create` function. As was mentioned earlier, this sets all thread attribute values to their default values.[17]   In general, the operating behavior of a thread is controlled by an attribute object of type `pthread_attr_t` if specified as the second argument to `pthread_create`. To give the reader a sense of the richness of a POSIX thread, we will now list all the attributes one can specify for it:[18]

- *detachstate*

  This attribute controls whether the thread is created in a joinable state, in which case the value of the attribute is `PTHREAD_CREATE_JOINABLE`, or in a detached state, in which case the value of the attribute is `PTHREAD_CREATE_DETACHED`. The former is the default value. If a thread is created in a detached state, thread coordination cannot be achieved by invoking a function like `pthread_join` on it.[19] Additionally, whereas a thread created in a detached state immediately frees up the resources occupied by it when the thread runs to completion, a joinable thread will not do so until `pthread_join` is called for it. For example, the thread ID (which is the first argument to `pthread_create`) and the exit status of a joinable thread are retained until some other thread calls `pthread_join` on it. (Therefore, it is imperative that `pthread_join` be called

---

[16]The call to `pthread_create` shown here is meant to illustrate the basic syntax of the function call. This function, as all other "pthread" functions, returns an error code, which is 0 for successful completion and some nonzero value in case of failure. For functions returning error codes, it is a good programming practice to trap the returned value and to then print out any error messages by using a library function like `strerror(errorcode)` that returns a string corresponding to its argument.

[17]As an alternative to NULL for the second argument, the default-value initialization of all thread attributes can also be specified by using an object of type `pthread_attr_t` on which the function `pthread_attr_init` has been invoked, as we do in the program `ThreadBasic.c` of this section.

[18]These are reproduced from the man pages for LinuxThreads by Xavier Leroy, who is also the original developer of LinuxThreads.

[19]Like Java's `join` whose use was illustrated in Section 18.1, `pthread_join` suspends the calling thread until the called thread has run to completion. In addition to not being callable on a detached thread, `pthread_join` can also not be called on a daemon thread. A daemon thread, like the garbage collection thread in Java, runs in the background and the termination of a program is not predicated upon the daemon thread running to completion. We will show an example later in this section that uses `pthread_join`.

for each joinable thread to avoid memory leaks.) It is possible to dynamically change this attribute for a previously created joinable thread by calling
`pthread_detach(pthread_t threadID)` on it.

- *schedpolicy*

  This attribute selects the scheduling policy to be used for the thread. Its value
  can be SCHED_OTHER for regular, nonrealtime scheduling, or SCHED_RR for
  realtime, round-robin, or SCHED_FIFO for realtime first-in first-out. The default
  value is SCHED_OTHER. The realtime policies are available only to processes that
  carry superuser privileges. The scheduling policy of a thread can be changed
  after the thread is created by invoking `pthread_setschedpolicy`.

- *schedparam*

  This sets the scheduling priority for the thread. It is only meaningful for realtime
  scheduling policies. The default value of this attribute is 0. The scheduling
  priority of a thread can be changed after the thread is created by invoking
  `pthread_setschedparam`.

- *inheritsched*

  This attribute indicates whether the scheduling policy and scheduling parameters for a newly created thread are to be determined by the values of the attributes
  `schedpolicy` and `schedparam`, or should they be inherited from the parent
  thread. The two values for this attribute are PTHREAD_EXPLICIT_SCHED and
  PTHREAD_INHERIT_SCHED. The former is the default.

- *scope*

  This attribute defines the scope to be used for resolving the scheduling con-
  tention. The issue here is whether the thread priority should be relative to
  all other processes competing for time on the processor, or relative to just the
  other threads in the same process. The POSIX standard specifies two values
  for this attribute: PTHREAD_SCOPE_SYSTEM and PTHREAD_SCOPE_PROCESS.
  The former is the default, which says that a thread must compete with all other
  processes for time on the processor. Linux only supports this default value.

The value of any attribute in the `pthread_attr` object can be set by invoking

```
int pthread_attr_setattrname()
```

and retrieved by

```
int pthread_attr_getattrname()
```

where the part of the function call that is underscored with small uparrows is to be
replaced by the name of the attribute. For example, to set the scheduling policy,

```
int pthread_attr_setschedpolicy( const pthread_attr_t* attr,
                                          int* policy )
```

and to retrieve the policy

```
int pthread_attr_getschedpolicy( const pthread_attr_t* attr,
                                              int* policy )
```

In both cases, the successful completion of the function calls is indicated by a return value of 0. In the second case, if the policy is what is specified by the second argument, the return value will be 0.

We will now show a simple program for illustrating thread creation. This program does the same thing as our first Java multithreaded program, ThreadBasic.java, of Section 18.1 and, like the Java program, suffers from some serious flaws that we will address next. Since our intent here is to focus on the basics of thread creation, we will be content with the default values for the thread attributes.

```
//ThreadBasic.c

#include <pthread.h>
#include <stdio.h>

void* print_message( void* );

main()
{
    pthread_t thread1, thread2, thread3;
    pthread_attr_t attr1, attr2, attr3;

    char* message1 = "Good ";
    char* message2 = " morning";
    char* message3 = " to";

    pthread_attr_init( &attr1 );
    pthread_attr_init( &attr2 );
    pthread_attr_init( &attr3 );

    pthread_create( &thread1, &attr1,
        ( void* (*)(void*) ) &print_message, (void *) message1);

    pthread_create(&thread2, &attr2,
        ( void * (*)(void*) ) &print_message, (void *) message2);

    pthread_create(&thread3, &attr3,
        ( void * (*)(void*) ) &print_message, (void *) message3);

    fprintf( stdout, "%s", " you!" );
    exit(0);                                              //(A)
}
```

```
// Function to be executed in each thread:
void* print_message( void* ptr ) {
    char* message;
    message = (char*) ptr;
    //  sleep( 2 );                                      //(B)
    fprintf( stdout, "%s", message);
    fflush( stdout );                                    //(C)
    pthread_exit(0);                    // terminates thread
}
```

If this program is stored in a file called `ThreadBasic.c`, it can be compiled by

```
gcc ThreadBasic.c -lpthread
```

One would think that the output of this program would be

```
Good morning to you!
```

but what you actually get would depend on the outcome of the race condition that exists in the program. And if you uncomment line (B) of the `print_message` function, the program will not at all behave as intended.

As was the case with the Java program of Section 18.1, the problem with this program is that the parent thread or the process in which `main` is being executed is racing to get to `exit(0)` in line (A) in competition with the child threads. If the three child threads are not done with their work by the time the main parent thread gets to executing `exit(0)`, the process will terminate, killing all the threads with it. Additionally, even if `main` did not complete its work before the child threads, there is no guarantee that the child threads would do their jobs in the order in which they are created. To accentuate the race between `main` and the three threads, you can uncomment line (B), which would cause the program to print out just *you!* and nothing else, as `main` would run to termination before the child threads can finish up.[20]

The program shown above can be partially fixed by using `pthread_join`. The fix shown here, meant to illustrate the usage of `pthread_join`, eliminates the race condition between the parent thread or the process running `main` and the child threads. As was mentioned earlier in this section, a call to the function

```
int pthread_join( pthread_t thread, void** status );
```

---

[20]The above program assumes that the `sleep` command puts an individual thread to sleep. That is the case with Linux, which was the environment on the machine on which the above program was tested. Also, note the importance of flushing the output buffer in line (C) in the function executed by the threads. If we deliberately introduce additional time delays between the different threads, you'd not be able to see the effect of those additional delays unless the output buffer is flushed in the manner shown.

makes the calling thread wait until the thread named in the first argument terminates either by calling `pthread_exit` or by being canceled. It is not uncommon to call this function with NULL for the second argument, as in the following invocation

```
pthread_join( thread, NULL );
```

if it is not desired to find out whether a thread terminated naturally by the invocation of `pthread_exit` or by being canceled. If the second argument to this function is not NULL, the value returned by the terminating thread is stored as a code in `status`. This value will either be the argument given to `pthread_exit` when it was invoked or the enumeration symbolic constant PTHREAD_CANCELED if the thread was canceled.

Here is the program:

```c
//ThreadBasicWithJoin.c

#include <pthread.h>
#include <stdio.h>

void* print_message( void* );

main()
{
    pthread_t thread1, thread2, thread3;

    pthread_attr_t attr1, attr2, attr3;

    char* message1 = "Good ";
    char* message2 = " morning";
    char* message3 = " to";

    int status1;
    int status2;
    int status3;

    pthread_attr_init( &attr1 );
    pthread_attr_init( &attr2 );
    pthread_attr_init( &attr3 );

    pthread_create( &thread1, &attr1,
        ( void* (*)(void*) ) &print_message, (void *) message1);
    pthread_create(&thread2, &attr2,
        ( void * (*)(void*) ) &print_message, (void *) message2);
    pthread_create(&thread3, &attr3,
        ( void * (*)(void*) ) &print_message, (void *) message3);

    pthread_join( thread1, (void*) &status1 );
```

```
        pthread_join( thread2, (void*) &status2 );
        pthread_join( thread3, (void*) &status3 );

        // optional code for processing status1, status2, status3

        fprintf( stdout, "%s", " you!" );
        exit(0);
}

// Function to be executed by each thread:
void* print_message( void* ptr ) {
        char* message;
        message = (char*) ptr;
        //  sleep( 2 );
        fprintf( stdout, "%s", message);
        fflush( stdout );
        pthread_exit(0);
}
```

18.10.1   Demonstrating Thread Interference with POSIX Threads

As was the case with Java multithreading, in addition to the race conditions, one also has to guard against thread interference. To demonstrate thread interference when using POSIX threads, we will show the following example that parallels the first Java example of Section 18.4 for illustrating thread interference.

As in the Java example UnsynchedSwaps.java, we launch four threads, each repeatedly modifying the two data members of a DataObject object, dobj, in such a way that the sum of the two data members should always add up to 100.

```
//UnsynchedSwaps.c

#include <pthread.h>
#include <stdio.h>
#include <time.h>

typedef struct {
  int dataItem1;
  int dataItem2;
} DataObject;

//initialization allocates memory for dobj:
DataObject dobj = { 50, 50 };
```

```c
void keepBusy( double howLongInMillisec );
void itemSwap( DataObject* dptr );
void test( DataObject* dptr );
void repeatedSwaps( DataObject* dptr );

main()
{
    pthread_t t1, t2, t3, t4;

    pthread_create(&t1, NULL, (void* (*)(void*)) repeatedSwaps, &dobj);
    pthread_create(&t2, NULL, (void* (*)(void*)) repeatedSwaps, &dobj);
    pthread_create(&t3, NULL, (void* (*)(void*)) repeatedSwaps, &dobj);
    pthread_create(&t4, NULL, (void* (*)(void*)) repeatedSwaps, &dobj);

    pthread_join( t1, NULL );
    pthread_join( t2, NULL);
    pthread_join( t3, NULL);
    pthread_join( t4, NULL);
}

void keepBusy( double howLongInMillisec ) {
    int ticksPerSec = CLOCKS_PER_SEC;
    int ticksPerMillisec = ticksPerSec / 1000;
    clock_t ct = clock();
    while ( clock() < ct + howLongInMillisec * ticksPerMillisec )
        ;
}
void itemSwap( DataObject* dptr ) {
    int x = (int) ( -4.999999 + rand() % 10 );
    dptr->dataItem1 -= x;
    keepBusy(10);
    dptr->dataItem2 += x;
}
void test( DataObject* dptr ) {
    int sum = dptr->dataItem1 + dptr->dataItem2;
    printf( "%d\n", sum );
}
void repeatedSwaps( DataObject* dptr ) {
    int i = 0;
    while ( i < 20000 ) {
        itemSwap( dptr );
        if ( i % 4000 == 0 ) test( dptr );
        keepBusy( 1 );          // in milliseconds
        i++;
    }
}
```

The logic of the above program is the same as that of the Java program
UnsynchedSwaps.java of Section 18.4; the reader is referred to the Java implementation for a more detailed explaination. The cause of thread interference also
remains the same. That the threads are stepping on one another is demonstrated by the
following output, which is similar to what we obtained with UnsynchedSwap.java:

```
100
99
101
101
100
100
99
98
101
102
104
106
96
99
100
103
102
101
96
103
```

18.10.2   MUTEX for Dealing with POSIX Thread Interference

Thread interference in POSIX threads can be eliminated by using a mutex lock. The
name mutex, an abbreviation of *mutual exclusion*, is one of the two thread synchronization primitives provided by POSIX, the other being the *condition variable* presented in the next subsection. The idea behind a mutex lock is that a shared resource
— such as a global variable — after it is locked by invoking pthread_mutex_lock is
accessible to only that thread which invoked the lock. The resource does not become
available to any other thread until the locking thread releases the lock by invoking
pthread_mutex_unlock.

In the following program, line (A) declares the identifier mutex as a mutex lock. To
initialize a mutex, we can either use the system supplied defaults, as we do in the commented out line (E), or we can declare a mutex attribute object for the purpose of initialization, as we do in line (B). The mutex attribute object is initialized to its defaults
by the invocation shown in line (C). In Linux, the mutex attribute object consists of
only one attribute — the *mutex kind*, which can either be PTHREAD_MUTEX_FAST_NP or

PTHREAD_MUTEX_RECURSIVE_NP, the former being the default value of the attribute.[21] The mutex kind determines what happens if a thread invokes pthread_mutex_lock on a mutex that it had locked previously. If a mutex is of the "recursive" kind, the invocation of the locking function succeeds. However, if a mutex is of the "fast" kind, the calling thread is suspended forever. For the recursive kind, the mutex records the number of times the thread owning the mutex has locked it through recursive calls. The owning thread must call the pthread_mutex_unlock function equal number of times before the mutex returns to the unlocked state. The kind of a mutex can be set by invoking

```
int pthread_mutexattr_setkind_np( pthread_mutexattr_t* attr,
                                  int kind )
```

and the kind of a previously created mutex can be examined by invoking

```
int pthread_mutexattr_getkind_np( pthread_mutexattr_t* attr,
                                  int* kind )
```

Both of these functions return 0 when they execute successfully. For the 'get' function, if the kind of a mutex is what is specified by the second argument, it returns successfully with 0.

Getting back to the problem of fixing thread interference in our earlier example of UnsynchedSwaps.c, we now place the vulnerable-to-interference parts of the code in the itemSwap and the test functions between the invocation pthread_mutex_lock(&mutex) and the invocation pthread_mutex_unlock(&mutex), as shown in lines (F), (G), (H), and (I). This way only one thread at a time will be able to execute these functions.

```
//SynchedSwaps.c

#include <pthread.h>
#include <stdio.h>
#include <time.h>

pthread_mutex_t mutex;                                      //(A)
pthread_mutexattr_t attr;                                   //(B)

typedef struct {
  int dataItem1;
  int dataItem2;
} DataObject;

DataObject dobj = { 50, 50 };
```

---

[21] The NP suffix means that it is a nonportable extension to the POSIX standard and should not be used in code meant to be portable.

```
void keepBusy( double howLongInMillisec );
void itemSwap( DataObject* dptr );
void test( DataObject* dptr );
void repeatedSwaps( DataObject* dptr );

main()
{
    pthread_t t1, t2, t3, t4;

    pthread_mutexattr_init( &attr );                            //(C)
    pthread_mutex_init( &mutex, &attr );                        //(D)
    // pthread_mutex_init( &mutex, NULL );                      //(E)

    pthread_create(&t1, NULL, (void* (*)(void*)) repeatedSwaps, &dobj);
    pthread_create(&t2, NULL, (void* (*)(void*)) repeatedSwaps, &dobj);
    pthread_create(&t3, NULL, (void* (*)(void*)) repeatedSwaps, &dobj);
    pthread_create(&t4, NULL, (void* (*)(void*)) repeatedSwaps, &dobj);

    pthread_join( t1, NULL );
    pthread_join( t2, NULL);
    pthread_join( t3, NULL);
    pthread_join( t4, NULL);
}

void keepBusy( double howLongInMillisec ) {
    int ticksPerSec = CLOCKS_PER_SEC;
    int ticksPerMillisec = ticksPerSec / 1000;
    clock_t ct = clock();
    while ( clock() < ct + howLongInMillisec * ticksPerMillisec )
        ;
}

void itemSwap( DataObject* dptr ) {
    int x;
    pthread_mutex_lock( &mutex );                               //(F)
    x = (int) ( -4.999999 + rand() % 10 );
    dptr->dataItem1 -= x;
    keepBusy(10);
    dptr->dataItem2 += x;
    pthread_mutex_unlock( &mutex );                             //(G)
}

void test( DataObject* dptr ) {
    int sum;
    pthread_mutex_lock( &mutex );                               //(H)
    sum = dptr->dataItem1 + dptr->dataItem2;
    printf( "%d\n", sum );
    pthread_mutex_unlock( &mutex );                             //(I)
}
```

```
void repeatedSwaps( DataObject* dptr ) {
    int i = 0;
    while ( i < 20000 ) {
        itemSwap( dptr );
        if ( i % 4000 == 0 ) test( dptr );
        keepBusy( 1 );              // in milliseconds
        i++;
    }
}
```

When a mutex lock is no longer needed, it can be destroyed by invoking pthread_mutex_destroy() with an argument that is a pointer to the mutex lock.

18.10.3   POSIX Threads: Condition Variables and the `wait-signal` Mechanism for Dealing with Deadlock

Using POSIX threads, potential deadlock can often be avoided by thread synchronization using condition variables. A condition variable acts like a signaling object. When a thread cannot continue execution because a certain data condition is not satisfied, it calls a special function that suspends the execution of the thread and at the same time sets up a signaling object known as a condition variable. And then later when some other thread is able to create the data conditions necessary for the first thread to proceed, the second thread signals the condition variable, enabling the first thread to try to regain its lock on the processor.

A condition variable is initialized by

```
pthread_cond_t cv;
cv = malloc(sizeof(pthread_cond_t));
pthread_cond_init( cv, NULL );                        //(A)
```

In general, the initialization is carried out by invoking

```
int pthread_cond_init( pthread_cond_t* cond,
                                pthread_condattr_t* attr ); //(B)
```

which initializes the condition variable cond using the attributes specified in attr. Default attributes are used if attr is NULL, as in line (A) above. The LinuxThreads implementation does not support any attributes for condition variables and ignores the second argument in the call to the initializer in line (B).

Apart from the initialization, the most commonly used condition variable related functions are

```
int pthread_cond_wait(pthread_cont_t* cond, pthread_mutex_t* mutex);
```

and

```
int pthread_cond_signal( pthread_cond_t* cond );
```

The first function, pthread_cond_wait, causes the unlocking of the mutex that is supplied to it as the second argument. This unlocking acts in the same manner as if a call was made to pthread_mutex_unlock. Additionally, and even more importantly, the thread execution is suspended until the condition variable cond is signaled, perhaps by the action of some other thread. It must be the case that the mutex that is unlocked by pthread_cond_wait was locked previously by the the same thread that calls pthread_cond_wait — the calling thread. When the condition variable is signaled, pthread_cond_wait re-acquires the lock (as per pthread_mutex_lock).

The thread state created by the execution of pthread_cond_wait can be thought of as the calling thread *waiting on the condition variable* that is the first argument to the function. The wait is for the condition variable to be signaled. In the meantime, the calling thread stays suspended.

A condition variable on which a thread is waiting is signaled by the execution of pthread_cond_signal by some other thread. It is possible for multiple threads to be waiting on the same condition variable. When such a condition variable is signaled, only one of those threads will be restarted. The POSIX standard does not say which one. If no threads are waiting on a condition variable that is signaled by some other thread, nothing happens.

If it is desired to simultaneously restart all the threads waiting on the same condition variable, the function to use is pthread_cond_broadcast:

```
int pthread_cond_broadcast( pthread_cond_t* cond );
```

Other condition variable functions that we do not present here are pthread_cond_timedwait and pthread_cond_destroy.

The program shown below is a POSIX threads version of the MultiCustomerAccount Java class of Section 18.6.[22] To make sure that there are sufficient funds in the common account before a withdrawal can take place, the program uses the wait–signal mechanism of POSIX threads. If the amount to be withdrawn is greater than the current balance, the following statement is executed in line (C) of the withdraw function:

```
pthread_cond_wait( &cv, &mutex );
```

where cv is the condition variable that is used in conjunction with the mutex lock. This statement causes the thread to relinquish its lock on the code block and places the

---

[22]The overall logic of the program MultiCustomerAccount.c of this section is the same as that of MultiCustomerAccount.java of Section 18.6. See the Java description for a more detailed explanation of the logic.

thread back in the wait state, where it waits for the condition variable to be signaled by the execution of

```
pthread_cond_broadcast( &cv );
```

by a depositor thread in line (A). When the signal is received, the waiting thread is put back in the running for time on the processor. When it starts executing again, the test in the while loop of line (B) causes it to recheck that the amount to be withdrawn does not exceed the new balance in the account. As long as this condition is not satisfied, it keeps on executing the wait function and relinquishing its mutex lock. But when the condition is satisfied, it goes ahead with the withdrawal. In this manner, the balance is never allowed to become negative.

```
//MultiCustomerAccount.c

#include <pthread.h>
#include <stdio.h>
#include <stdlib.h>
#include <time.h>

void keepBusy( double howLongInMillisec );

pthread_mutex_t mutex;
pthread_mutexattr_t attr;

pthread_cond_t cv;

typedef struct {
    int balance;
} Account;

Account* create_account();
void deposit( Account* a, int dep );
void withdraw( Account* a, int draw );
void multiple_deposits( Account* acct );
void multiple_withdrawals( Account* acct );

main()
{
    int i;
    int status;
    pthread_t depositorThreads[5];
    pthread_t withdrawerThreads[5];

    Account* account = create_account();

    pthread_mutexattr_init( &attr );
```

```c
    pthread_mutex_init( &mutex, &attr );
    pthread_cond_init( &cv, NULL );

    for ( i=0; i < 5; i++ ) {
        pthread_create( depositorThreads + i,
                        NULL,
                        (void*(*)(void*)) multiple_deposits,
                        account );
        pthread_create( withdrawerThreads + i,
                        NULL,
                        (void*(*)(void*)) multiple_withdrawals,
                        account );
    }
    for ( i=0; i < 5; i++ ) {
        pthread_join( *(depositorThreads + i), (void*) &status );
        pthread_join( *(withdrawerThreads + i), (void*) &status );
    }
}

Account* create_account() {
    Account* a = malloc( sizeof(Account) );
    a->balance = 0;
    return a;
}
void deposit( Account* a, int dep ) {
    pthread_mutex_lock( &mutex );
    a->balance += dep;
    pthread_cond_broadcast( &cv );                              //(A)
    pthread_mutex_unlock( &mutex );
}
void withdraw( Account* a, int draw ) {
    pthread_mutex_lock( &mutex );
    while ( a->balance < draw ) {                               //(B)
        pthread_cond_wait( &cv, &mutex );                       //(C)
    }
    a->balance -= draw;
    pthread_mutex_unlock( &mutex );
}
void multiple_deposits( Account* acct ) {
    int i = 0;
    int x;
    while ( 1 ) {
        x = rand() % 10;
        deposit( acct, x );
        if ( i++ % 100 == 0 )
            printf( "balance after deposits:  %d\n", acct->balance );
        keepBusy( 1 );
    }
}
```

```
void multiple_withdrawals( Account* acct ) {
    int x;
    int i = 0;
    while ( 1 ) {
        x = rand() % 10;
        withdraw( acct, x );
        if ( i++ % 100 == 0 )
            printf( "balance after withdrawals: %d\n", acct->balance );
        keepBusy( 1 );
    }
}
void keepBusy( double howLongInMillisec ) {
    int ticksPerSec = CLOCKS_PER_SEC;
    int ticksPerMillisec = ticksPerSec / 1000;
    clock_t ct = clock();
    while ( clock() < ct + howLongInMillisec * ticksPerMillisec )
        ;
}
```

Here is a portion of the output produced by the program. As the reader can see, the use of the wait–signal mechanism on the condition variable prevents the account balance from going negative. If a withdrawer thread wants to withdraw an amount that exceeds the balance in the account, it waits until the one or more depositor threads have created a sufficiently large balance in the account.

```
balance after deposits:  3
balance after withdrawals: 2
balance after deposits:  10
balance after withdrawals: 21
balance after deposits:  63
balance after withdrawals: 63
balance after deposits:  66
balance after withdrawals: 81
balance after deposits:  86
balance after withdrawals: 285
balance after deposits:  331
balance after withdrawals: 325
balance after withdrawals: 221
balance after deposits:  232
balance after withdrawals: 281
....
....
```

18.11   OBJECT-ORIENTED MULTITHREADING IN C++

While it is possible to use POSIX threads directly for C++ programs, there are now also available various object-oriented packages and stand-alone threading classes for this purpose. The C++ classes for threading are in most cases built on top of the POSIX threads, meaning that the threads created by the relevant C++ classes get compiled down into POSIX threads.

In this section, we will illustrate some of the C++ threading classes that come with the Qt library.[23] Qt provides a class `QThread` whose functionality is similar to the Java class `Thread`. A C++ class can be made multithreadable by extending `QThread` and overriding its `run` method. The code that needs to be executed in separate threads is placed in the `run` method. This code can be invoked for execution by calling the `start` method of `QThread`.

This is demonstrated by the following class, `HelloThreadWithJoin`, that gets executed in the same fashion as the Java class of the same name in Section 18.1. Note that what's accomplished by `join` for the Java case is accomplished by `wait` here. The thread in which `main` executes blocks when it encounters

```
ht1.wait();
```

until the thread on which `wait` is invoked, in this case the thread `ht1`, has run to termination (or was never started in the first place). The `wait` also takes an optional argument consisting of time in milliseconds that if elapsed from the moment the function is invoked will cause `wait` to return. The same is the case with the invocation `ht2.wait` and `ht3.wait` in the program.

```
//HelloThreadWithJoin.cc

#include <qthread.h>
#include <string>
#include <iostream>
using namespace std;
```

---

[23]For the examples shown in this section to work, you may have to reinstall Qt on your system if the original installation (for the GUI work in Chapter 17) was carried out without activating the support for multithreading. To reinstall Qt, first uninstall the existing version by going into the main Qt directory and executing

```
make clean
```

and then reconfigure and rebuild Qt by

```
configure -thread
make
```

```
class HelloThread : public QThread {
    string message;
public:
    HelloThread( string message ) { this->message = message; }
    void run() { cout << message; }
};

int main()
{
    HelloThread ht1( "Good " );
    HelloThread ht2( "Morning " );
    HelloThread ht3( "to " );

    ht1.start();
    ht2.start();
    ht3.start();

    ht1.wait();
    ht2.wait();
    ht3.wait();
    cout << "you!" << endl;

    return 0;
}
```

This program can be compiled with the following command line:

```
g++ -o HelloThreadWithJoin HelloThreadWithJoin.cc          \
    -I$QTDIR/include -DQT_THREAD_SUPPORT -L$QTDIR/lib -lqt-mt
```

Vis-à-vis the command-line compilation of Qt programs in Chapter 17, note the use of the macro QT_THREAD_SUPPORT for including multithreading support at compile time. Also note that now we are linking the program with the library libqt-mt that is automatically created when you install Qt with the multithreading option activated.

Our next example illustrates the use of QMutex class for suppressing thread interference by using mutex locks. This is a C++ version of the Java program SynchedSwaps.java of Section 18.5. In the code shown below, a mutex lock is used in the function itemSwap; that ensures that only one thread at a time will gain access to the code inside itemSwap. The function keepBusy inside itemSwap is supposed to simulate the condition of possible additional computing between the time instants when the two int data members of the DataObject class are changed in equal but opposite manner.

```
//SynchedSwaps.cc

#include <qthread.h>
#include <cstdlib>
#include <iostream>
#include <ctime>
using namespace std;

void keepBusy( double howLongInMillisec );

class DataObject : public QThread {
    QMutex mutex;
    int dataItem1;
    int dataItem2;
public:
    DataObject() {
        dataItem1 = 50;
        dataItem2 = 50;
    }
    void itemSwap() {
        mutex.lock();                                       //(A)
        int x = (int) ( -4.999999 + rand() % 10 );
        dataItem1 -= x;
        keepBusy( 1 );
        dataItem2 += x;
        mutex.unlock();                                     //(B)
    }
    void test() {
        mutex.lock();
        int sum = dataItem1 + dataItem2;
        cout << sum << endl;
        mutex.unlock();
    }
    void run() {}
};

DataObject dobj;

class RepeatedSwaps : public QThread  {
public:
    RepeatedSwaps() {
        start();
    }
    void run() {
        int i = 0;
        while ( i++ < 5000 ) {
            dobj.itemSwap();
```

```
            if ( i % 1000 == 0 ) dobj.test();
        }
    }
};

int main( )
{
    RepeatedSwaps t0;
    RepeatedSwaps t1;
    RepeatedSwaps t2;
    RepeatedSwaps t3;

    t0.wait();
    t1.wait();
    t2.wait();
    t3.wait();
}

void keepBusy( double howLongInMillisec ) {
    int ticksPerSec = CLOCKS_PER_SEC;
    int ticksPerMillisec = ticksPerSec / 1000;
    clock_t ct = clock();
    while ( clock() < ct + howLongInMillisec * ticksPerMillisec )
        ;
}
```

With the mutex lock in place, the program produces the following output:

```
100
100
100
100
100
100
100
100
100
100
100
100
100
100
100
100
100
100
100
100
```

However, if you comment out the mutex locks in lines (A) and (B), the output becomes the following, clearly showing that thread interference is taking its toll:

```
97
100
97
94
97
99
103
91
109
97
100
95
99
96
96
96
96
96
96
100
```

Qt also comes with a class QWaitCondition that can be used to keep multiple threads from getting into deadlocks in the same manner as the wait–notify mechanism of Java and the wait–signal mechanism for POSIX threads. QWaitCondition comes with the member function wait that works in a manner analogous to Object.wait for Java. When a thread executes this wait, the thread releases the mutex that must be locked prior to the invocation of wait. Such a thread stays dormant until another thread executes either wakeOne or wakeAll, the former for notifying one of the randomly selected waiting threads and the latter for notifying all waiting threads. The following program illustrates the use of the wait–wakeAll mechanism provided by the QWaitCondition class. This program is a C++ version of the MultiCustomerAccount.java program shown earlier in Section 18.6. We have five depositor threads and five withdrawer threads. If a withdrawer thread wishes to withdraw an amount that exceeds the current balance in the account, the thread must wait until the depositor threads have put sufficient money into the account.

```
//MultiCustomerAccount.cc

#include <qthread.h>
#include <cstdlib>
#include <iostream>
#include <ctime>
using namespace std;
```

```
void keepBusy( double howLongInMillisec );

QMutex mutex;
QWaitCondition cond;

class Account : public QThread {
public:
    int balance;

    Account() { balance = 0; }
    void deposit( int dep ) {
        mutex.lock();
        balance += dep;
        keepBusy( 1 );
        cond.wakeAll();
        mutex.unlock();
    }
    void withdraw( int draw ) {
        mutex.lock();
        while ( balance < draw ) {
            cond.wait( &mutex );
        }
        keepBusy( 1 );
        balance -= draw;
        mutex.unlock();
    }
    void run(){}
};

Account acct;

class Depositor : public QThread {
public:
    void run() {
        int i = 0;
        while ( true ) {
            int x = (int) ( rand() % 10 );
            acct.deposit( x );
            if ( i++ % 100 == 0 )
                cerr << "balance after deposits: "
                     <<  acct.balance << endl;
            keepBusy( 1 );
        }
    }
};

class Withdrawer : public QThread {
public:
```

```
    void run() {
        int i = 0;
        while ( true ) {
            int x = (int) ( rand() % 10 );
            acct.withdraw( x );
            if ( i++ % 100 == 0 )
                cerr << "balance after withdrawals:   "
                        << acct.balance << endl;
            keepBusy( 1 );
        }
    }
};

int main()
{
    Depositor* depositors[5];
    Withdrawer* withdrawers[5];

    for ( int i=0; i < 5; i++ ) {
        depositors[ i ] = new Depositor();
        withdrawers[ i ] = new Withdrawer();
        depositors[ i ]->start();
        withdrawers[ i ]->start();
    }
    for ( int i=0; i < 5; i++ ) {
        depositors[ i ]->wait();
        withdrawers[ i ]->wait();
    }
}

void keepBusy( double howLongInMillisec ) {
    int ticksPerSec = CLOCKS_PER_SEC;
    int ticksPerMillisec = ticksPerSec / 1000;
    clock_t ct = clock();
    while ( clock() < ct + howLongInMillisec * ticksPerMillisec )
        ;
}
```

18.12 CREDITS AND SUGGESTIONS FOR FURTHER READING

Section 18.6's multicustomer bank account example for illustrating Java's wait–notify mechanism for dealing with thread deadlock is based on Horstmann and Cornell's multicustomer example [27, pp. 101–111]. The example of data I/O between threads in Section 18.7 is a smaller version of a more thorough example provided by Horstmann and Cornell [27, pp. 113–115].

The Swing tutorial at `java.sun.com` [32] is an excellent source of information for all matters related to Swing, including issues related to multithreading and how to write thread-safe programs involving Swing components. That's where the reader will also find additional information on the `SwingWorker` class. The Swing examples shown in this chapter were inspired by the code in the on-line tutorial. For hardcopy resources on the multithreading issues related to Swing, the reader is referred to [26, 18, 52, 55].

With regard to POSIX threads, the type definitions and many of their elaborations were taken directly from the LinuxThreads man pages written originally by Xavier Leroy, the author of the LinuxThreads library [47]. The reader is referred to [11, 48, 49] for further readings on POSIX threads and to [40] for object-oriented C++ threads. Section 23.2 of the book by Stevens [53] is also a good introduction to the subject.

For multithreading in Qt, the best source is the on-line information at [29].

18.13 HOMEWORK

1. Write a clock program that displays an analog clock in which the second hand is updated every one second and the minute and the hour hands accordingly. Implement the timer part of the program as a thread that wakes up after every one second and gets the new time from the system. This thread can be a daemon thread. (A footnote in Section 18.10 explains what a daemon thread is.) For this exercise, you could declare your timer thread to be a daemon thread by

   ```
   Clock c = new Clock();
   Thread t = new Thread( c );
   t.setDaemon( true );
   ```

   assuming that the `Clock` object c is of type `Runnable`.

2. Write a multithreaded C++ program that solves the famous Dining Philosophers Problem. Your program should demonstrate how thread deadlock and starvation can be avoided by using mutex locks in conjunction with *condition variables*. The statement of the dining philosophers problem is:

   > Five philosophers are sitting around a round table, with one chopstick between each pair of philosophers. Each philosopher alternates between two states, THINKING and EATING, both for random periods of time. Suppose we represent each philosopher with one thread, the goal in solving this problem is to come up with a scheduling strategy so that all the philosophers get to eat for roughly the same time.

Obviously, only two philosophers can eat at one time. Moreover, a philosopher can eat only if both his/her two neighbors are not eating. Additionally, if it should happen that each philosopher has picked up one chopstick and is waiting for the other chopstick to be put down by a neighbor, we will have a deadlock. To see how we could get into a starvation situation for one of the philosophers, while only two philosophers can eat at any given time, it cannot be two adjacent philosophers. Let's say the philosophers are indexed 0, 1, 2, 3, and 4. Let's also say that 0 and 2 are eating. Let's assume that after 0 and 2 are done, 1 and 3 switch into the eating state. Now if after 1 and 3 are done eating, 0 and 2 resume eating, and so on back to 1 and 3, the philosopher 4 would end up starving.

19

Network Programming

This chapter shows how Java and C++ can be used for network programming based in the client–server model. Today it is probably the most commonly used model for communicating between applications running on different computers. It is also frequently used for establishing communication links between different applications running on the same computer.

In the client–server model, a server is usually a continuously running program that monitors a port for requests from other applications, called clients, wishing to communicate with the server through that port. The server and client roles apply only to individual communication links. That is, an application A can be a server with respect to application B's role as a client on one communication link. Yet, on a different communication link, application A could be a client to application B's role as a server.

Telnet service is a common example of the client–server model of communication. On the remote machine there is a constantly running program called `telnetd` (for telnet daemon) that monitors a designated port, port 23, for requests for telnet connections. When a client seeks such a connection, it runs a program called `telnet` that sends to the server machine a *socket number*, which is a combination of the IP address of the client machine together with the port number that the client will use for communicating with the server. When the server receives the client socket number, it acknowledges the request by sending back to the client its own socket number, meaning its IP address and the port on which it will communicate with the client.

In this chapter, we will first see how one can write client applications in Java to communicate with servers already in place. We will then show how one can set up both ends of a communication link. Next, we will show how C++ classes from the Qt library can be used for doing the same things.

19.1   ESTABLISHING SOCKET CONNECTIONS WITH EXISTING SERVERS IN JAVA

The following program is a client that seeks to connect to a server on port 80.[1] This port is usually monitored by the HTTPD servers (the HyperText Transmission Protocol Daemon program) on machines on which such servers are installed and running. In response to an appropriately formatted "GET" request received from a client on port 80, an HTTPD server can send back a web page whose URL is embedded in the request. Let's see how this can be done.

A client wishing to receive web pages from an HTTPD server that monitors port 80 constructs a socket by

```
Socket t = new Socket( webAddress, 80 );
```

The class Socket is defined in the package java.net. For example, if we wanted to download the raw ascii of the Purdue University web page, we would use the invocation

```
Socket socket = new Socket( "www.purdue.edu", 80 );
```

in our client program.[2] The Socket object thus constructed talks to the www.purdue.edu server on port 80 and delivers to it the client's "socket number," which consists of the IP address of the client and the port number being used by the client. The server acknowledges this request by sending back its own socket number, which is a concatenation of the IP address of the server and the port number the server will use for the connection with the client. The socket constructor throws the UnknownHostException if it is not able to establish a connection with the server.

---

[1]All communication in client–server links takes place through ports. The port numbers 0 through 255 are reserved for standard network services such as TELNET, FTP, FINGER, TFTP, ECHO, and so on. Port numbers above 255 can be used for more specialized user-created services.

[2]The Socket constructor call shown here is for establishing communication with a server using what's referred to as "a reliable, connection-based stream protocol," as in TCP (for Transmission Control Protocol). By appropriate handshaking with the destination machine, TCP ensures that a packet sent over a network was actually received at the destination. If the data was not received, it is re-transmitted. TCP is used by higher-level utility protocols such as Telnet, FTP (for File Transfer Protocol), SMTP (Simple Mail Transfer Protocol), rlogin (for remote log in), and so on. One can also construct a socket object that would permit communication based on the less reliable but faster datagram protocol, as used in UDP (for User Datagram Protocol). UDP is used by Trivial File Transfer Protocol (TFTP), the Remote Call Procedure (RCP), and so on. UDP is particularly suitable for those applications where missing packets can be tolerated, as for example in audio and video transmissions.

Once a client has established a socket link with the server, the data can be sent to the server and received back from the server on the link using essentially the same methods that are used for reading from files and writing into files on a local machine. The Socket class has two methods, getInputStream and getOutputStream, that return InputStream and OutputStream objects, respectively. Of course, when possible, for convenience you would want to convert the binary I/O stream objects into character I/O stream objects of type Reader and Writer.

```
OutputStream out = socket.getOutputStream();
PrintStream ps = new PrintStream( out, true );

InputStream in = socket.getInputStream();
InputStreamReader in_reader = new InputStreamReader( in );
BufferedReader br = new BufferedReader( in_reader );
```

The Reader object in_reader turns the bytes output by the InputStream object in into Unicode characters. By feeding these into the BufferedReader object br, we can invoke the efficient readLine method of BufferedReader to input one line of text at a time.

There is one more thing that needs to be mentioned in order to extract the raw ascii of a web page through a client socket. After establishing the socket communication link, the HTTPD server needs a precisely formatted request for the page. The format of this request is

```
GET http://....web-address... /HTTP/1.1\n\n

<------  256 chars ----->
```

where by web-address we mean a string such as *www.purdue.edu*. This string must be 256 characters long, with spaces occupying the positions not needed by the web address. In the following example, we synthesize this request in the char array urlArr.

```
//ClientSocket.java

import java.io.*;
import java.net.*;

class ClientSocket {
    public static void main( String[] args )
    {
        try {
            char[] urlArr = new char[256];
            String prefix = "http://";
            String webAddress = args[0];

            int i = 0;
            while ( i < prefix.length() ) {
```

```
                urlArr[ i ] = prefix.charAt( i );
                i++;
        }
        while ( i < ( webAddress.length() + prefix.length() ) ) {
                urlArr[i] = webAddress.charAt( i - prefix.length() );
                i++;
        }
        while ( i < 256 ) {
                urlArr[ i ] = ' ';
                i++;
        }
        String urlString = new String( urlArr );

        Socket socket = new Socket( webAddress, 80 );
        OutputStream os = socket.getOutputStream();
        PrintStream ps = new PrintStream( os, true );
        InputStream in = socket.getInputStream();
        InputStreamReader in_reader = new InputStreamReader( in );
        BufferedReader b_reader = new BufferedReader( in_reader );

        //format of GET request dictated by HTTP
        ps.print( "GET " + urlString + " /HTTP/1.1\n\n" );
        boolean more = true;
        while (more) {
                String str = b_reader.readLine();
                if (str == null) more = false;
                else System.out.println(str);
        }
    } catch( IOException e ) {
        System.out.println( "Error:    " + e );
    }
    }
}
```

When this program is executed by the call

```
java ClientSocket www.purdue.edu
```

the following is printed out on your screen:

```
HTTP/1.1 200 OK
Date: Mon, 03 Jan 2000 05:49:15 GMT
Server: Apache/1.3.9 (Unix)
Connection: close
Content-Type: text/html

<html>

<head>
```

```
<title>Purdue University - West Lafayette, Indiana</title>

<meta name=''keywords'' content=''Purdue University, Boilermakers, Boilers, \
College, higher education, West Lafayette, Indiana, public schools, United  \
States, academics, research, athletics, employment, professors, faculty,    \
technology, libraries, Ross-Ade Stadium, Mackey Arena, students, airport''>
<meta name=''AUTHOR'' content=''Rick DeLucio, Office of Publications,        \
Purdue University''>
<meta name=''ROBOTS'' content=''ALL''>
<meta name=''DESCRIPTION'' content=''This is the official website of Purdue \
University. It contains all known relevant information concerning the        \
university, the faculty, staff, and students.''>

<style type=''text/css''>
<!--
.roll { color: black; text-decoration: underline; text-transform: none;     \
letter-spacing: normal }
a.roll:hover { color: gray }-->
</style>

<BASE HREF=''http://www.purdue.edu/Purdue/''>
</head>

<body bgcolor=''white'' link=''black'' vlink=''#666666'' alink=''#ce9c00''>

. . . . . . . . . .
. . . . . . . . . .
```

Not all servers require that a client socket send them a specially formatted request in order to yield information. For example, if you construct a socket object in your program by connecting with port 13 of the "time-of-day" server maintained by the National Institute of Standards and Technology in Boulder, Colorado, by

```
Socket socket = new Socket( "time-A.timefreq.bldrdoc.gov", 13 );
```

you can get the time information directly by reading off the output stream as in the above program.

19.2   SERVER SOCKETS IN JAVA

We will now talk about the server end of a client–server communication link. This we will do with the help of a bare-bones chat-room program consisting of a chat server class, `ChatServer`, and a multithreadable client handler class, `ClientHandler`. We will show how a `ChatServer` is able to provide chat-room services to multiple clients simultaneously.

A server program constructs a server socket by invoking the `ServerSocket` constructor, as in the following statement

```
ServerSocket server = new ServerSocket( int portNumber );
```

Like the Socket class, the ServerSocket class is defined in the package java.net. The above invocation will cause a server program to monitor the port portNumber. For illustration, our ChatServer class shown below contains the following statement

```
ServerSocket server = new ServerSocket( 5000 );
```

in line (B). This will cause the server program to monitor port 5000. Another way of interpreting this statement is that it registers port 5000 for the chat server and binds the server to that port. While the chat server is in service, no other server will be allowed to use this port on the same machine.

There is also a two-argument version of the ServerSocket constructor whose second argument specifies the maximum number of clients allowed to connect to the server at one time. For example, the invocation

```
ServerSocket server = new ServerSocket( 5000, 10 );
```

says that no more than 10 clients will be allowed to connect with this server at any given time through port 5000.

Once a server is established by constructing a ServerSocket object in the manner shown above, the server program can be made to wait indefinitely for clients to connect by invoking

```
Socket socket = server.accept();
```

When a client connects on the designated port, this statement returns a Socket object that can then be used to establish a two-way communication with the client through the I/O stream objects that can be constructed from the socket. Each such socket can be handed off to a separate thread of a multithreadable client handler.

We show below the ChatServer class. We set up a server in line (B). Then, inside a forever loop, we invoke the accept method on server to enable any number of clients to connect with this server. Each socket delivered by accept in line (C) is handed off in line (D) to a new thread of ClientHandler. In line (E), each new client is pushed into the back end of the ArrayList container declared in line (A). Some sort of a list of all the clients is needed to broadcast each chat participant's words to the rest of the clients.

```
class ChatServer {
    public static List clientList = new ArrayList();              //(A)

    public static void main( String[] args ) {
        try {
            ServerSocket server = new ServerSocket( 5000 );       //(B)
            for (;;) {
                //wait for client to connect
                Socket socket = server.accept();                  //(C)
                System.out.print(
                        "A new client checked in:    " );
```

```
        ClientHandler clh =
                new ClientHandler( socket );           //(D)
        clientList.add( clh );                         //(E)
        clh.start();                                   //(F)
    }
  } catch( Exception e ) { System.out.println( e ); }
}
}
```

This brings us to the code for the `ClientHandler` class. This class has to serve the following purposes:

1. Its constructor must first establish the I/O streams and then, for convenience, the `Reader` and `Writer` objects for reading information sent by a client and writing information to the client.

2. It must print on a client's terminal a welcome message.

3. It must ask a client for a name that the client would want to use in the chat room for identifying himself/herself. It must pre-pend all the messages from a client with his or her name.

4. It must tell a client to type "bye" for signing off from the chat room.

5. Upon receiving a "bye" from a client, it must close the I/O streams associated with that client and also terminate the thread. When a client signs off, this information must be broadcast to all other clients.

6. When a client first signs in, it must print on the client's terminal all of the chat that has taken place up to that point.

7. Finally, and most importantly, it must broadcast each client's messages to all other clients.

Task 1 above, that is establishing the I/O streams, and so on, for a client socket, named `sock`, can be accomplished by statements like

```
PrintWriter out = new PrintWriter( sock.getOutputStream() );  //(G)
InputStream in_stream = sock.getInputStream();                //(H)
InputStreamReader in_reader =                                 //(I)
        new InputStreamReader( in_stream );
BufferedReader buff_reader =
        new BufferedReader( in_reader );                      //(J)
```

In line (G), we invoke the `getOutputStream` method on a client socket to construct a `PrintWriter` output stream for sending information to the client. Lines (H), (I), and (J) construct a `BufferedReader` input stream for reading the information received from a client. With the `PrintWriter` object `out`, the Tasks 2, 3, and 4 listed above can be taken care of simply by statements like:

```
out.println( "\n\nWelcome to the chat room");
out.println( "Type \"bye\" in a new line to terminate session." );
out.print( "Please enter your first name: " );
String userName = buff_reader.readLine();
```

When a new client signs in, Task 6 can be handled by the following code fragment at the beginning of the interaction with the client:

```
// chatStore is a static data member of type List for
// the class ClientHandler
if ( chatStore.size() != 0 ) {
    out.println( "Chat history:\n\n" );
    ListIterator iter = chatStore.listIterator();
    while ( iter.hasNext() ) {
        out.println( (String) iter.next() );
    }
    out.print("\n\n");
    out.flush();
}
```

Each message entered by a client is stored in the `ArrayList` object `chatStore`. When a new client first signs in, the `while` loop above prints out on the client's terminal the previously accumulated contents of `chatStore`.

With regard to Task 7, the following code takes care of displaying each client's message on the terminals of all other clients:

```
ListIterator iter = ChatServer.clientList.listIterator();
while ( iter.hasNext() ) {                                  //(K)
    ClientHandler cl = (ClientHandler) iter.next();
    if ( this != cl ) {                                     //(L)
        cl.out.println();
        cl.out.println( strWithName );                      //(M)
        cl.out.print( cl.userName + ": " );                 //(N)
        cl.out.flush();
    }
}
```

We go through all the clients stored in the list `ChatServer.clientList` one by one in the `while` loop in line (K). Since we do not want to send a message received from a client back to the same client, in line (L) we make sure that the current client is excluded from the loop. In line (M), we send the the string `strWithName` to all other clients; this string is merely the current client's message string pre-pended by his/her name. The purpose of line (N) is to make sure that new line on the other client's terminal screen has his/her name at the beginning.

Regarding Task 6, when a client sends "bye", this task can be handled by a statement block like

```
buffered_reader.close();
```

```
            out.close();
            sock.close();
```

Shown below is all of the source code. On the server side, you compile the program, and then run the server by

```
    java ChatServer
```

If a client does not have access to a GUI[3] for interacting with the chat server, he/she may still be able to participate in a chat through a simple telnet connection by typing the following string in a terminal window:

```
    telnet <internet name of your machine> 5000
```

If, for the purpose of experimenting with the code, you wish to connect to the server through multiple windows on the same machine on which you are running the server, you can create clients in separate windows by entering

```
    telnet  127.0.0.1  5000
```

in each window. The IP address 127.0.0.1, called the *local loopback address*, designates your local machine.

```
//ChatServer.java

import java.io.*;
import java.net.*;
import java.util.*;

public class ChatServer {
    public static List clientList = new ArrayList();

    public static void main( String[] args ) {
        try {
            ServerSocket server = new ServerSocket( 5000 );
            for (;;) {
                Socket socket = server.accept();
                System.out.print( "A new client checked in:    " );
                ClientHandler clh = new ClientHandler( socket );
                clientList.add( clh );
                clh.start();
            }
        } catch( Exception e ) { System.out.println( e ); }
    }
```

---

[3]A homework problem at the end of this chapter is about designing an applet that a client can download for a more pleasing interaction with the chat server shown here.

```
}

///////////////// class ClientHandler extends Thread ////////////////
class ClientHandler extends Thread {
    private String userName;
    private Socket sock;
    private static List chatStore = new ArrayList();
    private BufferedReader buff_reader = null;
    private PrintWriter out = null;

    public ClientHandler( Socket s ) {
        try {
            sock = s;
            out = new PrintWriter( sock.getOutputStream() );
            InputStream in_stream = sock.getInputStream();
            InputStreamReader in_reader =
                new InputStreamReader( in_stream );
            buff_reader = new BufferedReader( in_reader );

            // ask for user name
            out.println( "\n\nWelcome to Avi Kak's chatroom");
            out.println();
            out.println(
                "Type \"bye\" in a new line to terminate session.\n" );
            out.print( "Please enter your first name: " );
            out.flush();
            userName = buff_reader.readLine();
            out.print("\n\n");
            out.flush();
            System.out.print( userName + "\n\n" );

            // show to new client all the chat
            // that has taken place so far
            if ( chatStore.size() != 0 ) {
                out.println( "Chat history:\n\n" );

                ListIterator iter = chatStore.listIterator();
                while ( iter.hasNext() ) {
                    out.println( (String) iter.next() );
                }
                out.print("\n\n");
                out.flush();
            }
        } catch( Exception e ) {}
    }

    public void run() {
        try {
            boolean done = false;
```

```
        while ( !done ) {
            out.print( userName + ": " );
            out.flush();
            String str = buff_reader.readLine();

            if ( str.equals( "bye" ) ) {
                str = userName + " signed off";
                done = true;
            }
            String strWithName = userName + ": " + str;
            chatStore.add( strWithName );
            ListIterator iter =
                        ChatServer.clientList.listIterator();
            while ( iter.hasNext() ) {
                ClientHandler cl = (ClientHandler) iter.next();
                if ( this != cl ) {
                    cl.out.println();
                    cl.out.println( strWithName );
                    cl.out.print( cl.userName + ": " );
                    cl.out.flush();
                }
            }
        }
        System.out.println( userName + " signed off" + "\n\n" );
        buff_reader.close();
        out.close();
        sock.close();
    } catch ( Exception e ) {}
  }
}
```

19.3 ESTABLISHING SOCKET CONNECTIONS WITH EXISTING SERVERS IN C++

We will now show how C++ classes can be used for network programming in a manner very similar to Java. The goal of this section is to show a C++ program that works in the same way as the ClientSocket.java program of Section 19.1. This we will do with the help of the Qt classes for network programming.

The Qt library offers several C++ classes with the same high-level functionality as the Java classes we have used so far for network programming. For example, the class QSocket, like the Java class java.net.Socket, can be used to create a buffered TCP socket connection with a named server on a designated port. And the Qt class QServerSocket can be used to create TCP server sockets, like the java.net.ServerSocket class. Other Qt classes useful for network programming are QDns for asynchronous domain name server (DNS) lookup; QNetworkProtocol to serve as a base class for implementing new network protocols; QFtp, derived from QNetworkProtocol, that implements the FTP protocol; QUrlOperator for operating on hierarchical structures (like file systems) using URL's; and so on.

As mentioned already, the purpose of this section is to show a Qt program that does exactly the same thing as the Java program ClientSocket.java of Section 19.1. A client should be able to use the Qt program to set up a socket connection with a designated HTTPD server, to transmit to the server an appropriately formatted request for a web page whose address is embedded in the request string, and to then download the raw ascii of this web page.

The program shown below constructs a new TCP socket object in an idle state (not yet connected to the server) by invoking the QSocket constructor:[4]

```
QSocket* socket = new QSocket();
```

The socket thus constructed is connected to a named host by invoking

```
socket->connectToHost( qstr, 80 );   // asynchronous call
```

where the first argument, of type QString&, is the name of the server, and the second argument, of type Q_UINT16, is the port number on which a socket link is sought. QString is Qt's version of the string class from the C++ Standard Library and the type Q_UINT16 is Qt's 16-bit unsigned short integer.

The function connectToHost, like many other network related functions in the Qt library, works asynchronously, meaning that it returns before the designated operation has been completed. Whether or not a connection was really made and the state of that connection can be checked by trapping the signals emitted by a QSocket object.[5] It is the programmer's job to provide slots for processing these signals and for connecting the signals with their respective slots. After connectToHost is invoked, the signals emitted by a QSocket object are

---

[4]The constructor invocation shown is a default-argument version of the QSocket constructor whose prototype is

```
QSocket::QSocket( QObject* parent = 0, const char* name = 0 )
```

where parent and name arguments can be used in the same manner as in Chapter 17 for establishing parent–child containment relationships in a Qt program.

[5]See Chapter 17 for Qt's signal–slot mechanism.

```
    void hostFound()            // host lookup succeeded

    void connected()            // connection successfully
                                // established

    void connectionClosed()     // when the host closes the
                                // connection

    void delayedClosedFinished() // if you invoke close() to close
                                // a connection and there is
                                // buffered output data to be
                                // written, the socket object
                                // goes into the QSocket::Closing
                                // state and returns immediately
                                // from the call to close();
                                // the data will continue to be
                                // output until done  at that time
                                // this signal is emitted.

    void readyRead()            // means there is incoming data
                                // to be read; this signal is
                                // issued only once each time
                                // there is fresh incoming data
                                // to be read.

    void bytesWritten( int nbytes) // this signal is emitted when
                                // data is actually written to
                                // the network; the nbytes
                                // parameters says how many
                                // bytes were written.

    void error( int )           // an error occurred
```

With regard to the signal `delayedClosedFinished`, if a client invokes `close` on a TCP connection and there is still buffered output data to be written out, the `QSocket` object goes into the state `QSocket::Closing` and the output of the data continues. Since, like the `connectToHost` function, `close` is an asynchronous function, it returns immediately. So when a client program requests `close`, it is a good practice to check if the state of the connection has switched into `QSocket::Closing`. If that's indeed the case, you'd want to trap the signal `delayedClosedFinished` to determine the actual close of the connection.

The state of a `QSocket` object can be queried by invoking the function `state` on the object. A connection can be in one of the following states defined through an enumeration for `QSocket`:

```
    Idle        // if there is no connection

    HostLookup  // during DNS lookup
```

```
Connecting      // while a TCP connection is being established

Connection      // while there is an operational connection

Closing         // if client has invoked close() on a
                // connection, but there is still data in
                // the output buffer
```

The int argument of the error signal, error(int), that is emitted by a QSocket object can be processed by a programmer-supplied slot function to figure out the nature of the error. The different errors correspond to the following symbolic names defined through an enumeration:

```
ErrConnectionRefused        // if the connection was refused

ErrHostNotFound             // if the host was not found

ErrSocketRead               // if a read from the socket failed
```

The following program uses the QSocket class to establish a TCP connection with an HTTPD server. The program consists of the following three files:

```
ClientSocket.h
ClientSocket.cc
Makefile
```

The header file ClientSocket.h has the class declaration as shown below:

```
//ClientSocket.h

#ifndef CLIENTSOCKET_H
#define CLIENTSOCKET_H

#include <qsocket.h>
#include <string>

class ClientSocket : public QSocket {
    Q_OBJECT
    string wwwName;
    QSocket* socket;
public:
    ClientSocket( string wwwName );
    string constructHttpRequest();
    void socketClosed();
    ~ClientSocket();
public slots:
    void reportConnected();                                    //(A)
```

```
    void reportHostFound();                              //(B)
    void getWebPage();                                   //(C)
    void socketConnectionClosed();                       //(D)
    void reportError( int );                             //(E)
};
```

```
#endif
```

The implementation code is in the file ClientSocket.cc shown below. This code consists mainly of connecting the signals with the slots declared in lines (A) through (E) above and placing appropriate code in the slots. The signal hostFound is connected with the slot reportHostFound in line (F). All that this slot function, defined in line (M), does is to print out on the terminal a message that the hostname lookup was successful. More useful work is undertaken by the slot function reportConnected, defined in line (N), which first reports to us that a connection was successfully established with the server and then proceeds to send to the server a special string that elicits a web page from the server. The string transmitted to the server is the same as in the Java program ClientSocket.java of Section 19.1. When the web page sent by the server in response to the request from the client becomes available to the client, the QSocket object on the client side emits the signal readyRead. The getWebPage slot of line (O), connected to the signal readyRead in line (H), actually reads the incoming bytes one line at a time and displays them on the terminal screen through the following while loop:

```
    while ( socket->canReadLine() )
        cout << socket->readLine();
```

When the server closes the connection, the QSocket object emits the connectionClosed signal. Through the connection established in line (I), this signal fires up the slot function socketConnectionClosed defined in line (P), which eventually invokes the socketClosed function to terminate the client program. The testing that socketConnectionClosed carries out to check whether the state of the socket is Closing is unnecessary in this case because the server makes the web page available only after receiving the entire specially formatted HTTP request string. Since the client program does not transmit anything to the server after the request string, there will be nothing in the output buffer to cause the state of the socket to transition to Closing.

```
//ClientSocket.cc

#include "ClientSocket.h"

#include <qapplication.h>
#include <qsocket.h>
#include <string>
#include <iostream>
```

```
using namespace std;

ClientSocket::ClientSocket( string siteName ) : QSocket( 0 , 0 ) {
    wwwName = siteName;

    socket = new QSocket( );

    connect( socket, SIGNAL( connected() ),
            this,   SLOT( reportConnected() ) );              //(F)
    connect( socket, SIGNAL( hostFound() ),
            this,   SLOT( reportHostFound() ) );              //(G)
    connect( socket, SIGNAL( readyRead() ),
            this,   SLOT( getWebPage() ) );                   //(H)
    connect( socket, SIGNAL( connectionClosed() ),
            this,   SLOT( socketConnectionClosed() ) );       //(I)
    connect( socket, SIGNAL( error( int ) ),
            this,   SLOT( reportError( int ) ) );             //(J)
    QString qstr( wwwName.c_str() );
    socket->connectToHost( qstr, 80 );   // asynchronous call     //(K)
}

ClientSocket::~ClientSocket() {}

string ClientSocket::constructHttpRequest( ) {                    //(L)
    char urlArr[256];
    string prefix = "http://";

    int i = 0;
    while ( i < prefix.length() ) {
        urlArr[ i ] = prefix[ i ];
        i++;
    }
    while ( i < ( wwwName.length() + prefix.length() ) ) {
        urlArr[i] = wwwName[ i - prefix.length() ];
        i++;
    }
    while ( i < 256 ) {
        urlArr[ i ] = ' ';
        i++;
    }
    urlArr[255] = 0;
    string urlString( urlArr );
    string httpRequestString = "GET " + urlString + " /HTTP/1.1\n\n";
    return httpRequestString;
}
void ClientSocket::reportHostFound() {                            //(M)
    cout << "host found" << endl;
}
void ClientSocket::reportConnected() {                            //(N)
```

```
        cout << "connection established" << endl;
        string httpRequest = constructHttpRequest();
        int len = httpRequest.size();
        socket->writeBlock( httpRequest.c_str(), len );
}
void ClientSocket::getWebPage() {                              //(O)
        cout << "socket ready to read" << endl;
        int howManyBytes = socket->bytesAvailable();
        cout << "bytes available: " << howManyBytes << endl;
        while ( socket->canReadLine() )
            cout << socket->readLine();
}
void ClientSocket::socketConnectionClosed() {                 //(P)
        socket->close();
        if ( socket->state() == QSocket::Closing ) {   // delayed close
            connect( socket, SIGNAL( delayedCloseFinished() ),
                     this,   SLOT( socketClosed() ) );
        } else {
            // The socket is really closed
            socketClosed();
        }
}
void ClientSocket::reportError( int e ) {                     //(Q)
        cout << "error report from connectToHost" << endl;
        cout << "error id: " << e;
}
void ClientSocket::socketClosed() {
        cout << "Connection closed" << endl;
        exit( 0 );
}

int main( int argc, char* argv[] )
{
        QApplication app( argc, argv );
        ClientSocket* sock = new ClientSocket( argv[1] );
        return app.exec();
}
```

Shown below is a makefile for the program. It has the same structure as the makefiles for Qt programs shown earlier in Chapter 17. As the makefile shows, using the moc compiler we first carry out a meta object compilation of the header file ClientSocket.h to generate moc_ClientSocket.cc, which is then compiled with g++ to generate moc_ClientSocket.o. At the same time, the implementation code ClientSocket.cc is compiled into ClientSocket.o. Finally, we link moc_ClientSocket.o and ClientSocket.o to generate the executable ClientSocket. The makefile is executed by the command line

```
make -f Makefile_ClientSocket
```

```
#Makefile_ClientSocket

CC=g++

#for static and dynamic linking
LDLIBS=-L$(QTDIR)/lib -lqt

#for compilation
CFLAGS=-g -I$(QTDIR)/include

ClientSocket: moc_ClientSocket.o ClientSocket.o Makefile_ClientSocket
        $(CC) $(LDLIBS)  -o ClientSocket moc_ClientSocket.o         \
                                                ClientSocket.o

moc_ClientSocket.cc: ClientSocket.h
        moc -o moc_ClientSocket.cc ClientSocket.h

moc_ClientSocket.o: moc_ClientSocket.cc
        $(CC) -c $(CFLAGS) -O2 moc_ClientSocket.cc

ClientSocket.o: ClientSocket.cc ClientSocket.h
        $(CC) -c $(CFLAGS) -O2 ClientSocket.cc

clean:
        rm -f ClientSocket
        rm -f *.o
        rm -f moc*.*
```

The executable can be invoked in a command line like

```
ClientSocket www.purdue.edu
```

if you wanted to see in your terminal window the ascii content of the www.purdue.edu
web page.

19.4 SERVER SOCKETS IN C++ (Qt)

We will now show how you can establish in C++ a server socket bound to a specific
port in the same manner as we showed in Section 19.2 for Java. This we will do
with the help of the Qt class QServerSocket. As mentioned earlier in Section
19.2, a server uses a server-socket object to monitor a designated port for incoming

connection requests from clients. When a client request for a connection is received on the designated port monitored by the server, the server-socket object creates a new socket for communicating with the client. The server-socket then resumes its business of monitoring the designated port for fresh requests from other clients.

The rest of this section parallels Section 19.2 where we presented a Java chat server program to demonstrate the server side of the programming needed for a client–server link. As with the Java program, the chat server program in this section will consist of the main server class, ChatServer, and a ClientHandler class whose objects will keep track of the individual clients participating in a chat. The ChatServer is derived from the Qt class QServerSocket:

```
class ChatServer : public QServerSocket {
    // ....
public:
    vector<ClientHandler> clientVector;              //(A)
    ChatServer( int port );                          //(B)
    void newConnection( int socketFD );              //(C)
    ~ChatServer();
};
```

This makes every ChatServer object a QServerSocket object. As we did with the ServerSocket class in Java in Section 19.2, we can now construct a C++ server socket object by, say,

```
ChatServer* server = new ChatServer( 5000 );
```

if we wish for the server to monitor port 5000 for client requests.

While creating server socket objects in C++ with Qt and in Java entail very similar syntax, what it takes to get hold of the actual socket that a server will use for communicating with a client is different in the two cases. In Java, we invoked the accept method on a server socket object for this purpose; receipt of an appropriately formatted client request caused accept to spit out the socket. In Qt, this is achieved by providing an override definition for the virtual function newConnection(int socketFd). Through the mechanism of virtual functions — in the same manner that low-level events are handled in a Qt GUI program (see Chapter 17) — when a new client request for a communication link is received, the programmer supplied definition of newConnection(int socketFD) is automatically invoked with the argument set to a socket file descriptor for the new link. The ChatServer class has the following definition for this virtual function:

```
void ChatServer::newConnection( int socketFD ) {
    QSocket* socket = new QSocket();                 //(D)
    socket->setSocket( socketFD );                   //(E)
    ClientHandler* clh = new ClientHandler( socket, this );
    cout << "A new client checked in on socket FD "
        << socketFD << endl;
}
```

So, as shown in line (E), it is the `setSocket` function that, when invoked on an already constructed `QSocket` object of line (D), yields the socket that the server will use for communicating with the client. This socket is provided to the `ClientHandler` constructor. As with the Java program, there is a separate `ClientHandler` object for each client. All `ClientHandler` objects are stored in the vector data member `clientVector` shown in line (A) of the `ChatServer` class shown above. Part of the job of each `ClientHandler` object is to transmit its client's chat to all the other clients stored in the `clientVector` data member. Here is a partial definition of `ClientHandler`:

```
class ClientHandler : public QObject {
    // ...
    QSocket* handlerSocket;                                      //(F)
    QString* chatName;                                           //(G)
    QTextStream* os;                                             //(H)
    ChatServer* chatServer;                                      //(I)
    // ...
};
```

The data member `handlerSocket` in line (F) is the `QSocket` object constructed by the `ChatServer` for this client. Each chat participant must have a name that becomes the value of the data member `chatName` in line (G). The member `chatServer` in line (I) serves as a back pointer to the `ChatServer` object that constructed this `ClientHandler` object. The data member `os` in line (H) is an I/O stream that a `ClientHandler` object uses primarily for broadcasting the strings received from each client to all other clients.

In addition to the usual complement of constructors, the `ClientHandler` class must be provided with a copy constructor and a copy assignment operator so that the `ClientHandler` objects can be stored in the vector data member `clientVector` of the `ChatServer` class:

```
class ClientHandler : public QObject {
    // ....
    ClientHandler( QSocket* sock, ChatServer* cserver );
    ClientHandler();
    ClientHandler( const ClientHandler& cl );                   //(J)
    ClientHandler& operator=( const ClientHandler& other );     //(K)
    ~ClientHandler();
    // ...
};
```

As mentioned in Chapter 5, when an object is inserted into a container class, it is a copy of the object as constructed by the copy assignment operator that is actually stored.

Finally, in order to read the information coming through a client socket, the `ClientHandler` object must respond to the `readyRead` signal by invoking an appropriate slot function. This slot function in our case is named `readFromClient` in line (L) below. It is one of the two slot functions defined for ClientHandler, the other being reportError in line (M):

```
class ClientHandler : public QObject {
    // ....
private slots:
    void readFromClient();                                      //(L)
    void reportError( int );                                    //(M)
};
```

After a connection is established with a client and a ClientHandler object constructed for the client, all the interaction with the client takes places through the readFromClient function of the ClientHandler class. This function works in three different modes:

1. If chatName's value has not yet been set, use the first input supplied by the client as the chat name since this input will be provided in response to a specific request (for a chat name) from the server. After a new client has checked in and supplied his/her chat name, a message is broadcast to all the other clients to that effect.

2. If a client has typed "bye" on his/her terminal, that means the client wants to sign out. This requires closing the socket for this client and broadcasting a message to all the other clients to that effect.

3. Otherwise, broadcast the string received from the client to all the other clients.

4. Finally, make sure that a fresh line on the client terminal begins with his/her own chat name followed by a colon.

The program shown below consists of three files

```
ChatServer.h
ChatServer.cc
Makefile_ChatServer
```

The header file ChatServer.h declares the ChatServer and the ClientHandler classes:

```
//ChatServer.h

#ifndef CHATSERVER_H
#define CHATSERVER_H

#include <qserversocket.h>
#include <qsocket.h>
#include <qtextstream.h>
#include <qstring.h>
```

```cpp
#include <vector>
using namespace std;

class ChatServer;

class ClientHandler : public QObject {
    Q_OBJECT
    QSocket* handlerSocket;
    QString* chatName;
    ChatServer* chatServer;
    QTextStream* os;
public:
    ClientHandler( QSocket* sock, ChatServer* cserver );
    ClientHandler();
    ClientHandler( const ClientHandler& cl );
    ClientHandler& operator=( const ClientHandler& other );
    ~ClientHandler();
private slots:
    void readFromClient();
    void reportError( int );
};


class ChatServer : public QServerSocket {
    Q_OBJECT
public:
    vector<ClientHandler> clientVector;
    ChatServer( int port );
    void newConnection( int socketFD );
    ~ChatServer();
};
#endif
```

The classes are implemented in the ChatServer.cc file:

```cpp
//ChatServer.cc

#include "ChatServer.h"

#include <qapplication.h>
#include <iostream>
using namespace std;

ChatServer::ChatServer( int port ) : QServerSocket( port )
{
    cout << "Server monitoring port " << port << endl;
```

```
        if ( !ok() ) {
            qWarning( "Failed to register the server port" );
            exit( 1 );
        }
    }


    // You must provide an override implementation for
    // this method.  When a client requests a connection,
    // this method will be called automatically with the
    // socket argument set to the filedescriptor associated
    // with the socket.
    void ChatServer::newConnection( int socketFD ) {
        QSocket* socket = new QSocket();
        socket->setSocket( socketFD );
        ClientHandler* clh = new ClientHandler( socket, this );
        cout << "A new client checked in on socket FD "
            << socketFD << endl;
    }


    ChatServer::~ChatServer(){}


    ClientHandler::ClientHandler() {}


    // Copy constructor is needed since it is the copies of
    // the ClientHandler objects that will be stored in the
    // vector clientVector
    ClientHandler::ClientHandler( const ClientHandler& other )
        : handlerSocket( other.handlerSocket ),
          chatName( other.chatName ),
          chatServer( other.chatServer ),
          os( other.os )
    {}


    ClientHandler& ClientHandler::operator=( const ClientHandler& other ) {
        if ( this == &other ) return *this;

        cout << "ClientHandler assignment op invoked" << endl;

        if ( handlerSocket != 0 ) delete handlerSocket;
        handlerSocket = other.handlerSocket;
        if ( chatName != 0 ) delete chatName;
        chatName = other.chatName;
        if ( os != 0 ) delete os;
        os = other.os;
        chatServer = other.chatServer;
    }


    ClientHandler::ClientHandler( QSocket* socket, ChatServer* chatserver )
        : chatName(0),
```

```
        chatServer( chatserver ),
        handlerSocket( socket )
{
    os = new QTextStream( handlerSocket );

    (*os) << "Welcome to a chat room powered by C++\n";
    (*os) << ">>>>    Enter 'bye' to exit    <<<\n";
    (*os) << "Enter chat name: ";

    connect( handlerSocket, SIGNAL( readyRead() ),
             this, SLOT( readFromClient() ) );
    connect( handlerSocket, SIGNAL( error( int ) ),
             this,  SLOT( reportError( int ) ) );
}


// The destructor definition intentionally does not invoke
// the delete operator on any of the objects pointed to
// by the data members of a ClientHandler.  In this program,
// the most frequent invocation of the destructor is caused
// by the push_back statement in the readFromClient()
// function.  The push_back invocation causes the vector
// to be moved to a different location in the memory.  The
// memory occupied by the ClientHandler objects in the
// vector is freed by invoking the destructor.  Deleting
// the memory occupied by the socket and other objects
// pointed to by the data members of the ClientHandler
// objects would lead to disastrous results.
ClientHandler::~ClientHandler(){}

void ClientHandler::reportError( int e ) {
    cout << "error report from connectToHost" << endl;
    cout << "error id: " << e << endl;
}

void ClientHandler::readFromClient() {
    QSocket* sock = (QSocket*) sender();
    while ( sock->canReadLine() ) {
        QString qstr = sock->readLine();

        // This block is for the case when a new chatter
        // has just signed in and supplied his/her chat name.
        // The block sets the chatname of the ClientHandler
        // object assigned to this new user.  Next it pushes
        // the ClientHandler object for this new user in the
        // vector clientVector.  Subsequently, The block informs
        // all other current chatters that this new user has
        // signed in.
        if ( chatName == 0 ) {
            chatName = new QString( qstr.stripWhiteSpace() );
```

```
        chatServer->clientVector.push_back( *this );
        for ( int i=0; i<chatServer->clientVector.size(); i++ ) {
            if ( *chatServer->clientVector[i].chatName
                                         != *chatName &&
                 chatServer->clientVector[i].handlerSocket != 0 ) {
                QString outgoing = "\nMessage from chat server: "
                                  + *chatName + " signed in ";
                *chatServer->clientVector[i].os << outgoing;
            }
        }
    }

    // This block treats the case when a chatter wants
    // to sign out by typing "bye".  It broadcasts a message
    // to all the other chatters that this chatter is signing
    // off.  This block than closes the socket.  Note that
    // socket pointer is set to null in both the ClientHandler
    // object assigned to the exiting chatter and its copy the
    // vector clientVector.
    else if ( qstr.stripWhiteSpace() == "bye" ) {
        for ( int i=0; i<chatServer->clientVector.size(); i++ ) {
            QString outgoing( "\nMessage from the chat server: " +
                     *chatName + " signed off" );
            if ( *chatServer->clientVector[i].chatName
                                           != *chatName  &&
                 chatServer->clientVector[i].handlerSocket != 0 ) {
                *chatServer->clientVector[i].os << outgoing;
            }
        }
        handlerSocket->close();
        handlerSocket = 0;
        for ( int i=0; i<chatServer->clientVector.size(); i++ ) {
            if (*chatServer->clientVector[i].chatName == *chatName)
                chatServer->clientVector[i].handlerSocket = 0;
        }
    }

    // This is the normal case encountered during the
    // course of a chat.  The string typed in by a
    // chatter is broadcast to all the other chatters.
    // The string is pre-pended by the name of the
    // chatter who typed in the string.
    else {
        cout << *chatName << ": " << qstr << endl;
        qstr.truncate( qstr.length() - 2 );
        for ( int i=0; i<chatServer->clientVector.size(); i++ ) {
            if ( *chatServer->clientVector[i].chatName
                                         != *chatName &&
                 chatServer->clientVector[i].handlerSocket != 0 ) {
```

```
                        QString outgoing = "\n" + *chatName + ": " + qstr;
                        *chatServer->clientVector[i].os << outgoing;
                    }
                }
            }

            // A chatter's terminal always shows his/her own
            // name at beginning of a new line.  This way,
            // when a chatter types in his/her own message, it
            // is always on a line that starts with his/her
            //own name.
            for ( int i=0; i<chatServer->clientVector.size(); i++ ) {
                if ( chatServer->clientVector[i].handlerSocket != 0 ) {
                    QString outgoing = "\n" +
                        *chatServer->clientVector[i].chatName + ": ";
                    *chatServer->clientVector[i].os << outgoing;
                }
            }
        }
    }
}

int main( int argc, char* argv[] )
{
    QApplication app( argc, argv );
    ChatServer* server = new ChatServer( 5000 );    .
    return app.exec();
}
```

Finally, here is the makefile:

```
#Makefile_ChatServer

CC=g++

LDLIBS=-L$(QTDIR)/lib -lqt

CFLAGS=-g -I$(QTDIR)/include

ChatServer: moc_ChatServer.o ChatServer.o Makefile_ChatServer
        $(CC) $(LDLIBS)  -o ChatServer moc_ChatServer.o ChatServer.o

moc_ChatServer.cc: ChatServer.h
        moc -o moc_ChatServer.cc ChatServer.h

moc_ChatServer.o: moc_ChatServer.cc
        $(CC) -c $(CFLAGS) -O2 moc_ChatServer.cc
```

```
ChatServer.o: ChatServer.cc ChatServer.h
        $(CC) -c $(CFLAGS) -O2 ChatServer.cc

clean:
        rm -f ChatServer
        rm -f *.o
        rm -f moc*.*
```

You can run the executable `ChatServer` on the machine on which you wish to host the chat server. Chat clients can then connect with the server via `telnet` by entering the following string in their terminals:

```
telnet <name of server machine> 5000
```

assuming that the port being monitored by the chat server is 5000. For experimenting with the server program on a local machine, you can run the server in one window and clients in other windows using the loopback address for the local machine. In the client windows, you'd enter the following string to establish a connection with the server:

```
telnet 127.0.0.1 5000
```

19.5 SUGGESTIONS FOR FURTHER READING

The reader will find instructional the tic-tac-toe example in [17] to see how client–server communications can be used to set up a game that can be played with the different participants logged on different machines while the game server is running on yet another machine.

19.6 HOMEWORK

1. Write an implementation of the `ChatServer` class of Section 19.2 that uses a *nonstatic* version of the data member `clientVec`. You may do this by making the following changes to Java program of Section 19.2:

   - In the `main` of the `ChatServer` class, pass the server object to the `ClientHandler` constructor by

     ```
     ClientHandler clh = new ClientHandler(socket, this);
     ```

   - Add the following additional data member to the `ClientHandler` class

     ```
     ChatServer chat_server;
     ```

- Change the `ClientHandler` constructor so that it accepts the two arguments shown below:

```
public ClientHandler( Socket s, ChatServer c ) {
    try {
        sock = s;
        chat_server = c;
        // .....
```

- With all of the above changes, the `for` loop in the `run()` method of `ClientHandler` can be changed to:

```
for (int i = 0; i < chat_server.clientVec.size(); i++) {
  ClientHandler cl =
      (ClientHandler) chat_server.clientVec.elementAt(i);
  // ......
```

2. Write an applet program that elicits a piece of information from a client viewing the applet and then sends the information back to a server program running at the host that is the home of the applet. This homework is also an exercise in launching a `JFrame` object from an applet. Your frame should consist of a text-field and a button. When the client clicks the button, the information typed into the text-field should get transmitted back to the server.

3. Extend the `ChatServer` class of Section 19.2 so that clients can download a chat applet from your web page. When a new client checks in via the applet, the applet should show all the accumulated chat up to that time in the main applet window. The applet should also include a button that creates a separate window (a popup) for a client to input his/her contribution to the ongoing chat. This separate window should include a submit button that when pressed causes the text entered to show up in the main applet windows of all the participating clients.

20

Database Programming

When information is organized as rows and columns of a table, we have a database, at least a database in its simplest form. For reasons we will state shortly, a single table does not suffice for most applications and one must resort to multiple tables, each designed to represent optimally some aspect of the information. Large databases employ highly optimized representations for the tabulated information. These representations are often proprietary and hidden from the user of a database. What's provided to a user is a database driver that knows how to communicate with the tabulated information through the proprietary representations.

In this chapter, we will first briefly explain further the notion of a database and SQL, the Structured Query Language, that is now in widespread use for communicating with databases. This will be followed by an introduction to JDBC and how it can be used for creating a database and then retrieving information from it. JDBC, which although a trademarked name in its own right, is often thought of as an acronym for *Java DataBase Connectivity*, consists of Java's classes that can be used for directly invoking SQL statements on a database, retrieving the results when the statements call for retrieval, and analyzing the results. In order to be accessible via JDBC, a database must support what's known as a JDBC driver, or a bridge between JDBC and the driver native to the database.

Finally, we will show some C++ classes from Mysql++ for the same kind of database programming that is achieved with JDBC in Java.

20.1 RELATIONAL DATABASES

Consider, for example, a database for storing information on all the books in a library. Let's say that we want to store the following information on each book:

```
Title
Author
Year
ISBN
NumberOfCopies
Publisher
PublisherLocation
PublisherURL
PublisherRep
PublisherRepPhone
PublisherRepEmail
```

Let's assume that the library has 100,000 books that are published by, say, 100 publishers. For the sake of making a point, let's also assume that each publisher is represented equally well in the library. If we represented all the books in a single "flat" table with eleven columns, one for each of the items listed above, the information in at least three of the columns — those under the column headings "Publisher," "PublisherLocation," and "PublisherURL" — would be the same for the 1000 rows corresponding to each publisher. That obviously is not an efficient way to store the information. There would be too much "redundancy" in the table. Since it goes without saying that the larger the number of entries that need to made to create a table, the greater the probability of an error creeping into one or more of the entries, our table would be at an increased risk of containing erroneous information. The table with the column headings as shown above will also have redundancies with regard to the PublisherRep information.

Now consider an alternate design consisting of three tables, one containing information generic to each book, the other containing information generic to each publisher, and the third containing information generic to each publisher rep:

```
BookTable:
    Title   Author   Year   ISBN   PublisherID   PublisherRepID

PublisherTable:
    PublisherID   PublisherName   PublisherLocation   PublisherURL

PublisherRepTable:   PublisherRepID   RepName   RepPhone   RepEmail
```

where we have assumed that the PublisherRep might be specific to each book and that the same rep may represent multiple publishers. We now associate unique identifiers, possibly numerical in nature, in the form of PublisherID and PublisherRepID to "link" the main book table, `BookTable`, with the other two tables, `PublisherTable` and `PublisherRepTable`.

These three tables together would constitute a typical modern `relational` database. Given this database, we may now query the database for information that for simple queries can be extracted from a single table, but that for more complex queries may require simultaneous access to multiple tables. Here are examples of simple queries that can be fulfilled from just a single table:

```
Retrieve all book titles published in a given year.

Retrieve all book titles published by a given author.

Retrieve all publishers located in France.

Retrieve all publisher rep names.

etc.
```

and here are examples of queries that require simultaneous access to more than one table in the database:

```
Retrieve all book titles along with the name of
                        the publisher for each book.

Retrieve all books for which the designated
                        publisher rep is given.

Retrieve all book titles published last year along
          with the name of the publisher for each
          and the name of the publisher's rep.

etc.
```

Other possible interactions with the database could consist of updating the database as the library acquires additional books, modifying the entries, and so on.

Over the years, a command language called SQL for *Structured Query Language* (SQL) has come into widespread use for communicating with databases, especially the server-based databases.[1] Since JDBC and Mysql++ programs serve as interfaces to SQL, it is important to get a sense of the syntax of SQL before launching into the syntax of JDBC and Mysql++. JDBC and Mysql++ programs send SQL queries to a database, analyze the results returned by the database, and display these results in forms desired by the user.

---

[1]The desktop-based databases are usually accessed through graphical user interfaces.

20.2 THE MySQL DATABASE MANAGER

Our SQL examples in the next section and our Java and C++ programs later in the chapter use the MySQL database management system. MySQL, one of the most popular open source[2] SQL-based systems for relational databases, can be downloaded from `www.mysql.com`.

The MySQL database management system consists primarily of a MySQL server that can be accessed by a MySQL client for creating and using databases.[3] MySQL also comes with a "terminal monitor" interactive program `mysql` that can be used for executing command-line SQL statements. This program can also be used to run SQL statements in a batch mode in which you place multiple statements in a file and then tell `mysql` to execute the contents of the file.

The rest of this section introduces some of the basic terminology of communicating with a database, our interest being specifically in communicating with MySQL databases. We will define and provide examples for the terms *Driver Manager*, *bridge driver*, and *database URL*. We will use Java-related examples for the terms, but the terms have the same meanings when C++ classes from Mysql++ are used for accessing a database.

As mentioned already, one communicates with a database through a database driver. It is the driver's job to figure out how to reach into the row–column representations of the tables of the database and to retrieve or modify the information at prescribed locations. There are a number of drivers available for communicating with a MySQL database. A commonly used driver by Java programs is the open-source `MM.MySQL` driver.[4]   In the same vein, other database systems have their own drivers. Many

---

[2]Open source means that the source code for the software is available free and can be extended/modified without penalty to suit a particular need. Open source software is commonly made available under the GNU General Public License (GPL). This license, available from `www.gnu.org`, spells out what you can and cannot do with such software.

[3]If you have installed MySQL with default options on a personal Linux machine and you are just now becoming familiar with it, for the kinds of practice programs we will be discussing in this chapter you can start up the server daemon as root by invoking

```
safe_mysqld -Sg &
```

where `safe_mysqld` is a wrapper around the daemon executable `mysqld` that automatically invokes the proper options to use — unless they are overridden by command line options. The command line option Sg — which stands for "skip grant tables" — starts up the server without grant tables, giving all users full access to all tables. With default installation on a Linux machine, the database tables would ordinarily be stored in the directory `/var/lib/mysql`. The command

```
mysqld --help
```

shows all the options with which the daemon server program can be run. The following command when entered as root shuts down the server on a Linux machine

```
mysqladmin -u root shutdown
```

With default options, the server daemon will ordinarily monitor port 3306 for incoming connections.

[4]MM.MySQL is available free from http://mmmysql.sourceforge.net/

of these database systems, such as Access, dBase, DB2, Excel, Text, and so on, can be accessed with the ODBC (for Open DataBase Connectivity) driver that also understands SQL. While each of these database systems would have its own driver module, an ODBC driver would know how to "talk" to the product-specific drivers. A Java database program can communicate with all ODBC-accessible databases by using the JDBC-ODBC bridge driver.

Platforms that support database programming also usually provide a *driver manager* that knows about the various types of drivers commonly used today. For example, the `DriverManager` class in `java.sql` will load in all the drivers referenced in the "jdbc.drivers" system property that can be included in a file of pathname *.hotjava/properties* at the top level of your home directory. One also has the option of loading into a JDBC program a specific driver by an invocation such as the following which works for the `MM.MySQL` driver:

```
Class.forName( "org.gjt.mm.mysql.Driver").newInstance();
```

where the static method `Class.forName` returns the `Class` object associated with the class of name `org.gjt.mm.mysql.Driver`.

A driver manager can also help establish a connection with a database. Using the example the JDBC class `DriverManager` again, its method `getConnection` returns an object of type `Connection` defined in the `java.sql` package. The argument to the `getConnection` method is a specially formatted string that for MySQL is the name of the database. For example, if we want a Java program to make a connection with the MySQL database `test` that comes with MySQL installation, we'd need to make the calls

```
String url = "jdbc:mysql:///test";
Connection con = DriverManager.getConnection( url );
```

The string "jdbc:mysql:///test" is called a database URL (as opposed to the internet URL). If, on the other hand, we wanted a Java program to talk to an ODBC database, we could say

```
String url = "jdbc:odbc:myDatabaseName";
Connection con = DriverManager.getConnection( url );
```

If you are trying to reach a remote database over the internet, the database URL string may have to include the port number and other information, besides, of course, the internet address of the machine hosting the database.

20.3 SQL

One obviously cannot write a meaningful JDBC or Mysql++ database program without reasonable familiarity with SQL. This section explains the syntax of some of the commonly used SQL commands. It is obviously not possible to list here all of the different ways in which a client can interact with a database server using SQL, or even all of the commands that are supported by MySQL. However, we will give a sufficient introduction to SQL so that the reader can start writing useful JDBC and Mysql++ programs.

In what follows, we will first describe some basic SQL commands and list some of the more commonly used data types in SQL. This will be followed by two interactive terminal sessions for demonstrating how one actually uses SQL. The interactive sessions will introduce additional commands and functions of SQL.

Some Basic SQL Commands:

To get started with SQL, we will now explain the syntax of the following very commonly used SQL commands:

```
CREATE TABLE  : creates a new table with given column headings
INSERT        : inserts a new row in a table
SELECT        : retrieves entries from single or multiple tables
                with or without constraints on the entries
UPDATE        : changes table entries
```

Although, in keeping with the convention, we have shown the SQL commands in upper case, their usage is case insensitive. Let's look at a typical CREATE TABLE statement:

```
CREATE TABLE BookTable ( Title        CHAR(20),
                         Author       CHAR(20),
                         ISBN         CHAR(13) PRIMARY KEY NOT NULL,
                         PublisherID  INT,
                         PublisherRepID INT,
                         Year         INT,
                         NumCopies    INT )
```

This will create a database table with seven attributes, each corresponding to a separate column in the table. It also declares the data type of each attribute. The first three are of type CHAR(n), where n is the maximum number of characters that the column will hold. The last four are of type INT. With regards to the data types allowed, the SQL 92 specification recognizes the following general types:

- exact numerics

- approximate numerics

- character strings

- bit strings

- datetimes

- intervals

Within each of these general types, there are subtypes:

`exact numerics:` INTEGER (or, INT), SMALLINT, NUMERIC, DECIMAL

`approximate numerics:` REAL, DOUBLE PRECISION, FLOAT

`character strings:` CHARACTER or CHAR, CHARACTER(n) or CHAR(n), CHARACTER VARYING(n) or VARCHAR(n), NATIONAL CHARACTER(n)

`bit strings:` BIT, BIT (n), BIT VARYING (n)

`datetimes:` DATE, TIME, TIMESTAMP, TIME WITH TIME ZONE, TIMES-TAMP WITH TIME ZONE

`intervals:` INTERVAL DAY (is the difference between two datetime values)

SQL does not specify the precision associated with the different data types — that's left to the implementations. However, SQL does place some constraints on the relative precision of the related types. For example, the precision of `SMALLINT` can be no larger than that of `INT`. However, commonly a `SMALLINT` is represented by two bytes, and an `INT` is represented by four. A `NUMERIC` type has a fractional component, in addition to its integer component. For this type, precision refers to the maximum number of digits to be used for both parts together and *scale* refers to the number of digits to be used for just the integer part. For example, if you know that all your numbers in a column are going to less than 999.99, you could specify the data type for that column as `NUMERIC (5,2)`. If you don't specify the precision and scale, the system will use a default of 12 for precision and 6 for scale. The `DECIMAL` type is closely related to the `NUMERIC` type. While a `NUMERIC` type can be used to place a constraint on the largest value in a column, there is no such enforcement for a `DECIMAL` type. For a column type specified as `DECIMAL (5,2)`, a value such as `99999.999` will be acceptable.

The difference between `CHAR(n)` and `VARCHAR(n)` is that for the former the system will pad a string with blanks if the number of characters in the data string is fewer than n. No padding is used for the latter.

Getting back to the `CREATE TABLE` statement shown earlier, note that we declared the ISBN column to be `PRIMARY KEY NOT NULL`. A KEY is an attribute (meaning, a column heading) that can be used to uniquely identify a row in a table. For a system to access a row, it must have some unique way to identify that row. An attribute declared as a KEY is supposed to serve that function. If you know that no two rows in a table will have the same value for a given attribute, use that attribute as the `PRIMARY KEY` for the table. Characterization of a key as `PRIMARY` is supposed to distinguish it from its declaration as a `FOREIGN KEY`. When an attribute is declared to be a foreign key in a table, it informs the table that the key in question is a primary key in another named table.

So, by definition, an attribute declared to be a `PRIMARY KEY` will take unique values in the different rows of a table. Moreover, this attribute will never be allowed to be `NULL`. In that sense, the declaration `PRIMARY KEY NOT NULL` is redundant.

Another way to declaring an attribute to be a primary key is by using the UNIQUE label, as in

```
CREATE TABLE BookTable ( Title         CHAR(20),
                         Author        CHAR(20),
                         ISBN          CHAR(13)  NOT NULL,
                         PublisherID   INT,
                         PublisherRepID INT,
                         Year          INT,
                         NumCopies     INT,
                         UNIQUE( ISBN ) )
```

Sometimes it is not possible to identify an attribute that will take unique values in a table. In these cases, multiple rows can be declared to be NOT NULL, and the system will use a *composite key* based on all those rows. Of course, you have to be sure that the entries for those attributes will never be null.

After you have declared a new table with the CREATE TABLE command, you can start inserting information into it with the SQL command INSERT, as demonstrated by

```
INSERT INTO BookTable VALUES ( 'Noxious Fumes',
                'Sul Phuric', '3636-7737-10', 3, 101, 1935, 3 )
```

Each such invocation will enter a new row into the table BookTable. After a table is thus brought into existence, you can examine all its contents by the SELECT command, as in

```
SELECT * FROM BookTable
```

where * will cause all the columns of the table BookTable to be shown for every row. If you only wanted to see the table entries corresponding to the books published in year 2002, you'd say

```
SELECT * FROM BookTable WHERE Year = 2002
```

The following retrieval command shows how the information contained in two different tables of a database can be merged:

```
SELECT BookTable.Title,
       BookTable.Author,
       PublisherTable.PublisherName
FROM   BookTable, PublisherTable
WHERE  BookTable.PublisherID = PublisherTable.PublisherID
```

In the interactive sessions that follow, also note the use of the following SQL commands:

```
UPDATE
ALTER TABLE
```

```
DROP TABLE
```

for doing exactly what the command names imply.

Interactive Session 1:

We will now show an interactive session with a MySQL database that demonstrates how SQL can be used to create, query, and modify a database. (This is also a good way to practice SQL.) To start the interactive session, you'd need to invoke the MySQL terminal monitor that allows you to execute command-line SQL. If the database server is running on the same machine on which you will be executing command-line SQL, you may be able to start up the terminal monitor by simply entering in a terminal window the following[5]

```
mysql
```

If your request for a connection succeeds, you will see a welcome message on your terminal followed by prompt

```
mysql>
```

Now you are ready to type in your SQL statements.

In what follows, we will show the MySQL prompt `mysql>` flush with the left margin. A user's entries will follow such prompts. The information returned by the database will be shown with an offset from the left margin. All words that are all in uppercase are either SQL commands or SQL keywords. This is just a convention that makes it easy for a human to parse the SQL syntax, but, as mentioned before, SQL itself is case insensitive. *Bear in mind that a requirement of MySQL is that each SQL statement be terminated in either a ';' or '\g'.* The interactive session that follows will create a rudimentary relational database for the library example of Section 20.1.

One of the first things you'd need to do after firing up the terminal monitor is to tell MySQL which database you'd be using. We will assume that you'll use the "test" database that is supplied with the MySQL installation for testing purposes. To tell the database server that you'd be using the "test" database, you'd need to enter

```
mysql>  USE test;
```

Now enter the following SQL statement:

---

[5]If this does not work, you may have to supply a user name and a password. In general, if the database server is running on a remote machine for which you have access privileges, you can start up the terminal monitor on your local machine by

```
mysql -h hostName -u userName -p
```

where `hostName` is the name of the remote machine and `userName` the name you can use to enter that machine. This more general command will prompt you for a password.

```
mysql>   CREATE TABLE BookTable ( Title CHAR(20), Author CHAR(20),
            ISBN CHAR(13) PRIMARY KEY NOT NULL, PublisherID INT,
              PublisherRepID INT, Year INT, NumCopies INT );
```

MySQL allows a single SQL statement to be in multiple lines, but the portion of the statement in the last line must terminate in either a ';' or '\g'. If you want to review the structure of the table that was just created, you could now enter

```
mysql>   DESCRIBE BookTable;
```

MySQL will come back with

Field	Type	Null	Key	Default	Extra
Title	char(20)	YES		NULL	
Author	char(20)	YES		NULL	
ISBN	char(13)		PRI		
PublisherID	int(11)	YES		NULL	
PublisherRepID	int(11)	YES		NULL	
Year	int(11)	YES		NULL	
NumCopies	int(11)	YES		NULL	

SQL statements such as the following would now insert rows of information into this table:

```
mysql>   INSERT INTO BookTable VALUES ( 'Noxious Fumes',
                'Sul Phuric', '3636-7737-10', 3, 101, 1935, 3 );
```

```
mysql>   INSERT INTO BookTable VALUES ( 'Nasty Nabobs',
                'Dem Ented', '3636-9983-10', 2, 101, 1943, 2 );
mysql>   .....
```

As you are entering new rows into the table, at any time you can see the contents of the table by typing

```
mysql>   SELECT * from BookTable;
```

Assuming that you entered the previously shown two INSERT statements and three more (now shown), MySQL will respond to the SELECT command by returning the following for the contents of the BookTable:

Title	Author	ISBN	PID	PRID	Year	NumCopies
Noxious Fumes	Sul Phuric	3636-7737-10	3	101	1935	3
Nasty Nabobs	Dem Ented	3636-9983-10	2	101	1943	2
Nosy Nostrils	Lus Hairs	3687-9983-10	3	103	1998	1
Attila the Hun	Wus Nofun	3687-9944-98	2	101	1989	10
Hairy Hoods	Lo Lifes	4303-9944-98	3	101	1978	2
Dancing Dollies	Boggy Boogers	4303-0000-98	1	121	1986	1

where we have used the abbreviation PID for "PublisherID" and PRID for "PublisherRepID".

To expand on the interactive session in progress, let's now create a new table, PublisherTable, to hold information about the different publishers.

```
mysql>   CREATE TABLE PublisherTable ( PublisherID INT,
             PublisherName CHAR(20), PublisherLocation CHAR(20),
                             PublisherURL CHAR(20) );
```

If you want to see all the tables currently in the database, you can do so by entering

```
SHOW TABLES;
```

The server will come back with

Tables_in_test
BookTable
PublisherTable

To insert an item into the new table, PublisherTable, we will use the INSERT command as before:

```
mysql>   INSERT INTO PublisherTable VALUES ( 1,
             'Warring Warriors', 'New York', 'www.warriors.com' );
```

If we use a couple of more INSERT commands for this table, in accordance with the second and the third rows shown below, the command

```
Select * from PublisherTable
```

will then yield

PublisherID	PublisherName	PublisherLocation	PublisherURL
1	Warring Warriors	New York	www.warriors.com
2	WordSmiths	New Delhi	www.wordsmiths.com
3	WordMasters	New Brunswick	www.wordmasters.com

We need one more table for our example, which we create with the command

```
mysql>   CREATE TABLE PublisherRepTable ( PublisherRepID INT,
             RepName CHAR(30), RepPhone CHAR(12), RepEmail CHAR(20) );
```

Inserting items into this table as shown by the rows below, we get the following for its contents:

PublisherRepID	RepName	RepPhone	RepEmail
101	Rip Offer	2347626266	rip@wol.com
103	Hory Detalis	3527622776	hory@wol.com
121	Nuts Galore	1117232776	nuts@wol.com

With our three-table relational database in place, we are now all set to demonstrate complex queries to the database that require accessing more than one table. For example, the query

```
mysql>   SELECT BookTable.Title, BookTable.Author,
                        PublisherTable.PublisherName
         FROM BookTable, PublisherTable
              WHERE BookTable.PublisherID = PublisherTable.PublisherID;
```

returns

Title	Author	PublisherName
Dancing Dollies	Boggy Boogers	Warring Warriors
Nasty Nabobs	Dem Ented	WordSmiths
Attila The Hun	Wus Nofun	WordSmiths
Noxious Fumes	Sul Phuric	WordMasters
Nosy Nostrils	Lus Hairs	WordMasters
Hairy Hoods	Lo Lifes	WordMasters

We will next illustrate how you can use the UPDATE command to alter a table at any time. Often, any updates to a table would be conditional, meaning that a row would be updated only if it satisfied certain requirements. For example,

```
mysql>   UPDATE BookTable SET Author = 'Long Hairs'
                        WHERE Title = 'Nosy Nostrils';
```

Now if we enter again

```
mysql>   SELECT * FROM BookTable;
```

we get

Title	Author	ISBN	PID	PRID	Year	NumCopies
Noxious Fumes	Sul Phuric	3636-7737-10	3	101	1935	3
Nasty Nabobs	Dem Ented	3636-9983-10	2	101	1943	2
Nosy Nostrils	Long Hairs	3687-9983-10	3	103	1998	1
Attila the Hun	Wus Nofun	3687-9944-98	2	101	1989	10
Hairy Hoods	Lo Lifes	4303-9944-98	3	101	1978	2
Dancing Dollies	Boggy Boogers	4303-0000-98	1	121	1986	1

where we have again used the abbreviation PID for "PublisherID" and PRID for "PublisherRepID". Here is another updating of `BookTable` that shows how rows can be updated selectively:

```
mysql>    UPDATE BookTable SET NumCopies = NumCopies + 1
                                       WHERE Year > 1980;
```

Displaying `BookTable` now yields:

Title	Author	ISBN	PID	PRID	Year	NumCopies
Noxious Fumes	Sul Phuric	3636-7737-10	3	101	1935	3
Nasty Nabobs	Dem Ented	3636-9983-10	2	101	1943	2
Nosy Nostrils	Lus Hairs	3687-9983-10	3	103	1998	2
Attila the Hun	Wus Nofun	3687-9944-98	2	101	1989	11
Hairy Hoods	Lo Lifes	4303-9944-98	3	101	1978	2
Dancing Dollies	Boggy Boogers	4303-0000-98	1	121	1986	2

where, once again, we have used the abbreviation PID for "PublisherID" and PRID for "PublisherRepID". To close the session, we say

```
mysql>    QUIT
```

Interactive Session 2:

Our previous session showed the basic workings of SQL. We will now show SQL that demonstrates

- Entering multiple rows simultaneously into a table using a feature provided by MySQL.

- Using the command SELECT with the ORDER BY option to display an ordered version of a database table.

- Invoking the SQL *set functions* to calculate the various statistics of the numerical values in the individual columns of a database table.

- Modifying a table structurally with the ALTER command after it is created and populated with data.

We will use the database "test" for this session also. Since we have no further need for the tables we created in the previous session, we can drop them by

```
mysql>    DROP TABLE BookTable;
mysql>    DROP TABLE PublisherTable;
mysql>    DROP TABLE PublisherRepTable;
```

That should basically empty out the database "test". For the purpose of this interactive session, let's now create a new table `TestTable1` by

```
mysql>   CREATE TABLE TestTable1 ( Id INT PRIMARY KEY NOT NULL,
                          price DOUBLE(10,2) DEFAULT '0.00' NOT NULL );
```

If we now enter

```
mysql>   DESCRIBE TestTable1;
```

to review the structure of the table, we get back

Field	Type	Null	Key	Default	Extra
id	int(11)		PRI	0	
price	double(10,2)			0.00	

So `TestTable1` is a table with two columns, `id` and `price`, the former of type `INT` and the latter of type `DOUBLE`. To insert a row of information into the table, we can say

```
mysql>   INSERT INTO TestTable1 VALUES ( 127, 4.98 );
```

Let's now say that we have a large number of additional entries to make like those shown above. MySQL gives us a way to enter them all at one time in a single SQL statement. In order to demonstrate how that can be done, let's first delete the row just entered:

```
mysql>   DELETE FROM TestTable1 WHERE id = 127;
```

If this table contained multiple rows and we wanted to delete them all with one command, we could just say

```
mysql>   DELETE FROM TestTable1;
```

In either case, `TestTable1` is now empty. The following command will now enter multiple rows simultaneously into the table:

```
mysql>   INSERT INTO TestTable1 VALUES (127, 4.98),
                          (222, 22.22), (111, 11.11);
```

The command

```
mysql>   SELECT * FROM TestTable1;
```

will now return

id	price
127	4.98
222	22.22
111	11.11

If we want the displayed output to be ordered by price, we can say

```
mysql>    SELECT * FROM TestTable1 ORDER BY price;
```

Now the displayed output would be

id	price
127	4.98
111	11.11
222	22.22

Many useful operations on databases consist of determining the various statistics for the entries in the individual columns of a table. For the example at hand, we may wish to find out the average price charged for all the items in the database, the max price, the min price, and so on. Shown below is a SELECT command that computes such values from the `price` column of the above table and that also returns the number of non-null items in the `id` column:

```
mysql>    SELECT MAX( price ), MIN( price ), AVG( price ),
                  SUM( price ), COUNT( Id ) FROM TestTable1;
```

This returns

MAX(price)	MIN(price)	AVG(price)	SUM(price)	COUNT(Id)
22.22	4.98	12.770000	38.31	3

The functions such as MAX, MIN, and so on, are known as the set functions.

It is possible to modify the structure of a table after it has been created and populated with data. Let's say we wish to add a third column to `TestTable1` to keep track of the quantity of each item in the database. We could use the ALTER command for this, as in

```
mysql>    ALTER TABLE TestTable1 ADD quantity INT;
```

Now if we say

```
mysql>    DESCRIBE TestTable1;
```

we will get back

Field	Type	Null	Key	Default	Extra
id	int(11)		PRI	0	
price	double(10,2)			0.00	
quantity	int(11)	YES		NULL	

Examining the contents of the table after this structural modification

```
mysql>   SELECT * FROM TestTable1 ORDER BY price;
```

we get

id	price	quantity
127	4.98	NULL
111	11.11	NULL
222	22.22	NULL

An updating of this table with

```
mysql>   UPDATE TestTable1 SET quantity = 2 WHERE price > 10.00;
```

yields the following for TestTable1 in the database

id	price	quantity
127	4.98	NULL
111	11.11	2
222	22.22	2

20.4   JDBC PROGRAMMING: INVOKING SQL THROUGH JAVA

JDBC is a programming interface that communicates your SQL commands to a database, retrieves the results, analyzes the results in whatever way you want them analyzed, displays the results retrieved from a database, and so on.

This section shows two JDBC programs. The goal of the first program is to make the reader familiar with some of the more basic classes of the java.sql package. This we do by constructing a couple of database tables and then querying them, just as we did in our first command-line SQL session in the previous section. The goal of the second JDBC program is to show how information can be rapidly loaded into a database table from a file.

As we will show in our first example, all communication with a database is through the executeQuery method of Statement, a class in the java.sql package. A Statement object is constructed by invoking the createStatement method on an object of type `Connection`, which represents the communication link with the database. But, as mentioned earlier, at the very beginning one must first register an appropriate driver with the driver manager. Since we will be using a MySQL database, we would need to register the `mm.mysql.Driver` driver with the JDBC `DriverManager` by

```
Class.forName( "org.gjt.mm.mysql.Driver").newInstance();
```

This invocation results in an automatic registration of the driver with the JDBC `DriverManager`.

When a JDBC program queries a table with `SELECT`, the object returned is of type `ResultSet`, another class defined in `java.sql`. To display the information in a `ResultSet` retrieval, one must first figure out its structure, meaning the number of rows and columns in the retrieved object. All such structural information regarding a `ResultSet` object resides in the corresponding `ResultMetaData` object. For example, if `rs` is a `ResultSet` object, to figure out the number of columns in this object, we can say

```
ResultSetMetaData rsmd = rs.getMetaData();
int numCols = rsmd.getColumnCount();
```

One often does not need to know explicitly the number of rows in a `ResultSet` object. The operator `next`, when invoked on a `ResultSet` object, takes the flow of control automatically to the next row. Therefore, once we have figured out the number of columns in the `ResultSet` object `rs` as above, we can set up the following print loop to display all the contents of the `ResultSet`:

```
while ( rs.next() ) {
    for ( int i = 1; i <= numCols; i++ ) {
        if ( i > 1 ) System.out.print( " | " );
            System.out.print( rs.getString( i ) );
    }
    System.out.println( "" );
}
```

Here is the source code for the first example:

```
//DBFriends1.java

import java.sql.*;

class DBFriends1 {
    public static void main( String[] args )
    {
        try {
            Class.forName( "org.gjt.mm.mysql.Driver").newInstance();
            String url = "jdbc:mysql:///test";
```

```
Connection con = DriverManager.getConnection( url );
Statement stmt = con.createStatement();

stmt.executeQuery( "SET AUTOCOMMIT=1" );
stmt.executeQuery( "DROP TABLE IF EXISTS Friends" );
stmt.executeQuery( "DROP TABLE IF EXISTS Rovers" );

// new table (Friends):
stmt.executeQuery(
    "CREATE TABLE Friends ( Name CHAR (30) PRIMARY KEY, " +
                          "Phone INT, Email CHAR(30) )" );
stmt.executeQuery(
    "INSERT INTO Friends VALUES ( 'Ziggy Zaphod',
                      4569876, " + "'ziggy@sirius' )" );
stmt.executeQuery(
    "INSERT INTO Friends VALUES ( 'Yo Yo Ma', 3472828, " +
                                " 'yoyo@yippy' )" );
stmt.executeQuery(
    "INSERT INTO Friends VALUES ( 'Gogo Gaga',
                      27278927, " + " 'gogo@garish' )" );

//new table (Rovers):

stmt.executeQuery(
    "CREATE TABLE Rovers ( Name CHAR (30) NOT NULL, " +
                          "RovingTime CHAR(10) )" );
stmt.executeQuery(
    "INSERT INTO Rovers VALUES ( 'Dusty Dodo', '2 pm' )" );
stmt.executeQuery(
    "INSERT INTO Rovers VALUES ( 'Yo Yo Ma', '8 pm' )" );
stmt.executeQuery(
    "INSERT INTO Rovers VALUES ( 'BeBe Beaut', '6 pm' )" );

// Query: which Friends are Rovers ?
ResultSet rs = stmt.executeQuery(
    "SELECT Friends.Name, Rovers.RovingTime FROM Friends, "
        + "Rovers WHERE Friends.Name = Rovers.Name" );

ResultSetMetaData rsmd = rs.getMetaData();
int numCols = rsmd.getColumnCount();
while ( rs.next() ) {
    for ( int i = 1; i <= numCols; i++ ) {
        if ( i > 1 ) System.out.print( " | " );
            System.out.print( rs.getString( i ) );
    }
    System.out.println( "" );
}
rs.close();
con.close();
```

```
        } catch(Exception ex ) { System.out.println(ex); }
    }
}
```

To compile this program, you'd need to tell `javac` how to locate the database driver. If the driver is in a JAR file named `mm.mysql-2.0.7-bin.jar`, an invocation like the following should work

```
javac -classpath .:~/mm.mysql-2.0.7-bin.jar DBFriends1.java
```

You'd also need to specify the classpath for the `java` application launcher:

```
java -classpath .:~/mm.mysql-2.0.7-bin.jar DBFriends1
```

Of course, you'd need to make sure that the MySQL server is on and running before you run the above JDBC program. (See the footnote in Section 20.2 dealing with the starting and the stopping of the database server.) The output of this program is

```
Yo Yo Ma | 8 pm
```

Large databases can obviously not be created from within JDBC programs one row at a time. The information that you want to enter into a database is more likely to be found in the form of what's known as a *flat file*. For illustration, we may have the following information in a flat file called `Friends.txt`:

```
Doctor Cosmos    876-6547    zinger@zoros    68  0  73  galacticSoccer
Yo Yo Ma         838-9393    yoyo@yahoo      56  1  0   violaHockey
Zinger Zaphod    939-1717    dodo@dada       23  0  2   tennis
Bebe Beaut       84-83838    bebe@parlor     18  1  3   tennis
```

Each row of this text file has a name, a phone number, an e-mail address, age, whether or not married, number of kids, and the name of the favorite sport. The entries in each row are tab separated, but can also be supplied in what's known as the *comma separated values* (csv) form. You can also have flat files in which each field is given a fixed number of positions.

So let's say that we want a database system to read this flat file and create a `Friends` database. In some systems this can be done with the help of another text file, known usually as a database table's *schema*, which tells the system how to interpret the position of each data item in a row of the flat file. In MySQL, the same is most easily accomplished by first creating a table directly with the `CREATE TABLE` command and then invoking `LOAD DATA INFILE` to read in the data from the flat file into the database table.

The following JDBC program executes the MySQL statement `LOAD DATA INFILE` for the creation of two database tables named `Friends` and `SportsClub`. Whereas the table `Friends` is created from the flat file shown above, the table `SportsClub` is created from the flat file:

```
Hobo Hooter       45     hockey         4
```

```
Doctor Cosmos    68    galacticSoccer    9
Zinger Zaphod    23    tennis            2
Bebe Beaut       84    tennis           10
```

where the entries are in the following order: name, age, sport, and the level at which sport is played. For the query, the program executes the SQL statement SELECT ... WHERE to seek out friends who play tennis at the sports club.

```java
//DBFriends2.java

import java.sql.*;

class DBFriends2 {
    public static void main( String[] args )
    {
        try {
            Class.forName( "org.gjt.mm.mysql.Driver").newInstance();
            String url = "jdbc:mysql:///test";
            Connection con = DriverManager.getConnection( url );
            Statement stmt = con.createStatement();

            stmt.executeQuery( "SET AUTOCOMMIT=1" );
            stmt.executeQuery( "DROP TABLE IF EXISTS Friends" );
            stmt.executeQuery( "DROP TABLE IF EXISTS SportsClub" );

            stmt.executeQuery(
                "CREATE TABLE Friends ( Name CHAR (30) PRIMARY KEY, " +
                            "Phone CHAR (15), Email CHAR(30), " +
                                "Age TINYINT (3), Married BOOL, " +
                            "NumKids TINYINT (3), Sport CHAR(20) )"
            );
            stmt.executeQuery(
              "CREATE TABLE SportsClub ( Name CHAR (30) PRIMARY KEY, " +
                            "Age TINYINT (3), Sport CHAR(20), " +
                            "Level Char(20) )"
            );
            stmt.executeQuery(
                "LOAD DATA LOCAL INFILE 'Friends.txt' INTO TABLE " +
                                    " Friends" );
            stmt.executeQuery(
                "LOAD DATA LOCAL INFILE 'SportsClub.txt' INTO " +
                            " TABLE SportsClub" );

            // which of the Friends also play tennis at the club:
            ResultSet rs = stmt.executeQuery(
                "SELECT Friends.Name, SportsClub.Level FROM Friends, "
                  + "SportsClub WHERE "
                  + "Friends.Name = SportsClub.Name AND "
```

```
                + "Friends.Sport = SportsClub.Sport AND "
                + "Friends.Sport = 'tennis' " );

        ResultSetMetaData rsmd = rs.getMetaData();
        int numCols = rsmd.getColumnCount();

        while ( rs.next() ) {
            for ( int i = 1; i <= numCols; i++ ) {
                if ( i > 1 )
                    System.out.print( " plays tennis at level " );
            System.out.print( rs.getString( i ) );
            }
            System.out.println( "" );
        }
        rs.close();
        con.close();
    } catch(Exception ex ) { System.out.println(ex); }
    }
}
```

The program can be compiled and executed with the command line invocations similar
to those shown for the first example. The output of this program is

```
Zinger Zaphod plays tennis at level 2
Bebe Beaut plays tennis at level 10
```

20.5 Mysql++ PROGRAMMING: INVOKING SQL THROUGH C++

The open source Mysql++ is a C++-based programming interface for communicating
with a MySQL database.[6] Just like JDBC, Mysql++ can communicate your command
to a database and can retrieve, analyze, and display the results.

Basic to Mysql++ programming are the Connection, Query, and Result classes.
They play the same roles in Mysql++ that Connection, Statement, and ResultSet
classes play in JDBC. The Connection class gives you a connection with a database.
Its constructor can be invoked directly with the database name as the sole argument,
as in

```
Connection con( "myDatabase" );
```

---

[6]Its future releases are expected to work with SQL databases in general. Mysql++ is available from
http://www.mysql.com/download_mysql++.html.

where "myDatabase" is the name of a MySQL database on the local machine and if the database user name is the same as the login name. For accessing a database on a different machine or when the database user name is not the same as the login name and if a password is required for accessing the database, you'd need to invoke the Connection constructor with additional arguments. The prototype of the constructor is

```
Connection( cchar* db, cchar* host="",
                        cchar* user="", cchar* passwd="" );
```

Another way to establish a connection with a database is to first carry out a partial construction of a Connection object with the use_exceptions option turned on and to then separately establish a connection with the designated database:

```
Connection con( use_exceptions );
con.connect( "myDatabase" );
```

There is also available a 9-argument constructor for Connection that allows specification of a port, a socket, connection timeout, and so on. When a connection is established with the two-call invocation shown above, the connect method can also be invoked with up to four arguments, the additional arguments allowing specification of a hostname, a user name, and password.

Invoking the function query on a Connection object returns a Query object that can then be used to communicate SQL statements to the database:

```
Connection con( .... );
Query query = con.query();
```

A Query object behaves much like an output stream object in C++, such as cout. You can use the insertion operator '<<' to insert strings in a Query object. These strings will usually be SQL statements. How you get those SQL statements to execute depends upon whether or not their execution is supposed to return something. When an SQL statement fed into a Query object is not supposed to return anything — such as when inserting a new row into a table — the inserted statement can be executed by invoking the function execute on the Query object, as in

```
Query query = ....
query << ... SQL statement ...
query.execute();
```

If it is desired to reset the state of the Query object, the last call can also be of the form that includes the flag RESET_QUERY:

```
query.execute( RESET_QUERY );
```

On the other hand, when the SQL statement is supposed to return a result set, you need to invoke store, which causes execution of the SQL statement and retrieval of a result-set object of type Result:

```
Query query = ....
query << ... SQL SELECT statement ...
Result res = query.store();
```

A `Result` object is an STL-like container, supporting a random-access read-only iterator and array-like indexing. Each element stored in a `Result` object corresponds to a row of the result set and is again an STL-like container that also supports array-like indexing. Both the `Result` object and the rows stored therein as elements can be accessed via iterators. Since both the row elements of a result set and the elements inside each row can be accessed by array-like indexing, the result set can be thought of as a two-dimensional table directly addressable by a pair of indices, as in

```
Result res = query.store();
cout << res[2][5];
```

which would display the datum in the column indexed 5 of the result set row indexed 2.[7]

The example below, DBFriends1.cc, is a C++ version of the Java example DBFriends1.java shown earlier. The reader should note the parallels between the two. Note how, in the C++ version, we first construct an iterator to the result set. As we step through the allowed values for the iterator, we gain access to each row of the result set. We determine the number of column entries in each row, and then we invoke a loop to print all the entries out. Before printing out the contents of the result set, we also print out the column headings for the columns in the result set by invoking the names function on the `Result` object, as in

```
Result res = query.store();
...
cout << res.names(j);
...
```

for displaying the name of the *jth* column.

```
//DBFriends1.cc

#include <iostream>
#include <sqlplus.hh>
#include <iomanip>

int main()
{
    try {
        Connection con( use_exceptions );
```

---

[7]There are two different kinds of result sets in Mysql++: *dramatic result set* and *static result set*. The two-dimensional indexing shown can only be used for the former type.

```cpp
con.connect( "test" );
Query query = con.query();
query << "SET AUTOCOMMIT=1";
query.execute();
query << "DROP TABLE IF EXISTS Friends";
query.execute();
query << "DROP TABLE IF EXISTS Rovers";
query.execute();

// Friends table:
query << "CREATE TABLE Friends ( Name CHAR (30) "
      << "PRIMARY KEY, Phone INT, Email CHAR(30) )";
query.execute();
query << "INSERT INTO Friends VALUES ( 'Ziggy Zaphod', "
      << "4569876, 'ziggy@sirius' )";
query.execute();
query << "INSERT INTO Friends VALUES ( 'Yo Yo Ma', "
      << "3472828, 'yoyo@yippy' )";
query.execute();
query << "INSERT INTO Friends VALUES ( 'Gogo Gaga', "
      << "27278927, 'gogo@garish' )" ;
query.execute();

// Rovers table:
query << "CREATE TABLE Rovers ( Name CHAR (30) NOT NULL, "
      << "RovingTime CHAR(10) )";
query.execute();
query << "INSERT INTO Rovers VALUES ( 'Dusty Dodo', '2 pm' )";
query.execute();
query << "INSERT INTO Rovers VALUES ( 'Yo Yo Ma', '8 pm' )";
query.execute();
query << "INSERT INTO Rovers VALUES ( 'BeBe Beaut', '6 pm' )";
query.execute();

query << "SELECT Friends.Name, Rovers.RovingTime "
      << "FROM Friends, Rovers WHERE Friends.Name=Rovers.Name";

// The result set:
Result res = query.store();
cout << "Query: " << query.preview() << endl;
cout << "Records Found: " << res.size() << endl << endl;

Row row_rs;
cout.setf(ios::left);
Result::iterator i;
for ( i = res.begin(); i != res.end(); i++ ) {
    row_rs = *i;
    int numFields = row_rs.size();
    if ( i == res.begin() ) {
```

```
                for ( int j = 0; j < numFields; j++ )
                    cout << setw( 17 ) << res.names( j ) << "\t\t";
                cout << endl << endl;
            }
            for ( int j = 0; j < numFields; j++ )
                cout << setw( 17 ) << row_rs[ j ] << "\t";
            cout << endl;
        }
    } catch ( BadQuery& er ) {
        cerr << "Query Error: " << er.error << endl;
        return -1;
    } catch( BadConversion& er ) {
        cerr << "Conversion Error: Tried to convert \""
             << er.data << "\" to a \""
             << er.type_name << "\"." << endl;
        return -1;
    }
}
```

This program can be compiled by the following command line that can be conveniently placed in a shell script:

```
g++ -o DBFriends1 DBFriends1.cc -I/usr/include/mysql    \
            -lsqlplus -Wl,--rpath -Wl,/usr/local/lib
```

This assumes a standard installation of Mysql++ on a Linux machine. The output of the program is the same as for the Java example DBFriends1.java.

Our next example, DBFriends2.cc, parallels the JDBC example DBFriends2.java. This example, like the earlier Java example, creates two database tables by reading in the data from two flat files and then executes a more complex query compared to our previous Mysql++ example. The result set returned by the query is displayed in a manner that is exactly the same as before.

```
//DBFriends2.cc

#include <iostream>
#include <sqlplus.hh>
#include <iomanip>

int main()
{
    try {
        Connection con( use_exceptions );
        con.connect( "test" );
        Query query = con.query();
```

```
query << "SET AUTOCOMMIT=1";
query.execute();
query << "DROP TABLE IF EXISTS Friends";
query.execute();
query << "DROP TABLE IF EXISTS SportsClub";
query.execute();

query << "CREATE TABLE Friends ( Name CHAR (30) PRIMARY KEY, "
      << "Phone CHAR (15), Email CHAR(30), "
      << "Age TINYINT (3), Married BOOL, "
      << "NumKids TINYINT (3), Sport CHAR(20) )";
query.execute();

query << "CREATE TABLE SportsClub (Name CHAR (30) PRIMARY KEY,"
      << "Age TINYINT (3), Sport CHAR(20), "
      << "Level Char(20) )";
query.execute();

query << "LOAD DATA LOCAL INFILE 'Friends.txt' "
      << "INTO TABLE Friends";
query.execute();
query << "LOAD DATA LOCAL INFILE 'SportsClub.txt' INTO "
      << " TABLE SportsClub";
query.execute();

// which of the Friends also play tennis at the club:
query << "SELECT Friends.Name, SportsClub.Level FROM Friends, "
      << "SportsClub WHERE "
      << "Friends.Name = SportsClub.Name AND "
      << "Friends.Sport = SportsClub.Sport AND "
      << "Friends.Sport = 'tennis' ";

Result res = query.store();
cout << "Query: " << query.preview() << endl;
cout << "Records Found: " << res.size() << endl << endl;

Row row_rs;
cout.setf(ios::left);

Result::iterator i;
for ( i = res.begin(); i != res.end(); i++ ) {
    row_rs = *i;
    int numFields = row_rs.size();
    if ( i == res.begin() ) {
        for ( int j = 0; j < numFields; j++ )
            cout << setw( 17 ) << res.names( j ) << "\t\t";
        cout << endl << endl;
    }
    for ( int j = 0; j < numFields; j++ )
```

```
                    cout << setw( 17 ) << row_rs[ j ] << "\t";
                cout << endl;
            }
    } catch ( BadQuery& er ) {
        cerr << "Query Error: " << er.error << endl;
        return -1;
    } catch( BadConversion& er ) {
        cerr << "Conversion Error: Tried to convert \""
            << er.data << "\" to a \""
            << er.type_name << "\"." << endl;
        return -1;
    }
}
```

This program can be compiled by the following command line that can be conveniently placed in a shell script:

```
g++ -o DBFriends2 DBFriends2.cc -I/usr/include/mysql    \
            -lsqlplus -Wl,--rpath -Wl,/usr/local/lib
```

As before, this assumes a standard installation of Mysql++ on a Linux machine. The output of the program is the same as for the Java example DBFriends2.java.

20.6 SUGGESTIONS FOR FURTHER READING

A classic and standard reference for SQL and for relational database concepts is the book by Date [15]. The on-line documentation on MySQL at [35] contains a detailed tutorial. Same is the case with the on-line documentation for MySQL++ at [36].

20.7 HOMEWORK

1. Write a JDBC program that can serve as a front-end server to a MySQL database. Your JDBC server should perform the following tasks:

    (a) Establish a password-protected connection between a client and the database. The client must specify his/her username, password, and the database name.

    (b) Report back any error messages to the client if there is any error while connecting with the MySQL database and allow the client to try to reconnect repeatedly until the client enters "exit" as the username.

    (c) Execute each SQL statement received from the client and display the retrieved results to the client as necessary.

(d) Display on the client's terminal an error message if the SQL command is invalid.

(e) Continue receiving SQL statements from a client until "exit" is entered by the user.

[Suggestion: The Java implementation of the chat server program of Chapter 19 would be a good starting point for the program needed here.]

2. Write a C++ implementation for the previous problem using Mysql++ classes. [Suggestion: As with the previous problem, the C++ implementation of the chat server program of Chapter 19 would be a good starting point for the solution needed here.]

References

1. C. Alexander, S. Ishikawa, and M. Silverstein. *A Pattern Language, Towns, Buidlings, Construction.* Oxford University Press, New York, 1977.

2. K. Arnold and J. Gosling. *The Java Programming Language, 2nd ed.* Addison-Wesley, 1997.

3. J. L. Bentley and M. D. Mcllroy. Engineering a sort function. *Software Practice and Experience*, 23:1249–1265, November 1993.

4. H. Boehm. Space efficient conservative garbage collection. *Proceedings of the ACM SIGPLAN '93 Conference on Programming Language Design and Implementation, SIGPLAN Notices 28*, 6:197–206, June 1993.

5. H. Boehm and M. Weiser. Garbage collection in uncooperative environment. *Software Practice & Experience*, pages 807–820, September 1988.

6. G. Booch. *Object-Oriented Analysis and Design with Applications, 2nd, ed.* Addison-Wesley, 1994.

7. G. Booch, J. Rumbaugh, and I. Jacobson. *The Unified Modeling Language User Guide.* Addison-Wesley, Reading, MA, 1999.

8. G. Bracha, M. Odersky, D. Stoutamire, and P. Wadler. Gj: Exending the java programming langauage with type parameters. *Online tutorial available from http://www.research.avayalabs.com/user/wadler/pizza/gj/Documents/*, March 1998.

9. G. Bracha, M. Odersky, D. Stoutamire, and P. Wadler. Making the future safe for the past: Adding genericity to the java programming language. *OOPSLA 98*, October 1998.

10. F. B. Brokken. *C++ Annotations*. http://www.icce.rug.nl/documents/cpp.shtml, 2001.

11. D. R. Butenhof. *Programming with POSIX Threads*. Addison-Wesley, 1997.

12. E. Castro. *HTML 4 for the World Wide Web, Fourth Edition*. Peachpit Press, Berkeley, CA, 2000.

13. J. W. Cooper. *Java Design Patterns, A Tutorial*. Addison-Wesley, Reading, MA, 2000.

14. M. K. Dalheimer. *Programming with Qt*. O'Reilly, 1999.

15. C. J. Date. *An Introduction to Database Systems, 7th ed.* Addison-Wesley, 1999.

16. K. Dattatri. *C++, Effective Object-Oriented Software Construction*. Prentice-Hall PTR, 1996.

17. H. M. Dietel and P. J. Dietel. *Java, How to Program*. Prentice Hall, 1999.

18. R. Eckstein, M. Loy, and D. Wood. *Java Swing*. O'Reilly, 1998.

19. D. Flanagan. *Java in a Nutshell*. O'Reilly, 1997.

20. M. Fowler and K. Scott. *UML Distilled: Applying the Standard Object Modeling Language*. Addison-Wesley, Reading, MA, 1997.

21. E. Gamma, R. Helm, R. Johnson, and J. Vlissides. *Design Patterns: Elements of Reusable Object-Oriented Software*. Addison-Wesley, Reading, MA, 1995.

22. D. Goldberg. What every computer scientist should know about floating-point arithmetic. *ACM Computing Surveys*, 23:5–48, March 1991.

23. J. Gosling, B. Joy, and G. Steele. *The Java Language Specification*. Addison-Wesley, 1996.

24. J. Gosling, B. Joy, G. Steele, and G. Bracha. *The Java Language Specification*. http://java.sun.com/docs/books/jls/second_edition/html/j.title.doc.html, 2000.

25. A. Griffith. *GNOME/GTK+ Programming Bible*. IDG Books, 2000.

26. C. S. Horstmann and G. Cornell. *Core Java 2, Volume 1 – Fundamentals*. Sun Microsystems Press, 1999.

27. C. S. Horstmann and G. Cornell. *Core Java 2, Volume II – Advanced Features*. Sun Microsystems Press, 1999.

28. http://developer.java.sun.com/developer/onlineTraining/collections/index.html. Introduction to the Collections Framework.

29. http://doc.trolltech.com/2.3/threads.html. Thread Support in Qt.

30. http://doc.trolltech.com/2.3/tutorial.html. Tutorial: The 14 Ssteps.

31. http://grouper.ieee.org/groups/754/. IEEE Standard for Binary Floating Point Arithmetic.

32. http://java.sun.com/docs/books/tutorial/uiswing/index.html. Creating a GUI with JFC/Swing.

33. http://java.sun.com/j2se/1.3/docs/index.html. Java 2 SDK, Standard Editor Documentation.

34. http://www.gtk.org/tutorial. GTK+ 2.0 Tutorial.

35. http://www.mysql.com/. MySQL Documentation.

36. http://www.mysql.com/documentation/mysql++/index.html. MySQL++ Documentation.

37. http://www.roguewave.com/support/docs/stdref/index.cfm. Standard C++ Library Class Reference.

38. http://www.roguewave.com/support/docs/stdug/index.cfm. Standard C++ Library User Guide and Tutorial.

39. http://www.unicode.org. Unicode Home Page.

40. C. Hughes and T. Hughes. *Object-Oriented Multithreading using C++*. John Wiley, 1997.

41. ISO. International standard, Programming Languages – C++.

42. N. M. Josuttis. *The C++ Standard Library, A Tutorial and Reference*. Addison-Wesley, 1999.

43. A. C. Kak. *What is a Fail-Fast Iterator?* http://www.jguru.com/faq/view.jsp?EID=221988, Oct 2000.

44. A. C. Kak. *What is Stable Sorting?* http://www.jguru.com/faq/view.jsp?EID=225366, Oct 2000.

45. K. N. King. *C Programming, A Modern Approach*. W. W. Norton & Company, New York, New York, 1996.

46. D. E. Knuth. *The Art of Computer Programming, Volume 3 (Sorting and Searching)*. Addison-Wesley, 1998.

47. X. Leroy. *LinuxThreads*. http://www.pauillac.inria.fr/ xleroy/linuxthreads/ index.html.

48. B. Lewis and D. Berg. *Threads Primer: A Guide to Multithreaded Programming*. Prentice Hall PTR, 1995.

49. B. Lewis and D. Berg. *Multithreaded Programming with Pthreads*. Prentice Hall PTR, 1997.

50. S. Lippman and J. Lajoie. *C++ Primer, 3rd ed.* Addison-Wesley, 1998.

51. S. Meyers. *More Effective C++*. Addison-Wesley, 1996.

52. M. T. Nelson. *Java Foundation Classes*. McGraw-Hill, 1998.

53. W. R. Stevens. *UNIX Network Programming, Volume 1, Second Edition*. Prentice-Hall PTR, 1998.

54. B. Stroustrup. *The C++ Programming Language, 3rd. ed.* Addison-Wesley, 1997.

55. S. R. Weiner and S. Asbury. *Programming with JFC*. John Wiley, 1998.

Index